Essentials of Fiscal Sociology

Finanzsoziologie

Herausgegeben von Jürgen G. Backhaus

Band 5

Zu Qualitätssicherung und Peer Review der vorliegenden Publikation

Die Qualität der in dieser Reihe erscheinenden Arbeiten wird vor der Publikation durch den Herausgeber der Reihe geprüft.

Notes on the quality assurance and peer review of this publication

Prior to publication, the quality of the work published in this series is reviewed by the editor of the series.

Jürgen Backhaus (ed.)

Essentials of Fiscal Sociology

Conception of an Encyclopedia

PL ACADEMIC RESEARCH

Bibliographic Information published by the Deutsche Nationalbibliothek
The Deutsche Nationalbibliothek lists this publication in the Deutsche Nationalbibliografie; detailed bibliographic data is available in the internet at http://dnb.d-nb.de.

Library of Congress Cataloging-in-Publication Data

Essentials of fiscal sociology : conception of an encyclopedia / Jürgen Backhaus (ed.).
pages cm. — (Finanzsoziologie, ISSN 1610-059X ; band 5)
ISBN 978-3-631-61522-5
1. Economics—Sociological aspects. 2. Finance, Public—Social aspects. 3. Political sociology. I. Backhaus, Jürgen G., 1950-
HM548.E87 2013
306.2—dc23

2013037451

ISSN 1610-059X
ISBN 978-3-631-61522-5 (Print)
E-ISBN 978-3-653-02905-5 (E-Book)
DOI 10.3726/978-3-653-02905-5

PL Academic Research is an Imprint of Peter Lang GmbH.

Peter Lang – Frankfurt am Main · Bern · Bruxelles · New York · Oxford · Warszawa · Wien

This book is part of an editor's series of PL Academic Research and was peer reviewed prior to publication.

www.peterlang.com

Table of Contents

Introduction

In 2000 I accepted the Krupp Foundation Chair in Public Finance and Fiscal Sociology, and in 2001, we planned an annual conference in Fiscal Sociology, which had to be postponed because of September 11th. In the meantime every year on the Friday before the start of the winter semester in the city castle of Rudolstadt, the annual conference on Fiscal Sociology takes place. This book contains contributions to the last four of these meetings.

The Title of this book suggests that the compilation is so massive that the project of an encyclopedia needs to be discussed during the next meetings in October 2013.

Dana Ruoff turned what was heading towards a publishing disaster into a nice success – thanks.

Erfurt University,
Jürgen Backhaus

Fiscal Sociology: An Innovative Approach Of Citizenship And Democracy Design

Bénédicte Le Brun

Introduction: A Speciality That Opens Perspectives

Fiscal sociology stands at the crossing of several disciplines: economic sociology, sociology of the State, anthropology, political science, fiscal law, public law; it is also necessary to take into account some dimensions of regional development, social geography, economics, local economy... This list is quite long and so many points of view can not be synthetized. The pertinence of fiscal sociology is to give some framework to a field wich has been progressively shrouded in a cloud of complexities and autonomy.

Economic relations are human relations. If this definition is easy to understand and do not hurt logic, it can be difficult to maintain it in the analysis, so powerful are the economist speeches. Theses predominant[11] speeches tend to impose the now deeply-rooted idea that economy can only be explained by economy. Anthropological and sociological theories do not escape this exclusion from the economic field. The definition of the sociology field has been shrinking as sociologists delimit, refine and claim particularities. Yet sociology can not be limited, since all humanity life is social. The potential field of fiscal sociology is very large; its sociogenesis is one of its interesting aspects, in particular ideological sociogenesis (as Max Weber considers ideology[2]).

Fiscal sociology allows to go beyond rather irrelevant disciplinary rifts and also to open the analysis of economic connexions.

Fiscality As A Contribution To Collective Action

The French tax-system is complex, institutions are financed by various taxes (tax mix) that do not have the same roles, do not mobilize the same funds, and do not make pay same persons. If finances are centralized at the State level, other institutions exert public power and are endowed with fiscality. The financing modes

1 Leroy M. Pourquoi la sociologie fiscale ne bénéficie t'elle pas d'une reconnaissance institutionnelle en France? in: Année sociologique 53, n°1, (2003), pp. 247-274.

2 Weber M. Economie et société tome1: Les catégories de la sociologie (1922). Paris: Agora, 1995.

of these new institutional territories do not escape to complexity and to political stakes of financial indepedence. The decentralization of French public financing tells us a lot about the construction of territorial belonging and its ability to set the limit of some "us". Indeed, fiscality can be defined in a familiar language as the transfer of "my" money to "our" money. It's very hard to define exactly when it changes from private field to public field. A lot of persons anticipate a separate budget for taxes, money from such subsidy or from other sources is affected to this use. It is then put aside or assigned sometimes before being received: for example, some companies anticipate professional taxes far ahead in their accountancy. This observation echoes the social marking theory as defined by Zelizer[3]. A work hypothesis is that distinction between notions of "private" and "public" is a legal necessity but in sociology, it would be wise to understand it as a mode of building belonging. Going from "my" to "our", this money partly builds my place in the "us" and defines the "us" in connection with the "not us". Ever since, the financing mechanisms of public collectivities become a part of what makes the group. For example, paying value-added tax everyday without thinking about builds belonging differently from writing an income tax return or paying a tax based on the added value of work such as professional taxes.

In a context of ladder-like places of political decisions, various belongings are mobilized by decision-makers, "pays" (life fields), regions, states, European Union... with complex, hardly-readable financial mechanisms. The distinction between collective incomes depending on the origins of the money is now a geopolitic stake in France. The political actors of local collectivities claim autonomy and financial indepedence. This independence demand comes as opposed to the budgetary supervision of the State. Money is becoming a stake of independence.

Fiscality As A Tool Of Territorial Political Design

Fiscal sociology proposes a concrete approach of the organization of public action. The obligation to pay taxes is also an obligation to contribute to an institution; in the same time, compulsory levies are the result of democratic games and of the evolution of the place of various institutions in the political arena. The decentralization of public financing begun in the 80's in France is considered as stepping backwards by some actors: this is linked to the will of a greater control over expenses and to a problem of managing the responsibilities of public finances between state and local collectivities. Legal responsibilities for ill-spending or over-spending, and also responsibilities for making a too general expense, with

3 Zelizer V. La signification sociale de l'argent. Paris: Seuil (Liber), (2005), p. 348

an important societal impact. Some financial transfers to local collectivities are assigned to obligatory expenses, which leaves very little place for political decision-making. Actors claim a certain supremacy for each decisions level. But it is not expressed as such, speeches could be contradictory: the State is disparaged as the nasty centralizing force and yet actors deny the competition between the levels on the political organization ladder. In the facts, holding several official positions makes political actors mobilize various belongings according to the place they play a part in.

There is a gap between decentralization texts, law texts governing financial procedures and the way these texts are implemented. Each time a funnel redefines the reality of decentralization. Teritorries buildings come within the framework of identitary strategies interwoven in the political action. The claims of belonging to a territory and to the supremacy –even limited- of this territory become the stake of competence transfer to local collectivities. It deals with power, establishing this power. But not only power over people, also power to make an "us", a together. Thus, fiscality is very linked to the legitimacy of the institution and to the legitimacy of territories in public action. This refers to the identitary strategies of the actors and, particularly, their way of building social classification through territorial belonging.

Belonging is often associated with identity. Yet, this concept must be dealt with care because defining an identity amounts to tell what is and what is not, to enclose a whole, and to close it off from others. Therefore, studies consisisting in making typologies run the risk of contributing, even against themselves, to make social classifications. If defining transport users typologies can help urban policy to be more efficient, it is ineffective and also dangerous to use social classification such as "national identity" or "regional identity". Studying the exchange rather than the result of the exchange allows not to harden groups or to form some others, but to represent what builds hardenings. Money is one of these exchanges that shows and forms belonging. Because money is concrete, it is possible to establish a socio genesis of the rules, to establish a comparison between the rules and the actual practices, which is difficult to make with other more invisible types of exchanges such as idea exchanges. Identitary strategies do not necessarly come up in the same time as belonging, identity may come later, to suit a belonging imposed by a social classification or it may come before, and it is the hypothesis analyzed here, to legitimize an institution, its administrative system, its political decisions, etc.

This way of dealing with this question leads to take into account the compulsory feature of belonging; paying a tax, compulsory levies, is participating, even without one's will, to a collective action. Belonging is sometimes analyzed through the feelings it brings. Here again, the national, regional or local feeling is not always mobilized in the same time as the objective belonging.

Conclusion: An Important Lighting On Political Organization

Fiscal sociology allows us to shed a considerable light on the notion of citizenship. These particular economical relations that fiscal relations are lead to acknowledge money as an instrument not only of exchange but also of social classification and of legitimate domination building. When fiscality becomes complex and put taxpayers in relations with several levels of political decisions, its modes become a part of the territorial design.

References

Badie, B., Birenbaum, P. Sociologie De L'état, Paris: Grasset (Coll. « Pluriel »). (1991, Première Ed. 1979), p. 238.

Bayart, J.-F. L'illusion Identitaire. Paris: Fayard, (1996), p. 307.

Bouvier, M. Introduction Au Droit Fiscal Général Et Théorie De L'impôt. Lgdj – 5ème Édition.

Favret-Saada, J. Algérie 1962-1964, Essai D'anthropologie Politique. Saint-Denis: Bouchene, (2005), p. 117.

Gauthier, R.-F., Robert, A. D., L'école Et L'argent, Quels Financements Pour Quelles Finalités. Paris: Retz (Défis D'éducation), (2005), p. 175.

Halbwachs, M. La Mémoire Collective. Paris: Presses Universitaires De France, (1950), p. 170.

Leroy, M. Pourquoi La Sociologie Fiscale Ne Bénéficie T'elle Pas D'une Reconnaissance Institutionnelle En France? in: Année Sociologique, 53, N°1, (2003), pp. 247-274.

Leroy, M. La Logique Financière De L'action Publique Conventionnelle Dans Le Contrat De Plan État-Région. Paris: L'harmattan, (2000), p. 223.

Leroy, M. La Sociologie De L'impôt. Paris: Puf (Coll. « Que Sais-Je ? »), (2002), p. 125.

Noiriel, G. Etat, Nation Et Immigration, Vers Une Histoire Du Pouvoir. Paris: Belin (Coll. « Socio-Histoire »), (2001).

Simon, P.-J. La Bretonnité, Une Ethnicité Problématique. Rennes: Terre De Brume Édition/P.U.R., (1999), p. 209.

Zelizer, V. La Signification Sociale De L'argent. Paris: Seuil (Liber), (2005), p. 348.

The Making Of The Estonian Fiscal Constitution: Institutional Interests Versus Historical Constraints

Ringa Raudla

Abstract

This paper analyzes the making of the constitutional provisions pertaining to budgeting in the Estonian Constitutional Assembly (1991-1992). The Estonian case is used to test the conjectures derived from the existing literature on constitutional political economy. The case of Estonia indicates that although institutional self-interest of the framers played an important role in drafting the constitutional budget process provisions, there were also notable exceptions, represented by proposals of institutional self-binding by members of the Assembly. The case study also demonstrates the significance of the Estonian inter-war constitutions in shaping the fiscal provisions in the 1992 Constitution.

1. Introduction

Constitutional political economy is a branch of political economy that examines how constitutional rules are chosen and what their impacts are[1]. Though initially constitutional political economy was primarily a 'normative endeavour interested in legitimising the state and its actions in terms of fairness, justice, or efficiency', in which the constitution was viewed as a social contract, then by now, the research program has clearly expanded and includes an increasing number of works of positive analysis[2]. Although the branch of positive constitutional political economy that is concerned with constitutions as *explananda* (focusing on factors that shape the adoption of a constitution) is still in its early stages of development, it has received increasing attention (owing to constitution-making in the European Union, among other factors) in recent years[3]. Of particular inter-

1 Buchanan, J. M. The Domain of Constitutional Economics. Constitutional Political Economy, 1, 1, (1990).Buchanan, J. M. Post-Socialist Political Economy. Selected Essays, Cheltenham: Edward Elgar, (1997).
Voigt, S. Positive Constitutional Economics: A Survey. Public Choice, 90, 1-4, (1997).
Voigt, S. Explaining Constitutional Change. A Positive Economics Approach. Cheltenham: Edward Elgar, (1999).
Voigt, S., Wagener, H-J. Introduction. (2002), in Voigt. S., Wagener', H-J. (eds) Constitutions, Markets and Law. Recent Experiences in Transition Economies. Cheltenham: Edward Elgar, (2002).

2 Voigt, S., Wagener, H-J. Introduction. (2002), in Voigt. S., Wagener', H-J. (eds) Constitutions, Markets and Law. Recent Experiences in Transition Economies. Cheltenham: Edward Elgar, (2002), p. xv.

3 Notes: 1

est have been the following questions: How do the types of actors involved in constitution-making, their preferences and the constraints they face influence the resulting *content* of the constitution?

As a result of intellectual affinity between constitutional political economy (CPE) and public finance, fiscal aspects of constitutions have received extensive attention in constitutional political economy. In particular, the literature has focused on constitutional provisions concerning balanced budget requirements, tax and expenditure limitations, borrowing restrictions and debt ceilings. Hitherto, however, the main focus of research has been on the *impacts* of these provisions rather than on their emergence. The studies that have regarded fiscal constitutional provisions as *explananda* have been, for most part, concerned with provisions that have been added to *existing* constitutions rather than analyzing how constitutional provisions pertaining to budgeting come about when an *entire* constitution is written afresh (for example, after a regime change)[4]. Furthermore, despite growing attention to budget procedures as factors explaining fiscal outcomes[5], there have been no studies that would have explored how constitutional provisions pertaining to *budget process* (regulating the preparation, adoption and implementation of the public budget) come about in the constitution-making process. This article seeks to fill this gap by making use of fiscal sociological approach. It will first put forth an analytical framework for examining budgetary constitutional provisions as *explananda*: by drawing on the hypotheses concerning constitution-making in general, a list of conjectures is put forth. Subsequently, these conjectures are tested with the case study of constitution-making in Estonia in 1991-1992.

Estonia is a particularly interesting case for constitutional political economy and fiscal sociology for a number of reasons. First, Estonia stands out for its commitment to fiscal discipline[6], which is a major concern for CPE. Since a number of studies have attributed the commitment to fiscal discipline in Estonia to its

---

4 Notes: 2

5 See: Hallerberg, M., von Hagen, J. Electoral Institutions, Cabinet Negotiations, and Budget Deficits in the European Union. In Poterba', J. M. & von Hagen, J. (eds) Fiscal Institutions and Fiscal Performance. Chicago: University of Chicago Press, (1999).
Hallerberg, M. Domestic Budgets in a United Europe: Fiscal Governance from the End of Bretton Woods to EMU. Ithaca: Cornell University Press, (2004).
Hallerberg, M., Strauch, R., von Hagen, J. The Design of Fiscal Rules and Forms of Governance in European Union Countries. European Journal of Political Economy, 23, (2007).
Hallerberg, M., Strauch, R., von Hagen, J. Fiscal Governance: Evidence from Europe. Cambridge: Cambridge University Press, (2009).

6 See, for example: Mulas-Granados, C., Onrubia, J., Salinas-Jimenez, J. Do Budget Institutions Matter? Fiscal Consolidations in the New EU Member States. Eastern European Economics, 47, (2009).

budgetary institutions[7], the factors influencing the emergence of budgetary institutions in Estonia should be of particular interest for constitutional political economy[8]. Second, the form of constitution-making – the Constitutional Assembly that included members of the existing legislature (the Supreme Council) and delegates from the Estonian Congress – lends itself to analyzing the effects that different kinds of participants can have on the content of the constitution.

The main sources of information for analyzing the emergence of the budget process provisions in the 1992 Constitution were different draft constitutions submitted to the Constitutional Assembly, the previous Constitutions of Estonia and verbatim records of the plenary sessions of the Constitutional Assembly. In addition, the published memoirs of the participants in the Constitutional Assembly and archival materials on the work of the Constitutional Assembly have been used for compiling the case study. The paper is organized as follows. Section 2 outlines the theoretical propositions on fiscal constitutional provisions as *explananda*. Section 3 gives an overview of how the budget process provisions in the Estonian Constitution came about and section 4 tests the theoretical conjectures with the Estonian case. Section 5 concludes.

2. Theoretical Propositions

The existing theoretical and empirical works in positive constitutional political economy have put forth a number of hypotheses concerning the effects of the constellation of actors involved, their motives and the constraints they face on the resulting content of the constitution[9]. Although these conjectures have not been formulated with specific reference to fiscal provisions, one can deduce more specific formulations from these general hypotheses.

Zapal, J., Schneider, O. What Are Their Words Worth? The Political Plans and Economic Pains of Fiscal Consolidations in the New EU Member States. Eastern European Economics, 44, 5, (2006).

7 7 Gleich, H. The Evolution of Budget Institutions in Central and Eastern European Countries. Bonn: University of Bonn, (2002).
Fabrizio, S., Mody, A. Can Budget Institutions Counteract Political Indiscipline? Economic Policy, 21, (2006).
Mulas-Granados, C., Onrubia, J., Salinas-Jimenez, J. Do Budget Institutions Matter? Fiscal Consolidations in the New EU Member States. Eastern European Economics, 47, (2009).

8 Raudla, R. Evolution of Budgetary Institutions in Estonia: A Path Full of Puzzles? Governance, 23, 3, (2010b).

9 This and the next paragraph draws on Raudla, Ringa, Explaining constitution-makers' preferences: The cases of Estonia and the United States. Constitutional Political Economy 21(3), (2010), p. 249-269.

Analogously to other constitutional provisions, *constitutional preferences* of the framers can be expected to play a major role in the resulting constitutional provisions pertaining to budgeting. Constitutional preferences would be shaped by *constitutional theories* and *constitutional interests* of the participants in the constitution-making process[10]. According to Vanberg and Buchanan[11], constitutional theories are a person's predictions about the prospective outcomes of alternative rules; constitutional interests are his or her subjective evaluations of the expected outcomes of the rules. Constitutional interests, in turn, can be carried by personal, institutional, and partisan interests[12], the prevalence of which would be influenced by the make-up of the constituent body. Elster[13] argues that when the constitution-making body coincides with the existing legislature (or is a sub-committee thereof) and / or other branches of government are involved, institutional self-interest would play an important role in constitution-making: the framers would be inclined to enhance their own position in the constitutional framework, at the expense of other organs of state[14].

Assuming institutional self-interest of the members of the constituent body, one can conjecture that if the framers are also members of the existing legislature, the parliament will be attributed a more important role in the budget procedure *vis-à-vis* the government and the president or other state institutions. Conversely, if the president, the government or other institutions are involved in the constitution-making process, they will seek to promote a greater role of their respective institutions in budget process.

Analogously to constitutional review, framers can be conjectured to be 'predisposed against limiting themselves, particularly in the form of oversight by other actors'[15] in the area of budgeting. Hence, when framers come from exist-

---

10 Vanberg, V., Buchanan, J. M. Interests and Theories in Constitutional Choice. Journal of Theoretical Politics, 1, (1989), 1.

11 Ibid.

12 Elster, J. Constitution-Making in Eastern Europe: Rebuilding the Boat in the Open Sea. Public Administration, 71, (1993), 1-2.
Elster, J. Forces and Mechanisms in the Constitution-Making Process, Duke Law Journal, 45, (1995), 2.
Elster, J. The Constitution-Making Process. In Pardo, J. C., Schneider, F. (eds) Current Issues in Public Choice. Cheltenham: Edward Elgar, (1996b).
Elster, J. Ways of Constitution-Making. In Hadenius, A. (ed.) Democracy's Victory and Crisis. Cambridge: Cambridge University Press, (1997).

13 Ibid.

14 See also Schnellenbach (2004), Geddes (1996), Frye (1997), Smithey and Ishiyama (2000), Ginsburg (2002), Romeu (2006), Benoit (2004), Benoit and Schiemann (2001), Benoit and Hayden (2008).
Notes: 3

15 Smithey and Ishiyama (2000), p. 171.

ing governing institutions or hope to be elected to the legislature or government in the post-constitutional phase, they can be expected to be reluctant to impose *substantive* constitutional limitations (in the form of balanced budget rules, for example) or strong *procedural* limitations (like supermajority requirements) on decisions concerning budgeting.

To the extent that the constituent body is made up of groupings clearly identified with particular parties, partisan interests are likely to play a role in constitution-making, alongside with institutional interests[16]. With regard to the role of partisan interests in the design of constitutional provisions concerning budgeting, one can conjecture that representatives of small parties are likely to argue for an active role of the legislature in budgeting, since that would preserve the possibility for parties outside the governing majority to provide input for the state budget during legislative proceedings. Members of large parties, conversely, may favor budgetary procedures that give the executive extensive powers and constrain the amendment rights of the legislature, given that this would give the government in office more leeway and discretion to pursue its budgetary policies. At the same time, even members of larger parties, expecting to be in opposition at least part of the time in the future, may want to preserve the rights of opposition parties to participate actively in shaping the state budget.

Alongside the preferences of the actors involved in constitution-making, the constraints they face can be assumed to play a role in influencing the content of the constitution. The literature on CPE has paid particular attention to two constraints: time limits and previous constitutions. Analogously to other provisions in the constitution, it can be conjectured that if the time-limit for designing the constitution is tight, there would be little space for constitutional innovation concerning provisions on budgeting and taxation and the framers would be inclined to draw extensively upon past institutional arrangements and provisions in the previous constitutions of the country[17]. Salzberger and Voigt[18] argue that especially in Central and Eastern Europe, the historical constitutions of these countries, which are often symbols of national pride or unity, can be expected to have amounted to an essential constraining force in constitution-making[19]. Thus, one can conjecture that provisions on budgeting are likely to have been taken over from the previous constitutions as well.

16 See Voigt, (2004), Mueller, (1996), ch. 21; Elster, (1993), Schnellenbach (2004), Benoit (2004), Benoit and Schie-mann (2001).

17 McFaul, M. Institutional Design, Uncertainty, and Path De-pendency during Transitions: Cases from Russia. Constitutional Political Economy, 10, 1, (1999), p. 30-31.

18 Salzberger, E. M., Voigt, S. On the Delegation of Powers: With Special Emphasis on Central and Eastern Europe. Constitutional Political Economy, 13, 1, (2002), p. 26.

19 See also Elster, Offe and Preuss (1998).

The conjectures that will be tested with the Estonian case are hence the following:

Conjecture 1: The members of the constituent body who are also members of the existing legislature will seek to grant the parliament a more important role in budget procedure compared with the roles of the government and the president or other state institutions.

Conjecture 2: If the president or the government or other institutions are involved in constitution-making process, they will seek to promote a greater role of their respective institutions in budget procedure.

Conjecture 3: The framers who come from existing governing institutions or expect to be elected to the legislature or government in the post-constitutional phase will be reluctant to adopt substantive constitutional limitations or strong procedural limitations for decisions concerning public finance.

Conjecture 4: Representatives of small parties will argue for an active role of the legislature in budgeting. Members of large parties will favor budgetary procedures that give the executive extensive powers and constrain the amendment rights of the legislature.

Conjecture 5: The constitutional provisions on budgeting will be taken over from the previous constitutions of the country.

3. The Making Of Constitutional Provisions Pertaining To Budgeting In The Estonian Constitutional Assembly

The Estonian Constitutional Assembly (CA) that prepared the 1992 Constitution of Estonia had 60 members: 30 from the Supreme Council and 30 from the Estonian Congress. Altogether, five draft constitutions were submitted to the Assembly. The main competing drafts were the draft of Jüri Raidla and his team (putting forth a more presidential system) and the draft of Jüri Adams (putting forth a more parliamentary system by mending the 1920 Constitution of Estonia with some more balanced provisions and incorporating some provisions from the 1938 Constitution). The CA chose the draft of Adams as the basis for further deliberations. During the subsequent sessions (taking place between September 1991 and April 1992), this draft was revised and the final version was approved in a referendum in June 1992. For more extensive discussions on constitution-making in Estonia[20].

Three of the draft Constitutions submitted to the Constitutional Assembly by 1 October 1991 included a separate chapter called 'Finance and the State Budget' and, on the whole, dedicating a separate chapter to the issues of public finance

20 See Taagepera (1993, 1994), Pettai (2001), and Raudla (2009, 2010a).

was seen as reasonable[21]. In the Constitution adopted in 1992, there are altogether 12 articles pertaining to the state budget. Five of them are brought out in the chapters on the *Riigikogu* (ch. 4), the Government (ch. 6), Legislation (ch. 7), and the rest in chapter 8, called 'Finance and State Budget'.

Article 65 sub-point 6 stipulates that the *Riigikogu* shall pass the state budget and approve the report on its implementation, sub-point 10 states that on the proposal of the Government the *Riigikogu* will decide on borrowing by the state and on the assumption of other proprietary obligations by the state. Article 87 states that the Government shall prepare the draft of the state budget and submit it to the *Riigikogu*, administer the implementation of the state budget and present a report on the implementation of the state budget to the *Riigikogu*. Article 104 stipulates that the State Budget Act and Acts pertaining to foreign and domestic borrowing and to proprietary obligations of the state can only be passed and amended by a majority of the membership of the *Riigikogu*. Article 106 establishes that, *inter alia*, issues regarding the budget, taxation and financial obligations of the state shall not be submitted to a referendum. Article 110 states that laws that establish state taxes and the state budget shall not be enacted, amended or repealed by a decree of the president.

In a separate chapter called 'Finance and the State Budget' (ch. 8), budget procedure is outlined in more detail. Article 115 states that the *Riigikogu* shall pass as a law the budget of all state revenue and expenditure for each year (section 1); the Government of the Republic shall submit a draft state budget to the *Riigikogu* not later than three months before the beginning of the budgetary year (section 2); and, on the proposal of the Government, the *Riigikogu* may pass a supplementary budget during the budgetary year (section 3). Article 116 requires that if a proposed amendment to the state budget or to its draft has the effect of decreasing estimated revenue or increasing expenditure or reallocating expenditure, the proponent of the amendment has to append financial calculations to the proposed amendment that demonstrate the sources of revenue necessary to cover the expenditure (section 1). Section 2 requires that the *Riigikogu* shall not eliminate or reduce expenditures in the state budget or in its draft that are prescribed by other laws. Article 117 states that the procedures for the drafting and passage of the state budget shall be provided by law. Article 118 stipulates that the state budget passed by the *Riigikogu* shall enter into force at the beginning of the budgetary year and if the *Riigikogu* does not pass the state budget by the beginning of the budgetary year, expenditure of up to one-twelfth of the expenditure of the preceding budgetary year may be made each month. Article 119 establishes that if the *Riigikogu* has not passed the state budget within two months after the beginning of the budgetary year, the president shall declare extraordinary elections to the *Riigikogu*.

21 Notes: 4.

In addition, in the chapter on the Auditor General, Article 135 provides that the Auditor General shall present to the *Riigikogu* an overview on the use and preservation of state assets during the preceding budgetary year at the same time as the report on the implementation of the state budget is debated in the *Riigikogu*. In the chapter on local government, Article 154 states that expenditure related to duties of the state imposed by law on a local government shall be funded from the state budget. Table 1 provides an overview of the sources of the different articles pertaining to budgeting and taxation in the 1992 Constitution of Estonia.

Table 1: Sources of fiscal constitutional provisions in the 1992 Constitution of Estonia[22]

Provision	Source
Article 65 sub-point 6	1920 Constitution, 1938 Constitution, complemented by Raidla's draft
Article 65 sub-point 10	1920 Constitution, 1938 Constitution
Article 87	1920 Constitution, complemented by Raidla's draft
Article 104	1920 Constitution, complemented by Raidla's draft
Article 106	1920 Constitution, 1938 Constitution
Article 110	1938 Constitution
Article 115 Section 1	1920 Constitution, 1938 Constitution
Article 115 Section 2	1938 Constitution
Article 115 Section 3	Raidla's draft
Article 116 Section 1	1938 Constitution, Adams' draft, modified by the Assembly
Article 116 Section 2	1938 Constitution
Article 117	Raidla's draft
Article 118	1938 Constitution
Article 119	Adams' draft, Raidla's draft
Article 135	1938 Constitution
Article 154	Raidla's draft
Article 157 Section 2	Adams' draft

22 Source: Author's comparisons

When comparing the final version of the Constitution with the drafts submitted to the Assembly, it is clear that most of the provisions pertaining to budgeting came from the draft submitted by Raidla's team (despite the fact that the draft of Adams was taken as the basis for the work of the Assembly). The only provisions that were in a similar form in the draft of Adams were Article 115 section 2, Article 116 section 1 and Article 119. When presenting his draft to the Assembly, Adams admitted that he was not a specialist in economics and that he had used Raidla's draft for coming up with the deadlines for the budget procedure[23]. Aaskivi[24] points out that when the third committee (in charge of the chapter on public finances) was working, it always had both drafts together on the table; on many occasions, the solutions and the wordings were compared and the best one used.

The articles in Raidla's draft, in turn, came for most part from the previous constitutions of Estonia. Article 65 sub-point 6 existed in a similar form in the 1920 Constitution and in the 1938 Constitution; only 'approving the report on the implementation of the state budget' was added by Raidla's team. Also, the 1920 Constitution said that the *Riigikogu* would approve the making of loans and the 1938 Constitution added that the Government would make a proposal for it. The addition 'other proprietary obligations by the state' was proposed by Raidla's team. The provision that the Government would submit the draft state budget was taken from the 1920 Constitution and Raidla's team added that the Government would also 'administer the implementation of the state budget and present a report on the implementation of the state budget to the *Riigikogu*'. Article 106 was taken from the 1920 Constitution; it was also in the 1938 Constitution. Article 110 was taken from the 1938 Constitution. The provisions pertaining to the budget procedure in chapter 8 of the Constitution have for most part been taken over from the 1938 Constitution. Article 115 section 1 was taken from the 1938 Constitution (a similar provision existed also in the 1920 Constitution); the word 'all' was added by Raidla's team. Section 2 of Article 115 was similar in the 1938 Constitution: it was stated that the Government has to submit the draft state budget 70 days before the beginning of the next budgetary year. Section 3 was added by Raidla's team. Article 116 section 1 is discussed at length below. Section 2 was taken from the 1938 Constitution. Article 117 was added by the team. Article 118 and 135 were taken from the 1938 Constitution. Articles 119 and 154 were added by Raidla's team.

For most part, the discussions on provisions concerning budgeting were confined to what was brought up in Raidla's draft. Thus, the initial drafts set the

23 Note: 5.

24 Aaskivi, Ü. Mälestused Põhiseaduse Assambleest. [Memories from the Constitutional Assembly], (2002), in Pärnaste, E. (ed.) Põhiseaduse Tulek. Kogumik [The Birth of the Constitution], Tallinn: Justiitsministeerium, Kirjastus SE&JS, (1997), p. 125.

frame for discussions and the Assembly did not add very much with regard to issues pertaining to the state budget. The only article that was 'new', in the sense that it was added to the Constitution during the debates of the Constitutional Assembly, was Article 104. This article was not included in the draft Constitution that was adopted in December 1991 but was included as a result of the public discussion. Many protest letters were concerned with the low quorum requirement for the *Riigikogu* (set at one-fourth in the draft of December 1991) and suggested higher quorum requirements, varying from one-third to nine-tenths[25]. Also, several letters were concerned with the fact that only a simple majority was required for passing legislation and the requirement of absolute majority was suggested. Given that the Assembly was reluctant to introduce a higher quorum requirement (in the final version of the Constitution, Article 70 stipulates that the quorum for the *Riigikogu* shall be provided by the *Riigikogu* Procedure Act), a 'compensation' for that was offered: an absolute majority requirement was set for a list of important acts, including the State Budget Act (the organic budget law) and acts pertaining to foreign and domestic borrowing and to proprietary obligations of the state.

Most of the budget process provisions that were included in the final version of the Constitution did not give rise to debates in the Constitutional Assembly. In fact, most of the debates regarding the state budget concerned articles that were included in the initial drafts but were eventually left out of the Constitution. The issue giving rise to most controversies in the Assembly was whether and how relations between the state budget and the legislation should be provided for in the Constitution, and, in particular, whether those introducing new legislation should bring out the implications it would have on the budget.

The 1938 Constitution, which was also submitted as one of the drafts for initial discussion, included an article stipulating that the draft acts of legislation (initiated by members of parliament) that bring about additional expenditures in the budget or reduce or abolish state revenues have to be accompanied with financial calculations, showing what the source of revenue for covering the costs would be. In addition, those drafts could only come to debate in the parliament after receiving consent from the Government. With regard to the state budget procedure itself, it was stipulated that the parliament could increase expenditures and introduce new revenues to the state budget only after receiving consent from the Government. The same provisions (together with the stipulation that calculations need to be appended if the act brings about *reallocation* of expenditure) were included in the draft Constitution submitted by the working group of Raidla. A similar provision (but without the requirement to receive the consent from the

25 Põhiseadus ja Põhiseaduse Assamblee (1997), p. 722.

Government) was also included in the draft Constitution submitted by Adams and it was worded as following: 'For all draft acts and amendments to the budget that increase the expenditures or decrease the revenues the initiators have to append financial calculations to the proposed amendment, which demonstrate the sources of revenue necessary to cover the expenditure.' The draft of Adams, however, did *not* require receiving prior consent from the Government when parliament wanted to increase expenditures or reduce revenues during the readings of the state budget in parliament.

The relation between legislation and state budget came up for the first time at the third session of the Assembly (on 27 September 1991), when the draft of Raidla's working group was discussed. Hallaste pointed out that the provision according to which all draft acts that have budgetary implications should be accompanied with cost calculations (and indications of which revenues would be used to cover these costs) and all such drafts would need to secure the consent of the Government, would reduce the role of the parliament in legislation to zero and turn the *Riigikogu* into a puppet parliament, since all drafts would increase or redistribute costs. Raidla answered that such a requirement is necessary, because the Government has a more comprehensive overview and more information of the factual situation of the budget than the parliament. Therefore, he emphasized, the draft acts that have budgetary implications should be under Government's control, so that only such decisions would be adopted that can be feasibly implemented[26].

Since Raidla's draft was not taken as the main basis of the Assembly's discussions, the subsequent discussions did not focus on Government's consent but on the need to append financial calculations to *all* legislative drafts. The main provision that was debated upon during subsequent sessions was whether initiators of draft legislation have to append the financial calculations when the act would have implications for the budget. This issue was discussed altogether at five different sessions of the Constitutional Assembly. The main proponent of this provision was the vice chairman of the third committee of the CA Kalju Koha (also the head of the Economic Affairs and Budget Committee of the Supreme Council) and the main opponent of it was the chairman of the third committee Illar Hallaste (from the Estonian Congress, but also a member of the Supreme Council). The suggestions made to the Assembly by the third committee reflected the internal developments in the committee: the recommendations varied depending on who had been present at the meetings of the committee and who had been chairing the meeting. For most part, although the chairman was against this provision, the committee as a whole supported the requirement.

26 Põhiseadus ja Põhiseaduse Assamblee (1997), p. 80.

At the sixth session of the CA, Hallaste pointed out that it would be better to abolish this requirement and suggested that the financial calculations should be done instead by the Government, when putting together the following year's budget. At the same session, Koha explained why the requirement of appending financial calculations should still cover *both* the amendments to the state budget and draft acts. He pointed out that during the preparation of the state budget, the spenders have to present their cost estimates and there is a discussion over how much money they receive. He argued that the same logic should apply to all acts that bring about costs: before the parliament passes an act, it should know how large the costs brought about by this act are[27].

The lengthiest discussion on that issue was held during the 20th session. First, Liia Hänni (delegate of the Supreme Council) pointed out that the redaction committee doubted the practicality of this requirement, since at the beginning of the legislative process it may be difficult to evaluate what the budgetary implications of the act are. She stated that such a restriction would amount to an unnecessary filter in the legislative process and make the legislative process too cumbersome, by bringing about lengthy discussions on whether the prognoses about the costs are correct. In his answer, Koha emphasised that the budget is the second most important document in the life of the state (after the Constitution), because it would concern all inhabitants of Estonia and form the basis for implementing domestic and foreign policies. He argued that the budget is a very precise document: it is submitted by the Government, behind whom there is a huge apparatus that makes the calculations of expenditures and revenues. He stated that the constraining condition is necessary in order to prevent populism in the passage of laws: 'When we change a tax law, some expenditure would remain outstanding. This cannot be done in a populist way and therefore it is necessary that those who initiate an act prove that the act does not change the structure of the expenditures and, if it does, where funds would be taken to cover the expenditures'[28].

After Koha's speech, Tiit Käbin (delegate of the Supreme Council) pointed out that although the principle of such a requirement is correct, it should not be stipulated in such an absolute way in the Constitution. He brought an example of declaring an emergency situation and how it would be absurd, if the resolution were to be accompanied with exact calculations. To that Koha answered, 'Even when an emergency situation is declared, we still have to take a decision on which expenditures have to be curtailed. ... We cannot make a decision that we have an emergency situation and simply spend'[29].

27 Põhiseadus ja Põhiseaduse Assamblee (1997), pp. 186, 190.

28 Põhiseadus ja Põhiseaduse Assamblee (1997), pp. 667-8.

29 Ibid., pp. 668-669.

Peet Kask (delegate from the Supreme Council) pointed out in his subsequent speech that, in reality, it would be difficult to verify whether the calculations satisfy the conditions set out in such constitutional provision. As he put it: 'Formally, these calculations can be required and a piece of paper, on which a number is written, is a calculation.' He argued that if a certain legislative draft entailed a danger of hurting the state purse, the Government or a respective minister would bring up this issue anyway. In his opinion, it should be the task of the minister to demonstrate that the draft act hurts the budget and to provide the appropriate calculations, instead of making the one initiating the act responsible for providing the calculations. He admitted that while the principle in itself is acceptable, it requires more detailed specification in further acts and it should not be such a categorical requirement for all initiators of draft acts[30].

In the following speech, Ülo Uluots (delegate from the Supreme Council) brought an example of discussions on supplementary budget in the Supreme Council:

> A rather innocent-looking proposal came from the assembly room, but, at a closer inspection, it turned out that this would instantly imbalance the budget. ... But because our reglement, which is for us a like a constitution, allowed it, the Supreme Council had to work for two additional days in order to balance the budget again.

He claimed that the requirement to append financial calculations is necessary for preventing such populist proposals. He suggested that perhaps after three or four years such an article could be abolished (after the organic budget law has been passed), but until then it should be provided for by the Constitution[31].

Kalle Jürgenson (delegate from the Estonian Congress) argued against this provision by pointing out that a draft act goes through several readings, during which the experts have time to review it and find out whether the act fits in the framework of the existing budget or not; if it does not, this question would be taken up by the budget committee. He added, 'I do not think that a legislator should be required to do calculations regarding fields that may be rather alien for him.' Valeri Kois (member of the Economic Affairs and Budget Committee of the Supreme Council) also argued against this provision,

> We often have situations in the Economic Affairs Committee in which the Committee wants to make changes to a Government project. Then the representatives of the Government start contravening and ask questions about money: where to take the money from and where to put it. Since the Government already has the whole information, they have a very strong weapon. If we put this provision into the Constitution, we cannot do anything with them[32].

---

30 Põhiseadus ja Põhiseaduse Assamblee (1997), p. 669.

31 Ibid., pp. 669-670.

32 Põhiseadus ja Põhiseaduse Assamblee (1997), p. 670.

Following this discussion at the 20th session, the Assembly voted against this provision (it received 21 votes against and 6 votes in favor) and it was left out of the Constitution. What remained was the requirement that if a proposed amendment to the *state budget* or to its *draft* has the effect of decreasing estimated revenue or increasing expenditure or reallocating expenditure, the proponent of the amendment has to append financial calculations to the proposed amendment, which demonstrate the sources of revenue necessary to cover the expenditure. For the rest of the legislation, this requirement did not apply anymore.

Most of the delegates who were involved in the discussions over this requirement were members of the Supreme Council[33] and, as could be seen, the arguments of the different delegates clearly reflected their own experiences with legislation and state budget in the Supreme Council and their conceptions of the balance of powers between parliament and cabinet in legislative activities[34]. The remarks made by Kois, for example, mirror very clearly the power fights going on between the Economic Affairs and Budget Committee of the Supreme Council and the Government, which contributed to his reluctance to give the Government an additional tool for exerting its power[35]. The speech by Uluots, on the other hand, mirrored the frustration with the messy proceedings of the state budget in the Supreme Council. Still, the arguments presented by Koha (who was the chairman of the Economic Affairs and Budget Committee of the Supreme Council) were more strongly driven by constitutional theories about how relations between the state budget and legislative activities should look like.

With regard to Article 119 (stating that if the *Riigikogu* fails to pass the state budget within two months after the beginning of the budgetary year, the president shall declare extraordinary elections to the *Riigikogu*), Adams, when introducing his draft, admitted that this was inspired by recent experiences in the Supreme Council. He noted that although most of the constitutions in Europe appear to assume that the legislature would not run into trouble with adopting the budget in due time, the Estonian practice had shown otherwise[36]. The redaction committee proposed at the 16th session (on 22 November 1991) to soften this provision and to leave it up to the president to decide whether extraordinary elections would be declared or not, instead of foreseeing it as a compulsory move. Although such a 'softer' provision was included in the draft Constitution at first, it was again changed back to the original formulation in February 1992 (as a result of the recommendations of the local expert team). The final version states that the 'president declares' – rather than 'may declare' – extraordinary elections, if the

33 Notes: 6.

34 Notes: 7.

35 Notes: 8.

36 Põhiseadus ja Põhiseaduse Assamblee (1997), p. 142.

Riigikogu has not passed the state budget within two months after the beginning of the budgetary year.

Another debate that touched upon the state budget concerned the issue of whether the establishment of certain parliamentary committees should be fixed by the Constitution. At the seventh session, Uluots pointed out that two committees should be brought out by the Constitution: the budget committee and the legal committee. He feared that, otherwise, political games may end in a situation where there is no budget committee or legal committee[37]. Ülle Aaskivi (a member of the third committee) stated that the third committee had discussed this issue and although the idea seemed attractive at first, then, as a result of further deliberations, the committee had voted against that provision. Juhan-Kristjan Talve stated that since the competences of the budget committee would not be specified in the Constitution, just mentioning the committee would remain rather abstract and hence unnecessary. Vello Saatpalu argued that the future parliament would be clever enough to establish such committees on its own initiative. Andres Tarand argued that it is difficult to foresee what kind of committees would be needed in 25 years, for example, and it should be the task of the *Riigikogu* to organize its work in a way it considers appropriate. Hando Runnel, however, emphasized, 'Some statesmen have said that the right of budget is the main right of the representative body.' He pointed to two tendencies that might threaten this right: 'one tendency that says that the budget should be put together by the government and another that says that parliament is useless in that process'. Therefore, in his view, fixing the budget committee in the Constitution was practical and not redundant[38]. The issue was voted upon and received 8 votes for and 25 against and was hence left out of the Constitution.

With regard to Article 115, the Constitutional Assembly decided amend the draft of Adams draft and use the formulation from Raidla's draft (entailing the word 'all'), resulting in the wording 'The *Riigikogu* shall pass as a law the budget of *all* state revenue and expenditure for each year.' At the 18th session, Hänni explained that the word 'all' was considered to be necessary, because the state should not have extra-budgetary revenues or expenditures[39]. It can be argued that adding the word 'all' added to Article 115 mirrored framers' dissatisfaction with the opacity of existing state budgets. For instance, the expenditure side of the 1990 state budget included only 14 items; 37% of the expenditures were planned for 'financing the national economy' without further details. Further, the transparency of the budget was reduced by complicated interrelations between the

37 Notes: 9.

38 Põhiseadus ja Põhiseaduse Assamblee (1997), pp. 266-7.

39 Ibid., p. 554.

budget of Estonia and the budget of the Soviet Union. As Tang and Nilgo[40] point out, because of the interrelations with the Soviet budget, it was almost impossible to know the total expenditures or revenues in any given year. The arguments in favor of requiring the initiators of draft acts to append budgetary calculations (indicating the sources for financing the act), repeatedly brought up by Koha, reflected his dissatisfaction, as a head of the Economic Affairs and Budget Committee of the Supreme Council (responsible for evaluating the budgetary implications of the proposed draft acts), with the proceedings of draft acts in the Supreme Council at the time.

Although in general the arguments presented by foreign experts played a significant role in work of the CA[41], the foreign experts paid only scant attention to constitutional provisions concerning budgeting and the deliberations on the provisions concerning the budget process did not refer to the opinions submitted by some foreign experts[42].

4. Testing The Conjectures

The Estonian case for most part corroborates Conjecture 1, implying that if the members of the assembly are members of an existing legislature, they will seek to grant the parliament a more important role in the budget process compared to the executive branch. The 1992 Constitution of Estonia does indeed attribute an important role to the legislature in the budgetary process. Although the Government submits the draft budget, the *Riigikogu* has the right to change the document before approving it. Further, the role of the president regarding the budget is explicitly limited: the Constitution stipulates that presidential decrees cannot concern the issues of the state budget or the State Budget Act. An important provision concerning the budgetary powers of the *Riigikogu vis-à-vis* the Government is Article 65 sub-point 10, stating that on the proposal of the Government, the *Riigikogu* will decide on borrowing by the state and on the assumption of other proprietary obligations by the state. This provision entails clear constraints on 'independent' borrowing by the executive and requires all loans to be approved by the legislature. As could be seen from the overview in section 3, most of the members of the Assembly were reluctant to constrain the *Riigikogu*'s role in making the budget and rejected the provision allowing Government's veto on amendments to the budget and on draft acts that have implications for the

40 Tang, P., Nilgo, H. Budget Reform. In Lugus, O., Hachey, G. A. (eds), Transforming the Estonian Economy. Tallinn: Estonian Academy of Sciences, Institute of Economics, (1995), p. 92.

41 See Raudla (2009, 2010a).

42 Notes: 10.

budget. Also, many members of the Assembly – apart from some notable exceptions – considered it problematic to restrict the legislators by requiring them to show budgetary implications and sources of financing for the draft acts that they initiate. Since many delegates of the CA had a legislative background or could see themselves as future members of the parliament, they were reluctant to endorse a requirement that would have clearly constrained the initiation of draft acts by members of the parliament. As could be seen from the discussions of the Constitutional Assembly, the members of the Assembly were afraid that this requirement would constrain legislative freedom and give the Government an informational advantage in discussing draft acts.

At the same time, however, the Estonian Constitution imposes some clear constraints on the legislature in the budget process, providing evidence against Conjecture 1. In particular, Article 116, requiring the amendments to the draft budget to be offsetting, and Article 119, implying high costs of failing to pass the budget for the legislature (extraordinary elections), can be considered to constrain the powers of the *Riigikogu vis-à-vis* the Government. As the discussion above shows, this puzzle can at least partly be explained by the heritage of the 1938 Constitution: it was an important source of inspiration for public finance provisions in Raidla's draft, which played a major role in shaping the public finance provisions in the final version of the Constitution. Since the 1938 Constitution gave very strong powers to the executive, the 'borrowed' provisions pertaining to budgeting carried some of the legislative constraints also over to the 1992 Constitution. At the same time, there were some framers who supported self-binding provisions of the legislature, inspired by constitutional theories of budgeting and experiences with legislative problems of budgeting.

The Estonian case also provides some evidence for Conjecture 2. The representative of the executive, Minister of Justice Jüri Raidla sought to attribute stronger budgetary powers (including veto power on legislative amendments to the budget and on draft acts with budgetary implications) to the Government in his draft. The need to secure Government's consent would have significantly increased the power of the Government at the expense of the *Riigikogu*. The 'theory' underlying the provision requiring the Government's consent in Raidla's draft was that the Government is better informed about the implications of the different acts for the budget and the Government's consent would secure the feasibility of the proposals. To what extent this preference was inspired by the team's fondness of the 1938 Constitution, to what extent by institutional self-interest, is difficult to ascertain, but the provisions in Raidla's draft were *perceived* to represent the institutional self-interests of the executive by the members of the Assembly and were rejected as such. At the same time, the draft constitution proposed by Raidla entailed clear limitations of the executive power *vis-à-vis* the legislature: Article

65 sub-point 10 prevents the Government from taking independent decisions on state loans; this can be regarded as evidence against Conjecture 2.

The Estonian case also offers evidence for Conjecture 3: the majority of the framers came from existing governing institutions or expected to be elected to the legislature or government in the post-constitutional phase and the resulting constitution does not entail substantive constitutional limitations (e. g., balanced budget rules) or strong procedural limitations (like supermajorities for acts concerning public finance). The constraints embodied in provisions on public finance in the 1992 Constitution of Estonia are only procedural (rather than substantive) and, as such, relatively moderate: an absolute majority is required for the organic budget law and framework laws pertaining to borrowing, but not for the organic tax law or specific tax laws. Provisions concerning substantive constraints were not proposed by any member of the Assembly. Although the German Basic Law has often been cited as one of the main examples for the Estonian Constitution, establishing a 'golden rule' in borrowing (as it exists in the German Basic Law) never came up in the discussions of the CA[43].

The testing of Conjecture 4 is somewhat complicated in the Estonian case, given that the party system was still in an embryonic phase of development. Since there was a large number of parties and party-like organizations, it would have been the interest of the representatives of all these parties to argue for a stronger role of the legislature in budgeting. There were, however, also framers who supported more stringent constraints on legislature in issues concerning public finance. Such divergence may also reflect the fact that at this stage of transition, the parties (or party-like organizations in Estonia, like in several other post-communist countries, were characterized by internal divisions and did not always act as unitary actors with regard to institutional choices[44].

Conjecture 5, suggesting that the provisions on budgeting are likely to be taken over from the constitutions that were in force in the pre-communist period was clearly confirmed in the Estonian case. Two-thirds of the provisions pertaining to budget in the 1992 Constitution were taken from the 1920 and 1938 Constitutions. The importance of the time constraint in constitution-making was also confirmed in the Estonian case. The very short deadline set by the Supreme Council meant that draft constitutions had to be submitted very fast and the Assembly had to work very swiftly. Given the time pressure, the structure presented in the winning draft Constitution changed very little and the additions that were made came chiefly from the main competing draft. Both of the draft constitutions that influenced the final outcome had a separate chapter on finance and the state budget.

43 Notes: 12.

44 See, for example, Ishiyama (1993, 1997).

In both drafts, the provisions in this chapter were rather brief. Bringing up new articles for that chapter would have been the task of the third committee. Given that besides the chapter on finance and the state budget, the third committee had to deal with very important chapters concerning the parliament, government and legislation, it had to prioritize. Naturally, the issues regarding the parliament and government received much more attention. Since the draft of Adams was very vague on the exact duties and powers of the legislature, government and the president[45], it was seen as needing extensive revision, which in turn left less time for discussing the chapter on finance and the state budget. Thus, a further conjecture for the theoretical framework could be: if there is a specific committee in the constitutional assembly, focusing on the issues of public finance, there would be a larger number of more specific provisions pertaining to budgeting.

5. Conclusion

In the theoretical approaches of constitutional political economy, institutional self-interests of the framers are conjectured to play a major role in drafting the constitutional provisions. It is expected that actors involved in constitution-making attempt to design such political institutions that would enable them to exercise power to the greatest possible extent in the post-constitutional phase. As the Estonian case study demonstrates, institutional self-interest did indeed play some role in the design of the provisions concerning the budget process: the legislature-oriented Constitutional Assembly attributed extensive budgetary powers to the *Riigikogu* and opposed a number of proposals that would have enhanced the power of the executive in the budget process or constrained the legislators, while the representatives of the executive sought to attribute more extensive powers to the executive in the budget process.

At the same time, as the discussions of the Constitutional Assembly indicate, there were a number of framers, who, despite being members of the existing legislature, advocated the imposition of somewhat stricter constraints on future legislators. Such proposals for self-binding were driven by constitutional theories concerning budgeting and the problems that the proponents of such constraints had experienced in legislative budgeting. Also, even in the draft constitution proposed by the member of the executive, there were a number of provisions that strongly constrained the powers of the executive in budgeting. Thus, the Estonian

45 Pettai, V. Estonia: Positive and Negative Institutional Engineering. In Zielonka, J. (ed.) Democratic Consolidation in Eastern Europe. Vol 1, Institutional Engineering. Oxford: Oxford University Press, (2001), p. 122.

case of constitution-making indicates that alongside institutional self-interests of the framers, the constitutional theories and lesson-drawing from previous experiences can play an important role in shaping the budget process provisions in the constitution. In other words, constitutional choices are also influenced by preferences derived from 'general interest' (or general welfare) and not only by 'self-interest' considerations, to use Benoit's[46] distinction of different kinds of preferences shaping institutional choices.

The literature of constitutional political economy has argued that previous constitutions would amount to important constraints in the making of a new constitution. The Estonian case indeed corroborates the importance of the inter-war constitutions in shaping the constitutional articles pertaining to budget procedure: two-thirds of the pertinent articles were taken over from the constitutions adopted in 1920 and 1938. Besides being a 'constraint', one can argue that the historical constitutions served as important models and major 'focal points' for the framers[47]. The symbolic importance of the inter-war constitutions – and the break they represented from the communist regime – contributed to the willingness of the members of the Assembly to transfer provisions from these documents into the new Constitution. It is especially noteworthy that despite the differences between the political regime created by 1938 constitution and the regime adopted in 1992, a number of provisions on budgeting were taken over from the 1938 constitution[48].

The discussions of the Constitutional Assembly also indicate that when the framers have already been involved in legislative and governmental budgeting, constitutional theories concerning budget process put forth during the discussions of the constituent body draw extensively on the preceding experiences, and the solutions offered will be oriented to existing problems. Indeed, one has to agree with Holmes and Lucky[49] in that constitutions tend to be retrospective documents rather than prospective ones, 'designed to solve the most pressing problems of the past, not the future'.

Acknowledgements

Research for this article was carried out with the financial support of the Mobilitas Grant of the European Social Fund (Grant no. MJD43). The author would like

46 Benoit, K. Models of Electoral System Change. Electoral Studies, 23, (2004), 3.

47 See Schelling (1960), cited in Elster (1992).

48 Notes: 11.

49 Holmes, S., Lucky, C. Storm over compatibility. East Euro-pean Constitutional Review, 3, 1, (1994), pp. 121-122.

to thank Jürgen Backhaus, Helge Peukert, Gerhard Wegner, Mark Peacock, Wolfgang Drechsler, and participants at the 6th Erfurt Conference of Fiscal Sociology (October 13, 2006) and at the 20th Consecutive Workshop in Law and Economics, Erfurt (April 4-5, 2007). This paper is also a revised version of chapter 3 of the author's doctoral dissertation *Constitution, Public Finance, and Transition* (Peter Lang, 2010).

Notes

1. For discussions on constitution-making in the European Union, see Magnette and Nicolaidis (2004), Crum (2004), and Bohman (2004), among others.
2. In particular, the factors behind the decisions to add fiscal constitutional provisions to an existing constitution have been considered. Most of the studies exploring this issue have focused on the U.S. states and, among the factors behind fiscal constitutional choices, the following ones have received particular attention: the antecedent fiscal balances, tax burden, debt level, fiscal preferences of the electorate and the existence of direct democracy mechanisms (see, *inter alia*, Helland 2000; Gordon 2008; Kousser, McCubbins, and Rozga 2008; Poterba 1996). The two studies that have analysed the making of fiscal constitutional provisions in the context of drafting an entirely new constitution are Tang (1991) for the Hong Kong Constitution, and Brennan and Pardo (1991) for the Spanish Constitution. These studies, however, have primarily a normative orientation and do not seek to test any specific hypotheses.
3. In his discussion over the factors driving institutional choices, Benoit (2004), for example, distinguishes between preferences derived from self-interest and from general interest. The self-interest derived preferences, in turn, can be driven by policy seeking, office seeking or personal gain considerations of the institutional designers. Although Benoit's (2004) discussion is concerned with choices made with regard to the electoral system, similar arguments can be made with regard to other institutional choices as well.
4. In presenting his draft Constitution, Ando Leps pointed out that although Raidla's draft had a separate chapter on the state budget, then, in his opinion, the 'whole budget buffoonery' would require a separate act and should not be outlined in the Constitution *(Põhiseadus ja Põhiseaduse Assamblee* 1997, p. 113). That, however, was not a prevailing position among the delegates.
5. Also, given that Adams had a very short time to prepare the draft and that his focus in drafting the proposal was on giving larger powers to the parliament

(in comparison with Raidla's draft), it is understandable that he could not focus on the aspects of public finance in greater detail.

6. Also, in the third committee that discussed the topic of finance and budget, six members out of seven were members of the Supreme Council (although some of them had been elected by the Estonian Congress).
7. On the whole, as can be seen from the verbatim records of the sessions of the Supreme Council, the members were becoming increasingly dissatisfied with the situation that the Council itself lacked capacity to draft laws and had to rely primarily on legislative drafts coming from the Government.
8. The Economic Affairs and Budget Committee was the committee in the Supreme Council that, *inter alia*, dealt with issues pertaining to budgeting and taxation. The Rules of Procedure of the Supreme Council required that all legislative proposals that have implications for the budget have to be commented upon by the Budget and Economic Committee. This committee was also responsible for looking through and coordinating the amendments to the draft budget in the legislative budget procedure.
9. This proposal might have been inspired by the fact that in the Supreme Council there was no *separate* committee on budgeting or taxation. The Economic Affairs and Budget Committee dealt, in addition to other issues of economic policy, with budgeting and taxation.
10. Provisions on budget procedures were commented on only by two foreign On the one hand, Ragnemalm (from Sweden) noted in his written opinion on the draft constitution that the requirement to append financial calculations to all draft acts is unrealistic (Archival document no. RA-23-24-1-5, p. 123). On the other hand, Carcassonne (from France) remarked that the provisions in the draft constitution would not protect public finances sufficiently. He argued that calculations appended to legal acts are usually unimpressive and the indications of the sources of finance may turn out to be economically absurd. He suggested that in order to avoid demagogy in difficult situations, it would be better to leave only the Government the right to increase expenditures or even to decrease expenditures, like it is stipulated in the constitutions of France and Germany. (Archival document no. RA-23-24-1-5, p. 150)
11. Another possible explanation for this omission is that the concept of balanced budget prevailing at the time was a merely a 'formal' notion. The State Budget Act (passed in 1989) required the Government to submit a balanced budget to the parliament, but the list of budget revenues also included loans, which meant that the budget would always be 'balanced'. An alternative explanation is that since the constitution-making took place amidst economic crisis, introducing a balanced budget requirement (in its real sense), a golden

rule or a debt limit would have been perceived as unwanted constraints in a tight fiscal situation.

12. As discussed in Raudla (2010a,b), such provision-copying continued with the organic budget law as well. In the State Budget Act, adopted in 1993, a number of provisions had been copied from the framework law for budgeting, enacted in 1938.

References

Aaskivi, Ü. Mälestused Põhiseaduse Assambleest. [Memories from the Constitutional Assembly], (2002), in Pärnaste, E. (ed.) Põhiseaduse Tulek. Kogumik [The Birth of the Constitution], Tallinn: Justiitsministeerium, Kirjastus SE&JS, (1997).

Archival document no. RA-23-24-1-5. Estonian State Archive. Eesti Vabariigi Põhiseaduslikule Assambleele esitatud ekspertide arvamused. [The opinions of experts submitted to the Constitutional Assembly of the Republic of Estonia].

Benoit, K. Models of Electoral System Change. Electoral Studies, 23, 3, (2004), pp. 363-389.

Benoit, K., Hayden, J. Institutional Change and Persistence: The Origins and Evolution of Poland's Electoral System 1989-2001. The Journal of Politics, 66, 2, (2008), pp. 396-427.

Benoit, K., Schiemann, J. W. Institutional Choice in New Democracies: Bargaining Over Hungary's 1989 Electoral Law. Journal of Theoretical Politics, 13, 2, (2001), pp. 153-182.

Bohman, J. Constitution Making and Democratic Innovation. European Journal of Political Theory, 3, 3, (2004), pp. 315-337.

Brennan, G., Pardo, J. C. A Reading of the Spanish Constitution (1978). Constitutional Political Economy, 2, 1, (1991), pp. 53-79.

Buchanan, J. M. The Domain of Constitutional Economics. Constitutional Political Economy, 1, 1, (1990), pp. 3-20.

Buchanan, J. M. Post-Socialist Political Economy. Selected Essays. Cheltenham: Edward Elgar, (1997).

Crum, B. Politics and Power in the European Convention. Politics, 24, 1, (2004), pp. 1-11.

Elster, J. Making Sense of Constitution-Making. East European Constitutional Review, 1, 1, (1992), pp. 15-17.

Elster, J. Constitution-Making in Eastern Europe: Rebuilding the Boat in the Open Sea. Public Administration, 71, 1-2, (1993), pp. 169-217.

Elster, J. Forces and Mechanisms in the Constitution-Making Process. Duke Law Journal, 45, 2, (1995), pp. 354-396.

Elster, J. The Role of Institutional Interest in East European Constitution-Making. East European Constitutional Review, 5, 1, (1996a), pp. 63-65.

Elster, J. The Constitution-Making Process. In Pardo, J. C., Schneider, F. (eds) Current Issues in Public Choice. Cheltenham: Edward Elgar, (1996b).

Elster, J. Ways of Constitution-Making. In Hadenius, A. (ed.) Democracy's Victory and Crisis. Cambridge: Cambridge University Press, (1997).

Elster, J., Offe, C., Preuss, U. K. Institutional Design in Post-communist Societies: Rebuilding the Ship at Sea. Cambridge: Cambridge University Press, (1998).

Fabrizio, S., Mody, A. Can Budget Institutions Counteract Political Indiscipline? Economic Policy, 21, (2006), pp. 689-739.

Frye, T. A Politics of Institutional Choice: Post-Communist Presidencies. Comparative Political Studies, 30, 5, (1997), pp. 523-552.

Geddes, B. Initiation of New Democratic Institutions in Eastern Europe and Latin America. In Lijphart, A., Waisman, C. (eds) Institutional Design in New Democracies: Eastern Europe and Latin America. Boulder: Westview Press, (1996), pp. 15-41

Ginsburg, T. Economic Analysis and the Design of Constitutional Courts. Theoretical Inquiries in Law, 3, 1, (2002), pp. 49-86.

Gleich, H. (2002) *The Evolution of Budget Institutions in Central and Eastern European Countries* (Bonn, University of Bonn).

Gordon, T. M. The Calculus of Constraint: A Critical Review of State Fiscal Institutions. In Garrett, E., Graddy, E. A., Jackson, H. E. (eds) Fiscal Challenges: An Interdisciplinary Approach to Budget Policy. Cambridge: Cambridge University Press, (2008), pp. 271-289.

Hallerberg, M. Domestic Budgets in a United Europe: Fiscal Governance from the End of Bretton Woods to EMU. Ithaca: Cornell University Press, (2004).

Hallerberg, M., von Hagen, J. Electoral Institutions, Cabinet Negotiations, and Budget Deficits in the European Union. In Poterba, J. M., von Hagen, J. (eds) Fiscal Institutions and Fiscal Performance. Chicago: University of Chicago Press, (1999), pp. 209-232.

Hallerberg, M., Strauch, R., von Hagen, J. The Design of Fiscal Rules and Forms of Governance in European Union Countries. European Journal of Political Economy, 23, 2, (2007), pp. 338-359.

Hallerberg, M., Strauch, R., von Hagen, J. Fiscal Governance: Evidence from Europe. Cambridge: Cambridge University Press, (2009).

Helland, L. Fiscal Constitutions, Fiscal preferences, Information and Deficits: An Evaluation of 13 West-European Countries 1978-1995. In Strauch, R., von

Hagen, J. (eds) Institutions, Politics and Fiscal Policy. Dordrecht: Kluwer Academic Publishers, (2000), pp. 107-138.

Holmes, S., Lucky, C. Storm over compatibility. East European Constitutional Review, 3, 1, (1994), pp. 120-122.

Ishiyama, J. T. Founding Elections and the Development of Transitional Parties: The Cases of Estonia and Latvia, 1990-1992. Communist and Post-Communist Studies 26, (1993), pp. 277-299.

Ishiyama, J. T. Transitional Electoral Systems in Post-Communist Eastern Europe. Political Science Quarterly, 112, 1, (1997), pp. 95-115.

Kousser, T., McCubbins, M. D., Rozga, K. When Does the Ballot Box Limit the Budget: Politics and Spending Limits in California, Colorado, Utah, and Washington. In Garrett, E., Graddy, E. A., Jackson, H. E. (eds) Fiscal Challenges: An Interdisciplinary Approach to Budget Policy. Cambridge: Cambridge University Press, (2008), pp. 290-319.

Magnette, P., Nicolaidis, K. The European Convention: Bargaining in the Shadow of Rhetoric. West European Politics, 27, 3, (2004), pp. 381-404.

McFaul, M. Institutional Design, Uncertainty, and Path Dependency during Transitions: Cases from Russia. Constitutional Political Economy, 10, 1, (1999), pp. 27-52.

Mulas-Granados, C., Onrubia, J., Salinas-Jimenez, J. Do Budget Institutions Matter? Fiscal Consolidations in the New EU Member States. Eastern European Economics, 47, 1, (2009), pp. 60-91.

Pettai, V. Estonia: Positive and Negative Institutional Engineering. In Zielonka, J. (ed.) Democratic Consolidation in Eastern Europe. Vol 1, Institutional Engineering. Oxford, Oxford University Press, (2001), pp. 111-138.

Põhiseadus ja Põhiseaduse Assamblee. Koguteos. [The Constitution and the Constitutional Assembly. Anthology]. Tallinn: Juura, Õigusteabe Aktsiaselts, (1997).

Poterba, J. M. Budget Institutions and Fiscal Policy in the U.S. States. The American Economic Review, 86, 2, (1996), pp. 395-400.

Raudla, R. Constitution, Public Finance, and Transition: Theoretical Developments in Constitutional Public Finance and the Case of Estonia. Frankfurt am Main: Peter Lang, (2010a).

Raudla, R. Evolution of Budgetary Institutions in Estonia: A Path Full of Puzzles? Governance, 23, 3, (2010b), pp. 463-484.

Raudla, R. Explaining Constitution-Makers Preferences: The Cases of Estonia and the United States. Constitutional Political Economy, 21, 3, (2010c), pp. 249-269.

Romeu, F. R. The Establishment of Constitutional Courts: A Study of 128 Democratic Constitutions. Review of Law and Economics, 2, 1, (2006), pp. 103-135.

Salzberger, E. M., Voigt, S. On the Delegation of Powers: With Special Emphasis on Central and Eastern Europe. Constitutional Political Economy, 13, 1, (2002), pp. 25-52.
Schelling, T. The Strategy of Conflict. Cambridge: Harvard University Press, (1960).
Schnellenbach, J. The Evolution of a Fiscal Constitution When Individuals are Theoretically Uncertain. European Journal of Law and Economics, 17, 1, (2004), pp. 97-115.
Taagepera, R. Estonia: Return to Independence. Boulder: Westview Press, (1993).
Taagepera, R. Estonia's Constitutional Assembly, 1991-1992. Journal of Baltic Studies, 25, 3, (1994), pp. 211-232.
Tang, P., Nilgo, H. Budget Reform. In Lugus, O., Hachey, G. A. (eds) Transforming the Estonian Economy. Tallinn: Estonian Academy of Sciences, Institute of Economics, (1995), pp. 92-111.
Tang, S. Fiscal Constitution, Income Distribution and the Basic Law of Hong Kong. Economy and Society, 20, 3, (1991), pp. 283-305.
Vanberg, V., Buchanan, J. M. Interests and Theories in Constitutional Choice. Journal of Theoretical Politics, 1, 1, (1989), pp. 49-63.
Voigt, S. Positive Constitutional Economics: A Survey. Public Choice, 90, 1-4, (1997), pp. 11-53.
Voigt, S. Explaining Constitutional Change. A Positive Economics Approach. Cheltenham: Edward Elgar, (1997).
Voigt, S., Wagener, H-J. Introduction. In Voigt. S., Wagener, H-J. (eds) Constitutions, Markets and Law. Recent Experiences in Transition Economies. Cheltenham: Edward Elgar, (2002), pp. xiii–xxi.
Von Hagen, J., Harden, I. Budget Processes and Commitment to Fiscal Discipline. European Economic Review, 39, 3-4, (1995), pp. 771-779.
Zapal, J., Schneider, O. What Are Their Words Worth? The Political Plans and Economic Pains of Fiscal Consolidations in the New EU Member States. Eastern European Economics, 44, 5, (2006), pp. 6-37.

Europe's Fiscal Constitution

Auke. R. Leen

1. Introduction

In a public consultation paper, the European Union (EU) asks its citizens and Member States to come up with ideas how to reform the EU Budget. The key research challenge of our paper – to answer the consultation paper – is to give a novel angle from the point of fiscal sociology and Austrian economics towards the selection among the alternative budgetary powers made available to the EU.

We do suggest guidelines for exclusion and inclusion of provisions in the EU-Budget that are not prizes captured in negotiations, often partisan struggles, between the Member States. The focus is on the normative evaluation of quasi-permanent budgetary institutions and their tasks. We do also suggest that such a constitutional framework creates trust and facilitates a robust democratic debate. The emphasis is not, as is usually the case based on a benevolent EU, to enhance economic efficiency (making the EU "work better") and / or to increase the equity of budget rules. We will put to test a different approach: an analysis that we define by the limits it places on the powers of Brussels, an egoistic despot, to "tax and spend". Though the model of a budget-maximizing Leviathan-like EU bureaucracy, a discretionary agency, may seem extreme, the norms laid down may possible prove acceptable as embodying a minimax strategy: to ensure that the best remains a possibility by guarding against the worst.

2. Background And Approach To The Problem

Since the rejection of the draft Constitutional Treaty in 2005 by French and Dutch voters, a revision of the budgetary powers of the EU is a priority. If, the "no" of the French and Dutch citizens was a revolution, the truth counts that at least halve of all historic revolutions were fiscal revolutions[1]. Hence the 2007 consultation call by the Commission is, in the words of Dalia Grybauskaite (European Commissioner for Financial Programming and Budget), a "unique, may be once-in-a-lifetime opportunity", to discuss a fundamental review of the EU Budget[2].

1 Nef, R., Lob des Non-Zentralismus, Sankt Augustin: Academia Verlag, (2002).

2 European Commission: Communication from the Commission. Reforming the Budget, Changing Europe. A public Consultation Paper in view of the 2008/2009 budget re-view,

In 2011 the Commission will come up with a final reform proposal for the next Financial Framework (2014 and onwards). In the mean time the Commission asks Europeans and the Member States for their completely "open and no taboo" opinion on the reform of the EU budget: a wide-ranging review of all aspects of EU spending and resources.

The road suggested in the Commission's consultation paper, just as the approach after the rejection of the draft Constitutional Treaty, can be a very toilsome process inside the realm of partisan (Member States') advocacy. Solidarity, for instance, has to be bought with financial pet projects for individual Member States. Or, alternatively, budget reform is discussed by the direct application of abstract ethical norms in a vacuous (without a model of governmental-political behavior) institutional setting.

Moreover, fiscal decision-making is often based on the rule that policies have to pose as little resistance as possible for the majority that must approve of them. The feeling, often, dominates that someone else pays[3]. In the four years before 2005, no member of the US congress has on total voted for a reduction in government outlays, though the rhetoric to speak of fiscal discipline was on the rise[4]. A situation, probably, that is not much different for Europe. Besides, in general, it is most likely that possible rates of government spending will always be higher than the revenue from the taxes legislatures are willing to impose on their constituents[5]. This since decisions on the spending side of the budget are made independently of the decisions on the taxing side. Ever growing government tasks and a growing government budget and corresponding taxation are the result.

The paper shifts the grounds for the debate on the reform of the EU budget towards an authentic fundamental review: it focuses on the choices among quasi-permanent constraints (within which alternatives should the EU's budgetary powers be exercised) and not, as is usually the case[6], on choices within given constraints. The paper adopts a rule-based perspective on the EU Budget: we do choose budgetary rules of which we know that such institutions, once selected, will remain in being over an indeterminately long sequence of budgetary periods. We should take literally Grybauskaite remark about an "once-in-a-lifetime possi-

---

Brussels, 12.9.2007, SEC (2007) 1188 final.

3 Spicer, M. W. On Friedrich Hayek and Taxation: Rationality, Rules, and Majority Rule. National Tax Journal, Vol. 48, No. 1, (1995).

4 Dircksen, J. Vote Tally Report 108-2. *NTUF Policy Paper* 156, (2005), www.ntu.org.

5 See Buchanan (1980, 2000).

6 ECB, The EU budget: How much scope for Institutional Reform? European Central Bank, Occasional Paper Series, no. 27, April (2005).
ECFIN workshop, The role of fiscal rules and institutions in shaping budgetary outcomes: proceedings from the ECFIN workshop. Economic Papers, nr. 275, (2007).

bility". The rules are quasi-permanent and long-lived. Members States are unable to predict with precision what their position will be at any particular moment in the future. In particular, they are presumed to be unable to identify their position (a veil of ignorance) either as payer or as spending beneficiary in a sequence of separate budgetary periods. History shows that these kinds of debate about a framework for political action, not an instrument thereof, have been possible and fruitful[7].

Our research is a normative activity. It is not discussed in traditional constitutional law, which mostly looks at existing positive law[8]. In public finance, however, the whole problem seems to have no place either. It is typical something that is often considered to be too vague; it is to be described as fiscal sociology[9]. Primarily, the method used to discuss constitutional limitations cannot be empirical. There is a clear difference between our empirical knowledge of decision-making within a given framework and discussions about the framework itself. To discuss the latter is like speculation. In that realm, hypotheses are only conceptually refutable.

3. Fiscal Sociology And Austrian Economics

The EU fiscal system has three segments. The first segment is the EU budget. The second one is the harmonization of the national tax systems. The third is the coordination of the budget policies of the Member States through EU's fiscal rules, e. g., the Pact on Stability and Growth and the Maastricht convergence criteria. This paper concentrates on the first segment. Cultural, political (3.1), and economic (3.2) reasons make it difficult to have fiscal decision-making re the EU budget in the sense of an all-out democratic process on a broad spectrum of EU tasks.

---

7 Buchanan, J. M., Choice, Contract, and Constitutions. Indiana-polis: Liberty Fund, (2001). Elster, J. Arguing and Bargaining in the Federal Convention and the Assemblée Constituante. Center for the Study of Constitutionalism in Eastern Europe, Working Paper no. 4, August, (1991).

8 Kinneging, A. De Europese Grondwet, het staatsrecht en de constitutionele theorie. In: Cliteur, P., Franken, H., Voermans, W., eds. Naar een Europese Grondwet, Den Haag: Boom, (2004), p. 130.

9 Backhaus, J. Fiscal Sociology: What for? American Journal of Economics and Sociology, Jan. (2002).
Backhaus, J. Fiscal Sociology: Guest editor's introduction. Journal of Economic Bahavior & Organization, Vol. 59 (2006).

Fiscal policy and democracy are hard to reconcile. It is an almost impossible combination to ask for. To understand and solve this problem we do need the approach of fiscal sociology: a fusion of economics and sociology. It is (a change of) socio-political rules we are looking at. How can social order be established and preserved? A fiscal constitution must accommodate not only Member States with different constitutions and different economic and political systems, but also with different histories, cultures and socio-political visions[10]. We can identify the burden of taxation as the focus of research in fiscal sociology. Fiscal sociology is a science that became necessary after the twentieth century separation of economics, sociology, politics and law, with the resulting lacunae. Large comprehensive studies, which once characterized the activities of leading social scientists, became de-emphasized.

In the middle of the previous century, Friedrich Hayek[11] wrote that democracy can only under very restricted conditions be transposed to a supra-national organization. A little later, his American counter-ego Milton Friedman said the same. If you apply both ideas to the situation in Europe, we have to conclude that the EU is not only missing the necessary homogeneity to form clear policy goals in a democratic way, but it misses as well the stimuli not to waste money.

Why is it so hard to expect concrete policy goals and fiscal constraint from the European parliament – the most democratic institution of the EU? Of course, very general objectives (e. g., prosperity for everyone) will be easy to agree on. After that, however, it becomes difficult. Concrete objectives will be difficult to formulate. The countries of the EU differ too much in culture, history and economic development. Every choice supposes a balancing of the pros and cons (cp. Hayek[12]. The recently weakened Services Directive of 2006, e. g., is supposed to show the social face of the EU. No worker from Eastern Europe, however, will be glad with the "social protection" of the revised directive or the "social clause" in the new Treaty of Lisbon (2007). Within a relatively homogeneous country like the Netherlands, however, the original directive would be no problem. Every plumber from the north of the Netherlands is welcome in the south. Likewise, the Netherlands, e. g., is supporting with a low price of gas a national pride: the

---

10 Backhaus, J. Fiscal Sociology: Guest editor's introduction. Journal of Economic Bahavior & Organization, Vol. 59 (2006).

11 Hayek, F. A. Freedom and the Economic System, Public Policy Pamphlet, No. 29, Chicago: The University of Chicago Press, (1939).
Hayek, F. A. The Economic Conditions of Interstate Federalism. In: Individualism and Economic Order, London: Routledge and Kegan Paul, (1949), pp. 255-272.

12 See Hayek (1944), (1986), p. 168.

agriculture of vegetables in greenhouses in the west of the country. However, the very same solidarity for a, e. g., Spanish national pride is something completely different. The same goes for the other way around.

Hence, if a parliament cannot give and agree on policy objectives, the European Commission remains de facto the administration. Often below the guise that it concerns only a technical affair. That is hard to maintain. Over a change in policy, no matter how technically it does look like, the parliament belongs to decide. Moreover, also the Commission has to do with the various wishes of the Member States that do make up the members of the Commission.

Besides that, large countries will never transfer their economic power to Brussels. The course of events re the reformation of the Pact on Stability and Growth is characteristic thereof. It is naïve to expect the same reforms if a few small countries had broken the rules. Therefore, we can expect that, e. g., the new rule on decision-making by the way of a qualified majority, to be introduced in 2014, based on the double majority of Member States and people, 55 % of the Member States representing at least 65 % of the Union's population, is violated if it should be of a disadvantage to large countries.

The EU, also, has hardly any incentives not to waste money. The best guarantee not to waste money is that the same person both owns and does spend the money[13]. For then we can expect that you loan on the penny and sees to it that you do get value for your money. Members of parliaments or commission members, however, do spend others men's money, on behave of, often again, other men. That is almost a guarantee for ineffective and inefficient spending. Of members of a local parliament we can expect some restraint in spending the taxpayers' money of their own citizens. What to think, however, of an Eastern-European member of the EU-parliament who does spend the money of West-European taxpayers at projects in Eastern Europe? To satisfy the members of parliament of Western-European countries pork-barrel legislation will rise. Not much different as is presently the case in the US where the support of congressional representatives has to be bought with financial presents (pet projects) for their local constituents. In short, we will see more signs along the roads that state, "This project has been realized with the help of the EU". A project, if the Member State had to decide and pay for itself, it would not have spent the money on.

In sum, cultural and political differences make it difficult to have a fiscal constitution in the sense of an all-out democratic process in which majorities do decide. We can transpose democracy to a supra-national organization only under

13 Friedman, M. and R. Free to Choose. Harmondsworth: Penguin Books, [1979], (1981), p. 146.

very restricted conditions[14]. It is, however, the popular thing to do[15]. The solidarity and trust that is necessary for concrete policies within the EU is very tenuous. Even within one country if things do differ like language (Belgium), religion (North-Ireland) or economic development (North and South-Italy) solidarity is hard to find. All of these situations do characterize the situation within the European parliament. Policies, no matter how good the intentions behind them, which are possible for each of the countries separately, are no option for the EU as a whole. Europe lacks the necessary homogeneity; priorities cannot be set. To transfer authority and hence policy to Brussels has its limits. Hence, of an (in the future) democratically chosen Chinese parliament with its approximately 3000 members we can expect more priority setting then by the 751 members of the European parliament. China with its fifty minorities but overwhelming majority of almost 95 per cent Han Chinese is more a unity then the 27 members of EU are.

3.2 Economic Differences

Why does the new Treaty of Lisbon (2007) set out individual freedom as one of the core values of the EU? It is a good in itself. We can only make real choices based on individual freedom. Freedom is also essential to develop as a moral being. Man is first and for all a spiritual being. The choices, e. g., we make to help other people, have to be taken in freedom.

Individual freedom is also a necessity for our economic order: the market economy. Not only, quite visible, the climate and the physical characteristics of the Member States do differ, but, less visible, though of more importance, also men in their preferences and knowledge do differ. A market economy, as has been emphasized by the Austrian-born economist Hayek, is to make optimal use of those differences in knowledge[16]. Hence, the problem in a market economy is not to give the central authorities, be it Brussels or a local government, all the extra knowledge it needs to pursue policy. The problem is to give each individual all the extra knowledge he needs, mostly in the form of price (profit) signals, so he can decide for himself how to pursue his own goals. In this way, society does make

14 Gillingham, J. European Integration 1959-2003. Superstate or New Market Economy. Cambridge: Cambridge University Press, (2003).
Gillingham, J. Design for a New Europe. Cambridge: Cambridge University Press, (2006).

15 Leonard, M. Democracy in Europe. How the EU can survive in an age of referendum. Essays Centre for European Reform, (March 2006).
Verhofstadt, G. De Verenigde Staten van Europa, Manifest voor een nieuw Europa. Antwerpen: Houtekiet, (2005).

16 Hayek, F. A. Law, Legislation and Liberty. London: Routledge & Kegan Paul, (1982), Volume 1.

use of often-unique knowledge of local circumstances and preferences that do differ in time. Knowledge that is difficult to centralize. An idea as valid for individuals as for countries and has found its expression in the idea of subsidiarity[17].

Hayek describes the market process as one of learning by discovery. We are looking at the core of Austrian economics. In Austrian economics knowledge dissemination and the discovery thereof are of central importance. Endogenous change in the ends-means relationship – says Israel Kirzner, building his theory as Hayek did – is possible with the entrepreneurial element in each individual market participant: alertness. Alertness is "the propensity [...] toward fresh goals and the discovery of hitherto unknown resources"[18]. A disequilibrium situation points to market ignorance. From it emerge profitable opportunities, alertness exploits. Alertness gives a more realistic image of human action (and hence real choice) and makes possible the description of the market as a unified discovery process. "[The] 'alertness' view of the entrepreneurial role rejects the thesis that if we attribute genuine novelty to the entrepreneur, we must necessarily treat entrepreneurially generated market events as not related to earlier market events in any systematic way. The genuine novelty [...] attribute[d] to the entrepreneur consists in his spontaneous discovery of the opportunities marked out by earlier market conditions (or by future market conditions as they would be in the absence of his own actions)" [...] "[These] entrepreneurial discoveries are the steps through which any possible tendency toward market equilibrium must proceed"[19].

A market economy makes room for human freedom and uses existing knowledge the best[20]. Hence we should make decisions re rules on an as decentralized level as possible. The economic way to solve problems when sovereignty sharing by the way of a complete harmonizing of all rules is impossible is to apply the concept of mutually recognition of differences[21]. In a market exchange, strong differences of opinion are taken care of in a peaceful way. Subsidiarity, an orga-

---

17 Backhaus, J. Das Subsidiäritatsprinzip als Baustein einer entstehender Europäischen Verfassung. (2001).

18 Kirzner, I. M. Competition and Entrepreneurship, Chicago: University of Chicago, Press, (1973), p. 34.

19 Kirzner, I. M. Discovery and the Capitalist Process. Chicago: University of Chicago Press, (1985), pp. 11-12.

20 Hayek, F. A. Law, Legislation and Liberty. London: Rout-ledge & Kegan Paul, (1982), Volume 1.
Buchanan, J. M. Liberty, Market and State. Brighton: Wheatsheaf Books, (1986).

21 Backhaus, J. Das Subsidiäritatsprinzip als Baustein einer entstehender Europäischen Verfassung, (2001), p. 9.

nizing and enforceable principle is congruent with the market[22]. In a sense, competition between local authorities or Member States, where there is freedom of movement, provides experimentation with alternative models that is conducive to growth. It resembles the market economy best[23]. Subsidiarity has remained a part of the new (reformed) European Treaty of Lisbon. It states that we should only shift powers to Brussels when Member States themselves cannot achieve the same results[24]. From this principle, which we can also describe as economic federalism[25], flows the responsibility of the Member States to provide the legal conditions under which the citizens can accumulate wealth in order to satisfy their needs themselves.

In sum, in the last centuries the goal of a market economy in which everyone aims at his own interests and uses his own knowledge has been a basic economic value in Europe. For James Buchanan this is all a part of the superiority of the Western value system[26]. In the 19e century John Stuart Mill already wrote, "it is now recognized, though not till after a long struggle, that both the cheapness and the good quality of commodities are most effectively provided for by leaving the producers and sellers perfectly free, under the sole check of equal freedom to the buyers for supplying themselves elsewhere"[27]. John Maynard Keynes spoke in similar words a century later, "The advantage to efficiency of the decentralization of decisions and individual responsibility is even greater, perhaps, than the nineteenth century supposed; and the reaction against the appeal to self-interest may have gone too far"[28].

4. Constititutional Political Economy

In constitutional economics, we define the rules of the socio-economic-political game. We have to make two sorts of constitutional decisions. First, we must choose from possible constitutional (so-called higher law) rules. Behind a veil of ignorance, countries and people choose electoral and non-electoral constitutional

22 Ibid.
Apolte, T. Die eigentümliche Diskussion um Zentralisierung und Dezentralisierung in der Europapolitik. Perspektiven der Wirtschaftspolitik, 5(3), (2004), pp. 271-291.

23 Hayek, F. A. The Constitution of Liberty. London: Routledge, (1960), p. 230.

24 See: Treaty 2004, Title III, Article I-11, cp. Treaty, 2007.

25 Inman, R. P., Rubinfeld, R. P. Rethinking Federalism. The Journal of Economic Perspectives, Vol. 11, No. 4. (Autumn, 1997).

26 Buchanan, J. M. Restoring the Spirit of Classical Liberalism. Notes from FEE, (July 2005), p. 1.

27 Mill, J. S. On Liberty. Harmondsworth: Penguin Books, [1859], (1974), p. 164.

28 Keynes, J. M. The General Theory or Employment, Interest, and Money. New York: Harcourt, [1937], (1964).

rules. No one knows his future position. (Of all the Member States, Germany broke the rules of Pact on Stability and Growth. Though beforehand, Germany was a most unlikely candidate.) It is at this initial constitutional decision stage, where we choose the basic fiscal arrangements, that citizens not only can really control the state, but widespread public agreement is possible[29]. This since the prospect for general agreement changes dramatically if we allow for some introduction of ignorance and / or uncertainty into the Member States' calculus. The prospects of agreement relate directly to the predicted length of life of the tax reform. Then we will tend to opt for rules that are "fair". Hence the measures to be discussed below are meant not just for the upcoming, 2013, sixth financial framework but "forever". Besides, it is always easier to secure agreement on a set of rules than to secure agreement for example on who is our favorite player. The tone of the discussions is theoretical and argumentative. Gains for all members are real.

Second, we have to state rules for day-to-day policies within the framework. Making decisions by majority ensures the workability of the political process. The tone of the discussions is one of weighting up interests and bargaining[30]. Ordinary politics, post constitutional choice, tends to be conflictual. The reformed EU treaty, however, gives unanimous consent a smaller role, without making the distinction between the just-mentioned two sorts of decisions.

Part of the difficulty of our answer is constitutional illiteracy. We have to shore up constitutional understanding: the choice by individuals, who are related one to another in an anticipated set of interactions, of a reciprocally binding constraint[31]. Rules and institutions rather than outcomes should be the focus. In general, orthodox public finance, with its emphasis on the direct application of normative criteria to tax arrangements, does not give us an understanding of observed fiscal processes in the EU nor is it a basis for improvement on grounds that are acceptable to the taxpayers. As we do test in this paper, the logic of a constitutional approach can give such an interpretation, just as it gave an analytic interpretation of the popular tax revolts sweeping across the U.S. in the late 1970s. A constitution contains a principle-based limitation of the role of government in society and defines the basic rules for ordinary politics. A constitution is a framework for political action, not an instrument for action[32].

29 Brennan, G., Buchanan, J. M. The Power to Tax, Analytical Foundations of a Fiscal Constitution. Indianapolis: Liberty Fund, (1980), (2000).

30 Elster, J. Arguing and Bargaining in the Federal Convention and the Assemblée Constituante. Center for the Study of Constitutionalism in Eastern Europe. Working Paper no. 4, (August, 1991).

31 Rawls, J. A. A Theory of Justice. Oxford: Oxford University Press, (1971).

32 Elster, J. Ulysses Unbound. Cambridge: Cambridge Uni-versity Press, (2000), p. 100.

There are no unique constitutional solutions; several combinations of electoral and non-electoral rules are possible. In this paper, we first look at the tasks the EU has to do, and second we look at the way fiscal policy is decided. If political and cultural differences do exist (3.1), and freedom of choice and free initiative of citizens is important (3.2), limiting constitutional rules do make sense. Which reform of the EU budget is necessary? We can look back and learn from history. We look at what did shape the American fiscal constitution[33]. If the problem is to carry over tasks to supranational authorities, as is the case in new Treaty of Lisbon, we do feel protected if these supranational authorities can act on two provisions. Firstly, and, for James Buchanan, most importantly, on provisions that lay out the (limited) range and scope of activities that are appropriately to be undertaken (4.1)[34]. Secondly, on provisions that state a bicameral fiscal (constitutional) framework (4.2)[35].

4.1 Limiting The Tasks Of The EU

If the problem is how to establish a limited government, we can look at the constitution of the U.S. In the U.S., two authorities are of interest: the authorities in each of the states and the federal government in Washington. Is that not too much government? Not if both authorities compete with each other in the sense that they each have their own branch of power. We can guard a branch if a constitution does support us. As has been said by James Madison, one of the founders of the American constitution, in the U.S. constitution the central authorities do have little and limited and the states do have many and large competences[36]. The former has powers related to foreign policy and national defense. The latter has powers related to the criminal justice system and the protection of the family. In the EU Treaty of Lisbon, however, the opposite seems to be the case: there seems to be little that does not fall under the jurisdiction of Brussels. The Treaty describes tasks that the EU has to do under all circumstances (e. g., customs, competition and monetary policy, fishing, trade and the internal market policy), tasks

---

33 Dam, K. W. The American Fiscal Constitution. The Uni-versity of Chicago Law Review, Vol. 44, Nb. 2, (1977).

34 Buchanan, J. M. Choice, Contract, and Constitutions. Indiana-polis: Liberty Fund, (2001), p. 442.

35 Nef, R. Lob des Non-Zentralismus. Sankt Augustin: Aca-demia Verlag, (2002).

36 Markman, S. Constitutional Myths and Realities. Imprimis, Vol. 34, Number 8, (August, 2005).

that can be appropriated if necessary (e. g., environmental policy and consumer protection) and tasks the EU supports (e. g., tourism)[37].

Power, however, wants more power, all to the good or to the bad. Hence, every possibility, how artificially, the EU will use to enlarge it. The manner of subsidizing activities, for instance., enormously enhances the influence of the EU. Suppose the EU gives a subsidy of 50 % to a certain activity. That is almost blackmail; no local government, in their good mind, is opposed to it. For the local authorities the gains of the activity has to be only halve of the total costs[38]. The pressure to accept the subsidy is enormous. Even, however, if the given task for the (federal) central authorities is small, as, e. g., described in the U.S constitution, for insterstate trade. Just as the EU-authorities do have a stake in border crossing interests. That, however, is a license for government involvement, at least in the US, in approximately everything. Look at what did happen in the US. The federal authorities may not meddle with agriculture in the separate states. Yet – with the rule and power of the authority over interstate trade in hand – it states how many acres in the separate states have to remain wasted. How can the federal authorities motivate this? A farmer did grow grain on his "wasted" land and fed the grain to his cattle. At first site, no interstate trade seems to take place. The Supreme Court, however, did argue that if the farmer had not grown grain on his wasted land, he would have bought it. He, also, influenced the price of grain on the market and so interstate trade[39].

In general, federalism in the US is (1) the division of powers of government between the national government and the states. (2) the separation of powers in which each branch of the national government---the legislative, the executive, and the judicial branch---has distinct responsibilities, yet is subject to the checks and balances of the other branches. In addition, (3) there is the principle of limited government in which the national government is constrained to exercise only those powers set forth by the constitution[40].

In sum, even if there is a clear separation of powers and limitation of tasks, as in the US, central government often grabs the possibility to enlarge its powers. What then can we expect of the description of tasks in the (revised) EU treaty? There seems to be little that does not fall directly or indirectly under the jurisdiction of Brussels. The EU has tasks to do under all circumstances (e. g., customs, competition and monetary policy, fishing, and internal market policy), tasks that

37 See: Treaty (2005, 2007).

38 Edwards, C. Downsizing the Federal Government. Washing-ton: Cato Institute, (2005).

39 Snyder, J. R. Unrestrained Appetites, Unlimited Government. The Freeman: Ideas on Liberty, (May 1998).

40 Markman, S. Constitutional Myths and Realities. Imprimis, Vol. 34, Number 8, (August, 2005), p. 2.

can be appropriated if necessary (e. g., environmental policy and consumer protection) and tasks it supports (e. g., tourism)[41]. The just-stated possibility of subsidizing activities enormously enlarges the influence of the EU. See how acute the gold rush response is with "matching" grants. In general, also EU-tasks, in principle, are many and hard to control by a democratic decision-making process. A process in which everyone thinks that other people do pay for a certain policy and changing majorities have to be bought, time and again. An ever-increasing government budget might be expected.

4.2 The Institutional Structure Of Fiscal Decision-Making

For Hayek it is necessary to create a Legislative Assembly (upper house) that states the rules and a Governmental Assembly (ordinary legislature or parliament) that administrates within those rules[42]. A new and differently elected and organized Legislative Assembly should draw up semi-permanent fiscal rules, and should not be subject to influences of particular groups. In the EU, however, there is an intentional combination, the decision-making (institutional) triangle, of the European Commission, the European Council and European Parliament. All of whom state what the budget is and make the policy within it[43]. Consequently, the proposed change in policy of the EU from unanimity to majority rule is no effective constraint on the exercise and growth of EU power[44].

Constitutional economics is both thinking outside the box and back to basics. For the EU it is scientifically largely uncharted territory. Hayek's model of bicameralism for fiscal powers for example, to my knowledge, has never been part of any political agenda. It is thinking outside the box of mainstream public finance[45].

41 See Treaty (2004, ep. 2007).

42 Hayek, F. A. Law, Legislation and Liberty. London: Routledge & Kegan Paul, (1982), Volume 3.

43 See Treaty (2004, 2007).
Scharpf, F. W. The Joint-Decision Trap Revisited. Journal of Common Market Studies, Vol. 44, No, 4, (2006) pp. 845-64.
Thomson, R., Hosli, M. Who Has Power in the EU? The Commission Council and Parliament in Legislative Decision-making. Journal of Common Market Studies, Vol. 44, No. 2, (2006).

44 Brennan, G., Buchanan, J. M. The Power to Tax, Analytical Foundations of a Fiscal Constitution. Indianapolis: Liberty Fund, (1980), (2000).
Baldwin, R., Widgrén, M. Council voting in the Constitutional Treaty: Devil in the details. CEPS Policy Brief, No. 53, (July 2004).

45 Blankart, C. B. Öffentliche Finanzen in der Demokratie, München: Franz Vahlen, (1991).
Rosen, H. S., Windisch, R., Oberdieck, E. Finanzwissenschaft I, München: Oldenbourg Verlag, (1992).
Enderlein, H., eo. The EU Budget. How Much Scope for Institutional Reform? European Central Bank, Occasional Paper Series, no. 27, (April 2005).

In due course, the separate "taxation chamber" can even grow into an institution where all legislation in the EU is made independently from the direct policy use of it. For Buchanan the European constitution is an opportunity, EU citizens need to grasp, for going back to constitutional basics[46]. The constitutionalist mindset, however, that says that persons owe loyalty to the constitution rather than to the government, is (has become) foreign to European thinking[47]. The idea that there are, or should be, any limits on the powers of the government has largely passed from the contemporary scene. This lack of a constitutional mindset is also part of the problem this research program has to tackle.

Of central importance is that constitutionalism can be the core of fiscal constraints in which subsidiarity (the primary liability for the solution of problems lies with the smallest functional unit) and the consent of free individuals (trust), two of the main problems of the EU, are of central importance.

5. Conclusion

In general, the EU-budget hovers between one that redistributes money between members and one that achieves certain EU-wide policies. The budget is the cause of many of the bitterest arguments between the Member States. Often, the objective of spending seems to be to achieve acceptable net balances rather than agreed policy. It has been said that the EU budget has never been used as a means to meet the objectives of the Union but rather as a negotiating tool for its members[48].

If fiscal dissatisfaction in the EU is the result of a growing tendency in which majorities do decide, and hence does give changing majority coalitions political authority, within that framework we can never solve the problem. There is another possibility. Form the point of view of constitutional economics and fiscal sociology two things are necessary. One, we need a fiscal constitution on the bases of a clearly enumerated list of tasks for the EU. Second, we have to split fiscal powers: the establishment of a separate legislative branch of the EU that does state the principles of taxation and another branch that makes policy inside those rules. Presently, however, often majority by means of the European Commission and

46 Buchanan, J. M. An American Perspective on Europe's Con-stitutional Opportunity. Cato Journal, Vol. 10, No. 3, (Winter 1991), pp. 619-629.
Buchanan, J. M. Europe as Social Reality. Constitutional Political Economy, 7, (1996a), pp. 253, 256.

47 See Buchanan, 1996b, 2003, cf. Weiler, 1996; Shaw, 2000; Bermann, 2004; Bellamy, 2006.

48 Figueira, F. How to Reform the EU Budget? Going Beyond Fiscal Federalism. Utrecht, (2006).
Eppink, D-J Europese Mandarijnen, Achter de schermen van de Europese Commissie. Tielt: Lannoo, (2007), p. 190.

the European Parliament does set the fiscal rules as well as does make policy inside those rules on a seemingly endless list of possible tasks.

In the wake of the demise of the proposed Constitution, instead of the present non-constitutional approach, a model fiscal constitution for the EU budget can become an agenda-setting focal point for a new scientific research program (constitutional economics and fiscal sociology) and future EU policy. A fiscal constitution is a means proportionate to the problem at hand. A fiscal constitution (1) can be a real possibility. In history, constitutional debate has always been possible and fruitfu. (2) it creates trust between the states. A shared framework facilitates a robust democratic debate. (3) it makes subsidiarity a real possibility. The market economy functions within a limited government. And (4) it substitutes for improving the morals between Member States. Just as the market economy does the same by steering self-interested human behavior within a constitutional order of private property.

In sum, this paper shows how we can use the reformed new EU-budget by imposing constraining rules to promote solidarity and trust in the setting of an EU-Leviathan. Instead of emphasizing efficiency, to up-date goals and means, and / or to aim at greater fairness the paper shifts the emphasis to the making of authentic rules: the design of possible constraints on a revenue-maximizing EU. Because of their voluntary consent (an internal criterion based on the desires of the Member States themselves) it is acceptable to the Member States that are to be subject to it. No external criteria, and hence no agreement over the goodness or badness of these criteria used, e. g., allocative efficiency or equal treatment for equals, are necessary. The shared framework of a model EU-budget (politically independent fiscal rules) creates trust and social cohesion between the Member States, the European Parliament, Commission, and Council of Ministers. It facilitates a robust democratic debate within a consistent, transparent and reliable policy and legislation framework. Member States can anticipate making appropriate behavior adjustments, including those made over a long–term planning period. The paper gives the analytical arguments in support of two appropriately designed budgetary measures (moderately permanent features) re the up-coming EU Budget Review: a clear limitation of tasks and a split in budgetary powers.

References

Apolte, T. Die eigentümliche Diskussion um Zentralisierung und Dezentralisierung in der Europapolitik. Perspektiven der Wirtschaftspolitik, 5(3), (2004), pp. 271-291.

Bachhaus, J. Das Subsidiäritatsprinzip als Baustein einer entstehender Europäischen Verfassung. (2001).
Backhaus, J. Fiscal Sociology: What for? American Journal of Economics and Sociology, (Jan. 2002).
Backhaus, J. Fiscal Sociology: Guest editor's introduction. Journal of Economic Bahavior & Organization, Vol. 59 (2006), pp. 457-459.
Baldwin, R., Widgrén, M. Council voting in the Constitutional Treaty: Devil in the details. CEPS Policy Brief, No. 53, (July 2004).
Bellamy, R. The European Constitution is Dead, Long Live European Constitutionalism. Constellations, Volume 13, No. 2, (2006), pp. 181-189.
Bermann, G. A. Editorial: The European Union as a Constitutional Experiment. European Law Journal, Vol. 10, No. 4, July, (2004), pp. 363-370.
Blankart, C. B. Öffentliche Finanzen in der Demokratie. München: Franz Vahlen, (1991).
Brennan, G., Buchanan, J. M. The Power to Tax, Analytical Foundations of a Fiscal Constitution. Indianapolis: Liberty Fund, (1980), (2000).
Buchanan, J. M. Liberty, Market and State. Brighton: Wheatsheaf Books, (1986).
Buchanan, J. M. An American Perspective on Europe's Constitutional Opportunity. Cato Journal, Vol. 10, No. 3, (Winter 1991), pp. 619-629.
Buchanan, J. M. Europe as Social Reality. Constitutional Political Economy, 7, (1996a), pp. 253, 256.
Buchanan, J. M. Federalism and Individual Sovereignty. Cato Journal, Volume 15, Number 2-3, (Fall/Winter 1996b), pp. 259-275.
Buchanan, J. M. Choice, Contract, and Constitutions. Indianapolis: Liberty Fund, (2001).
Buchanan, J. M. Public Choice. Politics without Romance. Policy, Vol. 19, No. 3, (Spring 2003), pp. 13-18.
Buchanan, J. M. Restoring the Spirit of Classical Liberalism. Notes from FEE, (July 2005).
Dam, K. W. The American Fiscal Constitution. The University of Chicago Law Review, Vol. 44, Nb. 2, pp. 271-320.
Dircksen, J. Vote Tally Report 108-2, NTUF Policy Paper 156, (2005), www. ntu. org.
ECB, The EU budget: How much scope for Institutional Reform? European Central Bank, Occasional Paper Series, no. 27, (April 2005).
ECFIN workshop, The role of fiscal rules and institutions in shaping budgetary outcomes: proceedings from the ECFIN workshop, Economic Papers, nr. 275, (2007).
Edwards, C. Downsizing the Federal Government, Washington: Cato Institute, (2005).

Elster, J. Arguing and Bargaining in the Federal Convention and the Assemblée Constituante. Center for the Study of Constitutionalism in Eastern Europe, Working Paper no. 4, (August, 1991).

Elster, J. Ulysses Unbound, Cambridge: Cambridge University Press, (2000).

Enderlein, H., eo. The EU Budget. How Much Scope for Institutional Reform? European Central Bank, Occasional Paper Series, no. 27, (April 2005).

Eppink, D-J Europese Mandarijnen, Achter de schermen van de Europese Commissie, Tielt: Lannoo, (2007).

European Commission: Communication from the Commission. Reforming the Budget, Changing Europe. A public Consultation Paper in view of the 2008/2009 budget review, Brussels, 12.9.2007, SEC (2007) 1188 final.

Figueira, F. How to Reform the EU Budget? Going Beyond Fiscal Federalism. Utrecht, (2006).

Friedman, M. and R. Free to Choose. Harmondsworth: Penguin Books, [1979], (1981).

Gillingham, J. European Integration 1959-2003. Superstate or New Market Economy Cambridge: Cambridge University Press, (2003).

Gillingham, J. Design for a New Europe. Cambridge: Cambridge University Press, (2006).

Hayek, F. A. Freedom and the Economic System. Public Policy Pamphlet, No. 29, Chicago: The University of Chicago Press, (1939).

Hayek, F. A. The Economic Conditions of Interstate Federalism. In: Individualism and Economic Order, London: Routledge and Kegan Paul, (1949).

Hayek, F. A. The Constitution of Liberty. London: Routledge, (1960).

Hayek, F. A. Law, Legislation and Liberty. London: Routledge & Kegan Paul, (1982).

Inman, R. P., Rubinfeld, R. P. Rethinking Federalism. The Journal of Economic Perspectives, Vol. 11, No. 4. (Autumn, 1997), pp. 43-64.

Keynes, J. M. The General Theory or Employment, Interest, and Money. New York: Harcourt, [1937], (1964).

Kinneging, A. De Europese Grondwet, het staatsrecht en de constitutionele theorie. In: Cliteur, P., Franken H., Voermans W., eds. *Naar een Europese Grondwet,* Den Haag: Boom, (2004).

Kirzner, I. M. Competition and Entrepreneurship. Chicago: University of Chicago, Press, (1973).

Kirzner, I. M. Discovery and the Capitalist Process. Chicago: University of Chicago Press, (1985).

Leonard, M. Democracy in Europe. How the EU can survive in an age of referendum. Essays Centre for European Reform, (March 2006).

Markman, S. Constitutional Myths and Realities. Imprimis, Vol. 34, Number 8, (August, 2005).
Mill, J. S. On Liberty. Harmondsworth: Penguin Books, [1859], (1974).
Nef, R. Lob des Non-Zentralismus. Sankt Augustin: Academia Verlag, (2002).
Rawls, J. A. A Theory of Justice. Oxford: Oxford University Press, (1971).
Rosen, H. S., Windisch, R., Oberdieck, E. Finanzwissenschaft I. München: Oldenbourg Verlag, (1992).
Scharpf, F. W. The Joint-Decision Trap Revisited. Journal of Common Market Studies, Vol. 44, No, 4, (2006), pp. 845-64.
Shaw, J. Process and Constitutional Discourse in the European Union. Journal of Law and Society, Vol. 27, No. 1, (March), pp. 4-37, 2000.
Snyder, J. R. Unrestrained Appetites, Unlimited Government. The Freeman: Ideas on Liberty, (May 1998).
Spicer, M. W. On Friedrich Hayek and Taxation: Rationality, Rules, and Majority Rule. National Tax Journal, Vol. 48, No. 1, (1995), pp. 103-112.
Treaty establishing a Constitution for Europe, Official Journal of the European Union C-310, Volume 47, 16 December 2004; *Treaty of Lisbon*, Official Journal C-306, Volume 50, 3 December, 2007.
Thomson, R., Hosli, M. Who Has Power in the EU? The Commission Council and Parliament in Legislative Decision-making. Journal of Common Market Studies, Vol. 44, No. 2, (2006), pp. 391-417.
Verhofstadt, G. *De* Verenigde Staten van Europa, Manifest voor een nieuw Europa. Antwerpen: Houtekiet, (2005).
Weiler, J. H.H. European Neo-constitutionalism: in Search of Foundations for the European Constitutional Order. Political Studies, XLIV, (1996), pp. 517-533.

Cognitive Dissonance And Taxpayer's Discipline

Vladimir Boguslavskiy

Abstract

This article uses interdisciplinary approach mainly from the side of social and cognitive psychology to explain phenomena of corruption and shadow economy distribution as consequences of individual choices made in the station of anomie. In the situation of widespread anomie norms possessed by individual stop to control their behavior thanks to system of collectively legitimized excuses. Excuses in turn are designed to reduce psychological discomfort called cognitive (dignity) dissonance when a person chooses utility against of value. The research among a group of Russian entrepreneurs revealed, on one hand, strong evidence of dignity dissonance, and three types of excuses used for it's reduction, on the other. This proves that Russians possess norms of honest taxpayers despite negative historical experience, although dwell in the station of anomie.

Introduction

Among the range of problems of economical development that the orthodox economics is unable to explain is high level of shadow economy and corruption. These two are seemed to be an integral part of social-economic reality in many developing and transition countries. Economists elaborate methods to assess the level of shadow economy in order to include it into real GDP estimation. For nowadays the array of method has been developed starting from simple calculation of difference between stated numbers (cost minus gain) and finishing statistical models like Cash demand based or LISREL type[1]. It is difficult to imagine any economy with high tax evasion and low corruption. These two phenomena perfectly correlate and are connected, in turn, with low GDP per capita the way it is difficult to define – weather mentioned phenomena reasons or consequences of poverty.

The best expression explaining their connection would be "vicious cycle". Institutionalists point out on bad conditions for accumulation of capital and development. And institutes, in turn, have to be financed by individuals interested in, namely through tax contributions. But what happens when the number of "free riders" overcome the number of those agree to pay? Does this mean that the ship will not go? It will go, because at least one person needs it to be called "the ship" having all attributes of, like sails and cannons and able to float the see –

1 Schneider, F., Enste, D. The Shadow Economy: An International Survey. Cambridge University Press (2003).

this person is captain. The captain can be called president, or King or "Narodni Komissar" or Fuhrer and the ship is the state.

The leader of the state is not the only person interested in proper performance of it's institutions but he / she or they (as government) are only people, whose responsibility for the state is direct. In the absence of consensus between "riders" and "payers" though this may be the same individual the government has to design aggressive stimuli for the population like total nationalization used by Stalin (Dzugashwilli) and bolsheviks or "Lebensraum" conception implementation by Hitler. John Hobson traced this process though exemplifying not that dramatic development of pre-WWI biggest imperial states[2]. The reasoning presented above calls for consideration how microsociologycal phenomena shape macro-performance of a social structure.

Making the last sentence the departure point we can proceed firstly considering how actually institutions come into life of an individual using inspirations from interdisciplinary rainbow of social psychology of economical behavior and economical psychology of conventions, and showing why norms are central category of social relations, particular type of which are economic relations. Then, taking the example of shadow economy in broad sense of the world, we'll consider how the station of anomie distributes. Using Kosewski's definition of anomie, situation of temptation and dignity dissonance, we'll show social –psychological conditions necessary for it. Further consider special cases of anomie is 'economical anomie' on the example of not following by the population the norms of honest taxpayer, and the resulting widespread tax evasion among high income categories of taxpayers in Russia. The conception of social capital, that became popular for it's explaining social-economical development power, we'll employ in connection with the logic of anomie, where provide data on the low level of civic participation in Russia associated with low tax discipline and offer possible solution. We'll review results of qualitative survey with classifying three types of excuses helping to neutralize dignity dissonance arising because of choice in favor of utility instead of value.

Norms as economical category and their violation consequences.

Real economical interaction is among people having values and inclinations, that can be stated with scientific precision thanks to works of Tversky[3], Kahneman (Noble Prize in Economics 2002) and others. In the series of experiments on cognitive psychology of economical behavior they proved existence of "mental models" different from rational egoism of "economical man" in capacity of the

2 Hobson, John M. The wealth of states: a comparative sociology of international economic and political change. Cambridge University Press, (1997).

3 Tversky A, Kahenman D. Judgement under uncertainty: heuristics and biases: Biases in judgments reveal some heuristics of thinking under uncertainty. Science 185, (1974), pp. 1124-29.

basis of economical interactions[4]. In various situation actors are trying to notice familiar traits, regular expectations, and use standard patterns of thinking and stereotypes to work out strategies of action. These standards are influenced by assessing of what others are going to do, what worked in the past and imagination of the subject about general trend of things. These patterns of action are dynamic and change through analysis of interaction and reaction on effects caused by. The economic sociology of conventions, as enhancing introduction into by Beamish[5], contributes into the discussion with following proposition that we can adapt here:

1. Market forces work around categories that have been socially established', thus particularly taxpaying culture does not emerge within new markets. Contrary, in western civilization capitalism was developing thanks to gradual lowering barriers and prohibitive taxes of feudalism epoch.
2. Actors possess common definition of acceptable ways of action when coming to the market'. Thus legitimacy of tax collection by government either exist as the category of social reflection or not. If the taxes are considered as "costs" or "non production loss", then a law abiding individual striving for profit maximization will contribute considerable resources to "tax optimization" or tax avoidance, the resources otherwise be spent for growth of production or before tax profit.
3. Actors seek excuses of their actions in order they look as proper from all points of view of their community'. Excuses enable individuals to act without deep analysis of social correctness of their behavior thus to achieve psychological comfort.

The 3rd point calls for more scrutinized analysis. Psychological comfort that actors seek, may also be named "cognitive consonance" the notion inspired by conception of "cognitive dissonance" elaborated and based on experiments by Festinger who pointed out on situations when a person experiences internal discomfort from perception of controversy between 'cognitions' or elements of knowledge. When a person gets into the situation where experiences cognitive dissonance, his mental activity is directed on reduction of it by mean of cognitive combination between these 'elements of knowledge' or cognitions[6]. Latter his findings were subject of empirical and theoretical development into 'Communication Theory'. One of productive offsprings of Communication Theory is work of polish social psychologist Marek Kosewski, who applied it for the situation of "temptation".

4 See Fischhoff, Kahenman and Tversky (2000), Slovic et al. (1979), Tversky and Kahenman (1974).

5 Beamish T. D., Biggart N. W. The economic sociology of conventions: habit, custom, practice, and routine in market order. Annual Review of Sociology, Vol. 29., (2003).

6 Festinger, L. A theory of cognitive dissonance. Evanston, IL: Row, Peterson, (1957).

Temptation is the situation when a person faces two alternatives, one of which is to follow own convictions, another is to obtain an utility or benefit. The clue element of "temptation" is that a person can not do both – to follow convictions or norms and "to get the thing"[7].

From the viewpoint of social psychology individual norms and values are not the product of isolated development, but a kind of reflection of socially approved norms, values and models of behavior, although it does not eliminate possibility of inborn perception of rightfulness as Rogers[8] following Durkheim states[9]. Although there exists legal mechanisms of delinquent behavior punishment, all of them are effective only thanks to norms abidance by majority of citizens or members of big group establishing state.

In the aspiration to emancipate human action and individuality from boundaries of existing traditional society, the early researchers of, strive to escape from study of basic social determinants of behavior that are norms. The norms being not explored always presented on the background of social theories[10]. It was usually referred to on the occasion of distributed disobedience to, like Durkheimian 'anomie' growth. Norms unlike ideologies were treated as something that goes without saying to the extent that professor of ethics Adam Smith in his book on moral sentiments wrote about well known 'invisible market hand' that, taken out from the context, became the banner of classical economist for elaboration social theory free from any notion of norms. The long time methodological neglect of social especially economical scientists to the norms is conditioned by kind of rational approach towards phenomena that draws no attention until cause considerable problems. The problem of shadow economy and corruption did not generate attention before it started to generate considerable loss of budgets for developing and some of developed countries. On the other hand, this class of economic phenomena can be related to general deviance, and is problem of criminology. Criminology as we'll see later is changing, and becoming more concerned with 'analysis of situations and their interpretations'[11].

Most probably the general trend of social sciences on humanization achieved criminology as well. Besides this, societies gradually learn not to commit 'funda-

7 Kosewski M. Ludzie w sytuacijach pokusy i upokorzenia. Warszawa: Wiedza Powszechna, (1985).

8 See Rogers (1964).

9 Kosewski M. Ludzie w sytuacijach pokusy i upokorzenia. Warszawa: Wiedza Powszechna, (1985).

10 Therborn G. Back to Norms! On the Scope and Dynamics of Norms and Normative Action. Current Sociology, November Vol. 50 (6), (2002).

11 Birkbeck, C. & LaFree G. The Situational Analysis of Crime and Deviance. Annual Review of Sociology, 19, (1993).

mental attribution error' the term from social psychology referring to inclination of people to explain behavior of other people by their inner characteristics, not search for objective or situational influences. Nowadays the shift in criminology means differing between 'criminality' and 'crime'. The former relates more to personal biography factor analysis the later – to the consideration of the situation and it's interpretation by the actor.

Situational approach theorists when considering criminal cultures as within prisoners so acting criminals, noticed presence of a lot of aspirations of members, especially most advanced in hierarchy towards following internal group norms and ethos[12 13]. Though not without definite material interest, for most junior gang members, participation in was the way to realize their need for dignity, based on following particular moral standards. Similarly considering tax evasion as a kind of norm violation activity, as our preliminary research result indicates, it is productive to treat distribution of the practices as a kind of 'anomie'.

What happens when the norms are not followed on bigger scale then negligible one? The situation emerged called "anomie" that the term author Durkheim measured by indices of crime and punishment rate[14]. In majority of developing and transition as well as in some developed countries there is similar phenomena of "economical anomie" that is high level of tax evasion expressed in rates of shadow economy. According to the estimations done on the basis of Russian middle class incomes and tax evasion preferences, the structure of tax evasion contributions on PIT (Personal Income Tax) in 2005 was as shown on figure 1. It should be taken into account that Russia has one of the lowest PIT in Europe with flat rate is 13 %. So the calculation does not include evasion from united social tax including social, medical and obligatory pension contributions amounting 30 % of wage fund.

12 Short J. F., Strodtbech F. L. Group Process and Gang Delinquency. Chicago: University of Chicago Press, (1965).

13 Kosewski M. Ludzie w sytuacijach pokusy i upokorzenia. Warszawa: Wiedza Powszechna, (1985).

14 Horton, J. The Dehumanization of Anomie and Alienation: A Problem in the Ideology of Sociology. British Journal of Sociology, Vol. 15, (1964).

Figure 1. Russian PIT evasion within different high income groups of the population in 2005[15].

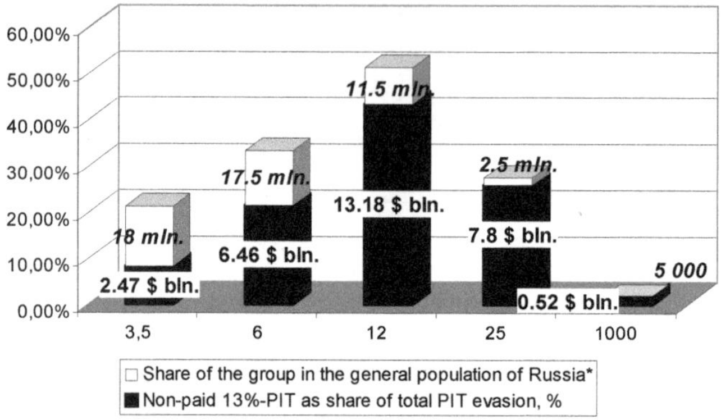

* On the pillars are quantities in absolute characters (i. e. 18 mln. persons)
** Axis X shows income in the group as: thousand US$ per month per person.

There is no need to explain the consequences of such performance for Russian economy, the only remark is that corruption is functionally and through vicious cycle pattern connected with high tax evasion.

Institutional characteristics recently occurred in the focus of attention for their explanation power in economical development indicators. However the next step is to explore what the institutions compile in terms of micro-sociology and social psychology of economical behavior and what is the dynamics of basic elements of public opinion on important issues, creating the institutions. Corruption and tax evasion for Russia and other European societies consequences are examples of institutions empowered by economical anomia – special kind of anomia definition of which will be given in the next section after the theoretical review.

Economical Anomie

High level of shadow economy and corruption in some European countries are not natural for their cultures, these negative phenomena are the consequences of distribution of 'excuses' within social groups concerned. Further we will explain why this situation can be qualified as 'anomie'.

The word 'anomie' belongs to Durkheim he used for considering human behavior leading to suicide, but as Kosewski states, translation of this world as

15 Source: Author.

"normlessness" is incorrect. Merton also refers to this phenomena, causing negation of norms but rests the responsibility for anomia mostly on external by reference to individual action forces[16].

'Anomia as social phenomena means that in particular sectors of socium, it's classes or strata, keeping to the norms becomes considered as unnecessary, though before was contrary.'[17] On the one hand it is difficult to trace when it happens, one can always rise the question – did they really follow these norms ever? Corruption and black market existed in Soviet Union, sometimes were inbuild institutions inevitable for 'the plan' execution. On the other hand, the norms always existed as well through communist times and after.

'Relatively to an individual, anomie appears the way that suddenly, previous methods of achievement of purposes became non-adequate to situational abilities. While new means are not created or unpleasant for the actor.'[18] For Durkheim norms are social barriers that limit horizon of personal aspiration. Personal aspiration is inborn quality transforming into different forms of tangible assets, if possessing of these assets considered by society as indicators of individual progress on the way to perfection. Thus aspiration of individual can be transformed into unlimited wealth accumulation that, in turn, can not satisfy an individual deprived of social norms, leads, by Durkheim, to disappointment and possibly suicide. Durkheimian viewpoint is partly confirmed by experiments on consumer satisfaction where consumers, who were given for choice 6 sorts of an item, proved to be more satisfied then those who had 30 of it[19]. This effect was also called "freedom terrany"[20].

In terms of economical upheaval of recent history of transformation Merton's description is relevant for many citizens of socialist countries, previously enjoying stable employment. Later had to search for new sources of income like trade, early treated as 'speculation' – illegal activity, so it naturally is not to be connected with execution of duty by reference to the state that is taxpaying. The same is true for corrupt officials who faced decline or wages relatively the prices and consequently lowering of social status non-compliant to power endowed.

The contra argument can be that in socialist time many of the same employees did not hesitate to abuse their position if not threatened by serious punishment. This is true about widely distributed phenomena of theft of materials, instru-

16 Merton R. K. Social Theory and Social Structure. New York: Free Press of Glencoe, (1957), p. 146.

17 Ibid.

18 Ibid.

19 Iyengar, S. S., Lepper, M. R. Rethinking the role of choice: A cultural perspective on intrinsic motivation. Journal of Personality and Social Psychology, 76, (1999).

20 Mayers D. G. Social psychology, 7th ed. McGraw Hill, rus. transl. 'Piter', (2005).

ments and ready products from factories by workers to the degree that new members of working collective had to take part in symbolical steal otherwise risking to be ostracized. The same tendencies were in government structures in forms of monopolistic corruption headed by the communist party regional chiefs[21]. Thus there is a lot of evidence that transition to market did not change much for corrupt individuals, which thanks to new conditions received possibility to perform larger scale public property theft transactions.

Merton treats anomia as both – station of mechanism of a subject activity regulation and as quality of activity performed in the station of anomia. It is useful explanation of why vicious cycle of corruption and tax evasion exists. They both as we'll see later reinforce each other since based on the same mechanism of elaboration of excuses.

Kosewski's conclusion on anomia is different from Merton's, though more linked to Durkheim's. The main object of research of Kosewski is situation of temptation (see above), since norms do still exist in the consciousness of those involved in corruption and tax evasion, violation of them for the sake of material benefit generates cognitive or 'dignity' dissonance. To reduce it the only way is to use excuse. Every deviant group has its own system of excuses. Universalization of the excuses all over society brings about emergency of anomie. Thus, anomia, is not absence of norms but distribution of excuses preserving values (such as honesty, responsibility, patriotism etc.) to be connected with activity[22].

Economical anomie is characterized by presence of norms in the consciousness of actors involved into economical transactions however 'normless' the activity can seem, what enables them to do it is distribution excuses preserving norms of controlling actions.

Norms In Taxation

The function of norms is to connect values with acts and there is always the dilemma – the more general the norm is – the more difficult to connect it with particular activity, but the more detailed it is – the more difficult to connect it with concrete value, hence making it vulnerable to manipulation. The example may be 'honesty' as a value, let's say that the norm connected with means – "if you participated in gaining some good together, you must share it equally

21 Kordonski S. Transformation of administrative market, www.libertarium.ru., (2001).

22 Kosewski M. Ludzie w sytuacijach pokusy i upokorzenia. Warszawa: Wiedza Powszechna, (1985), p. 73.

among all of you". Let's guess two people found one orange and one of them want's to eat it now – another want's to spare it for tomorrow. In this case it becomes difficult to distribute the norm directly to the case so one who is more strongly can use force to execute his own strategy.

On the other hand, the norm can state "if you find an orange then you must cut it in parts and distribute it immediately to all who took part in". So what if we found melon? Or what if we all wish to consume it tomorrow?

Orthodox economics dealing with problems of Robinson left alone on an isle does not even go into the question, and for example, positing 'taxation' only with the word 'burden'. This is what the future business elite studies in universities and this is why it will be difficult to convince them that tax rate above Laffer's optimum – 25% is reasonable. What clear is that the Laffer's theory provides business community with effective excuse to evade tax or at the best to avoid it, though for the budget result will be the same negative.

Business community from developing and transition countries permanently complain on complexity of tax legislation, that every year become more and more overwhelmed by changes. Parliaments and fiscal organs are engaged in endless race with the best minds of tax advising society elaborating more and more advanced methods of avoidance if not evasion. Until recently the best way to combat dishonest methods was specifications or making norms more precise, prescribing how they should be applied in peculiar situation. Actually it is not necessary if a taxpayer knows that the state expects from him to pay certain share of income, received in the situation with all signs of similarity. But a taxpayer always has a temptation to say "What about melon? It is said here only about orange..." If this was the case – the legislator could state in the rule "...all fruits and vegetables...". But there always be a smart biologist (lawyer or tax adviser) who will draw attention of the court that melon is berry.

The relatively effective solution of the problem was found cooperatively by fiscal organs and business communities in UK and Australia. They designed special kind of normative acts called "Charters" which are not obligatory from the angle of civil or common law and thus do not need excessive particularization of clauses. The same way many of these acts contain in the content of articles a lot of preferences and appeals to values. For example, "in order to provide honest treatment" or "we, citizens of... with full responsibility" etc. History of this kind of documents dates back to 'Magna Charta of year 1215'. First modern days Citizens Charter appeared in UK in 1991, By March 1994 there were officially 38 different individual government charter documents, in 1997 there were 40 main charters and over 10,000 local charters that were of purely local origin. According to estimations there were over 200 national charters in the UK though the number of local charters goes closer at around 10,000 by year 2003[23]. The important meaning of this kind of act is confirmed by the fact that model charters are distributed through UN development program[24] as well as OECD target action[25] (OECD, 2004).

Another example of this kind of normative document is 'code of ethics' for definite professional social group. Within the framework of Russian Tax Administration Modernization Program (TAMP-II) of World Bank (the first part (TAMP-I) started in 1991) the tender announced in 2006 for execution of work on compiling Code of Ethics (CE) or Russian tax administration employee[26] This document is expected to embrace more wide range of situation and motivations, which arise in everyday life of tax collecting body public servant in order to address to his self-comprehension as member of the collective with high social status. Thus, in many cases, introduction of CE to improve conduct of the group under concern will be effective to the extent of how high the status of the group is.

Russian tax administration employees are considered as other budget employees, that, in conditions of low tax discipline leaves to the government only two opportunities: to pay all state budget employees (like teachers, doctors, etc.) relevant wages, say from oil money, generating inflation pressure on the economy, or consent on marginalization of these social groups and growth of corruption within. Eventually there is one more solution of rather business character – to refer to privatization of public sector. For Russia it will be difficult since 65 % of population live below social survival minimum and will not be able to finance these necessary services. What about tax administration the effective would be either full range 'tax farming'[27] or it's 'soft' variant that is giving material stimulation to inspectors collecting more or punishing more with fines. The first 'hard' variant is difficult to implement in a democratic state by political and ideological reasons, the 'soft' variant often generates taxpayer's dissatisfaction with 'two zealous profit seeking' inspectors, who often look for easy victims and avoid powerful people auditing.

---

23 James, S., Murphy, K., Reinhart, M. The Taxpayers' Charter: A case study in tax administration. Journal of Australian Taxation, (2006) (in press), http://ctsi.anu.edu.au/-publications/taxpubs/Murphy.James.JAT.pdf.

24 UNDP, (2002).

25 OECD Committee of Fiscal Affairs Forum on Tax Administration (2003), Taxpayers' Rights and Obligations – Practice Note. GAP002 Available from the OECD website and accessed on 6 May 2004.

26 Available on Russian on FNS site www.nalog.ru.

27 Under 'tax farming' tax collecting body receive right to collect taxes in particular segment of society on it's own. Sometimes it is required to contribute amount of taxes expected in advance, then working for surplus as it was in ancient Rome, the well known case is biblical 'publican'.

The only way remained is to rely on gradual introduction of institutional instruments including Code of Ethics, improving material base (computers, infrastructure, etc.), changing selection procedures[28]. The growth of real wages in public sector is planned to be 15 % at inflation of 12 %, so now the government is concerned in lowering the inflation in order to achieve higher budget employees real wages growth.

The more general norm is the closer it to the value and specialization of makes it not always able to regulate all situations. The law can not be set in so general form that would appeal only to values but special kind of normative acts can execute this important function. However to establish these Charters active participation of communities, especially local communities is inevitable. Participation in turn is one of the main items of social capital.

Social Capital And Economical Development – What Is First And How?

Social nature of the norms appears also in being of social capital, the recently emerged notion with growing explaining power, to the degree that is considered as one of the most important assets, responsible for social – economical progress and level of development of concrete region. Another relevant for our analysis associated category of social development would be 'networks'. Unlike social capital, it is used mostly not as territorial characteristics but as local asset of particular social group.

There are different definitions of 'social capital'[29] but the most important variables of it – trust and participation. The positive influence of on taxpaying discipline[30] is combined with causal effect on level of economical development[31]. Although Amartia Sen did not use this notion directly, there is a lot of similarity in conditions of society needed for effective public choice[32] and definitions of social capital.

---

28 According the new Russian legislation on public service in the council, taking final decision on hiring, the share of experts from outside the concerned organizations has grown (university professors, public representatives) and amount 25 %. This share is expected to grow.

29 For more comprehensive review see Social capital Critical Perspectives. Ed. Stephen Baron John Field and Tom Shuller Oxford University Press 2000.

30 Feld, L. P., Frey, B. S. Trust Breeds Trust: How taxpayers are Treated. CESifo Working Paper 322, Munich, (2000).

31 Ballarino G., Shadee H. Civicness and Economic Performance. A longitudinal Analysis of Italian Provinces, 1980-2000. European Sociological Review Vol. 21 Number 3, July, (2005), pp. 243-257.

32 Sen, A. K. Collective Choice and Social Welfare. San Fransisco, (1970).

Hence the lack of social capital can be responsible for slow economical development at least in it's official part. The table 1 shows results of survey conducted by Institute of Complex and Social Research of Russian Academy of Science on participation of Russians in social life. It indicates not only actual but also potential participation or level that is expected to be achieved in the nearest future.

Table 1. Actual and potential participation of Russians in social life[33].

Participated %	The form of participation	Ready to participate, %
23,4	Collective accomplishment of commonly used infrastructure (houses, play grounds, etc.)	43,8
10,0	Targeted local actions participation.	16,4
3,8	Self-government participation.	6,5
10,2	Humanitarian relief collection	27,9
9,0	Election companies participation.	8,9
5,9	Labor circles participation.	9,1
2,8	Meeting and trade union strikes participation	4,4
2,7	Charity, NGO, remedial actions and other funds participation.	10,2
1,0	Local political party participation.	1,9
1,8	Religious organizations participation	2
0,6	Others kinds of participation	0,5
58,3	*Didn't do any \\\ I'm not going to !*	*37,5*

As is seen from the table the participation is very low, and what is more important almost 40 % of population is not going to take part in social activities. Unfortunately the respondents were not ranged by income but the fact that in Russia 40 % of population live below poverty level generates additional support to connection of poverty and social capital low level.

This connection is not single sided, as Ballarino and Shadee inspired by their countryman, author of famous research on social capital taking example of Italy, Putnam, found that, for example, economical growth has stronger causal influence on social capital. In summary their findings contain the following[34]:

33 Source: IKSI RAN.

34 Ballarino G., Shadee H. Civicness and Economic Performance. A longitudinal Analysis of Italian Provinces, 1980-2000. European Sociological Review Vol. 21 Number 3, July, (2005).

1. Civic Participation and economical development are connected in long term period but independent in short term period.
2. Civic Participation (CP) improvement causes economical growth in the time span of 20 years, where economical indicators improvement causes CP to grow two times faster then vice-versa.
3. The more traditional and possessing less democratic culture society has weaker connection between CP and economy.

This findings allows to shed light on why non-democratic development can become more effective in boosting the very democracy if only has purpose to achieve economical growth and has definite limitation in time. How much time the country may need differs considerably, it also relevant for new members of European Union as seen from the table 2.

Table 2. New EU members and 'old 15': economical development gap bridging[35].

Country	Year when the economy growth has first time exceeded average EU –15 growth rate	Average growth rate from the first exceed up to 2002, %	The number of years needed for achievement of average GDP per capita of EU-15	The number of years needed for achievement of GDP per capita of Greece
Bulgaria	1995	-3,1	N/A	N/A
Czech Republic	1993	0,1	657	75
Estonia	1995	2,7	34	19
Lithuania	1995	2,6	36	19
Latvia	1996	4,3	25	12
Poland	1992	2,9	31	20
Rumania	1993	-0,3	N/A	N/A
Hungary	1993	2,1	29	7
Slovakia	1994	1,3	58	25
Slovenia	1993	2,4	14	Achieved in1998

The success of China and improvement in Russian economic development after president Putin reforms makes many Russian economists to treat beneficially 'strong hand' approach. Athough there is always threat that the condition of

35 Source: Kaminski Antoni. Z., Kaminski Bartlomiej (2002:180).

limitation of such policy in time will not be executed, then economical growth will bring about overconcentration of power in the hands of government creating temptation to misuse it.

Thus high tax discipline and low corruption as the feature of society with high social capital is achievable with economical growth. On the other hand, the reverse dependence can also be used, the needed social-psychological parameters of target social groups like middle class and businessmen can be improved with the help of approach originating from French researcher on organizations Michel Crozier's 'culture management'.[36]

Dignity Dissonance Of Russian Tax Evaders.

The only known way of influence on social values is to use social marketing, information campaign or 'propaganda' however negative the latter sounds. At any rate 'propaganda' is similar to any instrument in the hand of a human – it can destroy or create. Pratkanis and Aronson compare it with electrical current that can be dangerous and fascinating and useful simultaneously for us depending on what we know about it[37]. From advertising agencies and political technologists to cheaters of all kinds – the use of persuasion designed according to proved to be effective rules is widespread. Development of social psychology and cognitive psychology experiments give powerful tools for changing values. If so then why not to contribute more resources for social marketing to get socially beneficial results?, We'll illustrate research results which can be first steps in the future project on lowering of level of tax evasion in Russia using Kosewski's conceptions of anomia, temptation and cognitive or 'dignity' dissonance.

However not followed many norms violated in connection with tax evasion still present in the consciousness of Russian population. In USSR time people in Russia did not actually pay taxes, the only experience about, was negative and connected with expropriation of private property. In 1920th just after Civil War communists victory, in order to restore economy, private business activity allowed, then gradually through increase of taxation, government acts and confiscation was liquidated by the 1930th. The only semi-private form of legal business activity remained were cooperatives. Another example associated with taxation in historical memory of Russians was Chrushev's (the incomer after Stalin) tax on fruit trees on private lands. This tax introduction caused demolition of fruit

36 Crozier Michel The Bureaucratic Phenomenon. The University of Chicago Press Phoenix Books, (1967).

37 Pratkanis A. R., Aronson E. Age of Propaganda: The Everyday Use and Abuse of Persuasion. W. H. Freemand and Co.NY, (2001).

gardens all over the Russia and is used as an example of voluntarism and absurdity of communist rulers. Historical pathway offers confirmation of absence of any culture of taxpaying among Russians. The difference is with the results of our research.

If Russians did not have cultural norms of taxpaying then they would not be in the station of anomia about it. That means taxpaying would not exist as the norm, thus, a person required to pay tax would follow rationally and assess power of tax collector to punish him for disobedience. If the probability to punish is low, then a taxpayer will not pay tax, evade it, and if asked by third *disinterested* party about motives of his action, he without any negative emotions would explain it by low probability of detection. That would be in the world of econometrics – not in the world of people.

None of surveyed Russian entrepreneurs were 'rational' in 'economic man' sense, all of them experienced cognitive dissonance. All confessed in tax evasion, started to explain their action either from attacks on government policy or conditions of their activity, corruption etc. The most 'rational' of them seek confirmation of their action rationality from the interviewer.

According to Kosewski who used similar paradigm for analysis of criminal behavior, a person in the situation of anomia is trying to reduce cognitive dissonance of choice against values by:

- impugning the weight of damage caused, trying to find positive side effects of his action;
- manipulating by balance of responsibility between himself and others[38].

All of these methods to reduce cognitive dissonance were used by respondents in interviews, that allowed to classify excuses of entrepreneurs into tree main category.

- Excuses based on general 'life philosophy' views, similar to first group of two given by Kosewski. For instance a respondent said that government should not have too much money since it'll cause warfare race and military conflicts. Those who demonstrated ignorance in purpose of taxation the same way doubted justice of taxation system at all.
- Excuses based on negative *indirect experience* with activity of those identified as users or managers of collected funds. This includes corruption cases known from media, wrong financial decisions of statesmen, stories from the life of other people known to the respondent.

38 Kosewski M. Ludzie w sytuacijach pokusy i upokorzenia. Warszawa: Wiedza Powszechna, (1985), p. 49.

– Excuses based on negative *direct experience* with activity of those identified as users or managers of public funds. This includes cases of corruption of local authorities that the respondent was victim of, claims on wrong treatment of him by tax administration officials, group polarization – division on 'we – entrepreneurs' and 'tax-tax collectors', failing of representatives of state to execute their functions for the benefit of concrete taxpayer.

Presence of cognitive or 'dignity' dissonance gives evidence that evading taxes Russian entrepreneurs succumb to temptation and consequently experience cognitive or 'dignity' dissonance because of violation of social norms. Trying to reduce it elaborate excuses, which legitimize through mates support. Thus theoretical propositions of Kosewski about anomia, temptation and dissonance confirm in the case of taxpaying. An informational campaign can make it's target excuses to lay them bare and to generate dignity dissonance in order to preserve taxpayers to succumb temptation and chose utility against value.

Conclusion

Norms are in the core of social processes having economical interaction as part a case of. Both economical sociology of conventions and revelations in cognitive psychology give evidence to it. For analysis of behavior violating the norms we used conception of deviant behavior of Marek Kosewski. Kosewski's conception is one of productive offspring of 'Communication Theory' and comprises definition of factors of situational analysis which are: anomie, situation of temptation and dignity dissonance. Mostly inspired by field criminological observation this conception is relevant for tax evasion and corruption as well since gives report on cognitive forces defining individual behavior in the situation of temptation with two alternatives: moral value or private utility. Choice of utility generates dignity dissonance so a person feels cognitive discomfort, the only way to reduce it is to design system of excuses. Distribution of excuses within a social group brings about anomie – when norms still exist but do not control behavior. Economical anomie is particular case of anomie manifesting itself in high level of tax evasion as it is shown by example of Russia.

The more detailed norms are the more farther they are from values. The less detailed norms are the more difficult to use them as direct regulator of behavior. The same is true about norms of a tax code that is now the field of fight between legislators and tax avoidance scheme designers. However there is the class of normative act as Citizens Charters proved to be effective regulating tool combining advantages of both – moral philosophy and legal act. Another possible solution is – code of ethics, although it's 'working' only if the group concerned has high social status. To make both these instruments effective the definite participation rate is required. It will be difficult to realize in countries with low social capital like Russia. One of the way to increase it is to achieve sustainable economical growth even though in combination with political stability with less democratic content. Another possibility is to use reverse connection between social capital and economical development and through propaganda to influence level of participation.

As qualitative research proved despite grave historical experience with the taxation Russians possess inner honest taxpayer norms and experience cognitive dissonance when evading taxes. Three standard types of excuses used to reduce this dissonance are generally compatible with Kosewski theory, so making the target of informational campaign the excuses it is possible to improve taxpayer's discipline.

References

A First Look at Communication Theory. ed. by Em Griffin, McGraw-Hill, Inc, (1997).

Beamish T.D., Biggart N.W. The economic sociology of conventions: habit, custom, practice, and routine in market order. Annual Review of Sociology, Vol. 29, (2003).

Ballarino G., Shadee H. Civicness and Economic Performance. A longitudinal Analysis of Italian Provinces, 1980-2000. European Sociological Review Vol. 21 Number 3, July, (2005), pp. 243-257.

Birkbeck, C., LaFree G. The Situational Analysis of Crime and Deviance. Annual Review of Sociology, 19, (1993), pp. 113-37.

Citizen's Charters: Selected Examples. United Nations Development Program, (2002).

Crozier, M. The Bureaucratic Phenomenon. The University of Chicago Press Phoenix Books, (1967).

Esteller-More, A. Is there a Connection Between the Tax Administration and the Political Power? International Tax and Public Finance, 12, (2005), pp. 639-663.

Feld, L.P., Frey, B.S. Trust Breeds Trust: How taxpayers are Treated. CESifo Working Paper 322, Munich, (2000).

Festinger, L. A theory of cognitive dissonance. Evanston, IL: Row, Peterson, (1957).

Fischhoff, B. Understanding long-term environmental risks. J. Risk and Uncertainty 3, (1990), pp. 315-30.

Hobson, J. M. The wealth of states: A comparative sociology of international economic and political change. Cambridge: University Press, (1997).

Horton, J. The Dehumanization of Anomie and Alienation: A Problem in the Ideology of Sociology. British Journal of Sociology, Vol. 15, (1964), pp. 283-300.

Iyengar, S. S., Lepper, M. R. Rethinking the role of choice: A cultural perspective on intrinsic motivation. Journal of Personality and Social Psychology, 76, (1999), pp. 349-366.

James, S., Murphy, K., Reinhart, M. The Taxpayers' Charter: A case study in tax administration. Journal of Australian Taxation, (2006) (in press). http://ctsi.anu.edu.au/-publications/taxpubs/Murphy.James.JAT.pdf.

Kahenman, D, Tversky, A. Choices, Values, and Frames. New York: Cambridge Univ. Press, (2000).

Kaminski, A. Z., Kaminski, B. Korupcja Rzadow Wydawnictwo TRIO. Warszawa: Institut Studiow Politycznych Polskiej Academii Nauk, (2002).

Kordonski, S. Transformation of administrative market. (2001), www.libertarium.ru.

Kosewski, M. Ludzie w sytuacijach pokusy i upokorzenia", Wiedza Powszechna, Warszawa.

Mayers, D. G. Social psychology. 7th ed. McGraw Hill, (2005), rus. transl. "Piter".

Merton, R. K. Social Theory and Social Structure. New York: Free Press of Glencoe, (1957).

OECD Committee of Fiscal Affairs Forum on Tax Administration. Taxpayers' Rights and Obligations – Practice Note. (2003), GAP002 Available from the OECD website and accessed on 6 May 2004.

Pratkanis, A. R., Aronson, E. Age of Propaganda: The Everyday Use and Abuse of Persuasion. W. H. Freemand and Co.NY, (2001).

Schneider, F., Enste, D. The Shadow Economy: An International Survey. Cambridge University Press, (2003).

Sen, A. K., Collective Choice and Social Welfare, San Fransisco, (1970).

Short, J. F., Strodtbech, F. L. Group Process and Gang Delinquency. Chicago: University of Chicago Press, (1965).

Slovic, P, Fishhoff, B, Lichtenstein, S. Rating risks. Environment 21, (1979), pp. 14-20.

Therborn, G., Back to Norms! On the Scope and Dynamics of Norms and Normative Action. Current Sociology, November Vol. 50 (6), (2002), pp. 863-830.

Tversky, A, Kahenman, D. Judgement under uncertainty: heuristics and biases: Biases in judgments reveal some heuristics of thinking under uncertainty. Science 185, (1974), pp. 1124-29.

Property, Social Order, And Public Finance

Richard E. Wagner

Abstract

This paper probes an alternative approach to the theory of public finance, where the state is treated as an order and not as an organization. Hobbes-like formulations of the generation of order are replaced by Aristotelian-like formulations where property and state are coeval and grounded in human nature. The theory of public finance is correspondingly construed as a facet of social theorizing and not as a facet of systems design, and with the domain of welfare economics conceptualized in terms of a theory of fiscal sociology and not in Paretian fashion.

Property, State, And Tectonic Political Economy

This paper is concerned with the object we denote as state and its relationship to those other objects we denote as economy and society, or, alternatively, market. In short, state is conceptualized as an order and not an organization, and the activities of state are treated as latent in human nature and emerging out of interaction among people[1]. State and market are conceptualized as coeval, in contrast to the Hobbes-like formulations where individuals subsequently form states. Property is never wholly private or wholly collective, but rather always resides in some mixed status that invariably entails margins of contestability that generates a tectonic political economy of varying degrees of turbulence.

Hobbesian Agonistics

It is a common analytical device to treat the formation of states or other political entities as resultants of people's prior rights of private property. Within this Hobbes-like orientation, what is a puny and insecure form of private property may be strengthened by pooling some of those rights to form a state. If strengthening does result, people will value what remains in their bundle of property rights more highly than they valued the full bundle before the state was established. Whether the post-state residual bundle is truly more valuable than the pre-state bundle depends on various types of considerations that are explored in this literature concerning this presumptive leap from anarchy,

1 Wagner, R. Fiscal Sociology, and the Theory of Public Finance: An Exploratory Essay. Cheltenham UK: Edward Elgar, (2007).

as illustrated by such works as Tullock, Buchanan, de Jasay, Morris, Young, Gordon and Barzel[2].

These formulations start with adults whose property is insecure because they lack confidence that other people will leave their property alone. The resolution to this presumed prisoner's dilemma is to create a state to provide security. As is well explored in this literature, this formulation raises the ancient problem of who guards the guardians: a state that can secure rights of property by keeping the peace is also one that can use its police power to abridge those rights. One problem these efforts face was articulated nicely by Emile Durkheim[3] in his objection to Herbert Spencer's treatment of society as a contractual formation. Durkheim pointed out that the ability of people even to think in terms of contracting with one another is to presume the existence of the society that contracting is thought to form. The ability to think of contract, after all, presumes that the participants possess that modicum of commonality that we denote as society. The parties to a contract constitute a society before they contract; contract follows society, it doesn't lead it. The problematic feature of the Hobbes-like formulations was expressed particular clearly by Norbert Elias[4], though it recurs back to Aristotle. Adults don't arrive at adulthood while living alone. They do so while living in groups, mostly families these days though the historical record presents many forms. While individuals comprise society, the structured formations that individuals generate through their interactions with one another serve to create, shape, and regulate patterns of individual action and conduct. Habits of heart and mind are formed before adulthood, which, however, is not to deny that they can continue to evolve once adulthood has been reached.

In a somewhat related vein, Liam Murphy and Thomas Nagel[5] argue that conventional discussions of how states redistribute income among people are off base because those discussions presume individual and not collective ownership as the point of departure. Their alternative conceptual window reverses the Hobbes-like sequence by invoking collective ownership as the point of departure, and with individuals allowed through collective action to withdraw some collective property for their personal use. Thus the state does not redistribute, but rather changes the terms of withdrawal. Nagel and Murphy have, I believe, done a fine service in bringing into the analytical foreground the relationship among property, people

2 See Tullock, G. (ed. 1972), Buchanan, J. M. (1975), de Jasay, A. (1985), Morris, C. W. (1998), Young, H. P. (1998), Gordon, S. (1999), Barzel, Y. (2002).

3 Durkheim, E. The Division of Labor in Society. London: Mac-millan, 1893 [1933].

4 Elias, N. The Civilizing Process. New York: Pantheon Books, (1982).
Elias, N. The Society of Individuals. Oxford: Basil Blackwell, 1939 [1991].

5 Murphy, Liam and Thomas Nagel, The Myth of Ownership. Oxford: Oxford University Press, (2002).

and societies or states, even if their sequence is as incoherent as the Hobbes-like sequence.

Property, Market, And State

Within an emergent ontology that treats both individuals and society as real objects[6], questions arise concerning the relation between the two[7]. The pure logic of a market economy explores the notion of an unhampered market economy. This is an ideal-typical construction and not an effort to represent reality. An unhampered market economy describes human interaction when all action is governed wholly by private property and freedom of contract and association. Not only is such an arrangement non-existent, it is also impossible within its own logic, which has nothing to do with overcoming Hobbes-like problems of predation. It has to do rather with Durkheim-like issues. Starting from a world where all rights of property are held privately so that no attribute of commonness remains to be found, it is impossible for two parties to trade without violating private property. Whether a vendor approaches you by email, by telephone, or by direct visitation, rights of private property are bring abridged. To be sure, we don't think if it this way, but this is because we have internalized recognition that the world we experience is not partitioned into mutually exclusive domains of private property, nor could it be. Action in society requires some irreducible element of commonality which lubricates action in society, but at the same time generates scope for conflict.

Property denotes proper-ness (or propriety) in conduct. From where do the requisite notions of properness arise, it can be asked? From other people it can be answered, as conveyed by the regulative patterns on individual conduct that emerge out of societal formations. For the most part, people accept such regulative patterns as second-nature, though not fully and with differences arising among people in the extent of their acceptance. This is hardly surprising, for without contestation there would be stagnation and not development, for conflict is valuable for fomenting societal change, which, of course, is not to claim that conflict is always beneficial[8].

Property, market, and state all derive from the confrontation between human nature and scarcity. Universal private property is impossible, but so is universal common property. Universal private property would allow no contact between

6 Wagner, R. Choice, Catallaxy, and Just Taxation: Contrasting Architectonics for Fiscal Theorizing. Social Philosophy and Policy 23, (2006).

7 My orientation in this regard is similar to that expressed by Tony Lawson (1997).

8 Coser, L. A. The Functions of Social Conflict. New York: Free Press, (1964).

or among people, so markets could never emerge. The emergence of markets requires spheres of commonality, not the least of which is language, the generation of which is not a private activity. Universal commonality would allow no exchange because exchange requires private property. Some mixture of private and common is the only theoretical-historical possibility.

To be sure, I don't use state to denote what we mean today by the concept of the nation-state. The nation-state, with its territorially-based claims has come about only over the past few centuries, but states as authority outside of oneself are universal. Properness of action is invariably determined by other people. In most cases most of the time, we internalize that sense of propriety and don't feel particularly constricted by it. Private property limits one's freedom of action, but common property does not, but for the most part we sense that private property contributes to good order, but not always and not for everyone.

The main point, though, is that what constitutes properness, and thus property, in individual action is determined through societal processes of some sort. Those processes, moreover, are grounded in conflict that becomes resolved in a way that leads to some redefinition or clarification of the constituents of property. Claims of property arise only in the presence of scarcity; indeed, scarcity is just another name for conflict, regardless of whether that conflict is manifest or suppressed. To hold some property right today is thus no guarantee to hold it tomorrow. You will hold it tomorrow only if no one complains about your holding it today. If someone does complain about your conduct today, whether you continue to hold the right to act in that manner tomorrow will depend on how that conflict is resolved, and with that resolution having almost nothing to do with your preference in the matter.

Displeasure And Institutional Arrangements For Mitigating Conflict

Suppose a putrid aroma from a nearby factory sometimes hangs in the air[9]. People who live, work, or play in the vicinity are displeased with this situation, often intensely so. This displeasure will manifest itself in some form. Indeed, there are many forms of possible manifestation. The Coase-inspired[10] gloss on this situation keeps the conflict within the market arena by conceptualizing resolution through market exchange. As we know, the factory can either try to secure per-

9 Water pollution could have provided an alternative illustration, as exemplified by Jürgen Backhaus (1999).

10 Coase, R. H. The Problem of Social Cost. Journal of Law and Economics 3, (1960).

mission from the residents to spew putrid air or the residents can try to convince the factory owners to shift to some costlier process of production that sweetens its airborne emissions before releasing them. The Coasian resolution uses a market process to resolve the conflict within the market.

While the Coase-inspired literature is right to note that this conflict can be resolved within the market, other arenas for resolution are also present within society. Whereas a systems design approach to public finance might be used to argue for market-based or state-based approaches to conflict resolution, a social-theoretic approach would treat the particular approach taken as an emergent feature of societal processes. While the Coasian formulation brings closure to what is otherwise an open societal setting, the actual paths to conflict resolution are limited only by the imagination of the participants; social theorizing within a framework of open concepts must be open to all such acts of imagination. The conflict might be resolved within the market, but it need not. The challenge for social theorizing, as against systems design, is to acquire insight into the variable historical forms through which conflicts are resolved, as against arguing for market-based resolutions as superior to other forms of resolution.

The conventional theoretical posture is for the theorist to theorize from a vantage point that stands outside the object of theorization. An alternative posture is to theorize from inside the object of theorization. Such theorizing from the inside looking out is to seek to render social processes and institutions intelligible in terms of people formulating and pursuing plans, and with the meaning of human action rendered sensible in this manner[11].

With respect to the concrete situation being considered here, we may assume that the stench is sufficiently putrid that those who live nearby are intensely irritated. The irritation with the aroma is apparent from conversation in stores and on streets, from newspaper editorials, and from numerous other sources. With the factory located in the neighborhood, we may assume that the people who work there are from the neighborhood as well. Must it not be embarrassing for them to work for such a disgraceful outfit? Such employees may find their circle of friends constricting, or portending such a result should they remain employed there.

It is easy enough to envision market-generated resolution of the conflict. To keep its labor force in the presence of the growing stench, the factory will probably have to pay employees more to compensate them for the loss of friendships. It is entirely conceivable that it would be less expensive for the factory to clean and sweeten its emissions than to pay its employees enough to compensate for their loss of friendships.

11 Lachmann, L. Capital, Expectations, and the Market Process. Kansas City: Sheed Andrews and McMeel, (1977).

When social processes are modeled from the inside-out, it becomes quickly apparent that societies also contain other processes for conflict resolution. As the stench worsens, some employees of the factory might find their homes sprayed with paint and their lawns littered with garbage. Complaints subsequently filed with the Chief of Police, moreover, might not bring satisfaction because no apprehensions are made. Indeed, the complainants might have suspected this when they noticed that the Chief wears a mask to work to reduce the degree of putridity of the air he breathes. While the factory will have to pay even higher compensating differentials, property rights will be in the process of changing as the conflict is spilling into other societal arenas and forums.

The connections that run through a society are numerous and dense in places, and can lead in truly surprising directions. Non-market forms of organization, moreover, often have a structure that works against the free riding that is often thought to plague collective action. To keep the numbers small, suppose the area has 100 families. This is large enough to give credence to the free rider argument. Thus if someone were asked to imagine getting the 100 families together to determine contributions to make to buy aroma abatement equipment for the factory, it is plausible that a good deal of free riding would result, and with the extent of free riding rising with the number of participants. Life in society, however, does not generally unfold in this manner, as society is not encountered as a formless mass but as a structured network of connections and relationships.

Leadership and entrepreneurship are generally in play, and part of the entrepreneurial challenge is to construct networks of relationships that offset potential free riding. A far likelier scenario would begin with some prominent citizens who had heard many expressions of irritation as well as bearing their own. They could take the conflict to the marked by talking with the factory CEO and working out an agreement. But they needn't do so, and perhaps they might have tried and were rebuffed.

Within this alternative context, suppose the 100 families fall pretty naturally into a dozen or so neighborhoods of around eight or nine families each. The prominent citizens who spoke with the factory CEO live in those neighborhoods. They have parties for their neighbors where they discuss the situation (though these are far from the first discussions they have had about the stench). Through this process pledges and commitments are made. There is no guarantee that everyone will participate and that free riding will be avoided, but we do know that much collective action gets organized through these kinds of processes, processes that often contain mixture of consent and duress, and with the duress occurring not at the point of a gun but through the fear of being regarded as a free-loader and of being shunned.

What is set in motion in any case is preparation for legislative and judicial action as alternative approaches to resolving the conflict that has arisen. The alternative processes and channels that I have described—gossip, parties, discussion groups, and editorial writing – require time to develop momentum. If such conflict is resolved as it buds, so to speak, it seems more likely to remain within the market sphere than to surface in other arenas. The aforementioned alternative processes involve people in establishing connections with one another. The establishment of a connection, as illustrated by a discussion group entails a fixed cost to create that particular networked relationship. Once established, that network can be maintained at lower cost. The longer such conflicts fester, the more fully such alternative processes will emerge, and which in turn surely supplies momentum to efforts to take those conflicts to non-market forums to exploit complementarities in the associated processes of conflict resolution. Legislatures and courts come increasingly into the picture as the conflict simmers, due to reconfigurations in the networks of human relationships and association set in motion by the conflict.

States As Orders And Not Organizations

Contemporary scholarship mostly treats the state as an organization, and analogizes states to firms. My alternative point of departure treats the state as an arena of interaction, just as market denotes an arena of interaction. Among other things, tectonic turbulence arises at the various boundaries where the two arenas and the actions they contain rub against one another. The market is the arena where people don't raise complaints about actions undertaken by other people. The propriety of individual actions is not questioned; those actions are governed by the framework we denote as private property. The state is the arena where the propriety of individual action is questioned, and in consequence individual action is bent to conform to the resulting societal articulation of propriety[12]. There are actually several such societal arenas, all of which involve the transformation of third party desires into first party actions.

This ontology, wherein both individuals and society have real existence, though at different levels, is conformable with a bivalent characterization of human nature. One feature of human nature is a desire for autonomy in action, which maps into private property and human relationships governed by private property. The other feature can be expressed variously as a desire for solidarity or a need for connections with others, and in any cases maps into some form of socially-constituted commons. What particular form is a historical matter that is distinct from the underlying, universal quality that informs all such sentiments.

12 In referring to societal articulation, I am working with an ontology that treats society as a real object, though certainly not as some sentient, acting creature.

State is the term I use to express this universal quality, in distinction to the many particular forms through which this quality can find and has found historical expression. With state as an order whose foundation resides in human nature, just as does market, the location or establishment of particular enterprises within the state follows entrepreneurial actions just as does the establishment of enterprises within the market. State and market denote arenas of interaction within society, and with that interaction reflective of and emergent from human nature.

Figure 1 illustrates what I have in mind. The vertices denote enterprises and the edges denote connections among the enterprises. The circles denote enterprises that are established within the market according to the framework of private property. The squares denote enterprises that are established within the state according to the institutional framework for collective property that is in place. This graph of relationships is incomplete, which is a graph that maps comfortably into notions of localized and particularized knowledge. Furthermore, Figure 1 shows only relationships among enterprises. An alternative hypergraph sketch could show another plane with customers and clients, and with connections running from that plane to the enterprise plane. Figure 1 is just an abstract representation of a snapshot. A later snapshot would show a different graph. The transformation from the former to the latter graph is the province of entrepreneurial activity.

Both market and state activity emerge out of entrepreneurial action. Moreover, state-based enterprises as well as market-based enterprises act within society and not on or over society. This, I believe, is a significant distinction, one that is perhaps best clarified by historical illustration. Consider the American adoption of Prohibition in 1919. If state acts on society, Prohibition would have converted the United States into an alcohol-free zone. Prohibition changes the rules of the game, so subsequent action proceeds in some alcohol-free manner.

We know that Prohibition didn't work this way (see, for instance, Miron and Zwiebel[13] and Thornton[14]). It led to some reduction in the total volume of alcohol consumed, but it also led to changes in the forms in which alcohol was consumed by increasing the use of distilled beverages which are easier to conceal. It also led to shootings to resolve commercial disputes, to bribery, and to commercial espionage. These consequences are easy to understand when it is recognized that state enterprises can only act within and not on society. Prohibition was not a rule that created an alcohol-free America. It was a rule that empowered designated state-supported enterprises to apprehend people who were caught in possession

---

13 Miron, J. A., Zwiebel, J. Alcohol Consumption during Pro-hibition. American Economic Review, Proceedings 81, (1991).

14 Thornton, M. The Economics of Prohibition. Salt Lake City: University of Utah Press, (1991).

of alcoholic beverages. The effect of this rule change enters society at particular nodes within the societal nexus, and the subsequent impact of that change depends on how it spreads throughout the societal nexus. Furthermore, something doesn't spread just because it is articulated; it spreads because there are people who are actively pushing its spread. Connections, moreover, run in two directions. A police officer might be empowered to make arrests for possession, and might also like alcohol himself. In short, any articulation of state policy does nothing to change anything. Change always starts at some state-supported node, but how extensively it spreads is an emergent result of interaction and not a result of policy choice.[15]

Bureaucratic Free Enterprise: Tullock And Mises Amplified

With state construed as an order or complex system and not an organization, we enter a situation where there is not one locus of sovereignty where action in the name of state can be either initiated or withheld. What we have is what Gordon Tullock[16], in amplifying and extending Ludwig von Mises[17] described as bureaucratic free enterprise. If state denotes an arena and not a firm, it is an arena that contains many distinct firms, as illustrated by Figure 1. To be sure, the Tullock-Mises notion of bureaucratic free enterprise was articulated in the context of the state as a firm, only one that had grown so large that it became uncontrollable. Hence, individual units within the state apparatus practiced a form of free enterprise. Once the state is construed as an order and not an organization, a form of free enterprise becomes recognized as the ordinary mode of operation and not some aberration.

Plans are action directed at future objectives. Entrepreneurial plans provide the propulsive energy through which societies generate their own transformation. It is straightforward to characterize entrepreneurship within the market, for it is induced by beliefs about profits that can be captured by seizing tomorrow by initiating a plan today. Entrepreneurship within the state arena has the same formal

15 It makes a big difference in this regard whether state in-jections have general or only partial support within the population. When support is general, mere articulation can pretty much spread the change. Traffic control is a good illustration of this. With other measures, however, where state actions gives advantages to some people and imposes disabilities on others, as illustrated by Prohibition, societal consequences emerge through interaction and will generally have effects quite at variance with what would have happened had mere articulation been sufficient, or nearly so, to generate the called-for changes in individual action.

16 Tullock, G. The Politics of Bureaucracy. Washington: Public Affairs Press, (1965).

17 Von Mises, L. Bureaucracy. New Haven, CT: Yale University Press, (1944).

character, for the effort to replace less desired states with more desired states is a universal quality of human action; indeed, we couldn't even recognize ourselves if it weren't true.

The substance of state-based entrepreneurship must take shape differently from that taken by market-based entrepreneurship, due to differences in the forms of property and property-based relationships in the two settings. Profit simply signifies that gains from trade have been captured. Within the market, much of that capture takes the form of capital appreciation. Within the state arena, however, there can be no capital appreciation. The absence of capital appreciation is a historical feature that accompanies the absence of transferable ownership within the state arena. The search for gain, however, is a universal feature of humanity. Within the state arena, profit must be captured in other forms than capital appreciation.

Refer again to the enterprise map represented by Figure 1.That map depicts eight market-based enterprises and six state-based enterprises, to reflect some rough correspondence with various aggregate measures of market and state activity. The pattern of connections shown in Figure 1 has a story to tell that reflects a presumption about the capture of profit from state-based enterprises. Each market-based enterprise has connections with multiple other market-based enterprises. This is sensible, as all such enterprises exist within a chain of transactions, providing output to some enterprises and receiving input from other enterprises.

The pattern of connections is different with state-based enterprises. As shown in Figure 1, state-based enterprises establish connections with market-based enterprises but not with other state-based enterprises. This is not to suggest that such connections aren't ever created, but is only to note that they are rare. Connections between state-based and market-based enterprises can be important conduits by which profit is extracted from state-based enterprises. A state-based enterprise that had no connections with market-based enterprises would be unable to appropriate profit from its activities. The nonprofit status of state-based enterprises does not eliminate profit but only changes the concrete forms it takes. Those forms, moreover, are surely myriad. As an abstract matter, profits can be transferred through market-based enterprises either by increasing the prices paid for inputs or reducing the prices charged for outputs. Which form this transfer of profits takes, moreover, will depend on the identity and position of the genuine owners and sponsors of any particular state-based enterprise.

Economists are, of course, accustomed to thinking of profit in monetary form. This is the normal form within market-based arrangements, due to the alienability of property. Nonprofit forms of enterprise surely offer greater scope for nonmonetary forms of profit extraction, in addition to indirect extraction through market-based enterprises. One seemingly growing form of such extraction could perhaps be described as a form of sport whose popularity has grown with increasing wealth: meddling with other people. When most people had to work 14 or so hours a day for six days a week to support themselves, they had little time or energy for meddling. It's now a different matter, as work takes only about half the time it formerly took. The week is as long as ever, of course, so people must find other things to do with their time. Some people spend more time in athletic forms of sporting activity, as reflected in the growing membership and participation of gymnasiums and health clubs. Other people spend more of that released time in non-athletic forms of sporting activity, as reflected in the growth in an enormous array of interest group activity. While I am confident that a significant portion of interest group activity represents investment in the search for profit, I am also confident that a significant portion represents a desire to participate in sporting activities in a collective setting of some sort. Indeed, it is probably the union of both that gives them political salience, as a form of Baptist-and-bootlegger story[18].

Tectonic Societal Landscapes

The enterprise map presented in Figure 1 appears placid because its medium of presentation leaves no alternative. Yet life within the enterprise sea charted by Figure 1 cannot be placid. Ordinary contract among holders of private property is generally placid as both parties gain through trade. It must be different with relationships that cross the boundaries between the two forms of enterprise. Relationships between market-based enterprises are normally placid, but relationships between market-based and state-based enterprises will often be accompanied by turbulence. Alternatively, to change to a landscape metaphor, the surface that connects market-based enterprises can be reasonably characterized as continuous and twice differentiable, but the surface that connects state-based and market-based enterprises will contain tectonic regions.[19]

This reference to tectonics brings to mind Maffeo Pantaleoni's[20] treatment of parasitical political pricing, which is discussed in Wagner[21]. Pantaleoni developed

18 Yandle, B. Bootleggers and Baptists in Retrospect. Regulation 22, (1999), pp. 5-7.

19 Young (1991) describes tectonic politics in a related context. In a similar vein, Jason Potts (2000) distinguishes between integral and non-integral geometries, only he refers to market relationships generally. I don't dispute Potts' formulation in this respect, but I want to place the focus on the different forms of relationship among alternative forms of enterprise.

20 Pantaleoni, M. Considerazioni sulle proprieta di un sistema di prezzi politici. Giornale degli Economisti 42, (1911).

21 Wagner, R. Parasitical Political Pricing, Economic Cal-culation, and the Size of Government: Variations on a Theme by Maffeo Pantaleoni. Journal of Public Finance and Public Choice 15, (1997).

his model with reference to two bazaars. One bazaar denoted the ordinary market arrangement. The other bazaar denoted a politically organized bazaar where prices were political and not market prices. The exact character of political prices depends on the tax system that is used. For instance, a tax that is in proportion to income creates a system of political pricing where prices rise in proportion to income. People with lower incomes would pay lower prices in the political bazaar, while people with higher incomes would pay lower prices in the market bazaar. The movement of customers would set in motion various changes in the bazaars, because the loss of buyers who were charged higher prices by the political bazaar would erode the ability of the political bazaar to offer lower prices to other buyers.

At this stage, the analysis can proceed in any of several directions, only one of which will be considered here. The creation of the political bazaar violates market conformability as this was articulated initially by Walter Eucken[22] and as examined in the essays collected in Leipold and Pies[23], as well as Vanberg[24]. It does not change the universal applicability of economic law but only changes the course it takes through society. What happens subsequently is a course of development that can be rendered intelligible as a playing out of the societal tectonics that is set in motion by the injection of political pricing into a society[25]. The low prices that enterprises inside the political bazaar offer to some buyers are made possible by the high prices those enterprises charge to other buyers. If people who are charged high prices take their business to enterprises located in the market bazaar, the viability of enterprises located within the political bazaar will be threatened. This possibility sets in motion clashes of interest within the society, and those clashes can play out in any number of ways. However they might play out, they are intelligible features of the non-optional character of economic law.

It is surely noteworthy that in their treatise on *Crime and Human Nature*, James Wilson and Richard Herrnstein[26] limited the crimes they treated to what they called "natural crimes." These were things like murder, robbery, theft, rape, and incest. The crimes those didn't treat could reasonably be called "political crimes" to denote that they represented efforts within a political regime to suppress forms of activity that supporters of that regime want to suppress. Legisla-

---

22 Eucken, W. Grundsätze der Wirtschaftspolitik. Tübingen: J. C. B. Mohr, (1952).

23 Leipold, H., Pies, I. (eds.) Ordnungstheorie und Ordnungs-politik: Konzeptionen und Entwicklungsperspektiven. Stutt-gart: Lucius & Lucius, (2000).

24 Vanberg, V. Ordnungstheorie as Constitutional Economics: The German Conception of a 'Social Market Economy. ORDO 39, (1988).

25 It is also a course of development that was illustrated nicely by the American experience with Prohibition, and is also illustrated nicely by various contemporary experiences of a similar sort.

26 Wilson, J., Herrnstein, R. Crime and Human Nature. New York: Simon and Schuster, (1985).

tion, however, can't repeal natural law any more than a surfer on a board can repeal physics. Natural crimes have no defenders, and even guilty parties know they are wrong and try to avoid detection.

The situation is different with political crimes. For instance, such a straightforward activity as buying and selling stock is criminal under a wide variety of circumstances even though many and perhaps most people see nothing wrong in doing so without filing notice or asking permission from some regulatory agency. Just because a legislative assembly or regulatory agency seeks to prevent such trades doesn't make them wrongful to many or perhaps even most people. It means instead that people should be cautious, and in many cases will be inventive in developing new forms of contract and enterprises that will allow otherwise proscribed transactions to go forward. This situation will in turn induce governing officials to spy on ordinary citizens. This in turn, would seem to transform a "we" into an "us and they." By this, I mean that public officials morph from being people who help to facilitate commerce to being people who week to take on some lordship position over society, by replacing contract-based relationships with status-based relationships.

It is instructive in this regard to consider Martin Buber's[27] distinction between two ideal-typical patterns of relationship. One type is of I-It form and the other is of I-Thou form. It is straightforward enough to assert that I-It refers to relationships between people and inanimate objects while I-Thou refers to relationships between people. As ideal types, this is what the terms signify. I-Thou are relationships grounded in the mutuality of engagement, while I-It are relationships grounded in detachment. They each have their proper spheres, and to some extent Buber is concerned to clarify those spheres. But beyond this, Buber is also interested in the feedback effects that are exerted when an I treats a Thou as an It.

There would seem to be some connection between Buber's formulation and those advanced by both Pantaleoni and Eucken, or at least I will try to sketch such a connection. I-Thou relationships are between equals, and with both parties acting within a framework of mutuality and respect. I-It relationships arise when one person regards the other not also as a subject but as an object to be acted upon and manipulated. Market-based relationships seem typically to be of the I-Thou form, where the focus of the conversation between the parties is on whether they can arrange something that will be for their mutual benefit.

By contrast, political relationships seem often to involve significant elements of I-It relationships. It is instructive to compare how government agencies and private businesses handle similar security concerns regarding personal identification. It is now illegal throughout the United States to renew driver's licenses

27 Buber, M. I and Thou. New York: Scribner's, (1958).

online, as renewal now requires personal visits, sometimes multiple visits, reflecting the detachment of I-it relationships. In contrast, banks and other financial institutions deal with the same concerns and situations, and handle them in generally friendly and engaging ways with their customers.

Economists have often claimed that state-based enterprises are more costly producers than market-based enterprises, though the empirical claims in this regard have a good deal of ambiguity. Whatever the strength of those empirical claims, they have analytical cogency on their side. That analytical cogency, however, focuses on technical efficiency in combining inputs, by arguing that residual claimacy gives stronger incentive to achieve least-cost combinations than is present when residual claimacy is absent. Buber calls our attention to a different dimension of human existence, where we can ask whether the organizational arrangements we generate can influence the people we become and the ways we relate to one another. The treatment of people as objects and not as subjects is surely more prevalent within state-based enterprises than within market-based enterprises, and may thus present another reason for seeking to restrain the sphere of state-based activity within society, even though that sphere will not and, indeed, cannot dissolve.

In Closing

This paper has sought to envision the state through an alternative analytical window, one that conceptualized states as orders and not as organizations. A wholly market economy organized exclusively through private property is as much a historical impossibility as is a wholly collective economy. We necessarily live with a mixed framework of property-governed relationships, and this mixture is accompanied by tectonic turbulence at various boundaries where relationships organized within different zones of action come into contact. The extent of that turbulence at any historical moment, moreover, is not an object of direct choice but is an emergent feature of complex societal processes whose control may range between difficult and impossible.

The turbulence of this unavoidably mixed framework, moreover, confronts us with a continuing dilemma regarding the maintenance of social relationships based on mutuality and respect. On the one hand, the inequalities that arise through market success tend to feed the vanities by exaggerating individual accomplishment relative to what is really due to the supporting nexus of relationships. On the other hand, political action creates positions of lordship in place of relationships of mutuality, thereby transforming I-Thou relationships into I-It relationships.

Figure 1: Emergent Map of Market and State Enterprises

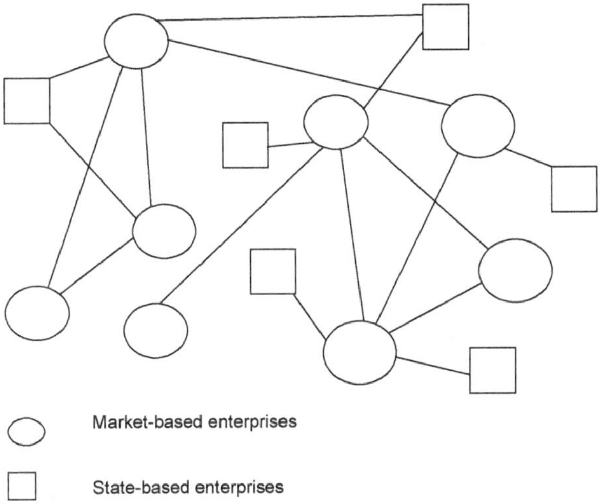

References

Backhaus, J. Land Rents and Ecological Crisis: The Case of the Oder River Valley. American Journal of Economics and Sociology 58, (1999), pp. 249-52.

Barzel, Y. A Theory of the State. Cambridge: Cambridge University Press, (2002).

Buber, M. I and Thou. New York: Scribner's, (1958).

Buchanan, J. M. The Limits of Liberty. Chicago: University of Chicago Press, (1975).

Coase, R. H. The Problem of Social Cost. Journal of Law and Economics 3, (1960), pp. 1-44.

Coser, L. A. The Functions of Social Conflict. New York: Free Press, (1964).

de Jasay, A. The State. Oxford: Basil Blackwell, (1985).

Durkheim, E. The Division of Labor in Society. London: Macmillan, 1893 [1933].

Elias, N. The Civilizing Process. New York: Pantheon Books, (1982).

Elias, N. The Society of Individuals. Oxford: Basil Blackwell, 1939 [1991].

Eucken, W. Grundsätze der Wirtschaftspolitik. Tübingen: J. C. B. Mohr, (1952).

Gordon, S. Controlling the State: Constitutionalism from Ancient Athens to Today. Cambridge: Harvard University Press, (1999).

Lachmann, L. Capital, Expectations, and the Market Process. Kansas City: Sheed Andrews and McMeel, (1977).

Lawson, T. Economics and Reality. London: Routledge, (1997).

Leipold, H., Pies, I. (eds.) Ordnungstheorie und Ordnungspolitik: Konzeptionen und Entwicklungs-perspektiven. Stuttgart: Lucius & Lucius, (2000).

Miron, J. A., Zwiebel, J. Alcohol Consumption during Prohibition. American Economic Review, Proceedings 81, (1991), pp. 242-47.

Mises, L. von Bureaucracy. New Haven, CT: Yale University Press, (1944).

Morris, C. W. An Essay on the Modern State. New York, Cambridge University Press, (1998).

Murphy, L., Nagel T. The Myth of Ownership. Oxford: Oxford University Press, (2002).

Pantaleoni, M. Considerazioni sulle proprieta di un sistema di prezzi politici. Giornale degli Economisti 42, (1911), pp. 9-29 and 114-33.

Potts, J. The New Evolutionary Microeconomics: Complexity, Competence, and Adaptive Behaviour. Cheltenham, UK: Edward Elgar, (2000).

Thornton, M. The Economics of Prohibition. Salt Lake City: University of Utah Press, (1991).

Tullock, G. The Politics of Bureaucracy. Washington: Public Affairs Press, (1965).

Tullock, G. (ed.) Explorations in the Theory of Anarchy. Blacksburg, VA: University Publications, (1972).

Tullock, G. (ed.) Further Explorations in the Theory of Anarchy. Blacksburg, VA: University Publications, (1974).

Vanberg, V. Ordnungstheorie as Constitutional Economics: The German Conception of a 'Social Market Economy'. ORDO 39, (1988), pp. 17-31.

Wagner, R. Parasitical Political Pricing, Economic Calculation, and the Size of Government: Variations on a Theme by Maffeo Pantaleoni. Journal of Public Finance and Public Choice 15, (1997), pp. 135-46.

Wagner, R. Choice, Catallaxy, and Just Taxation: Contrasting Architectonics for Fiscal Theorizing. Social Philosophy and Policy 23, (2006), pp. 235-54.

Wagner, R. Fiscal Sociology, and the Theory of Public Finance: An Exploratory Essay. Cheltenham, UK: Edward Elgar, (2007).

Wilson, J., Herrnstein, R. Crime and Human Nature. New York: Simon and Schuster, (1985).

Yandle, B. Bootleggers and Baptists in Retrospect. Regulation 22, (1999), pp. 5-7.

Young, H. P. Individual Strategy and Social Order: An Evolutionary Theory of Institutions. Princeton: Princeton University Press, (1998).

Young, R. A. Tectonic Policies and Political Competition. In Albert Breton (et al. eds.) The Competitive State (Dordrecht: Kluwer Academic Publishers), (1991), pp. 129-45.

The Sociological Theory Of Fiscal Illusion And The Laffer Curve. Reflections On An Italian Case

S. Fedeli and F. Forte

Abstract

The first section of the paper is devoted to the theory of fiscal illusion by Amilcare Puviani and to the several fiscal illusion hindering the rational perception of the Laffer curve. In the second section, we consider the relevance of these fiscal illusions for the Italian two tier regime of labour contracts, introduced in the 1997-2001 period by means of partial liberalization and reduction of the social security contributions and payrolls (SC). The reform had important positive effects both on employment and on SC revenues, although with a time lag as for the Laffer effect. This Laffer effect is overshadowed by fiscal illusion due to the fact that the SC revenue, in spite of the great increase of employment bringing new SC revenue, was lower than in previous periods, due to the persisting difficulties of the labour market. Laffer effects emerged *only in comparison with the revenues in the absence of the reform.* In this comparison, an increase in employment occurred also for the labour contracts with high SC burden, not liberalized by the reform, likely because of bundling effects. A collateral fiscal illusion diminishing the appreciation of the positive fiscal effects of the reform lies in the fact that the lower SC paid on the new flexible labour contracts originated lower pensions rights. The claim that "because of the reform" part of the workers would get "lower pensions", however, overlooks the fact that, without the reform, most of the new employment would have not taken place and there would have not been any legal and economic basis for pensions.

Keywords: Fiscal sociology, fiscal illusion, Laffer Effect, Social Security contributions, Labour market liberalization.

JEL Codes: H79, Z13, E24, E62, J38.

Section I

1. *Reflections, in terms of Puviani's theory of political and fiscal illusion, about the critical points and the ambiguities of Laffer curve and about the reasons of a "taboo" against it.*

In the great tradition of Italian fiscal sociology (Mc Lure, 2007), three great figures emerge: Vilfredo Pareto, Maffeo Pantaleoni and Amilcare Puviani. In this paper, we focus on the seminal contribution of Amilcare Puviani on the political and fiscal illusion, also considering Pareto seminal contribution on "derivations" and "residue" in connection with fiscal illusion.

Amilcare Puviani (1903), in his seminal book, defines political illusions and fiscal illusions as wrong perceptions of the reality. They are classified in the two broad categories of positive and negative illusions. The positive illusions consist in perceiving as existing phenomena that do not exist. The negative illusions consist in not perceiving the existence of phenomena that exist. The theoretical background of Puviani's theory of fiscal illusion is in a public choice perspective. Indeed, Puviani considers the fiscal illusions as a component, perhaps the main component (but not the only important one), of the political illusions, which in a democracy may hinder the correct public choices of the citizens. In principle, taxes, by their level and quality, should be adopted by the governments in such a way that their marginal pain equalizes the marginal benefit obtained by their expenditure. However, because of the fiscal illusions on both the revenue and the expenditure sides, often, over taxation and over spending take place. Puviani recognizes that the opposite cases, of under taxing and under spending, may also take place because of fiscal illusions over stating the negative effects of taxes and under stating the benefits of public spending. Nevertheless, he tends to consider these cases rather secondary because normally politicians are interested to increase the size of the government and, thus, tend either to promote fiscal illusions that hide the negative effects of taxes and emphasize the positive effects of the spending or to conceal the real amount of revenues needed to balance the budget in order to gain popularity and power. Generally, Puviani's theory of fiscal illusion has been employed to explain over expansion of taxes or changes of taxes that, without diminishing the fiscal burden, appear to do so.[1] It may also be applied to the suggestions of the Keynesian fiscal policy of deficit spending as a way to increase employment, GDP and national welfare. Indeed, according to Buchanan and Wagner (1977), here there is a fiscal illusion because the perception of the burden of inflation and of public debt is lower than the true burden and lower than that of taxes.[2]

Puviani's theory of political and fiscal illusions, to our knowledge, has never been used to explain why the Laffer effects of tax cuts, motivated by supply side considerations, are systematically viewed with suspicion from the stand point of fiscal soundness. Nevertheless, the connection between the theory of fiscal illusion by Puviani and the Laffer curve is supported by several reasons. A first reason has to do with the existence of two "critical points" in the relation between the increases in tax burden and tax revenue: one beyond which the revenue does not increase and another beyond which the revenue decreases. Accordingly, a weak and a strong Laffer effect should be distinguished. The overlooking of the hidden explanatory variable of both effects, consisting in the increase of the eco-

1 For a brief review of the literature on fiscal illusion see Forte (2005, p.119).

2 See Buchnan and Wagner (1977), especially from paragraph on "Fiscal perception and Tax Institutions" up to the end.

nomic activity taxed, due to the reduction of tax burden, may lead to a political undervaluation of the *economic and social relevance* of the Laffer effect and of the meaning of a weak Laffer effect. A typical case is that of the tax on labour in relation to unemployment. A second possible reason of illusion may be that deriving from focusing only on the level of the tax rate while often the value of the taxable matter is paramount for the change in the burden in relation to a possible Laffer effect. This may be the case of the reduction of the unit burden of *ad valorem* taxes on factors of production and products when a liberalization reduces their prices. A third reason of fiscal illusions arises from the time lags of the Laffer effects. A fourth, particularly important, has to do with the difficulty of tracing Laffer effects when the ratio of revenues to GDP under a high tax burden and severe regulations is diminishing and the strong Laffer effect may attenuate the diminution. A fifth reason of tax illusion [3] may be the artificial reduction of the perception of the burden of the tax, that reinforces the "drive to contribute", caused by the ignorance or imperfect feeling of the tax shifting. A sixth reason of fiscal illusion it is the taboo ("residue" in Pareto's sociological theory) about the virtuosity of balancing the budget to protect from the tendency of the democracies to run deficits. This taboo or "residue" determines the non logical belief ("derivation" in Pareto's terminology) that reducing taxes always means to *permanently* reducing revenues.[4] Because of so many tax illusions hindering a rational perception of the effectiveness of the Laffer curve, it may be difficult to convince the public about the merits of policies bringing about delayed-hidden Laffer effect.

If taxes are the prices of public services, why people should believe that increases of these prices always increase the revenue of the Treasury, while this is not the case with market prices in monopolistic conditions? The Laffer curve with its shape intends to respond to this question: after a maximum, the increase of the tax burden implies a reduction of revenues, precisely as in the monopoly case of the market economy. A further reflection, however, shows that, conceptually, and perhaps also in the reality, there must be two *critical points*[5] on this tax

3 This explicitly considered by Puviani.

4 On the definition of "derivations" and "residue", in Pareto's sociology as "non logical action", see Pareto (1906), Chapter 2, Pareto (1923) and McLure (2007, Ch. 3, especially from p.44 and followings). Fiscal illusions in Paretian analytics are a subclass of the non logical actions (see Forte, 2005). They *may* be "derivations" from "residues" or may be con-caused by them, but they do not need to have this origin, as a reflection on the cases dealt with in the text easily shows.

5 The theory of "critical points" in economics, set forth by Emanuele Sella (1914 and 1916), has been subsequently applied by Luigi Einaudi (1949, III Part, pp. 138-46) to social institutions as the family or a monastic order, to social behaviour as the use of mass media (with reference to radio, because television was not yet diffused in the post war Italian society) and to political-

revenue curve. The first is the point beyond which an increase of a given tax or the general increase of tax burden does not increase the revenues, i. e., it causes a zero change of revenues. Let us call this effect a "weak" Laffer effect. The second critical point is that beyond which the revenues do decrease. Let us call it a "strong" Laffer effect. Lack of clarification about the relevance of both critical points may create an illusion – a negative political illusion in Puviani's terminology – against the relevance of the weak Laffer effects. Take the case of a tax on labour – the theme on which we focus in section II. If, by reducing the burden of the tax on labour, one gets a zero loss of revenue but increases employment, this is an important economic and social achievement and even if there is a minor loss of revenue, only a partial weak Laffer effect, that policy, likely, deserves to be pursued.

The Laffer curve, as it is normally presented, appears as a simple dual relation between the size of the revenue and the size of the tax burden on the considered taxable matter. The focus on this dual relation, overshadows the change in the units of taxable matter either in physical units or in money value, i. e. the explanatory variable of the Laffer curve, which makes the theorem obvious and not paradoxical (see figure 1, which shows the three dimensional Laffer curve, with the bold dotted line representing the average tax rate that maximises tax revenues for different level of employment)[6]. Lack of consideration of the explanatory variable behind the Laffer curve, may create a negative illusion about the relevance of the economic and social effects of the policy change leading to the reduction of the burden. This may be the case with a policy of liberalization and de-taxation of labour that leads to a great increase in employment of young people, females, workers in the less developed regions.

---

economic institutions. He distinguishes two critical points: the first beyond which an increase of the doses of the given rules or habits does not increase the utility and the second beyond which an increase causes a net diminution and, going on, a ruin. The application to the Laffer curve implies a correction of it, changing it from a simple parabolic curve to a curve with a plateau and then decreasing, initially smoothly, then rapidly or with a kink.

6 Notice that, in figure 1, for low level of employment the average tax (tax burden) that maximises the revenues is much higher than that maximising revenues for higher levels of employment.

Figure 1. Three dimensional Laffer curve

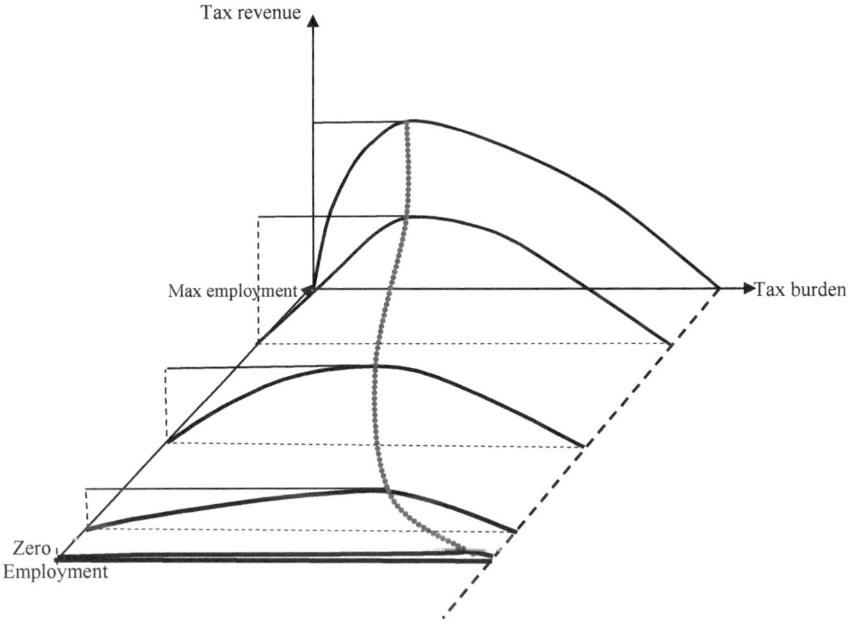

Another illusion may hinder a full appreciation of the relation between the change in the amount of revenue and the change in the tax burden shown by the Laffer curve. Normally this curve is presented in terms of the relation between the rate of reduction of given taxes and their fiscal revenue. However, the burden of a tax does not merely vary with a change in its rates. The taxable basis is also extremely important. Sometime governments practice a combination of positive-negative tax illusions reducing the rates of a tax, but broadening its taxable basis, so that its burden appears to be lower than before (but, in the reality, it may be unchanged or even increased). And the governments may gain popularity because of the lack of perception of the actual extent of the effects of the broadening of the tax basis. On the other hand, when a government deregulates a given set of factors of production or of products so that their prices go down and their supply and demand increase, there may be a similar illusion, in the opposite direction, that may lead to ignore the Laffer effect implicit in this policy. Indeed, if this set of factors or products is burdened with *ad valorem* taxes either direct or indirect, the reduction of the prices before the tax due to the competition automatically leads to a lower amount of tax per unit of supply reducing the average and marginal costs. The expansionary effects of liberalizations on the supply side are often caused by hidden Laffer effect of this kind.

Puviani defines as "drive to contribute" the moral force that induces the citizen to approve the given tax burden because the citizen, possibly by an illusion, values the pain less than the benefit deriving from the related public expenditure. The excess of the perceived benefit over the perceived burden constitutes the quantitative measures of the degree of the drive to contribute. When the taxpayer fears that the personal loss of utility brought from the tax is greater than the personal benefit of the related expenditure there is a "counter drive to contribute" measured by the excess of one's perception on the other.

Among the tax illusions, Puviani mentions those related to the fact that taxes are shifted and people may see who nominally pays them but not who really bears their burden. Taxes for social security, which mostly are nominally paid by the employers, may be shifted forward through a decrease in the demand for labour. The working class may easily be under the illusion that taxes for social security paid by the employers are chiefly a burden for them. On the other hand, they know that the benefits of the social security services flow to them. In particular, they appreciate the benefits of the pensions. Therefore, there may easily be, for workers, a great drive to contribute: i. e., a conventional wisdom among the workers, their unions and the socially oriented politicians to oppose any form of reduction of the social security contributions and payrolls (hereby SC) by lowering either their rates or their taxable basis. Obviously, the bureaucracy of the social security institutions has an interest in maximizing SC revenues. If all of them, are under the above illusion about the real burden of these taxes, they may oppose a tax cut, fearing that this may reduce the funding for social security expenditures. On the other hand, employers, who perceive the pain of SC in terms of burden on their costs of production and do not perceive their benefits from the increased protection of the workers, may be in favour of the reduction, even if they reduce the SC revenues, because they are under a strong counter drive to contribute. If politicians seek popularity, they may promote these cuts, claiming illusory Laffer effects.

When one considers important changes in important components of the tax system, and/or of the aggregate tax burden on all taxpayers in relation to the aggregate tax revenues, a hidden explanatory variable, behind a possible Laffer curve of a reduction in these burden, is the change in GDP. Thus, in order to assess the existence of weak and strong Laffer effects, one has to consider two different scenarios: the first assumes that the change of GDP is exogenous, so that the two critical points, relating to the changes in tax (and regulatory) policies may be unambiguously defined by reference to the ratio of the considered tax revenue to GDP, even if its dimension does changes through time; the second considers the effects on GDP of the different policies, so that the two critical points must be determined for the tax revenue after the new policy as a share of the GDP, which would have existed without the new policy, in comparison with the revenue in the absence of the new policy as share of the GDP obtained without the new policy.

For the sake of simplicity, in our empirical test of the Laffer effect for a policy of reduction of SC *cum* partial liberalization of labour market, we have adopted the assumption of exogenous GDP. However, likely the new policy had some positive effect on the rate of growth of GDP, therefore, likely, a hidden Laffer effect has been overlooked. Part of the bad reputation of the Laffer effect must be explained by the illusion that taxes have no economic effect on GDP. *This causal relation is not apparent.* If a policy of tax cuts, without change in the budgetary deficit or surplus,[7] i. e., without a Keynesian effect, generates a GDP increase, it may have a Laffer effect also under a diminution of the tax revenues/GDP ratio. One may not understand that the reasons why the ratio of tax revenues to GDP has diminished after the tax reduction is not that the tax revenues have diminished but that GDP has increased. On the other hand, one cannot argue that all public expenditures need to grow at the GDP rate, as if there was a sort of entitlement to a constant share of GDP for public expenditures. The claim may have a merit for the wages of public sector, and partially for pensions (in so far as they are linked to GDP growth), but not for the purchase of goods and services of the public administration, for health expenditure and net public investments in so far as, here, the law of productivity may work. Interests on public debt and expenditure for gross investment, replacing the old infrastructure are related to the past expenditure.

In recent times, a new kind of fiscal illusion has emerged in terms of Keynesian policy, i. e., the illusion that a policy of deficit spending by increasing the aggregate demand may generally or, at least, frequently, increase the level of economic activity and, therefore, the level of employment, of GDP and, after a while, the size of Government revenues, in such a way that the initial loss of revenue is recovered. This is not the place to discuss the limits of this policy, but it is obvious that they exist and that trespassing them may be dangerous in terms of monetary stability and sustainability of the public debt burden.

Even if the theory of the Laffer effects of tax cuts is different from the Keynesian theory of tax cuts as a deficit spending policy, because it assumes invariant budgetary effects, they are frequently confused. Thus, there are good motivations in a prejudice against the Laffer curve, when it is employed to reinforce the fiscal illusion that deficit spending has generally marvellous effects. Politicians

7 Actually also without changes in the size of the aggregate demand due to Haavelmo theorem's effects.

may abuse of this doctrine to practice easy fiscal policies to keep power and gain popularity. Similarly – Puviani argued – Governments frequently like practicing positive fiscal illusions, to increase their power and/or gain popularity by over assessing their revenues, and negative fiscal illusions, by undervaluing their expenditures, thus, engaging in new grandiose projects that please their supporters, which they finance by issuing public debt or merely by inflationary issuance of money. Against these practices of unsound finance, the rule has been developed that any additional expenditure or reduction of taxes should be financed by a corresponding increase of other taxes or/and by a reduction of other expenditures. The rule, in our opinion, act as a sort of taboo, similar to those against eating pork meat in some religion. The belief in it may help to prevent "infections". As noted above, the Laffer theorem is only true when some critical point has been trespassed. The evidence of this fact is not easy at all. A Government, that claims that it can finance the reduction of a tax merely with the revenue obtained by that reduction may be often suspected of practicing a positive political illusion in order to gain easy popularity. Even in the most favourable cases the full recovery of the revenue lost, in comparison with the situation without tax cut, is not immediate. It may require surrounding favourable circumstance and may frequently take some years, maybe several.

3. Buchanan's "delayed Laffer effects", the "public choice trap" for politicians and fiscal illusions

So far we have exposed several aspects in which the theory of political and fiscal illusions is relevant for the Laffer curve's debate. Let us now consider additional aspects which we have faced in a research on the revenues' effects of the policy of partial liberalization and reduction of the SC in Italy in the 1997-2001 period.

James Buchanan [with Dwight R. Lee (1982a and 1982b) and with Geoffrey Brennan (1985)] argues that Laffer effects take place with a substantially delayed effect because the increase of the object of taxation enticed requires time. This seems particularly true in the area of the reduction of tax burdens connected with a partial liberalization of the labour market. It takes some time for the firms to take advantage of the new opportunities by reorganising or/and beginning new activities. Because of the delay, a trap may emerge for the public choices of the Government. After the tax cut, in the immediate, tax revenues are likely to decline and only later they may increase above the level that they could have reached if the rates had not been reduced. Politicians who need to show the positive outcomes of their policies within the end of the legislature may, thus, be caught into a trap, because they may not be able to demonstrate that the tax cuts were rational in the Laffer curve sense. The expression "rational" leads us to the public choice assumption implicit in Buchanan's model. To analyze the logic of the Laffer curve one has to consider the fact that a bigger revenue with a lower tax implies a bigger taxable basis and that normally this implies a better situation for taxpayers, because they are left with a greater room for their choices. Therefore, it is rational for the Government to collect the same amount of revenue on a bigger than on a smaller taxable basis.

The role of the elasticity of demand and supply through time is crucial, in Buchanan's approach, to the full success and the political workability of the policy. Buchanan and Lee (1982a and 1982b), in their theoretical work, focused on the role of the elasticity of demand in the case of a commodity tax and, therefore, on the adjustment through time of consumers' demand in case of a tax cut. Buchanan and Brennan (1985), in their successive shorter treatment of the issue, considered the case of a reduction of the income tax like that undertaken in the US in the early '80s, mentioning, among others, the time required to adjust the investments to the new tax situation: i. e., the time lags in the supply of productive activities related to the demand for and supply of capital as factor of production. The reasoning may be easily extended to the time lags of demand for and supply of labour.

In this respect, however, another aspect may easily come into play. While the time lag, for the full increase of the demand, may be a market economy adjustment process related to commodities and investments, the case may not be the same for labour services whose market, in industrial countries with "welfare institutions", is normally submitted to extensive regulations. Here, without liberalization, the increase of the demand for labour due to a tax cut may be hindered by the rigidity of labour supply so that liberalization may be helpful in obtaining the Laffer effect through time. Recall that liberalization, allowing for substantially lower wages, automatically includes a substantial reduction of tax burden on labour, as for SC and income taxes because these are *ad valorem* taxes (with the income tax being an *ad valorem* progressive tax), thus reducing substantially the average and marginal cost of labour, even if the rates of these taxes were unchanged.

If all the Laffer effects were immediate, in order to asses them, one could make a comparison between the likely revenue without the tax reduction during the year or in the incoming year and the likely revenue with the new policy. The aggregate and disaggregate parameters of national accounts determining the taxable basis may be easily deductible in both cases by the projection of the existing trend in the absence of policy changes and under the policy changes. But how to measure the delayed Laffer effects, if any, in the frame of a policy that requires time to fully develop its own effects? In principle, assuming that there is a "normal" behaviour of the revenue of the considered tax, one should confront it with the real behaviour of revenue. Indeed the existence of delayed Laffer effects could be captured by comparing the ratio of the revenue to GDP after the new policy with the ratio of the revenue of the considered tax to GDP *before the new policy,* under the assumption that without it, that ratio would have been constant. Nevertheless, ratios of taxes to GDP do change through the economic cycle. They jump when the cycle is upward and remain stable or increase slightly in phases of moderate stable growth, they decrease when the cycle is going down and in case of stagnation that generates losses both for the firms and in terms of unemployment. However, there may be time lags in the cycles of tax revenues, with respect to the business cycles, due to the different delays in tax collection on the different taxable basis and to their different degree of flexibility. Here, there is a large room for fiscal illusions about the effects of the changes in tax policies.

Puviani, as we have already seen, classifies fiscal illusion in the two broad categories of positive and negative illusions. We can use this basic distinction to consider the fiscal illusion related to delayed Laffer effects, through the economic cycle. Let us suppose that the delayed effects of a given policy of (labour) partial liberalization and related tax burden reductions take place when the economic cycle is going downward. Here the ratio of taxes to GDP tends to diminish as effect of the cycle. The hypothetical Laffer effects then may consist in a reduction of the pace and of the dimension of this diminution. But because a diminution is taking place, people cannot perceive the fact that, due to the delayed effect of a policy previously undertaken, it is smaller than otherwise. Thus, because of a negative illusion, this hidden Laffer effect may not be perceived. Let us now suppose that the delayed Laffer effects of the new policy take place in an upward economic cycle. Here the state of the world is characterized by an increase of the ratio of taxes to GDP. Thus, there may be two causes of that increase: the present *clearly observable* cause (consisting in the upward cycle) and the past cause (consisting in a delayed Laffer effect). People tend to perceive as cause this fact of the present and to ignore those facts of the past, for two reason. Because those facts of the past cannot be observed and because the policy changes with Laffer effects are not periodically recurring events. As David Hume as explained, causal relations are deducted by the constant relation between a given fact and other facts following them. Thus a "positive" illusion easily takes place by imputing entirely to the economic cycle the increase of the ratio of the considered tax to GDP and a negative illusion takes place about the delayed Laffer effect of the policy undertaken in past years.

However, this is not the end of the story, at least for the case we are considering of SC. Indeed, as previously noted, one needs to distinguish two types of situations: those in which the ratio to GDP of the considered tax, under unchanged policy, is stable or increasing, and those of a declining ratio. This second case is the most critical, even if it may not be the most common. Indeed the excess of tax and regulatory burdens in a setting of international competition may lead to a long run reduction of employment, so that the ratio of SC to GDP may have a long run tendency to shrink because the unit wages do not increase at the same pace as the unit revenues from other factors of production and, notwithstanding that, more capital and less labour would be employed. The considered policy of SC reductions cum (partial) liberalization of the labour market then may alleviate the decline rather than reversing it. Here, a new type of fiscal illusion may emerge, which we may term as strong fiscal illusion, because more difficult to overcome than the others. Frequently, the decline of the ratio of SC to GDP is contrasted by broadening the taxable basis by various devices and a positive illusion may emerge about the constancy of the ratio of SC to GDP. Thus, the diminution of the ratio may be imputed to the policy of labour market liberalization and SC reductions, which, actually, have the effect of moderating the trend.

Section II

1. *The possible Laffer effects of the Treu reform of labour market in Italy: Simulation of the employment, unit labour costs, SC unit costs to obtain the hypothetical revenue in the absence of the reform.*

The fiscal illusion about a Laffer effect is the topic that we consider in this section with reference to the reform of the labour market in the period 1997-2001 undertaken by Tiziano Treu, Minister of Labour of the Italian Government. The reform introducing new flexible types of labour contracts mostly characterized by substantially reduced SC rates had been mainly motivated by employment purposes, which indeed were accomplished by the government as the figures in tables 1 show. The policy of new atypical labour contracts taxed with lower SC rates was done partly by an *ad hoc* legislation and partly by allowing an extensive application of the *coordinated continuative labour contracts*, legally defined as "semi subordinated" labour contracts also known as "co.co.co.", with SC reduced rates. Initially, the SC rate due was 10 %, while the SC rates for the ordinary subordinate labour contracts were more than 40 %. Subsequently the SC rate has been increased to 18 %. Employment greatly increased *after the adoption of this policy*, thus, reversing a trend. However, the principle *"after hoc propter hoc"* applied to public policy may lead to a typical case of social illusion. One may correctly argue that part of the new employment in the atypical labour contracts took place at expense of a reduction of the employment in the standard labour contract and that some increase of the atypical labour would have also taken place without the reduction of the SC rates. The additional SC revenue obtained with the atypical labour contracts derived from the "discrimination" of the labour market realized, by dividing it into two segments: one with high unit wages and high SC burden and the other with cheap labour and small SC burden.

Table 1. Atypical jobs in Italy in 1997 and in 2001

	1997	2001	2001-1997	Rate of increase
Permament-PartTime	635	919	284	44.7
Temporary-Full-Time	779	1045	266	34.1
Temporary-Part-Time	340	469	129	37.9
Semi-subordinated	1277	2113	836	65.4
Total	3031	4546	1515	182.1

Source Altieri and Otieri (2003)

The effects for the Government's SC revenues by this discriminated labour *plus* SC policy are similar to those for the sales of a monopoly firm applying prices discrimination to its product by market segmentation. By assessing the hypothetical SC revenue in the absence of these policies we take out the fiscal illusion of a positive Laffer effect that could emerge considering all the SC revenue obtained from the new cheap labour as a true additional revenue.

Indeed, as already noted, part of this new cheap employment might replace an employment of more expensive type that could have been taken place in the absence of the discrimination. The same occurs with a firm that adopts a price discrimination: the entrepreneur has to assess whether the policy adopted increases his gross sales and not merely the amount of units of goods sold. However, one must be careful in pursuing this analogy. A supermarket that adopts price discrimination by reducing the price of given commodities with a policy of "sales" often increases its total sales also for the commodities sold at normal price, because it attracts more consumers. Similarly, the policy of a two tier labour market with two different segments of labour costs made of high unit wages and high unit SC and low unit wages and low unit SC costs may create new high-cost employment, together with a lot of low-cost employment, by making the firms more competitive and therefore able to expand their supply. The final result can only be ascertained *by conjecture* on what would have happened if the two tier labour-SC policy had not be adopted. An econometric analysis is then needed, to find this hypothetical outcome.[8]

8 Since not only the atypical but also the typical jobs increased after the Treu reform, it has been maintained that the creation of atypical jobs has acted as a pre-condition to the creation of

We have done this in an *ad hoc* research in Fedeli, Forte and Zangari (2008) with a standard macroeconometric model applied to the Italian labour market with data from 1980 to 1996, to assess the hypothetical level of employment for the period 1997-2001. The macroeconometric model considers the following variables: (the log of) employees in the market sector, as expressed in LSU (Standard Labour Unit); (the log of) productivity given by the ratio between (log of) GDP at constant prices (1995), and (log of) employment; (the log of) unemployment rate; (the log of) real labour cost per capita at constant prices. This set of variables has been tested for cointegration, and then has been tested to check whether one or more long run attractors do exist for the system. The results signal the existence of one long run relationship between the variables, which is suitable for dynamic forecasting.[9] On this basis, we estimated the trend of the *per capita* average wage in the hypothetical employment situation, for the 1997-2001 period. We then calculated the per capita SC revenue for the years 1997-2001 by multiplying the hypothetical per capita wage of each year by the SC rate of 1996, net of the health-social security contribution, which had been abolished, but actually replaced by a somewhat higher regional tax.

To minimize the employment effects of the considered policy, one might raise a typical political illusion argument, i. e., that a substantial part of the increase of employment in 1997-2001 took place because of the improved rate of growth of the Italian GDP in that period. The macroeconomic model adopted to simulate the hypothetical employment in Italy in this period, in the absence of the Treu reform, does not allow this conclusion.[10] Actually, the actual average rate of GDP growth in the considered period has been only about 2%. There was an improvement in the international conditions, but these effects on Italian GDP via exports, if any, were not enough to produce rates of GDP growth in line with those of Italy – say, of the second half of the'80s – *incorporated in the econometric simulation of employment in absence of Treu reform.*

In order to asses the hypothetical SC revenues in the absence of the Treu reform, we considered the SC legal rates of 1996, to be applied to the wage bill estimated in the absence of Treu reform. These rates are legally split into two parts: the

---

stable typical employment (see for example Banca d'Italia, various years). But this is a mere "post hoc propter hoc" conjecture.

9 The model follows the macroeconometric methodologies by Jacobson et al. (1997), Marcellino and Mizon (1997, 2000), Bruggemann (2001). Notice that in the model, dealing with the employment of the *private sector*, we left out the sub sector of self-employed or autonomous workers, which includes a great number of (small) entrepreneurs and VAT registered traders professionals.

10 It embodies the macroeconomic setting characterised by fiscal and monetary policies much more permissive than those after the entrance of Italy in the European Monetary Union.

amount nominally bearing on the employers, the biggest share of the total, which may nourish the fiscal illusion of the workers that most SC are a mere burden on the employers, and the smaller share, nominally bearing on workers. The SC bearing on employers underwent to an abrupt reduction of 5.26 % between 1997 and 1998, as a consequence of the mentioned abolition of the 6.26 % SC charge for the National Health-care Service. The reduction of 1 % was imputed to the rate levied on workers. However, this was a typical operation of fiscal illusion, entering in those classified by Puviani as illusions deriving from replacing an old unpopular tax with a new tax presented as an improvement on the former, because it appears different. Employers had to bear a Regional tax on value added of income-type named IRAP,[11] whose real burden in labour was equivalent or greater than the old SC of 6.26 % devoted to the National Health-care Service. Its nominal minimum rate was 4.25 %, but the reduction in comparison to its effective burden was a mere illusion, because the taxable basis did not consist of the gross wages, but of the gross wages *plus social security charges due by the employers*. Furthermore, while SC were deductible from the costs of the firm, IRAP is not.[12]

In order to measure the true Laffer effects we have measured the hypothetical employment (thousands of LSU) of the market sector in the absence of Treu law (see Fedeli, Forte and Zangari 2008).[13] The difference between the actual employment and the hypothetical employment without the new policies begins to emerge in 1997 and displays its relevance at an increasing pace in the subsequent years. In particular, in order to obtain the SC revenue appropriate for the simulation, Fedeli, Forte and Zangari (2008) multiplied the hypothetical employment of each year by a hypothetical per capita SC. The latter measure is obtained by considering the hypothetical unit labour cost in the absence of reform obtained by simulating the trend of wages of the standard typical labour contract in that period. A correction has been done to take into account the fiscal illusion due to the fact that a share of SC has been transformed in a regional tax of different nature, but of equivalent or greater burden. Therefore, we took the 1996 legal average SC rates (that was 48.98 %) and subtract the 6.26 percentage points of the abolished SC rate for health, replaced by the equivalent rate of Regional tax thus, obtaining a hypothetical level of 42.72 %. Knowing that, in 1996, with a rate of 48.98 %,

11 That is, Imposta Regionale sulle Attività Produttive (i. e. Regional Tax on Producutive Activities).

12 While the SC rates are deductible from the taxable basis of the personal income tax and corporate tax, the labour component of IRAP cannot be deducted. This benefit implied a tax saving of about 2 % of the official SC rate. Thus, the 6.26 % SC rate abolished, on average, was actually smaller than the 4.25 % IRAP rate.

13 Both the estimated hypothetical employment and labour costs are subject to wide confidence intervals.

the average SC revenues per thousand workers were 8.7 millions of euros, we infer that, with a rate of 42.72 %, the average SC revenues per thousand workers would have been 7.59 millions of euro. The latter figure, for the period 1997-2001, has been assumed to grow with the rate of inflation plus the rate of growth of real wage as forecasted by our simulation with respect to 1996. The effective SC implicit average rates, obviously, differ from this hypothetical rate because of the increasing number of atypical labour contracts with lower rates. They go down continuously from 1997 to the subsequent years, with a jump of about 1 percentage point in 1999 and a less pronounced reduction in the other years.

2. The results

As one can see, the Laffer effect results clear in figure 2, showing the difference between the effective and hypothetical revenues as share of GDP (also for the lower and upper bound of the simulation), over the five considered years. In other words, it is only in the comparison with the SC revenue in absence of the reform that a strong Laffer effect does emerge in the considered period.

Figure 2. H-Laffer differential effect of the Treu reform (including upper and lower bound of the point estimates)

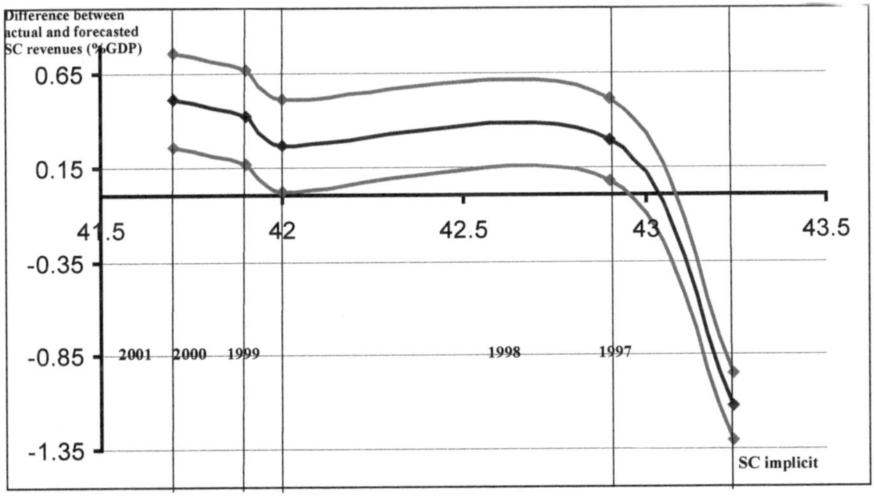

Remember that to have a Laffer effect one needs merely to have a revenue equal to that that one could have had without the considered reduction of tax burden. If the revenue obtained with the tax reduction, in the simulation, appears greater and this outcome persists through the years, one may argue that *a strong Laffer effect* has emerged.

The excess of the effective revenue over the hypothetical revenue, in 1999 is smaller than in 1998 and actually very small for the upper bound of the simulation. The explanation lies in the reduction of the average SC rate from 1997-1998 to 1999 of about one percentage point not matched by an equivalent increase in the taxable basis. Employment did increase substantially over the hypothetical level, but not enough to counterbalance the effect of the rate of reduction. Aside the case of 1999, there is always a differential among the real and the two hypothetical curves signalling a strong *(i. e. > 0)* Laffer effects and this effect increase through time. However, as we have seen, the confidence intervals of the simulation giving the hypothetical employment are quite wide. In other words, if we take the upper limit of the simulation, the differential signalling a Laffer effect (in percentage of GDP) is very small for 1998 and 1999. Only in the subsequent years the differential becomes clear and increasing as percentage of GDP also for the upper bound of the simulation, by an important percentage value of GDP. Therefore it requires time to have a clear and consistent *strong* Laffer effect.

One might argue that, after all, the Laffer effect exists also with a 0 result, i. e. when the actual revenue with the tax reduction is equal to that without the tax. However, we are comparing a real result with a hypothetical one: when the Laffer effect takes place, as in our case, under a situation of declining share of SC revenue to GDP, a powerful fiscal illusions operates to hide the Laffer effect. For the Laffer effect to emerge, it has required an econometric exercise on statistical data that not everybody may be prepared to accept as a basis of reliable knowledge in the political debate on fiscal policy when the result is a decline of the ratio of revenue to GDP. In Paretian terms, one may say that the belief that tax revenues always increase at least as the GDP, so that they generally are at least a constant share of GDP, is a "derivations" of the "residual" belief that taxes are generally either favourable or neutral to the growth of the taxable matter as a share of GDP.

In the case of SC having the role of financing future pensions, one may object that the fact that the per capita revenues, in our case, did fall, implies lower pensions, so that the Laffer effect is a mere illusion. However, this argument is based on the illusion, consisting in considering as existing a fact that does not exists. Indeed, the units of labour that shall have "lower pensions", without the lower wages with lower SC contributions, would have been unemployed and therefore would not have had the right to a pension at all. Those who argue that this policy reduces the future pensions are under the illusion or deceive the others because it actually creates the premises to increase the future pensions.

III Final remarks and conclusion

It may appear paradoxical that economist as James Buchanan who is furiously against the Keynesian profligacy are also praying a Lafferian gospel. But one cannot confuse the Laffer curve with the Keynesian deficit spending. The former is a supply side policy that does not imply any fiscal deficit to work, the latter is a policy assumed to work because of the assumption that an increase in the aggregate demand, generated with public deficit, may increase the ex post savings and investments, which, according to Buchanan, is a dangerous fiscal illusion. On the other hand, Puviani observed that a strong drive to contribute is essential for governments interested to finance an increased public spending trend without the risks of inflation. The discovery that lower taxes may bring more revenue may appear dangerous to those who are in favour of "big governments" because it may substantially weaken the drive to contribute. The thesis that a big government is always a good thing from the distributional point of view may lead to believe that it must also be good from the production point of view. In the common belief if something appears just it must also have good economic consequences. This belief that, in Pareto's terminology, may be defined as a "derivation" may lead to the illusion, hard to be dispelled, that it is always possible to get more revenue by increasing taxes. This may happen in the short term. Indeed, if the Buchanan' theorem of the delayed Laffer effects is true, it must also work in the reverse. Thus, taxes may easily increase beyond the long run maximum level of the Laffer curve. Obviously, then a room for tax cut with (delayed) Laffer effects is opened. The effects may be reinforced when liberalization increases the elasticity of supply and if a two tier policy is adopted, as in the case examined: the Laffer effect may be reinforced by the virtues of a policy similar to that of price discrimination in market economy. On the other hand, when the taxable basis is declining as a share of GDP, also because of its excessive tax burden, the Laffer effect of the tax reduction may also imply a share of the revenue of the considered tax to GDP lower than that of the past. Thus a double fiscal illusion may overshadow the Laffer effects: the delay of its manifestation and its appearance only by means of a comparison with the simulated trend of the revenue in the absence of that policy. This was actually the case for the Laffer effect by the Treu labour reform of 1997 in Italy.

In this case the time lag has been shorter than that considered by Buchanan in his theory of the "trap" of the delayed Laffer effect for politicians who adopt a policy of tax reduction thinking of the Laffer curve. The reason of the shorter lag in our case is likely to lie in the peculiar elasticity of the supply due to the fact that a two tier policy was adopted. So that the liberalization of the labour supply and the reduction of the SC tax burden affected only part of the supply and also the supra marginal employment with higher wages and SC burden increased, through a "bundle effect". This may be an interesting lesson on optimal taxation theory. On the other hand, this Laffer effect is particularly interesting in the area of fiscal illusions also because it relates to SC for pensions. While the lower SC through the Laffer effect provided the economic and legal basis for higher future pension rights,[14] many people, in good faith, claim the opposite. This happened because they are under illusion that without the lower tax burden, the employment level would have been the same.

Thus, a set of fiscal illusions created a political trap here to blur the effectiveness of such policies in terms of public revenues and social security rights and for politicians aiming to policies that give immediately perceivable positive results the trap relating to the Laffer effects may be broader than that specified by J. M. Buchanan.

References

Altieri G., and C. Otieri (2003), *Terzo Rapporto sul Lavoro Tipico in Italia:verso una stabilizzazione del precariato?*, IRES (CGIL), Roma.

Banca d'Italia, *Relazione Annuale*, Anni 1990-2001

Bruggemann, R. (2001), *Sources of German unemployment: a structural vector error correction analysis,* mimeo, Berlin University, available at: http://ise.wiwi.hu-berlin.de/~brueggem/research/unempl.pdf

Buchanan J. M. and D. R. Lee, (1982a) *Tax Rates and Tax Revenue in Political Equilibrium,* Economic Inquiry re-edited in J. M. BUCHANAN, Collected Works, Volume 13.,(2000) Politics as Public Choice, Indianapolis, Liberty Fund p.466-4

Buchanan J. M. and D. R. Lee, (1982b) *Politics, Time and the Laffer Curve*, Journal of Political Economy.

Buchanan J. M. and G. Brennan (1985), *The Reason of rules.* Constitutional Political Economy.

Buchanan J. M. and Wagner (1977), *Democracy in Deficit,* The Political Legacy of Lord Keynes, London, Academic Press

14 Assuming that the new employment lasts through time.

Einaudi L. (1949) *Lezioni di politica sociale*, Torino, Bocca.

Fedeli, S., F. Forte and E. Zangari (2008) *"An Econometric Analysis of the Employment and Revenue Effects of the Treu Reform in the Period 1997-2001"* Rivista di Politica Economica, Gennaio-Febbraio 2008, pp.215-248.

Forte F. (2005), *Fiscal and monetary Illusions and the Maastricht Rules*, in Backhaus J. (ed.), Essays in Fiscal Sociology, Berlin, Peter Lang.

Jacobson, T., A. Vredin, and A.Warne (1997), *Common trends and hysteresis in Scandinavian Unemployment*, European Economic Review 41, 1781-1816

Marcellino, M. and G. E. Mizon, (1997), *Wage, prices, productivity, inflation and unemployment in Italy 1970-1994,* Mimeo, European University Institute.

Marcellino, M. and G. E. Mizon, (2000), *Modelling shifts in the wage-price and unemployment-inflation relationships in Italy, Poland and the UK*, Economic Modelling 17, 387-413

Mc Lure M. (2007), *The Paretian School and Italian Fiscal Sociology,*London, Palgrave Macmillan

Ministero del Lavoro (2003) *Rapporto di Monitoraggio sulle Politiche Occupazionali e del Lavoro,* Roma.

Ministero del Tesoro (1990-2001) *Relazione sulla Situazione Economica del Paese,* Roma.

Pareto W. (1906), *Manuale di Economia politica,* Milano, Società Editrice Libraria

Pareto W. (1923), *Trattato di Sociologia Generale*, 2nd ed. Firenze, Barbera, 1st ed. Firenze, Barbera 1916.

Puviani A. (1903), *Teoria dell'illusione finanziaria,* Palermo, Sandron. New Italian edition (1973) with an "Introduction" by F. Volpi, Isedi, Milano. German edition (1960), *Illusionen in der Offentlichen Finanzwissenschaft,* Berlin, Duncker& Humboldt with an "Introduction" by E. D'Albergo.

Sella E. (1914), *La concorrenza. Sistema e critica dei sistemi,* Vol, I, Torino, Bocca.

Sella E. (1916), *La concorrenza. Sistema e critica dei sistemi,* Vol II, Torino, Bocca.

Wagner R. E. (1976), *Revenue Structure, Fiscal Illusion and Budgetary Choices,* Public Choice, 25.

Constitution And The Development Of Organic Budget Law In Estonia

Ringa Raudla

Abstract

The paper examines the impact of the 1992 Constitution on the development of the organic budget law in Estonia since 1993. The case study argues that the Constitution of Estonia has played a significant role in shaping the major changes made to the organic budget law. As a result of the constitutional review procedures and constitutional deliberations in the parliament, the budgetary autonomy of the constitutional institutions has increased. While amendments made to the organic budget law have augmented the budgetary powers of the cabinet and constrained the role of the parliament, the Constitution has had a mitigating impact on both of these tendencies, preventing the adoption of more extreme solutions.

1. Introduction

A growing body of literature in the field of constitutional political economy is concerned with how constitutions impact on budgetary policies and outcomes. A large number of studies have focused on the influences of constitutional features (parliamentarism versus presidentialism, proportional versus majoritarian electoral rules, and unicameral versus bicameral legislatures) on budgetary choices (levels of expenditure, taxation, budget deficit and public debt)[1]. Another stream of literature examines the impacts of constitutional fiscal rules (for example, balanced budget provisions, borrowing restrictions and debt limits) on budgetary outcomes.[2] A third line of research discusses the importance of budgetary institutions – usually outlined in organic budget laws – in explaining budgetary discipline. Budgetary institutions are a set of rules that guide the decision-making process in formulating, approving and implementing the budget. They can be seen as the "rules of the game" that shape the interaction of the participants involved in budget-making process by distributing strategic influence among them and regu-

1 For reviews of the existing literature see, *inter alia*, von Hagen (2002), Persson and Tabellini (2004), Berggren and Kurrild-Klitgaard (2002), and Congleton and Swedenborg (2006).

2 For overviews, see, for example, Krol (1997), Kirchgässner (2001), and von Hagen (2002, 2003).

lating the flow of information[3]. Buchanan[4] has noted that the rules governing the budgetary process could be interpreted as "essentially constitutional documents"; Berggren and Kurrild-Klitgaard[5] view them as part of the "extended" constitution. In a similar vein, Molander[6] notes that the choice of budgetary rules is "similar in kind to constitutional choice in general, with all the complications that go with it".

So far, however, limited scholarly attention has been paid to the *interaction* between the constitution and the development of budget institutions (or the organic budget law). Given the importance attributed both to constitutions and issues of public finance by constitutional political economy it is certainly important to ask whether and in what way a constitution can play a role in shaping the organic budget law. Here, fiscal sociological approach can certainly aid the analysis by providing insights to the dynamics of the development of budgetary institutions in a holistic way that takes into account the contextual factors, interactions between the political actors and the meanings attributed to evolving budgetary institutions by participants in the political process.

For exploring the role of constitutions in shaping the organic budget law, studying the countries in Central and Eastern Europe (CEE) can be considered to be particularly fruitful, given the presumably important role played by constitutions in this region.[7] McGregor[8] notes that constitutions in CEE countries "play a critical role in channelling political activity" and "the outcomes of many struggles over power and policy can be traced to the general and sometimes even specific influence of the constitutions". He argues that constitutions are espe-

---

3 Stein, E., Talvi, E., Grisanti, A. Institutional Arrangements and Fiscal Performance: The Latin American Experience. In J. M. Poterba, and J. von Hagen (eds.) Fiscal Institutions and Fiscal Performance. Chicago: University of Chicago Press, (1999), p. 118.
Hagen, J. von Fiscal Rules and Fiscal Performance in the European Union and Japan. Monetary and Economic Studies March, (2006), p. 47.

4 Buchanan, J. M. Why Do Constitutions Matter? In Berggren, Niclas, Karlson, Nils and Nergelius, Joakim (eds.) Why Constitutions Matter. New Brunswick: Transaction Publishers, (2002), p. 7.

5 Berggren, N., Kurrild-Klitgaard, P. Economic Effects of Political Institutions, With Special Reference to Constitutions. In N. Berggren, N. Karlson, J. Nergelius, Joakim (eds.) Why Constitutions Matter. New Brunswick: Transaction Publishers, (2002).

6 Molander, P. Budgeting Procedures and Democratic Ideals: An Evaluation of Swedish Reforms. Journal of Public Policy 21(1), (2001), p. 29.

7 Hence, examining the effect of constitutions on legislation in CEE countries could be seen as 'most favourable' case study design, in the sense that if constitutions do not exert an influence on important framework legislation in a CEE country (or countries), they can be expected to exert even less influence elsewhere.

8 McGregor, J. P. Constitutional Factors in Politics in Central and Eastern Europe. Communist and Post-Communist Studies 29(2), (1996), p. 148.

cially important in CEE because they provide "a firm anchor" in defining proper political behaviour, in the context where the experience with "normal politics" is lacking[9]. In a similar vein, Calvert and Johnson[10], drawing on Brown[11], Offe[12], and O'Donnell and Schmitter[13], argue that consti-tutions in CEE play an important role in resolving complex coordination problems in a situation where the entire political world is "in flux", the "the very parameters of political action" are contested, and there are intense struggles to impose "new political definitions"[14]. They suggest that constitutions can mitigate these problems by offering possible "hinges for interpretation"[15] in a situation where strategic conflicts among political actors concern not only competing interests but also "competing interpretations"[16]. Hence, examining the effect of constitutions on legislation in CEE countries could be seen as "most favourable" case study design, in the sense that if constitutions do not exert an influence on important framework legislation in a CEE country (or countries), they can be expected to exert even less influence elsewhere.

Given the lack of studies focussing on the interactions between a constitution and an organic budget law, there is a need for an exploratory case study that would examine these dynamics. Choosing the case of Estonia can be justified on several grounds. Estonia is often considered to be the exemplary country in Central and Eastern Europe with regard to fiscal discipline (expressed in balanced budgets and low levels of accumulated debt). In addition, comparative studies of the budget institutions in CEE point to Estonia as having the kind of budget institutions that are most conducive to budgetary discipline[17] with regard to the ability to overcome the common-pool resource problems in budgeting by provid-

9 Ibid., p. 151.

10 Calvert, R. K., Johnson, J. Interpretation and Coordination in Constitutional Politics. Working Paper No. 15. W. Allen Wallis Institute of Political Economy, University of Rochester, (1998).

11 Brown, J. F Hopes and Shadows: Eastern Europe After Communism. Durham: Duke University Press, (1994).

12 Offe, C. Varieties of Transition: The East European and East German Experience. Cambridge: Polity Press, (1996).

13 O'Donnell, G., Schmitter, P. Transitions from Authoritarian Rule: Tentative Conclusions about Uncertain Democracie. Baltimore, MD: Johns Hopkins University Press, (1986).

14 Calvert, R. K., Johnson, J. Interpretation and Coordination in Constitutional Politics. Working Paper No. 15. W. Allen Wallis Institute of Political Economy, University of Rochester, (1998), p. 1.

15 Ibid., p. 4.

16 Ibid., p. 1.

17 Gleich, H. Budget Institutions and Fiscal Performance in Central and Eastern European Countries. European Central Bank Working Paper Series, Working Paper no. 215, (2003). Yläoutinen, S. Fiscal Frameworks in the Central and Eastern European Countries. Finnish Ministry of Finance Discussion Paper No. 72, (2004).

ing for centralised and coordinated mechanisms for budget preparation, adoption and implementation.

The main question asked in this paper is: How has the 1992 Constitution shaped the development of the organic budget law in Estonia? In answering this question, a number of sub-questions will be addressed. First, which mechanisms of constitutional review have played an important role in the development of the organic budget law and in what directions have they influenced the development of the law? Second, in what way have the questions about the constitutionality of particular provisions shaped the legislative proceedings of the organic budget law? To what extent has the legislature resorted to auto-limitation in anticipation of constitutional review procedures? To what extent has the legislature put forth constitutional constructions when discussing the organic budget law? Third, what were the motives behind the constitutional interpretations and constructions offered: To what extent were the actors driven by self-binding considerations, to what extent by partisan and institutional self-interests?

In order to answer these questions, the case study draws on the legislative records (verbatim reports of the plenary debates and protocols of the committee meetings), the decisions of the Constitutional Court, the Chancellor of Justice and the President, and media articles discussing the organic budget law in Estonia. The paper proceeds as follows. In the second section, the theoretical framework of the study is outlined and some tentative conjectures (to be tested with the case study) offered. The third section gives an overview of the development of the organic budget law in Estonia. The fourth section analyses the role of the Estonian Constitution in shaping the organic budget law, and the last section concludes.

2. Theoretical Framework

The constitution can shape the making and development of an organic budget law in different ways. First, the constitution has a straightforward impact when the constitutional provisions pertaining to budget process are integrated in the organic budget law. The constitutional provisions on budget process, however, are rarely precise enough to provide a full content for the organic budget law. Therefore, the constitutional provisions have to be specified and further aspects added when the organic budget law is drafted. Second, as suggested by Haller-

Fabrizio, S., Mody, A. Can Budget Institutions Counteract Political Indiscipline? Economic Policy 21(48), (2006).

berg and von Hagen[18], the choice of budgetary institutions is likely to be influenced by the form of government – whether it is a single-party majority government or a multi-party coalition government – which in turn is influenced by the electoral system[19]. Hallerberg and von Hagen[20] argue that if a more coordinated budget process is sought for, single-party governments are more likely to opt for a "delegation approach" where the minister of finance is given extensive powers in coordinating the preparation of the budget, whereas multi-party coalition governments are likely to choose a "fiscal contracts" (also called a "commitment") approach, where the fiscal goals for the budget are established collectively by the cabinet. Thus, the electoral system outlined in the constitution can indirectly influence the basic choices made with regard to the organic budget law. Third, the constitution can shape the organic budget law by providing a framework for evaluating enacted or proposed provisions in the organic budget law on the grounds of constitutionality. Even if the constitution is silent on, for example, the exact role of the cabinet or the minister of finance in budget procedure, the respective provisions in the organic budget law can be considered and assessed in the light of the constitution. In addition to constitutional provisions pertaining directly to the issues of budgeting, other constitutional articles can be evoked for evaluating, contesting and defending provisions in the organic budget law.

There are two main mechanisms through which the constitution can exert an influence in this third mode. First, the constitution can shape the organic budget law (or any other law, for that matter) through an official process of constitutional review, where the constitutional court (or an equivalent) assesses the constitutionality of the contested provisions, strikes down unconstitutional legislation and indicates how the law should be changed in order to be in compliance with the constitution. This effect – called the "downstream" or "remedial" effect by Favoreu[21]

---

18 Hallerberg, M., von Hagen, J. Electoral Institutions, Cabinet Negotiations, and Budget Deficits in the European Union. In J. M. Poterba, and J. von Hagen (eds.) Fiscal Institutions and Fiscal Performance, Chicago: University of Chicago Press, (1999).

19 Duverger, M. Political Parties, Their Organization, and Activity in the Modern State. New York: Wiley, (1954),.
Rae, D. The Political Consequences of Electoral Laws. New Haven: Yale University Press, (1967).
Taagepera, R., Shugart, M. S. Predicting the Number of Parties: A Quantitative Model of Duverger's Mechanical Effect. American Political Science Review 87(2), (1993).

20 Hallerberg, M., von Hagen, J. Electoral Institutions, Cabinet Negotiations, and Budget Deficits in the European Union. In J. M. Poterba, and J. von Hagen (eds.) Fiscal Institutions and Fiscal Performance, Chicago: University of Chicago Press, (1999).

21 Favoreu, L. The Constitutional Council and Parliament in France. In C. Landfried (ed). Constitutional Review and Legislation. An International Comparison. Baden-Baden: Nomos Verlagsgesellschaft, (1988), p. 103.

and “immediate, direct, or formal” effect by Stone Sweet[22] – is often considered as the most obvious one and has received the most extensive scholarly attention.

In addition to constitutional review exercised by courts, the analytical framework that is concerned with the effects of a constitution on legislation should consider the role of other “constitutional watchdogs” or “guardians of the constitution” that may play an important role in supervising the constitutionality of laws and initiating constitutional review proceedings. The functions of a constitutional watchdog can be performed by a president in promulgation of the laws, an ombudsman or a legal chancellor or some other body that is *formally independent* of the parliament. The roles of the president and the legal chancellor (or public defender or an equivalent institution) can be considered to be of particular importance, provided that these bodies have been specifically entrusted with the task of constitutional supervision.

Alongside the “institutionalised” venues of constitutional review or the “first face” of constitutional power[23], a constitution can shape a law already *before* the adoption of a law by legislature, by influencing the proceedings of the law through “constitutional deliberations” during the legislative debates. Pickerill[24] has defined “constitutional deliberation” as “reflection and debate over constitutional issues that rise in the context of specific legislation”, which encompasses “interpretation, construction, and other forms of discourse and reflection over the meaning of constitutional provisions and powers”. In other words, the constitution can play a role by framing the legislative debates on the organic budget law and by providing a source of arguments for the proponents and opponents of particular provisions. Indirect influence of a constitution can be observed “by tracing legislation through the policy process to determine how and why it is altered as a result of constitutional argument”[25]. Here, again, it would be analytically fruitful to divide the influence of the constitution into two different forms.

First, it can take the form of “indirect” authority of the constitutional court – what Stone Sweet calls “pedagogical, indirect, or feedback effect”[26] or “auto-limitation”[27],

22 Stone Sweet, A. Governing with Judges. Oxford: Oxford Uni-versity Press, (2000), p. 63.

23 Whittington, K. E. Constitutional Theory and the Faces of Power. In K. D. Ward and C. R. Castillo (eds.) The Judiciary and American Democracy: Alexander Bickel and the Counter-majoritarian Difficulty and Contemporary Constitutional Theory. Albany: State University of New York Press, (2005).

24 Pickerill, J. M. Constitutional Deliberation in Congress: The Impact of Judicial Review in a Separated System. Durham, NC: Duke University Press, (2004), p. 28.

25 Stone, A. Judging Socialist Reform. The Politics of Coordinate Construction in France and Germany. Comparative Political Studies 26(4), (1994), p. 447.

26 Stone Sweet, A. Governing with Judges. Oxford: Oxford Uni-versity Press, (2000), p. 63.

27 Ibid., p. 76.

Favoreu[28] terms "upstream or preventative effect", and Whittington[29] views as the "second face" of power[30] of the constitutional system. "Auto-limitation" is "the exercise of self-restraint on the part of the government and its parliamentary majority in anticipation of an annulment by the constitutional court"[31]. Auto-limitation can be observed when the government and parliament take decisions during the legislative process that "sacrifice initially held policy objectives" with the aim to "reduce the probability that a bill will either be referred to the court, or be judged unconstitutional"[32]. The mechanisms of "auto-limitation" or the "power of anticipation" or the "second face of power" can also come into play in parliament's relations with other institutions of constitutional review[33].

Second, a constitution can exert an influence through *constitutional constructions*. Constitutional arguments can shape deliberations on legislation and make certain options more or less feasible depending on how they appear to fit with the constitutional provisions – independently of the threat of referral and the anticipation of what the court's decision would be. Interpreting the constitution and pointing to possible unconstitutionality of certain provisions can add weight and legitimacy to the arguments (presented in the parliamentary discussions) about why they should be removed or changed.[34] Fisher[35] has noted that "[j]ust as it is

---

28 Favoreu, L. The Constitutional Council and Parliament in France. In C. Landfried (ed). Constitutional Review and Legislation. An International Comparison. Baden-Baden: Nomos Verlagsgesellschaft, (1988), p. 104.

29 Whittington, K. E. Constitutional Theory and the Faces of Power. In K. D. Ward and C. R. Castillo (eds.) The Judiciary and American Democracy: Alexander Bickel and the Countermajoritarian Difficulty and Contemporary Constitutional Theory. Albany: State University of New York Press, (2005).

30 For the original formulation of the concept of 'second face of power', see Bachrach and Baratz (1962, 1963).

31 Stone Sweet, A. Constitutional Courts and Parliamentary De-mocracy. West European Politics 25(1), (2002), p. 94.

32 Ibid.

33 See: Cameron, C. M. Veto Bargaining. Presidents and the Politics of Negative Power. Cambridge: Cambridge University Press, (2000).

34 Legislative constitutional interpretation in the US context has been discussed by Katyal (2001), Peabody (1999, 2004), Fisher (1985), Whittington (1999, 2002), Tushnet (1999), Devins (1996), and Pickerill (2004). For most part, these studies have been carried by normative rather than positive considerations; the main questions addressed in these works have been whether the legislature *should* be involved in constitutional interpretation, how it should do that, and what the advantages of legislative constitutional interpretation are. Still, some authors have sought to take a more positive stance, e. g. by looking at how frequently constitutional deliberation takes place, what factors are conducive to it and how it can be characterised. In the European context, the literature concerned with judicial politics and judicialisation of politics has also discussed the effects of the constitution on legislative debates (see Landfried 1984; contributions in Landfried ed. (1988); Stone Sweet 2000, 2002).

35 Fisher, L. Constitutional Dialogues: Interpretation as Political Process. Princeton: Princeton University Press, (1988), p. 6.

a mistake to study constitutional law solely from the standpoint of court decisions, so would it be misleading to treat constitutional interpretation as simply the interactions between the judiciary and the other branches. Government operates within a political culture that presses its own brand of constitutional law." In a similar vein, Whittington argues that "[a]lthough the history and practice of judicial review have obviously influenced the effect of the Constitution on politics, the Constitution also operates more directly on political actors, without the mediation of the courts or the creation of amendments"[36]. He puts forth and elaborates on the concept of "constitutional construction" that supplements other methods of determining the meaning of the constitution and plays an important role in the political (especially legislative) arena. He argues that "[p]olitical actors can be expected to bring a different set of concerns and interests to bear on the Constitution, leading to a much more contested and rather different process of constitutional deliberation than a simple reliance on judicial interpretation would allow"[37]. Whittington emphasises that "constitutional constructions are often made in the context of political debate"[38] and "by altering the discursive space of politics, a successful construction makes certain policy options more difficult to realize"[39]. Whittington[40] also remarks (based on the analysis of the debates in the U.S. Congress) that those who advocate a given construction expect to benefit from it: self-interest is an inherent part of the arguments compiled by various government actors seeking to construe the constitution so as to favour their own institutional position. In a similar vein, Peabody[41] has advocated going beyond the conventional legal interpretive modalities when analysing constitutional interpretation in a parliamentary setting and adopting a broader view of what counts as constitutional analysis, including an explicitly political form of legislative constitutional interpretation. Peabody[42] suggests, based on his study of constitutional interpretation in the U.S. Congress, that interpretation in the legislature is informed by constituent interests and policy concerns.

---

36 Whittington, K. E. Constitutional Theory and the Faces of Power. In K. D. Ward and C. R. Castillo (eds.) The Judiciary and American Democracy: Alexander Bickel and the Counter-majoritarian Difficulty and Contemporary Constitutional Theory. Albany: State University of New York Press, (2005), p. 2.

37 Whittington, K. E. Constitutional Theory and the Faces of Power. In K. D. Ward and C. R. Castillo (eds.) The Judiciary and American Democracy: Alexander Bickel and the Counter-majoritarian Difficulty and Contemporary Constitutional Theory. Albany: State University of New York Press, (2005), p. ix.

38 Ibid., p. 6.

39 Ibid., p. 219.

40 Ibid., p. 212.

41 Peabody, B. G. Congressional Constitutional Interpretation and the Courts: A Preliminary Inquiry into Legislative Attitudes, 1959-2001. Law and Social Inquiry 29, (2004).

42 Ibid., p. 167.

In addition to different forms of constitutional debate, the frequency and saliency of constitutional issues in legislative debates has been discussed. The empirical studies of the United States and European countries point to diverging evidence. In the continental European countries constitutional issues come up frequently in legislative debates (see contributions to Landfried ed. 1988)[43], as a result of the abstract constitutional review by the court and the right of the legislative minority to refer the legislation to the court (e. g., in France, Spain and Hungary). In the context of the U.S. Congress, Pickerill[44] argues that "the incentives of the institution and democratic lawmaking are not favourable for encouraging routine constitutional deliberation"[45] and the evidence confirms that constitutional issues come up only rarely in congressional debates. He argues, however, that under certain circumstances legislators are likely to be more attentive to constitutional issues and engage in constitutional deliberation[46]. First, issues of constitutionality are likely to come to the forefront when the law is controversial and has strong opposition: the opponents of the draft law may use arguments of unconstitutionality as a reason for voting against it. Further, constitutional issues are likely to be taken up during the debates when the act concerns some "pet issue" of a particular legislator[47].. In addition, Pickerill argues, constitutional issues are more likely to surface in legislative debates when the Supreme Court has acted recently or frequently on the issue under discussion[48]. Peabody[49] also discusses factors that make the issues of constitutionality salient for legislators. He argues that legislative awareness of constitutional issues is highest when they bear on the benefits of their constituencies and concern the relations of the legislature to other branches government[50]. In other words, the legislators are likely to give greatest attention to constitutional areas close to their constituent or institutional interests.

With regard to making predictions about the influences of the constitution on the organic budget law in CEE in general and Estonia in particular, a number of conjectures can be advanced, based on the existing theoretical and empirical literature. First, because of the importance of the organic budget law in hammering

43 Some contributors note even that it has become 'excessive', see Rubio Llorente (1988, p. 145), Landfried (1988b), p. 161.

44 Pickerill, J. M. Constitutional Deliberation in Congress: The Impact of Judicial Review in a Separated System. Durham, NC: Duke University Press, (2004).

45 Ibid., p. 64.

46 Ibid., pp. 64-66.

47 Ibid., p. 144.

48 Ibid., p. 66.

49 Peabody, B. G. Congressional Constitutional Interpretation and the Courts: A Preliminary Inquiry into Legislative Attitudes, 1959-2001. Law and Social Inquiry 29, (2004).

50 Ibid., p. 138.

out the institutional powers of the different branches of government, its implications for the "division of powers" between the legislative majorities and minorities, and the significance of the budget for the constituents of the legislators, constitutional arguments are likely to play an important role in legislative discussion over the organic budget law. Second, given that the constitutional courts have been functioning for a relatively short time, legislators are likely to face greater uncertainty with regard to how the court would view the organic budget law, were it to be submitted for constitutional review.[51] This, in turn, should lead to attempts of legislators to interpret the constitution themselves, rather than just guessing the possible decision of the court.

Since the organic budget law can be considered to be a part of the "extended" constitution, some questions that are usually asked of constitution-making processes can be asked in the context of the making of organic budget law as well. Drawing on the existing body of research in constitutional political economy addressing that issue – in particular the works of Elster[52] – important questions in this context would be: 1) To what extent has the making of the organic budget law been driven by institutional self-interest of the political actors involved? 2) To what extent have the different institutions involved in the making of the budget law been willing to engage in self-binding? 3) To what extent have the changes reflected partisan interests? As Molander[53] has noted, "[t]he choices associated with the design of budgetary institutions reflect classical, or even existential, dilemmas of self-binding". At the same time, he reminds us, "binding others rather than oneself is perhaps the overarching goal in the context of practical constitutional politics".

The theoretical framework outlined in this section will be taken as the structure for analysing the Estonian case. It should be noted, of course, that analysing official decisions and legislative debates does not give a full picture of how the

51 This statement, however, should be qualified with regard to some countries in CEE. In Hungary for example, the constitutional court reviewed more than 600 laws and struck down about one-third of them in 1990-1995 (Bond 2006).

52 Elster, J. Making Sense of Constitution-Making. East European Constitutional Review 1(1), (1992).
Elster, J. Strategic Uses of Argument. In K. Arrow et al. (eds.) Barriers to Negotiated Resolution of Conflicts. New York: Norton, (1995a).
Elster, J. Forces and Mechanisms in the Constitution-Making Process. Duke Law Journal 45(2), (1995b).
Elster, J. The Role of Institutional Interest in East European Constitution-Making. East European Constitutional Review 5(1), (1996).
Elster, Jon Deliberation and Constitution Making. In J. Elster (ed.): Deliberative Democracy. Cambridge: Cambridge University Press, (1998).

53 Molander, P. Budgeting Procedures and Democratic Ideals: An Evaluation of Swedish Reforms. Journal of Public Policy 21(1), (2001), p. 29.

constitution has shaped the organic budget law since some of its effects may have taken place during the process of its initial drafting in the Ministry of Finance and the consultation rounds with other ministries where the legal specialists have had a chance to comment on the law and propose changes. Still, one can argue that the most controversial issues do surface in the course of the parliamentary debates and inter-institutional discussions, hence justifying the focus on these arenas.

3. Development Of The Organic Budget Law In Estonia

The first State Budget Act (the organic budget law or the framework law for budgeting) of the independent period in Estonia was passed in June 1993 and came into force in January 1994. Shortly after the Act had come into force, the preparations for amending it started in the Ministry of Finance. Based on experiences of other countries and recommendations made by the international financial institutions, changes were constantly made to the draft, which in turn prolonged the preparation process. The new State Budget Act was initiated by the Government in June 1997. It was then discussed at six different sessions of the parliament and was eventually passed on 27 January 1999. The President did not promulgate it, however, on the grounds that some provisions in the Act violated the Constitution. After the Riigikogu (the Estonian Parliament) made some of the recommended changes to the Act, the President promulgated it. In June 2001 substantial amendments to the Act were initiated, but when put on final vote in December 2001, they did not get enough votes. In February 2002, for most part the same amendments were proposed again and were passed in April 2002. The President did not promulgate the amended Act, on the grounds of unconstitutionality. After the *Riigikogu* had made changes to the Act, it did not receive enough votes (falling short of one vote). In June 2002, the amendment Act was initiated again (accommodating some of the arguments of the President), it was passed on 20 June 2002 and the President promulgated it. As can be seen already from this brief overview, the organic budget law of Estonia has given rise to several constitutional disputes. Therefore, the constitutional debates within and between the political institutions can be expected to have played at least some role in how the controversial provisions of the Act evolved.

With regard to contents, the organic budget law has gone through a number of significant changes. The 1994 State Budget Act outlined a budget process where the preparation phase was very centralised (with the minister of finance having very extensive powers), the adoption phase entailed only few constraints on the legislature, and the implementation phase was relatively centralised. As a result of the changes made to the State Budget Act in 1999 and 2002, the role of the Minister of Finance in the preparation phase of the budget process has been weakened, while the powers of the cabinet in setting the targets and negotiating the budgets have been increased. At the same time, a number of constraints have been imposed on the legislature when amending the budget in the adoption phase. The implementation phase has become more centralised and the Finance Ministry's control over the use of budgetary appropriations increased.[54] In other words, the delegation approach employed in the preparation phase has been gradually replaced by contracts approach. At the same time, the adoption phase has become to embody an increasing number of elements characteristic to the delegation approach, while a number of delegation elements have been added to the implementation phase, alongside with some contracts elements.

4. The Role Of The Constitution In The Development Of The Organic Budget Law In Estonia

4.1. Provisions Pertaining To The Budget In The Constitution

As pointed out in section 2, the most straightforward influence of the constitution on the organic budget law would be to provide a list of articles pertaining to the state budget and the budget process, which would in turn be incorporated into the organic budget law. In the Estonian Constitution adopted in 1992, there are altogether twelve articles pertaining to the state budget. Five of them are brought out in the chapters on the *Riigikogu* (ch 4), the Government (ch 6), and Legislation (ch 7) and the rest in a chapter called "Finance and State Budget".

Article 65 sub-point 6 stipulates that the *Riigikogu* shall pass the state budget and approve the report on its implementation, sub-point 10 states that on the proposal of the Government the *Riigikogu* will decide on borrowing by the state and on the assumption of other proprietary obligations by the state. Article 87 states that the Government of the Republic shall prepare the draft of the state budget and submit it to the *Riigikogu*, administer the implementation of the state budget, and present a report on the implementation of the state budget to the *Riigikogu*. Article 104 requires that the State Budget Act and acts pertaining to foreign and domestic borrowing and to proprietary obligations of the state can only be passed and amended by a majority of the membership of the *Riigikogu*. Article 106

54 For a more detailed review on the changes made to the organic budget law, see Raudla (2010a, ch. 7). For a discussion on the development of the budgetary institutions in Estonia in general, see Raudla (2010b).

requires inter alia that issues regarding the budget, taxation, financial obligations of the state shall not be submitted to a referendum. Article 110 states that laws which establish state taxes and the state budget shall not be enacted, amended or repealed by a decree of the President of the Republic. In a separate chapter called "Finance and the State Budget" (ch. 8) the budget procedure is outlined in more detail. Article 115 states that the *Riigikogu* shall pass as a law the budget of all state revenue and expenditure for each year (section 1); the Government of the Republic shall submit a draft state budget to the *Riigikogu* not later than three months before the beginning of the budgetary year (section 2); and on the proposal of the Government, the *Riigikogu* may pass a supplementary budget during the budgetary year (section 3). Article 116 requires that if a proposed amendment to the state budget or to its draft has the effect of decreasing estimated revenue or increasing or reallocating expenditure, the proponent of the amendment has to append financial calculations which demonstrate the sources of revenue necessary to cover the expenditure (sec 1). Section 2 requires that the *Riigikogu* shall not eliminate or reduce expenditure in the state budget or in its draft which is prescribed by other laws. Article 117 stipulates that the procedures for the drafting and passage of the state budget shall be provided by law. Article 118 states that the state budget passed by the *Riigikogu* shall enter into force at the beginning of the budgetary year and if the *Riigikogu* does not pass the state budget by the beginning of the budgetary year, expenditure of up to one-twelfth of the expenditure of the preceding budgetary year may be made each month. Article 119 states that if the *Riigikogu* has not passed the state budget within two months after the beginning of the budgetary year, the President of the Republic shall declare extraordinary elections to the *Riigikogu*. In addition, in the chapter on the Auditor General, Article 135 stipulates that the Auditor General shall present to the *Riigikogu* an overview on the use and preservation of state assets during the preceding budgetary year at the same time as the report on the implementation of the state budget is debated in the *Riigikogu*. In the chapter on local government, Article 154 states that expenditure related to duties of the state imposed by law on a local government shall be funded from the state budget.

Most of these articles – for example the stipulated deadlines for the budget process in Aarticle 116 section 1 – have been integrated in the organic budget law. Still, most of these articles only set out very general contours – for example that the Government prepares the budget and the *Riigikogu* passes is – which give very little guidance as to how the budget process should look like. Therefore, these articles had to be translated into more specific provisions. Before analysing the constitutional controversies that arose during the debates on the organic budget law, a brief overview will be given of the mechanisms of constitutional review in Estonia.

4.2. Mechanisms Of Constitutional Review In Estonia

The Estonian Constitution provides for three different institutional venues of constitutional review: 1) the President when proclaiming laws; 2) the Chancellor of Justice when reviewing the consistency of legislation with the Constitution; 3) the Supreme Court when resolving constitutional review decisions of the President, the Legal Chancellor, and courts.[55]

The Constitution accords the President (the ceremonial head of the state with a list of executive duties, but separate from the Government) with the powers of ex ante constitutional review of pending legislation. The President may refuse to proclaim a law passed by the *Riigikogu* and return the law to the parliament for a new debate and decision. If the *Riigikogu* passes the law unamended, the President can either proclaim the law or propose to the Supreme Court to declare the law unconstitutional. If the Supreme Court declares the law constitutional, the President of the Republic has to proclaim the law.

The second venue for constitutional review is the Chancellor of Justice, who can exercise abstract review. The Chancellor of Justice is an independent institution and is elected by the parliament for a seven-year term. As stipulated in the Constitution, if the Chancellor of Justice finds that legislation passed by the legislative or executive powers or by a local government is in conflict with the Constitution, he or she shall propose to the body which passed the legislation to bring the legislation into conformity with the Constitution within twenty days. If the body does not comply, the Chancellor of Justice will propose to the Supreme Court to declare the legislation invalid.[56] In addition, the Chancellor of Justice can be engaged in constitutional review through consultative review during the proceedings of the legislation in the parliament. The members of the parliament can turn to the Chancellor of Justice with interpellations.[57]

What makes constitutional review in Estonia special compared to other CEE countries and in Western Europe is that Estonia does not have a separate con-

---

55 For more detailed discussions on constitutional review in Estonia, see Maruste and Schneider (1996, 1998) and Roosma (1998, 2001). For an analysis of the making of the Estonian constitution, see Raudla (2010c).

56 The office of Chancellor of Justice in Estonia has also received attention in the academic literature (see Järvelaid (2001) for an overview). See also Maveety and Pettai (2005) for the discussion on the relationship between the Chancellor and the Supreme Court. They show that in most cases the Constitutional Review Chamber has agreed with position taken by the Chancellor of Justice.

57 As Hänni (2002) notes, this opportunity has been actively used by the members of the opposition; for example, only in spring 1999, 27 interpellations like that were submitted by the members of the opposition, compared with 2 interpellations from the members of the coalition parties.

stitutional court[58]. The highest court of general jurisdiction – the final appellate court – also fulfils the functions of a constitutional court. While the opinions of President and the Chancellor of Justice with regard to constitutionality are by nature recommendations, the decisions of the Supreme Court are binding for the legislature. The issues of constitutional review in Estonia would be usually decided by the Constitutional Review Chamber, which consists of nine judges who serve as members of Supreme Court (and at the same time are members of other specialised chambers as well) and are elected by the Supreme Court *en banc* for the term of five years.

4.3. The Role Of Constitutional Review And Constitutional Deliberations In The Development Of The Organic Budget Law

The aim of this section is to analyse how the Constitution has shaped the organic budget law of Estonia through the mechanisms of constitutional review and constitutional deliberations. The analysis will be presented by taking up the issues in the organic budget law which have dominated the constitutional debates in the parliament.

4.3.1. Increasing The Budgetary Autonomy Of Constitutional Institutions

One of the most important constitutional debates on the organic budget law concerned increasing the budgetary autonomy of constitutional institutions (i. e., the *Riigikogu*, the Supreme Court, the President, the Legal Chancellor, and the State Audit Office) by reducing the powers of the Minister of Finance and the Government in budgetary negotiations with these institutions.

The question of establishing a different kind of budget procedure for some state institutions came up first in November 1995 and was proposed by a member of parliament Arvo Junti (Centre Party); it was discussed by the *Riigikogu* from October 1996 until June 1997. The draft foresaw that a different procedure for compiling the budget proposal would be applied for the *Riigikogu* and the Supreme Court (compared with the procedure applied to other state institutions) and it would have significantly increased the budgetary autonomy of these two

58 Salzberger, E., Voigt, S. On the Delegation of Powers: With Special Emphasis on Central and Eastern Europe. Constitutional Political Economy 13, (2002), p. 37.
Sadurski, W. Legitimacy and Reasons for Constitutional Review After Communism. In W. Sadurski (ed.) Constitutional Justice, East and West: Democratic Legitimacy and Constitutional Courts in Post-Communist Europe in a Comparative Perspective. The Hague: Kluwer Law International, (2002), p. 163.

institutions. It was proposed that 1) the Minister of Finance would not establish ceilings for budget proposals to be submitted by the *Riigikogu* and the Supreme Court; 2) the budget proposals of these two institutions would be included in the draft state budget as a result of negotiations between the representatives of the Ministry of Finance, after the Minister of Finance has approved them; 3) if no agreement is achieved or the Minister of Finance does not approve the budget proposals, the proposals would be submitted to the Finance Committee of the *Riigikogu*, which would decide on the size of these budgets (but subject to the constraint that it cannot *increase* the sum that was stipulated in the original budget proposal submitted); 4) the Government has no right to leave out sums foreseen for the *Riigikogu* and the Supreme Court in the state draft budget. If it does not consider the sums foreseen for these institutions in the budget to be reasonable, it will make a suggestion to change them together with the draft budget submitted to the *Riigikogu*.

In the explanatory note to this draft act and in his presentation to the plenary assembly of the parliament, Junti explained that the budget procedure outlined by the existing organic budget law violated the constitutional principle of separation of powers by giving the executive too extensive powers and thereby subjecting the legislature and the judiciary to the executive in compiling the budget. Thus, he emphasised that the proposed changes would allow a more complete realization of the principle of separation of powers stipulated in the Constitution, by giving the parliament and the judiciary the right to decide more autonomously over their own budgets. Both the initiator of the draft act and the Chairman of the Finance Committee Jürgen Ligi (Reform Party) referred to specific examples from the preceding years, when the officials from the Ministry of Finance had unilaterally changed the sums in the budget request of the *Riigikogu* and sometimes even the Minister of Finance had not been informed about them. Junti also stated that in preparing the draft law he had drawn upon the examples of other countries – for example, Germany, Sweden, Finland and Hungary. He added that in Spain, such a specific procedure had even been established by the constitution[59]. Ligi also agreed that the existing arrangements put the Minister of Finance higher than the parliament, and such an arrangement would enable the executive to impose political pressure on legislative and judicial powers if it wanted to[60].

At the second reading of the act, Rait Maruste, the Chairman of the Supreme Court, was invited to give his opinion. Maruste emphasised the importance of the principle of the separation of powers and pointed out that the Estonian Constitution is one of few constitutions where this principle is clearly spelled out. Thus,

59 *Riigikogu* Verbatim Record, 8 October 1996, 22 October 1996.

60 *Riigikogu* Verbatim Record, 8 October 1996.

he stated, the legislative, executive and judicial powers should be separated. He emphasised that the Government should play the role of *coordinating* the preparation of the budget but should not be able to *dictate* the conditions for the *Riigikogu* and the Supreme Court. Maruste also noted that such a change in the organic budget law was necessary for facilitating the development of democratic institutions in Estonia and for overcoming the tendency (prevalent in transition countries) of an excessively strong executive – a relic of the totalitarian regime[61].

Interestingly, several members of the parliament argued *against* increasing the budgetary autonomy of the parliament and the Supreme Court. Liia Hänni (Moderates), for example, referred to the existing organic budget law, which required a balanced budget, and argued that if the judiciary and the legislature submit their budget proposals independently, then, in order to balance the overall budget, the executive might have to cut its own expenditures, which, in turn, would imply a clear weakening of the executive in the budget process. Jüri Adams (Pro Patria Union), who had been the author of the draft Constitution that had become the basis for discussions in the Constitutional Assembly in 1991-1992, noted that the Estonian Constitution requires a balanced budget and argued that the Government would be in a difficult situation when the budget requests of the *Riigikogu* and the Supreme Court unbalance the budget[62].

The amendments that would have increased the budgetary autonomy of the *Riigikogu* and the Supreme Court were not passed, since in June 1997, the Government submitted a new draft organic budget law to the parliament and the initiator of the draft act decided to withdraw the proposal from the proceedings, arguing that these issues should be solved together with the new organic budget law. In addition, it became clear during the proceedings of the Act that the Government was opposed to these changes[63]. Although, not surprisingly, this proposal had been initiated by a member of the opposition, the most vocal opponents of this provision were also members of the opposition. One would have expected the opposition members to argue *in favour* of such a provision, given that it would have enabled the parliament to have more control over its own budget, but the opposition members considered the overall budget balance to be more important than the budgetary autonomy of the parliament and they were therefore willing to maintain the extensive budgetary powers of the executive *vis-à-vis* the legislature.

The provisions proposed by Junti were not included in the first version of the new organic budget law passed on 27 January 1999, but the same issue – although

61 *Riigikogu* Verbatim Record, 22 October 1996.

62 *Riigikogu* Verbatim Record, 20 May 1997.
In fact, the 1992 Constitution does not explicitly require a balanced budget.

63 *Riigikogu* Verbatim Record, 20 May 1997.

in an extended form – was taken up by President Lennart Meri, who decided not to promulgate the State Budget Act on the grounds that several provisions in it were unconstitutional (Resolution No. 507, from 17 February 1999). For most part, the objections of the President concerned the provisions that gave the Government (and the Minister of Finance) too extensive powers *vis-à-vis* the constitutional institutions in the budget process. His main objection was that the same procedure for drafting, implementing and reporting on the budget that applies to the ministries applies to the constitutional institutions (i. e., the *Riigikogu*, the President, the State Audit Office, the Legal Chancellor and the Supreme Court) as well. The procedure in the adopted act foresaw that: 1) the Government would set (based on the proposal from the Minister of Finance) upper ceilings for the budget requests of the constitutional institutions; 2) the Minister of Finance has the right to change or delete the sums in the budget proposals; 3) in the case of disagreement between the Minister of Finance and a constitutional institution the dispute is solved by the Government; 4) the Government has a right to change or delete the expenditures in the budget requests of the constitutional institutions. The President argued that such a procedure would violate the principle of separation and balance of powers stipulated in Article 4 of the Constitution. He argued that the Act would make the constitutional institutions dependent on the Government and the Minister of Finance and hence violate the principle of the rule of law. Further, the President claimed that such a procedure would endanger the realization of constitutionally stipulated rights and duties of the constitutional institutions, since by assessing the expediency of expenditures, the content of the *decisions* of these institutions could be indirectly evaluated.

The resolution of the President was discussed both in the Constitutional Committee and the Finance Committee of the *Riigikogu*, and the opinions were presented in the plenary session of the parliament. The Constitutional Committee agreed with the President's argument that it would be unconstitutional to have the same procedures for constitutional institutions as for ministries. As the Chairman of the Constitutional Committee Tiit Käbin (Reform Party) explained at the plenary session, especially the Finance Minister's right to change or delete the sums in the budget requests of the constitutional institutions could be seen as going against the principle of the separation of powers. He added, "As we know, in practice, these sums are not changed or eliminated by the Minister of Finance himself but by some officials from the Ministry of Finance." The Finance Committee, however, remained ambiguous on the issue. The Chairman of the Finance Committee Kalle Jürgenson (Pro Patria Union), when presenting the opinion of the Committee at the plenary session, stated that it was debatable whether the Government can influence the decisions of the constitutional institutions by influencing the budget[64].

64 *Riigikogu* Verbatim Record, 14 April 1999.

Still, by the next reading of the Act, the Finance Committee suggested special arrangements for the constitutional institutions (which were also incorporated into the new version of the act): if during the budget negotiations between the Minister of Finance and the constitutional institution no agreement is reached, only the Government (and not the Minister of Finance) has the right to change the sums in the budget request and it has to motivate the decision in the explanatory note to the draft state budget submitted to the *Riigikogu*.

Thus, it can be argued that the Constitution played an important role in increasing the budgetary autonomy of the "constitutional institutions". Appealing to the special role attributed to the constitutional institutions by the Constitution and evoking the constitutionally stipulated (though a very vague) notion of the separation and balance of powers allowed the President to achieve the respective changes in the organic budget law. The arguments of the President were eventually accepted by the *Riigikogu* and, as a result, changes were made to the law that would have otherwise not been included in it. This controversy is a clear example of auto-limitation by the Estonian parliament. If the *Riigikogu* had not made the changes to the organic budget law, the President would have taken the Act to the Supreme Court. Fighting for the budgetary autonomy of the constitutional institutions was one among the several battles that the President undertook in protecting his institution from the *Riigikogu* and the Government; the previous decisions of the Supreme Court regarding the powers of the President had agreed with the President. In addition, if the issue had reached the Supreme Court, there would have been clear incentives for the Court to the support the President, since the Court itself was one of the constitutional institutions whose budgetary autonomy was in question. The remarks by the Chief Justice of the Supreme Court during the discussion on a similar issue in 1996 also indicated that the Court would have been likely to find the organic budget law unconstitutional. Thus, the mechanism of auto-limitation played a significant role here: the *Riigikogu* could anticipate that it would lose the case in the Supreme Court, were it to pass the law unamended. Although some of the members of the parliament (especially from the Finance Committee) sought to contest the constitutional interpretation of the President, the majority of the legislature agreed with his interpretation and did not seek to offer alternative constructions of the notion of the separation and balance of powers.

It is also appropriate to ask here to what extent the debate – framed in constitutional terms – was motivated by institutional self-interest. In many ways, the decision of the President could be seen as having been motivated by the desire to increase the autonomy of his institution in compiling the budget. It is interesting to note that the issue of giving more autonomy in compiling the budget proposal had already had been considered by the *Riigikogu* itself in 1995. It was inspired by problematic relations between the Government and the parliament and hence reflected institutional self-interest of the parliament. But, as could be seen from the discussions on the organic budget law in October 1996, several members of the parliament did not support such changes, since they were afraid of the implications that such changes would have for budget discipline. Thus, when the President took the question up, it was not an entirely new issue on the agenda. It might have well been the discussions on granting the *Riigikogu* and the Supreme Court more extensive budgetary autonomy in 1996-1997 that inspired the President to proceed with this issue in 1999. In other words, the pursuits of institutional self-interest by the parliament in 1996 "boomeranged" three years later and led to the extension of budgetary autonomy for all constitutional institutions.

4.3.2. Parliament Versus The Cabinet In The Budget Process Limiting The Amendment Power Of The Parliament In The Budget Process

As a result of the changes made to the organic budget law since 1994, the amendment powers of the parliament have been constrained. The constraints that were *actually* incorporated to the Act, however, were relatively mild compared to several *proposals* that were made either in the draft law or in the course of the legislative debates. The provisions that sought to constrain the role of the parliament in the budget process more extensively were rejected by members of the parliament on the grounds of alleged unconstitutionality.

One of the main issues that was debated during the readings of the State Budget Act in 1997-1999 was a question that had been brought up in the discussions of the Estonian Constitutional Assembly in 1991-1992 as well: To what extent should the *Riigikogu* have the right to make changes to the draft budget and should Government consent be received before making the amendments[65]? In February 1998, a motion to amend the organic budget law was made by a member of opposition Heiki Kranich (Reform Party)[66], according to which the *Riigikogu* could only make amendments to the draft budget after receiving consent from the Government. This proposal gave rise to heated discussions in the *Riigikogu* and the MPs held widely diverging opinions on whether this provision would be constitutional or not.

There were several members of the *Riigikogu* who clearly supported this proposal and viewed it as conforming to the Constitution. If in the initial phases of the debate the supporters came primarily from an opposition party (Reform

---

65 The Constitutional Assembly decided to leave out a proposed provision that would have required Government consent on the amendments to the draft budget (see Raudla 2010, ch. 3).

66 Kranich had also been minister of finance for six months in 1994.

Party), then in the later phases, members of the coalition parties started supporting it as well. At the first debate on the issue, Kalev Kukk (Reform Party) argued, referring to the Constitution, that the task of the Government is to *prepare* the budget and the task of the *Riigikogu* is to *pass* the budget, and the way *Riigikogu* had made changes to the budget in the previous years had amounted to interference with the executive authority. Valve Kirsipuu (Reform Party) pointed out that the Constitution does not say anywhere that the *Riigikogu* can *make changes* to the budget; to the contrary, Article 65 Section 6 says that the *Riigikogu* shall pass the state budget and approve the report on its implementation. She added that preparing the budget requires thorough analysis by the Ministry of Finance, which could easily be rendered meaningless by the motions to amend the draft budget by the *Riigikogu*. She argued that the way the *Riigikogu* had dealt with the state budget in 1997, for example, was not normal for a democratic state.

Another member of the parliament, Liia Hänni (Moderates), who had been a prominent member of the Constitutional Assembly, argued that although the Constitution does not give an answer to the question of how exactly the budget procedure should look like, there are still some footholds. She emphasised that it has to be analysed what the general constitutional principle of the separation and balance of powers means in the particular context of Estonia. She suggested that if the state has a strong parliament and developed democracy, it would be conceivable to employ the model used in Germany, where the Government puts together the budget and the parliament simply agrees or disagrees with it. She emphasised that a strong parliament, where the governing coalition is able to control the government, can afford the luxury of not changing the budget submitted by the Government. She argued, however, that the *Riigikogu* was not yet strong enough to give the Government so much freedom and doing that would endanger the Estonian democracy. Eiki Nestor (Moderates) pointed out that giving the parliament the right to say only "yes" or "no" to the budget submitted by the Government is characteristic to presidential systems. To this, Kukk answered that Germany, which is even less presidential than Estonia, also uses a system that limits the rights of the parliament to make amendments to the budget submitted by the government. The Chairman of the Finance Committee Olev Raju (Coalition Party) stated that the general position of the Committee was that although this provision would not directly violate any article in the Constitution, it could go against the *context and ideology* of the Constitution[67].

By the next reading (8 April 1998), the disputed amendment proposal was modified by Kranich, and the role of the *Riigikogu* Finance Committee was added. Thus, the proposed provision stated that those amendment proposals to

67 *Riigikogu* Verbatim Record, 11 February 1998.

the draft budget that the Government has not agreed with *and* the Finance Committee has not consented to, cannot be put on vote. The Finance Committee of the *Riigikogu* supported this provision. The Minister of Finance Mart Opmann (Coalition Party), when presenting the draft act in the *Riigikogu*, argued that this amendment would enable the Government to fulfil the goals it has set. He pointed out that the experience of the previous years had shown that during the passage of the budget in the parliament, not only the structure but also the size of the expenditures had been changed; this meant that the Government's plan of economic policy had been changed without thorough prior analysis. He emphasised that the provision that would limit the right of the parliament to make amendments to the draft budget would preclude such situations. He added that in putting together the draft State Budget Act, the organic budget acts of Germany and Finland had been used as examples[68].

This proposal, again, gave rise to debates over constitutionality. Liina Tõnisson (Centre Party) asked the Minister of Finance, "What kind of a principle of democracy is this proposal based on?" In his answer, the Minister noted that the approach so far had been "unrestrictedly democratic" and referred to year 1993, when one particular MP had made 102 amendment proposals to the draft budget during one reading. The Minister also brought out that the experience with the amendments made to the draft budget in the past showed that the amendments had often not been justified and the Government had had to revert these amendments. As an answer to the question by Siiri Oviir (Centre Party) – "What constitutional provision is this amendment in compliance with?" – the Minister of Finance admitted that he did not know. The question of constitutionality was also taken up by Raju. He stated that he had consulted with the Supreme Court judges (he admitted though that he did not know whether they were members of the Constitutional Review Chamber). Although the judges could not issue written opinions on draft legislation, they had been willing to give him their opinion unofficially (since they had been together at university). The judges he had consulted thought unanimously that such a restriction was in compliance with the Constitution, since the Constitution stipulates that the proceeding of the budget in the parliament is a special procedure and a special procedure can be made different from the general procedure[69].

Kranich, who had made the proposal to limit the amendment powers of the *Riigikogu*, addressed the question of whether the procedure for the budget should be different than for other acts. Kranich emphasised that the budget should be seen as the plan of the government, which it submits to the *Riigikogu*, presents

68 *Riigikogu* Verbatim Record, 8 April 1998.

69 *Riigikogu* Verbatim Record, 8 April 1998.

it thoroughly, answers exhaustively to all questions and asks whether *Riigikogu* thinks it is a financial document, on the basis of which the Government can govern. He also emphasised, "In deciding over this issue, we should not think of the current situation and belonging to opposition. All members might belong to a governing coalition in the future, and for such a situation, one would want to have a strong backing and the ability to govern based on the budget that was planned. Therefore, we have to look further into the future."[70]. Still, when put on vote, this provision was not supported. Instead, a "softer" version of the legislative constraint was adopted, stating that motions to amend, which are submitted after the suspension of the second reading of the draft state budget shall not be put to a vote if they are not supported by the Government and not accepted by the Finance Committee of the *Riigikogu.*

It is noteworthy that the first proposal for restricting the amendment rights of the parliament in 1998 was not brought up by the Government or by MPs from the governing coalition but by a member of opposition. At first, the members of the governing coalition were even sceptical of it, although they did, indeed, support it at the next reading. Thus, it can be argued that the proposal made by Kranich (and supported by a number of members) did reflect a will of institutional self-binding. The proposal of self-binding was certainly facilitated by the personal experience of Kranich in the executive, the antecedent experiences of the *Riigikogu* with budgeting, and the examples from Germany and Finland. Other participants in the debate, however, were driven by institutional self-interests: the Government eventually supported the proposal, the Finance Committee supported the proposal only after it had been included as a veto power alongside the Government, and the majority of the parliament was against it (at least in 1998). Still, in 2002, the majority of the legislature supported the constraint according to which motions to amend the draft state budget cannot cause a state budget deficit, an increase in the deficit or a reduction in the surplus, partly reflecting the desire of institutional self-binding by the parliament, partly the institutional self-interest of the Government, partly the partisan interests of the Reform Party to maintain fiscal discipline and follow conservative fiscal policies. Vocal objections to these proposals came in particular from the MPs who were in the opposition. The interest of the opposition in maintaining the amendment rights of the parliament is particularly strong, since the amendments (or amendment proposals) to the budget is an important way of signalling to the constituents the work done for them.

These debates also point to an interesting example of an attempt to use the reverse of "auto-limitation". The arguments by Raju show that the anticipated

70 *Riigikogu* Verbatim Record, 8 April 1998.

decision of the Supreme Court can also be used to *facilitate* the adoption of a provision that is suspected to be unconstitutional by other members of the legislature. The unofficial opinion of the Supreme Court judges served as rhetorical means to persuade other legislators of the constitutionality of the contested provision.

Constitutional arguments were used by all actors in the debate to corroborate their viewpoints. Given that the Constitution is very vague on the division of work between the legislature and the executive with regard to the budget, both proponents and opponents of the provision limiting the amendment rights of the parliament could evoke arguments of constitutionality. Although it can be argued that it was not necessarily the alleged unconstitutionality of the proposed provision *itself* that led to leaving it out from the Act in 1998 (but the institutional self-interest of the legislators), the arguments of unconstitutionality provided rhetorical ammunition to its opponents and made the decision to appear more legitimate.

Binding The Draft State Budget To Issue Of Confidence

In addition to the organic budget law, some aspects of the budget procedure are stipulated in the *Riigikogu* Rules of Procedure Act[71]. Shortly before the adoption of the negative supplementary budget in June 1999, a significant change was made to the Rules of Procedure Act, allowing the Government to bind the draft state budget to an issue of confidence. The 1994 Rules of Procedure Act had hitherto explicitly forbidden the use of that procedure in the budget process. This provision came about a result of constitutional review. After the opposition had submitted more the 500 motions to amend during the debates on the negative supplementary budget in June 1999 (signalling the intended use of obstructionism, which did indeed take place some days later), the Chancellor of Justice notified the *Riigikogu* that the provision in the Rules of Procedure Act forbidding the binding of the draft state budget to an issue of confidence was unconstitutional, since the Constitution provided no limitations with regard to what kind of draft acts can be bound to an issue of confidence. As a result, an amendment to the Rules of Procedure was passed less than a fortnight later, allowing *all* draft acts to be bound to an issue of confidence. Given that the amendment was enacted very fast, it would have allowed the coalition to bind the draft negative supplementary budget (under discussion) to an issue of confidence; this would have meant that those motions to amend the draft act not supported by the Government would not have been put on vote in the parliament. In anticipation of that, the opposition stopped filibustering and the supplementary budget was passed.

71 This paragraph draws on Raudla, R. The Evolution of Budgetary Institutions in Estonia: A Path Full of Puzzles? Governance 23(3), (2010), p. 463-484.

During the parliamentary deliberations on the proposed provision, the members of opposition argued that the timing of the letter of the Chancellor of Justice was obviously advantageous to the governing coalition and was clearly addressed to the proceedings of the negative supplementary budget in the parliament. It was pointed out that this provision in the Rules of Procedure had been in force for five years and it was suspicious that its unconstitutionality was only brought up then. In defending the provision, Liia Hänni (Reform Party), the Chairman of the Constitutional Committee, stated that the fact that the Rules of Procedure violated the Constitution only became evident because of the obstructionist tactics of the opposition, which made it impossible to proceed with the draft supplementary budget in a normal way. She emphasised that it was an important role of the Chancellor of Justice to bring up issues of unconstitutionality that have risen from the *actual context*[72].

Several opposition members argued that allowing the Government to bind the draft state budget to an issue of confidence would be unconstitutional. Edgar Savisaar (Centre Party) argued that the same logic that is expressed in the Constitution concerning acts that cannot be submitted to a referendum should apply to binding the draft acts to an issue of confidence. He stated that since the list of acts that cannot be put on referendum includes acts pertaining to the state budget, the Government should not be allowed to bind the passage of the budget to an issue of confidence. Savisaar also pointed out that by binding the draft budget to an issue of confidence, the Government would assume the role of a legislature and this would violate the principle of the balance of powers, which would be dangerous to development of democracy in Estonia[73]. The opposition also criticised the fact that the governing coalition wanted to change the rules of the game in the middle of the game: to use the amended procedure to continue the proceedings of the draft supplementary budget. Changing the procedure for the purpose of passing one particular act was seen as undemocratic[74]. Despite the objections of the opposition, the amendment was passed.

Introducing a provision that allow the Government to bind the passage of the state budget to issue of confidence is a clear example of how the Constitution

72 *Riigikogu* Verbatim Record, 15 June 1999.

73 Similarly, Sven Mikser (Centre Party) noted in a media article that since the state budget can not be submitted to a referendum, giving the right to the Government to push the budget through the parliament would further reduce the voice of the people in budgetary deliberations (Mikser 1999). Mikser also argued that Article 117 of the Constitution, stating that the procedures for the drafting and passage of the state budget shall be provided by law, indicates that the Constitution allows restrictions to be made to the budget procedure (including the restriction that an issue of confidence can not be used).

74 *Riigikogu* Verbatim Record, 15 June 1999.

was evoked to serve the pressing political needs of the governing coalition. If the coalition parties had initiated the change of the Rules of Procedure Act themselves, they would have had a lower leverage in justifying the change, because it was clearly connected to the desire to pass the supplementary budget. Since the proposal came from the Chancellor of Justice, who is considered to be a neutral guardian of the Constitution, the proposal had more weight and legitimacy. Introducing this provision reflected clearly a partisan interest rather than the institutional self-interest of the parliament. The coalition parties in the parliament were willing to *increase* the power of the Government and *reduce* the power of the parliament in budget process in order to achieve pertinent partisan policy goals (restoring fiscal balance).

The Concept Of "Government Budget" And How Detailed The Budget Should Be

An important constitutional issue that came up in the proceedings of the organic budget law in 2001 was the question of how detailed the classification of expenditures in the state budget should be. The draft acts amending the organic budget law initiated in 2001 and 2002 sought to introduce the concept of "Government budget", which would be adopted *after* the *Riigikogu* passes the annual state budget and which would additionally classify the categories of expenditures in the budgets of individual ministries. The "Government budget" implied that the budget submitted to the parliament would contain more general classifications, which would be additionally sub-divided by the Government itself after the adoption of the budget in the parliament. As pointed out in the explanatory note to the draft act, the purpose of this amendment was to change the level of decision-making: to "give more authority to the level that has the most information" and to stop the practice that the *Riigikogu* decides on the internal structure of the operating expenses.

Again, this proposal gave rise to extensive debates in the parliament. While it was supported by the majority of the Finance Committee and the members of the coalition parties, it was considered to be unconstitutional by the opposition and the President. The main argument of the opponents was that the "Government budget" violates the constitutional principle of the balance of powers by reducing the transparency of the budget and by giving excessive powers to the Government.

Jaanus Männik (People's Union), Vice Chairman of the Finance Committee, the most vocal opponent of the concept of Government budget, asked from the Minister of Finance, "Which articles in the Constitution allow that the state budget contains only general contours and aggregate sums, and the actual expenditures are determined by regulations of the Government?" The Minister of Finance Siim Kallas (Reform Party) answered that the Constitution does not say how the budget classification should look like[75]. When asked the same question at the next reading of the draft, Kallas argued that the draft act had been discussed with legal experts and the Constitutional Committee of the *Riigikogu*, and no violation of the Constitution had been found[76]. In his speech at the first reading of the draft act, Männik stated that this provision would clearly violate the Constitution, since the Constitution says nothing of a "Government budget" but says that *all* state revenues and expenditures are enacted as a law by the parliament[77]. At the second reading, Männik added that the "Government budget" violates the Constitution and the principle of parliamentary democracy, since it is the constitutional *obligation* of the *Riigikogu* to decide on the expenditures and enact them as a law; therefore, it should not delegate these decisions to the executive[78]. Tiit Toomsalu (United People's Party of Estonia) also brought up the issue of constitutionality in his speeches and argued that the Estonian Constitution foresees a parliamentary system, but the concept of "Government budget" would lead towards a state where the executive power dominates[79]. Similar arguments as those pointed out by the members of the opposition against the notion of "Government budget" were also brought up by President Arnold Rüütel in his resolution not to promulgate the State Budget Act[80].

The Constitutional Committee of the *Riigikogu* agreed for most part with the arguments of the President, while the Finance Committee did not agree. The Chairman of the Finance Committee Meelis Atonen pointed out that the Constitution says nothing on the extent of the classification of revenues and expenditures[81]. Still, the organic budget law adopted in June 2002 did *not* include the concept of the Government budget anymore. Instead, a more ambiguous version was proposed (and eventually adopted), stipulating that more detailed classification of expenditure in the state budget (according to the economic content) can be done *either* in the state budget *or* by the Government after the budget has been passed, and that on the basis of a reasoned proposal made by the Minister of Finance, the Government of the Republic may further classify expenditure incurred by the ministries.

75 *Riigikogu* Verbatim Record, 5 December 2001.
76 Ibid., 19 December 2001.
77 Ibid., 5 December 2001.
78 Ibid., 19 December 2001.
79 Ibid., 5 December 2001.
80 Resolution No. 153, from 6 May 2002.
81 *Riigikogu* Verbatim Record, 14 May 2002.

At the readings of the re-initiated organic budget law in June 2002, the main issue debated was the question of whether the changes made to the Act removed the alleged conflicts with the Constitution that the President had pointed out. Atonen (the initiator of the draft) asserted that the problems the President had pointed out had been removed from the draft[82]. The Chairman of the Finance Committee Jürgen Ligi even argued that the previous draft had not been unconstitutional either; the governing coalition had not considered the arguments of the President very convincing but had still been willing to come half the way and to make some changes as a compromise[83]. The members of the opposition who had opposed the idea of "Government budget" asserted that the new draft law had just made cosmetic changes but had not the changed the content of the Act with regard to the Government's authority to further classify the expenditures. Jaanus Männik, the main opponent of the Act, argued that the new draft act still violated the Constitution[84]. Janno Reiljan (People's Union) pointed out that this Act would give an absolute power to the governing coalition and to prevent the control by the opposition: the opposition would know what is in the budget only after the Government has classified it, but then it would be too late for any changes by the *Riigikogu*[85]. Arvo Sirendi (People's Union) argued that the "unavoidable condition of democracy is that the supreme authority knows in detail what is going on in the state", and that the Constitution says clearly that the Government *prepares* the budget and the *Riigikogu adopts* it[86]. Ligi argued that the Act was not in conflict with the Constitution and that the *Riigikogu* could still decide on what level of detail the expenditures have to be written in the budget. He emphasised, however, that from the point of view of the users of the money, flexibility would allow greater efficiency[87]. Männik pointed out that half of the members of the parliament had a different understanding of the Constitution and that this conception should be assessed by the Supreme Court. Despite the contentions by the opposition, the provision allowing additional classification of items was included in the Act that was passed on 20 June 2002. This time, the President did not contest these provisions.

In summary, as a result of the alleged unconstitutionality, the concept of "Government budget" as such was abandoned and a more ambiguously worded version (in essence still allowing the classification to be done by the Government, but also mentioning the opportunity for the parliament to do it) was adopted. On

82 Ibid., 18 June 2002.

83 *Riigikogu* Verbatim Record, 20 June 2002.

84 Ibid., 18 June 2002, 20 June 2002.

85 Ibid., 18 June 2002.

86 Ibid., 20 June 2002.

87 Ibid., 18 June 2002.

the whole, these debates indicate that since the Constitution contains only very general provisions on what the roles of the *Riigikogu* and the Government in the budget process are, it was easy – by both sides of the dispute – to appeal to the same constitutional provisions. It is interesting to note that the parliamentary majority was willing to increase the budgetary powers of the Government and to reduce the powers of the parliament. In part, this attempt of self-binding (against future interference with the details of the budget) was driven by the desire to make the execution of the budget more flexible. On the whole, however, the high level of detail had been advantageous to the members of the *Riigikogu*, since an extensive break-down of the expenditures allowed them to make very specific amendment proposals during the legislative proceedings of the budget and, in that way, demonstrate to their constituents that they had at least *attempted* to stand up for them. Another question is: why was the President so concerned with protecting the power of the *Riigikogu* against that of the Government? In part, this may have to do with the fact that the President had been a member of the party (People's Union) that was in opposition and whose members were the most vocal opponents of the concept. It is also noteworthy that while during the debates in 2001, the People's Union and the Centre Party were against increasing the power of the Government (and thus the governing coalition) in the budget-making, then after the shift in the coalition, as a result of which the Centre Party became part of the governing coalition in January 2002, the members of this party started supporting the concept of the Government budget.

Altogether, the debates on the budgetary roles of the Government *vis-à-vis* the legislature law can be summarised as following: the Government sought repeatedly to increase the power of the executive in the budget process and the parliamentary opposition endeavoured (together with the President) to prevent the reduction of the parliament's role in the budget process by evoking constitutional arguments. At the same time, there were also clear exceptions to this pattern: the proposal introducing Government veto on legislative budgetary amendments came from a member of opposition and the Chancellor of Justice supported increasing the authority of the budgetary powers of the executive *vis-à-vis* the legislature.

5. Discussion And Conclusions

In sum, the Constitution has played an important role in shaping the organic budget law in Estonia. In addition to constitutional articles that have been incorporated in the organic budget law, the Constitution has influenced the development of the law through mechanisms of constitutional review and by framing the legislative discussions on the law. As a result of the constitutional review by the president and constitutional deliberations in the parliament the budgetary autonomy of constitutional institutions was increased. Ensuing from the constitutional review by the Chancellor of Justice, the budgetary powers of the Government were increased by giving it the right to bind the passage of the state budget to issue of confidence. At the same time, constitutional deliberations circumscribed the extent to which the budgetary powers of the Government were increased and it did not go as far as the Government had desired: the concept of Government budget was abandoned and a more ambiguous version of it adopted and the Government was not given the right to veto parliamentary amendments at the first readings of the state budget. The role of the parliament in the budget process has also been influenced by the interpretations and constructions of the pertinent articles. As a result of constitutional deliberations and constitutional review, the budgetary amendment rights of the parliament were constrained – although not to the extent desired by some actors. Altogether, the Constitution has played a balancing role by not allowing the budgetary powers of the executive to become excessive or the powers of the legislature too constrained.

The analysis above indicates that the most important mechanism of constitutional review on the debates on the organic budget law so far has been that of the President. Although the Chancellor of Justice has generally been very active in Estonia, his role in the development of the organic budget law was limited to bringing up binding the passage of the state budget to issue of confidence. Although the organic budget law itself has not been discussed in the Constitutional Review Chamber of the Supreme Court, auto-limitation by the Riigikogu – the guesses of how the Court would decide, were the President to take the contested budget laws to the Court – played a role in the Riigikogu's reaction to the President's protests and influenced its willingness to make the amendments suggested by the President. As Hänni[88] notes, the Supreme Court has, in general, in its decisions, protected the right of the President to carry out its constitutional functions without excessive interference from the Parliament. In addition, the Supreme Court has given the right in constitutional cases to the President. (e.g., in the period 1992-2001, out of the eight cases that the President took to the Supreme Court, the Court agreed with the President in seven cases). Also, by evoking the argument of protecting the budgetary autonomy of the constitutional institutions, the President could appeal (at the same time as protecting its own institution) to safeguarding the budgetary autonomy of the Supreme Court itself. In that way it is understandable that the members of the Riigikogu were during the disputes in 1999 fairly convinced they would lose the case if it were referred to the Supreme Court.

88 Hänni, L. Põhiseaduse mõju poliitilisele otsustusprotsessile. [The Effects of the Constitution on Political Decision Process] Riigikogu toimetised 5, (2002).

Even though the legislative opposition in Estonia does not have the right to refer a bill for constitutional review in the Supreme Court, on several occasions the opposition used the explicitly worded call for auto-limitation, saying that otherwise the Court will invalidate the provisions. Several times the members of opposition "threatened" the majority with the claim that the President would not promulgate the Act because of unconstitutionality. That shows that "auto-limitation" can take place not only in reference to the constitutional review by the Court but also by other institutions of constitutional review. Further, it demonstrates that even in countries where the opposition does not have referral rights to the constitutional court, it can use other institutions of constitutional review to sustain their calls for auto-limitation.

As conjectured in section 2, constitutional issues came up *frequently* at the parliamentary discussions over the organic budget law. Indeed, a large portion of the debates over the organic budget law was dominated by constitutional deliberation. Also, as conjectured in section 2, the political actors – the members of the parliament, the cabinet members, and the President – used the text of the Constitution to support their own partisan and institutional interests. The proposal of Junti in 1996 reflected institutional interests of the parliament. The plea to increase the budgetary autonomy of constitutional institutions certainly reflected the institutional self-interest of the President to have more budgetary autonomy for his institution. The proposals to constrain the right of the parliament to make amendments to the draft budget were rejected by the majority of the parliament (during the discussions in 1998-1999), reflecting the desire of the parliament not to cede its budgetary powers. The Finance Committee agreed to support the constraints on parliamentary amendment rights after it had been included as a gatekeeper alongside the Cabinet.

In addition to institutional self-interests, partisan interests were reflected in most of the constitutional disputes. As could be seen in the discussions during 2001 over different proposals that sought to constrain the role of the legislature and increase the role of the executive, the members of the opposition sought to demonstrate unconstitutionality of these proposed provisions. In addition, amid the disputes in 2001-2002, the President sought to protect the role of the parliament (and in particular the role of the opposition) vis-à-vis the Government in the budget process. The President's concern with protecting the role of the parliament and the opposition is likely to have been related to the fact that he had been a presidential candidate of one of the parties in the opposition. The partisan interests were also reflected in the fact that a party (the Centre Party) that had been against the concept of "Government budget" when it was in the opposition, started supporting it once it was in the governing coalition. The dispute over the right of the Government to bind the passage of the budget to issue of confidence was perhaps the clearest example of how alleged unconstitutionality was used as a means for serving short-term partisan interests (the adoption of the supplementary budget) in the face of the obstructionist tactics of the opposition.

There were some proposals, however, that went beyond institutional and partisan self-interest, and reflected the will of "self-binding". The proposals to constrain the parliament's right to amend the budget in 1998 were made by a member of the opposition (and supported by some other members of the opposition), appealing to the desire to improve the rationality of the budget process. The proposal of parliamentary "self-binding" was certainly facilitated by the personal experience of the proponents of this proposal in the executive branch. In addition, these proposals were inspired by specific and recent experiences of budgeting in 1997, when the parliament had lost "self-control" and increased the volume of the budget by a significant amount. Also, self-binding concerns came to the fore in the discussions in 1995-1996 over granting more budgetary autonomy to the *Riigikogu* in the preparation phase of the budget process. Motivated by the concerns of maintaining budget balance, a number of opposition MPs called for not granting the parliament (and the Supreme Court) more extensive freedom in compiling its own budget proposal. In other cases, however, the "self-binding" provisions of the parliament (e. g., the provisions allowing the Government to have a more important role in classifying the expenditures, introduced in 2002) came about as a decision of the coalition parties, reflecting – in addition to the desire to increase the efficiency and flexibility of the budget process – the wish to increase the power of the coalition at the expense of the opposition parties. The parties in the coalition are usually able to pursue their goals through the cabinet, which can explain their readiness to limit the role of the parliament to a certain extent.

Altogether, the exploratory case study of Estonia shows that the constitution can play a substantial role in influencing the development of an organic budget law and shape it through different mechanisms, especially through constitutional review and legislative constitutional deliberation. Further comparative studies on this issue are certainly called for in order to make systematic evaluations of the interactions between the constitution and the budgetary institutions. As this paper demonstrates, taking a fiscal sociological approach to explore these interactions can provide useful insights for understanding these dynamics and it has a potential to contribute to constitutional political economy, by bringing forth issues that have so far been neglected in the existing literature.

Acknowledgements

Research for this article was carried out with the financial support of the Mobilitas Grant of the European Social Fund (Grant no. MJD43). The author would like thank Jürgen Backhaus, Kenneth Kriz, Richard Wagner, Helge Peukert and Enrico Schöbel and participants at the 7th Erfurt Conference of Fiscal Sociology for their useful comments on earlier versions of this paper. This paper is also a revised version of chapter 9 of the author's doctoral dissertation *Constitution, Public Finance, and Transition* (Peter Lang, 2010).

References

Bachrach, P., Baratz, M. S. Two Faces of Power. American Political Science Review 56(4), (1962), pp. 947-952.

Bachrach, P., Baratz, M. S. Decisions and Nondecisions: An Analytical Framework. American Political Science Review 57(3), (1963), pp. 632-642.

Berggren, N., Kurrild-Klitgaard, P. Economic Effects of Political Institutions, With Special Reference to Constitutions. In N. Berggren, N. Karlson, J. Nergelius, Joakim (eds.) Why Constitutions Matter. New Brunswick: Transaction Publisher, (2002).

Bond, J. Concerning Constitutional Courts in Central and Eastern Europe. International Public Policy Review 2(2), (2006), pp. 5-25.

Brown, J. F. Hopes and Shadows: Eastern Europe After Communism. Durham: Duke University Press, (1994).

Brünneck, A. von Constitutional Review and Legislation in Western Democracies. In C. Landfried (ed.) Constitutional Review and Legislation. Baden-Baden: Nomos Verlagsgesellschaft, (1988).

Buchanan. J. M. Why Do Constitutions Matter? In Berggren, Niclas, Karlson, Nils and Nergelius, Joakim (eds.) Why Constitutions Matter. New Brunswick: Transaction Publishers, (2002).

Calvert, R. K., Johnson, J. Interpretation and Coordination in Constitutional Politics. Working Paper No. 15. W. Allen Wallis Institute of Political Economy, University of Rochester, (1998).

Cameron, C. M. Veto Bargaining. Presidents and the Politics of Negative Power. Cambridge: Cambridge University Press, (2000).

Congleton, R. D., Swedenborg, B. Introduction: Rational Choice Politics and Political Institutions. In R. D. Congleton and B. Swedenborg (eds.), Demo-

cratic Constitutional Design and Public Policy, Analysis and Evidence. Cambridge: MIT Press, (2006).
Devins, N. Shaping Constitutional Values: Elected Government, the Supreme Court and the Abortion Debate. Baltimore: Johns Hopkins University Press, (1996).
Duverger, M. Political Parties, Their Organization, and Activity in the Modern State. New York: Wiley, (1954).
Elster, J. Making Sense of Constitution-Making. East European Constitutional Review 1(1), (1992), pp. 15-17.
Elster, J. Strategic Uses of Argument. In K. Arrow et al. (eds.) Barriers to Negotiated Resolution of Conflicts. New York: Norton, (1995a).
Elster, J. "Forces and Mechanisms in the Constitution-Making Process. Duke Law Journal 45(2), (1995b), pp. 354-96.
Elster, J. The Role of Institutional Interest in East European Constitution-Making. East European Constitutional Review 5(1), (1996), 63-65.
Elster, J. Ways of Constitution-making. In A. Hadenius (ed.) Democracy's Victory and Crisis. Cambridge: Cambridge University Press, (1997).
Elster, Jon. Deliberation and Constitution Making. In J. Elster (ed.): Deliberative Democracy. Cambridge: Cambridge University Press, (1998).
Elster, J. Ulysses unbound. Cambridge: Cambridge University Press, (2000).
Fabrizio, S., Mody, A. Can Budget Institutions Counteract Political Indiscipline? Economic Policy 21(48), (2006), pp. 689-739.
Favoreu, L. The Constitutional Council and Parliament in France. In C. Landfried (ed). *Constitutional Review and Legislation. An International Comparison.* Baden-Baden: Nomos Verlagsgesellschaft, (1988).
Fisher, L. Constitutional Interpretation by Members of Congress. North Carolina Law Review 63, (1985), pp. 707-47.
Fisher, L. Constitutional Dialogues: Interpretation as Political Process. Princeton: Princeton University Press, (1988).
Fisher, L. Separation of Powers: Interpretation Outside the Courts. Pepperdine Law Review 18, (1990), pp. 57-93.
Fisher, L. Constitutional Conflicts between Congress and the President. 4th ed. Lawrence: University Press of Kansas, (1997).
Gleich, H. Budget Institutions and Fiscal Performance in Central and Eastern European Countries. European Central Bank Working Paper Series, Working Paper no. 215, (2003).
Hagen, J. von Fiscal Rules, Fiscal Institutions, and Fiscal Performance. The Economic and Social Review 33(3), (2002), pp. 263-284.
Hagen, J. von Fiscal Rules and Fiscal Performance in the European Union and Japan. Monetary and Economic Studies, (March 2006), pp. 25-60.

Hallerberg, M., Hagen, J. von Electoral Institutions, Cabinet Negotiations, and Budget Deficits in the European Union. In J. M. Poterba, and J. von Hagen (eds.) Fiscal Institutions and Fiscal Performance. Chicago: University of Chicago Press, (1999).

Hänni, L. Põhiseaduse mõju poliitilisele otsustusprotsessile. [The Effects of the Constitution on Political Decision Process] Riigikogu toimetised 5, (2002), pp. 82-87.

Järvelaid, P. Das Institut des Justizkanzlers in Estland: Geschichte und Gegenwart. Osteuropa Recht 5, (2001), pp. 365-374.

Katyal, N. K. Legislative Constitutional Interpretation. Duke Law Journal 50, (2001), pp. 1335-1394.

Kirchgässner, G. The Effects of Fiscal Institutions on Public Finance: A Survey of the Empirical Evidence. Discussion Paper no. 2001-15, University of St. Gallen, (2001), http://www.fgn.unisg.ch/org/fgn/web.nsf/SysWebRessources/VWA_2001_15/$FILE/0115.pdf (last retrieved 1 January 2010).

Krol, R. A Survey of the Impact of Budget Rules on State Taxation, Spending, and Debt. Cato Journal 16(3), (1997), pp. 295-307.

Landfried, C. Bundesverfarsungsgericht und Gesetrgeber. Baden-Baden: Nomos Verlagsgesellschaft, (1984).

Landfried, C, Introduction. In C. Landfried (ed). Constitutional Review and Legislation. An International Comparison. Baden-Baden: Nomos Verlagsgesellschaft, (1988a).

Landfried, C. Constitutional Review and Legislation in the Federal Republic of Germany. In C. Landfried (ed). Constitutional Review and Legislation. An International Comparison. Baden-Baden: Nomos Verlagsgesellschaft, (1988b).

Maruste, R., Schneider, H. Constitutional Review in Estonia – Its Principal Scheme, Practice and Evaluation. In R. A. Müllerson and F. Fitzmaurice and M. Andenas (eds.) Constitutional Reform and International Law in Central and Eastern Europe. The Hague: Kluwer Law International, (1998).

Maveety, N., Pettai, V. Government Lawyers and Non-judicial Constitutional Review in Estonia. *Europe*-Asia Studies 57(1), (2005), pp. 93-115.

McGregor, J. P. Constitutional Factors in Politics in Central and Eastern Europe. Communist and Post-Communist Studies 29(2), (1996), pp. 147-166.

Mikser, S. Libe tee. Teerull, demokraatia ja usaldus. Postimees 18.06.1999.

Molander, P. Budgeting Procedures and Democratic Ideals: An Evaluation of Swedish Reforms. Journal of Public Policy 21(1), (2001), pp. 23-52

O'Donnell, G., Schmitter, P. Transitions from Authoritarian Rule: Tentative Conclusions about Uncertain Democracies. Baltimore, MD: Johns Hopkins University Press, (1986).

Offe, C. Varieties of Transition: The East European and East German Experience. Cambridge: Polity Press, (1996).

Peabody, B. Nonjudicial Constitutional Interpretation, Authoritative Settlement, and a New Agenda for Research" Constitutional Commentary 16(1), (1999), pp. 63-90.

Peabody, B. Congressional Constitutional Interpretation and the Courts: A Preliminary Inquiry into Legislative Attitudes, 1959-2001. Law and Social Inquiry 29, (2004), pp. 127-175.

Peabody, B. Congressional Attitudes toward Constitutional Interpretation. In N. Devins and K. E. Whittington (eds.) Congress and the Constitution. Durham and London: Duke University Press, (2005).

Persson, T., Tabellini, G. Constitutions and Economic Policy. Journal of Economic Perspectives 18(1), (2004), pp. 75-98.

Pickerill, J. M. Constitutional Deliberation in Congress: The Impact of Judicial Review in a Separated System. Durham, NC: Duke University Press, (2004).

Rae, D. The Political Consequences of Electoral Laws. New Haven: Yale University Press, (1967).

Raju, O. Riigikogu roll riigieelarve kujundamisel. [The Role of the Riigikogu in Designing the Budget] Riigikogu toimetised 7, (2003), pp. 113-118.

Raudla, R. Constitution, Public Finance, and Transition: Theoretical Developments of Constitutional Public Finance and the Case of Estonia. Frankfurt am Main: Peter Lang, (2010a).

Raudla, R. Evolution of Budgetary Institutions in Estonia: A Path Full of Puzzles? Governance, 23(3), (2010b), pp. 463-484.

Raudla, R. Explaining Constitution-Makers Preferences: The Cases of Estonia and the United States. Constitutional Political Economy 21(3), (2010c), pp. 249-269.

Roosma, P. Constitutional Review under 1992 Constitution. Juridica International 3, (1998), pp. 35-42.

Roosma, P. Development of Constitutional Review in Estonia. Revue de Justice Constitutionelle Est-Europeenne 2, (2001), pp. 283-323.

Rubio Llorente, F. Constitutional Review and Legislation in Spain. In C. Landfried (ed.) Constitutional Review and Legislation. An International Comparison. Baden-Baden: Nomos Verlagsgesellschaft, (1988).

Sadurski, W. (ed.). Constitutional Justice, East and West: Democratic Legitimacy and Constitutional Courts in Post-Communist Europe in a Comparative Perspective. The Hague: Kluwer Law International, (2002).

Sadurski, W. Legitimacy and Reasons for Constitutional Review After Communism. In W. Sadurski (ed.) Constitutional Justice, East and West: Democratic

Legitimacy and Constitutional Courts in Post-Communist Europe in a Comparative Perspective. The Hague: Kluwer Law International, (2002).
Salzberger, E., Voigt, S. On the Delegation of Powers: With Special Emphasis on Central and Eastern Europe. Constitutional Political Economy 13, (2002), pp. 25-52.
Stein, E., Talvi, E., Grisanti, A. Institutional Arrangements and Fiscal Performance: The Latin American Experience. In J. M. Poterba, and J. von Hagen (eds.) Fiscal Institutions and Fiscal Performance. Chicago: University of Chicago Press, (1999).
Stone, A. The Birth of Judicial Politics in France. The Constitutional Council in Comparative Perspective. New York: Oxford University Press, (1992a).
Stone, A. Abstract Constitutional Review and Policy Making in Western Europe. In D. W. Jackson and C. N. Tate (eds.) Comparative Judicial Review and Public Policy. Westport and London: Greenwood Press, (1992b).
Stone, A. Judging Socialist Reform. The Politics of Coordinate Construction in France and Germany. Comparative Political Studies 26(4), (1994), pp. 443-469.
Stone Sweet, A. Constitutional Dialogues: Protecting Human Rights in France, Germany, Italy and Spain. In S. J. Kenney, W. M. Reisinger and J. C. Reitz (eds.) Constitutional Dialogues in Comparative Perspective. London: Macmillan, (1999).
Stone Sweet, A. Governing with Judges. Oxford: Oxford University Press, (2000).
Stone Sweet, A. Constitutional Courts and Parliamentary Democracy. West European Politics 25(1), (2002), pp. 77-100.
Taagepera, R., Shugart, M. S. Predicting the Number of Parties: A Quantitative Model of Duverger's Mechanical Effect. American Political Science Review 87(2), (1993), pp. 455-464.
Tushnet, M. Non-Judicial Review. Harvard Journal on Legislation 40, (2003), pp. 453-492.
Vanberg, G. Abstract Judicial Review, Legislative Bargaining, and Policy Compromise. Journal of Theoretical Politics 10(3), (1998), pp. 299-236.
Vanberg, G. Legislative-Judicial Relations: A Game-Theoretic Approach to Constitutional Review. American Journal of Political Science 45(2), (2001), pp. 346-361.
Whittington, K. E. Constitutional Construction. Divided Powers and Constitutional Meaning. Cambridge, MA: Harvard University Press, (1999).
Whittington, K. E. Extrajudicial Constitutional Interpretation: Three Objections and Responses. North Carolina Law Review 80(3), (2002), pp. 773-851.
Whittington, K. E. Constitutional Theory and the Faces of Power. In K. D. Ward and C. R. Castillo (eds.) The Judiciary and American Democracy: Alexander

Bickel and the Countermajoritarian Difficulty and Contemporary Constitutional Theory. Albany: State University of New York Press, (2005).
Yläoutinen, S. Fiscal Frameworks in the Central and Eastern European Countries. Finnish Ministry of Finance Discussion Paper No. 72, (2004).

Public Services As Productive Factors – An Italian View

Giuseppe Eusepi

1. Fiscal Archeology Or Searching For Precursors?

The Italian School of Public Finance was not at all a homogeneous body of doctrine. In particular, there were two strands – one essentially 'democratic', the other a non-democratic, or ruling class, strand that should not be neglected since it produced significant analysis and outstanding results.

Overall, the Italian School of Public Finance embodied dozens of scholars and, at least, about one hundred books and papers. To attempt a complete treatment would require more time than a paper affords. A task of the sort has in any event already been fulfilled by James M. Buchanan at the end of the fifties[1].

This paper has a more limited task of critically examining only the democratic strand of the Italian School. This body of thought maintained that the logic of market and exchange ought to be extended to the state, although somewhat cautiously. If this school was an inspiration for the extension of the idea of contract to the state, then De Viti de Marco must be given some of the credit for laying the foundations of the contractarian approach.

A final remark before entering the substance of my paper. De Viti wrote in Italian, on subjects and with methods outside the mainstream of his discipline. His *Principles*[2] is a marvel of scholarship. Yet, the language barrier has given rise to adverse selection. The fact that De Viti is unknown abroad is a glaring example of this. When ideological motivations or simply misfortune add to language barriers, alas, no professional forum for the exchange of ideas exists.

To outline the logic of tax-price or fiscal price in Antonio De Viti de Marco's work involves going back to the origins of the Italian School of Public Finance that was at its full flower between 1880-1940. This leap backward may lay oneself open to a twin criticism: that of toying with a sort of *fiscal archeology* and that, only partially different, of providing fashionable ideas with a respectable antiquity. Supposing this to be the judgment of the reader, there is no denying the healthy dose of wisdom that can be drawn from this great theorist in public finance.

In his essay on De Viti de Marco, Steve[3] warned against scholars whose scope is that of fitting out their works with precursors. I shall try to demonstrate that

1 See James M. Buchanan (1960).

2 A. De Viti de Marco (1936).

3 S. Steve (1997) e (2002). Of the same tenor Einaudi (1953).

dealing with De Viti de Marco in 2007 does not mean at all either toying with fiscal archeology, or being fatally fascinated by precursors. Even in Italy very few scholars who were trained in the De Viti's or Einaudi's books are still alive and only to those few would this address sound like "reminiscences". I am convinced that those who appreciate De Viti de Marco hardly run the risk of making out of him a precursor of whatever fashionable theory. The role of precursor is unfit for a first-class scholar as De Viti de Marco was. I think his contribution to the understanding of fiscal matters is so internally consistent and exhaustive that it represents an indispensable basis for a true democratic reform in contemporary public finances[4]. And, in fact, De Viti's contribution was anything but a work with potentialities only.

2. The Public Finances: An Extension Of Economic Science To State Theory

Until about the mid-eighties of the nineteenth century when De Viti de Marco was beginning his scientific career, the Marginalist school was commonly assumed to be synonymous with economic science also in Italy[5]. Unlike the Anglo-Saxon tradition that almost totally ignored the role of the state, the state had long occupied a central role in the Italian School of Public Finance. It is no surprise, then, that in Italy the Marginalist theory was extended to the state and found rich expression in economic writings, especially in Mazzola[6] who remains the most conspicuous example.

Even in the Mazzola case, however, we cannot speak of a mere extension of the Marginalist model to the state, precisely because in Mazzola's treatment public needs and public goods are complementary to, and mingle with, private or final goods. Yet, Mazzola suggested that the choice about resource allocation in both private and public goods is dependent on the individuals' marginal evaluations. In so doing he failed to see that complementary needs and goods emerge in and are satisfied through the political market, and that political decision-making is incompatible with marginal adjustments. To see this, note that votes, unlike market prices, do not allow *market adjustments* and hence they are not instrumental to choices. We can speak of a choice only if we think of "the majority" as a single actor, and not as the aggregation of individual evaluations. So ultimately one must conclude that there are substantial reasons for maintaining that Maz-

4 See G. Vitaletti (1996).
5 See P. Barucci (1972).
6 U. Mazzola (1890).

zola can be regarded as a Marginalist: although he emphasizes the mediating role played by the state, he offers no analysis of the distinguishing features of political markets.

3. Public Services As Productive Factors

Two years before the publication of Mazzola's book, De Viti de Marco had published *Il carattere teorico dell'economia finanziaria*[7] where he set forth the propositions on which he had worked for forty years and that led to the final version of *Principî dell'economia finanziaria*[8]. De Viti's approach was simply incompatible with the Marginalist view of the state. As is well-known, in the Walrasian construction, the state was an artificial appendix added to the economic system after it had already reached its general equilibrium. To Walras the state was nothing more than an equation closing the model.

De Viti made the assumption that the state is one of the productive factors like land, capital and labor. In so doing, he emphasized that an independent economic equilibrium could not be conceived as pre-existing the state. The state is as important as the other three productive factors traditionally used in political economy. To achieve a sort of semantic consonance with Sraffa's notion of basic goods, De Viti's state could be defined as a "basic factor". Like Sraffa's basic goods, De Viti's basic factor was ever present in private goods and services, though it was not as tangible and easily identifiable as land, capital and labor. It was, in fact, a pervasive institutional or organizational factor. Even though the semantic consonance with Sraffa accounts for the state as an essential factor, it would, however, hide an equally important component of De Viti's conception of the state, namely the non-objectivity of the productive contribution involved. When considering the proper function of the state, De Viti defined it as a necessary organizational factor, best conceived as a constitutional factor or as a public good *tout court*. As a result of this viewpoint three different types of states (or, in other terms, three different types of constitutions and roles for the state) emerge:

1. tutorial-altruistic;
2. monopolistic-egoistic; and
3. co-operative

In order to check whether De Viti's three schemes are related to three separate roles we need to see whether there is considerable substance behind each of them,

7 Cf. A. De Viti de Marco (1888) and S. Steve (1997).
8 A. De Viti de Marco (1936).

or whether they are just useful steps he conflated into one heuristic tool for developing his *optimal* state. I interpret De Viti's argument to be that, in order for the state to operate as a productive factor within the context of an exchange economy, an appropriate constitution must be in place. And I see this argument as De Viti's strong point. To corroborate my interpretation there is a glaring although indirect proof. The conception of the sate as a *tutorial* state, which has played such a large role in post-war II economic policies, was briefly sketched in his earlier 1888 work, but completely omitted in the latest version of his *Principles*. This is important to note because the tutorial function as the rationale for the state provided the very web and texture of what was to become the benevolent despot paradigm that has been the central object of criticism by Public Choice scholars.

The tutorial state not only raises problems of democratic legitimacy, but it ends up by describing an extreme Hobbesian paradigm. And, in fact, the alleged "altruism" of the tutorial state turns out to be a surreptitious ploy to support the political survival of the despot at a minimal cost[9].

The monopolistic-egoistic model is retained in the final version of the *Principles* because De Viti was only too well aware that the coercive component (protective state in Buchanan's terms) is ever present even in the most democratic of institutions. These democratic institutions De Viti labeled as the co-operative state. And, in fact, the protective (not tutorial) state co-exists with the state as provider of public goods and services. What has to be emphasized here is that the coercive power component, whether altruistic or egoistic, is amenable to a fiscal model that is revenue maximizer in nature and that assumes the ability-to-pay principle and its related sacrifice theories as equality criteria.

At this juncture, I want to dispose of the idea that there is anything of interest in De Viti's discussion of the various version of sacrifice theories. Not only because interpersonal utilities cannot be compared, but essentially because what matters in taxation is the contribution that the state as an organizational factor secures for its individual taxpayers[10]. On this basis, public expenditures rather than taxation offer valuable insight into the organization factor. As is well-

9 G. Brennan, G. Eusepi (2000).

10 The following excerpt clearly illustrates De Viti's critique of the ability-to-pay principle and his unreserved support of the benefit principle or value-countervalue principle. 'One [the ability-to-pay principle] is proper to those who build up their edifice under arbitrary assumptions increasingly extended up to the point of stating that a tax is an act of the sovereign will of the state, totally divorced from any economic content grounded on the exchange between taxes and public services'.....the other [that based on the benefit principle] is proper to those, who starting from the exchange relationship between taxes and public services, build up their edifice on the natural game of economic forces and reduce arbitrary assumptions to the minimum in order to reach a safer political equilibrium', [own translation] A. De Viti de Marco (1953), p. 118.

known, the ability-to-pay principle considers the tax side only; in so doing the state behaves in an arbitrary way, unless the ability-to-pay principle is assumed to be objectively measurable. By whom? And how? In reality, if reasons based on political or ideological motivations are excluded, the only real reason for the ability-to-pay principle to have taken and still take "the lion's share", also in contemporary fiscal systems, was clearly identified by Morgenstern[11]. According to him, the popularity of the ability-to-pay principle has to be ascribed rather to its ambiguities, which allow anyone to use this principle either in a destructive or supportive way in the assessment of the distribution of the tax burden, than to its alleged objectivity. In sum, the Marginalists' view of the state was incompatible with De Viti's logic and so was the ability-to-pay principle.

It was De Viti's contention that the state is an organizational factor. The overriding principle of his philosophy is that the state, as provider of public goods and services, should supply goods and services that are productive for all members of the community. That is so precisely because state services are demanded by all individuals. According to De Viti, the productivity of public services can, at least in principle, be tested at an aggregate level by comparing the productivity of equal amounts employed in public services and in privately ones respectively. The proposition to be tested could be put as follows: Would the present value of future income flows increase, decrease, or remain unchanged by an incrementally variation in the amount of public expenditures?[12] Central to De Viti's logic was the idea that the state spends *differently* from individuals. Accordingly, the hypothesis of equality in future income flows has to be discarded. In sum, present values of future income flows may be either increased or decreased by a state acting as a productive factor. This is an interesting way of assessing the efficiency properties of public decision-making.

Yet, his conclusion that public choices might be more efficient than the market ones is illuminating in understanding why De Viti rejected the minimal state hypothesis. My interpretation is corroborated by De Viti's extension of the *minimum means* approach to public services. This extension, however, strikes a jarring chord. The last forty years of studies on government failures and bureaucratic behaviors have shown how the *minimum means* constraint can be finessed by the government via fiscal illusion. Such fiscal illusion is not created exclusively by the maneuvering of politicians. Bureaucracy too plays an active role in creating and widening fiscal illusion due to its informational advantages on costs[13].

11 O. Morgenstern, 'Antonio De Viti De Marco' in Studies <In memoriam> of Antonio De Viti de Marco. collected by Professor Ernesto D'Albergo of Roma, University of Bari, Cacucci, s. d. pp17-19.

12 See J. M. Buchanan (1960).

13 On this point see G. Eusepi (2006).

4. The Contractual State As A Basis For Tax-Prices

To gain a better understanding of dualism, it is useful to refer to Buchanan's treatment of this issue. More than fifty years ago, Buchanan thought of dualism as the distinguishing element in the Italian School of Public Finance and made use of it to create a watershed between the Italian doctrinal body in public finance and the Anglo-Saxon fiscal tradition. The two trends of thought are equally well described by the two opposite views on fisc: the benefit principle or tax-price and the ability-to-pay principle with the related sacrifice theories.

Yet, if we want to go a step ahead we have to clarify the concept of dualism. As Buchanan explicitly emphasized, dualism is not attributable to any dual vision of the world, but to the contractualist view of the state. De Viti de Marco, was the first and even yet the only one after Ferrara, to offer a coherent defense of this view and apply it to fiscal matters in an innovative way.

It is the contractual vision of the state rather than Einaudi's subsequent relevant analytical justifications, that makes the so-called "hailstorm tax" incompatible with De Viti's paradigm. The "hailstorm tax", in fact, is conceived as a tax stemming from a non-democratic political setting where citizens and the state are morally unequal. More generally, the logic of a tax-price is incompatible with all versions of the sacrifice theory and, hence, with the ability-to-pay principle, the success of which can, as already mentioned, be best ascribed to its ambiguities.

In a nutshell, De Viti's dualism is of the institutional kind. His monopolistic state is the polar alternative to the cooperative state and mimics the Hobbesian context *lato sensu*. That is why De Viti de Marco has paid little attention to the monopolistic state and to the related fiscal system. He conceived of it, in fact, as an institutional alternative jeopardizing the co-operative state. Founded on the sacredness of moral equality between citizens and the state, his co-operative state was his highest theoretical achievement.

Concluding on this point, we can say that De Viti de Marco's contractual constitution, which the co-operative state hinges upon, is exactly the appropriate process to make the absolute or monopolistic state unfeasible. This was the ground for making tax-price central in the decision-making process on matters of public finances. The whole decisional scenario in the co-operative state is conceived by De Viti de Marco as being made-up of two separated, although related, contracts – a point emphasized in particular by Steve[14].

The first contract applies to goods and services that are *specific*, and is between consumers and producers (state, local governments). Here the logic of the tax-price follows the market logic since demands are genuine. In this case prices of

14 Cf. A. De Viti de Marco (1953), especially Ch. VII and S. Steve (1997).

public goods are properly viewed as "season tickets"[15]. Moreover if the government sets prices below market prices there would be excess demand resulting in a misallocation of resources in the long run. The reason why De Viti insisted on cost coverage through fiscal prices was to be understood by economists much later. Only after World-War II, it became clear why fixing inappropriate toll fees gives rise first to highway crowding and then congestion, but also to an excess in road transportation investments *vis à vis* rail transportation.

The second contract, the one between the community of taxpayers and the state represents De Viti de Marco most original feature. In the case of a general public good, the individual demand is unknown, and according to De Viti a solution can be reached presumptively only. He outlines two presumptive hypotheses:

1. All members of the community consume general services for the survival of the community itself (think, for example, of the constitution of a state, its external defense and its domestic security.)
2. The individual income produced can be taken as the best proxy for that individual's demand of public goods.

Rigorously speaking, the concept of fiscal price or tax-price should be related only to general public goods and services. In a context of the sort, there would not be any explicit role for the demand – although it might be said that the demand for a constitution as a meta-rule emerges anyway and such a constitution would be a general public good that citizens-taxpayers demand.

This is a critical point because, with the sole exception of the constitution itself for which the unanimity test was appropriate, all other collective decisions were to be taken on a majoritarian basis and, hence, depended on the expected utility of the majority. Using the Marginal utility theory to fix prices for general public goods was to De Viti at once impossible and necessary, exactly because one faces presumptive, not genuine demands. I shall come back to this point further below. Without any possibility to define the demand, De Viti assumed that the income produced is a proxy to determine the demand for public goods and suggested that the proportional income tax is the best parameter to approximate the tax-price of his co-operative state. The assumption that the proportional tax is a criterion that best approximate prices stems from De Viti's view that public services are productive factors. Since the state is a productive factor, each unit of income produced has a built-in tax. As a consequence, if one unit of income escapes taxation it produces undue charges on the other units of income that are taxed. Hence, according to De Viti, the equity principle requires that a proportional tax, not a progressive one, should be the best analogue for price. It is this point that best

15 Cf. J. M. Buchanan (1960), (1999).

shows De Viti's critique of utility theories based on the ability-to-pay principle. His view of income as a parameter to evaluate the demand of public goods and services explicitly incorporates the expenditure side: the ability-to-pay principle simply omits it.

Since for the ability-to-pay principle the expenditure side is immaterial, equity can be pursued only through taxation and its sacrifice theories – whether the sacrifice is equal, proportional or minimal-aggregate. In such a context, the optimal tax cannot but be a poll tax for the simple reason that such a tax does not give rise to substitution effects. Any sacrifice theory was incompatible with De Viti's theory that public goods and services are productive. It is exactly this that makes room for tax-prices. At the most, the Marginal utility theory might supply the solution for assessing prices for *specific* public goods and services. But marginal utility theory is unfit for assessing prices for general public goods and services. In the latter case, because individuals do not choose directly, the productivity of public services cannot be measured according to the Marginal utility parameters. It is true that the impossibility to apply the Marginal utility theory for calculating costs and benefits at an individual level highlights the difference between tax-price and market price, but equally the tax-price entirely retains its theoretical appeal as a basis for public financing.

In a sense, the concept of presumptive demand as deriving from individual income seems to rescue the price logic to some extent although via a political process, and a correspondingly heavily nuanced explanatory power. Political decisions, in fact, incorporate an *arbitrary* component. De Viti de Marco was aware of this and tried to reduce its potential destructive impact on tax-price. Not only did he manage to reduce "presumptions" to the minimum, but he also suggested possible "correctives". "In short one might say that each taxpayer pays his tax bill now, not only to satisfy his present need, but also his future needs"[16]. [own translation]

At this point the difference between De Viti and Mazzola is evident. Mazzola believed that the mechanism underlying the equilibrium between public and private use of an income unit is an opportunity cost calculation at an individual level, which, however, has to be aggregated.

Yet, the absence of a political market as an aggregating mechanism gave rise to Wicksell's reaction. Wicksell's critiques would be inappropriate if extended to De Viti who writes:

"There is no doubt that our income is the measuring rod for all our consumptions, be they present or future, individual or collective. It is axiomatic that our consumptions are proportional to our incomes. The proportionality criterion,

16 A. De Viti de Marco (1953), p. 116.

however, holds at an aggregate level only, but not at an individual level"[17]. [own translation]

De Viti fully realized, among other things, that in democracies choices are majoritarian in nature and the median voter is pivotal while the opposition's votes have no impact. He reached the conclusion that the equilibrium resulting from public choices is at an aggregate level, but not at each individual's level in the community[18]. Since choices are taken in the political market and not at an individual level, the logic of a utility chain is broken unless one resorts to an utterly abstract scheme. In such a framework the one who decides to produce and the one who decides to consume are the same individual. This is the reason why De Viti introduces his co-operative state where the use of the unanimity principle embodied in unanimous choice explicitly restores the logic of market exchange to the political market.

5. The Logic Of Tax-Price: Feasibility Problems

In the real-world fiscal systems, which have at the most a faint likeness to De Viti's co-operative model, the provision of general public services involves a somewhat arbitrary element that, following De Viti, could be labeled as the "presumptive" un-productivity of these goods for the minority. There is a puzzle here. On the face of things, De Viti's price logic requires that the minority should not be required to pay for the public services it consumes, because the minority has not expressed a demand for them.

However, it is exactly the generality of the service that prevents the price logic from being coincidental with the logic of the tax price. If there were such a coincidence only the decision-making majority would bear the entire cost of the general public service.

In such a way, however, the democracy rule would be twisted because the majority would be charged also with the service burdens of the goods consumed by the minority. So interpreted, the principle "who decides pays" turns out to be a paralogism! The tax price logic suggests that the minority has to pay despite its suffering the damage represented by "the difference between the amount of the tax bill he pays and the lower amount that he was willing to pay"[19]. [own translation]

17 Ibid., p. 115.

18 Cf. J. M. Buchanan (1960), especially sections 3 and 4.

19 A. De Viti de Marco (1953), pp. 124-125.

The excerpt from De Viti helps clarify why to someone the tax-price logic might appear incompatible with the logic of the market. In my opinion, this is only a distinction of degree. In the market, private demand and consumption are coincidental while in fiscal economy "General public goods are consumed also by those who have not demanded them"[20]. [own translation]

The polar case of the co-operative state that assumes all political decisions to be taken with a unanimous consent cannot be fitted to real-world fiscal systems. De Viti himself was aware of the feasibility problems inherent in his scheme. The most glaring consequence is that the co-operative state scheme cannot have a predictive value at all because it cancels out all conflicts arising from majoritarian rules. As De Viti brilliantly suggests, the fact that in real-world fiscal systems, increases in public expenditures are demanded by those who do not pay for taxes and vice-versa is revealing of this conflict.

It was De Viti's ambition to eliminate this conflict that caused him to seek for an optimal tax-system in his co-operative state. This change in perspective requires that the analysis should move from a purely normative to a more positive sphere -- from a system dictating which norms the state should follow in order to have a system in equilibrium where individual freedom is as large as possible within the limits of reciprocal compatibilities, to a system that seeks to explain how the state behaves in reality. In this new perspective, the logic of the tax-price – although divorced from the Marginal utility theory – emerges once again, but here for the purpose of eliminating externalities. As De Viti saw it, these externalities are the result of "presumptive" demands rather than genuine demands within the political market. Hence, the criteria for setting tax-prices are chosen by individuals (politicians) who are different from actual consumers.

In a context of the sort, it is necessary to search for a mechanism representing the closest substitute for price. A genuine price mechanism cannot work in a world of indirect "presumptive" demands that, in turn, originate from income levels only presumptively. Public services as productive factors involve the possibility of imputing a distributive quota, as is the case of labor and capital mentioned in section 3 above. But when public services are general, one has to face the problem of how to determine an appropriate tax-price.

According to De Viti a proportional income tax would not only meet vertical and horizontal equality criteria because each unit of income produced would be charged with an equal tax bill, but such a tax would also indirectly determine the level of public services through the role that tax-prices play in the political pro-

20 Ibid. (1888), Ch. III, par. 5.

cess, provided that a fiscal constitution prevents the government from resorting to debt financing[21].

6. Conclusions

I conclude where I began. In my view, the Italian School of public finance – specifically in the democratic version exemplified by the work of De Viti de Marco – is both of enormous historical interest and considerable contemporary relevance. There is, as I have argued, the argument for proportionality in the income tax rate structure as a mechanism for moderating the exploitation of minorities under necessarily majoritarian political processes. But there is the more general insistence that the study of public finance requires an explicit attention to politics – a point the force of which mainstream Anglo-Saxon public economics has really begun to acknowledge only with the rise of Public Choice scholarship within the last thirty years or so.

References

Barucci, P. The Spread of Marginalism in Italy (1871-1890). The History of Political Economy. vol. IV, n.2, (1972), pp. 512-532.

Brennan, G., Eusepi, G. Hobbesian And Contractarian Constitutions. paper presented at the European Public Choice Society, Siena, (April 2000).

Buchanan, J. M. <La Scienza delle finanze>: The Italian Tradition in Fiscal Theory. In *Fiscal* Theory and Political Economy. Selected Essays. Chapel Hill: The University of North Carolina Press, (1960).

Buchanan, J. M. The Demand and Supply of Public Goods. The Collected Works of James M. Buchanan, Vol. V, Indianapolis: Liberty Fund, (1999).

de Viti de Marco, A. Il Carattere Teorico dell'Economia Finanziaria. Roma: Pasqualucci, (1888).

de Viti de Marco, A First Principles of Public Finance. translated from the Italian by Edith Pavlo Marget, New York: Harcourt Brace and Co., Inc, (1936).

de Viti de Marco, A. Principî di Economia finanziaria. 3rd ed. Torino: Einaudi, (1953).

---

21 What maintained in the text seems not to be in line with the so-called democratization of public debt that according to De Viti would result in an automatic debt extinction. It is worth noting, however, that resorting to debt is a way used by governments to partially hide tax-prices. Debt financing is, thus, a typical example of fiscal illusion.

Einaudi, L. Saggi Bibliografici e Storici Intorno alle Dottrine Economiche. Roma: Edizioni di Storia e Letteratura, (1953).

Eusepi, G. Public Finance and Welfare: From the Ignorance of the Veil to the Veil of Ignorance. Journal of Economic Behavior and Organization. Vol. 59, (April 2006), pp. 460-477.

Mazzola, U. I Dati Scientifici della Finanza Pubblica. Roma: E. Loescher, (1890).

Morgenstern, O., De Viti de Marco, A. in Studies <In memoriam> of Antonio De Viti de Marco. collected by Prof. Ernesto D'Albergo of Roma, University of Bari, Cacucci, (1890), pp. 17-19.

Steve, S. La Finanza di Antonio De Viti de Marco. In Scritti vari, Milano: Ciriec, Franco Angeli, (1997), pp. 353-367.

Steve, S. Gli Studi di Finanza Pubblica: qualche aspetto della tradizione italiana. Economia Pubblica, (2002).

Vitaletti, G. Ipotesi per un sistema fiscale basato sul principio del beneficio. In A. Fossati, S. Giannini (eds.), Nuovi sistemi tributari. Milano: SIEP, Franco Angeli, (1996), pp. 49-81.

Privatization And Labour In South Asia: Some Issues In Fiscal Sociology

Nalin Bharti / Gopal Ganesh

Abstract

Privatization as a policy supports the government to balance the fiscal problems but at the same time it creates social problems in terms of worker's uncertainty, unrest and job loss. Paper finds the current trends in privatization especially in relation to post privatization impact on labour in India, Bangladesh and Sri Lanka. It has also observed that reactive labour restructuring has been the norm and pro-active restructuring has been hardly practiced in all the three economies. The Paper advocates strongly pro-active labour restructuring since all these economies are facing alarming labour unrest due to privatization. It warns that unless privatization programme design in these countries are taken into account such strategies for pro active labour restructuring, may make the policy of privatization end up being abandoned. The field dependent and field independent study concentrates on the role of the State to serve the purpose of privatization with certain social obligation for workers in dual preference economies of South Asia.

1. Privatization: An Introduction

Privatization practically presents the transfer of assets and service functions from public to private hands. It may be the partial or total transfer of enterprises from public to private ownership. As such, it is the precise reverse of nationalization. The sale of public assets, the introduction of competitive tendering deregulation and the establishment of surrogate markets within public sector organizations are examples of the generic policy referred to as 'privatization'. In a broader sense, Privatization, means giving private actors a greater role in decisions about what, where and how to produce goods and services. A great deal of experience has now accumulated regarding this process. Some of it shows the great potential that privatization has for increasing productivity, income and welfare. It has come to symbolize a new way of looking at society's needs, and a rethinking of the role of government in fulfilling them. It means relying more on society's private institutions and less on government to satisfy the needs of the people[1].

A pervasive dissatisfaction with the performance of public enterprises (PE) is at the heart of the appeal for privatization to the policy makers in developing countries. The public-enterprise sector which were either expanded or remained the same size in almost all countries from the Second World War through the 1970s conversely, either contracted or remained the same size in most of the

1 See Heald 1985, Hanke 1987, Bos 1991, Ahmed et.al 1994, Savas 1987.

countries in the 1980s and early 1990s[2]. Dissatisfaction from PEs was at the peak during 1970s.In 1980s because of the poor performance of PEs, a large number of reform exercises suffered a setback all over the world. However it caused fast privatization in 1990s. "The 1980s may have been named the decade of merger and acquisition, leveraged buy-outs, and junk bonds, but the 1990s are likely to be known as the decade of privatization and market economy"[3]. In post 1990s PEs's became less relevant for the world economy.

Privatization appeared on the world scene in the 1980s, as a result of intensive scrutiny of the role of the public enterprises in developed and developing countries[4].

Many policy makers were disenchanted with the fact that a large number of public enterprises were making losses[5]. They were not the ideal hybrids combining the strength of the public and private sectors; usually they ended up combining the worst of both. They failed to maximize the greatest good, or did so at high cost. The PE sector absorbed a large share of governments' budgets in the form of subsidies and capital flows. Governments ran into severe financial problems in the 1980s and experienced inability to raise loans at home and abroad. This forced them to look at radical options for turning around PE performance. This consisted of two major initiatives: (a) PEr reform and (b) Privatization. It also helped international financial institutions such as the International Monetary Fond (IMF) and the World Bank which also insisted upon PE Reform to begin with and later upon Privatization as a method of making public enterprises perform satisfactorily. In so far as developing countries are concerned, the move for privatization has been due to the imperative need to correct macro economic imbalances in the public sector and balance of payments constraints.

2.1 Privatization In South Asia

Public enterprises in South Asia came into existence primarily due to the economic condition of newly independent countries. Just after the independence from colonial regimes, governments felt that the public sector would be the means of enhancing industrial growth as well as employment. It is true that during the

2 Galal, A., Jones L., Tandon P., and Vogelsang I. (ed.) Welfare Consequences of Selling Public Enterprises. Oxford University Press, 1994.

3 Amnuay, V. Privatization:Financial choice and Opportunities. International Centre for Economic Growth Publication, California, 1992.

4 More than two decades ago Heald 1985 claimed that the world embraces many different policies, having quickly become established as a piece of shorthand. The wide verity of policies and measures included under its umbrella are portrayed as being part of a movement in favour of 'rolling back' the state in the names of freedom and efficiency.

5 More recently Wagner 2006 admits that the problem that the public enterprise faces is the higher cost of production due to its technical inefficiency.

40's and 50's, not a single independent nation in South Asia was in a position to depend only on the private sector for industrial growth. Even in 1971, when Bangladesh became independent, the Government there nationalized almost 92% of the enterprises left by the Pakistani owners.

Countries in South Asia had resorted to nationalization for achieving their goals of providing quick growth with social justice and increasing employment. These had also been in tune with the political environment of these countries. The private sector was perceived as profit making and exploitative and the public sector as the vehicle of progress. In many countries, the public sector alone was capable of investing substantial funds for infrastructure development. Initially, nationalization did help in increasing industrial production and employment. But, in the 80's, it was realized by most of the South Asian nations that the public enterprises had become a burden on the State, incurring substantial losses and redundancy. These led to efforts at public sector reform, but since most of these efforts were neither sincere nor sustained, they failed. Privatization of public enterprises is the direct outcome of the failure of public sector reforms.

South Asia represents a huge working population. The idea of public enterprises was very much motivated by the feeling that Public Enterprises will be the source of employment generation. The country study represents the fact that a sound number is still employed by this sector. The worker's protest against privatization is more or less because of loosing social safety nets and the uncertainty of employment. It is quite obvious that in an alarming unemployment in this region workers unrest is a major question for the policy makers. The State which has started PEs as the employment generator itself is ready to finish their employment. In such a policy turn in all three mixed economies of south Asia (India., Bangladesh and Sri Lanka) which has discussed in this paper, the issue of *Fiscal Sociology* is quite prominent. The country study provides the detailed status of linkages between workers and privatization in these economies.

2.1.1 The Era Of Public Enterprises In India

Speedy economic development with social justice became the priority for the Government with the advent of Independence in 1947. The State was perceived to be the driving force for this purpose. The Industrial Policy Resolution of 1948 stressed the importance of the active role of the State in development of industries. This philosophy was also enshrined in the Indian Constitution[6].

6 For instance, Article 38 of the Directive Principle of State Policy states that the State shall strive to promote the welfare of the people by securing and protecting as effectively as it may a social order in which justice--social, economic and political – shall inform all the institutions of economic life.

In December 1954, the Indian Parliament passed a resolution proclaiming that 'socialist pattern of society' as the objective of the State[7]. Consistent with this policy, the successive plans gave higher priority to industrialization in the public sector. The Industrial Policy Resolutions of 1977 and 1980 also envisaged public enterprises as means of socializing the means of production in strategic areas.

Industrial Policy Resolutions since 1948 have divided industry into three groups. The first consisted of those relating to defence, heavy industry, mining, aircraft, air and rail transport, communications and power. These would remain in the public sector. The second consisted of a category, which would be open to public and private sectors. The third consisted of those which were left to the private sector in areas like consumer goods etc. However, in practice, public sector expanded into consumer good areas such as hotels and tourism and as a result of take over of sick private sector units. Until 1991, therefore, public sector was a holy cow.

Successive governments in India kept acquiring more and more loss- incurring private enterprises in the name of employment protection and thereby substantially increased the size of the public sector. It would not be wrong to say that, by this method, governments converted private bankruptcy into public debt. Thus, India pursued for almost four decades, a path of development in which public sector was expected to be the engine of growth. Public Sector had thus scaled the commanding heights of the Indian economy up to 1991. This was also perhaps necessitated by the lack of entrepreneurship in the Indian industry and the then leadership's abiding faith in socialistic pattern of society. The concept of mixed economy or dual preference economy, where public and private sector would both receive their due importance gradually resulted in preference for the public sector in all areas of infrastructure activity. Reservation of certain sectors for the public sector further accentuated this preference. For instance, prior to July 1991, 17 industries were reserved for the public sector. These were in crucial areas such as power, petroleum, Iron & steel, coal, railways, mining, airlines, roads, ship-building, telecommunications etc.

---

7 The Industrial Policy Resolution of 1956 stated that 'the adoption of the socialist pattern of society as the national objective, as well as the need for planned and rapid development require that all industries of basic and strategic importance or in the nature of public utility services should be in the public sector. Other industries which are essential and require investment on a scale, which only the State, in the present circumstances, could provide, have also to be in the public sector. The State has, therefore, to assure direct responsibility for future development of industries over wider areas'.

2.1.2. Public Sector Performance In India

Over a period of time, public enterprises have exhibited a number of problems such as low productivity, poor project management skills, overmanning, lack of technology upgradation, inadequate attention to research and development, and low priority to human resource development requirements. These problems and other economic compulsions have forcibly led the government to reappraise its approach to the public sector. In terms of net value added, the public sector enterprises constitute a sizeable share among all major industry groups. From just 5 enterprises with investment of Rs.29 crores in 1950-51, the public sector has expanded in size and stature to 240 enterprises (230 operating enterprises) with investment of Rs. 3,24,632 crores at the end of March 2002. These include 149 enterprises engaged in manufacturing/producing goods and 81 enterprises rendering services. Out of these 230 operating public sector enterprises, only 119 were profit-making as of March 2002. Profits of profit making enterprises totaled Rs.36,432 crores. As many as 119 enterprises made losses amounting to Rs. 10,387 crores at the end of March 2002. Cumulative losses of public sector enterprises total a massive Rs.69,932 crores. Overall rate of return on capital employed (net profit to capital employed) in these public sector enterprises was of the order of only 6.67% in 2001-02[8].

Despite huge investment in the public sector, the Government is required to provide more funds every year to the public enterprises. The public sector equity base of about Rs. 40, 000 crores has yielded dividend of Rs. 39,720 crores during the last twelve years. However, Government had to invest a further sum of Rs. 1,00,127 crores during this period in the form of equity (Rs. 46,508 crores), plan loans (Rs. 35,691 crores), and non-plan loans (Rs 17,928 crores), besides providing for Voluntary Retirement Scheme(VRS). The average rate of return on the Government investment for these years works out from 1% to 7.66% (Disinvestment Policy and Procedures, 2001).

Besides contributions towards equity and grant of loans, Government also supports PSEs by extending guarantees for loans and waivers. Compared to the total investment, the dividend declared is negligible. Huge amounts of hidden subsidies go into maintaining unviable / weak public sector units. This may be in the form of loans converted into equity or loans written off or fresh infusion of funds for revival of weak/sick units, or waiver of dues whether they are in the form of loans, interest or penal interest. During last ten years, the total amount of

8 Public Enterprises Survey. 2001-2002, Vol. 1, Ministry of Heavy Industries and Public Enterprises, Government of India, New Delhi.

subsidies to PSEs amounted to Rs. 1, 83, 896.4 Crores (Rangarajan Committee on Disinvestment of Shares in Public Sector Enterprises, 1993).

Already 175 public sector enterprises (74 CPSEs and 101 SPSEs) are with the Board for Industrial and Financial Reconstruction (BIFR). Many more would land in the lap of the BIFR, if measures are not taken expeditiously to restructure them to function on commercial lines.

2.1.3. Economic Reforms In India

India's economic reforms since 1991 were the result of serious financial crisis. By the middle of 1991, India's foreign exchange reserves were barely adequate for two weeks' imports. This became the cause for market liberalization measures in 1991[9]. It was only in 1991 that a fresh look was taken at the philosophy of public sector dominance. The Industrial Policy Resolution of July 1991 made a sobering appraisal of the role of the public sector in the country's economic development. It took note of the problems such as over manning, lack of technological upgradation, inadequate attention to R&D, human resource development and low return on investment. It also took note of the dilution of the original concept of public sector due to take over of many sick units of the private sector and the diversification into consumer goods and service sectors. The Policy Resolution also promised to move towards privatization and resolved to review the portfolios of public investment of industries which have a low technology base and which operate in inefficient and unproductive areas and vacate those areas where private sector has sufficient expertise and resources. The areas reserved for PEs were reduced to 8 from 17. However, the list has since been progressively reduced with the result that from December 2002, only three areas viz. Atomic Energy, Mineral specified in Atomic Energy (Control Production and Use) Order, 1953 and Railway Transport continue to be reserved.

2.1.4. Disinvestment In India

Disinvestment initially was resorted to in selected public sector units through selling small percentages of equity to financial institutions. Later, the C&AG found the methodology followed for disinvestment to be defective, since it had resulted in gross under valuation of the work of the shares disinvested.

The Rangarajan Committee on Disinvestment (1993) advocated that target ownership in all units which operated in areas reserved for public sector should normally be 51 % and 26 % in exceptional cases; in others, it could go down

9 Sachs, J. D., Varshney, A., Bajpai, N. (eds) India in the era of Economic Reforms. Oxford University Press, 1999.

to zero. The Disinvestment Commission (1997) recommended strategic sale of public sector units in order to meet the weaknesses of the units and make them non-efficient. Following these reports, Government embarked on a Policy of Disinvestment by which disinvestment could go up to 74% in generality of cases and even up to 100% where necessary. The Disinvestment Policy also resolved to use the proceeds for meeting expenditure on social sector schemes, restructuring public enterprises and reduction of public debt. The aforesaid Policy also stated that interests of workers would be fully protected and a social safety net would be provided to them (Ministry of Disinvestment, 2003). From 1999-2000 to 2002-03, the Government succeeded in disinvesting 51% or more equity in 36 public sector enterprises and netted Rs. 11,344 crores. Previously, Government had netted Rs. 19,573 crores from 1991-92 to 1999-2000 from sale of minor shareholdings in 39 public sector enterprises. The stark difference was that whereas earlier, Rs. 2793 crore of equity was sold; in the latter period, only Rs. 894 crore work of equity was sold to garner better realization.

Disinvestment through the strategic sale method has raised the value of PSE listed stocks. This has benefited all those who had invested in PSE stocks, such as retail investors and financial institutions. Government has not only benefited from increased realization from disinvestment (as opposed to negligible dividends it had received from the PSEs), but it has also benefited from increased dividends from residual shareholding in privatized PSEs.

The companies that had been privatized have done exceptionally well (with the exception of VSNL). For instance, in Paradeep Phosphates, which was a losing concern, losses came down by Rs.170 crores in the first year after Privatization. In IPCL, profits nearly doubled in the first year after Privatization.

The efficiency of privatized enterprises improved significantly after privatization, as in the case of MFIL, where sales registered almost 100% increase. Considerable improvement in labour productivity has been registered through labour restructuring and technological improvements. For instance, in Paradeep Phosphates, production increased nearly three times in the space of one year after privatization. Share prices of listed PSEs generally went up immediately after privatization (e.g. CMC).

Workers who were retained in the privatized enterprises generally benefited from better working conditions, and increase in salaries and allowances. But there have been complaints of harassment of labour by the managements, increase in efficiency standards for payment of incentives and 'persuation' to take VRS. Workers who took VRS are generally poorer, since they have spent the compensation money or social functions like marriages.

2.1.5. *Privatization And Workers In India*

One of the major fears of privatization is the potential loss of present and future employment. The relative decline of employment in the private sector and the growth of public service employment in the 1970s and 1980s may have further strengthened the notion that jobs in the public sector are more secure. Public sector employment accounts for nearly two-thirds of the 7 per cent formal sector employment in India, which has virtually stagnated in relative terms over the past two decades. In the wake of liberalization public sector employment has actually showed a negative rate of growth. The report of the Fifth Central Pay Commission and other reports prepared by the Task Forces headed by GeethaKrishnan, Rakesh Mohan and Montek Singh Ahluwalia on government employment, railways and employment policy respectively, have pointed out the need to reduce redundant workforce in government, railways and public sector enterprises. It is true that PSEs are overstaffed. One could, however, differ on the extent of redundancy. Various methodologies have been adopted for estimating redundancy. These have placed redundancy between 18 % to 25 %[10].

In India, even without privatization, employment situation has been very critical and rather gloomy. Post disinvestment employment position in 9 divested enterprises, 12 ITDC hotels and a unit of Hotel Corporation of India, show that from an initial employee strength of 43,433 at the time of disinvestment, 4390 employee separation has taken place. During the same period, 1050 fresh appointments have also taken place resulting in a net reduction in work force by 3340, which is around 7.69 per cent of the employees' strength at the time of disinvestment. In CMC, employment has increased from 3119 at the time of disinvestment to 3544 due to fresh recruitments. BALCO with a net reduction of 1425 and Modern Food Industries Ltd. with a net reduction of 889 account for 69 per cent of the overall net reduction in employment. Detailed position in respect of employment in these PSEs is given in the following Table 1[11]:

10 Gupta, S.P. The Role of National Renewal Fund in Economic Restructuring. In National Renewal Fund – A Look Ahead (ed.) M. L. Nandrajog, ILO, New Delhi, 1998, pp. 183-184.

11 Source: Reply of Minister of Disinvestment to Rajya Sabha Starred Question No.418, 10th April 2003 as presented in Naib, S., 2004: Disinvestment in India: Policies, Procedures, Practices, Sage Publications, New Delhi.

Table 1. Details of Employment Pattern – Pre- and Post-Disinvestment.

PSE	Disinvested in	Employees at the Time of Disinvestment	Attrition				Fresh Recruits	Not Change	Present Position
			Retirement	VRS	Others	Total			
MFIL	Jan 2000	2037	79	853		932	43	-889	1148
BALCO	Mar 2001	6436	361	1099	159	1619	194	-1425	5011
CMC	Oct 2001	3119	11	-	122	133	558	425	3544
HTL	Oct 2001	1138	134	-	77	211	1	-210	928
VSNL	Feb 2002	2902	49	-	85	134	1	-133	2769
IBP	Feb 2002	2200	2	-	2	4	-	-4	2196
PPL	Feb 2002	1149	16	137	22	175	3	-172	977
HZL	Apr 2002	8322	8	177	34	219	41	-178	8144
IPCL	May 2002	13536	62	-	79	141	6	-135	13401
ITDC (10 hotels)	2001-02	1798	9	730	81	820	178	-642	1156
HCI (Centaur Mumbai)	Apr 2002	796	--	-	2	2	25	23	819
Total		43433	731	2996	663	4390	1050	-3340	40093

These changes in employment have to be viewed in light of the fact that there has been a uniform decline in employment amongst all PEs irrespective of whether they have been divested or not. Apparently, decline in employment was also due to the fact that PEs were facing competition. A study[12] on the impact of market structure on employment divided the disinvested PSEs till 1999-2000 into two groups: those which are functioning in competitive environment (25 enterprises) and those which are operating in monopoly environment (13 enterprises). It was found that the employment declined in the post-divestiture period for the complete sample of 38 enterprises, as well as for the enterprises operating in competitive environment. As post-liberalization pressure increased on the PSEs, a number of them resorted to restructure labour strength through VRS. The surprising result was that in monopoly enterprises, there was an increase in average employment during this period.

The managements of privatized enterprises have resorted to payment of handsome compensations to induce labour to opt for VRS. They have no responsibility to provide any non-monetary safety net for retrenched workers, such as training in entrepreneurship, assistance in job search etc. Recent privatizations have thrown up innumerable problems for retrenched labour of privatized enterprises. Some of them have been forced to literal penury through unemployment and family exploitation for gaining compensation money.

It may, therefore, be desirable that Government does the labour restructuring in a systematic manner prior to privatization not only by providing for monetary compensation but also through non-monetary safety nets such as retraining, rede-

12 Naib, S., Partial Divestiture and Performance of Indian Public Sector Enterprise Economic and Political Weekly, XXXviii (29), 2003.

ployment, entrepreneurship development and job assistance. This would ensure that Government obtains a proper price for its stake during privatization and at the same time take care of workers' interests.

Protection of employees interest forms an integral part of the disinvestment process. The Government is committed to protect the interests of all the workers. A number of protections are available to the employees under various labour laws. These labour laws are applicable to the company irrespective of whether it is in the Public Sector or in the Private Sector. Besides this, employee protection is ensured through incorporation of suitable clauses in the shareholders' agreement, specifying that the strategic partner shall not retrench any of the employees of the company for a period of one year. Further, in the event of any reduction of the strength of the company's employees the strategic partner shall ensure that the company offers its employees an option to voluntarily retire on terms that are not, in any, manner, less favourable than the VRS applicable before disinvestment. This, however, does not prevent the privatized managements from downsizing numbers through VRS programmes. Labour alleges that various methods are used to force workers to avail VRS. Some of them include increase in efficiency standards and transfers to other far-away units or posting labour in areas where they have no expertise. It has been found that in recent privatizations in India, workers had not been taken into confidence about the need to disinvest and how their interests would be taken care of. This has led to labour's perceived sense of dissatisfaction about disinvestment and the fear that their days would be numbered under privatized managements. Usually, no retraining is provided to VRS optees to enable them to pursue other employment after availing VRS. This is an area where Government could do considerable work and obtain worker's co-operation for disinvestment.

Privatization in India can therefore be termed as a partial success, since distributional and welfare objectives have not been fully achieved. As yet, increased investments expected from the strategic buyers have not materialized. The firms have made profits due to better co-ordination of activities, utilization of spare capacities and downsizing of labour and elimination of wastages. Only when increased investments take place in the privatized enterprises and expansion / diversification are undertaken will there be prospects of greater employment and greater benefit to the consumers and peripheral development.

The new Coalition Government, which assumed power at the Centre in May 2004 onwards, has wound up the Disinvestment Ministry and stopped strategic sales of PSEs. It has also promised not to disinvest in profit making PSEs. This has put a break to the tremendous pace of privatization that India witnessed during 199-2004. During 2005-10, government has left the idea of setting revenue targets from disinvestment and during this period government has also changed the methodology of strategic sale into the method of partial disinvestment through minority sale.

3.1. *The Era Of Public Enterprises (1956-1960) In Sri Lanka*

Although Sri Lanka achieved independence in 1948, it did not have a strong entrepreneurial economy till about 1956. There were no major changes in the classic dual economy, with the export-oriented plantation sector separated from the large peasant subsistence sector till 1956. Even State involvement in productive areas of the economy was insignificant. Public sector policy was reviewed in early 1950s by the Government of Sri Lanka and by the World Bank in 1952. These reviews suggested caution in expanding the scope of public sector activity. A law was enacted in 1955 called the Government Sponsored Corporations Act, 1955 to privatise public corporations in stages. In 1956, Sri Lanka made a conscious decision to march towards industrialization. This was perceived as a means of restructuring the economy in order to get away from the economic dependence of exports. The Government Sponsored Corporations Act, 1955, was succeeded by the State Industrial Corporations Act, 1957, paving the way for establishment of Public Enterprises in the economy. This was followed by a drive for nationalizing private companies under the 1957 Act. Many of the activities such as public road passenger transport services, insurance, petroleum distribution, port cargo handling, leading local banks and several trading activities were nationalized. These measures were thought necessary to transform an economy dominated by plantations to an industrial one.

The period 1960 to 1970 saw continued proliferation of PEs. Over twenty private companies were nationalized during a period of twenty years (1957-77). This proliferation assumed startling proportions during 1970-1977 with the nationalisation of plantations in 1975 which itself was a follow-up of the Land Reforms Act, 1972. Several legislative measures such as the State Trading Corporations law also prompted the quick setting up of public enterprises. The Business Acquisition Act (BAA) of 1971 accelerated nationalisation of private sector businesses. The public sector's role in production and distribution in the agricultural sector expanded rapidly during 1970-77. By 1977, a major proportion of Sri Lanka's economic activity was either controlled or regulated by the State. The large increase in the government's direct control over trade and commerce since 1970 resulted in the rapid expansion of the public sector. The size of the public sector increased from about 21 % of GNP in 1970 to 24 % in 1977, and employment in this sector increased from a cadre of 135,019 in 1970 to 617,033 in 1977[13].

13 Karunatilake HNS Public Enterprise and the Private Sector, Sri Lanka Economic Journal, Vol. 1, No.2, 1986 and Karunatilake HNS The Economy of Sri Lanka, CDSS, Colombo, 1987.

3.2. Performance Of PEs In Sri Lanka

By mid-70s, there was substantial evidence to show that most PEs were highly inefficient[14]. The continued growth of PEs to serve political interests perhaps increased the inefficiencies and had spill over effects, such as increased cost of raw materials and intermediate goods.

The United National Party, which came to power in 1977, decided to liberalise the economy and abolish most of the import controls and foreign exchange restrictions, slashing subsidies and opting for more realistic exchange rates. The acts of liberalisation were the introduction of private sector in external and internal trade in competition with State Trading Corporations, lifting of monopoly rights of manufacturing, introduction of private trade in paddy milling and rice trading, etc. By the mid-1980s, some public enterprises found it extremely difficult to compete with imported goods in the liberalized scenario; their performance fell far below expectations, and the progressive decline in efficiency and productivity made it increasingly necessary to provide more tariff protection, which was contrary to the liberalization mantra. This also necessitated state subsidies, which subsequently became an enormous burden on the government budget. In his 1985 budget speech, the Minister of Finance stated "Unfortunately some public corporations are becoming an intolerable burden on the budget and the people of the country. Unless we do something immediately to improve their efficiency, the implications for the future are likely to be serious"[15].

3.3. Economic Reforms And Privatiztion In Sri Lanka

The guiding principle of Sri Lanka's economic policies since 1977 has been to lower the level of State intervention in the economy. The Government has also pursued a consistent and accelerated programme of privatization of public enterprises. Although Sri Lanka liberalized its economy in 1977, it was only a partial liberalization in the overall sense. A substantial liberalization took place in the area of regulations and controls, but the State's role in the economy remained significant. It has been estimated that in the mid-1980s, the state controlled about 40 percent of the manufacturing sector's value-added production. The Government did not repeal the BAA until 1988, but used it to take over three enterprises during the 1977-87 period.

---

14 Ministry of Finance, Budget Speech, Government Press, Colombo, 1985.

15 Ministry of Finance, Budget Speech, Government Press, Colombo, 1987.

3.3.1. *Privatization Policy In Sri Lanka*

It was only in 1987 that full scale privatization featured in the policy package. However, Sri Lanka did take initiatives for the privatization of management of selected state enterprises, deregulation of selected commercial activities, and the partial or full privatization of some parts of PEs after reorganizing them into subsidiaries. These transactions were very small and were sold practically by private placement. Hence, there was hardly any public protest. Many PEs such as the State Fertilizer Corporation, Tobacco Industries Corporation, and a few spinning and weaving mills and silk mills, which were unprofitable, were closed down during this period[16]. However, no serious attempt was made to fully privatize the PEs during 1977-88. However, partial disinvestment, liquidation of management contracts and franchising etc. took place during 1983-88 with considerable degree of success. These initiatives, in the early years, were not referred to as Privatization. This could be perhaps due to the fact that no transfer of assets to the private sector took place. Privatization was not seriously tried till 1987, though some groundwork was done during the previous decade. Privatization was announced as a State Policy for the first time in the 1987 Budget Speech of the Finance Minister[17]. During 1987-89, the privatization process consisted of three phases viz (1) conversion of corporations and government--owned business units (GOBUs) into public companies, (2) restructuring viable public companies and (3) privatization of selected public companies. However, from 1989, all these phases were merged into one step viz. conversion, immediately followed by divestiture, in the case of small PEs, and into two steps, viz. conversion and privatization / restructuring, in the case of larger PEs, particularly in textiles.

The period 1987-90 saw the beginning of the privatization phase. In August 1987, a Presidential Committee for Privatization (PCP) was set up. This Commission recommended that those State Enterprises carrying on the functions of a commercial nature should be disinvested[18].Those enterprises, which are not profitable, should be given priority for disinvestment in the privatisation programme in the first phase. The Commission also laid down the following criteria for choosing the enterprises for privatisation:

They should be small enough to be disinvested in the domestic market and
They should not be security sensitive.

16 Ministry of Finance, Budget Speech, pp 43-44, Government Press, Colombo, 1987.

17 Kelegama, S. in Anthony Bennett (ed): How does Privatization Work? Routledge, London, 1997.

18 Ibid.

3.3.2. Peopleization Policy (1989)In Sri Lanka

The Presidential Committee on Privatization was discontinued in 1989 with the election of the U.N.P. Government, which canvassed for a privatization programme named 'peoplisation' to attract the imagination of the lower and middle class voters. The idea was to emphasize the freedom that was to flow from the privatization policy. Basically, the objectives were:

to reduce the fiscal burden and permit the industries to raise funds from the capital market;
to increase competition and efficiency which would, in turn, introduce technology, modernisation and better consumer awareness;
to provide share ownership; and create an enterprise culture[19].

The programme reflected the Government's objective of broad- based share ownership wherever possible, though it was recognised that private corporate investors would have to assume management control of the public enterprises and that issues were not the most appropriate form of disinvestment. The Government embarked on an ambitious programme of privatisation and new institutional arrangements were put in place to facilitate the process.

A major change of economic significance effected during 1992 was the privatization of State-owned tea, rubber and coconut plantations. Of the 502 Government owned plantations, 449 were handed over to 22 private management companies with the objective of increasing productivity and quality while reducing the overheads in the plantation sector. While the productivity of the plantation sector has increased as a result of the private sector management, government subsidies to this sector too have declined considerably.

Sri Lanka's privatization programme covered the major sectors of the economy viz., industry, agriculture, and services. In the industrial sector, 15 public enterprises had already been fully privatized by February 1992. Before the end of 1992, another 29 PEs were to be privatized. In agriculture, privatization of the management of the plantation sector was well under way. In the services sector, the bus transport subsector had already been privatized (Karunatilake, 1986). By the end of 1993, the majority shareholdings of 35 public enterprises had been divested and another 30 were in various stages of divestiture· Between December, 1989 and mid-August, 1994, there were 43 public enterprises, which were privatized yielding over Rs. 12 billion. This amounted to 8% of GDP and 18% of State revenue. Privatisation proceeds came from both domestic (Rs. 5.25 billion)

19 Kelegama, S. Privatization: The Sri Lanka Experience, Research Studies. Public Enterprises Series No.1, Institute of Policy Studies, 1992.

and foreign (Rs.4.07 billion) sources in addition to public share floatation (Rs.2.5 billion).

3.3.3. Public Enterprise Reforms Commission (1995)

In 1995, the Public Enterprises Reforms Commission (PERC) was set up under Act No.l of 1996 to advise and assist the government on reforms of public sector enterprises and other related matters. The primary role of the Commission was to reform the public sector and other public enterprises leaving the government free to address its social agenda. Till date, it is the PERC which is implementing the privatisation programme in Sri Lanka. It has been fairly successful in carrying out equity sale of public corporations to investors.

3.3.4. Progress Of Privatization

Between March 1995 and June 2001, 44 PSEs were privatized with proceeds of around Rs.43.4 billion. During 2002, Government was able to divest 12 percent of its stake in SLT (Rs. 3.2 billion) through an offer for sale on the Colombo Stock Exchange. Foreign investors subscribed to 16 percent of the share issues, while the balance was taken up by domestic retail investors and state and private institutions. Overall, privatization proceeds in the year 2002 amounted to Rs. 5.7 billion against a target of Rs. 21 billion.

3.4. Privatization And Workers In Sri Lanka

3.4.1. Retrenchment Of Workers

PEs were largely overstaffed since employment had been given mainly under political patronage but also as a means of reducing unemployment. Recruitment procedures were comparatively easy in the semi-skilled and unskilled categories and hence surplus labour was usually found in the ranks of labourers, clerical and other allied grades rather than in management or executive grades. Workers employed a high sense of security, since labour laws were fairly rigid on their protection. The Termination of Employment Act (1971) required private sector employers of 15 or more employees to obtain the written consent of the employee or the approval of the Labour Commissioner for terminating the services of employees on non-disciplinary grounds. This may have given rise to the practice of the private sector managements to remove employees on fictitious disciplinary grounds and to refrain from recruitment of employees. Workers who were retrenched were paid compensation at different rates, depending on the bargaining ability of trade unions. One of the reasons advanced for the Government's more to privatize without labour downsizing was Govt.'s inability to pay increasing compensation packages. The privatized managements frequently had to pay compensation at rates higher than the last package agreed by the Labour Commissioner in order to remove more employees. These compensation packages proved to be detrimental to the companies' financial position. The Voluntary Retirement Schemes were aimed at reducing the number of employees without considering their usefulness. Frequently, therefore, talented workers had to be rehired at higher salaries in order to run the companies.

Sri Lanka, like all developing countries, has a large surplus of employees / labour in its public sector enterprises, due to political patronage. It has been estimated by Fiszbein[20] that the level of redundancy in public sector enterprises in Sri Lanka is nearly 50 % or more, as per studies conducted by experts.

Sri Lanka's labour laws are very stringent in the sense that no retrenchment is allowed without the express permission of the Labour Commissioner. In most cases, retrenchment was voluntary. However, involuntary retrenchments took place before 1st May 1992. Involuntary dismissals did take place before that date, especially in cases where PEs were divested by asset liquidation route rather than the strategic sale of ongoing concerns. When the government failed to remove the surplus labour through VRS, forced retrenchment was occasionally used, as this was possible under the Establishment Code. The leading Trade Union at that time viz. the Jathika Sevaka Sangamaya (JSS), resented this and consequently, on 1st May 1992, the President of Sri Lanka announced an employment guarantee for all public sector employees until they attained the age of 55 years. This put an end to all involuntary retrenchment by the State.

According to a recent study, estimated number of workers laid off in the first wave of privatization varies from the Labour Ministry's figures of 18000-20000 (around 25000 by the end of 1992) to the Employers' Federation figures of around 35,000 and the JSS's claim of 50,000 persons. It could be, therefore, safely assumed that the number of retrenched non-plantation workers could be between 25,000 and 50,000 between 1993 and 1994.

An accurate estimation of the magnitude of employment losses as a result of privatization is impeded by the absence of reliable data on total pre-privatization employment. However, the data available with the Institute of Policy Studies in Sri Lanka (given in Table 2) shows the extent of job losses due to privatization:

20 Fiszbein A, Labour Retrenchment and Redundancy Compensation in the State Owned Enterprises: The Case of Sri Lanka. Internal Discussion Paper, The World Bank, South Asia Division, 1992.

Table 2. Retrenchment in Selected Public Enterprises: 1995 to 2003 (average employment)[21].

Enterprise	Year of Privatization	Pre- privatization	Post privatization	Change
Sri Lanka Telecom Ltd. (SLTL)	1997	7,599	8,499	900
Sri Lankan Air Lines Ltd. (SLAL)	1998	4,358	4,908	550
Colombo Gas Company Ltd. (CGCL)	1995	646	292	-354
National Development Bank (NDB)	1993	188	311	123
Caltex Lanka Ltd.(CLL)	1994	320	275	-45
Bogawantalawa Plantations Ltd. (BPL)	1992	20,031	16,501	-3530
Lanka Ceramics Ltd. (LCL)	1992	4,082	2,021	-2,061
Lanka Salt Ltd.	1997	1,562	560	-1,002
Total				-5,419

From the above Table, it is clear that privatization caused net job losses of 5,419 workers in the eight firms surveyed with job gains recorded in three firms viz. SLTL, SLAL and NDB. Job gains in these three firms indicate expansion in company activities in the post-privatization period.

Job losses in four of the seven entities that were re-invested with the government under the Public Enterprise Rehabilitation Act No.29 of 1996 amounted to 5,660 as shown in the following Table 3:

Table 3. Retrenchment under the Public Enterprise Rehabilitation[22] *Act No.29 of 1996.*

Enterprise	Year	Job losses (No. of workers)
Kantale Sugar Industries Ltd.	1994	1,132
Lanka Loha Hardeware Ltd.	1997	460
Pugoda Textile Mills Ltd.	1999	2,800
Hingurana Sugar Industries Ltd.	2002	1,268
Total		5,660

21 Source: Institute of Policy Studies: Sri Lanka State of the Economy, 2003, p 84.
22 Source: Annual Reports of the Companies.

3.4.2 Share Ownership For Workers

Privatization has been opposed by trade unions, primarily because it is associated with labour retrenchment. However, after the strike of July 1980, the power of trade unions has undergone significant reduction. In order to overcome resistance of trade unions to privatization, the government of Sri Lanka had offered 10 percent of the shares free of charge to the workers. This enables the transformation of the employee to employee and part-owner; instead of salary alone, Worker would get salary and dividends. However, in actual practice, it has been found that workers' share had gone down from 10 per cent, since most employees sell off the shares when the share prices go up. The VRS also had its share of problems. When the VRS was operated in PEs, some of the most talented and experienced people left, while the most inefficient remained. This created practical problems in the running of the PEs.

3.4.3 Agreements On Employee Retention

In the second phase of privatization i. e. after May 1992, Sri Lanka's policy has been to obtain from prospective buyers a commitment to maintain existing levels of employment because it could no longer afford to pay the heavy compensation demanded by trade unions. It has been reported that employees' severance payments amounted to several times their annual salary.

This policy of leaving it to the private owner to deal with labour restructuring causes financial problems for the private sector owner. It is not easy for the private owner to lay off surplus labour. The Termination of Employment of Workmen Act of 1971 (TEWA) stipulates that an employer with 15 or more workers who wishes to terminate services of an employee with one or more years of service on non-disciplinary grounds, must obtain the written consent of the employee or the consent of the Labour Commissioner. The procedure is often a very lengthy one; sometimes it takes up to six months or more to get the consent of the Labour Commissioner. This may be perceived as a safety net mechanism for workers but it does not appear to be in the interests of labour, since employees are reluctant to hire workers that they would find unduly difficult to lay-off. (This is one of the reasons for less employment generation). Prospective bidder may become shy of bidding for enterprises, looking at the problems of laying-off surplus labour and this may affect the privatization programme itself. Moreover, trade unions also claim that private owners often lay off workers on false grounds of misconduct in order to get around TEWA. When Voluntary Retirement was used in the pre-privatization scenario, the government gave at least three months notice to the workers to decide. In the post-privatization scenario, the workers were given only roughly 2 to 3 weeks by the new owners to decide whether they wanted to take the compensation package and leave. In some cases, the deadline for the decision was extended indefinitely so that workers could leave the firm whenever they wanted (e. g. United Motors). The firm terminated this provision when the number of workers was brought down to the level deemed optimal by the management

Trade Unions feel that the existing provisions for appeal to Labour Tribunals against such wrongful lay off is hardly practical, looking at the enormous legal costs involved. The focus of pre-privatization labour restructuring has been on getting targeted number of workers down rather than on the structure / quality of employment. Nevertheless, in view of the difficulties faced by purchasers in labour restructuring, it appears that it would be better for firms to be downsized prior to privatization. This would increase investor interest and receipts for the government.

Kelegama and Salih rightly observe that "labour retrenchment should not be viewed in the context of privatization alone, but as part of the move to a market economy. Ad hoc retrenchment programmes that lack transparency, only increase information asymmetries and confusion, leading to a very uneven and inefficient public sector downsizing in a privatization programme."[23]

3.4.4 Compensation Schemes

Surplus labour in Sri Lanka was retrenched by Government through Voluntary Retirement Schemes which were backed by handsome compensation schemes, as recommended by the Presidential Committee on Privatization in 1987. The Presidential Committee on Privatization (PCP) was set up to develop policy guidelines on the privatization process. The PCP proposed *interalia* the following measures:

a) a monetary compensation package
b) pre-privatization retrenchment only on a voluntary basis
c) premature payment of gratuity to employees who opt to retire.
d) Offer only surplus workers retirement option and
e) Workers not in surplus only entitled to gratuity payment.

However, the PCP failed to comprehensively address problems such as targeting workers for retrenchment and estimating the type and amount of compensation package. A second Committee which was appointed to address these shortcomings in the PCP recommendations came up with a report setting out a

23 See Kelegama and Salih 1998.

formula for payment of compensation, called the *Bulumulla Formula*. However, the trade unions rejected this package in 1991, and Government then came out with two new formulae viz. the *Leather Products Company formula* and the *Ceramics Company formula*. These formulae were found to be more attractive than the *Bulumulla formula*.Some of these packages have been more attractive than the others. Hence, there has been confusion and distrust of privatization among the workers. The absence of a uniform package of compensation for retrenched workers did create unevenness and dissatisfaction among workers. However, the labour commissioner rejected the idea of a uniform package of compensation on the plea that the ability to pay compensation varied with each privatized enterprise. This, however, led to trade unions bargaining for the best compensation package. Basic monetary package – excluding gratuity, gifted shares, encashment of unutilized annual leave etc- increased from around 17 months salary to 53 months salary between 1989-97 for a 40 year old worker with 18 years of service. Many privatized firms could not afford to pay this package; instead they preferred to absorb the surplus labour. This has created considerable opposition to the privatization efforts. One reason for the resistance of labour to privatization is the absence of the labour absorptive capacity of the manufacturing sector in Sri Lanka.

The compensation packages adopted in Sri Lanka are based on the number of years of service, with employees with greater service periods getting more compensation. This discriminates against younger persons with lesser service and who belong to employment categories where job opportunities in the economy are scarce. This problem is made worse since effective, sustainable unemployment safety nets such as retraining or developing business skills which have been long overdue, have not yet received the attention of Government.

Though Sri Lanka succeeded both in restructuring labour prior to privatization up to 1995 and after privatization from 1996, there has been no programme to counsel or retrain VRS optees for alternative vacations. Many workers were reduced to penury after paying off debts / expenditure on social functions likes birth, marriages and deaths. Government of Sri Lanka has not been able to bring out necessary changes in policy to provide adequate social safety net for retrenched workers.

4.1 The Era Of Public Enterprises In Bangladesh

Bangladesh inherited a largely private sector dominated economy at the time of its liberation in 1971. But with the wholesale nationalization immediately after liberation, several thousand industrial, commercial and financial enterprises came under government control. As a result, the government's control over the fixed assets of the industrial sector shot up from 34% of pre-liberation period to 92% by 1972 (Dowlah, 1997). For the purposes of control, supervision and coordination of the aforesaid nationalized enterprises, several corporations were established under the provision of the President's order No. 27 of 1972. "This order effectively nationalized the industrial sector, fulfilling an Awami League promise made in a highly successful election campaign in mid-1970. The party's 'manifesto' had received widespread support from the public, who had seen nationalization of financial and industrial sectors as a way to forestall concentration of wealth in a few hands. This had been the general public sentiment even before the break up with Pakistan. At that time, the notorious 22 leading families of West Pakistan had dominated the concern. In 1972, it was directed at Bangladesh's own fledging industrial capitalist community."[24]

4.1.1 Performance Of Public Enterprises

PE sector grew rapidly in Bangladesh during the period 1971-75. The reasons for this spectacular growth were: first, historical circumstance (the government was forced to take possession of business abandoned by their former Pakistani owners at the time of liberation); and second, the political persuasion of the government of the time which nationalized industry, banks and other financial institutions. As a result, there were about 350 PEs by 1975[25].

However, PEs right from the beginning could not run efficiently and many of them ran into severe financial difficulties and serious management problems. Due to interference by the trade union leaders in the management of enterprises, excessive work force, inexperience and inability of the officials to act as efficient entrepreneurs, etc., besides various other reasons, accounted for a chaotic condition in the nationalized sector and became a burden for the government. The programme of nationalization in Bangladesh has been plagued by many problems. The absence of autonomy at the corporation and enterprise level and also the involvement of a large agencies in the decision making process have been mentioned by many as seriously limiting the operational efficiency of the public sector enterprises, mainly the nationalized industries in the post – independence Bangladesh[26].

24 Sobhan R. and Ahmad. M., Public Enterprises in Intermediate Regime: A Study in the political Economy of Bangladesh. BIDS, Dhaka, 1980.

25 World Bank, Bangladesh: Privatization and Adjustment, Re-port no. 12318-BD, Washington, 1994.

26 Alamgir M., Nationalized Industries of Bangladesh: Problems and Prospects. The Bangladesh Development Studies, 1974.

4.2 Privatization Of PEs In Bangladesh

4.2.1 The Era Of Gradual Denationalization

During the period of 1975-81 the government followed a policy of gradual denationalization. Some sectors were kept under state ownership, the rest were opened to domestic and foreign private capital investment. The provision of nationalization in the future was deleted; a tax holiday and other incentives were offered. Industrial financing institutions were directed to provide equity support to prospective industrialists[27].

Between 1975 and 1978, the government sold 116 enterprises to the private sector. A number of other measures designed to promote modern private industry were implemented, e.g., the reopening of the stock market in 1976, the establishment of the Investment Corporation of Bangladesh to provide bridge financing and underwriting facilities to the private sector and the abolition of restriction on collaboration between domestic private industries and direct foreign investment[28]. Bangladesh embarked on a major macroeconomic stabilization programme in the mid–1980s that coincided with the launching of Third Five Year Plan[29].

The imposition of military rule in early 1982 was followed by the adoption of the New Industrial Policy in June of the same year. Under this policy, large-scale denationalization occurred and in particular the jute and cotton textile mills, which had been taken over from Bangladeshi industrialists in 1972, were restored to their former owners. Of the 72 jute mills in the public sector on 30th June 1982, 34 (accounting for 38 % of production capacity) were denationalized by June 1985. Of the 52 cotton textile mills in operation in the public sector on 30th June 1982, 22 were denationalized within one year of the announcement of the New Industrial Policy[30].

In the six years of the Zia regime, a total of 255 PEs were divested or privatized in one way or another. Thirty of these were the last of the 'enemy' cum

---

27 Khan A. R. and Hossain M., The Strategy of Development in Bangladesh. Macmillan, London, 1989. To improve the performance of public enterprises, the government had implemented several measures over the past few years. In addition to denationalization of selected public enterprises, the government tried to improve the performance of the remaining enterprises through financial and physical rehabilitation and measures to improve management autonomy, pricing policies and performance monitoring. However, despite these measures, the financial performance of public enterprises continued to remain poor.

28 *Third Five Year Plan,* Planning Commission, Ministry of Planning, Government of the Peoples Republic of Bangladesh, Dhaka, 1985-90.

29 Khan A. R. and Hossain M., 1989, *The Stra-tegy of Development in Bangladesh,* Macmillan, London.

30 Binayak, S. Whether privatization: Results of an exploratory Survey of the Disinvested Industries in Bangladesh. Mimeo.

vested properties originally confiscated from Indians during the Pakistan period. Another 115 were small firms divested through the office of the Director General of Industries (DGI), similar to the small units unloaded during the Mujib's period.

Privatization and private sector development were advanced significantly during the period of President Zia (1975-81). The politics was basically liberal, but carried out with more caution than conviction. The emphasis on policy was more than its implementation and as with the predecessor government; no well-thought-out plan with coherent objectives was ever developed.

4.2.2 Extensive Divestiture / Privatization 1982-91 In Bangladesh

Ultimately the New Industrial Policy announced in 1982 by the government was a clear indictment of the mistakes committed by the erstwhile policy makers. In 1982, the New Industrial Policy envisaged a massive programme of disinvestment of public sector industrial units, especially in jute and cotton textile sectors. A second element of the reform included denationalization / disinvestments of banks and insurance companies. The decision to permit Bangladeshis to set up private commercial banks and specialized financial institutions with their own capital or in collaboration with foreign capital in 1977-78 effectively ended the monopoly of commercial banking by the Nationalized Commercial Banks (NCBs). In 1978, the decision was taken to breach the exclusive jurisdiction of the state over insurance company by permitting a number of private insurance companies to be set up in competition with the state sector (Zohir, 1996). It can be easily seen that the policy towards the entry of private sector through the divestiture policy had become the part of the government plan prior to 1980.

In NIP 1982, the government for the first time recognized the major role of private sector in the process of industrial development of the country. These policies were further strengthened in 1986. Under the PEs ordinance of 1986, substantial autonomy to adjust prices has been granted to public enterprises, except for those producing a small number of monopoly and sensitive items. The target of domestic resource mobilization in the public sector remained largely unfulfilled during the Third Plan period. An overly cautious fiscal management subsequently helped to reduce the budget deficit whose main brunt was borne by the public sector development progamme. A weak domestic demand resulted in a slacking of growth in the industrial sector, which had definite implications for a shortfall in domestic resource mobilization. In the midst of the stabilization programme designed to reduce external and fiscal deficit, the country experienced an unprecedented series of natural disasters. During the first four years (1985-89) of Third Five Year Plan (TFYP) a total of 35 public enterprises were disinvested and transferred to private sector in order to create confidence among private entrepreneurs. Implementation of the privatization programme for Manufacturing public Enterprises (MPEs) during 1981-82 to 1986-87 reduced the size of public sector significantly (about 40%). In addition to disinvestments, measures were also introduced to deregulate private investment sanctioning procedures, relax import control and to provide positive export incentives. These reforms contributed to improv the policy environment with beneficial effects on private sector industrial activities[31].

The Fourth Five Year Plan document stated that

> Under the denationalization amendment Ordinance of June, 1987 financially profitable enterprises of the public sector corporations are being divested retaining 51% share for the government, 34% for the general public and the remaining 15% to the PE employees. These are being managed as companies giving more managerial autonomy through the enterprises Board, where, five out of nine Board members are appointed by the Corporation in place of the government, three are appointed by the general public (share holder) and one by the employees, if they acquire at least 15% share allocated to them. This divestiture process will be continued and possibility of further improving it allowing improvement in the formation of strong capital market through this process will also be attempted during the Fourth Five Year Plan (FFYP). Large private sector participation in share holding, operation and management of public enterprises shall be explored during FFYP[32].

4.2.3 Slow Pace Of Privatization: 1991 Onwards

The industrial policy of 1991 which was formulated in the light of promoting a competitive market economy and which was further revised in 1992 laid down basic strategies required for industrial development of the country. All industries have now been opened up for private investment, both domestic and foreign except a selected few related to national security like arms and ammunition, nuclear energy, minting and security printing, mechanized extraction in the reserved forest and the railways[33]. GOB has recently recognized the need for further reform. The industrial policy of 1999 stated that the government is mindful of the fact that a continuous process of reform is necessary to propel the industrial sector of Bangladesh to take-off stage[34]. In the industrial policy of 1999, the government again admitted the fact that without reform nothing could be possible. Some objectives of this policy clearly indicated that government was keen to accelerate the process of PEs reform. These objectives were:

(i) To focus the role of the government as a facilitator in creating an enabling environment for expanding private investment;

---

31 *Fourth Five Year Plan*, 1991, Planning Commission, Ministry of Planning, Government of the Peoples Republic of Bangladesh, Dhaka.

32 Ibid.

33 *Fifth Five Year Plan*, 1997-2002, Document, Planning Commission, Ministry of Planning, Governmnet of Bangladesh, Dhaka.

34 Industrial Policy 1999, Government of Bangladesh, Dhaka.

(ii) To permit public undertaking only in those industrial activities where public sector involvement is essential to facilitate the growth of the private sector and / or where there are overriding social concerns to be accommodated; and
(iii) To enhance operational efficiency in all remaining public manufacturing enterprises through appropriate management restructuring and pursuit of market-oriented policies.

Many SOEs retain an important role in the economy even after recent privatization, particularly in the financial and energy sectors. Around 22 SOEs have been included in the current programs of privatization commission as of January 2010. Privatization policy in Bangladesh had a more regulatory envirenment but the results of previous privatization are important to be evaluated when Bangladesh has many more task of privatization on the way.

4.3 Privatization And Workers In Bangladesh

Labour interests are usually of the least concern in the agenda of privatization in Bangladesh. It is also surprising that the even after a host of labour laws, post privatization results failed to deliver any remarkable support for interests of labour. Large scale job losses resulting from lay-offs and retrenchment and closure of the privatized units after divestiture, and uncertainty about payment of adequate compensations etc. are the major concerns of the workers. All these remain truly real concerns in Bangladesh and tend to be aggravated by a relationship of mistrust persisting among labour, government and the private sector employers. The impact of closure of the privatized enterprises was found to have serious consequences as the aggregate loss of jobs due to closure alone was estimated to be 39,007 by Sen's study. The recently conducted study also estimates a 25 per cent decrease in employment after divestiture in 11 of the currently operating PEs out of a total of 13 privatized during 1991-96[35].

Privatization analysts like Berg and Berg calculated the employment loss of labour force in a single Company where in July 1993, the workforce was cut to 650 people from its previous level of 1200 workers. Again it was reduced from 650 to 350 and overtime has been also disappeared. (Berg and Berg, 1997) The contradiction starts in case of Kohinoor Chemicals Limited (KCL) when the president of the KCL said that there were not a great number of retrenchments. However findings of Berg and Berg do show a large number of retrenchments[36].

Table 4 shows that except Bangladesh Cycle Industries Ltd. all other recently privatized PEs had retrenched laboures. According to this Table average per cent-

35 Ahmed Mumtaz Uddin in Privatization in South Asia, Gopal Goshi (ed), ILO, New Delhi, 2000.

36 An Interview with KCL, President, 7th March, 2003.

age of retrenchment in these PEs is 30. These tables do not show any positive indication of privatization in relation to labour in Bangladesh.

Table 4. Change in Employment Status of the Currently Operating Enterprises after Privatization during 1991-96[37]*.*

Sl. No.	Name of the Enterprises	Employment		
		At the time of privatization	After privatization	Change in per cent
1.	Dhaka vegetable oil industries Ltd	525	295	-43.8
2.	Chittagong Cement Clinker and Grinding Co.Ltd.	318	252	-20.8
3.	Kohinoor Chemicals Co.	889	789	-10.2
4.	Kohinoor Spinning Mills ltd	1030	530	-48.5
5.	Bangladesh Cycle industries Ltd	119	800	672.2
6.	Barisal Textile Mills (New: Name 5R Ltd.)	1172	832	-29
7.	Style Fabrics & Embroidery Ltd. (Old Name: Zotime Fabrics)	61	50	-18
8.	Madaripur textile Ltd.	1056	742	-29.7
9.	Kishoregange Textile	1275	758	-40.5
10.	Eagle Box & Carton Mfg. Ltd	268	172	-35.8
11.	Quontum Pharmaceutical Ltd.	283	n.a.	n.a.
12.	Hamida Metal Industries Ltd.	Disappeared		
13.	Sharmin Textile Mills	6996	5229	-25.3

Average percentage of retrenchment in these PEs was 30 per cent. Table 5 and 6 (which is based on the BIDS findings) also presents a high number of retrenchments as it is evident from Table 5 below:

37 *Source*: World Bank: Privatization Experience in Bangladesh, 1991-96; World Bank (Vol. 1); Sep. 1997.

Table 5. Labour Restructuring after Disinvestment: Cohort Analysis for currently Running Enterprises[38].

	Before Disinvestment	After Disinvestment	% difference
No. of production workers	97048(89.3)	73711(89.50)	-24
No. of non-production workers	11597(10.7)	8643(10.5)	-25.5
Total number of workers and employees	108645(100)	82354(100)	-24.2

Note: The estimates are based on 112 privatized enterprises, which are currently running.

Table 6. Impact of Closure on Employment: Cohort Analysis for Currently Closed Enterprises[39].

	Before disinvestment	*After disinvestment*	*Difference*
No. of production Workers	35435	1066	34369
No. of non- production Employees	4884	246	4638
Total number of workers and employees	40319	1312	39007

These data do not show any positive indication of divestiture in relation to labour. BIDS study of divested industries (Tables 5 and 6) and World Bank's (Table 4) study of recently privatized 13 PEs have predicted a picture of high level of worker's retrenchment.

Labour unrest is a major issue in privatization process in Bangladesh. Privatization has created a sense of insecurity amongst the workers of the divested nationalized industries and commercial concerns owned by the government. Though in order to facilitate the privatization process the concept of *'golden handshake'* has been introduced where the workers have been offered substantial financial benefit in exchange for leaving the job yet this approach has not met with much success. The workers do not feel secure in leaving the present job and to seek out new job. Workers are apprehensive of the fact that in the event of privatization of the enterprises they would lose their jobs under the private management and would be secure by making necessary provisions in the instrument of transfer for continuity of their service. Unless the workers are taken into confidence and they cooperate, the process of privatization can not take place. Hence it is neces-

38 Source: BIDS survey of disinvested industries, 1997.
(Figures in percentage represent column percentages)

39 *Source*: BIDS survey of disinvested industries, Table shows a wide gap of workers retrenchment after disinvestment. This can be a most negative aspect of workers/employees concern.

sary to motivate the workers and give them a sense of economic security. It is indeed very difficult on the part of any elected government to take any decision, which would have adverse effect upon its popularity. The decision of privatization is not a very popular one since it would affect the interest of large number of workers in particular enterprises[40]. Most of the private entrepreneurs are not even interested in looking at the retrenched worker. The rate of getting employment for that poor labour is really very low. This is one of the most serious consequences of privatization[41].

New hopes like Voluntary Depature Scheme (VDS), Special Workers Fund (SWF), and other legal mechanisms also have not succeeded so far. The successes of disinvestment policy also depend on how the government is meeting the interests of the PEs privatization workers. The government should try to solve the conflict between workers and management before taking up privatization.

One major negative aspect of PEs in Bangladesh is that many of them are closed and some of them are on the verge of closing. On the other hand, reports go, more then 100 industrial units may be privatized or closed; which might mean retrenchment of about 75000 employees. Apart from this, measures for rationalization of manpower might be put into effect in many sectors[42].

Labour interest would occupy high priority in the privatization process if labour unions show strong commitment for labour welfare. In Bangladesh, labour unions are fractured and less committed. Even after the government of Bangladesh commitment to introduce ESOP in the industrial policy of 1999, the actual benefits have been limited.

The International labour Organisation has taken interest to assess the labour laws in the country in view of the fact that due to privatization, there has been large number of retrenchments. On the issue of lay- off and retrenchment the recent report of ILO has stated that

> Any factory that has completed not less than one year of continuous service is laid-off, he/she shall be paid by the employer compensation. For the first 45 days of the lay-off period during any calendar year, compensation shall be equal to half of the total of basic wages and dearness allowance, and the full amount of housing allowance. If the lay-off lasts, whether continuously or intermittently, for more than 45 days, compensation shall be equal to one fourth of the total of basic wages and dearness allowance, and the full amount of housing allowance for every subsequent period of 15 days or more. After the first 45 days of lay off, the employer may retrench a worker instead of laying off such a worker for any continuous period of 15 days or more. However, no compensation shall be payable to a laid-off worker if this worker: (1) refuses to accept any alternative employment on the same wages in the same

40 See Sobhan, 1997

41 Begum Ferdausa Ara in an Interview with author at Dhaka Chamber of Commerce and Industry (DCCI), 15 March 2003.

42 Bangladesh Observer, July 7, 2003, Dhaka.

establishment, or in any other establishment belonging to the same employer; (2) does not present himself/herself for work at the establishment at the appointed time during normal working 8 hours at least once a day if so required by the employer; or (3) such lay-off is due to strike in another part of the establishment No worker who has been in continuous service for more than one year in any establishment shall be retrenched unless:(a) the worker has been given one month's notice in writing, or has been paid wages for the period of notice;(b) a copy of such notice is sent to the Chief Inspector or his authorized officer; and (c) the worker has been paid compensation equivalent to thirty days' wages for every completed year of services or any part thereof in excess of six months' or gratuity, if any whichever is higher[43].

Some new government initiatives and commitments to the ILO can give a new hope to the workers and employees. New schemes like *golden handshake* financial compensation scheme introduced initially in Railways, BJMC and BTMC were the VDS, under which the terms of payment appeared to be generous and response from workers was also favourable. A PE employee with 30-year service would be entitled to five years pay as gratuity alone and thus the workers, response to VDS has been quite positive during 1991-93, especially in the Railway, Bangladesh Jute Mill Corporation (BJMC) and Bangladesh Textile Mill Corporation[44]. But the overall participation of labour in VDS is very less since only a very small number have served the enterprise for more than 30 years. Many Bangladeshi PEs were not even established 30 years ago.

In 1999, the GOB pledged that the workers interest would be taken care of through various policy packages. Government also favoured the practice of Employment Stock Option Programme (ESOP) through which employees will get benefits of buying shares of divested public enterprises (Industrial Policy 1999). In the Budget Speech 2002-03, Finance Minister also admitted

Government is sincere about the need to protect the legitimate interest of officers,employees and the labourers while implementing the privatization programme. To this end, I propose an allocation of Tk. 400 cr. To ensure disbursement of severance benefits payable to the concerned laboures, employees and officers. If necessary the allocation will be further enhanced[45].

However in the same financial year (2002-03), Government of Bangladesh (GOB) also planned for closure and divestiture of many public enterprises without considering its long run impact on the workers. Recent reports of the World Bank have stated that most of the training programme by the World Bank has not suc-

43 International Labour Organization (ILO) and Bangladesh Garment Manufacturers and Exporters Association (BGMEA), A Handbook on Relevant National Laws and Regulations of Bangladesh, 2003, Dhaka.

44 Ahmed M. U. in Privatization in South Asia, Gopal Goshi (ed), ILO, New Delhi, 2000.

45 Rahman S., Budget Speech, GOB, Ministry of Finance, Part- I, 2002-2003.

ceeded much since the support base from both side government as well as labour is less compared to other countries[46].

Even after the involvement of ILO and a host of labour laws, labour unrest is common in most of the nationalized and divested / privatized enterprises. The high level of corruption at the labour court, the workers' mistrust of trade unions, the discontinuity of democracy during the period 1975-1990 have all created a situation where the Government is left with a very limited choice in relation to its labour laws and Privatization. This provides opportunities for people who are keen on their personal growth at the cost of the huge work for Bangladesh. Implementation of Labour laws does not favour the world's poorest work force in the process of privatization. The question looms large is who will protect the interest of the workers where trade unions, government machinery and legal set up appear totally opposed to their interest. International agencies such as ILO and World Bank are also not in a position to protect the interest of the workers, since many of the pro active steps taken by these agencies have also failed. Even if Bangladesh has failed to structure the proactive labour restructuring in the era of democratic holiday (1975-1991)[47], the democratic period (1991 onwards) should have tried to protect the interest of the workers.

5. Linking Privatization, Workers And Fiscal Sociology In South Asia

Fiscal sociology is a field that deals with the wider ramifications of a state's fiscal activities that cannot readily be captured either by micro- or macroeconomic analysis or by financial institutional description[48]. There is considerable debate in political sociology about the degree to which the structure of the state apparatus influences policy making[49]. The debate in political sociology especially the role of *the state* also evoked issues in Fiscal Sociology in many ways. The concept of privatization is an interesting area to understand the downsizing the role of state (as a producer) and its impact on workers. Privatization is being attacked in various economies by workers.

46 World Bank, *Bangladesh: Privatization and Ad-justment*, Report no. 12318-BD, Washington, March 10. 1997.

47 During this period Bangladesh was not governed by any elected democratic government.

48 Backhaus J., Wagner R. (Ed) Handbook of Public Finance. Norwell Kluwer Academic Publishers, 2004.

49 Skocpol, T., 1985 as cited in *John L. Campbell,* The State and Fiscal Sociology, *Annual Review of Sociology*, Vol. 19, 1993.

Former World Bank economist Percy Mistry, in his research on privatization has concluded that, the somewhat ambitious claims made for privatization need to be scaled down and that it could even be counter productive, especially in smaller developing countries[50]. It is true that the role of the state is really changing and the fiscal discipline in terms of hardening the budget, cutting the subsidies has become the most important task for the state. The impact of those fiscal reforms is faced by the workers working in the PEs in developing countries. Privatization and its impact on workers is one of the most pressing issues in the field of Fiscal Sociology because it is somewhere understood by the policy makers that selling PEs is just the final exercise for the government. Labour restructuring is an integral part of privatization programmes. Sometimes, it highlights the overstaffing of the enterprise and as a result, speeds up labour downsizing which, in any case, was necessary.

Public enterprises were established as a part of the State's role to promote welfare of the people in South Asia. For this purpose governments in South Asia came out with different constitutional provisions and laws. The presidential order No.27 in 1972 in Bangladesh has helped fast nationalization of PEs. More or less in all three economies due to these act and constitutional obligation state became a producer and job provider and the issue of nationalization was linked with the issue of job creation.

Expenditure on PE were made through public money. But it is the sad part of the entire public sector reform in the all three economies of South Asia where workers are not having major stake. An interesting case can be presented from India where BALCO Workers Union wanted to have some part of the share in BALCO privatization but government never thought for this option. The 51 % of Companies share has been diluted to Sterlite Company. Supreme Court of India's judgment too admitted that the share dilution to Sterlite is valid and worker's demand is not valid. *Management Employ Buy Outs (MEBOs)* is one of the ways of privatization where the Public Sector shares can be diluted to the employees of the companies. MEBOs have not been a serious concern in these economies. This method of privatization is an interesting and important exercise which South Asia can practice.

Labour law in South Asia prevents workers' retrenchments in PEs.But labour law is not focusing issues involved in privatization. Many countries have proved better with the help of a clear cut privatization law. The absence of privatization law does make strong cases for protecting the interest of workers. Sri Lanka is the only country in the current study which has some experiences in privatization

50 Mistry, P. The Roots of privatization: Briefing notes for Current debates on public sector issues. Public Service International, France.

law. Both legal enactments viz. the Act 23 of 1987 and Act 24 of 1987 which deal with privatization do not mention concerns about the employees affected by the privatization process. The India the case of BALCO privatization is not the only case of ignoring the workers in privatization in South Asia. Data on retrenchment of workers in Sri Lanka and Bangladesh is enough to prove that workers are the last concern in the entire agenda of privatization.

Apart from this there is also a need to have a disinvestment / privatization fund which can be used to restructure the public enterprises or to enhance the skill of the workers for re-employment. Disinvestment fund has not been created in India even after the strong recommendation by the Disinvestment commission. The earnings through privatization are made for Budget expenditure in these economies. The issue should be re-examined by the government. Job loss because of retrenchment, VRS, closure of the enterprises in privatization ultimately breeds uncertainty for the workers. Workers should be the integral part of PEs reforms. The privatization exercises in South Asia should be more job providing. Workers should not be left without job. There is more to do for workers in privatization in South Asia.

5. Conclusion

The emerging trend in privatization and worker' concern in South Asia bring up pertinent issues in *Fiscal Sociology* to redesign the privatization programmes so that pro-active restructuring steps are taken to reduce hardship to the redundant labour and prevent adding to the growing unemployment; otherwise privatization policy may itself come under threat and may be abandoned. That would be a pity since it would amount to throwing out the baby along with the bathwater. South Asian economies such as India, Sri Lanka and Bangladesh, which are sizable dual preferences economies, need to focus on State sponsored welfare measures, such as workers' interest, this will be in its own interests to reduce its dependence on the public sector as a vehicle of progress.

Notes

1. The term *State Owned Enterprises (SOEs), Public Enterprises (PEs), Public Sector Units (PSUs) and, Public Sector Enterprises (PSEs)* are same in the meaning. Without making any change, this paper presents all terms in the same manner as it was presented in different reports and documents.

2. *Voluntary Retirement Scheme* (VRS) and *Voluntary Disposal Scheme* (VDS) are having same meaning in India and Bangladesh respectively.
3. Divestiture, divestment and Disinvestment are synonymous.

References

Ahmed, M. U. in Privatization in South Asia. (ed) Gopal Goshi, ILO, New Delhi, (2000), p. 27.

Alamgir, M., Nationalized Industries of Bangladesh: Problems and Prospects. *The Bangladesh Development Studies,* Vol. II, No. 3, 1974. p. 704.

Amnuay, V. Privatization:Financial choice and Opportunities. International Centre for Economic Growth Publication, California, (1992), p. 8

Annual Report, Kantale Sugar Industries Ltd., Sri Lanka, (1994).

Annual Report,Lanka Loha Hardeware Ltd., Sri Lanka, (1997).

Annual Report, Pugoda Textile Mills Ltd, Sri Lanka, (1999).

Annual Report, Hingurana Sugar Industries Ltd.,Sri Lanka, (2002).

Backhaus, J., Wagner, R. (Ed) Handbook of Public Finance. Norwell Kluwer Academic Publishers, Boston, (2004), pp. 521-542.

Backhaus, J. Fiscal sociology: Guest editor's introduction, Journal of Economic Behavior & Organization. Volume 59, Issue 4, (2006), pp. 457-459.

Backhaus, J. Fiscal Sociology: What for? American Journal of Economics and Sociology, (2002).

Backhaus, J. The state as a club: a perspective for public finance in a prosperous democracy. Journal of Public Finance and Public Choice, (1992), pp. 3-16.

BALCO Employees Union V. Union of India & Ors. Respondents, Transferred Case (Civil) No. 8 of 2001, Spreme Court of India.

Bangladesh Observer, July 7, 2003, Dhaka

Begum Ferdausa Ara in an Interview with author at Dhaka Chamber of Commerce and Industry (DCCI), (15 March.2003).

Berg, A., Berg, E. Methods of Privatization. Journal of International Affairs, (1997), p. 364.

Bös, D. Privatization: A Theoretical Treatment. Clarendon Press, Oxford, (1991), p. 2.

Budget Speech, Part- I, 2002-03, Ministry of Finance, Government of Bangladesh, Dhaka, pp. 37-38.

Disinvestment Commission, Report 1, Governmnet of India, (1997), p. 17-18.

Disinvestment Policy and Procedures, Department of disinvestment, Gov of India, (2001), p. 22-23.

Dowlah CAF Privatization Experience in Bangladesh 1991-96 Executive Summary. World Bank, Bangladesh, (1997), pp.vi-vii

Fifth Five Year Plan, 1997-2002, Document, Planning Commission, Ministry of Planning, Governmnet of Bangladesh, Dhaka, p. 301

Fiszbein, A. Labour Retrenchment and Redundancy Compensation in the State Owned Enterprises: The Case of Sri Lanka. Internal Discussion Paper, The World Bank, South Asia division, (1992), p.6.

Fourth Five Year Plan, Planning Commission, Ministry of Planning, Government of the Peoples Republic of Bangladesh, Dhaka, (1991), p.xi-8-15.

Galal, A., Jones L., Tandon P., and Vogelsang I., Welfare Consequences of Selling Public Enterprises Oxford University Press, (1994), pp. 13-14.

Gupta, S. P. The Role of National Renewal Fund in Economic Restructuring. In National Renewal Fund- A Look Ahead (ed.) M. L. Nandrajog, ILO, New Delhi, (1998), pp. 183-184.

Hanke, S. Privatization and Development. USAID, (1987), p. 4.

Heald, D. Privatization: Policies, Methods and Procedures. Asian Development Bank, Manila, (1985), p. 58.

Industrial Policy, Government of Bangladesh, Dhaka, (1999), p. 1.

Industrial Policy Resolution, Government of India, New Delhi, (1956).

International Labour Organization (ILO), and Bangladesh Garment Manufacturers and Exporters Association (BGMEA), A Handbook on Relevant National Laws and Regulations of Bangladesh. Dhaka, (2003), pp–7-11, Webster's New Collegiate Dictionary, 9th ed. (1983), p. 936

Karunatilake HNS Public Enterprise and the Private Sector. Sri Lanka Economic Journal, Vol. 1, No.2, (1986), p. 112.

Karunatilake HNS, The Economy of Sri Lanka. CDSS, Colombo, (1987), pp. 145-147.

Kelegama, S. Privatization, The Sri Lanka Experience, Research Studies. Public Enterprises Series No.1, Institute of Policy Studies, Colombo, (1992), pp 24-30.

Kelegama, S. in Anthony Bennett (ed) How does Privatization Work? London: Routledge, (1997), p. 166.

Kelegama S. and Salih R., Labour Retrenchment in a Privatization Programme: The Sri Lankan Experience Sri Lanka Journal of Social Sciences, Vol. 21, Nos. 1 & 2, 1998.

Khan A. R., Hossain M. The Strategy of Development in Bangladesh. London: Macmillan, (1989), p. 82

Leroy P. J., Pankaj Tandon, Ingo Vogelsang, Jones et al., Selling Public Entewrprises: A Cost-Beneift Methodology. London: The MIT Press, (1990), p. 162.

Ministry of Disinvestment, Policy and Procedures, September, 2001 to 27th May, 2004, p. 14-16
Ministry of Finance Budget Speech, Government Press, Sri Lanka, Colombo, (1985).
Ministry of Finance Budget Speech, Government Press, Colombo, (1987), pp 43-44.
Ministry of Finance and Planning Public Investment 1987-91, Colombo, (1987).
Ministry of Industries, Government of Bangladesh, Dhaka, (1976).
Naib S. Partial Divestiture and Performance of Indian Public Sector Enterprise Economic and Political Weekly. XXXviii (29), (2003), pp. 3088-3093.
Naib S. Disinvestment in India: Policies, Procedures, Practices. New Delhi: Sage Publications, (2004).
Mistry, P. The Roots of privatization: Briefing notes for Current debates on public sector issues. France: Public Service International, (1997), p. 10
Public Enterprises Survey, 2001-2002 Vol.1, Ministry of Heavy Industries and Public Enterprises, Government of India, New Delhi.
Raghavan. S. N. Public Sector in India: Changing Perspectives. Asian Institute of Transport Development, New Delhi, (1994), p 92.
Rahman S. 2002-03, Budget Speech, GOB, Ministry of Finance, Part- I.
Rangarajan Committee on Disinvestment of Shares in Public Sector Enterprises, Government of India, (1993).
Report of the Expert Group on Railways headed by Shri Rakesh Mohan (August 2001)- Planning Commission, New Delhi
Report of the Fifth Central Pay Commission, Ministry of Finance, Government of India, New Delhi, (1997).
Report of the Task Force on Employment Opportunities headed by Shri MSAhluwalia (July 2001) Planning Commission, New Delhi.
Reports of the Expenditure Reforms Commission headed by Shri Geethakrishnan (July 2000-September 2001)- Ministry of Finance, Government of India, New Delhi.
Sachs, J. D., Varshney, A., Bajpai, N.(eds) India in the era of Economic Reforms. Oxford University Press, (1999), pp. 1-2.
Savas, E. S. Privatization: The Key to Better Government. New Delhi: Tata Mc Graw-Hill Publication, (1987), p. 3.
Sri Lanka State of the Economy, Institute of Policy Studies, (2003), p. 84.
Sen, B. Whether privatization: Results of an exploratory Survey of the Disinvested Industries in Bangladesh. Mimeo, (1997), pp. 22-23.
Skocpol, T. 1985 as cited in John L. Campbell, The State and Fiscal Sociology, Annual Review of Sociology, Vol. 19, 1993 (1993), pp. 163-185

Smith, A. An Inquiry into the Nature and Causes of the Wealth of Nations, Modern Library, New York (reprint 1937), (1776).

Sobhan, R., Privatization in Bangladesh: An Agenda in Search of a Policy, Centre for Policy Dialouge,Dhaka,1997.

Sobhan, R. and Ahmad. M. Public Enterprises in Intermediate Regime: A Study in the political Economy of Bangladesh. BIDS, Dhaka, (1980), p. 122.

Third Five Year Plan, 1985-90, Planning Commission, Ministry of Planning, Government of the Peoples Republic of Bangladesh, Dhaka, p.v-3.

Wagner, R. States and the crafting of souls: Mind, society, and fiscal sociology. Journal of Economic Behavior & Organization, Volume 59, Issue 4, (2006), pp. 516-524.

World Bank, Bangladesh: Privatization and Adjustment, Report no. 12318-BD, Washington, (March 10 1994), p. i.

Zohir C. S. An Assessment of the Industrial Policy in Bangladesh: What Policies are We Talking About. BIDS Research Report No.142, (1996), p. 6.

Debating European Governance: An Institutionalist Assessment From The Viewpoint Of Political Economy And Fiscal Sociology

Alexander Ebner

1. Introduction

Following the failure of the constitutional project, the current state of European integration is informed by the need for implementing adequate governance structures that fit the enlarged European Union. In accounting for the dimensions of democratic participation, fiscal structures and state capacity, the matter of governance thus ranges among the most important topics of European integration. Indeed, it is safe to argue that institutional entrepreneurship in the formation of governance mechanisms will continuously shape the European policy agenda, as indicated by the German Chancellor's recent assessment of the German EU Presidency[1]. Yet the question remains, which types of strategic frameworks are actually available for pursuing these efforts. This hints at the decisive reform proposal of the Prodi Commission: the White Paper on European Governance. Published in 2001, it discusses major aspects of institutional reform in an enlarged Union[2]. Originally, it had been perceived as a statement of the Commission from the perspective of constitutional design, meant to advance the implementation of a European Constitution. However, it also provides a guideline for assessing the notion of governance as a strategic device in the institution-building efforts European integration is based upon. These aspects of building, reforming and transforming institutional frameworks have been highlighted most promisingly in the context of the various strands of institutionalist political economy. Its current revival also affects the research perspective of fiscal sociology. It explores the interdependence of states and markets as a reflection of exchange processes in the political-economic system, thus claiming that state activity is not to be viewed in isolation from society[3]. The state, its regulatory dynamics, its governance structures, and its fiscal profile can be considered as major research

1 Merkel, A., (2007), Speech to the European Parliament, Brussels, 27 June 2007. http://www.eu2007.de/en/News/-Speeches_Interviews/Juni/0628BKinEP.html.

2 Commission of the European Communities, (2001), *European Governance: A White Paper*, COM (2001) 428, Brussels: Office for Official Publications of the European Communities.

3 Wagner, R. Fiscal Sociology and the Theory of Public Fi-nance: An Exploratory Essay. Cheltenham: Edward Elgar, (2007).

objects of fiscal sociology that are viewed in their co-evolving relationship with the market sphere[4]. Fiscal sociology therefore addresses questions of legitimate political rule and efficient organisation that substantiate the matter of taxation in the evolution of modern states[5]. State-making, institution-building and the formation of markets feed back on each other in the adaptation of governance structures of both the public and private sector[6]. The case of European governance thus provides a most promising research area for fiscal sociology as a strand of institutionalist political economy.

From that perspective, exploring the debate on European governance requires a reconstruction of the governance discourse that was originally stimulated by the European Commission with its White Paper on European Governance from 2001. The first section deals with Commission's diagnosis of the state of European governance in the situation of the Post-Nice process of integration, addressing the prospects for institutional change and policy reform. The second section summarises related arguments on the future course of European governance, highlighting propositions for reorienting both policies and institutions in an enlarged Union. Finally, the third section seeks to evaluate the White Paper's statements in the context of related efforts in theorising on European governance, as stimulated by political economy and fiscal sociology. In conclusion, the assessment of the policy implications of the debate on European governance hints at the need for tackling state-society relations in their significant complexity and thus underlines the persistent relevance of interdisciplinary efforts in governance research.

2. European Governance As A Strategic Perspective On Institutional Reform

The notion of governance has evolved as a major element in the discourse on the prospects of European integration. As such, the matter of European governance designates controversies on the adequate institutional underpinnings of the integration process, framed by attempts to legitimise certain integration strategies

4 Ebner, A. Institutions, Entrepreneurship and the Rationale of Government: An Outline of the Schumpeterian Theory of the State. Journal of Economic Behavior and Organization, Vol.59, No.4, (2006a), pp. 497-515.
Marques, R. Fiscal Sociology: Setting a Research Agenda, Paper Presented at the Annual Meeting of the American Sociological Association, 14-17 August 2004, San Francisco.

5 Swedberg, R. Max Weber and the Idea of Economic Sociology. Princeton: Princeton University Press, (1998), p. 57-61.

6 Fligstein, N., Stone Sweet, A. Constructing Polities and Markets: An Institutionalist Account of European Integration, American Journal of Sociology, Vol.107, No.5., (2002).

and de-legitimise others[7]. The corresponding role of discourse in political and economic change has been outlined most prominently in the sociological works of Pierre Bourdiue's post-structuralist approach to *habitus*. According to Bourdieu, the set of possible discourses serves as an institutional constraint on the full scale of hypothetical options and possibilities, thus channelling strategic efforts for promoting change processes into distinct directions[8]. Accordingly, specific discourses may be said to structure the political domain in a paradigmatic manner, following the logic of an inclusion and exclusion of certain positions in the array of legitimate arguments. It is this characterisation of discourses, which informs a distinct discursive strand in the institutionalist line of reasoning in sociology and political science. It highlights the discursive dimension of institutions in shaping perceptions and understandings which are underlying the diverse orientations of public policy[9]. Thus, discursive institutionalism addresses those discourses, which shape the selective communication of ideas about legitimate political action[10].

Understanding the conceptual implications of the notion of governance, however, requires some specified elaboration. Governance as a topic of discourses on the reform of government and administration is rooted in the perception of a declining state capacity that is said to result from a fiscal crisis of the state in OECD economies since the 1980s, as expressed by the massive increases of budget deficits and public debt, also informing the debate on the policy impact of globalisation[11]. Accordingly, the fiscal structure of the public budget reflects the substance of governance mechanisms in a political-economic system. However, governance involves not only the public sector, but also the private sector and civil society as interactive components. Accordingly, form a governance perspective, public goods may be approached as multi-actor products, for various actors apart from the state are involved in coordinating their provision, in particular coming from the private business sector and the organisations of civil society[12].

---

7 Diez, T. Europe as a Discursive Battleground: Discourse Analysis and European Integration Studies. Cooperation and Conflict, Vol. 36, No.1, (2001), p. 5-6.

8 Bourdieu, P. Outline of a Theory of Practice. Cambridge: Cambridge University Press, (1977), p. 169.

9 Campbell, J. L., Pedersen, O. K. Introduction: The Rise of Neoliberalism and Institutional Analysis. In J. L. Campbell and O. K. Perdersen (eds.) The Rise of Neoliberalism and Institutional Analysis. Princeton: Princeton University Press, (2001), p. 6.

10 Schmidt, V. Give Peace a Chance: Reconciling Four (Not Three) 'New Institutionalisms'. Paper Presented at the Annual Meetings of the American Political Science Association, Philadelphia, PA, Aug. 31-Sept. 3, 2006.

11 Pierre, J., Guy Peters, B. Governance, Politics and the State. Houndmills: Macmillan, (2000), p. 52-53.

12 Kaul (2001), pp. 255-256.

In contrast to the notion of government with its hierarchical connotations, governance addresses reflexive self-organisation and rule-based, decentral steering capacities in the policy domain. Thus, the notion of governance differs from concepts of "political steering" that are the hallmark of an actor centered approach to policy-making. Indeed, governance is the key concept of an institutionalist perspective that deals with regulatory structures combining public and private, hierarchical and network forms of action coordination[13]. Moreover, in terms of its concern with both administrative efficiency and democratic legitimacy, governance is perceived as a cooperative steering approach that should allow for participation, transparency, efficiency and responsibility, quite in accordance with rule-guided procedures that have become prominent in discussions on the reform of government and administration under the moniker of "good governance"[14]. Thus, the notion of governance addresses the organisational conditions for reforming procedures of policy-making in government and administration on the basis of democratic principles, yet it is also concerned with the institutional inclusion of civil society and private sector in the interactive formulation and implementation of public policy[15].

These considerations provide the background for the Prodi Commission's White Paper on "European Governance", published on 25 July 2001. Its four chapters deal with reasons for a reform of the system of governance in the European Union, the principles of good governance, and distinct proposals for change that address the policy-related matter of involvement, regulation and delivery as well as the role of global governance as arguments for refocusing policies and institutions in a comprehensive reform process[16]. In this context, the Commission addresses the notion of governance in agreement with established interpretations from the discourse on reform strategies in government and administration, applied to the matter of European integration: "'Governance' means rules, processes and behaviour that affect the way in which powers are exercised at European level, particularly as regards openness, participation, accountability, effectiveness and coherence"[17]. These principles of good governance represent the conceptual core of the Commission's reform proposals and the underlying strategic outlook on the role of the state in the process of European integration. This exposed status of the

13 Mayntz, R. Governance Theory als fortentwickelte Steuerungstheorie? MPIfG Discussion Paper 04/1, Cologne: Max Planck Institute for the Study of Societies, (2004), p. 5-6.

14 Grindle (1997).

15 Kjaer, A. M. Governance, Cambridge: Polity Press, (2004), p. 3-6.

16 Commission of the European Communities, (2001), European Governance: A White Paper, COM (2001) 428, Brussels: Office for Official Publications of the European Communities, p. 2.

17 Ibid., p. 8.

notion of good governance is also prevalent in the presentation of the key concerns of the White Paper that are presented in its Executive Summary. Right from the outset, the White Paper argues that the complexity of policy formulation and implementation in the European Union is not adequately met by the established institutional set of governance structures and processes, thus contributing to a deepening crisis of legitimacy in its citizenry. The corresponding strategic outlook is characterised as follows: "Many people are losing confidence in a poorly understood and complex system to deliver the policies that they want. The Union is often seen as remote and at the same time too intrusive. (...) The White Paper proposes opening up the policy-making process to get more people and organisations involved in shaping and delivering EU policy. It promotes greater openness, accountability and responsibility for all those involved."[18]

By explicitly addressing a comprehensive array of institutions – involving central government, regions, cities, and civil society – the White Paper underlines an argumentation that perceives governance in a multi-actor and multi-level policy context. With regard to the resulting proposals for change, then, this orientation towards an institutional setting of multi-level governance that should contain a wider sphere of interactions with civil society is accompanied by an emphasis on the need for both legislative and non-legislative instruments. This perspective on governance as an institutional process is presented in terms of a renewal of the Community method of policy-making, which implies a flexibilisation of the separation of legislative and executive powers between Commission, Council and Parliament: "The Union must renew the Community method by following a less top-down approach and complementing its policy tools more effectively with non-legislative instruments"[19]. Accordingly, the flexible correspondence of governance profiles with the institutional mechanisms of deliberative democracy is taken to the fore. In particular, this aspect of public discourse and civil society involvement in the actual terrain of policy-making is reflected by the measures that are specified in the proposals for change. They involve measures of e-Governance provided by the Commission, accompanied by measures that should support interactions with regional and local governments as well as with organisations of civil society. Recommended means are multi-level dialogues among regional, national and Community levels in the policy process, local flexibility in implementing Community legislation, and the standardisation of more transparent consultation procedures, to be accompanied by improvements in the

18 Commission of the European Communities, (2001), European Governance: A White Paper, COM (2001) 428, Brussels: Office for Official Publications of the European Communities, p. 3.

19 Commission of the European Communities, (2001), European Governance: A White Paper, COM (2001) 428, Brussels: Office for Official Publications of the European Communities, p. 4.

preparation of policy results through diverse policy tools, simplified legal rules, more transparent external advice, and improved mechanisms for enforcement and regulation[20].

Moreover, well in addition to the matter of governance in terms of an institutional reform of policy processes, the White Paper refers to the matter of global governance in combination with the notion of good governance, interpreting both as concepts for a more effective international dialogue with governmental and non-governmental actors: "The Union should seek to apply the principles of good governance to its global responsibilities. It should aim to boost the effectiveness and enforcement powers of international institutions"[21]. This strategic orientation towards the international position of the EU is paralleled by a concern with refocused institutions in the division of responsibilities between Commission, Council and Parliament that should allow for increased policy coherence in accordance with established long-term objectives[22]. The latter aspect points to the projected renewal of the Community method as a key concern of the reform of the European system of governance, highlighting a separation of powers in which the European Commission makes specific legislative and policy proposals in its function as guardian of the Treaties, who represents the Community in international negotiations; whereas, fundamental legislative and budgetary acts are adopted by the Council of Ministers as representative of the Member States and the European Parliament as representative of the citizens. While the execution of policy is entrusted to the Commission and national authorities, the European Court of Justice enforces the rule of law[23].

This leads to the question of the Commission's perception of governance as a conceptual framework that should inform the reform of the institutional architecture of the European Union. According to the White Paper, the five principles of openness, participation, accountability, effectiveness and coherence are singled out as factors that underpin good governance and the changes proposed for the institutional reform of policy-making in the European Union, promoting democracy and the rule of law in the Union's setting of multi-level governance. Openness points to the matter of transparency in the formulation and communication of the various policies, paralleled by need for comprehensive participation in an inclusive mode of policy-making. Accountability then shapes the roles of EU institutions as well as national and regional governments and other participating actors in the legislative and executive processes, thus contributing both to the effectiveness of policies and the coherence of these policies and corresponding

20 Ibid., p. 4-5.
21 Ibid., p. 5.
22 Ibid., p. 6.
23 Ibid., p. 8.

action in the complex setting of a European Union its enlargement[24]. Moreover, these principles of good governance are said to reinforce decisive policy-related principles that result from the interpretation of the Treaties, namely proportionality and subsidiarity. They highlight the choice concerning the level at which policy action is actually to be taken as well as the selection of adequate instruments. In conclusion, due to the increasing complexity of the Union's policy agenda regarding both internal and external affairs, the corresponding mode of governance is need of a systematic adaptation towards more flexibility in practice: "This means that the linear model of dispensing policies from above must be replaced by a virtuous circle, based on feedback, networks and involvement from policy creation to implementation at all levels"[25]. With these concerns for civil society participation, then, the White Paper spells out specific proposals for change that need to be translated into detailed reform measures.

As put forward in the Commission's White Paper, the proposals for change regarding the reform of the institutional foundations of policy-making address four distinct points: first, the problems of participation and transparency as key concerns of the governance approach; second, the policy-related aspects of regulation and delivery that pinpoint the public good quality of policy-making; third, the external dimension of the reform process with regard to the matter of global governance; fourth, the strategic orientation of policy-reform and institutional change for the institutional matrix underlying European governance. Thus, even with regard to the discursive structuration of these proposals, the substantial comprehensiveness of the notion of governance, as taken to the fore by the Commission, becomes obvious. It ranges from democratic participation and deliberation over administrative efficiency to global governance. However, while that lack of conceptual specificity may reflect the multi-facetted character of the subject under consideration, it may also promote the realisation of contradictious interpretations.

Regarding the first aspect of an improved involvement of various actors in the process of policy-making, the argumentation of the White Paper takes its point of departure in references to the indispensable role of public debate, involving access to information as a requirement for the participation in communication among actors in the general public. At this point, the Commission is primarily viewed as a provider of knowledge and moderator of knowledge networks, based on information technology in terms of e-Governance[26]. Moreover, reflecting the

24 Ibid., p. 10.

25 Ibid., p. 11.

26 Commission of the European Communities (2001) European Governance: A White Paper, COM (2001) 428, Brussels: Office for Official Publications of the European Communities, p. 11-12.

knowledge-related complexity of multi-level governance, the local and regional level of democratic participation and government activity should be strengthened, paralleling national involvement under conditions of increased flexibility and coherence. This should involve an institutionalised dialogue with European and national associations of regional and local governments, including the Committee of the Regions, as well as by the experimental launching of target-based contracts in the implementation of EU policies[27]. In addition to that, the Commission emphasises the outstanding role of civil society in voicing citizen preferences by promoting structured feedback channels and in delivering collective goods that contribute to meeting these preferences. In this line of reasoning, then, the domain of civil society should include trade unions and employer organisations, from a neo-corporatist perspective actually denoted as social partners, who can reach binding agreements that may be turned into Community law, following the consultation mechanism of the EU platform of social dialogue. Moreover, nongovernmental organisations, professional associations, charities, grass-roots organisations, local and municipal organisations, yet also churches and religious communities are mentioned as constitutive components of civil society[28].

The advocacy of an inclusion of the organisations of civil society in the communication and deliberation networks of European policy making is combined with a hint at the procedural responsibilities that coincide with participatory rights. In particular, the aspects of accountability and openness are mentioned with regard to the possibility of governance failure due to the sclerosis of exclusive networks. As in the case of participatory strategies, technological means of e-Governance are outlined as levers of institutional change, in this case through supplying databases that should assist in the reorientation of the internal structures of civil society organisations towards the principles of good governance[29]. Moreover, the Economic and Social Committee is singled out as an institutional actor that should facilitate corresponding patterns of responsibility – while it is implicitly portrayed as an arena for producer-related interest groups. Indeed, the order of listing the various participants of that Committee speaks for itself, as the White Paper enumerates: "representatives of producers, farmers, carriers, workers, dealers, craftsmen, professional occupations, consumers and the general interest"[30]. Evidently, the potential tension between the interests of both the latter groups and all of the former is not considered to be relevant for further scrutiny.

In agreement with these considerations, the Commission takes up the matter of consultation as a feature of policy deliberation. Beyond the confines of demo-

27 Ibid., p. 12-14.

28 Ibid., p. 14-15.

29 Ibid., p. 14-15

30 Ibid., p. 15.

cratic dialogue with civil society organisations, the use of expert knowledge is taken to the fore as a major issue, which is also of concern for the European Parliament and its committees. At this point, the institutional advantage of a "reinforced culture of consultation and dialogue" is highlighted[31]. Yet the lack of transparency and openness that is potentially related with these network-based modes of European policy making is said to require counter-measures like public reviews of consultative procedures, accompanied by a code of conduct with minimum consultation standards that could even prepare the ground for partnership agreements between the Commission and civil society organisations, combining reform efforts in external and internal governance dimensions[32]. All of this points to the impact of issue-related networks in the domain of European policy making, which need to become more accessible for the general public[33].

The second line of reasoning that is associated with the White Paper's proposals for change highlights the need for improving the implementation of policies, that is, the corresponding modes of regulation and their actual delivery. The underlying argument suggests that EU policies and legislation are getting increasingly complex, thus slowing down the legislative process. Accordingly, policy execution by the Commission needs more attention, reflecting an appreciation of expert advice in informing these policies. Thus, a more efficient mode of policy-related regulation is envisaged, combining effective decision-making with differentiated policy instruments. These need to account for aspects like the relationship between formal rules and non-binding policy tools such as recommendations, guidelines, and self-regulation. Additionally, flexible instruments like framework directives are appreciated together with the primacy of primary legislative instruments that are concerned with basic rules, which should leave their detailed actualisation to the executive. This approach is also prevalent with regard to the notion of co-regulation as a means for combining legislative and regulatory action with actions commonly taken by concerned actors in line with their expertise, thus allegedly promoting rule compliance[34].

At this point, the Commission discusses the "Open Method of Co-ordination", which has evolved as a flexible approach to sector-specific EU policy-making among various Member States, primarily in the areas of employment creation and social policy. It denotes a mode of co-operation through the monitored exchange of best practice in the context of common targets and guidelines. As the institutional character of the "open method" with its state-centred practices ranges well beyond the executive competence of the Commission, it is treated with critical

31 Ibid., p. 16.
32 Ibid., p. 16-17.
33 Ibid., p. 18.
34 Ibid., p. 19-21.

distance, for it is said to potentially upset "the institutional balance" of European governance as defined in the Treaties – with the Commission as the decisive organ of centralised coordination and policy stimulation. Indeed, hinting at the established separation of powers as denoted by the "Community Method", it is argued that the "Open Method" should not be used when legislative action under the procedures of the Community method is possible[35]. However, this argumentation points to an exposed role for the Commission in reforming both the formulation and implementation of legal rules that is said to be indispensable due to the increasing institutional complexity following European enlargement. Indeed, the proposed reorientation of legislation by Council and Parliament towards basic issues should go hand in hand with simplified legal rules, involving the more extensive use of differentiated policy tools like framework directives and co-regulatory mechanisms. This should allow for an improved application of these rules by the regulatory agencies of the EU, promoting their capabilities in drawing on sector-specific knowledge. Moreover, as the application of European Union rules on the national level remains in the domain of the nation-states themselves, strengthening their administrative capacity in terms of good governance strategies is viewed as decisive in proceeding with the rule of law. In this setting, monitoring the application of Community law should remain a task for the Commission, underlining its role as a guardian of the Treaties with supranational competences[36].

3. The Commission's Reform Proposals And Methods Of European Governance

Proceeding with its reform proposals, the Commission explicitly addresses the matter of global governance, claiming that domestic reform will enhance international change and thus support the role of the EU as an actor with global reach[37]. As the reform proposals are directed towards a sustainable division of competences among the various organs and actors of EU multi-level governance, however, the White Paper goes on with discussing the need for refocused policies and institutions. Actually it is argued that refocusing policies would allow for identify

35 Commission of the European Communities (2001) European Governance: A White Paper, COM (2001) 428, Brussels: Office for Official Publications of the European Communities, p. 22-23.

36 Ibid., p. 23-25.

37 Commission of the European Communities (2001) European Governance: A White Paper, COM (2001) 428, Brussels: Office for Official Publications of the European Communities, p. 26-27.

more clearly the long term objectives of the EU: "These may, with the overall objective of sustainable development, include improving human capital, knowledge and skills; strengthening both social cohesion and competitiveness; meeting the environmental challenge; supporting territorial diversity; and contributing to regional peace and stability"[38]. In meeting these long term objectives, the Commission views itself as the decisive organ for initiating policy-related activities and steering the long-term agenda of European integration. Accordingly, the need for refocusing policies should promote the use of a revitalised Community method as an institutional framework that resembles a seemingly traditional yet controversial separation of powers between Commission, Council and Parliament: "Everyone should concentrate on their core tasks: the Commission initiates and executes policy; the Council and the European Parliament decide on legislation and budgets – whenever possible in Council using qualified majority voting, the European Council exerts political guidance and the European Parliament controls the execution of the budget and of the Union's policies"[39].

In particular, the Commission provides an assessment of its own function in the mechanism of European governance that underlines "Treaty tasks of policy initiation; execution; guardian of the Treaty; and international representation of the Community"[40]. The Council of Ministers is criticised for a lack of capacity in political leadership needed for arbitrating between sector-specific interests, allegedly facing the situation that the Union has moved from a "diplomatic process" of partly formal and partly informal bargaining procedures to a "democratic process" of rule-based, transparent negotiations among legitimised policy actors. The European Parliament and the parliaments of the Member States are then singled out for stimulating public debates on the course of European integration; a function that should accompany efforts in monitoring the execution of EU policies and the implementation of the budget. In doing so, policy-oriented control measures based on political objectives were to replace procedures of detailed accounting that would lack strategic considerations[41]. This should lead to a situation where simplified legislation could outline the basic terrain for the Commission's executive role, to be monitored by Council and Parliament. Thus, legislative practices should assist in restructuring the complex set of regulatory and management committees under the leadership of the Commission[42].

38 Ibid., p. 28.
39 Ibid., p. 29.
40 Ibid., p. 29.
41 Ibid., p. 29-30.
42 Commission of the European Communities (2001) European Governance: A White Paper, COM (2001) 428, Brussels: Office for Official Publications of the European Communities, p. 31.

Following these considerations, the White Paper finally outlines the course of European integration as an institutional process that is based on well established principles of good governance, namely openness, participation, accountability, effectiveness and coherence, which are said to promote the related principles of proportionality and subsidiarity, prominent within the conceptual framework of the Treaties[43]. Moreover, the principles of good governance are also interpreted as key concepts for promoting a political vision of multi-level governance in the European Union with the Commission as decisive organ for monitoring, guidance and political leadership. This orientation is also emphasised by the summarising enumeration of strategic thrusts that are said to promote the reform of policy making and policy implementation in the European Union. Generally, the proposals in the White Paper are said to contribute to the restructuring of the European Union's relationship with civil society, involving a code of conduct for consultation that addresses the matter of responsibility and accountability and by doing so enhances a public dialogue, which contributes to the openness of civil society organisations. A related topic is the potential for making use of the dispersed skills, capabilities and knowledge segments of regional and local actors. The proposals for reforming the mechanisms of European governance are thus to be interpreted as means for mobilising and using local knowledge for the purpose of the Community at large. In this line of reasoning, the European Union's multi-disciplinary system for communicating expert advice is to be made more transparent by opening it up to extended public debates[44]. Further topics in the governance agenda of the Commission are outlined by emphasising the need for establishing a more flexible mode of promoting EU policies, combining formal legislation with non-legislative and self-regulatory mechanisms. EU regulatory agencies should support these efforts by elaborating on sector-specific governance. Generally, a refocusing of the institutions of the European Union is taken to the fore. Yet these reform proposals are not necessarily linked with Treaty changes, for the Commission underlines the need for political leadership within the established framework: "Carrying these actions forward does not necessarily require new Treaties. It is first and foremost a question of political will"[45].

Also the implementation of the reform proposals should primarily yield a refocusing of the decisive institutions in the scheme of European governance, namely Commission, Council, and Parliament. The proposals are meant to strengthen the leadership role of the Commission by allowing for a more targeted use of the right of initiative, as the mechanisms of consultation and involvement should support

43 Ibid., p. 32.
44 Ibid., p. 33.
45 Ibid.

knowledge flows from other political institutions and civil society organisations. With EU legislation focussed on basic rules and regulations, Council and Parliament should be enabled to concentrate on long-run issues of political content in their legislative activities, while detailed operations are left to the executive, that is, the Commission. Therefore, the White Paper promotes strengthening the executive position of the Commission in a refocused separation of powers between the organs and actors of European governance[46]. In addition to the matter of competences among the organs of the European Union, the reconsideration of the mechanisms of multi-level governance in the process of European integration is said to require the effective involvement of national and regional organs and actors in the EU policy process, involving the formulation and implementation of adequate rules. A this point, the White Paper points to the need for intensified dialogue, institutional decentralisation as well as sustained co-operation between the involved administrations. Yet there is a second effect mentioned, which is oriented towards approaching national and regional governance organs as communicative transmission belts of the Commission, as they are designated for informing the relevant national and regional public about EU policies[47]. Implicitly, the Commission stylises itself as a nodal centre of communication networks with a European reach.

This self-assessment, as well as the underlying strategic orientation, is in line with the emphasis on a renewal of the Community method in the face of international governance challenges. Again, the Community method as a scheme for the separation of powers that is said to follow from the practice which has been established with the political formation of the Union, informed by the Treaty principles of subsidiarity and proportionality, is defined as follows: "This means ensuring that the Commission proposes and executes policy; the Council and the European Parliament take decisions; and national and regional actors are involved in the EU policy process"[48]. While the Commission argues in favour of the co-decision procedure that allows for taking joint decisions by Council and European Parliament, the Commission alone is to assume responsibility for executive action. Yet this scheme includes also an allocation of competences to the Union and the Member States, approached in terms of a vision of the future of "a Union based on multi-level governance in which each actor contributes in line with his or her

46 Commission of the European Communities (2001) European Governance: A White Paper, COM (2001) 428, Brussels: Office for Official Publications of the European Communities, p. 33-34.

47 Commission of the European Communities (2001) European Governance: A White Paper, COM (2001) 428, Brussels: Office for Official Publications of the European Communities, p. 34.

48 Ibid., p. 34.

capabilities or knowledge to the success of the overall exercise", involving rules for sharing competences on different levels of the governance system[49].

The actual implementation perspective of these proposals was directed towards the Laeken Council, which was followed by a process of constitutional design in the European Convention that should provide the conceptual horizon for institutional reform. According to the Commission, several of the topics regarding institutional reform, as addressed in the White Paper, have been taken up in the draft constitutional treaty. This involves the general reference to a renewed Community method, yet also the emphasis on the principles of good governance in Article I-50[50]. Indeed, the Commission's assessment of the Constitution speaks for itself: "The conclusion can therefore be drawn that the Constitution has incorporated the debate on the reform on European governance at the level of primary Union law"[51]. The current state of the constitutional project, however, provides decisive arguments for re-assessing the debate on the White Paper in terms of its strategic relevance – in particular with regard to the aspects of democratic participation and legitimacy, which have been identified as major problems in the failed ratification of the Constitution. Indeed, already the introductory remarks of the White Paper – pinpointing the fact that the Union is often seen as too remote and as too intrusive at the same time[52] – remain significant for current attempts of realigning strategies for institutional reform with the preferences of the citizenry.

In summary, the White Paper hints at the primary concern with institutional reform in the multi-level system of European governance by promoting principles like openness, accountability and responsibility. Regarding the aspects of participation, consultation and dialogue, the involvement of national, regional and local levels of policy-making is addressed, accompanied by a concern with the involvement of the organisations of civil society. In promoting flexible policy tools, paralleling a formalised role of expert advice, the corresponding policy framework should be made compatible with the principles of good governance. Yet underlying these concerns is also the search for a well defined separation of powers, as the Commission emphasises its executive role. This line of reasoning has been upheld quite rigorously in the Commission's subsequent interpretations of the White Paper: "The basic message was a simple one and is as topical now as it was then: we need to *govern ourselves better, together* – European institutions and Member States. We can do this *without changing the Treaty*, without necessarily waiting for the successful outcome of a new intergovernmental con-

49 Ibid., 34-35.
50 Ibid., p. 12-13.
51 Ibid., p. 14.
52 Ibid., p. 3.

ference[53]. Indeed, it is claimed that the Community method produces universal rules in support of legal certainty. The Commission then concludes on the dynamism of institutional reform in the setting of European governance: "Changing what is amenable to change, without necessarily awaiting a reform of the Treaties; and in doing so, safeguarding the conditions for legal certainty; clarifying ways in which the Treaties can be deepened, and thus facilitating reform of the Treaties: this is the basic element which has emerged from the concept of European governance"[54].

Again, in the view of the failed ratification process of the European Constitution, this emphasis on the possibility of institutional reform within the established set of Treaties is a decisive point in the Commission's position, as promoted by the White Paper. While Commission, Council and Parliament should improve their interactions in the established framework of the separation of powers, the most significant implications of the governance approach are said to address the European Convention and its preparations for laying the groundwork of a European Constitution, perceived in terms of a "quiet revolution"[55]. However, since the project of the European Constitution has run into major difficulties while the separation of powers remains subject to controversies, currently mirrored by conflicts on budget affairs, the long-run view on the EU policy agenda is shaped by the need for coping with the status of participatory democracy in European governance. This aspect hints first of all at the multi-level character of European governance, which has consistently shaped the Commission's further reflections on that topic: "European governance is about the principles and tools for decision-making within the context of the multiple layers of players and decision-makers in Europe — from the European Community, through the Member States, to regional and local authorities and private parties. The coexistence and intertwining of several governance levels clearly constitute unprecedented challenges"[56]. According to the Commission's viewpoint, thus, the matter of governance is primarily a matter of the exercise of power, as governance comprises of "any rules, processes and practices that affect the quality of how powers are exercised."[57]

---

53 Commission of the European Communities (2002c) European Governance: Better Lawmaking, COM (2002) 275 final, Brussels: Office for Official Publications of the European Communities, emphasis in original.

54 Ibid., p. 5.

55 Ibid., p. 5-6.

56 Commission of the European Communities, *Report* from the Commission on European Governance, Brussels: Office for Official Publications of the European Communities, (2003), p. 31.

57 Commission of the European Communities (2004) Report on European Governance (2003-2004), SEC (2004) 1153, Brussels: Office for Official Publications of the European Communities, p. 3.

Moreover, the matter of participation implies a reconsideration of interactions with the organisations of European civil society: "Interaction between the European Institutions and society takes various forms: – primarily through the European Parliament as the elected representative of the citizens of Europe; – through the institutionalised advisory bodies of the EU (Economic and Social Committee and the Committee of the Regions), based on their role according to the Treaties; – and through less formalised direct contacts with interested parties"[58]. According to related statements by the Commission, this perception of civil society addresses a variety of interested parties involved in the management of socio-economic affairs even beyond the "third sector" of civic activities: "So 'civil society organisations' are the principal structures of society outside of government and public administration, including economic operators not generally considered to be 'third sector' or NGOs"[59]. Yet apart from civil society involvement as a requirement of deliberative democratic legitimacy, the underlying concern with steering and regulation addresses the functional coordination of knowledge. Indeed, the inclusive participation of civil society actors in the procedures of European governance should promote knowledge flows to the benefit of the steering efforts of the EU executive, that is, the Commission. Similarly, as outlined in the White Paper, expert advice is addressed as means for mobilising specific knowledge segments in the wider context of policy making: "Expertise forms an integral part of a dynamic knowledge-based society. Specialist know-how and skills help create new opportunities that can boost competitiveness and enhance our quality of life[60]. Related problems of decision-making under uncertainty, also owing to technological complexity, require the accountability, plurality and integrity of expert advice, as echoed by reforms concerning the system of scientific committees in the areas of food safety and consumer protection[61].

58 Commission of the European Communities (2002a) Towards a Reinforced Culture of Consultation and Dialogue – General Principles and Minimum Standards for Consultation of Interested Parties by the Commission, COM(2002) 704 final, Brussels, 11.12.2002, Brussels: Office for Official Publications of the European Communities, p. 1.

59 Ibid., p. 6.

60 Commission of the European Communities (2002b) On the Collection and Use of Expertise by the Commission: Principles and Guidelines – Improving the Knowledge Base for Better Policies, COM(2002) 713 final, Brussels: Office for Official Publications of the European Communities, p. 1.

61 Commission of the European Communities (2002b) On the Collection and Use of Expertise by the Commission: Principles and Guidelines – Improving the Knowledge Base for Better Policies, COM(2002) 713 final, Brussels: Office for Official Publications of the European Communities, p. 3-4.

4. Debating The White Paper: Democracy, Legitimacy And Multi-Level Governance

What are the common concerns in these arguments on European governance – as promoted by the Commission's White Paper and the elaborations it has stimulated subsequently? So far, academic discourse has been mostly critical of the White Paper, still acknowledging its stimulating role for subsequent developments in the discourse on institutional reform. The neo-institutional approach, in particular, which analyses the dynamism of both the processes of policy making and changes in their institutional conditions, has been most relevant for discussions of European governance[62]. Indeed, it has been claimed that debates on European democracy and the Constitutional foundations of European governance have commonly emphasised good governance in terms of efficient performance, stressing the aspect of "output legitimacy", whereas more recent arguments have put an emphasis on democratic participation in terms of "input legitimacy"[63]. This distinction refers to a notion of output legitimacy as efficient political-administrative problem-solving in terms of "government for the people"; whereas input legitimacy denotes a political responsiveness to citizen's preferences in terms of "government by the people"[64]. Nonetheless, critical reconsiderations of the White Paper highlight its specific way of dealing with problems of input and output legitimacy, perceived in terms of the participatory accessibility of the process of policy making and the efficiency of its outcomes in a multi-level setting[65]. Basically, then, it has been suggested that the decisive problem of European governance is an implicit elitism combined with lacking democratic legitimacy, in particular regarding the self-stylised leadership role of the Commission. Instead, the need for more inclusive and participatory governance modes, as discussed in terms of the need for substituting output legitimacy by input legitimacy, requires a rule-based framework of democratic criteria[66]. Accordingly, the Commission's strategic neglect of an inclusive participation of democratic citizenship and

62 Kohler-Koch, B. Interdependent European Governance. in B. Kohler-Koch (ed.) Linking EU and National Governance, Oxford: Oxford University Press, (2003), p. 10-11.

63 Kohler-Koch, B. Interdependent European Governance. In B. Kohler-Koch (ed.) Linking EU and National Governance, Oxford: Oxford University Press, (2003), p. 4.

64 Scharpf, F. Problem-Solving Effectiveness and Democratic Accountability in the EU. MPIfG Working Paper 03/1, Cologne: Max Planck Institute for the Study of Societies, (2003), p. 2-3.

65 Cygan, A. The White Paper on European Governance – Have Glasnost and Perestroika Finally Arrived to the European Union? Modern Law Review, Vol.65, No.2, (2002), p. 231.

66 Kohler-Koch, B. The Commission White Paper and the Improvement of European Governance, in C. Joerges, Y. Meny and J. H. H. Weiler (eds.) Mountain or Molehill? A Critical Appraisal of the Commission White Paper on Governance, Jean Monnet Working Paper No.6/01. New York: Jean Monnet Program, (2001), p. 5-8.

organised civil society, favouring in its place a consultative feedback mechanism, is harshly criticised: "Participatory democracy is a bottom up process of raising voice rather than a top down one of granting consultation rights. This concept is clearly input-oriented and rests on a shared understanding that democracy is a social endeavour based on communication and social transaction"[67].

Even more than that, the Commission's proposals has been denounced as a centralist and even authoritarian attempt of "the creation of a benevolent dictatorship"[68]. However, this may suffice as a pointed characterisation of a conceptual trend in the White Paper's treatment of governance approaches, characterised by an implicit bias towards uniformity across the EU and accompanied by efforts in centralising competences for policy making with the Commission, as reflected by its promotion of the Community method[69]. In more cautious and defensive terms, it has been also claimed that the White Paper represents the Commission's efforts in countering the spread of cooperative ventures of Council and Parliament that would circumvent the Commission's authority through strengthening informal contacts in the framework of co-decision procedures[70]. This interpretation assesses the White Paper as an attempt of regaining an irreversibly decreasing role as centralist steering authority. This argumentation points towards the political economy of European governance with its distinct pattern of conflict and cooperation among political organs and interest groups. Indeed, the governance approach to European integration needs to account for the fundamental role of power relations and dependency aspects in policy making and the exercise of political rule[71]. Accordingly, Schmitter's definition of governance deals with aspects of credible commitment in political bargaining processes: "Governance is a method / mechanism for dealing with a broad range of problems / conflicts in which actors regularly arrive at mutually satisfactory and binding decisions by negotiating and deliberating with each other and co-

---

67 Kohler-Koch, B. Synthesis of the Debates, Presentation at the Conference Participatory Democracy: Current Situation and Opportunities provided by the European Constitution. Comité Économique et Social Européen, Brussels, 8-9 March 2004, p. 9.

68 Scharpf, F. European Governance: Common Concerns vs. The Challenge of Diversity. In C. Joerges, Y. Meny and J. H. H. Weiler (eds.) Mountain or Molehill? A Critical Appraisal of the Commission White Paper on Governance. Jean Monnet Working Paper No.6/01, New York: Jean Monnet Program, (2001), p. 7.

69 Scott, J., Trubek, D. M. Mind the Gap: Law and New Approaches to Governance in the European Union. European Law Journal, Vol.8, No.1, (2002), pp. 15-16.

70 Héritier, A. The White Paper on European Governance: A Response to Shifting Weights in Inter-Institutional Decision-Making. In C. Joerges, Y. Meny and J. H. H. Weiler (eds.) Mountain or Molehill? A Critical Appraisal of the Commission White Paper on Governance. Jean Monnet Working Paper No.6/01, New York: Jean Monnet Program, (2001), pp. 1-2.

71 Jachtenfuchs, M. The Governance Approach to European Integration. Journal of Common Market Studies, Vol.39, No.2, (2001), p. 258.

operating in the implementation of these decisions"[72]. The institutional domain of governance then includes innovative practices, based on repeated procedures of deliberative interaction involving the evolution of trust and mutual accommodation between organisations. Governance is thus more likely to contribute to the solution of persistently pressing legitimacy problems in European policy making than conventional practices of hierarchical government[73].

Pointing in a similar direction, Neil Fligstein argues that institutions and governance structures in market economies tend to feed back into economic activity and thus promote the symbiotic development of markets and polities as self-reinforcing fields that comprise of organisations which seek to structure their environment, being constrained as well as enabled by established institution. Viewed from that position, the European Union represents an evolving governance system that is based on the simultaneous construction of markets and polities. As such, it provides evidence for the parallel advance of "negative" and "positive" integration. Both are not mutually exclusive, but rather complement each other. At last, this suffices as a confirmation of the suggestion that market formation is based on extended regulations. Accordingly, well functioning markets require governance functions provided by the state as an external enforcer[74]. In the case of European integration, however, the decisive difficulty emerges from the fact that the supranational level of regulation only exhibits a state-like structure that lacks autonomy in terms of democratic legitimacy and fiscal capacity. Accordingly, patterns of European governance will have to differ markedly from the established governance structures that characterise the Member States.

The corresponding tendency of implementing new modes of governance in the European Union is well reflected by a perception of the Open Method of Coordination as a means for promoting "democratic experimentalism", that is, a mode of decentralised decision making based on networks that are oriented towards establishing common standards through deliberative processes[75]. Setting the complex legal and institutional underpinnings of European integration in the context of a more general trend in state transformation, thus, Charles Sabel argues that current patterns of change in governance may lead to a participatory

72 Schmitter, P.C. What is there to Legitimize in the European Union… and How might this be Accomplished? In C. Joerges, Y. Meny and J.H.H. Weiler (eds.) Mountain or Molehill? A Critical Appraisal of the Commission White Paper on Governance. Jean Monnet Working Paper No.6/01, New York: Jean Monnet Program, (2001), p. 4.

73 Ibid., p. 4-5.

74 Fligstein, N., Stone Sweet, A. Constructing Polities and Markets: An Institutionalist Account of European Integration. American Journal of Sociology, Vol.107, No.5, (2002), p. 1206-1210.

75 Eberlein, B, Kerwer, D. New Governance in the European Union: A Theoretical Perspective. Journal of Common Market Studies, Vol.42, No.1, (2004), p. 133-134.

form of democratic experimentalism, differing from established neo-corporatist practices of administrative states, as the administrative centre now tends to set general standards and provides infrastructures for local units, which are striving for their own goals, allowing for coordinated learning strategies that tap local knowledge, by doing so promoting public accountability[76]. In particular, this type of democratic experimentalism allows for combining local innovation and public accountability through the mutual coordination of public institutions as well as the drive for social learning in a coherent societal setting[77]. Applied to the European Union, then, the proposed mode of reflexive governance allegedly informs a new architecture of public rule making, which involves a procedure in which framework goals and related implementation mechanisms are set up jointly by the European organs and the Member States, while lower level units in the national and regional domain may advance these ends in accordance with local conditions and traditions. Thus, the subsidiarity principle remains decisive in the implementation of rules and regulations. Still, the lower level units are also held accountable for their performance, as they are subject to benchmarking, peer reviews and revision proposals. Crucially, this kind of experimental procedure implies that specific governance functions may be carried out by a variety of institutional means, which allows for an adaptation of jointly set policy propositions to local capabilities[78].

Accordingly, it seems that the notion of governance may be accompanied by conceptual proposals for an institutional devaluation of constitutional rules as a source of state sovereignty and political authority to the benefit of more flexible arrangements based on the capabilities of political entrepreneurship in defining the opportunity space of state capacity[79]. Such a view, however, is highly problematic, for constitutional rules need not imply a static view on state capacity. Even in a dynamic setting they come to define a consensual set of general rules that may promote political entrepreneurship and institutional innovation in a setting of constitutional search, experimentation and discovery. In this manner, constitutional rules are indispensable for the maintenance of an adaptively flexible institutional structure of governance mechanisms. Similar variants of the

---

76 Sabel, C. F. A (ed.) Quiet Revolution of Democratic Governance: Towards Democratic Experimentalism, in Organisation for Economic Co-Operation and Development. Governance in the 21st Century, Paris: OECD, (2001), p. 123.

77 Ibid., p. 142.

78 Sabel, C. F., Zeitlin, C. Learning From Difference: The New Architecture of Experimentalist Governance in the European Union. European Governance Papers No. C-07-02, http:www.connex-network.org/eurogov/pdf/egp-connex-C-07-02.pdf, (2007), p. 6-7.

79 Pierre, J., Guy Peters, B. Governance, Politics and the State. Houndmills: Macmillan, (2000), p. 83.

governance discussion are related with the arguments of deliberative democracy, arguing in favour of small-scale decision-making institutions and individual involvement in the political process in order to counter widespread alienation and estrangement in democratic systems[80]. However, the critique of this position hints at asymmetries in the capability for agenda setting, resulting in a distortion of the deliberative profile to the benefit of selected special interests[81].

This is a crucial aspect of the governance perspective at large. Apart from the multi-level interactions between the designated legitimate actors of the process of policy making, such a perspective involves the communicative inclusion of a variety of organisation representing the diverse interests within an evolving civil society in a transparent and accountable manner that combines legitimation and efficiency considerations. For instance, in more concrete terms, the case has been made for restructuring the European Economic and Social Council. As it represents functional interests with an emphasis on neo-corporatist arrangements on the national level of interest aggregation, it is said to lack from a pluralist representation of the more diverse interest groups in European civil society[82]. Thus, it is primarily the reference to multi-level governance in the Commission's White Paper that remains of utmost importance for addressing European governance in its current post-constitutional phase. Yet this perspective needs to be combined with an exploration of the institutional transformation of the nation-state in order to produce a viable analytical framework for further reconsiderations.

At this point, it may be useful to invoke Christian Joerges' outline of well-established governance modes in the European Union. In criticising Sabel's approach of experimentalist governance as a perspective that contradicts the norms and values of the rule of law, Joerges pinpoints the fact that various governance mechanisms have already become vibrant components of policy making on the European Union that are set apart from the Community method. These governance mechanisms contain the following components[83].

- The System of Comitology. The European system of committees is basically concerned with the implementation of Community law framework provisions that are most relevant in the administration and regulation of the Common Market, reflecting the negotiations among expert groups that make up certain committees in related regulatory domains.

80 Ibid., p. 139.

81 Ibid., p. 155-156.

82 Kohler-Koch, B. Synthesis of the Debates, Presentation at the Conference Participatory Democracy: Current Situation and Opportunities provided by the European Constitution. Comité Économique et Social Européen, Brussels, 8-9 March 2004, p. 15.

83 Joerges, C. Integration Through De-Legislation? European Governance Papers No. N-07-03, (2007), http:www. connex-network.org/eurogov/pdf/egp-newgov-N-07-03.pdf, p. 9-12.

- The Principle of Mutual Recognition. Following the European Court of Justice's paradigmatic *Cassis de Dijon* decision, the principle of the mutual recognition of national law has been singled out as a major stimulant for inter-jurisdictional competition. At least, an opening of national legal systems to viewpoints of other systems has been observed.
- The New Approach to Technical Harmonisation and Standardisation. In this operative framework, European law-making would be concerned with essential regulations whose actual content and implementation would be left to expert groups on the European and national level that regularly include non-state actors.
- The System of Agencies. In a regulatory manner, a set of European agencies has become relevant in the governance structures of the Common Market, exercising market-correcting functions on the basis of a semi-autonomous status in their working relationship with the Commission.
- The Open Method of Coordination. A multilateral coordination process that is based on benchmarking procedures and non-binding guidelines laid down by European Council, Council and Commission as means for promoting policy learning of the Member States in selected policy fields.

Taken together, all of these governance mechanisms are an outcome of institutional efforts in the regulation of the Common Market. Indeed, while integration through law had been dominant for long in the integration process, especially the Delors Commission's project of completing the Common Market had paved the way for regulatory schemes that would later on inform the "governance turn" of the Prodi Commission[84].

Thus, the persistent relevance of the Commission's White Paper on European Governance may be derived from the attempt of combining a problematical modification of the division of competences between the Community organs with actually pressing problems regarding the combination of administrative efficiency and democratic legitimacy in a setting of multi-level governance. Adding to that dimension of institutional complexity, the process of economic globalisation exerts adaptive pressures on national and regional governance modes. An influential diagnosis of the situation of the European political economy thus draws on fundamental asymmetry and legitimacy problems that result from an institutional competitive pressure for deregulation on the national level, which contrast with the need for supranational modes of correcting market failure. Indeed, in this line of reasoning, the national varieties of capitalist market economies will prevail in the foreseeable future, while European policy making needs to remain

84 Joerges, C., (2007), Integration Through De-Legislation? European Governance Papers No. N-07-03, http:www.-connex-network.org/eurogov/pdf/egp-newgov-N-07-03.pdf, p. 18.

consensual; whereas, attempts of establishing centralist modes of regulation on a European level, involving aspects like majority rule accompanied by the Community method, are viewed as a recipe for disaster[85].

In proceeding with this matter of institutional variety, the perspective of differentiated integration is put forward, owing to the need for coping with both input- and output legitimacy in the European Union, placed in a setting of indispensable supra-national solutions that can deal with the regulation and correction of cross-border externalities, among others[86]. The persistence of the institutional arrangements for economic coordination and power distribution that characterise the varieties of capitalist market economies still underlines the pointlessness in endorsing institutional convergence[87]. Europe is not to be envisioned as a hierarchical and unitary entity, endowed with institutional competences for wide ranging political steering as implicitly suggested by the White Paper. Rather, a viable political project of European integration needs to account for the persistence of the nation-state and thus for the requirement of establishing an inclusive mode of Europeanising identities that could be promoted by an array of transnational intermediary organisations[88]. In other words, adequate mechanisms of European governance need to cope with distinct governance styles in a setting of multi-level interactions that allow for both competition and cooperation in a common institutional framework[89]. For instance, a model of transnational pluralism in the European Union, as proposed by Streeck and Schmitter some time ago, would imply a type of disjointed pluralism and competitive federalism with differentiated regional, national and supra-national levels of interaction that cover diverse actors and interests[90]. Yet European governance becomes ever more complex due

---

85 Scharpf, F., (2001), European Governance: Common Concerns vs. The Challenge of Diversity, in C. Joerges, Y. Meny and J.H.H. Weiler (eds.) Mountain or Molehill? A Critical Appraisal of the Commission White Paper on Governance, Jean Monnet Working Paper No.6/01, New York: Jean Monnet Program, p. 4-5.

86 Scharpf, F., (2003), Problem-Solving Effectiveness and Democratic Accountability in the EU, *MPIfG Working* Paper 03/1, Cologne: Max Planck Institute for the Study of Societies, p. 17-18.

87 Boyer, R. How and Why Capitalisms Differ. MPIfG Discussion Paper 05/4, Cologne: Max Planck Institute for the Study of Societies, (2005), p. 23-25.

88 Kohler-Koch, B. The Commission White Paper and the Improvement of European Governance. In C. Joerges, Y. Meny and J.H.H. Weiler (eds.) Mountain or Molehill? A Critical Appraisal of the Commission White Paper on Governance. Jean Monnet Working Paper No.6/01, New York: Jean Monnet Program, (2001), p. 13-14.

89 Ebner, A. The Intellectual Foundations of the Social Market Economy: Theory, Policy and Implications for European Integration. Journal of Economic Studies, Vol.33, No.3, (2006b).

90 Streeck, W., Schmitter, P.C. From National Corporatism to Transnational Pluralism: Organized Interests in the Single European Market. In W. Streeck (ed.) Social Institutions and Economic Performance: Studies of Industrial Relations in Advanced Capitalist Economies, London: Sage, (1992), p. 227.

to the ongoing process of globalisation, as the nation-state is transformed into a complex structure of associations that confronts its capacity for economic regulation. The corresponding institutional architecture functions as a polycentric system that coincides with a drive for shared sovereignty in cooperation and integration[91]. However, in such a setting, the question of the democratic legitimacy of political rule prevails – and it is particularly pressing with regard to the options for the institutional reform of governance structures in the European Union[92].

At this point, at last, the matter of constitutional design and implementation comes to the fore once again. Viewed from the perspective of constitutional law and economics, it highlights the need for rules and regulations that structure the process of policy-making by establishing well-defined propositions for a separation of political powers and their bargaining relations[93]. Indeed, the underlying aspects of adapting political governance structures to changing economic conditions make the European Union a prime example of the trial-and-error procedures that characterise institution-building in general[94]. Augmenting these considerations with arguments from fiscal sociology, however, implies the transcending of the dichotomy of state and market in favour of an exploration of their interdependence with regard to the exchange processes in the political-economic system. Again, the aspect of legitimacy plays a decisive role in the corresponding stylisation of state-society relations that shape the actual profile of governance structures and institution-building. This is the actual background for the claim that state-making, institution-building and the formation of markets feed back on each other in the evolution of governance structures[95]. In particular due to its discursive impact, thus, the Prodi Commission's White Paper on European Governance may accordingly be interpreted as an exercise in the political construction of legitimate governance structures that comes together with the formation of statecraft[96]. After all, these aspects may contribute decisively to a more sub-

---

91 Cerny, P. G. Structuring the Political Arena: Public Goods, States and Governance in a Globalizing World. In R. Palan (ed.) Global Political Economy: Contemporary Theories, London: Routledge, (2000).

92 Kohler-Koch, B., Rittberger, B. Review Article: The 'Governance Turn' in EU Studies. Journal of Common Market Studies, Vol.44, No.1, (2006), p. 41-42.

93 Cooter, R. The Strategic Constitution, Princeton: Princeton University Press, (2000), p. 211-213.

94 Ibid., p. 235-236.

95 Fligstein, N., Stone Sweet, A. Constructing Polities and Markets: An Institutionalist Account of European Integration. American Journal of Sociology, Vol.107, No.5, (2002).

96 Wagner, R. States and the Crafting of Souls: Mind, Society, and Fiscal Sociology. Journal of Economic and Behavior and Organization, Vol.59, No.4, (2006).
Wagner, R. Fiscal Sociology and the Theory of Public Finance: An Exploratory Essay. Cheltenham: Edward Elgar, (2007).

stantial understanding of the institutional processes underlying the future course of European governance.

5. Conclusion

The Prodi Commission's White Paper on European Governance has provided key motives for the debate on the institutional reform that should accompany the process of constitution design and implementation in an enlarged European Union. Despite the failure of the constitutional process, the White Paper still stimulated a discourse on European governance that has come to designate controversies on the adequate institutional underpinnings of the integration process. Indeed, it is actually the persistence of intensified attempts at reform in a provisional institutional setting that underlines the current relevance of the original strategies outlined in the Commission's White Paper. Indeed, it refers to the continuous search for adequate governance structures that support both legitimacy and efficiency in the setting of European integration. In terms of discourse theory, it follows that the White Paper has contributed to a channelling of strategic efforts for promoting institutional change into certain directions, by doing so structuring the political domain through the provision of legitimate arguments and thus shaping a common understanding of reform requirements.

In summary, the White Paper hints at the primary concern with institutional reform in the multi-level system of European governance by promoting principles like openness, accountability and responsibility. Regarding the aspects of participation, consultation and dialogue, the involvement of national, regional and local levels of policy-making is addressed, accompanied by a concern with the involvement of the organisations of civil society. In promoting flexible policy tools, paralleling a formalised role of expert advice, the corresponding policy framework should be made compatible with the principles of good governance. Yet underlying these concerns is also the search for a well defined separation of powers, as the Commission emphasises its executive role. However, since the project of the European Constitution has run into major difficulties while the separation of powers remains subject to controversies, currently mirrored by conflicts on budget affairs, the long-run view on the EU policy agenda is primarily shaped by the need for coping with the status of participatory democracy in European governance.

The latter aspect especially underlines once again the weight of arguments emanating from institutionalist lines of political economy, and here in particular from the reasoning of fiscal sociology with its reconsideration of the institutional underpinnings of the activities of government and administration. The basic proposition of fiscal sociology, namely the claim that the analysis of fiscal affairs and other elements of state activity needs to take into account state-society relations in their full complexity, most obviously connects very well with the debate on European governance. Viewing European integration as a historically specific case of institution-building thus implies that the discursive perceptions and understandings of the involved actors on the legitimacy of political actions are to be taken into account.

References

Bourdieu, P. Outline of a Theory of Practicel Cambridge: Cambridge University Press, (1977).

Boyer, R. How and Why Capitalisms Differ. MPIfG Discussion Paper 05/4, Cologne: Max Planck Institute for the Study of Societies, (2005).

Campbell, J. L., Pedersen, O. K. Introduction: The Rise of Neoliberalism and Institutional Analysis. In J. L. Campbell and O. K. Perdersen (eds.) The Rise of Neoliberalism and Institutional Analysis. Princeton: Princeton University Press, (2001), pp. 1-23.

Cerny, P. G. Structuring the Political Arena: Public Goods, States and Governance in a Globalizing World. In R. Palan (ed.) Global Political Economy: Contemporary Theories. London: Routledge, (2000), pp. 21-35.

Commission of the European Communities (2001) European Governance: A White Paper, COM (2001) 428, Brussels: Office for Official Publications of the European Communities.

Commission of the European Communities (2002a) Towards a Reinforced Culture of Consultation and Dialogue – General Principles and Minimum Standards for Consultation of Interested Parties by the Commission, COM(2002) 704 final, Brussels, 11.12.2002, Brussels: Office for Official Publications of the European Communities.

Commission of the European Communities (2002b) On the Collection and Use of Expertise by the Commission: Principles and Guidelines – Improving the Knowledge Base for Better Policies, COM(2002) 713 final, Brussels: Office for Official Publications of the European Communities.

Commission of the European Communities (2002c) European Governance: Better Lawmaking, COM (2002) 275 final, Brussels: Office for Official Publications of the European Communities.

Commission of the European Communities (2003) Report from the Commission on European Governance, Brussels: Office for Official Publications of the European Communities.

Commission of the European Communities (2004) Report on European Governance (2003-2004), SEC (2004) 1153, Brussels: Office for Official Publications of the European Communities.

Cooter, R. The Strategic Constitution. Princeton: Princeton University Press, (2000).

Cygan, A. The White Paper on European Governance – Have Glasnost and Perestroika Finally Arrived to the European Union? Modern Law Review, Vol.65, No.2, (2002), pp. 229-240.

Diez, T. Europe as a Discursive Battleground: Discourse Analysis and European Integration Studies, Cooperation and Conflict. Vol. 36, No. 1, (2001), pp. 5-38.

Eberlein, B, Kerwer, D. New Governance in the European Union: A Theoretical Perspective. Journal of Common Market Studies, Vol. 42, No. 1, (2004), pp. 21-142.

Ebner, A. Institutions, Entrepreneurship and the Rationale of Government: An Outline of the Schumpeterian Theory of the State. Journal of Economic Behavior and Organization, Vol. 59, No. 4, (2006a), pp. 497-515.

Ebner, A. The Intellectual Foundations of the Social Market Economy: Theory, Policy and Implications for European Integration. Journal of Economic Studies, Vol. 33, No. 3, (2006b), pp. 206-223.

Fligstein, N., Stone Sweet, A. Constructing Polities and Markets: An Institutionalist Account of European Integration. American Journal of Sociology, Vol. 107, No. 5, (2002), pp. 1206-1243.

Héritier, A. The White Paper on European Governance: A Response to Shifting Weights in Inter-Institutional Decision-Making. In C. Joerges, Y. Meny and J.H.H. Weiler (eds.) Mountain or Molehill? A Critical Appraisal of the Commission White Paper on Governance, Jean Monnet Working Paper No. 6/01, New York: Jean Monnet Program, (2001).

Jachtenfuchs, M. The Governance Approach to European Integration. Journal of Common Market Studies, Vol. 39, No. 2, (2001), pp. 245-264.

Joerges, C. Integration Through De-Legislation? European Governance Papers No. N-07-03, (2007), http:www.connex-network.org/eurogov/pdf/egp-newgov-N-07-03.pdf.

Kjaer, A.M. Governance. Cambridge: Polity Press, (2004).

Kohler-Koch, B. The Commission White Paper and the Improvement of European Governance. In C. Joerges, Y. Meny and J.H.H. Weiler (eds.) Mountain or Molehill? A Critical Appraisal of the Commission White Paper on Governance. Jean Monnet Working Paper No. 6/01, New York: Jean Monnet Program, (2001).

Kohler-Koch, B. Interdependent European Governance. In B. Kohler-Koch (ed.) Linking EU and National Governance. Oxford: Oxford University Press, (2003), pp.10-23.

Kohler-Koch, B. Synthesis of the Debates, Presentation at the Conference Participatory Democracy: Current Situation and Opportunities provided by the European Constitution. Comité Économique et Social Européen, Brussels, 8-9 March 2004.

Kohler-Koch, B., Rittberger, B. Review Article: The 'Governance Turn' in EU Studies. Journal of Common Market Studies, Vol. 44, No. 1, (2006), pp. 27-49.

Marques, R. Fiscal Sociology: Setting a Research Agenda. Paper Presented at the Annual Meeting of the American Sociological Association, 14-17 August 2004, San Francisco.

Mayntz, R. Governance Theory als fortentwickelte Steuerungstheorie? MPIfG Discussion Paper 04/1, Cologne: Max Planck Institute for the Study of Societies, (2004).

Merkel, A. (2007) Speech to the European Parliament, Brussels, 27 June 2007. http://www.eu2007.de/en/News/Speeches_Interviews/Juni/0628BKinEP.html.

Pierre, J., Guy Peters, B. Governance, Politics and the State. Houndmills: Macmillan, (2000).

Sabel, C. F. A (ed.) Quiet Revolution of Democratic Governance: Towards Democratic Experimentalism, in Organisation for Economic Co-Operation and Development. Governance in the 21st Century, Paris: OECD, (2001), pp. 121-148.

Sabel, C. F., Zeitlin, C. Learning From Difference: The New Architecture of Experimentalist Governance in the European Union. European Governance Papers No. C-07-02, (2007) http:www.connex-network.org/eurogov/pdf/egp-connex-C-07-02.pdf.

Scharpf, F. European Governance: Common Concerns vs. The Challenge of Diversity. In C. Joerges, Y. Meny and J. H. H. Weiler (eds.) Mountain or Molehill? A Critical Appraisal of the Commission White Paper on Governance. Jean Monnet Working Paper No. 6/01, New York: Jean Monnet Program, (2001).

Scharpf, F. Problem-Solving Effectiveness and Democratic Accountability in the EU. MPIfG Working Paper 03/1, Cologne: Max Planck Institute for the Study of Societies, (2003).

Schmidt, V. Give Peace a Chance: Reconciling Four (Not Three) "New Institutionalisms". Paper Presented at the Annual Meetings of the American Political Science Association, Philadelphia, PA, Aug. 31-Sept. 3, 2006.

Schmitter, P. C. What is there to Legitimize in the European Union… and How might this be Accomplished? In C. Joerges, Y. Meny and J. H. H. Weiler (eds.) Mountain or Molehill? A Critical Appraisal of the Commission White Paper on Governance. Jean Monnet Working Paper No. 6/01, New York: Jean Monnet Program, (2001).

Scott, J., Trubek, D. M. Mind the Gap: Law and New Approaches to Governance in the European Union. European Law Journal, Vol. 8, No. 1, (2002), pp. 1-18.

Streeck, W., Schmitter, P. C. From National Corporatism to Transnational Pluralism: Organized Interests in the Single European Market. In W. Streeck (ed.) Social Institutions and Economic Performance: Studies of Industrial Relations in Advanced Capitalist Economies. London: Sage, (1992), pp. 197-231.

Swedberg, R. Max Weber and the Idea of Economic Sociology. Princeton: Princeton University Press, (1998).

Wagner, R. E. States and the Crafting of Souls: Mind, Society, and Fiscal Sociology, Journal of Economic and Behavior and Organization. Vol. 59, No. 4, (2006), pp. 516-524.

Wagner, R. E. Fiscal Sociology and the Theory of Public Finance: An Exploratory Essay. Cheltenham: Edward Elgar, (2007).

Pareto's sociological maximum of utility of the community and the theory of the elites

F. Forte and P. Silvestri

ABSTRACT

The paper deals with three interrelated Pareto's contributions to fiscal sociology of relevant contemporary importance, i. e., the maximum of utility of the community as a sociological process (Pareto II criterion of maximum welfare), the non logical actions consisting of derivations based on residuals and the theory of the elites. Pareto II welfare criterion of sociological maximization of individual utilities is compared with Pareto I welfare criterion, commonly known as Pareto criterion, introducing the process of valuations by the elite of the utilities of different social groups weighed according to their residuals. Derivations are essentials to persuade the masses to move to the points designed by the elite. The process is subject to the law of circulation of the elites which leads to different sociological equilibriums. The theories of the elites of Pareto and Mosca, criticized by Einaudi, are then compared. For a disenchanted analysis of the fiscal processes and designs, Pareto's sociology may still provide to the economist more than a help.

JEL Codes: H79
Keywords: Paretian sociological maximum, derivations, Pareto's sociological school, theory of elites, Einaudi vs Mosca.

I Introductory Remarks

1. According to Richard Wagner[1] there are two windows from which to look at public finance as a compound of fiscal phenomena. The first one, as exemplified by Antonio De Viti de Marco "Principles of economics of public finance" consists in trying to know how in real life fiscal phenomena do develop. The second exemplified by Henry Simons' work in the same area, in the same epoch, consists in designing the (best) policies leading to the achievement of the given model of government: which for him is the model of a public finance most appropriate for a free society with a free market. De Viti had a similar free society, free trade credo but his primary perspective, in the theory of public finance was different because he was looking at the process not at the design.

The two windows of Wagner may seem to coincide with the dichotomy between positive and normative economic analysis. But they differ from it, because more comprehensive as for the content of the two points of view. Indeed the positive analysis may be done, and is frequently done by the economists, merely consider-

1 R. WAGNER (2007), *Fiscal Sociology and the Theory of Public Finance. An Exploratory Essay,* Cheltenham, Elgar.

ing the effects of the decisions, without looking at the process by which are taken by the decision makers. The normative analysis may be done assuming a given social welfare functions or, more simply, assuming given objectives. The focus of Wagner's distinction is between the point of view of the *process* and that of the *design*, i. e. between the approach in terms of interactions among individuals and groups adopted by the Austrian-Italian-Swedish school of economics of public finance and subsequently by the public choice school and the axiomatic welfare economics school, sometimes defined as Paretian welfare economics. However there is a second reason why Wagner's distinction does not coincide with the familiar dichotomy between positive and normative economics. And it is that the process of public finance and its design may not be satisfactorily explained by the mere economic analysis. It may be fruitful to look at the public finance process and design also from the sociological and the political point of view. It is in this broader perspective that can be fully appreciated Wagner thesis that both windows offer a valid perspective but the second is less interesting than the first. Indeed he argues that an analysis of the process of public economics leads to less unrealistic picture of what can be done by designs imposed to the real processes. And actually a window from where to look at the process of public finance, broadened to include also the sociological and the political point of view may be more realistic. This was done in the first part of the other century, in Italy, by the sociological school inspired by Pareto and by the political school leaded by Griziotti[2], against the economic school of public finance leaded by De Viti De Marco and Einaudi. According to the Italian economic school, as it is well known, the micro economic laws that operate in the market process tend to operate also in public finance and this economic reasoning may be usefully employed in the general explanation of the equilibrium laws of the fiscal processes. According

2 At the origin of Griziotti political approach there was the economic-sociological approach of Giovanni Montermartini with his theory of the political entrepreneur and related theory of the different models of public economy offered by the different political entrepreneurs to the electorate. As one can see, this was an approach in term of process, in which there is a sociological component given by the different kinds of political entrepreneurs competing for the electorate and a political economy component consisting in the models of public economics offered to them. Because a democratic system with a majority rule is assumed, each model implies some redistribution in favour of the majority, but because the political entrepreneurs need to gain votes to get and maintain the political power and there is a competition among them, the political process implies also the pursuance of interests broader than those of the prevailing majority even not necessarily a "strong" Pareto welfare maximum of the community. i. e. a result in which every body has a net gain. See G. MONTEMARTINI (1900), "Le basi fondamentali della scienza finanziaria pura", translated in 1967 as "The fundamental principles of pure theory of public finance", in R. A. MUSGRAVE and A. T. PEACOCK(eds) (1967), *Classics in the theory of public finance*, London McMillan.

to the Paretian sociological school and to the political school of Griziotti[3] the mere economic reasoning based on the marginal utility of the individuals cannot explain fiscal decisions[4].

Pareto's main contributions to fiscal sociology are in his *Trattato di sociologia generale (Treatise of general sociology)* published in 1916[5]. However the foundations of his sociology are already present in his three books of a much earlier period: *Les systèmes socialistes* of 1902, *Cours d'Economie politique* of 1896-7 and *Manuale di economia politica con una introduzione alla scienza sociale* of 1906. In particular both the theory of the non logical actions and the theory of the (circulation of) elites (*"parte eletta"*) are clearly outlined in his *Manuale*[6]. The two interrelated Paretian sociological categories of "residuals" and of "derivations" which characterize the non logical actions appear with these names only in the *Treatise of General Sociology,* but their concepts are already present in the *Manuale.* However the *sociological* maximum of utility *of the community*, by which Pareto puts together these concepts in a systematic view of the sociological process of public economy, is presented only in a paper of 1913 and, subsequently transferred in the *Treatise of General Sociology*[7]. Yet Pareto's other collective maximum, the *economic* maximum of utility *for the community* (defined by him as maximum of ophelimity to underline its subjective nature) is already clearly presented in the *Manuale.* And as we shall see, even if the two maxima are intrinsically different, among them there are several conceptual connections. It must also be noticed that between the theory of élites and of the non logical actions in the *Manuale* and in *Treatise of General Sociology* there is an evolution about the sociology of public finances. Their process in both books is a non logical phenomenon (Pareto clarifies that, from his point of view, non logic is not illogic i. e. irra-

---

3 Which some authors tend to put together but do differ in several aspects and essentially because of the very different way to appreciate the irrational sociological factors. On this point see MCLURE (2007), Chapter 7, especially the paragraph "An assessment", pp. 130-135.

4 As we shall see below, however, for Einaudi this type of research would be useful in a second approximation, to complement the general theory which would be basically economic. And actually he gave some contributions to fiscal sociology as for the theory of elites, particularly with the paper L. EINAUDI (1936). "Il peccato originale e la teoria della classe eletta in Federico Le Play", in *Saggi bibliografici e storici intorno alle dottrine economiche,* Edizioni di storia e letteratura, Roma, 1953, pp. 307-344.

5 Translated into English as *The Mind and Society: A Treatise on General Sociology.* New York: Harcourt, Brace, Jananovich, 1935. Reprint, New York: Dover Publications, 1963. For a recent discussion of Pareto contributions to fiscal sociology in relation to the theory of general economic equilibrium and to the public choices theory see J. G. BACKHAUS and J. A. MAKS, (2006) *From Walras to Pareto,* New York, Springer US.

6 Translated into French three years later and into English only in 1971.

7 See PARETO (1913) "Il massimo di utilità per una collettività in sociologia". *Giornale degli Economisti e rivista di statistica i,* 1913, April, pp. 338-341.

tional), but in the *Manuale* the elites even pursuing their own interest first, *may* favour religious sentiments and ethical values that preserve the social order and the economic prosperity[8], as frequently happened in the past. In the *Treatise e*, without contradicting that positive role of the elites, Pareto's vision is synthesized like this by Busino (2000): "one reality alone is ever lasting: there is a stratification in political and social life, that of the ruling and of the ruled. It is essential oligarchic. Politicians promise radical change but as soon as they have won power they defend a society that has nothing to do with whatever they have promised. Then, social life is hell, cruelty is unending and social agents are victim of illusions and myths. Men have only a small light at their disposal, a single weapon with which to fight: science"[9].

2. Pareto's *economic* maximum of ophelimity for the community, currently known as the Pareto welfare criterion, which we may call Pareto I welfare criterion, and Pareto's *sociological* maximum of utility of the community, which we may call Pareto II welfare criterion, while at first sight are radically different, have many aspects in common and these may be constitute the interdisciplinary bridge between fiscal economics and fiscal sociology together with the theory of elites.

Pareto distinguishes ophelimity and utility. By "ophelimity" he means what is useful to an individual not from the point of view of the observer but from his own point of view and appears to the observer by his behaviour. Defined in a marginal sense is the pleasure that an individual derives from a certain quantity of a good when that quantity is added to a given amount of the same good that he already had. By contrast, for Pareto, "utility" is what the observer thinks is useful to the subject observed from his own (of the valuator) point of view. Cocaine may be viewed as giving ophelimity to the individuals making use of it, *by observing their behaviour,* as expressed in their demand for it and by its price. But a given valuator may judge it as giving disutility to the individuals who consume it because it damages their health and induce them to economic and social behaviours that may be considered negatively from some ethical belief. This, if the judgment is done by another subject, *in Pareto's view,* is a sociological concept, not an economic one, even when the disutility of cocaine is judged by the valuator with some objective parameter relating to health because the valuator in order to asses this negative utility and to compare with the other (negative and positive) utilities of the observed individual has to make use of own coefficient of transformation of his various ophelimities in homogeneous quantitative units of utility.

---

8 See PARETO *Manuale* (1906), Ch. II, § 56 ff.

9 G. BUSINO (2000), "The signification of Vilfredo Pareto's sociology", Revue européenne des sciences sociales", n. 117, 2000, p. 226.

And even more so when the total utilities of a given subject must be compared by the evaluator with those of other subjects.

Pareto measure of ophelimity does not need any use of similar quantifications by the observer, who may merely observe the behaviours tracing indifference curves relating to different combinations of couples of goods. By this methodology ophelimity is a mere subjective ordinal concept and the maximum of ophelimity for the individual consists in the situation in which he cannot increase is ophelimity by changing his choices, because the loss of the choice to which renounces is greater to the pleasure of the one which in this way he can do. The maximum of ophelimity for the community shall be achieve when the position reached is such that it is impossible to make any smallest movement from it giving a benefit or a damage of ophelimity to all the members of that community because any smallest movement from that position necessarily has the effect of giving a benefit of ophelimity to some member of the community while damaging the ophelimity of some other.[10]

A further clarification of the maximum of ophelimity for the community, as contrasted with maxima of utility may be achieved, by referring to the *Treatise on General Sociology*, where Pareto[11] distinguishing points P and Q and movements (from) P to Q and movements (from) Q to Q or to P.

Movements of a first type P are such that, while beneficial to certain individuals, are necessarily harmful to others. Movements of the second type Q are to the advantage or at the detriment of all individuals without exceptions ..."Consideration of the two types of points, P and Q, is of great importance in political economy.[12] When the community stands at a point Q that it can leave with resulting benefits to all individuals, procuring greater enjoyment for all of them, it is obvious that from the economic standpoint it is advisable not to stop at that point, but to move on from it as far as the movement away from it is advantageous to all. When, then, the point P, where that is no longer possible, is reached, it is necessary, as regards the advisability of stopping there or going on, to resort to other considerations foreign to Economics – One, then, might decide, on grounds of ethics, social utility or something else, which individuals it is advisable to benefit, which to sacrifice. But from the strictly economic stand, as soon as the community has reached point P it has to stop. That point therefore plays, in the phenomenon, a role analogous to that of the point where the maximum of individual

10 PARETO (1906) *Manuale*, Ch. VI, § 33.

11 PARETO (1916) *The Mind and Society: A Treatise on General Sociology*, Dover Publications, 1963, § 2128 and followings. We have made some small change, in the above quotation from this version in English of the original Italian text, to make it more readable.

12 PARETO (1935, 1963) *The Mind and Society: A Treatise on General Sociology*, § 2129, we follow the English translation with modification.

ophelimity is attained, at which, therefore, the individual stops. Because of that analogy it has been called[13] *point of maximum ophelimity **for** the community*. But, as usual, nothing is to be inferred from the etymologies of those terms (§ 2129)". According to Pareto a regime of competitive market economy is the most likely to lead to points close to a maximum of the type P. Therefore even if maximum of ophelmity for the community is a subjective notion, it is also an operational concept relevant to depict real situations. The presentation of the Paretian *maxima of ophelimity for the P community* and of the conditions to be satisfied to reach them, may be now done with the diagram of figure 1 drawn from Forte (2010, Figure 2.6 pag. 111).

FIGURE 1
MAXIMUM OF OPHELIMITY FOR THE COMMUNITY

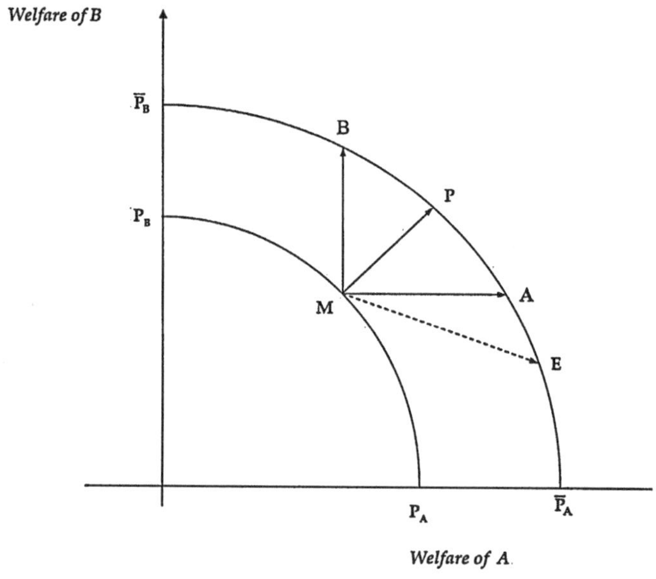

Figure 1

The diagram presents a Pareto frontier with points P on it traced for two individuals A (whose ophelimity may be measured on the X axis and B_x. (whose ophelimity may be measured on the Y axis) From a point M (which in the Paretian terminology is a point Q) inside the frontier where A has the welfare M_A (measured on the X) and B has the welfare M_B, (measured on the Y) it is possible for A and B to move to the set points P, on the frontier delimited by two straight lines, one horizontal that assures that B maintains the welfare that has in M (which is

13 Here PARETO refers to his *Manuale*.

measured on the Y axis) and the other vertical that assures that A maintains the welfare that has in M (which is measured on the X axis). The vertical straight line crossing the frontier in a point P_1 shall delimit the points on the frontier lower than P_1 that assure a net gain to A (in P_1 A has no gain and no loss).

The horizontal straight line crossing the frontier in P_3 shall delimit the points on the frontier higher than P_3 that that allow B to get a net gain (in P_3, B has no gain and no loss). Any movement forward from M within the straight lines MP_1 and MP_3 gives gains to both of them, and is a maximum of ophelimity for the community, because both members of it get a net gain of ophelimity. In all the movements from M on the straight line MP_1, there is no gain an no loss for A while all the gains go to B. The opposite happens for the movements from M on the straight line MP_3: here B gets no gain an no loss while all the gains go to A. A movement from M to point E, lower than P_3 where B suffers a loss of ophelimity and A gets a great gain would not satisfy the conditions required for a maximum of ophelimity for the community even if is on the Pareto frontier. However, as we shall see, it might be able satisfy the conditions of a sociological maximum of utility *for the community,* if the ruling class gives the same weight to the utility of A and of B (and even more likely if the ruling class assigns to the utility of A an higher weight) because likely – from the point of view of the elite ruling the community- the gain of marginal utility for A is greater than the loss of marginal utility of B.

3. As one can infer from the above presentation, Pareto in the *Treatise of General Sociology* considers the maxima of utility reached by a *sociological calculus* as deviations from the maximum of ophelimitiy due to interferences of the public sector in the free market and in the free behaviours of individuals in general. Here the theory of *elites* comes in to play. There is always a ruling class, consisting of those who form the government and those who support it, the two basic components of the elite that dominates in the society. They pursue the utility *of the community* mixing the utility of the members of the elite with that of the others in a unique whole to be maximized. By utility as distinct from ophelimity Pareto, however means, more generally, the perception of the welfare of others from the point of view of the person that judges it. One should not make the mistake[14] of believing that the difference derives from the fact that ophelimity is a narrow concept of egoistic utility while the sociological notion of utility is notion of individual welfare, incorporating a broader range of ends and values Not at all. Indeed for Pareto ophelimity, for the altruistic persons, may include not only the subjective welfare of the individual as considered by himself, *in relation to the most various ends* In this case it may also include the indirect utility that the

14 Done, for instance, by Amarthya Sen in his theorems about the impossibility of the Paretian liberal.

individuals feels in relation to the consequences of his behaviour on the welfare of the others and the utility that he fells by interdependency as for the welfare of the others of whom he cares. Thus ophelimity and utility *might became* intermixed concepts. The sociological aspect of the notion of utility derives from the fact that the judgment of the welfare of the others, is done from the point of view of those who value that welfare. When one feels indirect and interdependent utility in relation to the welfare of others, necessarily weighs the utility of different subjects by an intrinsically arbitrary operation And most individuals do it by a mixture of logical and non logical valuations, derived from sentiments and credence.

Moving now to the point of view of the elite in power or of someone who acts as if had to rule the community, there are two sociological maximum of utility (which we named Pareto, welfare criterion II) One is the maximum of utility for the community (Pareto welfare criterion II_I), which is parallel to the maximum of ophelimity *for the community* and the other is the maximum of utility *of the community* (Pareto welfare criterion II_{II}). The maximum of utility *for* the community (pareto criterion II_I) as the maximum of ophelimity *for* the community avoids any difference in weight as for the utility of the various individuals by the valuator. But the maximum of ophelimity *for* the community is such from the point of view of the individuals themselves, the maximum of utility *for* the community is such from the point of view of what the observer feels about the welfare of the considered individuals and groups Thus under this maximum too the observer shall find points P and Q. However they shall be sociological points obtained by an intrinsically arbitrary measure of the utilities and disutilities of the different "goods" for the given individual added together algebraically in an homogeneous quantity through intrinsically arbitrary coefficients of transformation.

The maximum of utility of the community (Pareto II welfare criterion) on the other hand, consists in adding together algebraically the maxima of utility of each member of the community by other transformation coefficients to get an homogeneous notion of utility for the community as a whole. This is *a fortiori,* a sociological concept, because, for Pareto, the community can be considered as an unitary being only in a sociological perspective. And here too there is a mixture of logical and non-logical valuations. The elite in power and those who wish to get the power, to conceal the fact that pursue their interest more than that of the others, must recur to "non-logical rationalizations of action that blend sentiment with logic in an ongoing manner"[15].

Pareto formalizes the II_{II} welfare criterion in a complex way that is worth of careful consideration because of the richness of sociological and economic implications.

15 See MCLURE (2007) pag. 45.

II The Sociological Maximum Of Utility Of The Community.

1. Pareto, in an article of 1913 on the maximum of utility for the collective in sociology [16] assumes first that each individual may have ophelimity not only from its own welfare but also from the utility that attaches to the welfare of others. Humanitarians, for instance, do not want that criminals be punished with heavy pains and feel diminished their own ophelimity if the welfare of the criminals (as assessed by the humanitarians by transforming the objective utility of the criminals by homogeneous coefficients that provide ophelinity to the humanitarians) is substantially damaged. The humanitarians thus shall assign to the criminals coefficients that limit their punishment and consequently damage the welfare of the victims. The humanitarians therefore, transported by their sentiments, tend to under asses the objective utility of the victims and shall (irrationally) assign low coefficient to them. We will have

(1) $dv=0=a_1df_1+a_2df_2$...where 1,2 are the individuals and df_1 are the variations of elementary utility 1,2. On the other hand a_1, a_2 are the coefficients which "serve to do the transition from the quantities df_2, df_3 ... which are objective and heterogeneous to the quantities a_2 df_2, a_3 df_3, ... which are subjective and homogeneous. Humanitarians 1,2, 3, who dislike to see criminals 4,5,6 in jail. giving not a thought to the victims 7,8 ...will assign high coefficients to the quantities df_4, df_5, df_6 [of individuals 4,5,6] and coefficients of approxi mately zero to the quantities df_7, df_8, [of individuals 7,8.]"

On the other hand the property owners damaged by the criminals shall make opposite valuations. They shall give coefficients close to zero to the utilities df_4, df_5, df_6 of the criminals 4,5,6 and high coefficients to the quantities df_7, df_8, of the victims 7,8.

"In that way, however, there are as many equations as there are individuals a_1', a_1'', a_1''' who feel the utilities of subjects 2, 3,4. Namely

(2) $0=a'_1\,df_1+a'_2df_2+a'_3df_3$
$0=a_1''df_1+a_2''df_2+a_3''df_3$
$0=a_1'''df_1+a_2'''df_2+a_3'''df_3$

And the heterogeneity eliminated from the quantities in the single equation turns up again in the quantities of the different equations"

16 PARETO (1913), "Il massimo di utilità per una collettività in sociologia". *Giornale degli Economisti e rivista di statistica,* 1913, April., reproduced in (1916) *Trattato di sociologia,* pag. 1470 of the English translation, footnote Pareto employs Greek letters.

Pareto therefore makes a second step, the transition from the individual ophelimities obtained from own ophelimity and from the utility of the welfare of the other individuals transformed in subjective ophelimity by their homogeneity coefficients to the utility for the community as considered by the given elites, by the employment of her second degree coefficients of homogeneity.

"To render these [ophelimities, as given in (2)] homogeneous they have to be multiplied again [by the given elites] by certain coefficients b_1', b_1", b_1"' ...determined with an objective purpose in view of the prosperity of the community, let us say. Suppose that the government believes that the prosperity of the community demands the extermination of criminals. It will then resign itself to inflicting pain on kind-hearted humanitarians [1,2,3]; it will, in other words, assign very low coefficients b_1'.b_1",b_1"' to their pains and fairly high coefficients b_1^{VII}, b_1^{VIII} to the pain of the victims [7,8] of the criminals. Now that, thanks to the coefficients the quantities corresponding to equation (2) have become comparable, their sum can be taken after they have been multiplied by b_1', b_1" .... and we get

(3) $0=M_1df_1+M_2df_2+M_3df_3+\ldots$[17]

The equation (3) will determine points of type P. A government that has fixed on the equation will have to carry the movement of the community until one of the points P is reached; and there it will stop, for if it went any farther it would become involved in self-contradiction, sacrificing people who it believes should not be sacrificed".

2. Pareto goes on arguing that "Even in the cases where the utility of the individual does conflicts with that of the community, the point of maximum of the first do not ordinarily coincide with points of maximum of the second". It is impossible to maximize simultaneously all the utilities of a subgroup of individuals member of a given group even when this maximization gives a benefit to the other members of the group, because this maximization reduces the maximum benefit for the entire group.

"Taking a given individual, let A being the extreme point representing strictest observance of every precept obtaining in his society; B another extreme point representing violations of precepts that are not recognized as absolutely indispensable; mnp the curve of utility of the individual who begins suffering a damage at A, then attains a benefit, which becomes greatest at n, the benefit thereafter diminishing and becoming a loss at B. Similarly let srv be the curve of the utility deriving to society from the fact that the considered individual gives a selective observance to the precepts according to their necessity. The social utility it is greatest at r. At the point q intermediate between A and B we get for the

17 The letters M stand for maximization

considered individual the maximum of utility *qn* ; at point t, also intermediate between A e B, there is the maximum of utility of the community *tr* obtained by the behaviour of the considered individual".

Pareto goes on "Instead of considering a single individual, one may take a number of individuals having approximately the same curve of utility, mnp. Then the curve of utility srv of the group to which the individuals belong will be the curve resulting from the conduct of those individuals" (Treatise § 2138).

In Figure 36, § 2138 of the book of Pareto,[18] the utility for the community is represented by the line mnp.

Here Pareto argues that if a given sub group of individuals that pursues the happiness rather than the duties violates the existing rules, they may reap a great benefit, while reducing the utility to the others, who are more respectful of the rules. The ruling class which weighs the utility of the considered subgroups to get the utility of the community, may reach the maximum of utility of the community in a point between q and t. Its maximum shall be close to r if its lead by an elite of pursuer of happiness who shall give much more weight to the utility of the first sub group. It shall be more close to n if lead by an elite of pursuer of the ethics of the duty.

Before coming to a second Pareto's example of maximization of the utility of the community given in this context, let us notice that here he is not considering choices by the elite of specific actions, but *of norms*. In one case the elite of pursuer oh happiness the norm consist in a mild respect of the existing rules, in the case of the elite pursuing the ethic of the duty, the norm consists in trying to enforce a greater respect of the rules.

Pareto makes another example of maximization of utility of the community by considering the change rather than the violation of the existing rules distinguishing by innovators (whom he also calls "*speculators*") who want reforms and "*rentiers*" who want to preserve the existing rules " Instead of mere violations of the norms obtaining in a society, we may consider transformations and reforms of them that take place in the society. In many cases t will be much closer than q to B [respect of existing rules]; in other words, as regards certain individuals, it will be advantageous to society that the reform be greater than the reform which would bring them the maximum utility. People who are already rich and powerful often times have little to gain from innovations. whereas society may benefit greatly by them. Or again for individuals inclined to quiet, unruffled living t will be much nearer than q is to b; in other words any innovation, however beneficial to society, will be distasteful and troublesome for them. For "speculators" on the

18 In the Italian crtitical edition of 1964 with Introduction of N. BOBBIO the Figure is at pag. 584 of the II volume.

other hand t stands much farther removed than q does from B –and "speculators" tend much more readily to change than is necessary for the good of society. If we go on considering the various categories of individuals in that way, we may find, needless to say, a certain amount of compensation in their conduct, so that, everybody pulling for himself, a position will result somewhere in the neighbourhood of point t, where the society maximum of utility is located". (Treatise, § 2139).

Two comments here need to be done. The first it is, again, that what Pareto present to us it in not a conflict among different actions envisaged by the dominant elite and by the opposing elite but a conflict among different institutional settings. The second it is that not all the elites are equally bad, even in the pessimistic general panorama that one can see from the sociological window of Pareto. Indeed when the "speculators" i. e. the innovators are in power the equilibrium position shall result closer to r than when the *rentiers* are in power, even if they t to maintain the power they must somewhat entice the ones who want to preserve their rents.

3. Pareto might be considered (and has been considered) the precursor of the Bergsonian-Samulesonian social welfare function currently adopted in the paternalistic approach to public economics from the window pursuing the optimization of the policy design.

Unfortunately, in this way the importance of Pareto II $_{II}$ welfare criterion, for the fiscal sociology window is missed. And actually this it is what frequently happened, also in Italy, where to ease the confusion there was the fact that Maffeo Pantaleoni had already theorized the difference between the maximization of the welfare from the point of view of the individuals and from the point of view of the government which judges and weighs the utility of them from its point of view or from the point of view of a parliament where prevails an average of individual interests.

But the true meaning of Pareto's theory of the maximum welfare of the community which has been presented only in his last big work, the *Treatise of sociology,* cannot be understood without considering the two theories of the elites and of the residuals and derivations. To understand the meaning of this Paretian collective welfare criterion one must operate a connection of it with the Paretian *development* of the theory of the elites *as political powers*. Actually here lies the focus of the choice process, as for the welfare maximization. Whichever is the elite who gets the power and dominates, the maximization of the utility of the community, for Pareto, is always – more or less – a non logic phenomenon. In it play a great role two basic sociological Paretian concepts: derivations and residuals, which represents a development of the theory of social equilibrium that he had traced in his *Manual of Political Economy.* Here sentiments i.e. The "residual states of the mind" that give origin to non logical actions, which mostly derive from religion, moral beliefs and legal habits, dominate the scene as the main factors of social stability and of improvement of the conditions of life, as well as of rupture and change of equilibrium. The sentiments and generally speaking the non logical actions enter in a mixture with the logical actions in a different measures depending from the social classes. In the lower, less cultured classes, which – at least originally – are also poor, the non logical actions brought about by the prevailing sentiments are dominant. In the elites the logical actions prevail. However they consciously and unconsciously do make appeal to sentiments i. e. non logical actions to capture the consensus of their supporters and of the other people. The fact that they do so does not mean that they always succeed in their purposes because it is difficult to make previsions in the area of sociological phenomena.

Derivations consist in a non-logical explanation of a social doctrine "that derive from residues and which seek to modify behaviour through persuasion"[19].

TABLE 1

THE PARETIAN CLASSIFICATION OF DERIVATIONS

I CLASS – Affirmations
Experimental or imaginary facts
Sentiments
Mixture of facts and sentiments
II CLASS- Authority
Authority of a person or of more persons
Authority of the tradition of usages and customs
Authority of a divinity
III CLASS- Accordance with sentiments or principles
Sentiments
Individual interest
Interest of the community
Juridical entities
Metaphysical entities
Supra natural entities
IV CLASS –Verbal Evidences
Indeterminate expression to indicate real things or indeterminate things
Expression that generates accessory sentiments
Expression with many accessory sentiments and an expression indicating different things
Metaphors, allegories and analogies
Dubious and Indeterminate expressions and expressions without content

Residuals are implicit or explicit sentiments and instincts or values that have non purely logical basis and while "some reasons for action, real or potential can

19 See MCLURE (2007), pag. 45

derive logically from this subjective residual ... more than often the reasons that derive from this residual are non-logical rationalisations of action that blend sentiment with logic in an ongoing manner"[20].

TABLE 2

THE PARETIAN CLASSIFICATION OF RESIDUALS

I CLASS-Combination Instincts
as
Combination of similar or opposite things
Similar things producing similar effects, rarely opposite
Mysterious operations of given things or acts
II CLASS- Persistence of Aggregates
as
Persistence of relation with other men and places
Family and community relations
Relations with places
Relations of social classes
Relation of living with dead peoples
III CLASS- Need to manifest own sentiments with external acts
as
Religious exaltation
IV CLASS- Residuals in relation with the sociality
as
Need of uniformity
Neo-phobia
Sentiment of hierarchy
Sentiments of the superiors
Sentiments of the inferiors
Need of social approval
V CLASS- Integrity of the individuals and of their dependence
as
Sentiments contrasting with the alteration of the equilibrium
Sentiments of equality of the inferiors
Restoration of the integrity of the individuals whose integrity has been offended
VI- SEXUAL RESIDUALS

As one can see from the sketch of the gigantic (and not always analytically unquestionable) classification of the residuals done by Pareto in his *Treatise of Sociology* offered in Table 2, the residuals lose any relation with systematic ethical axioms or juridical conventions which in Pareto's *Manual of Political economy* constitute the *a priori* basis of non logical actions together with sentiments. And as for the connection of the residuals with sentiments there is no attempt to classify them

---

20 See MCLURE (2007) pag. 45

in relation with the different kinds of sentiments. What emerges is their vastness, variety and fragmentation. So that non logical action are a sort of jungle

The actions of the ruling elites, therefore, are less non logical than the other people, because they need to have a broader view[21]. But when they make their process of maximization of the utility of the community they must take in consideration the jungle of residuals and derivations that pervade the individual functions of utility as for the arguments concerning their relation with the others. Furthermore they have at disposal an huge amount of residuals and derivation to come in power and to maintain the power.

4. To present the real maximization process that the elites pursue, therefore, Pareto in the *Treatise* proceeds by contrasting two abstract types of society:

1) A society where sentiments exclusively operate without any sort of reasoning;

2) A society where exclusively operate logical-experimental reasoning.

Two different ways to entice the community to reach the desired utility maximum may be presented the real and the imaginary "fantastic" utility maximum by referring to Fig 29, § 1869 in Pareto book. [22] But the derivations employed to entice the common opinion of the public tend to penetrate in the mind of the elites, so that their maximization of the collective utility becomes more and more non logical. Thus the elite shall not be able to reach i*ts own true maximum of utility.*

5. The sociological window, trough which Pareto was able to show a new land of fiscal sociology, because of its complexity and disorderly presentation, was hard to be utilized. On the other hand the interpretation of his own sociological theory of the maximum of utility of the community by Pareto, as a mostly "irrational" phenomenon while causing a sharp criticism by the Italian scholars who, as Einaudi, where pursuing and economic approach to public finance, disguised the interest in the scholars more interested of the interdisciplinary approach to the process of public finance.

Mauro Fasiani, a sharp economist, student of Einaudi, who did knew well the Paretian fiscal sociology[23], in his *Principles of public finance,*[24] tried to fill the gap left by De Viti De Marco and Einaudi, as for the theory of the monopolistic state, by a sociological analysis of it, mostly in terms of fiscal illusion, drawing more from the fiscal sociology of Amilcare Puviani than from the Paretian one

21 PARETO (1906), Ch. II, § 45

22 PARETO (1916), Ch. XI, § 1869 pag. 410 of the II volume of the Italian critical edition of 1964.

23 See M FASIANI (1940) "Contributi di Pareto alla scienza delle finanze", *Giornale degli economisti* translated as Pareto's contributions to the Science of Public Finance, in Mc Lure (2007) p. 206 and ff.

24 M. FASIANI (1951) *Principi di Scienza delle finanze,* Giappichelli Torino, Vol. I

with which he, however, was very familiar. The analysis remained incomplete, as the *Principles,* because of Fasiani's premature death. And the sociological analysis was presented only for the monopolistic model of state. One could draw the inference that is not relevant (even if in a lesser degree) also for a cooperative model, distorting its marginal equilibrium too. One may correctly argue that fiscal sociology may be relevant, in a second approximation to complete the economic approach, also in the cooperative model. Rent seeking is a typical case. And derivations may play a large role in them. We do not know how Fasiani could have dealt with these issues. Aldo Scotto, student of Fasiani, also familiar with the Paretian sociology, gave a stimulating contribution on a sociological theory of fiscal decentralization in terms of derivations, explaining it with the lack of homogeneity of the governing class, i. e. the Paretian elite[25]. This is done in the first pages of the paper *"Prime linee di un contributo alla teoria della finanza locale"*, where he considers the homogeneity of the elite as the primary factor influencing the grater or smaller fiscal decentralization. However, the focus of the analysis, in the remaining part of the paper is on the other factors. And in this light the paper appears a systematic anticipation of the successive theory of the fiscal federalism[26]

For Griziotti the sociological research may have an important place, in the analysis of the various political organizations representing the various social forces and interests that enter in the political equilibrium and in the shaping of the legal institutions and of their development[27]. But one needs to consider the institutions in which the interest of the different social groups are constrained and combined in the flow of overlapping generations. So that the analysis of the political process and the economic analysis lof aws are essential to understand the fiscal phenomena, and the sociological factors must be considered in connection with them. Obviously if the sociology of public finances was entirely about irrational processes as those of exploitation by the force or/and by manipulation of the masses by derivations it was not much relevant in an interdisciplinary approach

---

25 See SCOTTO A. (1950), "Di un indice di decentramento finanziario", in *Finanza pubblica contemporanea, Studi in onore di Jacopo Tivaroni,* BARI, LATERZA, and SCOTTO A. (1952). Prime linee di un contributo alla teoria della finanza locale", in *Studi in onore di Gino Borgata*, Bologna, Arti Grafiche, and the discussion of this contribution of Scotto to the Paretian fiscal sociology by Mc Lure (2007) chapter 9. In the paper *"Di un indice di decentramento finanziario"* the Paretian sociological instrumentation is merely confined to the three lines of note 1.

26 See A.FOSSATI (1993) "L'opera scientifica di Aldo Scotto", *Rivista di diritto finanziario e scienza delle finanze*.

27 On Griziotti own view of Pareto's fiscal sociology see B. GRIZIOTTI (1943), "Alla scuola di Wilfredo Pareto e Maffeo Pantaloni", *Rivista di diritto finanziario e scienza delle finanze*, 1943, translated in Mc Lure (2007) as B: GRIZIOTTI, "At the School of Wilfredo Pareto and Maffeo Pantaloni"

focusing on less capricious phenomena. To Griziotti and his older students therefore appeared more interesting to focus on public finance from another window, that of the economic and political analysis of fiscal law[28].

On the other hand Ernesto d'Albergo[29], after having named Pareto', maximum of utility of the community as Pareto II second welfare criterion to distinguish from the "first criterion" on which the Paretian welfare economics is based, applied Pareto II to represent the process of maximization of a social welfare function by a government aiming to maximize the national product. D'Albergo construct methodologically coincides with the Bergsonian representation of the social welfare function. However because the aim of the government process is the maximization of national product, as a way of pursuing the interests of the generality of peoples, its interpretation of the Pareto maximum of utility of the community may come close to the maximum of ofelimity for the community, by the assumed type of government objectives, thus offering an interesting link between the Paretian theory of economic welfare maximisation and the sociological analysis of welfare maximization under given assumptions about the ruling elite's behaviour. Indeed one may argue that in the long run, a ruling elite pursuing this objective, trough a competitive market economy and the application of the compensation criterion to avoid redistributions damaging the property rights, of some members of the community it is also pursuing a Pareto I welfare criterion, within the range of solutions that the starting points allows.

Emilio Giardina [30]presents an (economic) interpretation of the Paretian maximum of utility of the community based on the assumption that the political rulers take account of the fact that each individual considers together with his welfare that of others individuals. Thus the ruling elite tries to maximize a weighed sum of these individual welfare maxima, as viewed from the individual points of view. Therefore the choices of the ruling elite reflect the preferences of the individuals

28 As a younger student of Griziotti, focusing on public choices as an economic-political phenomenon, I believe that fiscal sociology is worth of being pursued to make the view of the fiscal process more comprehensive and more realistic both in its irrational an rational sociological aspects.

29 D'ALBERGO E. (1963), "Finanza pubblica e benessere. Oneri e vantaggi della frontiera dell'utilità", *Giornale degli Economisti*, D'ALBERGO E. (1963), "Finanza pubblica e benessere:ponderazioni necessarie di contrapposte grandezze edeniche ", *Giornale degli economisti*, D'ALBERGO E. (1963) "Finanza pubblica e benessere, riducibilità logica del modello paretiano di funzioni e schemi del welfare collegati con piani di bilanci finanziari", *Giornale degli Economisti*, D'ALBERGO E.(1964), "Finanza pubblica e benessere: validità attuale della genesi razionale italiana del massimo di benessere collettivo", *Giornale degli Economisti;* D'ALBERGO E.(1967). "Una identificazione di schemi per l'economia finanziaria", *Giornale degli Economisti.*

30 E. GIARDINA (1969), "Le scelte finanziarie e il massimo paretiano di utilità collettiva", in *Scritti in onore di Giordano dell'Amore*, Milano, Giuffrè.

member of the community. The ruling elite in doing so necessarily pursues the views of some majority, but fundamentally follows the individual ophelimities about the aggregation of the various interests.

III The theory of elites[31]

1. Even though one is used to attribute the genesis of the elite theory at the Italian school – Mosca, Pareto, Michels –, it is important to remember that these authors recognised (implicitly or explicitly, through indirect or direct quotations) the influence of other international scholars such as Taine, Ostrogorski, Bryce, Tocqueville, De Molinari, Sorel and Weber. The Italian school shared with these intellectuals the problem of the integration of the masses in the political society (and consequently the implicit contraposition between masses and elite).

Moreover, we can also put the elite theory into a wider frame, connecting it with the problem of the *authority*. In political sense, "authority" is the foundation of *legitimacy* of the *power* in general. In extreme synthesis, we can say that a power is legitimate when: a) it is based on the consensus (of the public opinion), renewed periodically through the elections; b) it is exercised in accordance with a fundamental law or constitution; c) through the constitution, the power is limited by the recognition of values, principles of justice and inalienable rights.

Focusing on the theme of the relationship between power and legitimacy of the power, the thesis that it is always a minority that governs, and that the power of this minority needs to be recognized and legitimated in order to be obeyed, it is not a theoretical novelty. Indeed, the true novelty, especially of Mosca and Pareto, is that they tried to lay the foundations of the political science in terms of a scientific study of power. Furthermore, the specificity of Pareto is that he tried to include the political reflections into his great and unique project of a System of general sociology.

Pareto formulates the theory of the elite (and the social stratification) by developing the economical-statistical scheme reached with the discovery of the income distribution curve. Starting from *Les systèmes socialistes*, and developing more and more his reflection up to the *Trattato*, the elite theory will become only an aspect, though important, of the social equilibrium and the social change (in which other variables are considered: «heterogeneity» and «social circulation», «residuals», «derivations», «interests»).

Pareto claims the scientific nature of the elites theory reconnecting it to the "principles of social-physiology" exposed in the *Course of political economy,*

31 This Section is written by P. SILVESTRI.

and, in particular, to the income distribution curve, that he considered a scientific constant, valid in every time and place. This constancy and validity depends "probably on the distribution of the physiological and psychological characters of men"[32].

From this standpoint, Pareto argues that the "characters" which mostly go together are the power and the wealth: "If men are distributed according to their degree of influence and according to their political and social power, in that case, in many societies, there will be, at least partly, the same men to occupy the same place, in such figure and in that of the wealth distribution. Classes called superiors are generally also the richest. These classes constitute the elected [*l'eletta*], an "aristocracy" (in the etymological sense: *aristos*)"[33].

The physical, moral and intellectual inequality among men is connected to one of the fundamental principles of the Paretian sociology, the principle of social *heterogeneity*.

This inequality depends on the diversity of indexes in the several branches of human activities, from which, at the same time, depends the emersion of the élite. In Pareto's words: the elite is «the class of those who have the highest indexes [*indici*] in the branch of their activity»[34]. These indexes refer to the natural (or hereditary) capacities of individuals.

The society is consequently divided into two layers: 1) lower and 2) superior (also in governed and governors, ruled and rulers). The lower layer is formed by the class which is not *elite* ["*classe non eletta*"]; the superior is further divided in (a) *elite* of government and (b) *elite* not of government.

From this perspective we can notice a difference between the *Socialist systems* and the *Treaty of Sociology*. In the first work the definition of the elite in terms of influence or power is coherent with a theory of the forms (or system) of governments, and it is linked to a particular political structure. In the *Treaty*, instead, the elite, defined in terms of individual superiority, is classified through psychological idealtypes. Here elites can be divided into two basic types, depending on whether within their members prevails one or the other of the two psychological characters (the so-called *residuals*): the instinct of combination, that is the inclination to innovate and invent, or the persistence of the aggregates, thus the inclination to stability and conservation.

Within this framework one of the principal factors that explains the social equilibrium and the social change is the *circulation of the elites*. The circulation takes place «when new elements, extraneous to the elite, becomes a part of it,

32 V. PARETO (1974), *I sistemi socialisti*, UTET, Torino, 1974, pp. 129-30.

33 Here, p. 20.

34 V. PARETO, *Trattato di sociologia*, § 2031, II.

bringing their opinions, their characters, their virtues, their prejudices». If the diversity of the extraneous elements ends up to be entirely assimilated by the elite, then one does not have circulation any more.

In any case, according to Pareto no social system last forever: "aristocracies do not last. It is incontestable that they, regardless their origins, disappear after a certain period. *History is a cemetery of aristocracies*"[35].

Under this point of view, we can notice that one of the problems of Pareto's politico-sociological theory has to do with his conception of the struggle (in particular of the struggle for power) and the social heterogeneity of values. In Pareto's vision the heterogeneity is so much structural and widespread that he is not able to conceive any form of mediation between governors and governed: the struggle for power is an endless struggle and the history is a «cemetery» of elites.

The following quotation is emblematic of his political realism, which seems more a kind of scepticism to us: «the true problem which humanity must solve, in order to have a *good government*, is: *how to entrust the power to those who are the best, avoiding that they abuse of it* ...». Pareto's answer is bitter: «the future society, even if communist, will be governed by an aristocracy or elite [...]. The liberal doctrine, when combines itself with that of the democracy and of the universal suffrage, is an optimist doctrine which supposes that the mob [*plebe*], obtaining the power via the extension of the vote, will not abuse of it to appropriate well-off citizens' goods. The experience of that doctrine was done in the XIX Century, and if we consider what happens in the most advanced democracies, we should reach to conclusions entirely different from the ones hoped. It is true that liberals partly expected that results, since they insisted in having a neutral government, not interfering in citizens' affairs. Their mistake is only in not having understood that, at the present stage of civilization, it was a utopia, and that in any case it was not allowed to hope that it would have been the people to set up such a government [...]. The new regime, of which the XIX Century was pregnant, now begins in the shadow of demagogy. One is not able to know what it will succeed in [...]. It is likely that it will not be a liberal regime; and this is because freedom never belonged and seems cannot belong to the extreme democracy. The freedom is a luxury [...]»[36].

2. All the three scholars which, according to McLure, are the main exponents of the Paretian school of fiscal sociology, Gino Borgatta, Guido Sensini, and Robert Murray[37], theorized a different model of the Paretian sociological maxi-

35 V. PARETO, *Treaty of Sociology* in the English version p. 82.

36 In BUSINO (1982) II Vol.

37 Murray, according to Borgatta (1920), does not belong to the Paretian school of sociology. Murray himself in his paper in Giornale degli Economisti of 1953 wrote that after his first attempt to systematize the principles of fiscal economics in *I problemi fondamentali*

mum of utility of the community, by a different type of elite. However they, for one reason or another, did not develop a theory of elites, nor did the empirical researches that the Paretian methodology would have required.

Roberto A. Murray developed a sociological theory of the elites in the years 1910-13[38] under the influence of Pareto's *Systemes Socialistes* and *Manuale di Economia Politica.* In the circulation of elites he distinguished two types of phenomena: transformations and substitution of elites, arguing that the most common of them is that of transformation by infiltration of new elements. The transformation mostly takes place because of extraordinary events. He further distinguished conservation and renewal of the elites. This second distinction lead him to follow the sociological dichotomy of Pareto of the two categories of rentiers and speculators. Subsequently, however in the public finance equilibrium as a political equilibrium he shifted to a political-economic theory of the elites in which the ruling class maximizes its utility by a logical economic behaviour at the expenses of the market economy agents[39]. Later on he published a new version of the model of the elite that acts logically to exploit the market economy and uses the non logical actions to realize its designs of exploitation and keep the power and the necessary consensus of the supporters[40].

Guido Sensini, on the other hand, in his sociological Paretian approach, modifies Pareto's view, distinguishing a government that acts in a strict logical way to achieve the maximum of utility of the collective, and a government that acts predominantly in non logical way pursuing the interests of the class that supports the government largely operating instinctively and the real governments that operate with a mixed behaviour[41]. But he did not elaborate on the theory of elites.

---

dell'economia finanziaria (Giornale degli Economisti 1912) by the Paretian sociology, in the subsequent researches, collected in the book *Le nozioni dello Stato, dei bisogni pubblici e dell'attività finanziaria* (Atheneum, Roma 1913), tried to show that true subjects of the fiscal activity are not the individuals as in the economic view or the groups and social classes, as in the sociological view, but the political entities, as in the political view (p. 282). GRIZIOTTI considered him among the followers of his political school.

38 See, R. MURRAY (1913), *Le nozioni dello stato, dei bisogni pubblici e dell'attività finanziaria,* Roma, Atheneum.

39 R. MURRAY (1914), *Principi fondamentali della scienza pura delle finanze,* Firenze, Carnesecchi, R. MURRAY (1915), "La scienza delle finanze, il diritto finanziario e la nozione di stato", *Giornale degli economisti,* translated as "The science of public finance, fiscal law and the notino of State", in MCLURE (2007).

40 Murray left the academic career in the twenties and re-entered in it in the fifties. He then wrote R. MURRAY (1952), *Lezioni di scienza delle finanze e diritto finanziario,* Pisa Pellegrini and R. MURRAY (1953), "Alcune osservazioni sui problemi della finanza pubblica come scienza politica", *Giornale degli economisti.*

41 G. SENSINI (1917), "Outline of theoretical Public finance", translation in MCLURE (2007) of "Prime linee di finanza teorica", in (1917) *Studi in onore di Tullio Martello,* Bari Laterza

3. Gino Borgatta[42] centred the process of sociological maximization of the utility of the community on the two types of potential elites, the speculators and the rentiers. However the work remained in its preliminary stage elaborated in two papers in an ambitious book written in the second decade of the XX century[43].

In the model of maximization of Borgatta the process is mostly non logical, not only as for the elite's behaviour with governed peoples, but also as for the process of government by the elite. This scholar, who had studied with Einaudi and then with Pareto, argued that "in its synthetic aspect the fiscal phenomenon is essentially sociological and as such cannot give rise to a search for its laws by deducing them from the (pure) economic hypothesis, or by treating them as a system of logical acts". Therefore he denied that "the fiscal phenomenon can be deduced by extending the (logical) *economic* property to the actions undertaken for the complete satisfaction of a set of needs of the individual, which, because of their social nature, require, or make more suitable, special forms of satisfaction through the public finance".

Borgatta denied De Viti De Marco's and Einaudi's theory according to which "the individual tends towards a position of equilibrium, where the marginal utilities of the goods used to satisfy needs – be they present or future, selfish or unselfish, public or private needs – are all equal"[44]. Einaudi reacted to this theory in his discussion of the determinants of fiscal choice in an essay of 1919 on the theory of tax amortization[45], in which he does a critical examination of the sociological or political theory of public finance. In this polemic with Borgatta[46], Einaudi argued that "It is true that the 'political' man does not cease of being egoistic. Therefore even if he may appreciate the advantages of the collective life and of

---

and G. SENSINI (1932), "La finanza sociologica", in G. SENSINI (1932), *Studi di scienze sociali*, Roma, casa Libraria Editrice italiana. After a period of sociological researches mostly of preliminary character, Sensini shifted more and more to studies of mathematical economics within the Paretian approach to the pure theory of general economic equilibrium.

42 G. BORGATTA (1920), "Lo studio scientifico dei fenomeni finanziari", *Giornale degli Economisti e Rivista di Statistica,* translated in MCLURE (2007) as "The Scientific Study of Fiscal Phenomena".

43 The Paretian – sociological criticism of the economic theory of public finance had been initiated by Borgatta in a book in private circulation in 1917 on the economic dynamics (G. BORGATTA 1919, *L'economia dinamica. Studio critico sui problemi dinamici nell'economia pura,* UTET, Torino). The book was never really published. Borgatta's interests shifted more and more to the economic aspects of public finance, with important researches on the measure of fiscal burden and other tax matters.

44 G. BORGATTA (1920) in MCLURE (2007) pag. 206.

45 L. EINAUDI (1919), *Osservazioni critiche intorno alla teoria dell'ammortamento dell'imposta e teoria delle variazioni nei redditi e nei valori capitali susseguenti all'imposta,* in Einaudi (1958), *Saggi sul risparmio e l'imposta*, Torino, Einaudi pp. 161-240.

46 Here pp. 201-202.

the prosperity of the government, he shall try to exploit the others, throwing on them the burden of taxes needed to finance the public services. Thus, this kind of researches – aiming to clarify the true calculus and the actions by which men actually allocate the tax burden and to cast light on the results of their attempts to enjoy the maximum of benefits with the minimum of the tax burdens – are of great utility. But these very useful researches should not start from the denegation of the truth of first approximation, that the use of the individual wealth to pay the taxes is a special case of the general law of the optimal allocation of the individual wealth, between the various goods. Rather, these researches must be addressed to correct and integrate this law. By doing so, one can see that this law is not[47] an abstract truth, which is so deformed by individual egotism and by the struggle between political groups and classes, that it seems never to happen concretely, but it is an objective that people are striving to achieve. Experience is persuading people more and more of the necessity of subjecting themselves to a common law. And furthermore they are being persuaded of the necessity to work consciously and voluntary on the creation of this common law, on its execution, on the procurement of the means able to make it active and fruitful. If this political awareness is not very widespread among the general public, felt by most people only in exceptional moments, it is undeniably growing, taking root in the human spirit and increasingly becoming an inspiration for the actions of *elected officials* and also for those of the governed multitudes. From an abstract scheme, useful as a guiding light for researchers and suited to classifying human actions, it is becoming, little by little, an objective to be achieved, a rule consciously desired and obeyed. It is the permanent rule that historically has always existed, although it has only gradually become able consciously to direct human actions. In comparison with it, the other rules of conduct seems transient, variable from time to time.

The purpose of the scientific research is to take into account both the permanent law, which from abstract and impalpable becomes more and more concrete and consciously observed, and special laws of every time and place. It would be certainly erroneous to deny these latter; but is not less serious the mistake of those who, for love of the concrete and truth, deny those truer realities which are the abstract ideas, the fundamental and simple strengths which really move men. Being afraid of abstractness they fall in bigger abstractness, which has never been

---

47 The paragraph that follows is quoted from Einaudi's "Introduction" to his *Contributo alla ricerca dell'ottima imposta, in Annali di Economia,* Milano, V, 1928-29, pp. 7-224, translated in L. Einaudi, *Contribution to the quest for an optimal tax*, in EINAUDI (2006), *Selected Economic Essays*, edited by Luca Einaudi, R. Faucci, R. Marchionatti, Palgrave Macmillan, p. 215.

imagined by those who always gave to their laws the value of first approximations subject to subsequent corrections and integrations».

4. While the theory of elites has a long history, in Italy the political-sociological theory of elites was first theorized by Gaetano Mosca. He, as Pareto, thinks that all the political communities, regardless of the government form, are ruled by an organized minority, which Mosca calls «political class» and Pareto «élite». This minority searches for and obtains the legitimacy and the obedience through the use of «political formulas» (Mosca), which seems to present a similarity with the Paretian «derivations». However Mosca thinks that the key to comprehend the social equilibrium and the social change, and, in particular, the rise and fall of big civilizations, must be found through the study of ruling classes.

For Mosca the "political class" or "ruling class" ("*la classe politica governante*") is the ruling minority of the society. Every politically organized society is characterized by the existence of an organized minority that rules, and a majority that is ruled. Mosca claimed that this fact is a "scientific invariance" or a scientific law supported by evidence from every place and period in history[48].

The «political formula» for Mosca is the body of doctrine, beliefs, «myths» or «dogma», or, in a wider and neutral sense, the ideology with which the ruling class tries to *justifies* its own authority and power and the need for other to *obey* it[49]. Examples of these doctrines are: "divine right", "traditional power", "force" (as an ideology), "heredity", "popular sovereignty". These «illusions», including religion or nationalist sentiments, are what keeps societies together. Mosca's analysis of «political formulas» focuses on the classical problem of the legitimacy of power, which he studied moving from his perspective of political *science* (accordind to Mosca the question of legitimacy taken from a *normative* point of view is a matter of political philosophy).

Though Mosca insisted on the scientific nature of his political theory, he could not avoid a prescriptive analysis of what ought to be the good government. He found it in the *mixed constitution*, in which the middle class plays a fundamental role. This analysis emerged in the second edition (1923), especially in the second book of the *Elementi di scienza politica*[50]. According to Mosca, not only the middle class has entrepreneurial capacities and a culture «superior to that of the other social classes»[51], but «the liberal principle finds the best conditions for his implementation when the electoral body is made up by a majority of that

48 G. MOSCA, *Teorica dei governi e governo parlamente,* in ID. (1982), p. 225.

49 G. MOSCA, *Elementi*, in ID. (1982), pp. 633-34.

50 Luigi Einaudi who, for the above seen reasons, was fiercely against the Paretian theory of the elites, promptly noticed this development of Mosca's theory of the elites as an important innovation. Both Einaudi and Mosca thought that the liberal state stood on the middle class.

51 G. MOSCA (1966), *The political class*, cit., p. 221.

second layer of the ruling class which forms the backbone of all big political organizations»[52]. Mosca could not avoid the "mith" of the middle class. This myth rooted in the faith (a very *topos* of 19th Century) about the capacity of the middle class of overcomin partisan interests: «if there is a social class – Mosca stated – able to renounce to its individual interest and have the calm and the open-mindedness needed to embrace and favour the general interest of the society, than it is the one in which a deep intellectual culture has strengthened the character, enlarged the horizons, developed the faculty to properly judge a social interest, the faculty to foresee and forestall; this class is the only one able to voluntarily sacrifice his present to avoid a future evil»[53].

In 1923, right when fascism had begun to threaten the constitutional liberties, Mosca was almost forced to re-evaluate the representative government: «representative regime» is superior because it is «able to canalize a huge sum of individual energies towards ends of collective interest without coercing or suppressing them; and has left them sufficient vitality so to achieve other big results»[54].

4. The theory of Pareto differs in many respects from that of Mosca[55], likely because of its origin from his reflection on the curve of distribution of wealth and also because of its intimate connection with his maximum of utility of the community. Truly both for Pareto and Mosca elites are a minority, but the Paretian elites are composed by individuals with superior talents in their activities, while in Mosca this is not a necessary requisite. Pareto's elites, made up of individuals who occupy the higher ranks in the curve of distribution of talents, are composed by two subgroups, a narrow one at the top and a broader one immediately below it. In Mosca there is not such stratification. Mosca's "political formula", by which the elite obtains and mantains power resembles very much the non logical actions of Pareto, however one cannot say that is made of residuals and derivations in the Paretian sense. The Paretian elite behaves by a mix of non logical and logical actions in its maximization process. Mosca's elites appear to pursue their objectives mostly by a political rationality. The biggest resemblance between Pareto's and Mosca's theory of elites is in the law of circulation of the elites. However, in Mosca the dichotomy between speculators and rentiers is replaced by a dichotomy between the middle class that is more suited to pursue the general interests by a democratic regime and the other classes. In any case, the two theories of élite of Pareto and Mosca have different origins. Mosca formulates his theory moving from juridical-constitutional and historical-political considerations.

52 Here, p. 261.

53 Quoted by P. FRASCANI (1969), p. 87.

54 G. MOSCA, *Elementi*, p. 1094.

55 See FEDELI and FORTE (2008) "Pareto's sociological theory of elites and the composition of the Italian parliament 1861-2007".

Pareto's theory of social equilibrium takes into account physics-mathematical as well as mechanical, economical, anthropological, sociological and historical considerations, and considers above all the dynamic aspect of societies. Mosca's theory appears more suited to describe and prescribe the conditions for the political stability than the conditions for the economic progress, while Pareto's theory appears more suited to analyze the conditions of the economic dynamics and the economic development.

5. Einaudi's theory of elites is, generally speaking, closer to that of Mosca than that of Pareto[56], though it took shape from his controversy with the Paretian sociological theory of the process of public finance presented by Gino Borgatta[57], as well as from his wider legal-political reflection.

Einaudi had commenced a long-lasting and constant speculation about the role of the political elite in a democracy, guided by his aspiration was to rebuild the liberal institutions compromised by the Great War and later destroyed by the Fascism. A first and fundamental synthesis of this speculation is offered in the book *La condotta economica e gli effetti sociali della guerra italiana* (1933), where Einaudi, from one hand, synthesizes the causes of the social disorder followed to the war and, on the other, traces the programmatic lines to rebuild a liberal society. In this regard, Einaudi identifies three fundamental issues: 1) the lacking of a ruling class able to "well-govern" the country, thus able to govern it in sight of the "good society", an ideal which for Einaudi is intrinsically liberal; 2) the necessity of reconstituting a stable and independent middle class from which should arise that ruling class; 3) the importance of public opinion as central institution of the liberal state and "place of mediation" between governors ad governed, a "place" in which the middle class should play a determinant role.

The importance that Einaudi attaches to the political class can be better understood recalling his recurring idealtipical opposition between Camillo Benso of Cavour, as liberal premier of the parliamentary government of the Kingodm of Piedmont in the middle of the nineteen century, and Giovanni Giolitti, liberal premier of the Italian parliamentary Government. In the first decade of the XIX century Cavour, who had a profound knowledge of the economic theory, is the ideal "progenitor" of what ought to be an aristocratic and independent political class; Giolitti is the real progenitor of a class of meddlers, bureaucrats and hustlers always ready to take advantage of the *res publica* for their own private ends.

56 In the dispute between Mosca and Pareto over who had first discovered the theory of elites, Einaudi came to the defense of Mosca. See L. EINAUDI (1934) "Dove si discorre di Pareto, di Mosca e anche di De Viti", *La riforma sociale*, XLI, reprinted in L. EINAUDI (1937), *Nuovi Saggi*, Einaudi, Torino.

57 G. BORGATTA (1920), translated in M. MCLURE (2007).

Discussing with Croce, who identified the «liberal government» with the Giolitti's government (the «political genius», according to the philosopher), Einaudi accused Giolitti to have reduced the art of good government to a mere «administration». As Einaudi stated, «one does not govern well without an ideal [...]. How can we imagine a politician who is a great one [...] without an ideal? And how is it possible to have an ideal and to pursue it if he does not know the needs and aspirations of the people which called him to govern and he does not know how to chose the means necessary to reach that ideal?»[58]. To state this in Weber's words (*Politik als Beruf*), «Three qualities are above all decisive for the political man: passion, sense of responsibility, farsightedness»[59]. These qualities are summarized by Einaudi in the "virtue" of prudence.

Nevertheless, for Einaudi it was a luck that, before the First Word War «the very representative classes of Italy – made of middle and little landlords, entrepreneurs, industrialists proprietary, merchants, very industrious artisans and, among a few meddlers, officials and bureaucrats devoted to the public good – still supplied the state with a good number of statesmen. Honest and laborious, they summarized the art of government into the formula "governing-well" the *res publica*, mutuating the model of "*good government*" from the wise and prudent way of managing their private life [here ment as *oikonomia*]»[60].

6. Though Einaudi had shared Mosca's *élites* theory, here his discourse becomes normative. It is probably because Einaudi could not be satisfied anymore, under the Fascism, with that kind of political realism according to which the relationship between the ruling class and the governed must be "scientifically" read as a pure power relation. However we might also think that Einaudi could not accept any more Mosca's idea that the governed «cannot but undergo» this power[61], neither that this relationship is a scientific «constant».

In an essay of 1936, reflecting on the «theory of the elected class in Frederic Le Play»[62], Einaudi definitively rejects the sociological conceptions of the political class. «Le Play's concept of "*élite*" must not be confused with the "ruling class" in the sense commonly widespread today». If for Pareto the «elected class or élite» includes «all those which were able to enter the governing class», «nothing is more disgusting to the spirit of Le Play than this mixture; for him the élite is the best [...]. A class which leads society to ruin, disorganization and decadence can be a "ruling" one, but not an élite»[63]. «It rarely happens, according to Le Play,

58 L. EINAUDI (1941), pp. 285-86.
59 M. WEBER (1919), *Politik as Beruf*, Munchen.
60 L. EINAUDI (1933), p. 400.
61 G. MOSCA (1982), p. 203.
62 L. EINAUDI, (1936), pp. 307-344.
63 Here, p. 318.

that the ruling class is also the elected class; but in those rare occasions in which the two classes become one, the foundations of a steady country are laid down for centuries»[64].

In that period Einaudi was in search for an ideal criterion of judgement, an «ideal schema» through which one can distinguish the good governors from the bad ones, the optimum state from the tyrannical one, the good government from the bad government. This is testified by the two last chapters of the book *Miti e paradossi della giustizia tributaria* [*Myths and paradoxes of fiscal justice*] significantly added (in 1940) to the previous edition. Einaudi become increasingly aware of this instance in the attempt to distinguish the «optimum tax» [«ottima imposta»] from the «"taille-tax"» [«imposta taglia»], a distinction which inevitably ended up to face the issue of power in order to distinguish those who govern in view of the common good from those who govern for its profit, the «finance of the *tyrannical government*» from the «finance of the *periclean polis*»[65].

Remembering «those epoches [in which] the *valentior pars* of the society played a fundamental role in the government decisions», Einaudi takes up the reflections on Le Play's thought. On this basis, he criticises a certain way of doing social and political science which, in order to find valid general laws in every time and place, does a pure statistical sampling of historical facts. «There is someone – among them he includes Marx, Pareto and Mosca – who divides the world into victims of oppression and oppressors, subject classes and ruling classes». In Einaudi's view that way of doing science «is false history and false theory. Facts should not be measured according to the extensions of time and place in which they happened, or according to the peoples who were actors and spectators of this facts»[66], for, by doing so, exceptional cases which, as such, are not included in the general laws, are cut out of history and theory. In other words, for Einaudi it is necessary to have a criterion of judgement and action on the basis of which to judge or guide the reality and not simply undergo it. «It does exists a hierarchy in the happened facts; and who cannot see it is not either historian or theoreticians». Therefore «the historian and theorist are not free to give [...] the same weight» to historical facts, or taxes, or fiscal systems. «Going beyond the rough cortex of the brute fact [...], it is necessary searching for the core idea, the ultimate end». So, «if we, for an instant, call "periclean" the "ideal fiscal system", and "daily" the current fiscal system working in the various times and places, I maintain that the historian and the theorist must look at periclean finance». This is because, «confronted to the other one, it is the judge and the executor of the high values of

64 Here, p. 319.

65 L. EINAUDI (1959), pp. 263 ss.

66 Here, p. 291.

justice»[67]. «Therefore I say that the very object of the financial "science" is not the precarious and contingent fact, but the ideal that the human reason admires when it looks to the current facts. The daily fact is the shade that fades away, the ideal is the only eternal reality»[68].

With the words which close the *Miti e paradossi della giustizia tributaria* Einaudi comes back again on the distinction between good government and bad government, and, respectively, between good governors and bad governors. «Any ruling class is able to get taxes coactively imposed. But the leader chosen by the *valentior pars* of the citizens [...] intends to raise the mortals from the city of man to the divine city, where the word "tax" [meant as a burden or imposition] is unknown, because *everyone knows the reason and the value of the sacrifice offered on the altar of the common good*»[69].

To know «*the reason and the value of the sacrifice offered on the altar of the common good*» is obviously something that goes beyond the mere economic calculus, which Einaudi previously considered a sufficient determinant of the fiscal choices[70]. It does imply that the citizens share a "vision of the world" consisting in that «common good», i. e. that citizens share given value judgements from which they derive the legitimacy of the fiscal power beyond the narrow paradigm of self interest.

In Einaudi's view, an essential character of the good governor would be the knowledge of the economic science with its laws, to be able to provide the "good government". Thus Einaudi refers to the work of Wicksteed (*The Common Sense of Political Economy Including a Study of the Human Basis of Econonomic Law*) as the «*treaty of good government*». Wicksteed, according to Einaudi, wrote the «*treaty of good government*» summing up the «common man's advice of good sense». «In private life it is useful to the man to study the elegant and admonishing ramifications of the choice theory, in order to avoid the unavoidable punishment of the ruin, of the failure, of the poverty, of the despair for himself and his children. Nevertheless, it is useful above all that the man in public life incarnates those laws [of economic science], because unfortunately the punishment for his mistakene choices falls [...] on the innocents»[71].

While for Pareto, obviously, all this would be a mixture of residuals and derivations giving origin to non logical actions, this Einaudi's view from a "process" window is intrinsically connected with his research from a "design" window of

67 Here, pp. 292-293.

68 Here p. 296.

69 Here p. 297.

70 In the above mentioned L. EINAUDI (1919).

71 L. EINAUDI, (1961), pp. 11-12.

the "optimal state" i. e. of the "good government", as an equilibrium model both of good society and of good rulers (shared by the citizens-taxpayers).

IV Concluding Remarks

The true meaning of Pareto's theory of the maximum welfare of the community which has been presented only in his last big work, the *Treatise of sociology,* cannot be understood without considering the theory of social equilibrium that he had traced in his *Manual of Political Economy.* Here sentiments, i. e. the "residual states of the mind" that give origin to non logical actions, which mostly derive from religion, moral beliefs and legal habits, dominate the scene. They are the main factors of social stability and of improvement of the conditions of life, as well as of rupture and change of equilibrium. The sentiments and generally speaking the non logical actions enter in a mixture with the logical actions in different measures depending from the social classes. In the lower, less cultured classes, which, at lest originally, are also poor, are dominant the non logical actions brought about by their prevailing sentiments. In the superior classes logical actions prevail. However they consciously and unconsciously make appeal to sentiments and instincts, i. e. to non logical actions to capture the consensus of their supporters and of the other people. The fact that they do so does not mean that they always succeed in their purposes. The reason is that, in the area of sociological phenomena, it is difficult to make previsions. Here comes in to play also the theory of the circulation of the elites as developed in the *Treatise of Sociology,* interconnected with the theory of the residuals and derivations.

Thus the Paretian theory of the sociological process of public economy is a complex made of three interconnected components. They are the theory of the maximum of utility of the community in sociology, the theory of the elites that actually perform this maximization or oppose the existing one, and, as a bridge among them, the theory of the non logical actions. This theory, in turn, leads us to the theory of the residuals and of the derivations and to the circulation of elites. The two main blocks of the Paretian public economy sociological process – i. e. the maximization of utility of the community and the elites that do this maximization, ruling the governments and those at the opposition – are linked together by non logical actions based on the "residuals" and derivations. The interests of the ruling elites and those of their supporters in the maximization have a greater weight than the interests of the opposing elites, and of all the others. But the social equilibrium may be obtained only letting the community to believe that what is really pursued by the ruling elite is their general interest. And this requires the continuous appeal to derivations and opens the way to the elites circulation.

This Paretian sociological view of the fiscal economy implies a pessimistic view of the process of fiscal choices, of the behaviour of the ruling elites and of that of the opposing ones. As a consequences also the judgement on the circulation of the elites is pessimistic. This unilateral view may non correspond to the real tendencies to equilibrium of the forces at work. And, as we have seen, it has raised harsh criticisms. However, the broadness of Pareto's sociological view opens the way to new developments of fiscal sociology together with a more careful consideration of the limits of the rational constructs of the social welfare functions – both as for the window of the fiscal process and for that of the policy design. The notion of national or general interest as guideline for this maximization, needs new reflections to connect Pareto I with Pareto II welfare criterion. Reflection on Pareto's fiscal sociology may be of great help in the researches in the area of the opportunistic behaviours and the pressure groups, and in that of the elites who make the fiscal choices. For the first group of theories, it may be of great help in complementing the current economic analysis with the sociological view about residuals and derivations. In the literature of the public choices there is a vacuum about their *political* actors. Indeed there is a rich theoretical and empirical literature on the voters behaviour, on elections and on bureaucracies and their behaviours. But the scientific literature on the political actors of public choice does not tell much, beyond the simplified proposition that their behaviour may be explained by their aim to be re elected, which does non clarify their ends and degree of rationality. Who they are, which skills they have, which ideologies, how these influence their re-election, which sociological and institutional factors influence the circulation of the political elites? The stimulus of the Paretian theory of the elites leads to open here a new window of empirical research.

Bibliography

Bachaus J. G. and Maks J. A (2006), *From Walras to Pareto,* New York, Springer US

Bobbio N. (1966), *Saggi sulla scienza politica in Italia*, Laterza, Roma-Bari

Bobbio N. (1972), *On Mosca and Pareto,* Librairie Droz, Geneve, Paris

Borgatta G. (1917), *L'economia dinamica. Studio critico sui problemi dinamici nell'economia pura*, UTET, Torino

Borgatta G. (1920), "Lo studio scientifico dei fenomeni finanziari", *Giornale degli Economisti* translated in M. McLure (2007) as " The Scientific Study of Fiscal Phenomena"

Delle Piane M. (1952), *Gaetano Mosca. Classe politica e liberalismo*, Esi, Napoli

Busino G. (2000), *The signification of Vilfredo Pareto's sociology*, in «Revue européenne des sciences sociales, 2000, n. 117, pp. 217-228

Busino G. (1989), *L'Italia di Wilfredo Pareto. Economia e Società in un Carteggio del 1873-1923,* Vol. I e II, Milano, Banca Commerciale Italiana

Busino G. (1975), *Guida a Pareto. Antologia per una teoria critica delle scienze della società*,, Milano, Rizzoli

D'Albergo E. (1963), "Finanza pubblica e benessere. Oneri e vantaggi della frontiera dell'utilità", *Giornale degli Economisti*

D'Albergo E. (1963), "Finanza pubblica e benessere:ponderazioni necessarie di contrapposte grandezze edeniche ", *Giornale degli economisti*

D'Albergo E. (1963), "Finanza pubblica e benessere, riducibilità logica del modello paretiano di funzioni e schemi del welfare collegati con piani di bilanci finanziari", *Giornale degli Economisti*

D'Albergo E. (1964), "Finanza pubblica e benessere: validità attuale della genesi razionale italiana del massimo di benessere collettivo", *Giornale degli Economisti*

D'Albergo E. (1967), "Una identificazione di schemi per l'economia finanziaria", *Giornale degli Economisti*

De Pietri-Tonelli A. (1935), *Mosca e Pareto, Rivista internazionale di scienze sociali,* anno XLIII, IV, Luglio

Einaudi L. (1914), *Osservazioni critiche intorno alla teoria dell'ammortamento dell'imposta e teoria delle variazioni nei redditi e nei valori capitali susseguenti all'imposta*, in EINAUDI L. (1958), *Saggi sul risparmio e l'imposta*, Einaudi, Torino

L. Einaudi (1919), *Osservazioni critiche intorno alla teoria dell'ammortamento dell'imposta e teoria delle variazioni nei redditi e nei valori capitali susseguenti all'imposta,* in Einaudi (1958), *Saggi sul risparmio e l'imposta*, Torino, Einaudi pp. 161-240.

Einaudi L. (1923), *Parlamenti e classe politica*, in «Corriere della Sera », 2 giugno 1923,riedited in (1960) *Cronache Economiche e Politiche di un trentennio,* VII, pp.

Einaudi L. (1928-9), "Introduction" to *Contributo alla ricerca dell'ottima imposta, in Annali di Economia, Milano*, V, 1928-29, pp. 7-224, translated in L. Einaudi, "Contribution to the quest for an optimal tax", in EINAUDI, *Selected Economic Essays*, edited by L. Einaudi, R. Faucci, R. Marchionatti, Palgrave Macmillan

Einaudi L. (1933), *La condotta economica e gli effetti sociali della guerra italiana,* Laterza – Yale University press, Bari

Einaudi L. (1934), *Prefazione* to A. de Viti de Marco, *Principi di economia finanziaria*, Einaudi, Torino pp. XV-XXVII

Einaudi L. (1934), "Dove si discorre di Pareto, di Mosca e anche di De Viti" *La riforma sociale* 1934, XLI, reprinted in L. EINAUDI (1937). *Nuovi Saggi*, Einaudi, Torino

Einaudi L. (1936), *Il peccato originale e la Teoria della classe eletta in Federico Le Play*, in *Rivista di Storia Economica* No. 2, 1936, in *Saggi bibliografici e storici intorno alle dottrine economiche*, Edizioni di storia e letteratura, Roma 1953, pp. 307-344

Einaudi L. (1941), Liberismo e Communismo, in ID. (1954), pp. 264-287

Einaudi L. (1954), *Il buongoverno. Saggi di economia e politica (1897-1954)*, edite by Ernesto Rossi, Laterza, Bari 1954

Einaudi L. (1959), *Miti e paradossi della giustizia tributaria,* Einaudi, Torino

Einaudi L. (1961), "*I consigli de buon senso*", in il Mondo, 28 November, pp. 11-12

Fasiani M. (1932-33), Der Gegenrwartige Stand der Reinen Theorien der Finanzwissenschaft in Italien, Zeitschfrit fur Ntionaleconomie

Fasiani M. (1940 and 2007), "Pareto's contributions to the science of public finance" translated from M. FASIANI (1940) "Contributi di Pareto alla scienza delle finanze", *Giornale degli economisti* in Mc Lure (2007)

Fasiani M. (1951), *Principi di Scienza delle finanze,* Giappichelli Torino, Vol. I.

Forte F. (1982), *Luigi Einaudi: il mercato e il buongoverno*, Einaudi, Torino 1982

Forte F. (2010), *Principles of Public Economics. A Public Choice Approach*, Cheltenham, Edwaed Elgar

Frascani P. (1969), *Gaetano Mosca e il mito della middle class, Critica storica*(Messina-Firenze), VIII

Giardina E. (1969), "Le scelte finanziarie e il massimo paretiano di utilità collettiva", in *Scritti in onore di Giordano dell'Amore*, Milano, Giuffrè

Griziotti B. (1943 and 2007), "At the School of Wilfredo Pareto and Maffeo Pantaloni translated in Mc Lure (2007) from B. GRIZIOTTI (1943) "Alla scuola di Vilfredo Pareto e Maffeo Pantaloni", *Rivista di diritto finanziario e scienza delle finanze*, 1943

Lombardo A. (1976), *Teorie del potere politico. Mosca e Pareto*, Bologna, Bon

Meisel James H. (1958), *The Myth of the Ruling Class: Gaetano Mosca and the Elite*, Ann Arbor, University of Michigan

Montemartini G. (1900 and 1967), "The fundamental principles of pure theory of public finance", translation of (1900) "Le basi fondamentali della scienza finanziaria pura" in R. A. MUSGRAVE and A. T. PEACOCK (eds) (1967), *Classics in the theory of public finance*, London McMillan

Mosca G. (1982), *Teorica dei governi e governo parlamentare*, in MOSCA 1982 *Scritti politici*, a. c. di G. Sola, vol. I, Utet, Torino 1982

Mosca G. (1932), *Lezioni di Storia delle istituzioni e delle dottrine politiche*, Castellani, Roma

Mosca G. (1939), *The Ruling Class*, New York, McGraw-Hill
Mosca G. (1966), *La classe politica*, edited by N. Bobbio, Laterza, Bari
Mosca (1982), *Scritti politici*, edited by di G. Sola, vol. I and II Torino, Utet
Murray R. (1914), *Principi fondamentali della scienza pura delle finanze,* Firenze, Carnesecchi
Murray R. (1915), "La scienza delle finanze, il diritto finanziario e la nozione di stato", *Giornale degli economisti*, translated as "The science of public finance, fiscal law and the notion of State", in Mc Lure (2007)
Murray R. (1952), *Lezioni di scienza delle finanze e diritto finanziario,* Pisa, Pellegrini
Murray R. (1953), "Alcune osservazioni sui problemi della finanza pubblica come scienza politica" *Giornale degli economisti*
Pareto (1980-1982), *Ouvres Complètes,* edited by G, Busino, Genéve, Librarie Droz
Pareto (1894), "Il massimo di utilità dato dalla libera concorrenza", Giornale degli economisti reprinted in PARETO (1982), *Ouvres Complètes,* edited by G, Busino, Genéve, Librarie Droz
Pareto W. (1897), "Il compito della sociologia fra le scienze sociali", reprinted in Pareto (1980), vol. 22, *Ecrites sociologiques*
Pareto W. (1896-07 and 1953 and 1971), *Cours d'economie politique, also as Corso di Economia Politica,* Torino, Einaudi, 1953 and Torino, Utet 19071)
Pareto (1901-2), *Le sistemes Socialistes,* reprinted in PARETO (1980), vol. 22, *Ecrites sociologiques* also Italian edition by Pareto (1902 and 1974) *I sistemi socialisti*, Torino Utet
Pareto W. (1906, 1971 and 2006), *Manual of political Economy,* New York, Kelley,translation of PARETO (1906), *Manuale di economia politica* on the second French edition, new edition of 1906 the Manuale di economia politica, by A. Montesano, A, Zanni and E. BRUNI, Milano, Egea
Pareto W. (1913), "Il massimo di utilità per una collettività in sociologia". *Giornale degli Economisti e rivista di statistica i,* 1913, April., reprinted in PARETO (1982), vol. 26, *Ecrites d'économie politique*
Pareto (1916 and 1935 and 1964), *The Mind and Society: A Treatise on General Sociology.* New York: Harcourt, Brace, Jananovich, 1935. Reprint, New York: Dover Publications, 1963., translation of PARETO W. (1916) *Trattato di Sociologia Generale,* new Italian edition 1964, Vol. I and II l: with Introduction of N. Bobbio, Milano, Edizioni di Comunità
Passerin D'Entrèves A. (1959), *Gaetano Mosca e la libertà*, Torino Artigianelli
Piovani P. (1950), *Il liberalismo di Gaetano Mosca*, in *Rassegna di diritto pubblico* III-IV
Ripepe E. (1974), *Gli elitisti italiani. Mosca Pareto Michels*, Pacini, Pisa 1974

Scotto A. (1950), "Di un indice di decentramento finanziario", in *Finanza pubblica contemporanea. Studi in onore di Jacopo Tivaroni*, Bari, Laterza

Scotto A. (1952), "Prime linee di un contributo alla teoria della finanza locale", in *Studi in onore di Gino Borgatta*, Bologna, Arti Grafiche

Sensini G. (1917 and 2007), "Outline of theoretical Public finance", translation in Mc Lure (2007) of (1917), "Prime linee di finanza teorica", in (1917) *Studi in onore di Tullio Martello*, Bari Laterza

Sensini G. (1932), "La finanza sociologica", in G. SENSINI (1932), *Studi di scienze sociali*

Sensini G. (1932), *Studi di scienze sociali*, Roma, casa Libraria Editrice italiana

Silvestri P. (2006), "Il buongoverno nel pensiero di Einaudi e Mosca: tra governo della legge e governo degli uomini", *Annali della Fondazione Luigi Einaudi*, XL.

Silvestri P. (editor) (2007), *Carteggio Einaudi-Mosca*, in *www.scuolaeconomiatorino.unito.it/* (section: "Corrispondenze") pp. 1-97

Silvestri P. (2008), *Il liberalismo di Luigi Einaudi o del Buongoverno*, Rubbettino, Soveria Mannelli

Silvestri P. (2008), "On Luigi Einaudi's liberal heritage", *History of Economic Ideas*, 1-2, pp. 245-252

Silvestri P. (2009), "Veritas, Auctoritas, Lex. Scienza economica e sfera pubblica: sulla normatività del Terzo", *Il pensiero economico italiano*, XVII, 2, pp. 37-65

Wagner R. (2007), *Fiscal Sociology and the Theory of Public Finance, An Exploratory Essay,* Cheltenham, Elgar

Weber M. (1919 and 1989), *Politik als Beruf*, Munchen, 1919, reedited with an "Introduction" by by R. Dahrendorf, in 1899, Reclam Universal-Bibliothek

Cameralistic Accounting And Management Information System In Public Administration

Gerhard Scheuerer

Abstract

Cameralistic accounting prevailed in public admin in the past and suffers from managing diversity of courses in admin. Cameralistic accounting is not fit for steering administrative production processes. Today, an interdisciplinary approach is necessary not only concerning fiscal objectives but including organizational and economical concepts. It will be established, that prevailing cameralistic accounting system is furthermore necessary and that there are additional needs in public admin for detailed business information and data on administrative production / output processes nowadays. A Management Information System is recommended that combines both: cameralistic accounting as well as continuous business information.

1. Introduction

Cameralism as science developed in the age of absolutism. In Germany, some differentiations are determinable compared with the international discussions on mercantilism at that time. Cameralism as state science had supremacy in scientific, political and practical governmental activities for a long time in Germany up to the mid of the 20th century. In the 1960s, a change of paradigm took place and industrial economic views on administrative practices in governmental authorities came in the limelight[1]. In Germany, different federal state universities of applied sciences have been founded to train as higher civil servants. Mainly economic and operational contents of teaching were added to the former predominant juridical training curricula. During ensuing period New Public Management developed, which is disputed in literature if this is an independent science or if this consists of a collection of different parts of economic theories[2].

Besides fulfilling the different tasks of a public admin, a very important point of administrative practice is the management. Nowadays, management comprises in our context peculiarities planning, organizing, staffing, leading and controlling an admin to accomplish pre-decided aims. These issues need efficient data which produce the information of the more or less actual status of administrative processes, concerning planning and steering flow of work and output as well as human resources. Cameralistic accounting has different aims compared with the aims of double bookkeeping as used in industrial and trade companies for a

1 For example in Germany: König (1970) and more up-dated: Hughes (2003).
2 Osborne (2010).

long time already. According to the International Public Accounting Standards (IPSAS), double bookkeeping uses, first Financial Reporting Under the Cash Basis of Accounting (Einzahlungs-/ Auszahlungsrechnung), and second Financial Reporting Under the Accrual Basis of Accounting (Aufwands- und Ertragsrechnung). The latter is not used in cameralistic accounting. Concerning above named issues of management, which are not part of cameralistic accounting, discussion came up to introduce financial reporting into cameralistic accounting[3]

2. Management Information System

For following considerations, we define a Management Information System in the broadest sense as a System for strategic and operative decisions as well as planning, steering and controlling output and human resources to catch optimal product quality and service quality as well as number and qualification of civil servants. Human resources are clearly necessary for an efficient and effective system producing output und services.

3. Cameralisic Accounting Vs. Management Information System?

3.1 Tasks, Objectives, Means Of Cameralistic Accounting And Of Management Information System

In the following we will describe shortly the common aspect of cameralistic accounting managing cash flow. Tasks of cameralistic accounting are to indicate receipts as well as expenditures of public admin. Objectives are to find out, if the agreed and specified budget of public admin is formally realized. In certain cases, budget of public admin connects upstream of Cost-Benefit Analysis. Means of cameralistic accounting are to supervise budget via rolls and controlling the budget.

In Germany, several federal states introduced an integrated system of cameralistic accounting and double bookkeeping in past years[4], which is named The New Finance System (Das Neue Finanzsystem). This System is criticized by some practitioners of local government[5] that the procedure is very expensive, time-consuming and systematic borderlines are overlapping in some cases. Criticism forgets gladly

3 For example in Germany: Budäus (1975); Eichhorn (1977).
4 Schöbel (2012).
5 For example: Lutz / Treber 2009.

the advantages with reference to strategic planning and operative decisions as to production processes und product quality.

Public administrative action has been criticized often in the past, especially their productivity and costs. Public Choice Theory bases on utility maximizing homo oeconomicus, identifies rent-seeking and recommends competition and privatization[6]. New Public Management designs alternatives for avoiding privatization and contributes to requirements and conditions of effective administration action[7]

Based on demands on modern admin, task of a Management Information System as defined above is to plan and steer the administrative production processes and outputs considering customer satisfaction as well as human resource management. There are three objectives of Management Information System:

1. Minimizing costs of production processes in the admin,
2. Managing human resources by modern standards and
3. Maximizing customer satisfaction.

To realize above named objectives there are several different means essential, in particular:

- Type of cost (Kostenart)
- Cost centre (Kostenstellen)
- Cost Unit (Kostenträger)
- Human Resource Management
- Total Quality Management
- Balanced Scorecard
- Regular Reports

3.2 Résumé of comparison

Comparing the objectives of cameralistic accounting and Management Information System as described, before we assess different setting of objectives: Cameralistic accounting tries to discover fiscal administrative objectives whereas Management Information System enables economic administrative objectives. A lean public administration has to realize a stronger orientation on customer satisfaction as well as decreasing production costs (simultaneous engineering)[8].

6 Buchanan (1996), McKenzie/Tullock (1984).

7 König / Beck (1997).

8 Gablers Wirtschaftslexikon (2011).

Those aims require both, cameralistic accounting and Management Information System.

3.3 New Public Management in practical experience

Aim of New Public Management (NPM) is a comprehension on economic principles of market orientation to realize greater cost-efficiency of public administration's operation sequences[9]. NPM streamed over many public admin throughout the world and is part of discussions on Good Governance. Upcoming of NPM resulted mainly from handsome lack of public budget resources, which prevails still today. This basic motive leads to problems of acceptance in practice. Employees think, the only reason of admin reform is to reduce their salary.

4. Coverage Of An Integrated Management Information System

Comparing the German public admin with coverage as specified below, there exist several components already, which are part of the cameralistic accounting for a long time. These components are fixed assets, accounting receipts, accounting expenditures, inventory and monitoring lists. Some other components exist alike for some years, but continuous improvements are necessary, i. e. admin resource planning to a wide extent, human resource management, task management, document management system, which has been pushed by electronic data processing during the last years, and time reporting system to a minor degree. Based on experiences of the author, in German and European public admin cost accounting, Total Quality Management Systems / Balanced Scorecard and Customer Relationship Management should be necessarily more completed.

In the following scheme a frame of components of a Management Information System (MIS) is drafted, which includes both cameralistic accounting and elements of NPM:

9 Current example: Osborne (2010), Kräkel (2010). In Germany, New Public Management is named New Steering Model (Neues Steuerungsmodell).

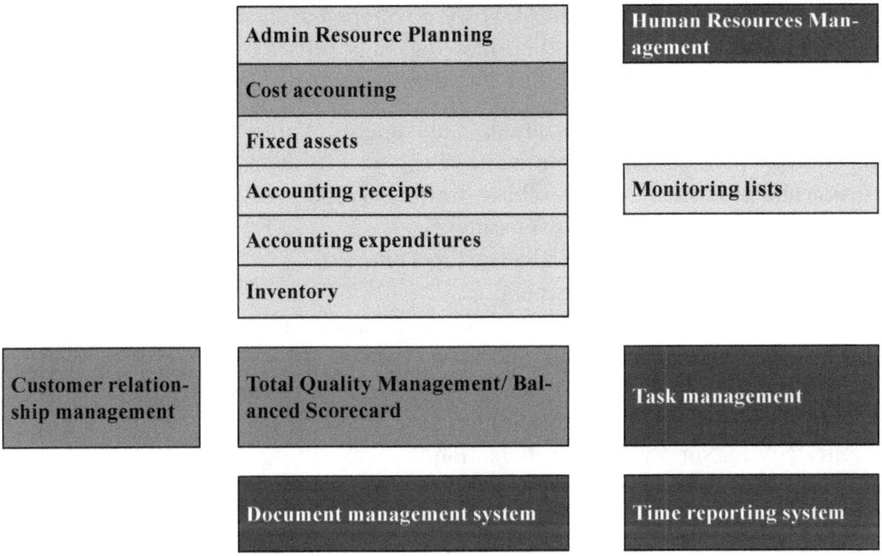

The proposed components of MIS, which are more and more common in public admin, will be described condensed in the following.

4.1 Cost Accounting

For implementing a MIS, cost accounting is an absolute requirement as common in the system of double bookkeeping. The following evidence is indispensable:

1. Cost type: which costs are emerged?
2. *Cost Centre*: where are the costs emerged?
3. Cost Unit: for what are the costs emerged?

These different costs take up products and services catalogue of the public admin for granted. Those indexes are difficult to establish without crossover.

4.2 Human Resource Management

Concerning comprehensive modern requirements on personnel work, Human Resource Management (HRM) seems to have been a poor cousin in some public admin in former times. When coming up awareness that staff training is indispensible in a changing working environment (mechanization of operational procedures) and attendant with NPM, HRM developed to an exceeding management business in public admin. In the following, only pillars of reasonable strategies will be enumerated, without going into details described in abundant literature[10]:

1. Strategy for current organizational adjustments (Vacancy Checks[11])
2. Strategy for electronic administrative use for loading and extracting information and produce managing tables, draft lists, reports concerning HRM, updating job descriptions and staff listings
3. Strategy for staff selection and staff recruitment
4. Strategy for career development
5. Strategy for staff training and professional qualification
6. Strategy for job rotation
7. Strategy for non-financial rewards (remuneration) based on results
8. Strategy for human resource planning
9. Strategy for survey on job satisfaction

Most practitioners will say: we have many of these strategies already. In reality, it lacks sometimes of written papers of the strategies including neutral individual support, which is necessary for discussions of in principle orientated future developments of tasks of the public authority.

4.3 Total Quality Management

Total Quality Management (TQM) has been developed out of original Japanese Quality Circles of the 1970s. TQM can be defined as comparison of continuous briefings on performance of admin processes and outputs with the needs and expectations of customers. In connection with public admin, it has to be attended that customers are the tax and fees payers! According to the International Organization for Standardization (ISO 9001), TQM is a quality management approach for an organization, which is

- Centered on quality
- Based on participation of all staff members and

10 Practical construction of the several pillars depends on laws and social culture in respective countries.

11 Vacancy check is a practical and tested proven organisation method to realise personnel needs assessments. Advantage for staff members is, that no employee is directly concerned. Only the unmanned activity area is of interest. Advantages for the admin are, first that developments of tasks and technique can be recognized as so to the organisational structure as well as to the organisation of workflow, and second that influence can be taken on the direction of the developments.

- Aiming long-term success through customers satisfaction as well as
- Benefits to all shareholders and to the society

In the following, only pillars of reasonable steps will be enumerated, without going into details described in abundant literature:

1. „Decision“ to carry out the administrative production
2. Preparation of the process organization
3. Strategy for data collection and document processing
4. Strategy for manufacturing final good
5. Customer Satisfaction Survey

In this context, the so called "7 W – Checklist"[12] is very helpful in praxis:

- What – is to do?
- Why – does he / she do it?
- Who – does it?
- What – has it to be done?
- When – has it to be done?
- Where – has it to be done?
- Why – is it not done in another way?

4.4 Balanced Scorecard

TQM as stated before should be completed by further grounded in consolidated findings depicting financial and organizational performances. For example, Balanced Scorecard (BSC) can help to support a comprehensive view of administrative business balancing financial objectives by customer (which are the tax and fees payers), process and output as well as employee‘s perspectives. In the following, only pillars of some reasonable steps will be enumerated, without going into details:[13]

1. Regular reports
2. Strategy for audits
3. Strategy for measuring and monitoring production processes / outputs
4. Strategy for management of non-conformities
5. Strategy for improvement actions

---

12 Kraus / Becker-Kolle / Fischer (2006)

13 Kaplan / Norton (2004)

BSC is similar to principles like Management by Objectives and ensures effective as well as efficient monitoring of strategy implementation.

5. Conclusion

The concept as characterized above in short lines demonstrates that further necessity exists to work with financial cameralistic system and that there are compulsory needs in public admin for additional business information and data on administrative production / output processes. Modern Public Admin is custodian of taxpayers! Therefore, acting persons in modern public administrative authorities have to realize cost-efficiency, effectiveness of labor as well as satisfaction of customers. For purposes planning and steering challenging production processes, human resources as well as customers satisfaction public admin demands unquestionable cost accounting verifying type of costs, cost centre and cost unit. These data constitute the basic specifications of a Management Information System, which tracks Human Resource Management and Quality Management including customers' satisfaction as well as job satisfaction.

In this essay, described requirements stand for a paradigm change and need many additional activities in public admin compared with mandatory regulations in former times. Of course, Management Information System as described above must be funded for the change management, but in the long term it will establish cost efficient and effective public admin as well as reducing public administrative expenditures.

References

Buchanan, James M. The Theory of Public Choice (Revised edition of: Theory of Public Choice 1972). University of Michigan Press, (1996).

Budäus, Dietrich Betriebswirtschaftliche Kostenrechnung im öffentlichen Bereich: Probleme und Schwachstellen der Praxis unter besonderer Berücksichtigung kommunaler Gebührenhaushalte in der Bundesrepublik Deutschland. In: Journal für Betriebswirtschaft, Bd. 33, Springer Verlag, Heidelberg, (1983), S. 168-183.

Eichhorn, Peter Kostendenken im öffentlichen Dienst. In: Öffentlicher Dienst. Festschrift für Carl Hermann Ule zum 70. Geburtstag. Hrsg. Klaus König, Hans W. Laubinger, Frido Wagener., Carl Heymanns Verlag, Köln, (1977), S. 33-51.

Gablers Wirtschaftslexikon; URL:http//wirtschaftslexikon.gabler.de/Archiv/ 54609/ lean-management-v5.html (2011)

Hughes, Owen Public Management and Administration: An Introduction. 3rd edition, Basingstoke U. K. (2003).

McKenzie, Richard B. / Tullock, Gordon: Homo Oeconomicus. Ökonomische Dimensionen des Alltags. Genehmigte Übersetzung der englischsprachigen Originalausgabe durch Jürgen Backhaus und Friedrich Schneider, Campus Verlag Frankfurt/Main, New York, (1984).

Kaplan, Robert S. / Norton, David P. Strategy maps : Der Weg von immateriellen Werten zum materiellen Erfolg. Aus dem Amerikanischen übersetzt von Péter Horváth, http://opac.uni-erfurt.de/DB=1/SET=6/TTL=32/MAT=/NOMAT=T/ CLK?IKT=1008&TRM=%§C&CVTOUR1%3E, Stuttgart, (2004).

König, Klaus Erkenntnisinteressen der Verwaltungswissenschaft. Duncker & Humblot, Berlin, (1970).

König, Klaus / Beck, Joachim Modernisierung von Staat und Verwaltung. Zum Neuen öffentlichen Management; Nomos Verlagsgesellschaft Baden-Baden, (1997).

Kräkel, Matthias Organisation und Management. 4., überarbeitete und erweiterte Auflage, Tübingen, (2010).

Kraus, Georg / Becker-Kolle, Christel / Fischer, Thomas Handbuch Change-Management: Steuerung von Veränderungsprozessen in Organisationen; Einflussfaktoren und Beteiligte; Konzepte, Instrumente und Methoden. Cornelsen Verlag Berlin, 2., überarbeitete Auflage 2006.

Lutz, Walter / Treber, Hagen Reformruine kommunale Doppik: Warum das neue kommunale Finanzwesen scheitern muss! Ein Vergleich von Doppik und Kameralistik; mb-Verlag Rheinfelden, (2009).

Osborne, Stephen P. (ed.) The new public governance?: Emerging perspectives on the theory and practice of public governance; London et al., (2010).

Schöbel, Enrico Double-Entry Bookkeeping in Municipal Finance: A Natural Field Experiment in Public Choice. In: Jürgen Backhaus (ed.): Two Centuries of Local Autonomy, Berlin, Heidelberg, New York: Springer, (2012), pp. 99-108.

Patenting Genetic Marine Resources: A Private Or A Public Choice?

Domenico da Empoli

1. The Convention on Biological Diversity defines *genetic resources* as "genetic material of actual or potential value" and *genetic material* as "any material of plant, animal, microbial or other origin containing functional units of heredity" (art. 2).

Activities related to marine genetic resources are quite recent and include three typologies: scientific investigation of the oceans and their biological processes; research and development or "bioprospecting" and exploitation.

At the current stage, various drugs, etc. derived from marine microorganisms (and in particular those extracted from the deep sea-bed) are now tested, apparently very successfully, in pharmacology for the treatment of cancer, tubercolosis, malaria and many other diseases. A number of patents in relation to development of biotechnology from deep-sea genetic resources has been granted already, not only in the domain of pharmacology, but also in the areas of chemistry, cosmetics, food and agriculture.

2. Considering the interest of these resources, a debate is currently going on in various international bodies (the United Nations Informal Consultative Process on the Law of the Sea, the meetings on the Convention on Biological Diversity, the United Nations General Assembly, the FAO, etc.) on the access to these resources and on the possible sharing of benefits from their exploitation (whether these benefits should be shared by the entire international community or only by the states, or by the individual firms with the capacity to exploit deep seabed genetic resources).

This debate includes two components: A) the issue of the current legal framework of the resources and B) the economic evaluation of its impact with some improvement suggestions.

A) The examination of the legal status of marine genetic resources requires the analysis of the rules provided by the UNCLOS (United Nations Convention on the Law of the Sea) on the resources beyond the national jurisdiction of the coastal states.

In particular, it is necessary to make sure whether these resources fall under the "common heritage of mankind" principle, which would mean that they cannot be freely used because they are under the jurisdiction of an international body, the International Seabed Authority. Otherwise, in absence of a precise obligation, the "freedom of the high seas" principle would apply and these resources could be exploited by anybody according to the "first come first served" principle.

The analysis of the complex system of UNCLOS on this matter seems to show that the principle of the "common heritage of mankind" only applies to the mineral resources of the deep seabed (polymetallic nodules, cobalt-rich crusts, polymetallic sulfides, methane hydrates).

Neither the UNCLOS rules dealing with scientific marine research (in Parts XIII and XIV of the Convention) apply to bioprospecting, since the provisions establishing the principle of freedom of marine research do not apply to commercial activities.

In conclusion, as to the UNCLOS, it appears that genetic resources of the sea bed have not been taken into consideration by the UN Convention on the Law of the Sea, which is understandable considering that during the Seventies and the early Eighties of last century the existence of genetic resources in the deep seabed was largely unknown.

Though the Convention for the Biological Diversity is more recent (1992), it also does not apply to the high seas genetic resources. In fact, indeed, the CBD's role is to regulate the use of genetic resources in zones under national jurisdiction, but it cannot extend its regulatory powers to the areas beyond national jurisdiction.

By consequence, currently there is no legal framework for collecting and exploiting seabed genetic resources, which means that to the exploitation of microorganisms in deep waters applies the "freedom of high seas principle".

B) As to the economic impact of this principle, it is necessary to verify whether there is any danger to face in this area a "tragedy of commons", that in this case might derive from two reasons: 1) the overexploitation of the genetic resources; 2) the possible damage to the environment.

As to 1), the overexploitation should not take place if the patent law will require, as it normally does –though the patent legislation of various countries is not yet fully harmonized- three criteria for granting patents: novelty, invention, and some industrial use. "Invention" is not to be mixed up with "discovery": in fact, the patent protects, in case of genetic resources, the drug whose component is the "discovered" microorganism. The Conventions on intellectual property rights (WIPO or TRIPS in the framework of WTO) recognize the right to patenting inventions based on genetic resources. But the microorganism as such shouldn't be patented, otherwise a problem (shortage) might emerge. And such a condition would certainly justify a strict regulation, with sharing of benefits and / or payment of royalties (maybe through the establishment of a special fund under the control of an international organization), as suggested on various occasions by developing countries.

As to 2), the actual preliminary stage of exploitation of seabed genetic resources does not allow to reach precise conclusions. However, the most updated study on this matter, by Arrieta, Arnaud-Haond and Duarte states that "bioprospecting of marine resources only requires the collection of a very limited amount of biomass for the initial gene or product discovery. Therefore, bioprospecting does not generally involve threats to biodiversity comparable to the large biomass removals involved in harvesting of marine resources for food"[1].

In spite of the reassurances, at this stage it appears convenient to rely on the principle of precaution.

3) In conclusion, this paper points out some of the main issues dealing with the management of deep seabed genetic resources. They require a very difficult balancing of private and social costs and benefits, in order to avoid discouraging industrial investments in this new and promising area and also not to restrict access to genetic resources for research purpose as well as for their exploitation. But the precautionary principle should be taken in due consideration.

References

Arrieta, J. M. – S. Arnaud-Haond – C. M. Duarte What Lies Underneath: Conserving the Oceans' Genetic Resources. in: Proceedings of the National Academy of Sciences of the United States of America, (2010), www.pnas.org/lookup/suppl/doi:10.1073/pnas.

Beslier, S. The Protection and Sustainable Exploitation of Genetic Resources of the High Seas from the EU's Perspective. The International Journal of Marine and Coastal Law, vol. 24, N. 2, (2009), pp. 333-341.

Eckert, R. D. The Enclosure of Ocean Resources – Economics of the Law of the Sea, Stanford, Hoover Institution Press, (1979).

Haefner, B. Drugs from the Deep: Marine Natural Products as Drug Candidates. (2003), www. Drugdiscoverytoday.com 8: 536-544.

Helfer, L. R. Using Intellectual Property Rights to Preserve the Global Genetic Commons: The International Treaty on Plant Genetic Resources for Food and Agriculture. In: Maskus, K. E. – Reichman, J. H. (eds.), International Public

1 Arrieta, J. M. – S. Arnaud-Haond – C. M. Duarte, 2010, 'What Lies Underneath: Conserving the Oceans' Genetic Resources', in: *Proceedings of the National Academy of Sciences of the United States of America*, www.pnas.org/lookup/suppl/doi:10.1073/pnas, p. 4.

Goods and Transfer of Technology Under a Globalized Intellectual Property Regime, (2005), pp. 217-223, Cambridge, Cambridge University Press.

International Foundation for the Law of the Sea, Symposium on Biodiversity and Genetic Resources of the Deep Sea, Hamburg, 29 September 2007.

Ostrom, E., Gardner, R., Walker, J. (eds.) Rules, Games, & Common-Pool Resources, Ann Arbor, The University of Michigan Press, (1994).

Kaul, I., Gruneberg, I., and Stern, M. A. (eds.) Global Public Goods – International Cooperation in the 21st Century, New York, Oxford University Press, (1999).

Leary, D. K. International Law and the Genetic Resources of the Deep Sea, Leiden-Boston, Martinus Nijhoff, (2007).

Scovazzi, T. Mining, Protection of the Environment, Scientific Research and Bioprospecting: Some Considerations on the Role of the International Sea-Bed Authority. In: The International Journal of Marine and Coastal Law, vol. 19, N. 4, (2004), pp. 383-409

United Nations University, An Update on Marine Genetic Resources: Scientific Research, Commercial Uses and a Database on Marine Bioprospecting, New York, U. N., June 2007.

Vaubel, R., Willett, T. D. (eds.) The Political Economy of International Organizations: A Public Choice Approach. Boulder, WestView Press, (1991).

The Pareto Sociological Theory Of The Elites And The Italian Parliament (1861-1928)

Silvia Fedeli and Francesco Forte

1. Introduction

The purpose of this paper is to test, in a fiscal sociology perspective, the relevance of the Pareto's theory of the members of the political class as elites, considering the composition of the Italian democratic parliament from the foundation of the Italian Kingdom in 1860 to 1928, the year of the last elected legislature before the Second World War. We focus on some of the main characters (e. g., age, level of education and profession, parties) of its members considering the legislatures under restricted suffrage up to those under quasi universal male suffrage.

Very important contributions to the sociological theory of the political class as elite have been offered by Vilfredo Pareto, in its three books, Le Sistemes Socialistes[1], Manuale di Economia Politica[2] and Trattato di sociologia[3]. This theory is particularly relevant for the fiscal choices because of its interconnections with his own sociological theory of the maximum of utility of the community and the economic theory of the public finance processes.[4]

The distinctive characters of the Pareto's theory of elites appear to be the followings.

a) The elites, meaning by this expression those who exert the economic and / or the political power and have superior roles in a given community or may succeed in these superior roles, as new elite, replacing an existing elite, are composed of individuals of superior talents in their own activity. The distribution of the qualities is similar to that of the wealth curve, with a campanula's shape, which implies that the elite is necessarily a minority, but the distribution of talents that enables to get the power does not (necessarily) coincide with that behind the existing wealth distribution.

1 Pareto (1901-1902)-

2 See Pareto, V. Manuale di Economia Politica Manuale di economia politica con una introduzione alla scienza sociale. Milano: Società Editrice Libraria, (1906), xii, p. 576 and further editions in 1909 and 1919.

3 For some odd reason its title in the English translation is *Mind and Society*.

4 See Forte and Silvestri (2009).

b) Each elite may be subdivided into two components, a small minority that actually rules the community and a larger minority which supports it; the ruling minority pursues its own interests and those of the supporting minority more than the interests of the others and particularly of those of the alternative elite(s).

c) Any individual and social group act via logical and non logical actions, driven by sentiments and beliefs in some ethical or religious credence. This cannot be avoided because the distinction between logical and non logical actions does not coincide with the distinction between experimental actions (i. e., those whose causal or interdependent nexus may be tested by experience) and non experimental actions. Thus, there are logical non experimental actions and non logical experimental actions. Individuals may easily consider true and valid the latter more than the former, because they are driven by sentiments and a priori beliefs which the experience cannot falsify. The non logical actions consists of derivations, i. e., principles, rules, actions *derived* from residuals not susceptible of experimental test. The elites, actual and potential, when belonging to activities that require the logic, as those of "ruling something", may be expected to have a more logical attitude than the other elites and the majority of the people in the relevant curves of talents.

d) However, in order to get the power and maintain it, the ruling elite, being a minority, needs to use the non logical actions, consisting in derivations to convince the majority that it is pursuing the good of the country and their interests. There may be an interaction between this way of ruling and the way the elite "reasons", i. e., between its mix of logical and non logical behaviour also in pursuing its own interests.

e) There is, also for this same reason, an inevitable decay of the elite in power and a replacement by other elites. Thus, there is a law of circulation of the elites which may be explained by three main causal factors: biological factors (age and other physical factors that cause the death), changes of the prevailing psychology – i. e., new cultural models – and decadence, in which the reduction of logical capacity and the submission to the non logic beliefs (derivations) of the opposing elites may play a paramount role.

f) Therefore, the circulation of elites takes place both inside the same type and between different types: one important classification of the types of elites is that between speculators and rentiers. The speculators, the first type of elites, in Pareto terminology consists of the individuals with a cultural model of risk taking. Therefore, they are the innovators and, among them, there are the entrepreneurs. The rentiers, the second type of elites, consist of individuals with risk adverse cultural models and, therefore, of people who are conservative against changes and innovations. Among them, we find those who like to survive by rents, not necessarily from real estate or from financial property, but also from a stable job in the public administration.

g) The social dynamic of the community is explained by the circulation of the elites, but there is also an interaction between cultural changes and changes of elites that shape the community.

h) However, the socio-economic equilibrium of the community may be characterized by excessive instability or by a static situation or by a stable development according to whether there is an absolute prevalence of the first type of elites and, hence, of the community over the second or the opposite situation or a combination of the first and the second type, with prevalence of the first, but not elimination of the second type of elites.

Many empirical researches of fiscal sociology might, thus, be done drawing from Pareto's theory of elites. Pareto himself, from his theory of the political elites, did draw pessimistic conclusion about the fiscal choices, because of the prevalence of non logic / demagogic behaviours of the political class in managing public money, particularly, with the advent of mass democracy. However, his theory of the maximum utility for the community developed in relation to his theory of elites does not necessarily lead to these results. Other authors, recognizing the imperfections of democracy, argue against the generalization of Pareto pessimistic conclusions (see, for example Forte and Silvestri, 2009). Here we shall not examine the choices of the Italian Parliament in the observed period, but the characteristics of its members as elite in power, in different disaggregations / subclasses, which, as one shall notice, do not give a negative picture their qualitative level.

2. Some Stylized Facts

On the basis of this Paretian theory of the elites, we now focus on the composition of the Italian democratic parliament, since the creation of the Italian State in 1861 to 1928 (on April, 6th 1924 there was the last general election, allowed by the fascist government). We concentrate on the chamber of deputies only, because, the Senators were appointed by the King under proposal of the head of the government.[5]

In the Paretian sense of a change of ideological residuals, it may be of interest to examine, first, whether and how much changes of this type affected the

5 The non elected chamber may, indeed, be considered as composed by members of the political elite ruling the public economy in so far as these bodies have a true decisional power, as it was certainly the case with the senate in the Kingdom of Italy. In this respect, a specific research shall be object of future analysis.

composition of the parliament. There are other important socio-cultural changes to be considered, interfering with the "non logical" scenario, as those dealing with the different degree of economic and social developments and with different moral attitudes. Furthermore, there are socio-cultural changes in the electorate affecting the types and degrees of non logical components of the voting choices, deriving from the different extension of the suffrage often related, not only to income, but also to degree of literacy. The degree of illiteracy, as shown in figure 1, declined over the period considered from the very high rate of 80% at the beginning of the Italian democratic system in 1861 to 55% at the beginning of the 20th century, to about 25% at the end of the period considered here. The women did not vote, not even when the quasi universal suffrage was introduced in 1913. As for men, the male illiteracy rate was about 70% in 1861, went down to about 50% at the beginning of the 20th century and was about 20% in the period of the last democratic elections. The degree of illiteracy is important for the composition and circulation of the political class, not only because, as observed, it affects the rationality of the electorate that chooses the politicians, but also because it influences the "supply" of the politicians who run for elections. Moreover, it is crucial for the extension of the suffrage.

Figure 1. Illiteracy in italy in Italy (1861-1931).

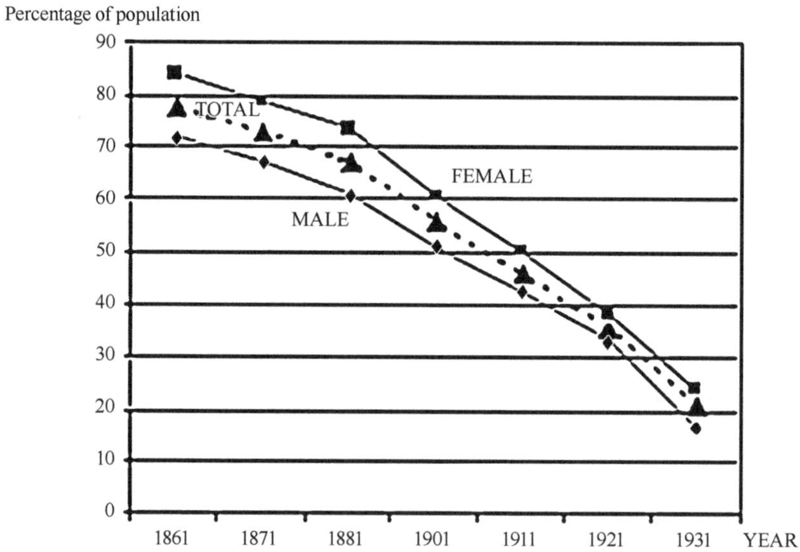

With respect to the extension of the suffrage, we shall divide the Monarchic epoch in six periods: the first, with restricted suffrage by level of income and literacy test until 1882; the second (from 1882 to 1892), with restricted suffrage and the right of vote to those who pay taxes and have at least two degrees of elementary education; the third, from 1892 to 1913, with the beginning of the Socialist movement[6] (socialism is one of the main source of the changes in residuals considered by Pareto); the fourth (from 1913 to 1919) with the (quasi) universal suffrage (voting right to men without literacy test) and proportional system with the mass parties and many minor parties; the fifth, after the first world war, from 1919 to 1924; and the sixth (the last legislature with the fascist government already in power) with the new electoral law giving a premium to the winning majority.

The determinants of re-election, as noted, are important to test the Paretian principle of "elites circulation" by means of a quantitative research on the composition of the Parliament in the different epochs. The re-election rates for both 2 and 3 consecutive legislatures of the elected representatives are reported in figure 2.

Figure 2. Re-election rate for 2 and 3 consecutive legislature of the representatives: Chamber of Deputies from 1861 to 1928.

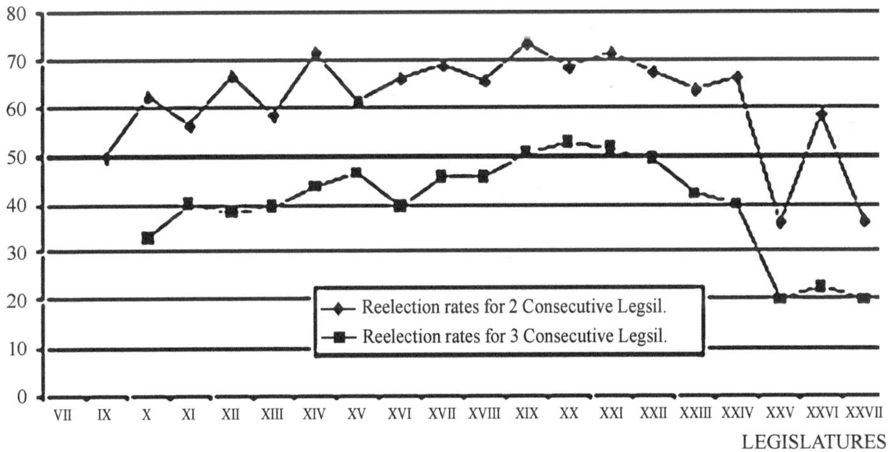

(♦ Reelection rates for 2 Consecutive Legsil.;
■ Reelection rates for 3 Consecutive Legisl.)

6 The Socialist party organized at national level was founded in a congress held in Genova in 1882 with the name PSI, Partito Socialista Italiano.

We have also classified the members of the Parliament on the basis of their education, prevailing profession, age and political affiliation.[7] If the members of parliament in general tend to have a relatively young age, it is clearly easy to enter the political arena and the law of circulation is quite pronounced so that the curve of talents selecting the elite does not seem much relevant. If, on the contrary, the members of parliament tend to have a relatively old age, the opposite occurs. In a Paretian perspective, the persistence over time, in different parties, of a relatively high age of the members of the elective Parliament signals that this political class is a true "elite", with its own curve of talents, forged by a previous career and reinforced in the parliament, so that there is a high re election rate. Every type of elite, in the Paretian theory is subject to the law of circulation through time. However, the persistence of high levels of education and of specific skilled and professional qualifications signals the persistence of characteristics that are relevant for the curves of distribution of talents required for those individuals, who compete for the election for the different parties, to be members of the new elites. The changes in levels and types of education and in professions signal the change of the characteristic relevant for the curves of talents of this political elite. The differences in education and profession, indeed, may influence the non logical / logical mix of the public choices. These differences may be relevant also in connection with the affiliation to different parties because of the differences in the curve of talents required to have success and survive in them. Different professions may be relevant for the curve of the talents of the different political parties, because of the different income classes, level of education and social status of their electorate and of the different presence in them of "rentiers" and "entrepreneurs" in the Paretian sense.

Let us start with the age. In the monarchic period, the age of the members of the chamber of deputies was generally high, ranging between 46.5 and 50 years – see figure 3 – with the only exception of the last legislature, the one already under the fascist regime in which the average age went down to about 43 years. Considering the different periods, with the exclusion of the last, the age was on the lowest value of the average in fifth period (beginning in 1919). The explanation lies in the socio political changes and in the deaths due to the war that originated a forced renewal of the political elites. The age's differences in question, however, are quite modest. The peak has been reached in the period of the introduction of the quasi universal voting right: clearly the age was a *pro* in the new more difficult election game with mass parties.

7 The Paretian distinction between dynamic communities, with a prevalence of innovative elites, and static communities, with prevalence of conservative elites, might also be relevant from the point of view of the comparison of the composition of the Italian Parliament as for the members elected in the Northern (dynamic industrialized) and Southern (static, less industrialized) regions. This shall be object of a future research.

Figure 3. Average age at the beginning of the legislature of the elected representatives: Chamber of Deputies from 1861 to 1928.

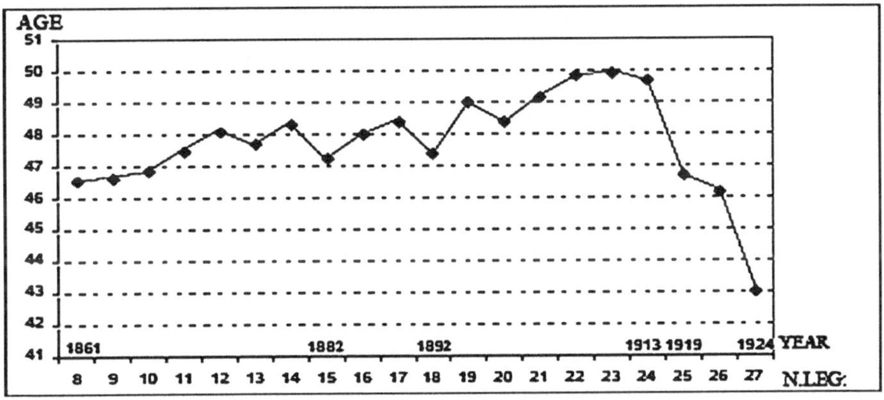

A further explanation of the high average age of the members of the Italian chamber in the monarchic period also lies in the high re-lection rates, shown in figure 2, from which it also emerges the remarkable correlation between the two variables. With the exception of few legislatures, at the beginning of the first period and in the last three ones, these re-election rates ranged between 62 % and 71 % for one re-election and from 39 % to 50.4 % for 3 or more consecutive legislatures. For the initial period, the likely explanation is in the process of selection of the incoming political elite. For the last three legislatures the likely explanation lies in the social destabilization of that epoch after the world war.

The political elite of the elected member of the parliament in the monarchic period looks as an elite also in the intellectual sense because of its high level of education as shown in figure 4. The share of the members of the Italian chamber with a university degree ranges from about 59 % at the beginning of the first period to about 78.6 % in the first legislature under the quasi universal suffrage in 1913. One cannot argue that the electoral law, introducing the quasi-universal suffrage, was the mere cause of that peak because the increase of the share of the elected member of the parliament with an university degree had persistently increased through the legislatures. It is noticeable that the change of the share of the electors on the total population from about 8 % to 27 % had not reduced the high share of the members of the chamber with university degree, but had reinforced it (with the exception of the two last legislatures considered here, already, under a strong fascist influence). An explanation of this fact is that the increased level of education in the population increased the level of education needed to enter in the political career, which, over the long period observed, required high intellectual talents for both the logical and the non logical components of the actions and also in the mass parties under the universal suffrage. Actually, in the three legislatures, after the world war with mass parties and universal suffrage, there was a gradual decline of the share of the members of the parliament with university degree (from a peak close to 80 % reached in the two last pre war legislatures to about 70 %).

Figure 4. Education of the elected representatives: Chamber of Deputies from 1861 to 1928.

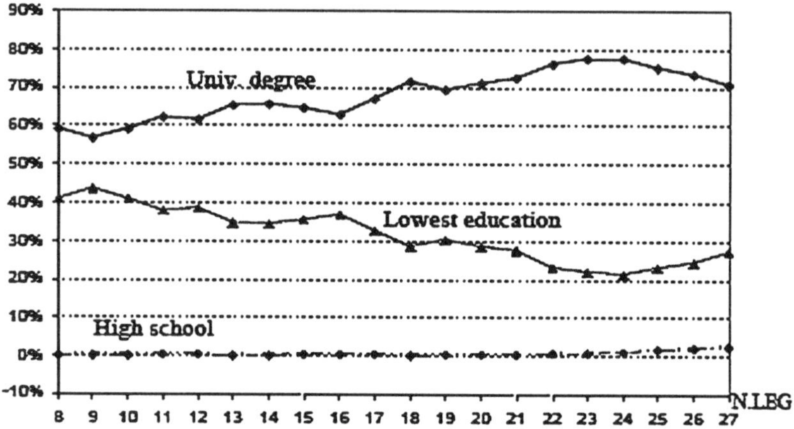

Table 1. Average age and education of the elected representatives grouped into legislatures having homogeneous electoral laws: Chamber of Deputies from 1861 to 1928.

Legislatures with homogeneous electoral laws	FIRST YEAR OF THE PERIOD	Average age	UNIVERSITY DEGREE	OTHER
VIII-XIV	1861	47.5	61.3%	38.7%
XV-XVII	1882	47.9	65.0%	35.0%
XVIII-XXIII	1892	48.9	73.3%	26.7%
XXIV	1913	49.8	78.6%	21.4%
XXV-XXVI	1919	46.5	75.8%	24.3%
XXVII	1924	43.1	72.4%	27.6%

An explanation of this phenomenon, which was present also for the left wing parties, lies in the types of socio-professional qualifications that were important for being elected. Tables 2 and 3 show the elected representatives grouped by prevailing professions, respectively, for each term and for groups of legislatures with homogeneous electoral laws. The most frequent socio-professional qualification of the members of the chamber was that in the juridical professions of "lawyers, notaries and judges", with a percentage that increased from 35 %, at the beginning of the first period, to 44 % in the first elections after the universal suffrage and then remained at about 40 %.

Table 2. The elected representatives grouped by prevailing professions: Chamber of Deputies from 1861 to 1928.

LEGISLA-TURE.	BEGIN-NING OF THE LEGISLA-TURE..	Lawyers/ notaries/ judges	Teach-ers	Entre-preneurs/ artisans/ traders	Archi-tects/ engineers	Doctors/ veterinar-ies/ chem-ists	Noble land-owners	Employ-ees / workers	Journal-ists / writers	Offi-cers	Others
VIII	1861	35.2%	11.4%	2.5%	4.4%	5.4%	16.8%	0.0%	2.8%	9.8%	11.7%
IX	1865	34.8%	10.0%	3.4%	2.8%	4.0%	16.1%	0.0%	3.4%	9.3%	16.1%
X	1867	33.9%	11.4%	3.3%	3.5%	3.6%	15.6%	0.0%	3.5%	8.3%	16.8%
XI	1870	38.3%	9.7%	3.5%	4.7%	2.9%	15.9%	0.0%	1.9%	8.1%	14.9%
XII	1874	37.9%	9.9%	3.9%	3.7%	4.3%	17.4%	0.2%	1.5%	8.1%	13.1%
XIII	1876	37.1%	11.7%	3.5%	4.3%	3.7%	15.1%	0.4%	1.2%	8.2%	14.9%
XIV	1880	36.3%	11.1%	2.4%	3.9%	3.5%	16.8%	0.4%	1.5%	7.5%	16.6%
XV	1882	34.7%	12.3%	3.1%	4.0%	3.2%	14.3%	0.5%	2.0%	8.7%	17.3%
XVI	1886	35.3%	10.1%	3.7%	4.8%	3.7%	13.1%	0.7%	3.0%	8.7%	17.0%
XVII	1890	35.7%	12.1%	4.7%	5.1%	3.6%	12.8%	0.8%	3.0%	8.9%	14.3%
XVIII	1892	38.6%	12.0%	5.4%	5.4%	4.2%	11.5%	0.2%	2.5%	6.7%	13.5%
XIX	1895	36.5%	12.2%	6.6%	5.9%	3.7%	12.7%	0.2%	2.7%	5.9%	13.7%
XX	1897	37.6%	13.0%	4.9%	5.5%	3.9%	14.5%	0.2%	3.4%	4.1%	13.0%
XXI	1900	37.9%	14.7%	6.1%	4.5%	4.6%	12.3%	0.5%	3.4%	3.9%	12.1%
XXII	1904	39.9%	14.5%	6.6%	4.7%	5.8%	10.6%	0.4%	3.5%	3.3%	10.7%
XXIII	1909	41.0%	13.2%	6.7%	5.2%	6.0%	10.8%	0.7%	3.4%	3.3%	9.6%
XXIV	1913	44.4%	13.5%	7.5%	4.1%	6.4%	10.0%	0.8%	4.1%	2.9%	6.4%
XXV	1919	41.5%	15.6%	5.5%	3.4%	7.3%	1.8%	5.7%	5.5%	1.2%	12.5%
XXVI	1921	41.5%	14.8%	5.5%	3.7%	5.1%	3.1%	4.8%	5.5%	0.9%	15.2%
XXVII	1924	39.7%	13.3%	7.4%	3.7%	3.9%	3.1%	4.0%	8.6%	4.0%	12.3%

Table 3. The elected representatives by prevailing professions grouped into legislatures having homogeneous electoral laws: Chamber of Deputies from 1861 to 1928.

Legislatures with homogeneous electoral lawsI	INITIAL YEAR OF THE PERIOD.	Lawyers/ notaries/ judges	Teachers	Entrepreneurs/ artisans/ traders	Architects/ engineers	Doctors/ veterinaries/ chemists	Noble landowners	Employees / workers	Journalists / writers	Officers	Others
VIII-XIV	1861	36.21%	10.74%	3.21%	3.90%	3.91%	16.24%	0.14%	2.26%	8.47%	14.87%
XV-XVII	1882	35.23%	11.50%	3.83%	4.63%	3.50%	13.40%	0.67%	2.67%	8.77%	16.20%
XVIII-XXIII	1892	38.58%	13.27%	6.05%	5.20%	4.70%	12.07%	0.37%	3.15%	4.53%	12.10%
XXIV	1913	44.40%	13.50%	7.50%	4.10%	6.40%	10.00%	0.80%	4.10%	2.90%	6.40%
XXV-XXVI	1919	41.50%	15.20%	5.50%	3.55%	6.20%	2.45%	5.25%	5.50%	1.05%	13.85%
XXVII	1924	39.70%	13.30%	7.40%	3.70%	3.90%	3.10%	4.00%	8.60%	4.00%	12.30%

It is of some interest the fact that the share of democratic representatives with a juridical professional qualification did increase with the extension of the voting rights to a greater share of the total population. As we shall see below, as for the high re-election rate of the members of parliament with this profession, the general explanation of their growing importance is the peculiar skill in combining logical and non logical factors "in defending a cause". And the more the electorate increases in size and its elitarian quality, in the narrow sense of this term, diminishes the more these skills are important. Another socio-professional qualification that has a constant increase from the initial period is that of teachers, mostly consisting of university professors. The share of elected members of parliament with this qualification increases from 11.4 % in the first legislature of the Kingdom of Italy to 14.7% in the 1900 elections, to remain around 13-14% afterward. Also the share of this professional qualification increases with the extensions of the voting rights, but unlike the juridical professions, the peak is not with the quasi universal suffrage, but in the post-war period, in which the spectrum of political ideologies appears broadened and fragmented. Professors' skills become increasingly important in politics with the increase of the relevance and differentiation of the ideologies in the political movements. Two other important socio-economic qualifications emerge in the political elite of the parliament of the monarchic period: the status of noble and/or landowner and the military profession. However, in both cases there is a declining trend. As for the nobles and landowners there is a first sharp decline with the end of the first period, then there is a more gradual decline but their share remains at the important level of 10% also with the quasi universal suffrage. The real fall takes place with the fifth period, after the world war. Clearly this phenomenon may be explained in Paretian terms with the declining influence of the rentiers in the electorate, after the initial period of quasi universal electoral suffrages. Career officers were about 10% in the first legislature of the new Italian Kingdom. The average of the first period is 8.47% and that of the second 8.77%. The great increase of the voting rights that took place in 1882 halved the share of the members of the military corps in parliament. The universal suffrage caused another diminution. The initial importance of the share of the career officers can be explained by the fact that the new Italian political elite partly came from the battles for the creation of the Italian independent state. The decline over time of the presence in parliament of the officers can be partly explained – in Pareto's terms – by the age factor affecting the original military elite. One may ask why there was not a renewal of the ranks of this elite in the political arena, given the importance of the army for the right wing parties. An explanation may be that the increase of the share of electors on the population made increasingly difficult for the officers to compete for the election because of their lack of political skills and flexibility suited to the political parties of a mass democracy. It might appear rather paradoxical that the world war made it irrelevant the share of the military career in parliament. In the post war period their presence in parliament was only 1%. This result has a likely Paretian biological explanation of the circulation of the elites: many of the best officers died in the war and the youngest ones had neither important military status nor political experience. Only in the last period, the career officers regained some importance, with a non irrelevant presence in the fascist-nationalist bloc, likely because the political experience and the military degrees of the young officials had grown.

Tables 4 and 5 below show the re-election rates for the member of the parliament grouped, respectively, by political affiliation only and by prevailing profession across the political group.

Table 4. Re-election rates for 2 legislatures of the elected representatives grouped by political affiliation: Chamber of Deputies from 1861 to 1928.

LEGISL.	BEGIN-NING OF THE LEGISL.	RIGHT	LEFT/ LIBER-ALS	ESTREME LEFT	PSI	PS Un	PSR	PCI	PRI	RADICALS	CATOL./ PPI
VIII	1861										
IX	1865	48.4%	48.5%								
X	1867	59.2%	69.0%								
XI	1870	54.7%	61.9%								
XII	1874	71.4%	61.8%	50.0%							
XIII	1876	68.7%	55.7%	40.0%							
XIV	1880	63.3%	75.3%	69.4%							
XV	1882	55.9%	64.9%	59.2%							
XVI	1886	57.7%	73.4%	63.0%	50.0%						
XVII	1890	70.9%	73.0%	59.6%	50.0%						
XVIII	1892	69.4%	67.4%	53.6%	55.6%						
XIX	1895	68.9%	83.3%	66.1%	58.3%						
XX	1897	60.8%	75.1%	67.1%	62.5%						
XXI	1900	82.0%	72.1%	67.9%	50.0%						
XXII	1904	75.2%	68.1%	67.2%	58.8%						
XXIII	1909	70.1%	71.8%	54.3%	48.9%						17.4%
XXIV	1913	56.8%	68.1%		39.2%						40.5%
XXV	1919		41.6%		17.9%		38.1%		44.4%	46.4%	14.9%
XXVI	1921		62.6%		56.9%		61.5%	62.5%	80.0%		62.9%
XXVII	1924		44.4%			41.7%		14.3%	28.6%		79.5%

Table 5. The elected representatives grouped by prevailing professions and parliamentary groups: Chamber of Deputies from 1861 to 1928.

LEG.	Parliamentary Groups	Lawyers/ notaries/ judges	Teach-ers	Entre-preneurs/ artisans/ traders	Architects/ engineers	Doctors/ veterinar-ies/ chem-ists	Noble landown-ers	Employ-ees / workers	Journalists /writers	Officers	Others
VIII	Total	35.2%	11.4%	2.5%	4.4%	5.4%	16.8%	0.0%	2.8%	9.8%	11.7%
VIII	Right	33.3%	11.9%	2.7%	5.8%	5.2%	19.4%		3.9%	8.2%	10.6%
VIII	Left	39.3%	14.9%	2.4%	3.0%	5.4%	9.5%		1.8%	11.3%	12.5%
IX	Total	34.8%	10.0%	3.4%	2.8%	4.0%	16.1%	0.0%	3.4%	9.3%	16.1%
	Right	33.1%	10.4%	2.2%	3.5%	4.8%	21.3%		4.3%	9.1%	11.3%
	Left	38.8%	10.5%	4.0%	2.5%	3.0%	10.0%		3.0%	10.4%	17.9%
X	Total	33.9%	11.4%	3.3%	3.5%	3.6%	15.6%	0.0%	3.5%	8.3%	16.8%
	Right	33.3%	11.1%	2.6%	4.4%	3.0%	21.5%	0.0%	3.7%	9.3%	12.6%
	Left	37.6%	11.7%	2.9%	3.3%	3.8%	9.6%		4.2%	8.4%	18.4%
XI	Total	38.3%	9.7%	3.5%	4.7%	2.9%	15.9%	0.0%	1.9%	8.1%	14.9%
	Right	32.2%	9.4%	3.5%	5.9%	2.8%	19.9%		2.8%	10.5%	12.9%
	Left	45.2%	10.2%	3.3%	3.7%	2.8%	9.8%		0.9%	7.0%	17.2%
	Extreme Left	52.7%	5.3%		10.5%	10.5%			5.3%	5.3%	10.5%
XII	Total	37.9%	9.9%	3.9%	3.7%	4.3%	17.4%	0.2%	1.5%	8.1%	13.1%
	Right	32.0%	9.7%	3.8%	5.0%	2.5%	23.9%		2.5%	10.1%	10.5%
	Left	43.7%	9.7%	3.8%	2.9%	5.0%	13.0%	0.4%	0.8%	5.0%	15.5%
	Extreme Left	41.2%	5.9%		5.9%	23.5%				11.8%	11.8%
XIII	Total	37.1%	11.7%	3.5%	4.3%	3.7%	15.1%	0.4%	1.2%	8.2%	14.9%
	Right	27.6%	11.5%	2.7%	6.7%	1.3%	28.2%		2.0%	8.1%	12.1%
	Left	41.0%	11.3%	4.2%	3.4%	3.7%	10.5%	0.6%	1.1%	7.1%	17.0%
	Extreme Left	36.2%	16.7%	2.8%	5.6%	16.7%	5.6%			8.3%	8.3%
XIV	Total	36.3%	11.1%	2.4%	3.9%	3.5%	16.8%	0.4%	1.5%	7.5%	16.6%
	Right	27.0%	11.4%	1.8%	5.4%	1.8%	26.9%		1.8%	7.8%	16.2%
	Left	40.0%	11.8%	3.3%	3.0%	3.6%	12.5%	0.7%	1.3%	6.2%	17.7%
	Extreme Left	47.2%	8.4%		5.6%	13.9%	5.6%			8.3%	11.1%
XV	Total	34.7%	12.3%	3.1%	4.0%	3.2%	14.3%	0.5%	2.0%	8.7%	17.3%
	Right	22.8%	11.8%	2.2%	8.8%	1.5%	20.6%		2.2%	11.8%	18.4%
	Left	38.1%	12.6%	3.3%	2.4%	3.0%	13.8%	0.6%	1.2%	6.9%	18.0%
	Extreme Left	46.9%	12.2%	2.0%	2.0%	10.2%	6.1%			8.2%	12.2%
	Socialist Party					33.3%		33.3%	33.3%		

XVI	Total	35.3%	10.1%	3.7%	4.8%	3.7%	13.1%	0.7%	3.0%	8.7%	17.0%
	Right	27.0%	9.8%	4.3%	9.2%	1.8%	17.2%		3.7%	9.8%	17.2%
	Left	38.5%	10.5%	2.9%	3.2%	4.2%	12.5%	0.6%	1.9%	7.7%	17.9%
	Extreme Left	43.5%	8.6%	4.3%	4.3%	4.3%	4.3%	0.0%	4.3%	6.5%	19.6%
	Socialist Party		16.7%			33.3%		33.3%	16.7%		
XVII	Total	35.7%	12.1%	4.7%	5.1%	3.6%	12.8%	0.8%	3.0%	8.9%	14.3%
	Right	29.8%	10.7%	5.0%	9.9%	2.8%	17.0%		5.0%	5.7%	14.2%
	Left	40.3%	13.0%	2.8%	3.5%	2.8%	12.3%	0.7%	2.1%	8.1%	14.4%
	Extreme Left	42.6%	14.9%	6.4%	4.3%	10.6%	2.1%		2.1%	4.3%	12.8%
	Socialist Party		12.5%	12.5%				25.0%	12.5%	37.5%	
XVIII	Total	38.6%	12.0%	5.4%	5.4%	4.2%	11.5%	0.2%	2.5%	6.7%	13.5%
	Right	29.8%	10.4%	7.5%	8.2%	3.0%	17.9%		4.5%	3.7%	14.9%
	Left	42.0%	12.0%	4.8%	4.8%	3.8%	11.0%	0.3%	1.0%	7.2%	13.1%
	Extreme Left	50.0%	14.3%	3.6%	5.4%	8.9%	1.8%		3.6%	5.4%	7.1%
	Socialist Party	22.2%	22.2%	11.1%		11.1%					33.3%
XIX	Total	36.5%	12.2%	6.6%	5.9%	3.7%	12.7%	0.2%	2.7%	5.9%	13.7%
	Right	30.5%	8.6%	7.3%	10.6%	1.3%	18.5%		3.3%	4.6%	15.2%
	Left	39.7%	11.9%	6.0%	4.0%	4.4%	13.1%	0.4%	1.6%	6.3%	12.7%
	Extreme Left	41.1%	17.8%	7.1%	7.1%	8.9%	1.8%		3.6%	3.6%	8.9%
	Socialist Party	16.7%	33.4%	16.7%		8.3%			8.3%		16.7%
XX	Total	37.6%	13.0%	4.9%	5.5%	3.9%	14.5%	0.2%	3.4%	4.1%	13.0%
	Right	33.5%	8.8%	6.2%	6.2%	2.1%	22.2%		4.1%	2.6%	14.4%
	Left	42.8%	15.3%	3.5%	3.9%	3.9%	12.7%		1.3%	4.4%	12.2%
	Extreme Left	38.6%	15.7%	5.7%	10.0%	8.6%	2.9%		5.7%	4.3%	8.6%
	Socialist Party	31.3%	18.8%	12.5%		12.5%		6.3%	12.5%		6.3%
XXI	Total	37.9%	14.7%	6.1%	4.5%	4.6%	12.3%	0.5%	3.4%	3.9%	12.1%
	Right	33.8%	8.8%	7.0%	5.2%	1.7%	19.8%		4.1%	4.7%	15.1%
	Left	43.1%	14.8%	5.3%	3.7%	4.5%	11.5%		1.6%	4.5%	11.1%
	Extreme Left	41.0%	20.5%	5.1%	7.7%	7.7%	2.6%		5.7%	2.6%	7.7%
	Socialist Party	31.3%	18.8%	9.4%	3.1%	12.5%		9.4%	9.4%		6.3%
		%									
XXII	Total	39.9%	14.5%	6.6%	4.7%	5.8%	10.6%	0.4%	3.5%	3.3%	10.7%
	Right	32.2%	10.1%	9.4%	5.4%	2.0%	18.1%		4.0%	5.4%	13.4%
	Left	44.5%	13.4%	5.9%	3.1%	6.7%	9.4%		2.0%	2.8%	12.2%
	Extreme Left	44.8%	18.0%	4.5%	10.4%	9.0%	1.5%		3.0%	3.0%	6.0%

	Socialist Party	38.2%	23.5%	5.9%		8.8%	2.9%	5.9%	14.7%		
	Catholics	16.7%	33.3%		16.7%		16.7%				16.7%
XXIII	Total	41.0%	13.2%	6.7%	5.2%	6.0%	10.8%	0.7%	3.4%	3.3%	9.6%
	Right	36.5%	10.9%	9.5%	5.8%	2.9%	19.0%		2.2%	4.4%	8.8%
	Left	43.6%	9.8%	6.4%	4.3%	7.7%	9.8%		3.0%	3.8%	11.5%
	Extreme Left	43.5%	21.8%	3.3%	7.6%	6.5%	5.4%		2.2%	2.2%	7.6%
	Socialist Party	40.0%	17.8%	4.4%		11.1%		8.9%	13.3%		4.4%
	Catholics	39.1%	17.5%	8.7%	8.7%		8.7%		4.3%		13.0%
XXIV	Total	44.4%	13.5%	7.5%	4.1%	6.4%	10.0%	0.8%	4.1%	2.9%	6.4%
	Right	38.9%	12.7%	7.6%	5.9%	0.8%	17.8%		3.4%	5.1%	7.6%
	Left	45.1%	8.8%	6.6%	4.4%	7.7%	10.4%		2.7%	4.4%	9.9%
	PRdissidenti	50.0%	12.5%	25.0%	12.5%						
	PRI	30.0%	20.0%	20.0%		10.0%			10.0%		10.0%
	RADICALI	53.2%	18.2%	2.6%	2.6%	13.0%	6.5%		1.3%	1.3%	1.3%
	PSI	37.3%	21.5%	7.8%	2.0%	11.8%		5.9%	9.8%		3.9%
	PSR	56.0%	16.0%	4.0%		4.0%	4.0%	4.0%	12.0%		
	SOC.IND	57.1%	14.3%	0.0%					14.3%		14.3%
	CATHOLICS	45.9%	13.5%	16.2%	5.4%		13.5%		2.7%		2.7%
XXV	Total	41.5%	15.6%	5.5%	3.4%	7.3%	1.8%	5.7%	5.5%	1.2%	12.5%
	PLD	50.4%	15.9%	7.1%	1.8%	5.3%	6.2%		3.5%	1.8%	8.0%
	PRC	51.8%	14.3%	1.8%	7.1%	17.9%					7.1%
	PRI	33.3%	11.1%	22.2%	22.2%	11.1%					
	PSI	27.9%	7.8%	7.9%	1.4%	8.6%		15.7%	10.7%		20.0%
	PSR	76.2%	23.8%								
	PPI	46.5%	17.8%	3.0%	5.0%	3.0%	1.0%	3.0%	3.0%	1.0%	16.8%
	PCI	22.2%	22.2%	11.1%				22.2%	5.6%		16.7%
	Mixed Group	30.8%	38.5%	7.7%	7.7%					7.7%	7.7%
	RINNOV	31.4%	25.7%		2.9%	14.3%	2.9%		14.3%	5.7%	2.9%
XXVI	Total	41.5%	14.8%	5.5%	3.7%	5.1%	3.1%	4.8%	5.5%	0.9%	15.2%
	PDI	41.4%	29.3%	7.3%	2.4%	12.2%					7.3%
	PLD	51.5%	7.6%	13.6%	3.0%	7.6%	4.5%		3.0%	1.5%	7.6%
	PSI	25.9%	13.8%	3.4%	1.7%	3.4%		13.8%	13.8%		24.1%
	PSR	69.2%	19.2%			3.8%			7.7%		
	PS UN	31.3%	12.0%	4.5%		7.5%		11.9%	7.5%		25.4%
	PPI	50.5%	15.3%	5.7%	2.9%	1.0%	1.0%	3.8%	4.8%		15.2%
	PCI	18.8%	18.8%	6.3%				18.8%	12.5%		25.0%
	DS	53.2%	17.2%	1.6%	7.8%	7.8%	1.6%				10.9%
	C.AGRARIO	15.4%	11.5%		11.5%	3.8%	30.8%		7.7%		19.2%
	Mixed Group	42.9%	10.7%	3.6%	10.7%		10.7%				21.4%

	PNF	31.1%	13.4%	6.7%	4.4%	4.4%	2.2%	6.7%	8.9%	8.9%	13.3%
	PRI	40.0%	20.0%	20.0%		20.0%					
XXVII	Total	39.7%	13.3%	7.4%	3.7%	3.9%	3.1%	4.0%	8.6%	4.0%	12.3%
	PLD	61.1%	11.1%	11.1%	11.1%	5.6%					
	PSM	22.7%	13.6%	4.5%	4.5%	9.1%	.	22.7%	13.6%		9.1%
	PSUN	50.0%	8.4%	4.2%		4.2%		4.2%	12.5%		16.7%
	PPI	46.2%	15.4%	5.1%	2.6%	2.6%	5.1%	2.6%	12.8%		7.7%
	PCI	19.0%	19.1%			4.8%		28.6%	9.5%		19.0%
	CONTADINI					25.0%					75.0%
	DS	60.0%	20.0%				10.0%				10.0%
	FD										100.0%
	LN	39.0%	12.4%	8.7%	4.2%	3.4%	3.7%	2.4%	8.4%	5.5%	12.1%
	OPP.COST	38.5%	46.2%						7.7%	7.7%	
	PRI	42.9%		14.3%		14.3%			14.3%		14.3%
	PARTITO SARDO	100.0%									
	SLAVI E TEDESCHI	50.0%									50.0%

BOX 1. LEGENDA

DS=Democrazia Sociale, i. e., Social Democracy
LN= Lista Nazionale, i. e., National List
OPP.COST:= Opposizione Costituzionale, i. e., Constitutional opposition
PCI= Partito Comunista italiano, i. e., Italian Communist party
PDI= Partito Democratico italiano, i. e., Italian democratic party
PLD = Partito Liberale Democratico italiano i. e., Italian liberal democratic party
PBF= Partito Nazionale Fascista, i. e., National Fascist Party
PPP= Partito Popolare Italiano, i. e., Italian Popular Party
PRdissidenti= Partito Repubblicano dei dissidenti, i. e., Italian Dissidents Republican party
PRC= Partito Radicale costituzionale i. e., Constitutional radicals' party
PRI= Partito Repubblicano italiano, i. e., Italian Republican party
PSI= Partito Socialista italiano, i. e., Italian Socialist party
PSM= Partito Socialista massimalista, i. e., Italian Maximalist Socialist party
PSR= Partito Socialista riformista, i. e., Italian Socialist Reformist party
PS UN.= Partito Socialista unitario, i. e., Italian Socialist Unitarian Party
RAD= Radicali, i. e., Radical party
RINNOV.=Rinnovamento, i. e., Renewal
SOC.IND.=Socialisti indipendenti, i. e., Independent Socialists
FD = Federazione Democratica, i. e., Democratic Federation
PNF = Partitito Nazionale Fascista i. e., National fascoist party
PARTITO SARDO=Sardinian Party
SLAVI E TEDESCHI = Slovenian and South Tiroler
CONTADINI = Farmers

Considering now the socio professional qualifications of the members of the different political movements in table 5, as expected, one can notice that the nobles and landlords are a much more important share in the right wing political elite than in the left wing parties and are important also in a typical party of the centre as the popular party (i. e., the Catholics). In the Paretian sociological approach one might expect that the "rentiers" are more important in the "conservative" parties of the right and of the centre. On the other hand, the fact that for a long period the officers are a share of the left at least as important as the share of the right wing may be explained with what we have observed before, i. e., that the political elite that had formed the new Italian state consisted, to a large extent, of patriots who had fight in the independence wars. A substantial part of them were members of the Garibaldi's volunteer army run by career officers of the various regions not yet belonging to the new monarchic state or by officers created by Garibaldi himself. These officers then entered the regular army of the new kingdom with the same degree. One can argue that the officers of this volunteer army, were a sort "dynamic" military elite of "speculator" in the Paretian sense; their "patriotic" and "quasi heroic" origin, for the electorate was a Paretian derivation with a powerful message.

The share of the members of the parliament with a juridical qualification is systematically greater in the left wing parties than in those of the right and of the centre. Their share in the right wing tends to diminish, while it tends to grow over time in the left wing parties with the growing importance of the left presence in parliament. In the extreme left, the share of members of parliament with a juridical qualification is close to half the total after the first extension of the suffrage and reaches 50 % at the beginning of the 1890s with the official creation of the socialist party. In it, the share of lawyers is initially much smaller than the average share in the parliament. However, with the growing presence of the socialists in the parliament, the share of socialists with a juridical professional qualification constantly increases to reach about the 40 % in 1913 with the universal suffrage law. After the war, with the political fragmentation of the parliament and the deep fragmentation of the socialists into two movements, the lawyers are about the 56 %. In the socialist reformist party they become about 70 %. The lawyers are also increasingly important in the catholic party, which, in turn, increased its importance, with the quasi-universal suffrage, as Popular Party, PPI. This was a party of centre: the share of PPI members of parliament with a juridical profession gradually increased from 40 % to 50 %. In the perspective of the Paretian mix of a logic and a non logic actions in the behaviour of the ruling elites one may argue that lawyers were better placed, in any political movement, because of their skill, given the need of building the institutions of the new state, in a period of intense economic and social transformations. However, they were much more important in the left than in the right and more important in the extreme left and in the irregular branches of the left than in the moderate left. For the extreme left parties the explanation of the prevalence of the lawyers among the members of the parliament may lie in the fact that they were defending the activists of these parties and of the unions in the courts. By performing this mission they had assumed a role of leading elites of these movements. For the socialist party, as mass organized party, there was and additional explanation for the importance of this profession: the daily activity of the lawyers in assisting unions and cooperatives in their contracts as well as the lawyers role in promoting the social legislation in the parliament. A similar explanation may be given for the great role of the members of parliament with a juridical professional qualification in the popular (i. e., the Catholics) party that was oriented to promote a moderate social and economic reformism. A different reflection may be employed to explain the growing presence of teachers (and, among them, of the university professors), particularly, in the left and centre parties: the role of providing them with ideologies. This role was likely growing because of the growing importance of the ideologies in the political movements, which took place along with the extension of the voting rights.

As one may expect the share of the entrepreneurs in the parliament grows through time with the economic growth of the country that increased the influence of the entrepreneurial class in the society. This may explain why the share of entrepreneurs in the XIX century doubled over the share of the two previous period. It is also important to note that this share increases with the quasi universal suffrage. One explanation could be that many peoples in the electorate may have considered entrepreneurs as better representing them because they know how to run a firm. A more convincing explanation may be the Paretian one, relating to the character of entrepreneurs as a dynamic elite of "speculators". In the new more dynamic political battles, they had good chances of being elected. The decline of their presence in the post war period may have a simple Paretian sociological explanation in the prevalence of non logic anti capitalist ideologies of that epoch, while obviously the recovered importance in the last period is related to the dislike of the anti capitalist ideologies. Workers never became an important share of the political elite. In the extreme left movements of the communists and of left wing socialists, they had a non irrelevant role still minor and only in the post war epoch, at the end of the democratic period. Likely this minor role, also in the parties whose electors were mostly workers, was due to their lower than average level education, which put them on the lowest part of Pareto's curves of distribution of talents. The share of journalist and writers increased from the early period to the last and tended to decrease in the right wing while growing in the left. The explanation seems to be that in the restricted suffrage period the main reason for them to have a place in the political elite was given by their popularity among the cultured people. The degree of literacy, at the beginning of the period, as seen, was quite low, even if growing. Their relatively greater place (even if very modest) in the right could be explained by the greater diffusion of literacy among the *leisure* class and by the fact that low income people had less money to spend on books and journals. The growth of the role of writers and journalists in the left wing parties and particularly in the socialist and the popular (catholic) party may be explained with the diffusion of the literacy and with the extension of the suffrage. They made important, among the masses, the political propaganda (by journals and pamphlets) and the politicians who were talented in this activity.[8]

3. The Empirical Analysis Of The Determinants Of The Circulation Of The Elites In The Italian Parliament

We now analyse the determinants of the circulation of the elites in the Italian parliament in the monarchic period by means of a count model. An event count is the realization of a nonnegative integer-valued random variable. We shall refer to the Poisson distribution and negative binomial distribution[9] given that our data

8 Benito Mussolini, before becoming the leader of the fascist movement was a popular left wing journalist, editor of 'Avanti', the newspaper of the socialist party and made an important contribution to the growth of popularity of the fascist as editor of its newspaper Il Popolo di Italia.

9 The Poisson probability distribution, $P(y \mid \mu) = e^{-\mu} \mu^{y} / y!$, assumes the same mean and variance (equidispersion) and that events are independent. Therefore, this distribution does not fit well in the presence of heterogeneity. The Poisson regression model incorporates observed heterogeneity into the Poisson distribution function, Var(yi|xi)=E(yi|xi)=μi=exp(xiβ). As μ increases, the conditional variance of y increases, the proportion of predicted zeros decreases, and the distribution around the expected value becomes approximately normal (Long 1997). The conditional mean of the errors is zero, but the variance of the errors is a function of independent variables, $\mathrm{var}(\varepsilon \mid x) = \exp(x\beta)$. The errors are heteroscedastic. Thus, the Poisson regression model rarely fits due to overdispersion (Long 1997; Maddala 1983). The negative binomial probability distribution is $P(y_i \mid x_i) = \frac{\Gamma(y_i + v_i)}{y_i!\Gamma(v_i)} \left(\frac{v_i}{v_i + \mu_i} \right)^{v_i} \left(\frac{\mu_i}{v_i + \mu_i} \right)^{y_i}$, where $1/v_i = \alpha$ determines the degree of dispersion and the Γ is the probability distribution. As the dispersion parameter α increases, the variance of the negative binomial distribution also increases, Var $(y_i \mid x_i) = \mu_i(1 + \mu_i / v_i)$. The negative binomial regression model incorporates observed and unobserved heterogeneity into the conditional mean, $\mu_i = \exp(x_i \beta + \varepsilon_i)$ (Long 1997). Thus, the conditional variance of y becomes larger than its conditional mean, E(*yi*|*xi*)=μ_i. which remains unchanged. When Var(*yi*|*xi*)>E(*yi*|*xi*), there is overdispersion.

Estimates of a Poisson regression model for overdispersed data are unbiased, but inefficient with standard errors biased downward (Cameron and Trivedi, 1998; Long, 1997). The likelihood ratio test for overdispersion examines the null hypothesis of α=0 (no-overdispersion). The LR statistic follows the Chi-squared distribution with one degree of freedom. If the null

set contains the count of the member of the parliament and the number of the re-elected members of the parliament. The latter variable shall be our dependent variable to explore the circulation of the elite in the monarchic period.

A preliminary picture of the dependent variable is given in tables 6 and 7. They show the re-election rates for 2 legislatures of the elected representatives grouped by prevailing profession, respectively for each individual term and for legislatures grouped by homogeneous electoral laws.

Table 6. Re-election rates for 2 legislatures of the elected representatives grouped by prevailing profession: Chamber of Deputies from 1861 to 1928.

LEGISL.	BEGINNING OF THE LEGISLATURE..	Lawyers/ notaries/ judges	Teachers	Entrepreneurs/ artisans/ traders	Architects/ engineers	Doctors/ veterinaries/ chemists	Noble landowners	Employees / workers	Journalists / writers	Officers	Others
VIII	1861										
IX	1865	58.7%	59.1%	47.1%	42.9%	50.0%	52.5%		41.2%	69.6%	12.5%
X	1867	54.9%	62.1%	57.9%	45.0%	57.1%	63.3%		65.0%	72.9%	57.7%
XI	1870	48.9%	73.0%	55.0%	48.1%	64.7%	45.1%		81.8%	70.0%	55.8%
XII	1874	63.1%	82.1%	66.7%	70.0%	60.9%	60.2%		62.5%	60.5%	64.3%
XIII	1876	60.5%	54.8%	45.0%	50.0%	76.2%	68.2%	50.0%	42.9%	54.3%	47.6%
XIV	1880	79.1%	74.1%	69.2%	76.2%	73.7%	72.2%	100.0%	66.7%	70.0%	62.9%
XV	1882	66.9%	62.2%	58.8%	54.5%	61.1%	64.6%	66.7%	63.6%	56.3%	61.5%
XVI	1886	62.6%	70.0%	52.4%	51.9%	52.4%	77.0%	75.0%	47.1%	77.6%	64.6%
XVII	1890	73.7%	68.2%	60.0%	66.7%	68.4%	63.2%	100.0%	81.3%	71.4%	73.7%
XVIII	1892	63.7%	71.0%	53.6%	71.4%	63.3%	65.0%	100.0%	69.2%	63.2%	61.4%
XIX	1895	70.7%	67.8%	64.7%	73.3%	57.9%	73.8%	100.0%	64.3%	80.0%	75.7%
XX	1897	68.0%	65.3%	73.1%	58.6%	66.7%	66.2%	0.0%	66.7%	77.3%	72.5%
XXI	1900	76.7%	64.3%	55.9%	76.0%	61.5%	84.1%	33.3%	84.2%	71.4%	69.1%
XXII	1904	65.0%	70.2%	69.4%	60.0%	56.2%	77.6%	100.0%	73.7%	72.2%	72.9%
XXIII	1909	64.5%	71.2%	73.0%	43.3%	63.6%	56.7%	25.0%	66.7%	75.0%	62.3%
XXIV	1913	66.2%	67.0%	56.4%	75.0%	51.5%	67.3%	75.0%	70.0%	66.7%	78.8%
XXV	1919	54.7%	41.3%	32.1%	35.3%	47.2%	77.8%	3.4%	34.6%	25.0%	7.9%
XXVI	1921	65.4%	66.4%	53.3%	50.0%	64.3%	41.2%	73.1%	63.0%	20.0%	48.2%
XXVII	1924	19.6%	40.8%	30.0%	30.0%	38.1%	29.4%	36.4%	31.9%	18.2%	28.4%

hypothesis is rejected, negative binomial regression model is preferred to Poisson regression model.

Table 7. Re-election rate for 2 consecutive legislature of the representatives by prevailing professions grouped into legislatures having homogeneous electoral laws: Chamber of Deputies from 1861 to 1928.

Legislatures with homogeneous electoral lawsl	INITIAL YEAR OF THE PERIOD..	Lawyers/ notaries/ judges	Teachers	Entrepreneurs/ artisans/ traders	Architects/ engineers	Doctors/ veterinaries/ chemists	Noble land-owners	Employees / workers	Journalists / writers	Officers	Others
VIII-XIV	1861	60.87%	67.53%	56.82%	55.37%	63.77%	60.25%	75.00%	60.02%	66.22%	50.13%
XV-XVII	1882	67.73%	66.80%	57.07%	57.70%	60.63%	68.27%	80.57%	64.00%	68.43%	66.60%
XVIII-XXIII	1892	68.10%	68.30%	64.95%	63.77%	61.53%	70.57%	59.72%	70.80%	73.18%	68.98%
XXIV	1913	66.20%	67.00%	56.40%	75.00%	51.50%	67.30%	75.00%	70.00%	66.70%	78.80%
XXV-XXVI	1919	60.05%	53.85%	42.70%	42.65%	55.75%	59.50%	38.25%	48.80%	22.50%	28.05%
XXVII	1924	19.60%	40.80%	30.00%	30.00%	38.10%	29.40%	36.40%	31.90%	18.20%	28.40%

The dependent variable reelection is also reported in table 8 showing the count of reelected member of the parliaments and its share of the total member in each legislature.

Table 8. The dependent variable reelection and the number of the member of the chamber of deputies in the monarchic period.

Legislature	Reelected members of the parliament for 2 times	% Reelected on the MEP	Members of parliament
VIII	.		443
IX	221	49.9%	443
X	307	62.3%	493
XI	279	56.6%	493
XII	338	66.5%	508
XIII	298	58.7%	508
XIV	364	71.7%	508
XV	311	61.2%	508
XVI	335	65.9%	508
XVII	351	69.1%	508
XVIII	333	65.6%	508
XIX	374	73.6%	508
XX	347	68.3%	508
XXI	363	71.5%	508
XII	342	67.3%	508
XIII	324	63.8%	508
XIV	336	66.1%	508
XV	189	35.9%	526
XVI	314	58.7%	535
XVII	194	36.3%	535

Table 9 reports the estimates of the determinants of the reelection in the monarchic period. In particular the results from negative binomial regression model and from a poisson regression model are reported.

Notice, first, that the number of observations is limited to 19 legislatures. Nevertheless, in spite of the limited number of observations, notice that the two models (poisson and negative binomial) reported show almost the same coefficient and standard errors, which suggest that the model is quite stable.

The variables tested in the model can be grouped as follows. (i) The professions and education of the member of the parliament (as depicted above); (ii) the extension of the suffrage as represented by the variable "N. voters" that is the share of citizen having the right to vote in Italy during the period considered. The latter variable is highly correlated with the degree of illiteracy in Italy shown in figure 1 and it is considered in order to capture in this context the relevance, if any of the electoral law which allowed us to distinguishing 6 different period. (iii) The age of the members of the parliament has been also tested. However, being highly correlated with the dependent variable, could not be used as a regressor.

Table 9. Count models' estimates of the reelection in the chamber of deputies in the monarchic period.

Poisson	regression			Negative	Binomial	regression	
Number	Of	obs=19		Number	Of	obs=19	
Wald	chi2(11)	=	176.21	Wald	chi2(11)	=	244.08
Prob	>	chi2=0		Prob	>	chi2=0	
Log pseudo-	Likelihood	=	-90.048	Log pseudo-	Likelihood	=	-87.702
Pseudo	R2	=	0.458	Pseudo	R2	=	0.1561
	Coef.	Std.Err.	Z		Coef.	Std.Err.	z
N. voters	0.0159	0.0047	3.4	N. voters	0.0166	0.0048	3.44
Lawyers	7.8551	3.0707	2.56	lawyers	8.1453	3.0776	2.65
Teachers	6.8555	3.4289	2	teachers	7.0746	3.4250	2.07
entrepreneurs	20.5899	7.4384	2.77	entrepreneurs	21.3979	8.1290	2.63
Architects/ engineers	6.0018	4.4014	1.36	Architects/ engineers	6.2156	4.4872	1.39
Doctors	10.1827	3.9624	2.57	doctors	10.2837	3.9817	2.58
Noble landowners	14.4598	3.5543	4.07	Noble landowners	14.8585	3.8136	3.9
Employees/ workers	5.5452	6.7743	0.82	Employees/ workers	5.5569	6.9378	0.8
Officers	5.3741	3.1675	1.7	officers	5.4671	3.2594	1.68
Others	16.4632	4.4780	3.68	others	17.0604	4.6806	3.64
University degree	2.4612	1.1102	2.22	University degree	2.4743	1.1312	2.19
_cons	-6.0449	2.9931	-2.02	_cons	-6.3875	3.1404	-2.03
				/lnalpha	-5.8239	0.4858	
				Alpha	0.0030	0.0014	

The variables resulting significant, all with positive sign, are the followings: the share of citizen having the right to vote; the professions of lawyers / notaries / judge, teachers, entrepreneurs, doctors, noble / landowners; the university degree. The professions of architects / engineers, blue and white collars, career officers are not significant.

It turns out that the re-election that might be considered as a limit to the circulation of the elites is unexpectedly affected by the increase in the share of voters on the population, e. g., the extension of the suffrage consolidates the elite in power. But Pareto's theory of the non logical components of the political choices of the voters provides an easy explanation of this phenomenon: in a mass democracy these non logical factors are more important than under very restricted suffrage and politicians in power can employ them to maintain their positions against the less known new comers.

The professions of lawyers/notaries/judge, teachers, entrepreneurs, doctors, noble/landowners also positively affect re-election. We have already mentioned the importance of the legal professions all over the considered period as well as of the teachers, mostly consisting of university professors, for strengthening the elite in power. In the perspective of the Paretian mix of logic and non logic actions in the behaviour of the ruling elites, one may argue that these categories were the best suited to the need of building the institutions of the new state, in a period of intense economic and social transformations. As for the university degree one may make a similar remark. Nobles and landowners in spite of their declining trend with the end of the first period, remained at the remarkable share of 10 % of the members of the parliament also with the quasi universal suffrage. Their real fall takes place with the fifth period, after the world war and, apparently, it was not enough to cancel their significance as elite in power. As for entrepreneurs, we already noticed that their share in the parliament grows through time with the economic growth of the country and also under the quasi universal suffrage law. Their decline in the post-war period due to the shift to anti capitalist ideologies of that epoch, does not reduce their relevance. The explanation for their persistence as elite in power, in Paretian terms, can be found in their dynamic character: even in the new more dynamic political battles, they had good and increasing chances of staying in power. As for doctors the persistence their popularity among the electors, that allows them to be re elected has a typical non logical Paretian explanation in the fact that, in their profession, they had shown their skills by taking care of the health of the people. This fact creates a faith in their talents and devotion to the welfare of the citizens also in politics, even if the two activities have different scope.

4. Conclusions And Suggestion For Further Research

The aim of this paper was twofold: to initiate a fiscal sociology analysis of the members of the political class that make the public economy decisions in parliament and to test the relevance of the Pareto's sociological theory of the elites, by an empirical research on the composition by age, level of education and profession of the Italian Parliament from 1861, the year of the first election of the chamber of deputies of the new Italian monarchic state to 1928, the year of end of the last elected chamber. The relevance of many principles deriving from Pareto's elites' theory emerged, showing a substantial continuity of characters, from the legislatures with restricted suffrage gradually broadened to those of quasi universal suffrage from the point of view the age, level of education and profession of its members, as a whole and by parties.

The member of the Italian parliament had, over the whole period, a relatively old age – between 46 and 50 years, with the only exception of the last legislature dominated by the new fascist coalition that determined a drastic circulation of political elites with the entrance in parliament of new class of politician. The relatively high age of the member of the Italian parliament in the monarchic democratic period signals that this high share of the political class, likely, was a true "elite", with its own peculiar talents that were formed through a career. This conclusion is confirmed by the constancy of the average high level of education of its members. The share of members of the Italian chamber with a university degree ranges from about 59 % at the beginning of the first period to about 78.6 % in the first legislature under the quasi universal suffrage in 1913. The change of the share of the electors on the total population from about 8 % to 27 % had increased the share of deputies with an university degree. An explanation of this fact is that the increased level of education in the population increased the level of education needed to enter in the political career, which, in that long period observed, required high intellectual talents both for the logical and the non logical component to be successful, even with the advent of the mass parties, under the universal suffrage. Actually in the three legislatures after the world war, before fascism with mass parties and universal suffrage there was a gradual decline of the share of the members of the parliament with an university degree from a peak close to 80 % reached in the two last pre war legislatures to 70 %. Likely, the decline in the intellectual level of the members of the parliament was a signal of the disintegration of that democratic political elite.

Considering the professions, it emerged that the share of the members of the parliament with a juridical qualification gradually increased from 35.2 % in the initial period to 44.4 % in 1913 under the universal suffrage, to go down after the war to 41 %-39.7 % under the new scenario of mass parties. In the perspective of the Paretian mix of logic and non logic actions in the behaviour of the ruling elites, one may argue that lawyers were better placed in any political movement, because of their skills joint with the need of building the institutions of the new state, in a period of intense economic and social transformations. However, the increase of the share of lawyers among the members of parliament until the first world war is related to the increase of importance of the left wing parties, where they were a greater proportion than in those of the right and of the centre. In the extreme left, the share of members of parliament with a juridical qualification is close to half the total after the first extension of the suffrage and reaches 50 % at the beginning of the ninety century. In the socialist party the share of lawyers at the beginning is much smaller than the average share in the parliament. With the development of the socialist party and the growing presence of the socialists in the parliament the share of socialists with a juridical professional qualification constantly increases to reach about the 40 % in 1913. After the war, with the political fragmentation of the parliament and the deep fragmentation of the socialists into two movements, the lawyers are about 56 %. Then in the socialist reformist party they become about 70%. The lawyers are also increasingly important in the catholic party, which did increase in importance, with the quasi-universal suffrage, as Popular Party. This was a party of centre: the share of PPI members of parliament with a law profession gradually increased from 40% to 50%. However, they were much more important in the extreme left and in the irregular branches of the left than in the moderate left. For the extreme left parties the explanation of the prevalence of the lawyers among the members of parliament may lie in the fact that they were defending the activists of these parties and of the unions in the courts, thus, assuming a role of guiding elites of these movements. A similar explanation may be given for the great role of the members of parliament with a juridical qualification in the popular (i. e. the catholic) party, oriented to moderate reformism. The second profession of the members of the parliament was that of teachers, with a growing presence particularly in the left and centre parties. Their role of providing the parties with ideologies was likely growing because of the growing importance of the ideologies in the political movements taking place along with the extension of the voting rights. Nobles and landlords are a much more important share in the right wing political elite than in the left wing parties and are important also in a typical party of the centre as the popular party (i. e. the catholic party). In the Paretian sociological approach one might expect that the "rentiers" are more important in the "conservative" parties of the right and of the centre. The fact that for a long period the officers are a share of the left at least as important as the share of the right wing may be explained by the fact that substantial part of them were the members of the Garibaldi's volunteer army. One can argue that they were a "dynamic" elite of "speculators " in the Paretian sense, and their "patriotic" and "quasi heroic" origin, for the electorate, was a Paretian derivation with a powerful message.

The share of the entrepreneurs in the parliament grows through time with the growing role in the country of this economic elite and their share increases under the quasi universal suffrage law. An explanation may be the Paretian one relating to the character of entrepreneurs as a dynamic elite. In the new more dynamic political battles, they had good chances of being elected. The decline of their presence in the post war period may have a simple Paretian sociological explanation in the prevalence of non logic anti capitalist ideologies of that epoch, while obviously the recovered importance in the last period is related to the dislike of the anti capitalist ideologies. Workers never became an important share of the political elite. Likely this minor role was due to the lower than average level education, e. g., they are in lowest part of Pareto's curve of distribution of talents. Journalist and writers increase their role from the early period to the last but tended to decrease in the right while growing in the left. This may be explained with the diffusion of the literacy and with the extension of the suffrage that made them important for the masses.

The re election rates increase with the increase in the share of voters on the population, e. g., the extension of the suffrage consolidates the elite in power. Pareto's sociological theory tells that, in a mass democracy, these non logical factors are more important than under very restricted suffrage and politicians in power can employ them better than the new comers.

The professions of lawyers/notaries/judge, teachers, entrepreneurs, doctors, noble/landowners also positively affect re-election. Nobles and landowners in spite of their declining trend remained at the remarkable share of about 10 % of the members of the parliament also with the quasi universal suffrage likely because of the relevance of the influence of "rentiers" in the social elite in Pareto sense. Their real fall took place after the world war when the "speculators", in Pareto sense, flooded the rentiers. As for entrepreneurs, their role increased through time with the economic growth of the country and with the quasi universal suffrage law, because of their dynamic nature as member of the Paretian class of "speculators". Their decline in the post-war period due to the shift toward anti-capitalist ideologies of that epoch. As for doctors the persistence their popularity among the electors, allowed them to be re elected. There was a typical non logical Paretian explanation: in their profession they had shown their skills by taking care of the health of the people. This fact creates a faith in their talents and devotion to the welfare of the citizens also in politics even if the two activities have different scope.

Further research in fiscal sociology is needed for the analysis of the political class as elite to test the other relevant sociological theories, to integrate them with the sociologically relevant economic theories and to extend the observations to more recent epochs and to observe also the political parties and governments. We shall pursue this aim in other researches, with a particular focus on their survival.

References

Cameron, C. e P. Trivedi Regression based test for overdispersion in the Poisson model Journal of applied econometrics, (1990), 46, pp. 347-364.

Cameron, C. e P. Trivedi Regression analisys of count data. Cambridge Univ. Press, New York, (1998).

Forte, F: The Law of Selection in Public Economy as compared to the Market Economy. Public Finance, 37, (1982), 2.

Forte F. and P. Silvestri Pareto's sociological maximum of utility of the community and the theory of the elites. Mimeo, (2009).

Long, S. Regression model for categorical and limited dependent variables. Sage Pubblications, Thousand Oaks, California, (1997).
Maddala, G. Limited dependent and qualitative variables in econometrics. Cambridge Univ. Press, New York, (1983).
Pareto, V. Manuale di Economia Politica Manuale di economia politica con una introduzione alla scienza sociale. Milano: Società Editrice Libraria, (1906), xii. Further editions in 1909 and 1919.
Pareto, V. Trattato di sociologia generale. Firenze: Barbera, 2 vol., (1916).
Pareto V. (1901-1902), Les systèmes socialistes: Cours professé à l'Université de Lausanne. – Paris: Giard & Brière, 1901-1902. Further ed. in 1926 *I sistemi socialisti*. – Milano: Istituto Editoriale Italiano, and 1917-1920.

A survival analysis of the circulation of the political elites governing Italy from 1861 to 1994

Silvia Fedeli and Francesco Forte

Abstract

We study the determinants of governments' survival in Italy from the unification to the end of the I Republic (1861-1994) – excluding the fascist period and the subsequent transitory institutional period, *"Constituente"* (1946-1948).

We test whether institutional features such as electoral systems, form of State and extent of suffrage had any effect on the survival of governments. We control for voting power of the parliamentary groups, number of parties represented in the parliament and size of the representative bodies.

Unlike the political economy wisdom, we show that, over the whole period, governments' survivals are inversely related to the plurality electoral system. The restricted suffrage and a high voting power of the leading parties reduce the risk of anticipated end of governments.

Keywords: Elites; Survival analysis; Electoral systems; Voting power, Political institutions.

1. Introduction

In this paper we analyze the "struggle for survival" of governments of the Italian democratic parliaments, from the creation of the Italian state (1861) up to 1994, with the exclusion of the fascist period (i. e., the legislatures from 1924 to 1945 in which the democratic institutions were absent and of the subsequent transitory institutional period, known as *"Constituente"*, lasting until 1948). We consider whether the survival of Italian governments was related to different electoral systems, to the voting power of the various political groups, to the number of parliamentary groups and to the size of the representative bodies. We also consider whether it was relevant for the government to be in a constitutional Monarchy, with an elective Chamber and a Senate appointed by the King as in the 1861-1924 period, or in a non presidential Republic, with two elective chambers as in the 1948-1994 period; and whether the extent of the suffrage had any effect.

In this respect, the political economy literature[1] is pervaded by the thesis that the *proportional electoral system is the main cause of political "fragmentation"* of the governance *via* the numerousness of parties in the government

1 See, for example, the surveys by Alesina and Perotti (1994) and Persson and Tabellini (2003).

coalitions, assumed to be a typical feature of the proportional electoral systems in contrast with the majoritarian electoral system. According to Alesina and Perotti (1994) "proportional, representational electoral system typically create multiparty systems and coalition governments; on the contrary, majoritarian systems lead to single party governments". Proportional representation also determines the short-life of governments because "governments durability is lower in representational systems characterised by coalition governments": by preventing the emergence of a leading-party the proportional electoral system implies higher fragmentation and short-living governments; this makes it difficult to reach an agreement on the governance and determines the delay of political decisions and actions. Roubini and Sachs (1989a and 1989b) argue that a short lived government only cares of the short horizon of the effects of its actions and it is induced to short-sighted policies which pre-empt the possibilities of the subsequent governments of pursuing their own different policies. According to Grilli, Masciandaro and Tabellini (1991), short lived governments and instability, caused by political fragmentation of coalitions of parties, prevent long run programs. Alesina and Perotti (1994)[2] argue that this type of situation might be irrelevant in calm periods, but becomes negatively crucial in critical situations such as those determined by economic shocks and subsequent crises. More recently, Persson and Tabellini (2003), with a panel including a huge group of countries from all the continents have found a number of peculiar effects determined by electoral rules. Countries under plurality electoral system cut taxes and spending ahead of elections, whereas countries with proportional electoral systems expand welfare programs in election years and further expand these programs in the years immediately following the elections. Furthermore, plurality reduces not only government ineffectiveness but also corruption by creating stronger incentives for politicians not to use their office for private gain.[3]

The above theories of fragmentation and instability basically supported by political economy scholars are not supported by sociologists and political scientists. Already in the '70s it was recognized that fragmented democracy can be as stable as the non fragmented (Lijphart, 1968). Sartori (1982) when asking why some democracy is stable and endures, whereas some other has difficult

2 Alesina and Perotti (1994) support their view on fragmentation on the basis of Drazen and Grilli (1993), Grilli, Masciandaro and Tabellini (1991).

3 One might argue that corruption is a function of the struggle for survival and, therefore, short living legislatures and governments, because of the higher frequency of the competitive struggle for their survival determine more corruption. Moreover, the struggle for survival might also imply policies of tax reduction to entice electors belonging to the right or welfare programs to entice the electors from the left.

life or dies, does not focus merely on fragmentation of the party system: this fragmentation, *per se*, does explain almost nothing unless it is considered in connection with polarization. Low polarization makes the governance of a democratic system viable even if its party system is fragmented, the structure of its own cleavages is segmented, and its own political culture is not homogeneous. According to Sartori fragmentation and multiplicity of parties do originate coalition governments, but governing coalitions are not necessarily unstable and unworkable. If coalitions are made up of similar/close political parties, which assure continuity, they might work satisfactorily. In this respect Laver (2000)[4] summarizes the key results obtained by political scientist as follows: (i) *Coalition governments* and even minority governments need not be weak and unstable. Both empirical and theoretical researches show that coalition governments can be stable equilibrium responses to electoral results by which no party has an absolute majority. Minority governments may also be stable equilibrium responses to particular government formation situations. The parties making up minority governments often tend to be quite large and quite central in policy terms. (ii) *Parties' policy* plays a remarkable role in the making and breaking of governments. There is a fear of coalition governments, considered anti-democratic, because citizens vote for parties at election time, but parties are forced by coalition bargaining to modify their policies after the elections if they want to get into office: both empirical and theoretical researches have shown that the resulting policy accommodations are almost invariably centripetal.[5] (iii) Both the formation and the durability of governments are heavily conditioned by the *institutional environment*.[6]

---

4 The wide political science literature on the formation and duration of governments basically follows two approaches. The first, essentially empirical (e. g., Blondel and Muller-Rommell, 1993; Browne and Dreijmanis, 1982; Lijphart, 1984; Pridham, 1986; Strom, 1985; Warwick, 1994), aims at singling out a set of variables relevant for the government duration in the real world. The second is characterized by *a priori* modelling of government formation. A first variant of the latter is "institution free" and aims at solving problems as the creation of a majority for an investiture vote (e. g., Axelrod, 1970; Grofman, 1982; McKelvey and Schofield, 1986, 1987; Peleg, 1981; Riker, 1962; Schofield, 1993). A second variant, developed within the "new institutionalist" approach, views the governments' formation process and governments' duration as a product of specific institutional rules (e. g., Austen-Smith and Banks, 1988, 1990; Baron, 1991; Huber, 1996; Laver and Shepsle, 1996; Lupia and Strom, 1995).

5 Parties may change their policies, but the beneficiary is almost invariably the median voter (see, e. g., Laver and Shepsle, 1996; Schofield, 1993). Coalition bargaining, therefore, can make more voters more happy than they were before (Austen-Smith and Banks, 1990; Baron, 1991, Huber, 1996; Laver and Shepsle, 1996, Schofield, 1993).

6 Amongst others, the institutional features analysed include the role of formal investiture votes (Strom, 1990); rules for choosing formateurs (Austen-Smith and Banks, 1988; Baron, 1991);

In section 2 we shall consider some stylised facts from the Italian democratic history on which basis we shall single out the variables of interest for the analysis of the Italian democratic parliament. In section 3, we empirically test the determinants of governments' length by means of survival analysis. Conclusions follow in section 4.

2. The determinants of governments' survival

2.1. Some stylised facts on the electoral systems in Italy

In Italy, since the creation of the parliament of the Italian Kingdom, in 1861, different electoral systems have been adopted. The pure uninominal electoral system, with some exception, was in place until 1919. After the interruption of the democracy, in the new republican period (since 1948) the pure proportional electoral system took place and lasted until the elections of 1994, when a hybrid form of majoritarian with a proportional share was introduced. But the electoral system changed again in 2006 into a hybrid form of proportional electoral system with a majority premium for the winning coalition. Therefore, for the analysis of the behaviour of the Italian parliament, only the sequence of governments since 1861 until 1994 allows us to properly test the propositions of the literature related to the role of electoral system. In particular, we analyze the sequence of the Italian governments in the nineteen democratic legislatures of the 1861-1924 monarchic period over 63 years (the elective chamber of deputies only, because the senate was non elective) and in the eleven legislatures of the Republic, from 1948 to 1994, i. e., over a total period of 109 years. Table 1 summarizes the basic features of the periods considered.

the role of confidence and no-confidence procedures (Huber, 1996); the rules of cabinet governance, in particular, the relationship between collective cabinet responsibility and individual ministerial responsibility for specified policy portfolios (Laver and Shepsle, 1996).

Table 1. The Italian Governments and legislatures: summary statistics

	Number of legislatures	Average duration of legislatures (in days)	Number of governments	Average duration of governments (in days)	Average duration of governments (subsequent governments with the same premier are joint)
MONARCHY (1861-1924) (pure plurality + mixed system-basically proportional)	19	1229	60	362	505
PURE PLURALITY SYSTEM	14	1227	48	350	494
PROPORTIONAL SYSTEM BY SCRUTINY OF LIST	5	990	12	412	550
REPUBLIC (pure proportional) 1948-1994	11	1525	47	322	504
PROPORTIONAL SYSTEM (mixed system + pure proportional)	16	1358	59	340	515

During the monarchic period, the pure majoritarian electoral system did last from 1861 to 1882, for seven legislatures, and from 1892 to 1919, for seven additional legislatures, with a total of 14 legislatures in 47 years, with an average survival of 494 days each).[7] In the 14 legislatures considered, there were 48 governments, on average, about 3 for each legislature. Under the quasi proportional system of the monarchic period (lasting from November 1882 to September 1892), there were 3 legislatures over 10 years, with an average survival of 1167 days each. The six governments survived on average 583 days. Under the proportional system with universal suffrage lasting about 4 years (from December of 1919 to January 1924), the legislature were 2 with an average survival of about 2 years each, and the governments were 6, with an average survival of about 8 months each. Overall, the non majoritarian periods (from November 1882 to September 1892, and from December 1919 to January 1924) had 5 legislatures in about 14 years, with an average survival of 990 days each, less than the survival of the legisla-

7 Of these legislatures, 4 were shorter than two years (IX legislature of 15 months – from November 1865 to February 1867 –; XII legislature of 23 months – from November 1874 to October 1876 –; XVII legislature of 21 months – from December 1890 to September 1892– ; XIX legislature of 21 months – from June 1895 to March 1897–).

tures under the majoritarian system (1227 days). There were 12 governments in 14 years, with an average survival of 412 days, slightly longer than that under the majoritarian system. Thus, in the monarchic period the majoritarian system determined a longer average duration of the parliaments in comparison with the proportional system, but the same did not occur for the survival of the governments, which is similar under the two electoral systems with a duration slightly longer for the governments under the proportional system. However, the plurality system gave these results in a period of 47 years of restricted suffrage. The results under the proportional system are an average of data of a limited period of 10 years under restricted suffrage and in an even shorter period of 4 years of male universal suffrage. Let us then consider the republican period of 46 years under the pure proportional system from April 1948 to April 1994. In this *long* period there were only two unusually short legislatures: the first from July 1976 to June 1979 and the second from April 1992 to April 1994. On average, the 11 legislatures in 46 years survived 1525 days, about 10 months less than the "physiologic" survival of 5 years set by the law. The number of governments, however, was 47 in 46 years, thus, confirming the average duration of the governments under the proportional electoral laws of the monarchic period.

Notice, however, that the number of governments as such, under the Italian parliamentary system, may be misleading because, *under the existing rule* both in the monarchic and the republican period, there is a formal change of government every time a given premier is charged by the head of state for "reshuffling" the cabinet, with some change of its composition, even if its political majority does not change. If one considered, as the same government, all the governments with the same prime minister succeeding to himself, into the same legislature,[8] under the plurality system the average survival of governments is 494 days, whereas under the proportional systems it becomes 515 days. Therefore, in the long run, an inverse relation seems to emerge between majoritarian system and governments' duration, in comparison with that under the proportional electoral system. Obviously, one might object that the majoritarian system we are considering was in place in a Monarchic period, mostly with limited suffrage. However, Monarchy and limited suffrage do not appear to be institutions adding instability to the governments. On the contrary, one might well argue that they have the opposite influence (see below). In any case, both with a pure formal and with a substantial definition of governments' duration, the thesis that the proportional system reduces the duration of governments and of parliaments has no empirical support

8 Notice, however, that according to Laver and Schofield (1991), the termination of a government would also be either the change of party membership of the cabinet, or the formal government resignation, or a change of the prime minister and election.

in the 109 years of the Italian democracy under consideration. And the same occurs for the related thesis that plurality electoral systems tend to generate long-life governments and parliaments. Other factors may, therefore, be relevant in explaining the different survival of governments and legislatures.

2.2. *The fragmentation of the Italian Parliament from 1861 to 1994 and the role of the political parties*

Duverger (1954) formulated a kind of "natural law of politics" according to which "dualism" in politics is natural. On this basis, quite often the West party-systems have been classified into two basic sytems – biparty and pluriparty – basically meaning that any system can be interpreted dualistically, by opposing, say, left to right, majority to opposition... and the like. On the other side, Sartori (1982) recognises that West Europe is often characterised by the "three party system".[9] In situations like the Italian, the main feature is a multi-polar system with the existence of a party (or group of parties) able to capture the opinion of the centre (not necessarily metrically between left and right). This situation does not allow the principle of alternate governments, but only semiperipheral reshuffling to the power.[10] According to this view, in Italy semiperipheral reshuffling has meant that the centre (the dominant party or a coalition of parties) has originally ruled without substitution. The extreme wing parties, in spite of their electoral weight (recall that the Communist party, PCI, in some legislatures got even 30% of seats), were almost never in the position of becoming ruling parties and the minor parties likely to be part of the ruling coalition had a minor influence and some time even for mere arithmetic reasons.[11]

9 That is, pluralism can be simple (biparty), moderate, extreme. Substantially, Sartori says that tracing the world back to a bipolar view is wrong and that Duverger excludes the existence of a "centre", only because centre parties are in contrast with his theory.

10 In other words, a biparty system allows alternate governments, a moderate pluralism allows alternate coalitions, extreme pluralism allows semiperipheral reshuffling, with the alternation limited to the minor parties only.

11 According to Sartori, in certain periods of the Italian history, the first consequence of this situation is an opposition without responsibility, because the opposition can never become majority. The further consequence might be that the likely allies of the main party are only (slightly) more responsible than the opposition, because only mere arithmetic reasons make them likely to become part of ruling coalition. Nevertheless, when in power the (minor) allies, being likely to become opposition again, because of the semiperipheral reshuffling, are less responsible of the government political action. In other words, for the minor parties, the lower the probability of becoming part of the ruling coalition, the higher the temptation of an irresponsible opposition. But, also, the higher the probability of becoming part of the ruling coalition, the higher the temptation of an irresponsible political action when in power.

In this context, any coalition of minor parties with the main party is possible *a priori.* One might object that this assumption is unrealistic, because there are parties ideologically idiosyncratic to each other. However, if one considers the Italian experience, in both the monarchic and republican periods, the coalitions of ideologically heterogeneous political groups were not rare under either electoral regime. The term "transformismo" was actually forged to design governments presided by right wing leaders[12] or with important right wing ministers and left wing majorities aided by right wing minorities and vice versa.[13] For the republican period, in the '70s the Democratic Christian party, DC, institutionalised a "grand coalition" with the Italian Communist Party, PCI, under the name of "historical compromise". The international political constraints made it impossible to have a national government with communist ministers, but they did not prevent a government with the PCI as "external support" to the majority.

Moreover, two important institutional factors relating to the functioning of the Italian Parliament must be considered to explain the semi-peripheral changes of the ruling coalition. Article 41 of the Statute of the Italian Kingdom stated that the "deputies represent the Nation in general and not the provinces in which they are elected. The electors cannot give them any agency constraint". Similarly, the article 67 of the Italian Constitution states that "every member of the Parliament represents the Nation and exerts his functions without agency constraints with the electors". According to the dominant traditional interpretation this principle allows the members of the parliament to vote disregarding their political (parliamentary) group. This possibility that emphasises the risks of losing power for a majority with a narrow margin over the majority quota – a feature quite independent of the type of electoral system. Another important principle of the Statute of Italian Kingdom allowing combinations amongst different political groups was that of the article 52, by which the vote both in the Chamber and in the Senate, in principle, was an open vote, but ten members could ask for secret ballots. A similar rule was adopted in the internal regulations of Chamber and Senate in the Italian Republic until August 1988. The secret ballot allowed the formation of various parliamentary coalitions, sometime different from that officially supporting the government in charge and rendered very difficult for the leading parties to rule without large majorities.[14]

If the above picture captures the main features of the Italian parliamentary system since 1861 to 1994, it seems to us that the proper way to analyse it is to

---

12 As the marquis Antonio Di Rudini three times in the XIX, XX and XXI legislatures.

13 Urbano Rattazzi – who was prime minister twice, in the VIII and X legislatures, of important right wing governments – was originally known as a person with left wing ideas.

14 The secret ballot principle, unrelated to the type of electoral system, originated the practice of the so called "snipers".

consider the parties' voting powers as determined by the Shapley-Shubik (S-S) index that measures the probability of any given voter of belonging to a winning coalition. Following the game theoretic approach underlying the S-S index of voting power,[15] we interpret the political groups represented (elected) in each branch of the Parliament as the players of a "*game to stay in power*" and assume that any political group – the players of the game – may combine opportunistically with any other, even disregarding their ideological differences.

Figure 1. The Shapley-Shubick index of the leading parties all over the considered period in the Chamber of Deputies (and Senate since 1948)

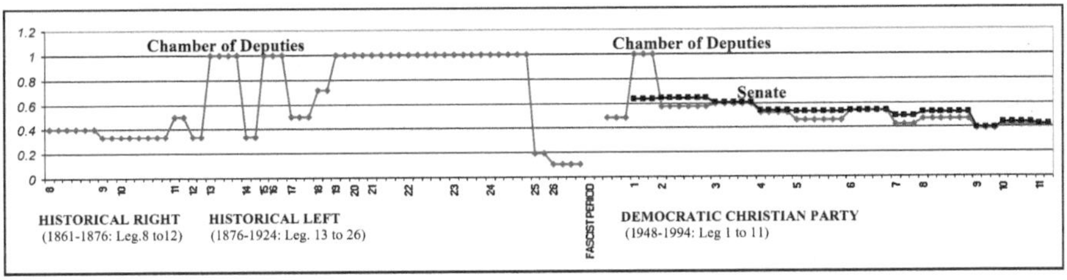

The notion of power of a player is referred to his ability to be the "last decisive" or marginal ("pivot") player of a winning coalition over all the possible coalitions.

Given the number of seats and, thus, the voting weights of each party represented in the Parliament in each legislature, the S-S indexes have been worked out for all the democratic Italian legislatures from 1861 to 1994. These values of the S-S indices are available from authors on request. Figure 1 shows the S-S power

15 The S-S index of voting power measures the chances of any party or player of being the pivotal member of a winning coalition as follows. Consider a n-players co-operative game defined by means of a characteristic-function, **v**: $A \rightarrow (0,1)$, where A is the set of all 2^n subset of the set of players N, (1,..,n) and **v** assigns to each subset $A \in$ **A** the value 1 if A is a winning coalition and 0 if it is a losing coalition. The S-S power index, S–S(i), for a player i can be defined as

$$\text{S-S(i)} = \frac{\sum_{i \in C, C \subset N} (c-1)!\,(n-c)!}{n!} [v(C) - v(C - \{i\})]$$

where the summation is taken over all coalitions C (consisting of c members), which i belongs to and '!' denotes factorial. A crucial role in the index is played by the permutations of players. We need to count for all 2^n coalitions the number of permutations of the remaining n-c members, i. e. only those cases in which $[v(C) - v(C - \{i\})] \neq 0$, that is, i is pivotal (his participation, as the last coming player, can change a losing coalition into winning coalition). In this sense, S-S(i) may be interpreted to represent both the possibility of measuring a player's power or "value" by the abstract probability that he is the pivotal member of a winning coalition and what a player should expect to receive, on average, under the assumption that his reward corresponds to his marginal contribution. See Shapley-Shubik (1954).

of the leading parties only (the biggest party in the government coalition) over the considered period. In the monarchic period, they are the Historical Right from 1861 (VIII legislature) up to 1876 (XII legislature) and the Historical-left from the XIII legislature (1876-1880) to XXVI legislature (1921-1924). Notice here that the monarchic period before the first world war was characterised by two leading parties: the historical right was formed mostly by free trade liberals, whereas the "historical" left, accepting some (protectionist) intervention of the state, was more open to the social reforms with a trend to the centre (as mentioned, the change of political positioning has been criticized as *"transformismo"*). In the Republican period, until 1994, only the Democratic Christian, DC, party had a dominant voting power. In this period the Senate became more relevant for government survival because the perfect bicameralism introduced by the Italian post-war Constitution entitled both branches to give the confidence vote to governments (see below).

Unlike the conventional view of fragmentation, the values of the S-S index of the leading parties over the considered period show that, in all the Italian legislatures, with few exceptions there was almost always a party with a S-S value dominant over the other parties in the elected branches of the Parliament. Even in the Republican period considered – often criticized for government instability –, in particular since 1948 up to 1976, the S-S value of the DC party was greater than 50%. In the subsequent legislatures the power of the DC declined, but an alternative majority without the DC was impossible. Moreover, with only two exceptions, all Presidents of the Republic belonged to DC. The two exceptions of a President belonging to the social democratic party, PSDI, and to the socialist party, PSI, were characterized by a strong alliance of these two parties with the DC in the government coalitions. This operated as a factor of stability.

However, the parties and their power in the Parliament change through time and their consideration may provide important insights of the duration of governments and legislatures. Therefore our analysis shall also consider two other elements. First, the *number of parties*, being cause of political fragmentation according to the dominant beliefs should reduce the lengths of governments and legislatures. Second, under the same perspective, also the *size of the assembly* (e. g., the number of parliamentary seats) might be considered a variable favouring the political fragmentation, being related to the number of members of the parliament to be convinced to support the Government. However, the opposite effect might also occur because both variables might reduce the voting power of the individual voter (either political group or member of the parliament) and, therefore, help the survival of the government in charge, when supported by a small majority.

2.3. *The form of state and the extension of the suffrage*

In addition to the electoral systems (plurality vs. proportional), to the number of political parties in the parliament, and to the size of the assemblies (i. e., number of seats), to the S-S voting powers as possible determinants of the duration of governments and legislatures, two other variables shall be considered. They are the form of state (monarchy vs. republic) and the extension of the suffrage (restricted vs. universal).

The question on whether the existence of monarchic or republican state influences the duration of governments is important for several reasons. First of all, in the monarchic period the leaders that should form the governments were appointed by the King and they had to count on the confidence vote of the King to which that of the parliament was added. There were two branches, but, unlike the republican constitution, in the monarchy, the Senate (not elective) was appointed by the King under proposal of the head of the government. The Senate could approve or veto the ordinary laws and the budget, but it had no power of approval and dismissal of government by a confidence vote, because this power belonged to the King only. Furthermore, the King could influence the Chamber with "a party of the King" crossing the distinction among the political groups. The President of the Republic according to the present Italian Constitution has limited powers, much smaller than those of a constitutional King and these powers are accurately defined.

Restricted *vs* universal suffrage might be relevant because the size of the electorate might have influenced the variation in the composition of the parliament because of a change of the active electorate. In 1860 (up to 1882) the electoral law was that in force in Piedmont in 1848: the right of vote was only for male over 25, owning an income of at least 40 liras and not illitterate. The right of vote was also deserved to those having university degree, to teachers, public officials and to members of few other professional activities, either in office or retired. This corresponded to an active electorate of about 7-8% of male and to about 2% of the total population. The law n.725, 7/5/1882 enlarged the suffrage to those whose education was limited to the firsts two (compulsory) years of elementary school or to the regimental school and to those contributing to the financial support of the state because of their jobs or their savings (i. e. by means of compulsory yearly taxation of 19.80 liras). The minimum age requirement for active electorate was reduced to 21 years. In 1894, the law n.286 allowed for the exclusion of a citizen from the electoral register for notoriety of acts against the public order, the article of the previous law that allowed the vote to those showing of being able of writing and reading is abolished. The laws n.655 (30/6/1912) and n.648 (22/6/1913) re-affirms the principle of ability to vote. The voting right is extended to male over 30 even illiterate, and to those having done the military service for a given period (the active electorate increased from about 8.3 % to about 23.2 % of the total population). The law n. 1985 16/12/1918 extended the voting right to male over 21 and to those who had been in the army.

3. Survival analysis of government

We study the determinants of the **Italian governments' duration** by means of survival analysis for which the outcome variable of interest is time until an event occurs. By time we mean days from the beginning of the follow up of an individual (government) until the event = anticipated end occurs. Although, ideally, both the beginning and the failure dates of governments should be known, censoring is a form of missing data problem that can be considered in this type of analysis. In particular, right censoring occurs for those cases whose beginning date is known but who are still "alive" when they are lost to follow-up. Here we shall assume that right censoring occurs for those governments "still alive" at the natural end of the legislature.

Survival models studying the time to the occurrence of an event, can be viewed as regression models in which the response variable is time.[16] Here we refer to the Cox proportional hazards, PH, model that gives an expression for the hazard at time t for an individual with a given specification of a set of explanatory variables X. The model can be expressed as follows

$$h\ (t,X) = h_0(t)\exp[\sum_i \beta_i X_i]$$

That is, the Cox model formula is the product of two quantities: the baseline hazard function, $h_0(t)$, and $\exp[\sum_i \beta_i X_i]$ e. g., the exponential expression to the linear sum (with X being a vector of variables modelled to predict an individual's hazard) that ensures that the fitted model will always give non-negative estimated hazard. The assumptions is that the baseline hazard is a function of t, but does not involve the predictors, in contrast to the exponential expression that might not

16 Warwick (1994) applies the survival analysis as for the formation and persistence of stable and effective government majorities in fragmented multiparty democracies. Across a diverse set of parliamentary systems from 1945 to 1989, he finds two relevant explanations of reduction of cabinet duration. One is the ideological diversity (or destabilizing effect of intra-coalition policy conflicts). The other is the bargaining complexity that leads to instability by the multiplicity of coalition options. Other characteristics, including economic conditions (unemployment and inflation), are also investigated. The main result is, however, that ideological diversity, more than bargaining complexity, does matter as a destabilizing factor of governments.

involve t if the predictors are time independent. If all the predictors are equal to zero the formula reduce to the baseline function.[17] The hazard function gives the instantaneous potential per unit time for the event to occur, given that the individual has survived up to time t, in contrast to the survivor function that focuses on not failing. Thus, the higher the average hazard the worse the impact on survival. Being a rate and not a probability the hazard ranges between zero and infinity.

3.1. Survival analysis of government duration by Cox PH model

The data set for the period considered contains the duration (in days) of each government. As mentioned, different definitions of government duration could be used. We refer to the *legal* notion of "new government" according to which the King or the President of the Republic registers than there is no longer a majority capable of expressing the existing government and charges a new or even the old premier to form a formally new government to get the confidence vote in the parliament even if sometime the new government is a "photocopy" of the previous one. This assumption helps in not to bias the results in favour of the proportional system that, as seen in table 1, in Italy shows a longer governments' length when subsequent governments are led by the same premier and the same coalition into the same legislature. The failure, under our assumption, is simply taken to be any legal end of government before the legal end of the legislature. Truncation (right censoring) occurs for the last government of a legislature lasting more than 1800 days. The analysis is carried on over the whole period for the Chamber of deputies and, in order to use all the available information, for the republican period we also analyse the government survivals in either branch.

The considered covariates for the Chamber of deputies from 1861 to 1994 (excluding the fascist period and the *"Constituente"*) and for Senate in the republican period only (from 1948 to 1994) are the following: the number of seats; the number of parties represented in the considered branch of the parliament; the Shapley-Shubik Index of voting power of the leading party; by means of dummy variables we distinguish the monarchic *vs.* the republican period, the restricted *vs.* the universal suffrage, the uninominal electoral system *vs.* the proportional system. For the political composition of the Parliament of the Kingdom we mainly

17 Notice that $h_{0g}(t)$ is an unspecified function and this allows the model, which uses a minimum assumptions, to be suitable for a wide variety of data situation. It is a "robust" model in that it closely approximate the result for the correct (parametric) model, that should be instead preferred only when we are sure of the correctness of the underlying distribution as for the estimated hazard ratio and survival curve. For a discussion of the actractiveness of the Cox model see Kleinbaum and Klein (2005).

refer to Malatesta (1940), who, however, gives only a broad political classification of the members of the parliament basically referred to their right or left "seat" in the parliament. A refinement of the classification of the parliamentary groups based on the parliamentary acts is in Piretti (1996) and in Bartolotta (1971). As for the republican period we refer to the official sources available, in particular La Navicella (2000 and 1985). Information about governments and legislatures durations are also available online at the official site of the parliament: www.parlamento.it. The variables related to the number of seats, the electoral system and the extension of the suffrage are built on the basis of the Italian electoral laws (most of which have been mentioned in section 2.3).

All the considered variables are reported in table 2 that shows their mean, standard deviation, minimum and maximum value over the considered periods grouped by governments and legislatures.

Table 3 reports the Cox PH estimates of the determinants (in terms of hazard ratio) of government duration in Italy from the unification to 1994 referring to the Chamber of deputies only. It turns out that the dummies capturing the republican period (as distinct from the monarchy) and the number of parties in the chamber are not significant. The extension of the suffrage and the Shapley-Shubik index of the leading parties are significant and present hazard ratio much lower than unit, with the lowest hazard being for governments with the highest voting power for the leading party. The number of seats is significant, but the hazard quite close to unity indicates no relation with duration of government. Finally, the plurality electoral system (as distinct from proportional) is significant with hazard ratio much higher than unity indicating the highest hazard for the duration of those government under plurality with respect to those under proportional electoral system.

Table 2. Summary statistics of the considered variables

Variable by Governments		Obs	Mean	Std.Dev.	Min	Max
(Chamber of Deputies from 1861 to 1994)						
Lenght of governments in days		107	344.72	262.856	8	1252
Lenght of legislatures in days		107	1414.96	424.829	452	2136
Restricted suffrage		107	0.45794	0.50057	0	1
Plurality electoral system		107	0.4486	0.49969	0	1
Republic		107	0.43925	0.49863	0	1
S-S index of the leading parties		107	0.60587	0.28004	0.101	1
Number of parties		107	7.70094	3.04747	3	14
Seats		107	551.495	62.8672	443	630
(Chamber of Deputies from 1861 to 1924)		0				
Lenght of governments in days		60	362.467	284.311	8	1252

Lenght of legislatures in days		60	1289.08	474.278	452	2136
Restricted suffrage		60	0.81667	0.3902	0	1
Plurality electoral system		60	0.8	0.40338	0	1
S-S index of the leading parties		60	0.6686	0.34089	0.101	1
Number of parties		60	6.21667	3.17881	3	14
Seats		60	499.633	23.9583	443	535
(Senate from 1948 to 1994)						
Lenght of governments in days		47	322.064	233.672	9	1058
Lenght of legislatures in days		47	1575.66	283.417	722	1874
S-S index of the leading parties		47	0.53598	0.07209	0.39762	0.64286
Number of parties		47	7.82979	1.10963	5	9
Seats		47	306.17	33.2084	243	342
(Chamber of Deputies from 1948 to 1994)						
Lenght of governments in days		47	322.064	233.672	9	1058
Lenght of legislatures in days		47	1575.66	283.417	722	1874
S-S index of the leading parties		47	0.5258	0.14134	0.38442	1
Number of parties		47	9.59575	1.37777	8	13
Seats		47	617.702	19.6047	574	630
Variables by Legislatures		**Obs**	**Mean**	**Std.Dev.**	**Min**	**Max**
(Chamber of Deputies from 1861 to 1994)						
Lenght of legislatures in days		30	1288.63	471.713	452	2136
Number of parties		30	7.4	3.21205	3	14
Restricted suffrage		30	0.53333	0.50742	0	1
Plurality electoral system		30	0.46667	0.50742	0	1
S-S index of the leading parties		30	0.61808	0.29678	0.101	1
Republic		30	0.36667	0.49013	0	1
Seats		30	544.467	60.8575	443	630
(Chamber of Deputies from 1861 to 1924)						
Number of parties		19	5.94737	3.02717	3	14
Restricted suffrage		19	0.84211	0.37463	0	1
Plurality electoral system		19	0.73684	0.45241	0	1
Lenght of legislatures in days		19	1151.63	482.282	452	2136
S-S index of the leading parties		19	0.67054	0.34305	0.101	1
Seats		19	501.79	21.9484	443	535
(Chamber of Deputies from 1948 to 1994)						
Number of parties		11	9.90909	1.57826	8	13
Lenght of legislatures in days		11	1525.27	359.66	722	1874
S-S index of the leading parties		11	0.52746	0.17126	0.38442	1
Seats		11	618.182	20.8702	574	630

Table 3. Government duration in the chamber of deputies 1861-1994, excluding the fascist period

```
Cox regression -- Breslow method for ties
No. of subjects        =          107
Number of obs          =          107
No. of failures        =          107
Time at risk           =        36885
Log pseudolikelihood   =   -390.89941
```

_t	Haz.Ratio	Rob.Std.Err.	z
SS lead. Party	.3428675	.0589748	-6.22
n.of parties	.9204824	.0486397	-1.57
Plurality E. S.	1.722632	.1519609	6.17
restr.suffrage	.4276038	.0605173	-6.00
Republic	.8058512	.1214506	-1.43
n.of seats	1.001974	.0008698	2.27

Figures 2 and 3 show the survival function of governments from the estimated model (estimated at the mean of covariates and at the values 0 and 1 of the electoral system, fig.2, and the extension of the suffrage, fig.3) in the period 1861-1994. It clearly emerges that the survival of the governments under the proportional electoral system clearly dominates that under uninominal electoral system and that the survival of the governments under restricted suffrage dominates those elected under universal suffrage.

Figure 2. The survival function from Cox PH regression system from 1861-1994 (for groups of governments distinguished by proportional and uninominal electoral)

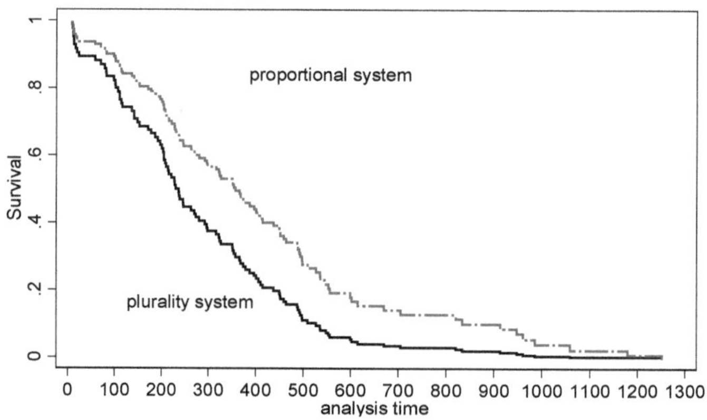

Figure3. The survival function from Cox PH regression system from 1861-1994 (for groups of governments distinguished by universal vs. restricted suffrage)

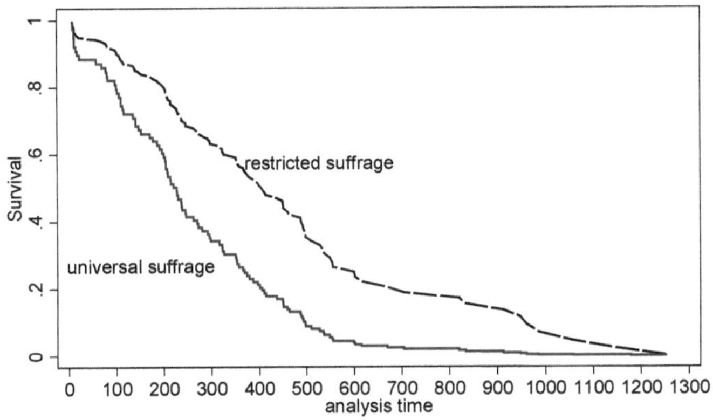

We now report separate estimates both for the monarchic period and republican period, for the latter, we also consider the role of the Senate.

Looking at the separate results for the pre-fascist legislatures (VIII to XXVI) – characterised by monarchy, plurality system (for all the legislatures excluding XV, XVI and XVII and XXV and XXI), restricted suffrage (since 1861 to 1913) followed by male universal suffrage (since XXIV legislature, 1913) – the results (table 4) confirm the negative relation between government survival and plurality system (the hazard ratio is about 1.61), as well as the positive relation between government duration and the high power in the parliament of the leading parties (the hazard ratio is about 0.37). The restricted suffrage, the number of seats and the number of parties are not significant. Figure 4 reports the survival function of governments from the estimated model (estimated at the mean of covariates and at the values 0 and 1 of the electoral system) in the period 1861-1924. It is interesting to notice that the curves in figure 4 have features similar to those of figure 2, in spite of the shorter period of proportional electoral system considered.

Table 4. government duration in the chamber of deputies 1861-1924.

Cox regression	--	Breslow method for ties
No. of subjects	=	60
Number of obs	=	60
No. of failures	=	60
Time at risk	=	21748
Log pseudolikelihood	=	-185.45451

_t	Haz. Ratio	Std. Err.	z
SS lead. Party	.3655316	.1211395	-3.04
n.of parties	1.04679	.1157771	0.41
plurality E. S.	1.610576	.2515561	3.05
restr.suffrage	1.084475	.4733566	0.19
n.of seats	.9987218	.0035455	-0.36

Figure 4. Government duration: The survival function from Cox PH estimates for groups of governments distinguished by proportional and plurality electoral system from 1861-1924

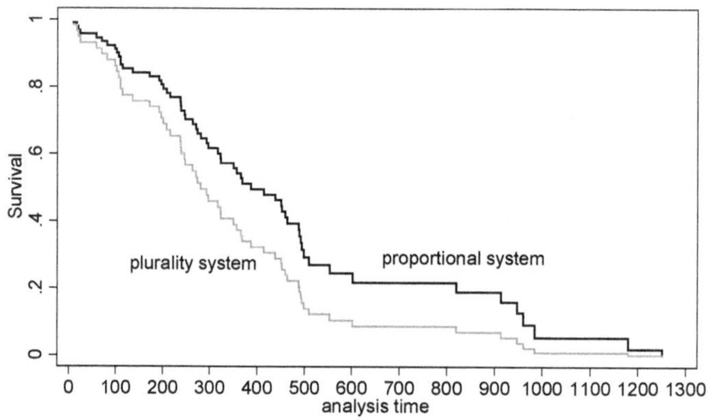

Even for the monarchic period alone, the empirical results are contrary to the common view that the plurality system favours the stability of the governments. The reason may be that under this system the individual personalities are more important than the political programs and the party's discipline. This obviously reduces the effectiveness of the voting power of the individual members of the parliament. On the other hand, the voting power of the leading party is still important for the survival of the governments, because the bigger this power the smaller the effect of a dissenting member (both in the parliament or in government's coalition). The number of seats in the Chamber of deputies is not significant as well as the number of parties that increased with the extension of the suffrage, also not significant. A likely explanation can be found in the fact that the organized parties together with the male universal suffrage entered into the scene only in the 20th century immediately after the two shocks of the first world war and of the subsequent inflation, and immediately before of the dictatorship.

Table 5 reports, for the post-fascist republican periods (1948-1994), the separate results for the Chamber of deputies and the Senate. The results show a different role played by the two branches of the parliament, over the same period, in determining government stability. This role results mainly driven by the political parties. On the one hand, in the Chamber of deputies, the government duration is positively affected by the number of parties and the S-S index of the leading party, whereas the number of seats is not significant. On the other hand, in the Senate, the only significant variable for government duration is the number of parties with hazard ratio lower than unity.

Table 5. Government duration in the chamber of deputies and senate in the republican period 1948-1994.

Chamber of deputies

```
Cox regression          --Breslow method for ties
No. of subjects         =        47
Number of obs           =        47
No. of failures         =        47
Time at risk            =     15137
                                             Wald chi2(3)   =   27.50
Log pseudolikelihood    = -134.21072         Prob > chi2    =  0.0000
```

_t	Haz.Ratio Rob.	Std.Err.	z
n.of parties	.7888244	.0448171	-4.18
n.of seats	1.008108	.0064362	1.26
SS lead. Party	.2233991	.0655302	-5.11

Senate

```
Cox regression          --   Breslow method for ties
No. of subjects         =    47
Number of obs           =    47
No. of failures         =    47
Time at risk            =    15137
                                             Wald chi2(3)  =  5.28
Log pseudolikelihood    =    -136.42882      Prob > chi2   =  0.1523
```

_t	Haz.Ratio Rob.	Std.Err.	z
n. of parties	.8824738	.05269	-2.09
n.of seats	.999991	.0053824	-0.00
SS lead. Party	.4837346	1.116238	-0.31

Thus, the empirical results for the two branches of the parliament considered separately confirm that the driving forces of the survival of the governments under the proportional system are related to the number of parties and, only in the Chamber of Deputies, to the voting power of the leading party. The reason for difference in the branches of the parliament is that the Chamber of deputies and the Senate have, not only a different number of seats and of parties represented, which determine different values of the S-S index of the leading party, but also different internal regulations that have been often considered cause of different support to the governments. In the Italian parliamentary tradition, the political arena *par excellence* is the Chamber of deputies, where, generally, a crucial defeat determines the end of a government. Moreover, given that the number of senators is about half that of the deputies, for the minor parties the chances of being represented tend to be very small. Furthermore, the marginal senators of the minor parties have reduced chances are of being re-elected. This may explain why in the senate the increase in the number of parties lowers the hazard ratio of the governments more than in the chamber.

4. Summary and conclusions

Referring to some institutional features of the Italian parliament and to the role of the political parties – as captured by the number of parties and by their Shapley-Shubik index of voting power of those represented in the Italian Parliament – we have analysed the Italian democracy (from the unification to the end of the first republic (1861-1994), with the exclusion of the fascist period and of the subsequent transitory institutional period known as "Costituente") as for the durability of the Italian governments. Our approach, based on survival analysis of government and legislature durations has given results, summarised in the table 7 in terms of hazard ratios, that differ from those prevailing in the political economy literature.

In the Chamber of Deputies, over the whole period considered, from 1860 to 1994, the survival of the governments is inversely related to the plurality system. Either the restricted suffrage or the Shapley-Shubik index of voting power of the leading parties takes hazard ratio strictly lower than 1. The institutional form of the state, parliamentarian republic *vs.* constitutional monarchy is not significant all over the period as well as the number of parties. The number of seats is significant, but the hazard ratio almost equal to 1 indicates no relation with government survival. Separate estimates of sub-periods give details on the longer term estimates: In the monarchic period the voting powers of the prevailing parliamentary group is significant with hazard ratio lower than 1, moreover the hazard ratio for the plurality electoral system is much greater than 1, in spite of the reduced period of the proportional counterpart. Proportional electoral systems, believed to be responsible to a tendency to short living governments, are not causing the same instability as the plurality systems. In this respect, notice that not even in the republican period alone, the "political game" depicted in terms of Shapley-Shubik index of voting power gave the (expected) picture of *fragmentation of the decisional powers.* Indeed, rather than a fragmented Parliament unable to produce a clear leading government because of the multitude of small political groups, it emerged a clear cut between the power of the main parties and those of all the other minor parties. Yet the role of parties (the increase of their number) becomes unexpectedly crucial in the estimates of the post war parliament which also consider the role of the senate.

Table 7. Summary of the results: survival analysis of government duration

	Chamber of Deputies (1861-1994)	**Monarchy: Chamber of Deputies (1861-1924)**	**Republic: Chamber of Deputies (1948-1994)**	**Republic: Senate (1948-1996)**
Plurality electoral system	**H. R.>1**	**H. R.>1**		
Number of parties	**N. S.**	**N. S.**	**H. R.<1**	**H. R.<1**
number of seats	**H. R.1**	**N. S.**	**N. S.**	**N. S.**
restricted suffrage	**H. R.<1**	**N. S.**		
Republic =1 after 1948 and 0 otherwise	**N. S.**			
S. S. index leading party	**H. R.<1**	**H. R.<1**	**H. R.<1**	**N. S.**

N. S. = not significant at 5 %
H. R. = hazard ratio

It is clear that, contrary to what has been often asserted, pure plurality reduces the chances of survival of governments in comparison with proportional system. Moreover a fractioned party system does not affect negatively the survival of governments. On the contrary, it plays a role in the period in which the party-system is consolidated.

However, admittedly, the governments in Italy had a short life under either system and the interruption of legislatures before the natural term occurred both in the monarchic and in the republican periods.

As seen, Alesina and Perotti (1994)[18] argue that short living governments may not be damaging in calm periods, whereas they become negatively crucial in

18 Alesina and Perotti (1994) support their view on fragmentation on the basis of Drazen and Grilli (1993), Grilli, Masciandaro and Tabellini (1991).

critical situations, such as those following an economic shock or an international crisis. However, at this stage of research, this thesis has not yet a *strong* empirical support for the Italian democracy both in the monarchic and in the republican period. The explanation might be found in the fact that those governments succeeding to each other, originated, for prolonged periods, from the same elite considered coherent in the long run. In some situation, perhaps the most critical, the ruling elite produced high-quality leaders. In the monarchic period the right-wing governments were constantly in power from 1861 to 1876, during 5 legislatures of about 3 years each with 11 different premiers for 15 different governments, each pursuing a similar liberal right-wing policy under the initial leadership of Cavour and of the leader of the economic and fiscal policy, Quintino Sella. These "short living" governments, ruling the new Kingdom of Italy, were facing a very critical fiscal situation because of the huge public debt inherited from previous states and the huge deficit of the public finances of the new unitary state. With a rigorous long run fiscal policy they were able to reduce the initial deficit, while undertaking important infrastructural public expenditures. In the subsequent period, the so called "historical left" (i. e., the left wing liberals) ruled from 1876 to 1890 over 7 legislatures, with 7 different prime ministers for 11 governments of the same orientation. In this period, the orientation of the fiscal policy was more permissive. On the other hand, from 1903 to 1914, a period of moderate liberal orientation, 8 different premiers succeeded to each other in 11 governments. This period, characterized by the first Italian economic miracle, was dominated by the figure (and political program) of Antonio Giolitti. In the Italian republic, in spite of its 47 government (on average, about 4 for each legislature), all the legislatures of the two post world war decades from 1948 to 1968, as noted by La Palombara (1988), showed a substantial political continuity, with DC always as a solid leading party. In this long period after a phase of pure "centrist" policy there was a cautious opening to a moderate centre left line. Thus, the "short living" centrist DC governments from 1948 to 1961 were able to fight the inflation, to restore the public finances and to create the conditions for a period of high economic growth that was called "economic miracle". The elite of the first period offered leaders as Alcide De Gasperi, Luigi Einaudi and Ezio Vanoni, respectively, in political, economic and fiscal matters. On the other hand, in the '60s, the centre left governments, with DC leaders and socialists in the government coalitions, were able to overcome the inflationary trend caused by the prolonged cycle of high economic expansion with neither a deflation nor a worsening of the ratio of the public debt to GDP: the ratio of state debt to GDP in the 1970 was still a mere 34 % as that of the previous decade. High deficits and high inflation appeared afterwards and the voting power of DC declined.[19] Governments, in spite of their duration, may have been weak because of the modest voting power of their majority. These observations, obviously, do not imply a preference for short living governments. Nevertheless a too prolonged stability, reduces the circulation of the political elites and may reduce the dynamic efficiency of the system. This may happen in a market economy with big firms dominating the market. The struggle for survival of the political elites governing the country, in a Schumpeterian perspective (Fedeli and Forte, 2011), must leave enough room for an efficient pursuance of their own programs both in emergency and in good periods. Yet, under short living governments, bureaucracies and interest groups may become more influential in the daily choices: legislation may become more complex, structural reforms may require more time to be accomplished and, in case, may become unduly complex. In sum, the circulation of the governing elites assures competition, as that of monopolies in the Schumpeterian theory, but their survival may assure dynamic efficiency and effectiveness. An equilibrium point has to be found as for the duration of governments. Indeed, governments shorter than the legislature appear an anomaly. Therefore, the question remains on the causes of the short living governments in Italy both under uninominal or proportional electoral systems both in the monarchic and in the republican period. If the electoral systems do not matter and the constitutional monarchy and the democratic republic do not matter either, other variables of institutional, sociological, political and economic nature have to be found. As for the institutional variables, the distribution powers between the head of the state and of the government, on the one hand, and the parliament, on the other, may be relevant. Under the Italian "parliamentary regime", in both the monarchic and the republican system, the head of the state must dismiss the government whenever the parliament denies it a confidence vote politically relevant and the head of the government has limited powers. A sociological factor that may explain the "Italian peculiarity" of short living government even with long living legislatures is the regional rivalry among the North, the Centre and the South an even among regions of these same three areas. It may be that under a federalist system the regional rivalries are reduced at the central state level because of the greater autonomy at the lower levels of government. A peculiar political factor present in the republican period has been the impossibility, for foreign policy reasons, for the biggest left wing party, the communist party, to guide a left wing government, before the fall of the Berlin wall. The left was thus split and only the major parties on the centre or on the right could form the governments. Among the economic factors for the short life

19 On the relation between the change in voting power of the dominant party and the change in deficit, see Fedeli and Forte (2003).

of Governments key macro economic variables, as the rate of inflation, the rates of unemployment and of economic growth have been found of scarce impact by Warwick (1994) who shows that the ideological diversity is the main destabilizing factor of governments. As for the Italian case, *prima facie*, one can note that there were short living governments with either low or high rates of unemployment, of inflation and of growth. Other explanations have been given in terms of game theory (see Laver 2003). Further research may be useful to throw light on the "Italian peculiarity".

References

Alesina, A., and A. Drazen (1991) *"Why are stabilization delayed?"*, American Economic Review, 82, 1170-1188.

Alesina, A. and R. Perotti (1994) *"The political economy of budget deficits"*, Imf Working Paper, 85.

Alesina, A. and H. Rosenthal (1995) Partisan Politics, Divided Government, And The Economy, Cambridge, Cambridge University Press.

Austen-Smith, D., and J. Banks (1988) "Elections, Coalitions, and Legislative Outcomes." American Political Science Review 82, 405-22.

Austen-Smith, D., and J. Banks (1990) *"Stable Portfolio Allocations."* AMERIcan Political Science Review 84, 891-906.

Axelrod, R. (1970) Conflict Of Interest: A Theory Of Divergent Goals With Applications To Politics, Chicago, Markham.

Baron, D. (1991) *"A Spatial Bargaining Theory of Government Formation in Parliamentary Systems"*, American Political Science Review 85, 137-65.

Barro, R. and V. Grilli (1996) European Macroeconomis, Mc GrawHills.

Bartolotta F. (1971) Parlamenti E Governi D'italia Dal 1848 Al 1970, Vito Bianco editore

Blondel, J., and F. Miiller-Rommel, eds. (1983) Governing Together: The Extent And Limits Of Joint Decision-Making In Western European Cabinets, London: Macmillan.

Browne, E..C., and J. Dreijmanis, eds. (1982) Government Coalitions In Western Democracies, New York, Longman.

Cox G. W. (1997), Making Votes Count: Strategic Coordionation In World's Electoral Systems, Cambridge University Press, Cambridge UK.

Diermeier, D. and R. Stevenson (1999) *"Cabinet Survival and Competing Risks"* American Journal Of Political Science 43, 1051-69.

Drazen, A., and V. Grilli (1993) *"The benefits of crises for economic reform"*, American Economic Review, 599-608.

Duverger, M. (1954), Les Parties Politique, A.Colin, Paris. (It.Ed. Duverger, M. (1961), I Partiti Politici, Comunita', Milano

Fedeli, S., and F. Forte (2003) *"The impact of the electoral system and of other political institutions on public debt and government's finances in Italy"*, in Economic Welfare, International Business And Global Institutional Change, R. Mudambi *et al.* eds. E.Elgar Publisher, pp. 36-80,.

Fedeli, S., and F. Forte (2011), "The law of survival of the political class: an analysis of the Italian Parliament (1946-2011) ", Working paper n.146 Dipartimento Di Economia Pubblica, Sapienza – Università di Roma: http://www.dipecodir.it/upload/wp/pdf/wp146.pdf

Grilli, V., Masciandaro D., and G. Tabellini (1991) *"Political and monetary institutions and public finance policies in the industrial democracies"*, ECONOMIC POLICY, 13.

Grofman, B. (1982) "A Dynamic Model of Protocoalition Formation in Ideological N-Space." Behavioural Science 27, 77-90.

Huber, J. (1996) Rationalizing Parliament: Legislative Institutions And Party Politics In France. New York: Cambridge University Press.

King G, Alt J. E., Burns N. E., and M. Laver (1990), *A Unified Model of Cabinet Dissolution in Parliamentary Democracies,* American Journal Of Political Science, vol.34 n.3

La Navicella (from 1949 to 2000) *I deputati e Senatori del parlamento repubblicano.* Serie pubblicata per ciascuna legislatura repubblicana. Roma-Milano-Catania.

La Navicella (1985) *Gli ex parlamentari della Repubblica.* [Prefazione di Vittorio Martuscelli], Pubblicazione dell'Istituto Nazionale dell'Informazione. Roma, Editoriale Italiana, 2000

La Navicella (2000) *1948-1998, Repubblica italiana : 50 anni di Parlamento, Governi, Istituzioni*, [Presentazioni di Nicola Mancino, Luciano Violante, Paolo Cabras] Pubblicazione dell'Istituto Nazionale dell'Informazione. Roma, Editoriale Italiana, 2000

La Palombara, G. J. (1988) Democracy Italian Style, Yale, Yale University Press.

Laver M.(2003), *"Government Termination"*, Annual Review of Political Science, 6, 23-40

Laver, M., (2000) *"Government Formation and Public Policy",* Political Science And Politics, 33, 21-23.

Laver, M. (1998) *"Models of Government Formation",* Annual Review Of Political Science 1, 1-25.

Laver, M., and N. Schofield (1990) Multiparty Government: The Politics Of Coalition In Europe, Oxford: Oxford University Press.

Laver, M., and K. A. Shepsle (1996) MAKING AND BREAKING GOVERNMENTS, New York: Cambridge University Press.

Laver M. and N. Schofield (1991), Multy Party Government. The Politics Of Coalition In Europe, Oxford University Press, Oxford.

Lijphart, A. (1968) *"Typologies of democratic system"*, Comparative Political Studies, 1.

Lijphart A (1994) *"Proportionality by Non-PR Methods: Ethnic Representation in Belgium, Cyprus, Lebanon, New Zealand, West Germany and Zimbawe"*, in Grofman B. and A. Lijphart (eds.) Electoral Laws And Their Political Consequences, New York, Agathon Press, second printing.

Lijphart, A (1984) *"Measures of Cabinet Durability: A Conceptual and Empirical Evaluation"* Comparative Political Studies 17, 265-79.

Lupia, A., and K. Strom (1995) *"Coalition Termination and the Strategic Timing of Legislative Elections"* American Political Science Review, 89, 648-65.

Malatesta, A. (1940) Enciclopedia biografica e bibliografica italiana : Ministri, deputati, Senatori dal 1848 al 1922, Milano, E.B.B.I., Ist. Editoriale Italiano B. C. Tosi S. A..

McCubbins, M. (1991) *"Party governance and US budget deficits: divided government and fiscal stalemate"*, in Politics And Economics In The Eighties, Alesina, A., and G. Carliner (eds.), Chicago, Chicago Universityy Press.

McKelvey, R. D., and N. Schofield (1986) *"Structural Instability of the Core"* Journal Of Mathematical Economics, 15, 179-98.

McKelvey, R. D., and N. Schofield (1987) *"Generalized Symmetry Conditions at a Core Point"* Econometrica 55, 923-33.

Peleg, B. (1981) *"Coalition Formation in Simple Games with Dominant Players"*, International Journal Of Game Theory 10(1), 11-13.

Persson, T. and G.Tabellini (2003) The Economics Effects Of Constitutions, The MIT PressCambridge, Massachusetts and London, England.

Piretti, M. S. (1996) Le Elezioni Politiche In Italia Dal 1848 A Oggi, Ed. Laterza, Bari

Pridham, G., ed. (1986) Coalitional Behaviour In Theory And Practice: An Inductive Modelfor Western Europe, Cambridge, Cambridge University Press.

Riker, W. (1962) The Theory Of Political Coalitions. New Haven: Yale University Press.

Roubini N. and J. Sachs (1989a) *"Government Spending and Budget Deficits in the Industrial Countries"*, Economic Policy, 8, p. 100-132

Roubini N. and J. Sachs (1989b) *"Political and economic determination of Budget Deficits in the Industrial Democracies"*, EUROPEAN ECONOMIC REVIEW, 33, p. 903-38.

Sartori, G. (1982) Teoria Dei Partiti E Caso Italiano, Sugarco, Milano, Italia.

Sartori, G. (1994) *"The influence of the electoral systems: Faulty laws or faulty method?"*, in Grofman B. and A. Lijphart (eds.) Electoral Laws And Their Political Consequences, New York, Agathon Press, second printing.

Schofield, N. (1993) *"Political Competition and Multiparty Coalition Governments."* European Journal Of Political Research 23, 1-33.

Shapley L. S. and M. Shubik (1954) *"A method for evaluating the distribution of power in a committee system",* American Political Science Review, 48, 787-792.

Strom, K. (1985) *"Party Goals and Government Performance in Parliamentary Democracies"* American Political Science Review 79, 738-54.

Strom, K. (1990) Minority Government And Majority Rule. Cambridge, Cambridge University Press.

Von Hagen, J. and I. J. Harden (1995) *"Budget Processes and Commitment to Fiscal Discipline"*, European Economic Review, 39(3-4), 771-79.

Warwick P., (1992), *Economic Trends and Government Survival in West European Parliamentary Democracies,* The American Political Science Review, Vol. 86, No. 4 pp. 875-887

Warwick, P. (1994) Government Survival In Parliamentary Democracies Cambridge, Cambridge University Press.

Fiscal Sociology And Public Choice

Jürgen Backhaus

ABSTRACT

In this paper, it is explained why fiscal sociology is gaining in importance again. The basic justification for fiscal sociology is provided by Pareto in his work on General Sociology. Samuelson in his efforts to establish the modern science of economics eliminated those aspects which he considered redundant. Yet, as the following example illustrates, fiscal sociological aspects matter. The 89 Russian Republics have tremendous difficulty to introduce a Financial Constitution and raising taxes. To the people of these republics it is not obvious what they get back in return. Therefore, something else is required in addition to taxes. In short, what we need is trust. Trust can be gained through emphasizing civic values, exemplary civil service, or religion, an aspect that has been worked out by Robert V. Andelson.

Introduction

Recently and only after the turn of the century, we have been able to witness a remarkable resurgence in an area of research which had long been neglected. In fact, the area of fiscal sociology does not even have a code for its classification in the Journal of Economic Literature (JEL) system.

In this essay, I briefly identify the recent literature and then try to explain its significance. In doing so, we have to begin with Paul A. Samuelson[1] who tried to make much of received public finance irrelevant. This effort at reduction also included the field of fiscal sociology. This effort stood in sharp variance with Pareto's project. Pareto[2] had tried to overcome disciplinary confines in economics in order to make room for the State in economic analysis. In this effort, Pareto was a precursor of Public Choice. The need for such a more inclusive analysis becomes particularly urgent when issues of constitutional and tax reform are to be considered. Here, there is a parallel to the emergence of constitutional public finance. In the end, a modern system of public finance requires for its practice the basic ingredients of civic society, *i. e.* agreed upon values and trust in its institutions. Andelson's[3] essay shortly to re-appear explores these realms.

1 Samuelson, Paul A., 'The pure theory of public expenditure', Review of Economics and Statistics, (1954), vol. 36, pp. 387-9; 'Diagrammatic exposition of a theory of public expenditure', *Review of Economics and Statistics*. 1955, vol. 37, pp. 350-6.

2 Pareto, Vilfredo, *Trattato di Sociologia Generale*, 1916; rev. French translation 1917; translated into English by Arthur Livingston as *The Mind and Society*, New York: Harcourt, (1935).

3 Andelson, Robert V, *Imputed Rights: An Essay in Christian Social Theory,* Athens: University of Georgia Press, (1971).

Richard Wagner's "exploratory essay"[4] takes the bull by the horns:

> "If the aim of market theorizing is to explain how people are able to generate generally orderly practices of activity when they relate to one another through private property, the coordinate aim of fiscal theorizing is similarly to explain how orderly patterns of activity emerge when people relate to one another in the particular form of collective property that constitutes a state".

The essay has eight chapters. After the first chapter on the architectonics, i. e. on how to set the whole thing up, the second gets right to the core: welfare economics is a contradiction in terms: how can we speak of "welfare" if the purpose is achieved on the basis of coercion. An "enterprise-based public finance" provides the key to redoing the dilemma. Property is often thought of as necessarily private. Yet conventions of professional economists in the US take place in hotels (not motels)[5]. The point is that hotels provide next to private rooms commons, the defining feature and main point of distinction and competition. The analogy fits federal republics well, but may frustrate colleagues working in such centralized environments as the Dutch or French. To top it, chapter three covers i. e. parliamentary assemblies as "catallactical arenas." With chapter four on political entrepreneurship Wagner returns to his roots, his very first article in Public Choice, then still called Papers on Non-Market Decision Making. Chapter five covers the economic organization of political enterprises: "People make connections, organizations don't"[6]. What comes as the claim on the residual in the private firm takes the form of revenue extraction in the public (ch. 5). The generation of tax complexity is part of the business (ch. 6). The issue of structure is appropriately dealt with in the crucial chapter seven with the contrast between federal and compound republics as ideal types. Finally, in chapter eight, Wagner defines fiscal sociology as a form of social agriculture – fiscal intentions are not only the result of human interaction, they also reflect the shapes of interests and sentiments[7].

The book by Fernández Cainzos[8] (published by the Research Institute of the Spanish Treasury) has a superbly clear structure. Six chapters cover the basics of

---

4 Richard E. Wagner, *Fiscal Sociology and the Theory of Public Finance: An Exploratory Essay*, (New Thinking in Political Economy Series), Cheltenham, UK, Edward Elgar, (2007), p. VIII.

5 In Europe, professional meetings of economists tend to take place in universities or town halls.

6 Richard E. Wagner, *Fiscal Sociology and the Theory of Public Finance: An Exploratory Essay*, (New Thinking in Political Economy Series), Cheltenham, UK, Edward Elgar, p. 121.

7 Richard E. Wagner, *Fiscal Sociology and the Theory of Public Finance: An Exploratory Essay*, (New Thinking in Political Economy Series), Cheltenham, UK, Edward Elgar, p. 180.

8 Cainzos, Juan Jesús Fernandez, *Sociología de la Hacienda Pública.*, Madrid, Spain, Ministerio de Economía y Hacienda, Instituto de Estudios Fiscales, 2006.

fiscal sociology (chs. 1 & 2), sociology of spending (ch. 3), and revenue collection (ch. 4), tax resistance (ch. 5) and fiscal illusion (ch. 6).

Pareto optimality is a household word in economics. Pareto's law on income distribution is a staple item in economics and often ignored by those in charge of economic policy. The Italian school Pareto had as a following in public finance and fiscal sociology has not been well documented before 2007. Michael McLure, the author of The Paretian School and Italian Fiscal Sociology,[9] does not only describe Pareto's influence on fiscal economic thought in the Italy of his time. Next to the ten chapters devoted to this task, he provides six more chapters which are, essentially, translations from the Italian documenting the kind of fiscal theorizing that Pareto instigated. Particularly fascinating in the light of modern developments are his thoughts on experimental economics.

II. Samuelson's Reduction

In order to achieve the famous reduction by which public finance could then be integrated into the simple menu of (general equilibrium) economics, Paul A. Samuelson applied a basic trick in logic: dichotomy. There are only two types of goods, private goods and public goods. The same calculus could be applied just with the exception that for public goods addition of utilities was required, not as in Walrasian markets the matching of individual bets so as to achieve an equilibrium.

How would this addition come about? The most basic desire of human people to see their individual desires fulfilled, also those that had come upon them through heritage, their aspirations and also needs, have been cast into a most simple mathematical process of addition.

This is where Arrow comes in. He took the challenge for what it was, postulated preferences on the part of citizens in a mathematical space and came to the conclusion that such a simple addition was not always logically possible – hence his paradoxon.

Here, two lines of thought come about. Tullock[10] embarked on the idea of exploring public choice. But others felt confident that Arrow's paradoxon was a possibility and would often not be relevant, certainly if great numbers (of voters) were involved.

---

9 New York, USA: Palgrave Macmillan, 2007.

10 Arrow, Kenneth J, *Social Choice and Individual Values*, New York: John Wiley and Sons 1951; Backhaus, Juergen and Richard E. Wagner, 'From Continental Public Finance to Public Choice. Mapping Continuity.', History of Political Economy, 2005, vol. 37, pp. 314-332; Tullock, Gordon, On Voting. A Public Choice Approach, Cheltenham: Edward Elgar, 1998.

In this way, the project of public economics came about. By reducing the State designed to overcome market failure,[11] the miracle was achieved to transform public finance into public economics and thus make it part of a mainstream.

You, the readers, are all in your right to ask the most obvious of why nobody said out loud: the Emperor has no clothes! The truth of the matter is: there was no little child in the profession.[12] Why did nobody simply point to the fact that the government cannot be imagined to act in a Walrasian paradigm?

It is probably always important for scholars to make their imprint within a certain paradigm. This is not a sign of impurity or timidity on their part. Research paradigms go with grants, and subsidies have to be paid also through the summer.[13] Yet, the mystery still remains, as Pareto's project had been launched decades before.[14]

III. Pareto's Project

What then was Pareto's purpose? In my possession is a collection of historical studies published under Pareto's name. It contains a preface in which the editor distances himself from the work. He could never have imagined, he says, of publishing a book in which he would just have collected historical studies, a clear steer at what came to be known as the Historical School.[15] Why did he disagree with this project published under his own supervision? This question can serve as a marker to explain what was to follow.

Take the recent American election process as one just example. Can Hillary Clinton with her plan on health care reform and now President Obama with his

11 Bator, Francis, 'The Anatomy of Market Failure.', The Quar-terly Journal of Economics, Vol. 72, No. 3. Aug. 1958, pp. 359-379.

12 When I was at the Public Choice Center in 1977/78, there was a presentation by J. M. Buchanan who was still intellectually struggling with the two Samuelson articles. He then went to take on the challenge with the notion of *Leviathan* (with Geoffrey Brennon). Brennon, Geoffrey and Buchanan, James M. *The Power to Tax.* Cambridge: Cambridge University Press, 1980.

13 American university teachers tend to be on nine-month-salaries.

14 Asking him about it, J. Buchanan showed me proudly his edition of Pareto's *Manual of Political Theory* (in French). Although he had spent so much effort on understanding the Italian classics, he proved not to know of Pareto's *Trattato.* – We were rather close, then, and he later said that he knew about the *Treatise* but didn't think much of it. This was after I had shown him my article 'Pareto on Public Choice.' *Public Choice*, Vol. 33, no. 1, pp. 5-17, 1978, which I had written for the purpose to honor him.

15 See Backhaus, Juergen, *Rediscovering the Historical Schools.* II Vols., Emerald Group Publishing Limited, 2005.

plan on health insurance reform[16] be described in terms of public or private goods? Certainly not. Public health provision would involve many private goods being provided publicly, but not as public goods. Health care is necessarily individually. Individual personal treatments have to be taken care of. But why publicly? This is a question that requires an answer beyond Samuelson. Hence Pareto's project.

Vilfredo Pareto, who had graduated from Torino with a (BA) thesis on the notion of the equilibrium in physics, spent most of his life as a railroad executive. All the while, he maintained an avid interest in politics and voiced his liberal views liberally in the business oriented press. Having received an inheritance he was able to retire and pursue a different career. He spotted the small University of Lausanne and persuaded the aging professor Walras there to suggest him to the city council as his successor. Everything happened according to plan. Pareto wrote up his lectures to his few students – he lectured in French, of course, but published in Italian, as there was his home market. His *Corso* is still very much what was to be expected at the time. His *Manuale*, however, is very different. It is here where Kaldor and Hicks claimed to have found the inspiration for what they called the *Pareto criterion.* The *Manuale* had an important mathematical appendix for the French edition meant to be a summary but susceptible to substantial misinterpretation if read without the benefit of the supporting text (in Italian).[17]

Although Schumpeter conducted a famous seminar on Pareto at Harvard, the mainstream reception of Pareto's work stopped with the *Manuale* and notably its French appendix. His main work, the *Trattato*, was published in English after the division between economics and sociology had become a *fait accompli* – the work was avidly claimed by the sociologists while most economists failed to see its value.

From the point of view of public choice or public finance, for that matter, the issue of how to model the State is at the center. Walras, of course, had to reduce the State to the role of an auctioneer. At this point, Walras and Pareto parted ways. Pareto became increasingly interested in the interdependence between the market and the State. While he perceived a lot of rational action in the market, he saw much less of this in the political arenas.

---

16 The health insurance system influences the health care delivery system by its decision of reimbursement of particular services, treatments, and pharmaceuticals, and this in turn can affect the availability of certain services and treatments in a particular country. Exploiting differences in health care delivery systems has given rise to the new phenomenon of health tourism. Impressively, old spas in Western Prussia and Galicia set up in the time by Prussian and Austrian administrators, after a long slumber, have come back to shiny new life in what is now Poland.

17 See Backhaus, Juergen, 'The Pareto Principle.', Analyse & Kritik, vol. 2, (Fall 1980), pp. 146-171.

Modeling an economy with an active State is more complex than the often discussed issue introducing money into the Walrasian system. The State is different from all other actors in the economy by its power to tax. While law abiding actors in the market require the consensus of their counterparts for transactions, the State does not. In fact, a tax is a payment required without any consideration, any stated purpose for which it might be used. So much leeway opens up opportunities for abuse. When they are systematically used, they can be modeled. This is Pareto's project. Actors at the different levels of government are described in their relentless efforts to convince, disguise, swindle, steal, bribe, bestow honors and receiving them and also perform exemplary civil service. These two sides of the world, shadow and light, bring Pareto's world to life.

This is very different from modeling the State as a *Leviathan*[18] whose voracious appetite is only checked by its desire to devour tomorrow no fewer resources than today. Pareto's State can also be benign, enlightened, civilized and civilizing, *i. e.* an example of good governance.

This is different, again, from Wicksell's vision of the State. Here,[19] the Crown pursues its dynastic interests and will to power[20] by persuading Parliament which holds the power to tax, to agree to projects that the Crown crafts so as to make them agreeable to the citizens whose consent it requires. While this model of the State appealed to Buchanan who made it popular, it is not Pareto's who would also have room for a monarch without any desire, just playing the flute. Mainly, however, Pareto distinguishes between lions and foxes, who use strength and wit respectively.

IV. TAX AND CONSTITUTIONAL REFORM

In Europe, we are currently confronted with many new States struggling for their recognition.[21] While, for instance in the case of the Kosovo (German: Amselfeld) the focus is on external recognition, the deeper and more important issue[22] is internal recognition by its citizens. Only if they can conceive of their State

18 James M. Buchanan, Brennan, Geoffrey, The Power to Tax, Cambridge: Cambridge University Press, (1980).

19 Wicksell, Knut, Finanztheoretische Untersuchungen, Jena: Gustav Fischer, (1896).

20 This is a term by Nietzsche. But the book under the same title is rather a falsification authored by his sister.

21 Look at Slovenia, Croatia, Macedonia, the Ukraine, and Russia itself with its 89 constituent republics. But also consider Germany's five new Federal States.

22 For instance, administrative practice in any area of public administration cannot be taught and thus transferred without considering the context, in which the administrative practice of one and the same procedure is to be deployed. For instance, executives I trained for the World

as legitimate will they be willing to pay taxes.[23] Legitimacy cannot be accomplished by a State perceived as a *Leviathan*. Legitimacy cannot be stolen, it must be earned.

The case can be illustrated for Germany. Recently, in the capital city of Erfurt, the mayoral direct election brought out only less than 31 % of the electorate. The Lord Mayor elected with a clear majority of this less than a third of the population obviously has a hard time bringing about worthwhile projects, getting developments approved (which require user fees and charges, not taxes) or conducting more than ceremonial politics.

The same applies almost everywhere we look at new States.[24] The States have to first earn trust before they can successfully embark on policy. This is despite the fact that some such States as Estonia, Slovakia, or Slovenia, have implemented well meant and amply provided economic advice and to good effect.

Political capital consists of trust and legitimacy. These are important ingredients for economic policy; hence they cannot be ignored in public oriented economic analysis – but they have been excluded as relevant items from the mainstream and thus the curricula of those schools who train future decision makers. This was Robert V. Andelson's project.

V. Trust And Religion

The book by Robert V. Andelson should also be interpreted as a contribution to fiscal sociology. When it appeared in 1971, it rather looked like a contribution to moral philosophy.[25] Andelson was by training a protestant minister, and served for decades as a professor of philosophy at Auburn University. The first sentence of his foreword, as well as subtitle of the book, reinforce the misunderstanding of the purpose of his book:

> "In our modern confusion about the meanings of words, most people are at sea when they come upon such terms as 'natural rights,' ' natural law,' 'rights of man,' 'human rights,' 'chartered rights of men,' and 'higher law.' Yet justice cannot be attained until a proper understanding of these terms is restored. Professor Robert V. Andelson's book is a courageous endeavor to renew the metaphysical foundations of natural rights. Knowing that all differ-

---

Bank from Slovakia and Romania would tell me distinctly different scenarios of how they would implement the one and the same practice I had just taught.

23 The term legitimacy has completely disappeared from public finance textbooks, although the concept is so crucial for taxation.

24 This is the focus of Leroy's comparative studies. Leroy, Marc, *Regards Croisés Sur le Système Fiscal: Allemagne, France, Italie, Russie*. Paris: L'Harmattan, (2005).

25 Robert V. Andelson, *Imputed Rights: An Essay in Christian Social Theory*, Athens: University of Georgia Press, (1971).

ences of opinion are theological at bottom, Mr. Andelson reaffirms the religious understanding of human nature, natural law, and natural right."[26]

After discussing the foundations of human rights in Part One, Part Two is devoted to the main message of the book, a realistic social utopia, called *The Community of Covenant*. This *Community of Covenant* is in fact a society based on the principles of Henry George.[27] The single tax on land to the exclusion of any taxes on capital or personal income or for that matter the effective demand of persons such as an excise tax or a Value Added Tax (VAT), leaves plenty of room for taxation, since land is residually defined (not capital, and not labor) as the original factor of production. This comes in many forms, I have detailed about two and a half dozen.[28] The ingenuity of the tax on land lies in its feature of facilitating tax avoidance. In his regular end of quarter Henry George Lecture, Robert V. Andelson once asked his students, which tax or charge they were happy to pay. They would not come up with the answer, so the professor gave it himself. He liked the parking charges at the university best. Anybody who wanted to avoid them, could by parking the car outside the university campus. Andelson, who used a cane, had a parking lot not far from the building.

The significance of this feature of Henry George's tax lies in the fact that by facilitating avoidance, it does not entail the typical excess burden of taxation. The excess burden of taxation is a social cost which arises out of the desire of the taxpayer to avoid the tax. It consists of two parts, *Tullock's Rectangle* and *Harberger's Triangle*.[29] For any amount of capital X in taxation, the taxpayer is willing to spend almost the same amount in order to avoid the tax. If X, the intended tax revenue, is levied on a particular production process, the entrepreneur will reconfigure the production process so as to avoid the tax, and this can result in inefficiencies almost as big as the amount of the tax avoided. Those inefficiencies will often remain in the economy as the established practice, even if the tax has long been repealed. *Harberger's Triangle*, on the other hand, shows the extent of production that has not taken place. The resources not used in the production process are likely not at all wasted, they rather have probably be used somewhere else and less efficiently. We just don't know what happened to them. Exploring the social reality of processes relating to *Tullock's Rectangle* and *Harberger's*

26 P. XI. The preface was written by Russell Kirk of Mecosta, Michigan.

27 *Progress and Poverty*, New York: Robert Schalkenbach Foundation, (1981).

28 See my 'Henry George's Ingenious Tax: A Contemporary Restatement.', *The American Journal of Economics and Sociology*, vol. 56, no. 4, (October 1997), pp. 453-474.

29 The Harberger triangle describes the welfare loss to society, when moving from a competitive situation to a monopoly, but the welfare loss to society from monopoly is much bigger than depicted by the Harberger triangle. Compare Gordon Tullock, 'The Welfare Costs of Monopolies, Tariffs and Theft.' *Western Economic Journal*. 5.3, (1967), pp. 224-232.

Triangle is the principle task of fiscal sociology. By proffering Henry George's tax constitution, from a human rights perspective, Andelson effectively probes an issue in normative fiscal sociology. This is why this essay reappears in this series, where it is more likely to be found, and valued, and read, for what it is.

The *Covenant* establishes the integrity of every member of the community, including his property. No authority whatsoever has a right to this property, and for that reason, taxes in the modern understanding of coerced payments without any service in return are impossible from a human rights point of view. In particular, state organized welfare services cannot be tax financed.

> "To assert that welfare services lie outside the proper competence of government is not to concede that they need be neglected or relegated to private individual performance. Why should it be taken for granted that things which individuals are unable, as individuals, to do for themselves, must, if they are to be done at all, necessarily be done through the coercive power of government?"[30]

Andelson explicitly criticizes Galbraith and his dichotomy of national life into "'public' (government) and 'private' (individual and commercial) sectors" as presenting a "false, truncated picture of the possibilities."[31] In Andelson's or Henry George's world, there is a very large and voluntary nongovernmental sector.

Andelson's *Covenant* stands in stark opposition to the mainstream view of a certain Harvard elite, also including Bator ("The Anatomy of Market Failure"),[32] which sees everything as the public, *i. e.* state purpose, which cannot be accomplished by individuals.

Those individuals who do not want to contribute their fair share to the covenant Republic are simply left to their own devices:

> "..., they may be left to defend themselves individually against predation the best they can, so long as they present no threat to the community in whose midst they live. If, however, they declare by word or deed aggressive war against the covenant, its adherents have no choice but to treat them as wild beasts to be forcibly restrained or, if need be, eliminated."[33]

Hence, there is coercion only in self defense, not in taxation. Andelson even goes further in emphasizing the right to resistance:

> "There is no special virtue attached to obedience to constituted authority or human law as such. The Declaration of Independence unequivocally asserts that the refusal to obey unjust laws or arbitrary rulers can be a duty under certain circumstances, and in this it but reiterates a theme earlier popularized by those sixteenth-century followers of Calvin to whom historians have applied the term 'Monarchomachists.' Where representative institutions obtain in

---

30 Andelson, *op. cit.*, p. 87.

31 Andelson, *op. cit.*, p. 87. The reference is to John Kenneth Galbraith, *The Affluent Society.* Boston: Houghton Mifflin, (1958).

32 *Quarterly Journal of Economics*, 72, (1958), pp. 351-79.

33 Andelson, *op. cit.*, p. 117.

fact as well as theory, the presumption is that those aggrieved should obey laws and rulers which they deem unjust, since avenues of peaceful change are open to them. But where an entrenched regime is able to perpetuate itself in power by means of the Hopkinsian strategy of 'tax, spend, elect,' or where it arrogates to itself advantages of propaganda, which make a mockery of the processes of consent, methods of persuasion cannot be depended upon to correct abuse, and militant resistance may be justified as a last resort."[34]

Education is of particular concern to Andelson:

> "Inasmuch as responsible decisions cannot be expected of an ignorant electorate, education becomes an auxiliary concern of any polity which incorporates a broad-based franchise. This means that the cost of such training as may be deemed essential for informed citizenship is a legitimate public charge. The taxpayer has no moral duty to subsidize either the aesthetic cultivation or the vocational preparation of the young; such subsidy is a parental responsibility. His just obligation is limited to the support of necessary education for citizenship."[35]

This education takes on the form of indoctrination.

> "Effective education for citizenship demands not merely that youth be drilled in civic facts and taught the fundamentals of valid reasoning. It demands, above all else, the cultivation of an attitude of dedication to the covenant, and of respect for the principles and the institutions whereby the covenant is actualized. This is to assert that effective education for citizenship is essentially a matter of moral indoctrination. But government, even on a local level, is the worst possible instrument with which to undertake this task."[36]

This means that effective education for citizenship is a common and in this sense public task, <u>not</u> to be entrusted to any form of government. Again, Andelson overcomes the artificial dichotomy between public= state and individual=private by postulating common institutions for essential purposes which are not state institutions.

Fiscal equalization is often considered an accomplishment of modern times, a cherished achievement to accomplish equality of opportunity, but Andelson notes:

> "As the 'equality of opportunity' in the full, literal meaning of the term, it, too, can be implemented only by means of inequality before the law. If government seriously undertakes to enforce equality of opportunity, it must go beyond preventing predation and the unequal advantages which arise therefrom, and seek to redress inequalities resulting from differences in native endowments. It can only do this by conferring special privileges on some of the expense of others, or by instituting artificial handicaps which penalize favorable heredity. The enforcement of equal *freedom* of opportunity, on the other hand, is a legitimate and essential function of public authority – a function which is not merely compatible with but which is required by the ideal of equality before the law."[37]

The difference between equality and justice is a recurring theme. There is a high tolerance for inequality. "A man's ability to pay should have no bearing upon his

---

34 Andelson, *op. cit.*, p. 121.

35 Ibid., p. 122.

36 Ibid., p. 122.

37 Ibid., p. 125.

eligibility to receive the benefits of law."[38] Not surprisingly, Andelson supports the benefit principle, but not as a principle of taxation, but correctly as a principle governing the levy of fees.

> "The benefit theory is also applicable in cases where a public service is provided not as a matter of compulsion but of convenience to the voluntary user. Insofar as roads and highways are maintained for purposes other than defense, gasoline taxes and toll fees fall into this category, as do parking meter fees, which are further justified as a species of ground rent. None of the above, however, can be classified as true taxes, but are rather public fees."[39]

The economist Heinrich von Stackelberg advanced the idea that taxes can be used to enforce the rules of competition; extra profits due to monopoly or oligopoly should be taxed away.[40] "The entire problem of apportioning the tax burden would be obviated if we could assume, as Henry George assumed with reason in his day, that indemnities for special advantages abstracted from the common stock of natural opportunity would, if set at the full market value of such advantages, be sufficient to defray the total costs of government's essential functions. Even in the light of today's expanded military budgets, this assumption need not be laughed out of court. Insofar as monopolistic privilege begets social evils which give rise to public expense, the indemnities, to the extent that they would extirpate such privilege, would concurrently reduce the need for public revenue."[41]

Finally, just as there is a right and even a duty to resist unjust authority, there is a duty or obligation to defend the innocent. He cites the famous case of Kitty Genovese, who was murdered while her neighbours looked on. "Their duty was not so much to the pathetic victim herself as to the covenant under which their common safety was presumptively assured."[42]

The freedom from coercion does not imply a free-for-all, but imposes duties as a precondition of justice.

VI. The Conclusion

Some fifty-five years ago, Paul A. Samuelson led the community of scholars in public finance astray. This has had fateful repercussions, as many European but also American universities now phase out their public finance positions; the discipline has lost relevance. This article tries to help in redressing the balance.

---

38 Ibid., p. 126.

39 Andelson, *op. cit.*, p. 127.

40 'Stackelberg's Concept of the Post-War Economic Order.' *Journal of Economic Studies*, vol. 23, nrs. 5/6, (1996), pp. 141-148.

41 Andelson, *op. cit.*, p. 129.

42 Andelson, *op. cit.*, p. 131.

References

Andelson, Robert V., Imputed Rights: An Essay in Christian Social Theory. Athens: University of Georgia Press, (1971).

Arrow, Kenneth J., Social Choice and Individual Values. New York: John Wiley and Sons, (1951).

Backhaus, Juergen, "Pareto on Public Choice." Public Choice, Vol. 33, no. 1, (1978), pp. 5-17.

Backhaus, Juergen, "The Pareto Principle." Analyse & Kritik, vol. 2, (Fall 1980), pp. 146-171.

Backhaus, Juergen, "Stackelberg's Concept of the Post-War Economic Order." Journal of Economic Studies, vol. 23, nrs. 5/6, (1996), pp. 141-148.

Backhaus, Juergen, "Henry George's Ingenious Tax: A Contemporary Restatement," The American Journal of Economics and Sociology, vol. 56, no. 4, (October 1997), pp. 453-474.

Backhaus, Juergen and Richard E. Wagner, "From Continental Public Finance to Public Choice. Mapping Continuity." History of Political Economy, 37, (2005), pp. 314-332.

Backhaus, Juergen, Rediscovering the Historical Schools. II Vols., Emerald Group Publishing Limited, (2005).

Bator, Francis, "The Anatomy of Market Failure." The Quarterly Journal of Economics, vol. 72, no. 3, (Aug. 1958), pp. 359-379.

Brennon, Geoffrey and Buchanan, James M., The Power to Tax. Cambridge: Cambridge University Press, (1980).

Cainzos, Juan Jesús Fernandez, Sociología de la Hacienda Pública.

Madrid, Spain. Ministerio de Economía y Hacienda, Instituto de Estudios Fiscales, (2006).

Galbraith, John Kenneth, The Affluent Society. Boston: Houghton Mifflin, (1958).

George, Henry, Progress and Poverty. New York: Robert Schalkenbach Foundation, (1981).

Kirk, Russell, "Foreword," in: Robert V. Andelson, op. cit., (1971), pp. xi – xiv.

Leroy, Marc, Regards Croisés Sur le Système Fiscal: Allemagne, France, Italie, Russie. Paris: L'Harmattan, (2005).

McLure, Michael, Vilfredo Pareto. Critical Assessments of Leading Economists. Vol. 1, Cunningham Wood, John and McLure, Michael, eds., Routledge, (1999).

McLure, Michael, The Paretian School and Italian Fiscal Sociology. New York, USA: Palgrave Macmillan, (2007).

Pareto, Vilfredo, Trattato di Sociologia Generale. 1916; rev. French translation 1917; translated into English by Arthur Livingston as The Mind and Society. New York: Harcourt, (1935).

Samuelson, Paul A., "The pure theory of public expenditure," Review of Economics and Statistics. Vol. 36, (1954), pp. 387-9.

Samuelson, Paul A., "Diagrammatic exposition of a theory of public expenditure," Review of Economics and Statistics. Vol. 37, (1955), pp. 350-6.

Schumpeter, Joseph A., History of Economic Analysis. New York: Oxford University Press, (1954).

Tullock, Gordon, "The Welfare Costs of Monopolies, Tariffs and Theft." Western Economic Journal, vol. 5.3, (1967), pp. 224-232.

Tullock, Gordon, On Voting: a Public Choice Approach. Cheltenham: Edward Elgar, (1998).

Wagner, Richard E., Fiscal Sociology and the Theory of Public Finance: An Exploratory Essay. (New Thinking in Political Economy Series). Cheltenham: Edward Elgar, (2007).

Wicksell, Knut. Finanztheoretische Untersuchungen. Jena: Gustav Fischer, (1896).

John R. Commons (1862-1945) On Constitution And Tax Assessment Procedure: A Classic In Fiscal Sociology

Enrico Schöbel

ABSTRACT

In his political economic essay on the "Taxation in Chicago and Philadelphia", published in 1895, John R. Commons analyses the tax assessment and tax compliance in case of the property tax. He demonstrates that the revenue is not just a question of the tax rate and the distribution of the tax burden but also a one of constitutional requirements and how the taxes are assessed by the authorities. Here Commons's article is re-examined from the perspective of subsequent Fiscal Sociology and with his later institutional economic writings in mind. The fiscal sociological method and his findings are discussed with regard to social provisioning of taxation and, in particular, the current political debate in case of professional tax advice.

1. Introduction

In his political economic essay on the "Taxation in Chicago and Philadelphia" John R. Commons[1] provides a comparative institutional economic analyses of the tax assessment and tax compliance in the two states. Considering the various actors, tax institutions, and social processes he actually explores a fiscal sociological field and applies a fiscal sociological approach to the issue of tax compliance. As a result, he corroborates the hypothesis that the property tax revenue is not just a question of the tax rate and the distribution of the tax burden but also a question of constitutional requirements and how the taxes are assessed. In conclusion he suggests a tax reform taking social action into account.

In modern democratic societies, for example USA and Germany, tax revenue stems to a large extent from income tax and general sales taxes. More than 50 % of declared income taxpayers consult a professional tax adviser while planning their tax liabilities and preparing their tax declarations. However, there are differences in the demand for assistance because of institutional diversity in national income tax regulations and procedures. In some countries, such as Germany, the professionals have self-regulated the market.

In this paper Commons's article is re-examined from the perspective of subsequent fiscal sociology and with his later institutional economic writings in mind to have another look at tax assessment and tax compliance. His findings of a

1 Commons, John R. Taxation in Chicago and Philadelphia, in: Journal of Political Economy, vol. 3, (1895).

social provisioning of taxation are reconsidered to beneficiate the current political debate on legal tax advice.

2. Fiscal Sociology And The Tax State

The tradition of Fiscal Sociology in Political Economy and Public Finance has been neglected for several decades but is rediscovered and revitalised at this time, in particular by Backhaus, McLure, Wagner, Fritz, Mikl-Horke, Schöbel, Peukert, Peukert, Prischnig, Ahrend, Martin, Mehrotra Prasad[2] and others. They all find the origins of fiscal sociology rooted in the historical dispute between Goldscheid[3] and Schumpeter[4] about the fiscal crisis of the tax state after the First World War.

Goldscheid[5] recommends examinations of conventional Public Finance issues by making use of fiscal sociology as a kind of method and identifies a particular area of fiscal sociological research. The opponent Schumpeter[6] in his plea for the tax state conforms Goldscheid's idea of a fiscal sociological method but combats his discordant political proposal for a state-run capitalism[7]. Fritz Karl Mann, who describes Goldscheid an emulous propagandist of fiscal sociology[8], condemns his narrow analytical investigation and suggests that public finance should be addressed more generally from a sociological perspective and not just based on

2 See Backhaus, Jürgen G., (2002), McLure, Michael (2003), McLure, Michael (2007), Wagner, Richard E. (2007), Fritz, Wolfgang; Mikl-Horke, Gertraude (2007), Schöbel, Enrico (2003), Schöbel, Enrico (2005), Schöbel, Enrico (2008), Peukert, Helge (2009), Peukert, Helge (2010), Peukert, Helge; Prisching, Manfred (2009), Ahrend, Julia Christin (2010) and Martin, Isaac; Mehrotra, Ajay K.; Prasad, Monica (2010).

3 Goldscheid, R. Staatssozialismus oder Staatskapitalismus: Ein finanzsoziologischer Beitrag zur Lösung des Staatsschulden-Problems. Leipzig, Wien: Anzengruber, (1917).
Goldscheid, R. Reine Vernunft und Staatsvernunft. Leipzig, Wien: Anzengruber, (1918).
Goldscheid, R. Sozialisierung der Wirtschaft oder Staatsbankerott: Ein Sanierungsprogramm. Leipzig, Wien: Anzengruber, (1919).

4 Schumpeter, Joseph A. Die Krise des Steuerstaats. Graz, Leipzig: Leuschner, Lubensky, (1918).

5 Goldscheid, R. Staatssozialismus oder Staatskapitalismus: Ein finanzsoziologischer Beitrag zur Lösung des Staatsschulden-Problems. Leipzig, Wien: Anzengruber, (1917).
Goldscheid, R. Staat, öffentlicher Haushalt und Gesellschaft. Wesen und Aufgabe der Finanzwissenschaft vom Standpunkte der Soziologie. In: Gerloff, Wilhelm; Meisel, Franz (eds.), Handbuch der Finanzwissenschaft, vol. 1, Tübingen: J.C.B. Mohr (Paul Siebeck), (1926).

6 Schumpeter, Joseph A. Die Krise des Steuerstaats. Graz, Leipzig: Leuschner, Lubensky, (1918).

7 See Blumenthal, (2007), p. 290 ff.

8 See Mann, (1934), p. 292.

the sociology of war and the peculiar issue of war finance. Herbert Sultan[9], who is well-known for his systematisation of sociological public finance[10], speaks of Goldscheid's sociological exaggeration of the public debt problematic in public finance, numerous grains of truth in his study, and a missing theoretical-systematising presentation. However, F. K. Mann, Sultan, Schumpeter, and other representatives of Political Economics make further use of the notion and emphasise the immanence of fiscal sociology in public finance.

In a later systematising article F. K. Mann[11] recommends a separation of public finance into the three divisions: fiscal theory, fiscal policy and fiscal sociology. Schumpeter[12] applies the fiscal sociological approach to the economic system of modern capitalism[13] and analyses social sources and social consequences of taxation[14]. As well as Schumpeter, F. K. Mann[15] distinguishes between method and field of research and classifies two types of fiscal sociological methods, analysing the impact of social, political, legal, and cultural circumstances on fiscal institutions on the one hand and examining how society, law, and public policy are influenced by fiscal institutions on the other hand.

In 1927 Otto Veit provides a fiscal sociological approach of understanding tax morality and identifies tax morality as being a fiscal sociological issue. Sultan commends Veit's analysis being an excellent fiscal sociological study[16] and agrees with other fiscal sociologists that it seems to be hasty to investigate taxpayers' behaviour towards taxation by generally supposing defence against taxation[17], as taken by F. K. Mann[18], who does not make a distinction between legal and illegal

9 Sultan, H. Finanzwissenschaft und Soziologie. In: Gerloff, Wilhelm; Neumark, Fritz (eds.), Handbuch der Finanzwissenschaft, 2nd ed., vol. 1, Tübingen: J.C.B. Mohr (Paul Siebeck), (1952), p. 70.

10 See Koch, (1981), p. 81 f.

11 Mann, Fritz Karl, Die drei Finanzwissenschaften. In: Finanzarchiv, vol. 30, (1972), pp. 1-13.

12 Schumpeter, Joseph A. Die Krise des Steuerstaats. Graz, Leipzig: Leuschner, Lubensky, (1918).
Schumpeter, Joseph A. Erbschaftssteuer. In: Der Deutsche Volkswirt: Zeitschrift für Politik und Wirtschaft, vol. 3.1, issue 4, (1928).
Schumpeter, Joseph A. Ökonomie und Soziologie der Einkommensteuer. In: Der Deutsche Volkswirt: Zeitschrift für Politik und Wirtschaft, vol 4.1, issue 12/13, (1929).

13 See Backhaus (2004), Ebner (2005).

14 See Martin, Mehrotra and Prasad (2010).

15 Mann, Fritz Karl, Finanzsoziologie. In: Beckerath, Erwin von, et al. (eds.) Handwörterbuch der Sozialwissenschaften, zugleich Neuauflage des Handwörterbuchs der Staatswissenschaften, vol. 3, Stuttgart et al.: Fischer, (1961), p. 642 ff.

16 See Sultan, (1923), p. 110.

17 See Sultan, (1931), p. 11.

18 Mann, Fritz Karl, Die Grundformen der Steuerabwehr. In: Jahrbücher für Nationalökonomie und Statistik, vol. 120 (III. Folge, vol. 65), (1923), p. 479 ff.

tax reduction. On account of practical experiences in the Prussian income tax administration, Behrnauer[19] sums up that taxpayers rather avoid taxation, take legal advice to interpret the law, and comply with legal requirements, than reduce taxes illegally by tax evasion.

In his fiscal sociological approach Veit[20] follows such a broader examination of taxation in a society. Tax compliance is not just the result of a subjective willingness to pay taxes but also determined by many other factors, such as social context, group belonging, political and cultural environment, public opinion, tax legislation, tax regulation, tax assessment, the use of the tax yield, and the fact if taxpayers can influence tax policy and public spending by voting. The fiscal sociological approach sheds light on the behaviour of the different types of individuals concerned, e. g. tax legislators, tax administrators, and taxpayers. Looking retrospectively at Behrnauer's practical experiences of the Prussian income tax, legal tax advisers should be added to the study. Nevertheless, Veit's thorough examinations are of immediate interest due to method and results[21]. The broader perspective was approached by one of the founding fathers of American (Old-) Institutionalism, John R. Commons, in a very early essay, which was not paid the same attention that his later work in Institutional, Constitutional, and Evolutionary Economics attracted, however, which should be revitalised to have another look at current debates in Public Finance and Fiscal Sociology.

3. John R. Commons (1895) On "Taxation In Chicago And Philadelphia"

In his political economic analysis of the "Taxation in Chicago and Philadelphia", John R. Commons[22] describes the tax system of the states Illinois and Pennsylvania in the first half of the 1890s. He finds differences not only in the substantial tax law but also in the procedural tax law and in the constitutional foundation of the tax system. As a result of his thorough analysis, he concludes that the technical design of taxation, its constitutional foundation and the tax assessment procedure are important.

19 Behrnauer, Friedrich, Der Streit um die Steuerhinterziehungen in Preußen. In: Jahrbücher für Gesetzgebung, Verwaltung und Volkswirtschaft im Deutschen Reich, vol. 34, (1919), p. 114.

20 Veit, Otto, Grundlagen der Steuermoral: Eine finanzsoziologische Studie. In: Zeitschrift für die gesamte Staatswissenschaft, vol. 83, (1927).

21 See Schöbel, (2003), (2005).

22 Commons, John R., Taxation in Chicago and Philadelphia. In: Journal of Political Economy, vol. 3, (1895).

Commons describes the legal institutional setting of the property tax system of the both of the states in the very detail. The property tax system at that time distinguishes personal property and corporate property. Later, personal property taxes were removed because of the tax authorities' difficulties at reaching the tax base, and other weaknesses. Injustice was recognised more and more often. Therefore, personal property tax revenue was replaced more and more by income tax revenue, which in the 20th century has become the major revenue source in modern democratic societies.

The reader obtains a general view of property tax figures, such as tax rates, "true" or "actual" value of property (according to the census), assessed value of property (assessed by the tax assessors), and tax revenue. The data originally stems from different sources, for instance the Census, the Pennsylvania State Secretary of Internal Affairs, the Pennsylvania Tax Commission, the Illinois State Auditor, the City Controller, and the Citizens' Association of Chicago. His own calculations add to the data set. Based on the data thus obtained, Commons searches for facts by the aim of understanding of how the property tax shapes individual behaviour through the assessment procedure in consideration of tax revenue.

First of all, Commons marks contrasts in the property tax system. Illinois has a uniform property tax law. The town, county, city, and state governments derive revenues from their respective rates imposed on the same assessment of local property. Consequently, all the assessed property in a tax district is uniformly taxed at the same rate. The Pennsylvania tax law differs from the equal treatment of property in Illinois. In Pennsylvania the different sources of revenue are distinguished and separated among the state and the local government. Revenues from personal and corporate property are due to the state, whereas revenues from real estate property are due to the local government. This regulation in Pennsylvania results in an unequal treatment of the distinguished kinds of property. Moreover, in Illinois all property is taxed with the exception of specifically exempted property, whereas the Pennsylvania tax law exempts all the property which is not specifically enumerated in the text of the law.

There is another dissimilarity which is highlighted by Commons in his description of the tax regulation. In Chicago (Illinois) tax assessors are independent and elected by the former towns over which the city has spread, whereas in Philadelphia (Pennsylvania) property is assessed by a centralised board of assessors. The assessors are appointed by a judge of the Common Pleas Court.

After marking contrast, Commons asks for the financial result of the property taxation in consideration of revenue. He finds several discrepancies which all provide the basis for his comparative analysis of assessment procedure and constitutional requirements of taxation. Disincentives from a specific institutional setting are demonstrated.

When comparing Cook county (the county around Chicago) instead of the city of Chicago itself with the city of Philadelphia there he states only little discrepancy. The county and the city of Philadelphia are found to be coterminous. However, in the comparing the cities of Chicago and Philadelphia he finds disparities reflected in the financial result. According to the census, the city of Chicago (Illinois) makes 31 % of the population and 30 % of the "true" value of property of Illinois in 1894. The city of Philadelphia (Pennsylvania) consists of only 20 % of the population and only 17 % of the property of Pennsylvania in 1894. Nevertheless, in Philadelphia there is raised 33 % of the state tax revenue, while in Chicago there is raised no correspondingly higher share, but only 31 % of the state tax revenue. In both states the assessed value of property is significantly below the "true" or "actual" value of the property according to the census. This points at a fiscal illusion. However, in view of the fact that the variations are not congruent, Commons addresses institutional setting of property assessment and constitutional foundation.

Obviously, the comparatively high Chicago city tax rates (in contrast to the relatively low state and county tax burdens) stimulate under-valuation of property. This means that the relatively high city tax burden is shifted to the honest. Commons corroborates the (long time before him developed and much later so called) idea of the Laffer Curve[23] while he states that the more important problem is not, what tax rate will maximise revenue, but at what tax rate the burden will be most equally distributed and the repressive effects of taxation be minimised. Undoubtedly, the high tax rates of Chicago exert pressure on the taxpayers to escape. Consequently, he suggest the superiority of the Pennsylvania property tax regulation in case of the exemption of particular kinds of property that are subject to taxation in Chicago but notoriously undervalued by the tax assessors or even concealed by the taxpayers.

4. Commons's Fiscal Sociological Approach Of Taxation

John R. Commons in his examination of tax pressure, repressive effects of taxation, and the different actors concerned moves towards the fiscal sociological approach of understanding tax compliance by Veit[24] and contemporary Fiscal

23 Laffer, Arthur C. Government Exactions and Revenue Deficiencies. In: Cato Journal, vol. 1, (1981).

24 Veit, Otto, Grundlagen der Steuermoral: Eine finanzsoziologische Studie. In: Zeitschrift für die gesamte Staatswissenschaft, vol. 83, (1927).

Sociology[25]. Commons explores repressive effects of taxation on industry and morals, but does not indicate a particular tax morality.

In addition, Commons anticipates constitutional political economic analyses on the issue of civic acceptance of taxation in modern democracy[26]. Buchanan[27] speaks of the relevance of taxpayers' temperature when taxpayers decide on escape. Commons analyses political representation of institutions in his book on "Proportional Representation", which was published in 1896, one year after his exploratory essay on "Taxation in Chicago and Philadelphia", and long time before civic acceptance of taxation has become an issue in Fiscal Sociology and Public Choice Theory[28]. The major difference: Commons (1895) addresses the property tax, whereas the latter primarily focus on income taxation.

In his book on "Legal Foundations of Capitalism", which is the first of his three most influential books in Institutional Economics, Commons[29] analyses market transactions by the distinction of different types of transactions. The two other influential books are "Institutional Economics"[30] (published in two volumes in 1934) and "The Economics of Collective Action"[31] by which he understands collective bargaining.

As a result of his historical institutional analysis brought forward in "Legal Foundations of Capitalism", he refuses the idea of a mechanistic provisioning of markets. His comparative institutional and evaluating method is clearly influenced by the empirical method of the German Historical School[32]. In the economic history he finds again and again that market transactions are socially embedded[33]. He states that institutions are set to restrain and to allow for economic transactions, whereas nowadays in New Institutional Economics institutions are almost defined by focusing only the restraints[34]. Commons also describes the development of institutions throughout history as being an evolutionary process and paved the way to an evolutionary economic approach.

25 See Schöbel (2003), (2005).

26 See Brennan and Buchanan (1980), Schöbel (2007).

27 Buchanan, James M. Taxpayer Apathy, Institutional Inertia, and Economic Growth. In: Journal of Public Finance and Public Choice, vol. 17, (1999).

28 See Schöbel (2008), (2010a).

29 Commons, John R. Legal Foundations of Capitalism. New York: The Macmillan Company, (1924).

30 Commons, John R. Institutional Economics. New York: The Macmillan Company, (1934).

31 Commons, John R. The Economics of Collective Action. New York: The Macmillan Company, (1950).

32 Peukert, Helge, Commons, John Rogers: Legal Foundations of Capitalism. In: Herz, Dietmar; Weinberger Veronika (eds.), Lexikon ökonomischer Werke, Stuttgart: Schäffer-Poeschel, (2006).

33 See Rutherford (1983), Ramstad (1986).

34 See Furubotn and Richter (1997).

Thus, Vanberg[35] in his review of Commons's work from a nowadays constitutional law and economics perspective speaks of a legal institutional framework that shapes transactions and that is defined by social action. However, Vanberg's wording could be misleading, because other than the German Ordoliberal School in Law and Economics (e.g. Walter Eucken), Commons does not search for an ideal orderly framework. He provides a positive instead of a normative analysis of institutions. His method is clearly empirical fact-finding when he searches for facts in the economic history.

The issue of the legal institutional foundation of social action in Commons's later books is already anticipated by himself in the essay on the "Taxation in Chicago and Philadelphia", which was published about thirty years before the appearance of his recognised book on "Legal Foundations of Capitalism". In addition to the issue of representation, he addresses the constitutional foundation of taxation in the fiscal federal system. His analysis discloses the disincentives from the fiscal federal system to the tax assessors and the taxpayers and identifies social sources and social consequences of tax developments.

5. Social Sources And Consequences Of Tax Developments

In his essay Commons[36] goes into more detail by analysing the application of the property tax law, in particular, the assessment of property in the both states compared. As mentioned above, property is assessed by the tax assessors significantly below the "true" or "actual" value according to the census. Henceforth, he speaks of under-valuation. On this basis of the data he concludes that the greater under-valuation in Chicago corresponds to the higher city tax rate of Chicago.

There is not only a greater extent of under-valuation in Chicago but also a greater temptation to undervalue, because under-valuation is cumulating. Due to the uniform property tax law in Illinois, which means that state, county, city, and town tax are based on the same property assessment, state, county, city, and town tax are saved. In this way Commons's comparative analysis points at constitutional requirements of taxation. Obviously, there are disincentives from the fiscal federal constitution of the uniform tax law in Illinois.

There is another disincentive from constitutional foundation outlined by Commons in his case study. In Chicago (Illinois) the election of the tax assessors induces competition between the assessors to undervalue the property, and so

35 Vanberg, Victor J. Institutional Evolution through Purposeful Selection: The Constitutional Economics of John R. Commons. In: Constitutional Political Economy, vol. 8, (1997).

36 Commons, John R. Taxation in Chicago and Philadelphia. In: Journal of Political Economy, vol. 3, (1895).

the property is much more undervalued in the city of Chicago than in the city of Philadelphia (Pennsylvania) where the centralised board of three assessors is appointed by a judge of the Common Pleas Court.

The Pennsylvania property tax system is criticised because of its administrative and technical complexity and heavy burdens on real estate. Besides, some weaknesses of other types of taxation, for instance income tax and special taxes, are pointed out.

Finally, Commons suggests a reform of the Chicago tax system and summarises: "The main obstacles to the reform of Chicago's tax system are the constitutional requirement of uniform laws and the state legislature elected by rural constituencies. State tax reform and city tax reform must come together. By separation of sources and a low tax on personalty both city and country would gain – the country by larger state aid to local expenses derived mainly from the city, the city by home rule, fairer valuations, larger state aid, and greater ability to bear the lower equalized personalty and corporate taxes."[37].

Commons demonstrates how institutions shape tax assessors' and taxpayers' behaviour. He distinguishes further groups of political actors, such as the state (government), the city, the county, the towns, the state tax auditor, the city tax controller, the Tax Commission, and the Citizens' Association, which all have impact on taxation by some means or other.

He finds that institutions on the one hand shape individual and group behaviour (for example, some taxpayers shift the burden to the honest), and that institutions on the other hand are created and developed by social action. From this point of view, the tax system can be reformed through social action, and indeed, Commons proposes a tax reform which is based on the results of his foregoing analysis of the tax assessors' and the taxpayers' behaviour. In his proposal he considers representation by taking the applicability of the law and the taxpayers' opportunity of escape from taxation into account. In summing up, his institutional economic analysis implies evolution of the institutions, and possibly anticipates his later work, but does not explicitly denote an evolutionary economic approach to the property tax law.

6. Professional Legal Tax Advice: A Current Political Debate

Since John R. Commons analysed property tax in Illinois and Pennsylvania, the tax law has become more and more complicated, especially the income tax law.

37 Commons, John R. Taxation in Chicago and Philadelphia. In: Journal of Political Economy, vol. 3, (1895), p. 460.

Income tax revenue has become the major source of public revenue in modern democratic societies, such as Germany and the United States of America. In the USA as well as in Germany more than 50 percent of the income taxpayers consult a professional tax adviser. However, there are fundamental differences in the income tax assessment procedures[38] and also in the provisioning of tax advice[39].

According to the self assessment principle, the taxpayers in the USA have to calculate their income tax obligations themselves and file their tax returns. Only a small proportion of all the tax returns for each year will be audited by the Internal Revenue Service (IRS). Instead of the self assessment principle, in Germany the tax offices have to investigate the taxable income and to assess the income tax obligation on the basis of the taxpayer's tax declaration and, if it is seen to be required, further information search. Taxpayers are obliged to cooperate for the official tax investigation and tax assessment procedure.

In the USA tax practitioners give professional tax advice. Most of them are attorneys and certified public accountants who are specialised in taxation. Tax practitioners are not licensed by the IRS but regulated by the Treasury Department, for instance, negligence in preparing the tax return is prosecuted. Due to the freedom of contract principle, there is no contractual liability as a matter of principle but liability can be agreed by contract. In spite of this, most personal income taxpayers cannot pay a tax professional. Tax practitioners typically have corporate clients. Therefore, most personal income taxpayers consult an income tax return preparer who typically does not have professional education and does not carry any liability. It is not unusual to see tax preparers advising non-compliance in case of ambiguous tax regulation[40].

In some OECD countries tax advisers are compensated on "value based" fee structures which are directly linked to the eventual success of the underlying tax scheme or to the amount of the claimed tax benefit (OECD 2008). In the USA "value based" fees are adopted. The United Kingdom revenue department HM Revenue and Custums and the tax authorities of the OECD countries Australia, Canada, Chile, France, India, Ireland, Japan, Mexico, The Netherlands, Spain, South Africa, and the USA see taxpayers encouraged not to comply with taxation. Therefore, the OECD (2008) proposal suggests that tax advisers should be requested to act as "tax intermediaries" between taxpayers and revenue bodies. This should lead to "a more constructive relationship" between them all three. However, Germany did not engage in the OECD tax intermediaries project.

38 Seer, Roman, Besteuerungsverfahren: Rechtsvergleich USA – Deutschland. Heidelberg: Verlag Recht und Wirtschaft, (2002).

39 Heuel, Carsten, Haftung für Steuerberatung: Eine rechtsvergleichende Untersuchung zum deutschen und US-amerikanischen Recht. Frankfurt am Main: Peter Lang, (2007).

40 See Klepper and Nagin (1989), Spilker, Worsham and Prawitt (1999).

Backhaus[41] argues that tax advisers had better self-regulate with the particular historical tradition of the profession in mind. His sketch of a fiscal sociological approach implies the social provisioning of the market for tax consultancy. Such an approach would conform Commons's idea of institutional evolution among competing societal groups[42].

The degree of liabilities is defining characteristics of the differences between the USA and Germany. In Germany tax advice is provided by authorised tax consultants, and as a rule it does carry liability[43]. The professionals have self-regulated the market for tax advice and tax preparation. The Chamber of Tax Consultants' professional code of conduct, the Tax Consultancy Act, the regulation of the tax consultants' tariff, and other regulations, have their seeds in the particular German historical tradition of the professions and the professional law[44]. Tax consultants are required to be specifically educated, qualified, assessed, and authorised, and there are liability and other requirements regulated in the professional law. The authorisation can be cancelled in case of serious violations of the obligations. On that legal basis, tax consultants run the risk of having their authorisation to be cancelled not only in case of advising illegal strategies of tax non-compliance but also as a consequence of other violations of their obligations. However, in view of increasing supervision and the OECD proposal, the taxpayer's agent seems to become more and more the tax authority's agent.

7. Conclusion

Currently, the role of tax advisers is critically discussed. The tax authorities of several OECD countries have engaged in the debate by initiating a project on tax intermediaries. In this essay the political economic study on the "Taxation in Chicago and Philadelphia" by John R. Commons[45] was reviewed from the perspective of subsequent fiscal sociology and his later institutional economic books in order to define a position from where the still ongoing debate can be critically looked at. This is revealing with regard to the social provisioning of the market for

41 Backhaus, Jürgen G. Neue Herausforderungen für den Berufsstand der Steuerberater durch das Risikomanagement in der Finanzverwaltung: Einführung und fiskalsoziologische Analyse. In: Deutsches wissen-schaftliches Institut der Steuerberater e. V. (ed.), Risikomanagement der Finanzverwaltung: Heraus-forderungen für den Stand der Steuerberater, Berlin: DWS-Verlag, (2009).

42 See Schöbel (2007), (2010b).

43 See Heuel (2007), Nickert (2008).

44 Niederer, Thomas, Die freie Berufsausübung als Steuerberater. Hamburg: Kovac, (2000).

45 Commons, John R. Taxation in Chicago and Philadelphia. In: Journal of Political Economy, vol. 3, (1895).

legal tax advice. The systematic analysis of social action, group context, political conflicts, constitutional foundation, and social consequences of tax assessment and tax compliance makes his essay a classic in fiscal sociology.

Acknowledments

The paper was presented at the 9th *Erfurt Conference on Fiscal Sociology* held at the Thuringian Court of Audit, City Castle Ludwigsburg, in Rudolstadt (Germany), Dec 4, 2009. The author is grateful to the organizers and participants for their comments.

References

Ahrend, Julia Christin, Fritz Karl Mann: Ein Pionier der Finanzsoziologie und der Theorie der Parafiski im Schnittfeld deutscher und amerikanischer Wissenschaftskultur. Marburg: Metropolis, (2010).

Backhaus, Jürgen G. Fiscal Sociology: What for? In: American Journal of Economics and Sociology, vol. 61, (2002), pp. 55-77.

Backhaus, Jürgen G. Neue Herausforderungen für den Berufsstand der Steuerberater durch das Risikomanagement in der Finanzverwaltung: Einführung und fiskalsoziologische Analyse. In: Deutsches wissen-schaftliches Institut der Steuerberater e. V. (ed.), Risikomanagement der Finanzverwaltung: Heraus-forderungen für den Stand der Steuerberater, Berlin: DWS-Verlag, (2009), pp. 13-15.

Backhaus, Jürgen G. Joseph A. Schumpeter's Contributions in the Area of Fiscal Sociology: A First Approximation. In: Journal of Evolutionary Economics, vol. 14, (2004), pp. 143-151.

Behrnauer, Friedrich, Der Streit um die Steuerhinterziehungen in Preußen. In: Jahrbücher für Gesetzgebung, Ver-waltung und Volkswirtschaft im Deutschen Reich, vol. 34, (1919), pp. 113-143.

Blumenthal, Karsten von, Die Steuertheorien der Austrian Economics: Von Menger zu Mises. Marburg: Metropolis, (2007).

Brennan, Geoffrey; Buchanan, James M. The Power to Tax: Analytical Foundations of a Fiscal Constitution. Cambridge: Cambridge University Press, (1980).

Buchanan, James M. Taxpayer Apathy, Institutional Inertia, and Economic Growth. In: Journal of Public Finance and Public Choice, vol. 17, (1999), pp. 3-10

Commons, John R. Taxation in Chicago and Philadelphia. In: Journal of Political Economy, vol. 3, (1895), pp. 434-460.

Commons, John R. Proportional Representation. New York: Crowell, (1896).

Commons, John R. Legal Foundations of Capitalism. New York: The Macmillan Company, (1924).

Commons, John R. Institutional Economics. New York: The Macmillan Company, (1934).

Commons, John R. The Economics of Collective Action. New York: The Macmillan Company, (1950).

Ebner, Alexander, Institutions, Entrepreneurship, and the Rationale of Government: An Outline of the Schumpeterian Theory of the State. In: Backhaus, Jürgen G. (ed.), Essays on Fiscal Sociology, Frankfurt am Main: Peter Lang, (2005), pp. 77-101.

Fritz, Wolfgang; Mikl-Horke, Gertraude, Rudolf Goldscheid: Finanzsoziologe und ethische Sozialwissenschaft. Berlin, Münster: LIT-Verlag, (2007).

Furubotn, Eirik G.; Richter, Rudolf, Institutions and Economic Theory: The Contribution of the New Institutional Economics. Ann Arbor: University of Michigan Press, (1997).

Goldscheid, Rudolf, Staatssozialismus oder Staatskapitalismus: Ein finanzsoziologischer Beitrag zur Lösung des Staatsschulden-Problems. Leipzig, Wien: Anzengruber, (1917).

Goldscheid, Rudolf, Reine Vernunft und Staatsvernunft. Leipzig, Wien: Anzengruber, (1918).

Goldscheid, Rudolf, Sozialisierung der Wirtschaft oder Staatsbankerott: Ein Sanierungsprogramm, Leipzig, Wien: Anzengruber, (1919).

Goldscheid, Rudolf, Staat, öffentlicher Haushalt und Gesellschaft. Wesen und Aufgabe der Finanzwissenschaft vom Standpunkte der Soziologie., in: Gerloff, Wilhelm; Meisel, Franz (eds.), Handbuch der Finanzwissenschaft, vol. 1, Tübingen: J. C. B. Mohr (Paul Siebeck), (1926), pp. 146-184.

Heuel, Carsten, Haftung für Steuerberatung: Eine rechtsvergleichende Untersuchung zum deutschen und US-amerikanischen Recht. Frankfurt am Main: Peter Lang, (2007).

Klepper, Steven; Nagin, Daniel, The Role of Tax Preparers in Tax Compliance. In: Policy Sciences, vol. 22, (1989), pp. 167-194.

Koch, Woldemar, Finanzsoziologie. In: Albers, Willi (ed.), Handwörterbuch der Wirtschaftswissenschaft, vol. 3, Stuttgart, New York: Fischer; Tübingen: Mohr; Göttingen, Zürich: Vandenhoeck & Ruprecht, (1981), pp. 97-106.

Laffer, Arthur C. Government Exactions and Revenue Deficiencies. In: Cato Journal, vol. 1, (1981), pp. 1-21.

Mann, Fritz Karl, Die Grundformen der Steuerabwehr. In: Jahrbücher für Nationalökonomie und Statistik, vol. 120 (III. Folge, vol. 65), (1923), pp. 497-523.

Mann, Fritz Karl, Beiträge zur Steuersoziologie. In: Finanzarchiv, Neue Folge, vol. 2, (1934), pp. 281-314.

Mann, Fritz Karl, Finanzsoziologie. In: Beckerath, Erwin von, et al. (eds.) Handwörterbuch der Sozialwissenschaften, zugleich Neuauflage des Handwörterbuchs der Staatswissenschaften, vol. 3, Stuttgart et al.: Fischer, (1961), pp. 642-648.

Mann, Fritz Karl, Die drei Finanzwissenschaften. In: Finanzarchiv, vol. 30, (1972), pp. 1-13.

Martin, Isaac; Mehrotra, Ajay K.; Prasad, Monica, The Thunder of History: The Origins and Development of the New Fiscal Sociology. In: Martin, Isaac; Mehrotra, Ajay K.; Prasad, Monica (eds.), The New Fiscal Sociology: Taxation in Comparative and Historical Perspective, Cambridge et al.: Cambridge University Press, (2010), pp. 1-28.

McLure, Michael, Approaches to Fiscal Sociology. In: European Journal of Management and Public Policy, vol. 2, (2003), pp. 32-42.

McLure, Michael, The Paretian School and Italian Fiscal Sociology. Basingstoke. Hampshire: Palgrave Macmillan, (2007).

Nickert, Cornelius, Die Haftung des Steuerberaters: Richtig handeln und Haftung vermeiden. Wiesbaden: Gabler, (2008).

Niederer, Thomas, Die freie Berufsausübung als Steuerberater, Hamburg: Kovac, (2000).

Organisation for Economic Co-operation and Development (OECD), Study into the Role of Tax Intermediaries, Paris: OECD, (2008).

Peukert, Helge, Commons, John Rogers: Legal Foundations of Capitalism. In: Herz, Dietmar; Weinberger Veronika (eds.), Lexikon ökonomischer Werke, Stuttgart: Schäffer-Poeschel, (2006), pp. 94-95.

Peukert, Helge, Rudolf Goldscheid: Menschenökonom und Finanzsoziologe. Frankfurt am Main: Peter Lang, (2009).

Peukert, Helge, Die große Finanzmarktkrise: Eine staatswissenschaftlich-finanzsoziologische Untersuchung. Marburg: Metropolis, (2010).

Peukert, Helge; Prisching, Manfred, Rudolf Goldscheid und die Finanzkrise des Steuerstaates. Graz: Leykam, (2009).

Ramstad, Yngve, A pragmatist's quest for holistic knowledge: The scientific methodology of John R. Commons. In: Journal of Economic Issues, vol. 20, (1986), pp. 1067-1105.

Rutherford, Malcolm, J. R. Commons's Institutional Economics. In: Journal of Economic Issues, vol. 17, (1983), pp. 721-744.

Schöbel, Enrico, Otto Veit (1898-1984) as a Fiscal Sociologist and his Fiscal Sociological Approach of Tax Morality. In: European Journal of Management and Public Policy, vol. 2, (2003), pp. 43-66.

Schöbel, Enrico, Otto Veit and Subsequent Developments of Tax Morality. In: Backhaus, Jürgen G. (ed.), Essays on Fiscal Sociology, Frankfurt am Main: Peter Lang, (2005), pp. 187-210.

Schöbel, Enrico, Lobbying on Taxation: A Neglected Aspect of Voting when Arguing Tax Compliance. In: International Advances in Economic Research, vol. 13, (2007), p. 110.

Schöbel, Enrico, Steuerehrlichkeit: Eine politisch-ökonomische und zugleich finanzsoziologische Analyse der Einkommensteuerrechtsanwendung und -befolgung in Deutschland. Frankfurt am Main: Haag + Herchen, (2008).

Schöbel, Enrico, Neue Politische Ökonomie. In: Gabler-Wirtschaftslexikon, 17th ed., vol. L-O, Wiesbaden: Gabler, (2010a), pp. 2187-2189, and online available at: http://wirtschaftslexikon.gabler.de/Definition/neue-politische-oekonomie.html.

Schöbel, Enrico, Self-Regulated Markets for Professional Legal Services: The Case of Tax Intermediaries. In: Journal of Economic Issues, vol. 44, (2010b), pp. 497-504.

Schumpeter, Joseph A. Die Krise des Steuerstaats. Graz, Leipzig: Leuschner, Lubensky, (1918).

Schumpeter, Joseph A. Erbschaftssteuer. In: Der Deutsche Volkswirt: Zeitschrift für Politik und Wirtschaft, vol. 3.1, issue 4, (1928), pp. 110-114.

Schumpeter, Joseph A. Ökonomie und Soziologie der Einkommensteuer. In: Der Deutsche Volkswirt: Zeitschrift für Politik und Wirtschaft, vol. 4.1, issue 12/13, (1929), pp. 380-385.

Seer, Roman, Besteuerungsverfahren: Rechtsvergleich USA – Deutschland. Heidelberg: Verlag Recht und Wirtschaft, (2002).

Spilker, Brian C.; Worsham, Ronald G.; Prawitt, Douglas F. Tax Professionals' Interpretations of Ambiguity in Compliance and Planning Decision Contexts. In: Journal of the American Taxation Association, vol. 21, (1999), pp. 75-89.

Sultan, Herbert, Art und Mass der Prognose der Steuerwirkungen, Antrittsvorlesung [inaugural lecture] am 18. Juli 1931, Recht und Staat in Geschichte und Gegenwart: Eine Sammlung von Vorträgen und Schriften aus dem Gebiet der gesamten Staatswissenschaften, vol. 86, Tübingen: J.C.B. Mohr (Paul Siebeck), (1931).

Sultan, Herbert, Die Staatseinnahmen: Versuch einer soziologischen Finanztheorie als Teil einer Theorie der politischen Ökonomie. Tübingen: J.C.B. Mohr (Paul Siebeck), (1932).

Sultan, Herbert, Finanzwissenschaft und Soziologie. In: Gerloff, Wilhelm; Neumark, Fritz (eds.), Handbuch der Finanzwissenschaft, 2nd ed., vol. 1, Tübingen: J. C. B. Mohr (Paul Siebeck), (1952), pp. 66-98.

Vanberg, Victor J. Institutional Evolution through Purposeful Selection: The Constitutional Economics of John R. Commons. In: Constitutional Political Economy, vol. 8, (1997), pp. 105-122.

Veit, Otto, Grundlagen der Steuermoral: Eine finanzsoziologische Studie. In: Zeitschrift für die gesamte Staatswissenschaft, vol. 83, (1927), pp. 317-349.

Wagner, Richard E. Fiscal Sociology and the Theory of Public Finance: An Exploratory Essay. Cheltenham, Northampton: Edward Elgar, (2007).

On the failure of European planning for less developed regions. The case of Calabria.

Francesco Forte
Cosimo Magazzino
Michela Mantovani

Abstract

This study analyzes the negative performance of Calabria's Regional Program 2000-2006, for the enhancement of cultural goods to attract tourism, as an example of the waste of resources in the regional planning under the EU-Italian complex planning procedure for economic convergence. The empirical analysis shows that the variables relating to cultural sites, education sites and sites with tourism or tourism potentialities had no significance or even negative influence. The most significant variable was the number of nonprofit organization present in the municipalities. A relevant part of the funds remained unspent for the purposes of the plan, and it was devoted to other destinations. After the program, the number of visitors and revenues from museum and archeological sites of Calabria was lower than before, while on average in Italy there was a great increase. On the other hand, tourism in Calabria experienced a differential increase, in spite of the waste of the funds of the European regional policy.

Keywords: cultural goods; tourism; public policies; public expenditure; Southern Italy.

JEL Classification: H4; R1; Z1.

1. Introduction

This study analyzes the negative performance of Calabria's Regional Operation Program (POR) 2000-2006. The program was devoted to projects for the enhancement of cultural goods to attract tourism, as an example of a waste of resources in the European Union's ambitious program 2000-2006, for the economic convergence of Europe's less developed regions with the developed ones (Community Support Framework, 2000-2006). The results of Calabrian POR, performed following the guidelines of the Council Regulation No. 1260/1999 of 21 June 1999, and of the related Italian Development and Plan, have been negative. The funds of 231 million Euro, which would activate a similar amount of co-financing, have been dispersed throughout the territory in 546 projects. Notwithstanding, the meticulous selection procedures used to establish the projects (many of those approved) resulted in significant inefficiencies: a large share of the projects were abandoned before completion, resulting in just 63 % of the funds allocated being spent. Despite the scale of resources mobilized (nearly 450 million of Euro in a region with 2 million of residents) both the flow of visitors to the cultural sites and, more generally, that of tourists to Calabria have not been enhanced. We show, by statistical analysis, how the variables that determined the allocation of the funds have been incoherent with the proclaimed objectives of valorization of cultural patrimony and the touristic promotion.

The study is divided in eleven sections. Section 2 provides a brief survey of economic literature on this issue. Section 3 provides background information on the POR 2000-2006 in Calabria. Section 4 gives an overview of the cultural heritage endowment of Calabria and of the implementation of the program. Section 5 presents the econometric methodology, the data set and the empirical results. Section 6 discusses some details of regression analysis. Section 7 demonstrates some statistical results about criminal hubs. Section 8 presents the impact of Calabria's POR project on both culture and tourism. Section 9 discusses coherent projects. Section 10 gives the concluding remarks and policy implications. Section 11 makes suggestions for future researches.

2. A survey of literature

In spite of the optimistic reports of the European Community, (Commission of the European Communities, 2009), in the literature on the European Regional Policies for less developed regions, those of the so-called Obiective 1 (Cini, 2003; 2007) predominate the research demonstrating disappointing results. Some authors argue that the results are poor in the case of regions with weak institutions and better in the other cases. However, the regions for whom the financial aid is justifiable are the less developed ones. And the weakness of the institutions is one of the main characters of the less developed regions belonging to advanced European countries. Basile, De Nardis and Girardi (2001) demonstrate that in spite of the huge amount of public aid to the poor regions of EU, the distribution of income, labour productivity and employment rates do not show a positive relation with the allocation of the EU structural regional funds, particularly in the Nineties. Boldrin and Canova (2001), argue that to a large degree these policies operated primarily as a transfer of funds with redistributive or assistance purposes rather than serving as agents to simulate or increase growth. Puga (2002) observe that, in spite of the large expenditures on European regional policies, the disparities remained or even widened, mainly because of factors connected with the location theory so that more emphasis should be placed on improving transport structures. Rodriguez Pose and Fratesi (2003) show that the returns to the investments in infrastructures and business support were not significant, and that only investment in education and human capital had positive and significant medium term returns. Ederveen, De Groot and Nahuis (2006) show that European structural funds were very largely ineffective in reducing regional disparities, with the exception of the regions where institutions are of a high quality. Bjorvatn and Coniglio (2006; 2007) maintain that generally – not only in Europe – policies to promote regional development very often have disappointing results and also connect such results with the weakness of institutions. In this case, targeted policies create rents that attract rent seekers, so that broad-based policies would be more appropriate. The targeted plans should be adopted for the regions with strong institutions. The first part of the conclusion appears reasonable; nevertheless, the second part is unconvincing. Indeed, where the institutions work well, it seems better to apply the general EU rules on competition, and leave to the market economy system the decision on which sectors can make best use of the subsidies supposedly given to compensate for the regional global externalities (Van der Beek, 2004). Eggert, von Ehrlich, Fenge and König (2007) analyze the impact of EU structural policy on the economic development of German regions between 1995 and 2004, arguing that the EU regional transfers speed up convergence, but have a negative impact on long run aggregate growth. Cappelen, Castellacci, Fagerberg and Verspagen (2003) argue that EU regional policies had significant and positive impact on growth of less developed European regions, and that the effects are much better in a more developed environment. It follows that the suggestion of improving the competence of the receiving environment appears rather *naïve* considering that the environment cannot be changed as long as the traditional social structures remain. Beugelsdijk and Eijffinger (2005) argue that the EU structural regional funds had a positive effect in the case of the poorer countries such as Greece, and they add that the less "clean" countries (i. e. those more corrupt) did not gain less economic growth from the structural funds. They add that many of those who receive the structural funds are not eligible and therefore use them inefficiently. In the Italian economic literature – see Giannola and Imbriani (2003), Lo Cicero and Reganati (2003), Viesti (2003; 2009), Viesti and Prota (2009) – there is a widespread consensus on the fact that the Italian public interventions for the development of Southern Italy failed, in a large part, to reduce the disparities between Centre-North and South. There is also consensus that the Regional funds did not fulfill their objectives. This occurred due to the complexity of the procedures and to other factors, as a relevant share of the funds was not allocated before the time limit, and it was diverted to other ends; moreover, the share of the funds that was utilized under the prescribed procedures was not properly allocated.

On the other hand, Loddo (2006) with a simplified econometric analysis argues that in Italy, in the period 1994-2004, the poorer regions have caught up with the richer regions, and that the European structural funds had a role in this convergence. However, agricultural funds had only a transitory positive effect, whilst the resources allocated had dubious effects from the distributional point of view and for the support of employment, education and the human capital. However, Vision & Value (2007) shows that in the period 2000-2001 the regions of Southern Italy featured in Objective 1 grew at a rate of 1.23% per year, while those of the Centre-North grew at a 1.24% rate, and EU-15 grew at the 1.96%. Similar results appear in Svimez (2009; 2010). While Cancelo, Faína and López-Rodríguez (2009) maintain that EU regional funds have been effective in promoting growth in the case of Galicia, a Spanish peripheral region in Objective 1. Borbalá-Szabó (2007) instead maintains that in Hungary the impact of the EU regional policies on economic growth have been disappointing. Ederveen and Gorter (2002), Edereveen, de Mooji, Gorter and Nahuis (2002), and Ederveen, de Groot and Nahuis (2006) provide an extensive econometric analysis to show mixed results both from the distributive and the growth perspectives, adding that the impact of these policies on national policies to reduce regional disparities has been negative. Tugores (2008), considering the EU-15 global macroeconomic results, concludes that the contribution of EU regional policy to the convergence among states is unquestionable for Spain, and it represented a factor for the Irish high growth. Nonetheless, there has not been a general a narrowing among regions inside these states. The critical issues are the possible distortions of the efficient assignment of resources and the risk that the resources placed at the service of cohesion may wind up in the hands of specific interests.

For Krueger (1974) this point leads to the consideration of rent seeking in terms of less developed economies, where rent seeking is the substitute to the missing stimulus to profit seeking. On rent seeking in EU regional policies see also Bjorvatn and Coniglio (2006; 2007). Outside EU, for rent seeking as a negative phenomenon in regional policies, see Zaostrovtsev (2003) for Russia, Dreger, Rahmani and Eckey (2007) for Iran, and Fisher (2006) for Africa. Golley (2007) reaches mixed conclusions on Chinese regional policies. For rich literature on rent seeking after the seminal works of Buchanan, Tullock and Niskanen see, more generally, for all Cogleton, Hillman and Konrad (2008).

In the specialized economic literature on cultural goods and on tourism, several contributions emphasize the importance of the cultural goods as attractors of touristic flows. See, for example, Goldoni, Rispoli and Troncon (2006), Colbert (2000), Kotler and Scott (1998), Nantel and Colbert (1992), Grossi and Debbia (1998), Diggles (1986), Hirshmann (1983). More generally, see Forte and Mantovani (2004), and Cooper *et al.* (1998).

The literature on the specific theme of this research – the Regional funds policies in the area of cultural goods and the development of tourism in Southern Italy – is not equally developed; however see Forte, Mantovani (2010), Mantovani, Skepys (2011), Spadaro (2010), Vision & Value (2007), and Ferrari and Cariola (2001).

3. Structure of EU Regional Policy 2000-2006 and Calabria's Operational Regional Program (POR) for cultural goods

The European Regional Policy, for the 2000-2006 program, has been implemented through a complex planning procedure, carried on in a number of stages[1], starting with Council Regulation No 1260/1999 of 21 June 1999, laying down general provisions on the Structural Funds. According to this Regulation, article 9, the Regional Programs of each Member State should follow the guidelines set forth in a development plan prepared by that Member State in light of the objectives referred to in Article 1 of the Regulation. This development plan should indicate the priority needs for attaining those objectives, together with the strategy, the planned action priorities, their specific goals and the related indicative financial resources. It follows that the Regional program should present the objectives individuated on the basis of the European Regulation and of the national development program, and should set forth the priorities to attain these objectives, the strategy to reach them, the planning actions priorities of the strategy and the specific goals, with the financial resources allocated to them. The general objectives of this planning are presented in article 1 of the Regulation with emphatic language, as follows "the Community shall contribute to the harmonious, balanced and sustainable development of economic activities, the development of employment and human resources, the protection and improvement of the environment, and the elimination of inequalities, and the promotion of equality between men and women". No clear priority emerges from this article.

Cultural development in connection with tourism is explicitly considered by Regulation 1260/99[2], among the objectives of the European Regional policy. The regulations state: "Whereas cultural development, the quality of the natural and the man-made environment, the qualitative and cultural dimension of life and the development of tourism contribute to making regions economically and socially more attractive in so far as they encourage the creation of sustainable

1 According to Article 9 "programming: means the organizing, decision-making and financing process carried out in a number of stages to implement on a multiannual basis the joint action of the Community and the Member States to attain the Objectives referred to in Article 1".

2 In paragraph 6 of the preliminaries to the articles.

employment". Here too, the language is nebulous and without any indication of priorities.

This task is devolved to the National Development Plan, which in the Italian case, for the less developed Regions consisted of QCS[3] 2000-2006 approved with the Decision 2050 of the European Commission of July 1, 2000. According to the guidelines of this Plan, each Regional Program of the Regions in Objective 1 should be divided into six axes:

- *Axis 1 – Enhancement of natural and environmental resources.*
- *Axis 2 – Use of local cultural and historical resources.*
- *Axis 3 – Human resource development.*
- *Axis 4 – Expansion and enhancement of local systems development.*
- *Axis 5 – Improving the quality of cities, local institutions and social life.*
- *Axis 6 – Strengthening of networks and service nodes.*

The guidelines of QCS 2000-2006 for Axis 2 suggest that the Southern Italy Regional Programs should focus not only on the most important cultural sites, but also consider the cultural patrimony diffused throughout the territory. Whilst this underlines the importance of cultural goods for the development of touristic activities, it adds that the program should also consider the cultural activities as "the entire cultural industry in the broad senses". However indicators of actions present the capacity of attracting touristic consumptions, and as indicators of results present the number of visitors to Museums.

Calabria's POR was approved by the Italian Government, in July 2000, and gained the approval of the EU Commission with Decision 2345 of August 8 2000. For this POR, as for any other regional POR of Objective 1, 50 % of the funds came from the budget of EU. Of this, nearly 60 % of funds came from by European Regional Development Fund (ERDF), which finances productive investment and infrastructure projects, with a further 20 % from the European Agriculture Guidance and Development (EAGGF), and the remaining 20 % of funds were administered by the European Social Fund (ESF). A residual 0.94 % of the EU funds came from Financial Instruments for Fisheries Guidance (FIFG). The remaining 50 % of (non-EU) funds came from the finances of the receiving country, in this case Italy. A share of 80 % was given by the Central Government, and the remaining 20 % was provided by the receiving Regions and by local programs. Therefore Calabria contributed to the POR for 10 % of its total funds. Private entities that presented projects had to be co-finance 50 % of the cost of the project. Those presented by the public entities were totally financed by the POR. But these projects could have been part of

3 QCS means "Quadro Comunitario di Sostegno", or "Communitarian Frame of Support".

broader projects financed for the remaining part by the public entity applying to the POR.

Axis 2, which is the object of our research, had an European endowment of 231 million Euro, and could mobilize additional Italian public finance resources of a similar amount, so that the total import of the public funds for the project would have been roughly 450 million Euro. It was subdivided in three "measures" pertaining to different kinds of projects, classified by their nature and by the subjects entitled to receive the funds.

- *2.1 Interventions for the preservation and valorization of cultural goods.*
- *2.2 Public services for the valorization of cultural goods.*
- *2.3 Development of entrepreneurial initiatives in these areas*[4].

Measures 2.1 and 2.3 were administered by the Regional Department of Tourism because cultural goods were financed mainly as an attractor of tourism.

The program, following article 9 of Council Regulations No. 1260/1999, was constructed in a "gothic style", by four goals, with five programmatic strategies for each goal and seven specific actions, each articulated in a number of sub-actions.

The four goals were described in an emphatic and vague language as follows:

a) Construction of networks for the enjoyment of cultural and historical heritage, in accordance with already planned network initiatives, and to identify meaningful property at the regional level on which to focus project resources in order to conserve, protect, and enhance.

b) Generate managerial services of both public institutions and private entrepreneurs to meet the demand of residents and tourist for cultural heritage resources.

c) Qualify and support the training of technical and scientific figures tied to the heritage and cultural tourism sector, primarily for cultural management (organization of cultural institutions and utility companies) and management services for the dissemination of local knowledge (tour services).

d) To develop companies and organizations (public and private, profit and non-profit, cultural foundations) relating to the conservation, enhancement, and management of the development of services that combine the benefits of tourism with cultural resources.

4 Project funds for development of entrepreneurial initiatives are granted within the limits of the *de minimis* rule.

Each of the four goals had to be implemented by the following program strategies:

a) Concentrating resources around cultural emergencies, identified as key exploitable resources.
b) Enhance regional cultural identities through the wide range of arts, entertainment, and culture for social and economic development.
c) Provide the region with infrastructure resources, including "horizontal" factors such a knowledge and training of cultural heritage.
d) Create an interconnected function system to strengthen the cultural whole (the network of archeological areas, coastal castles, regional libraries, *etc.*).
e) Fostering entrepreneurship in innovated private management services.

The five program strategies then had to be realized by seven types of actions.

a) Enhancement of the archeological heritage of Ancient Greece.
b) Establish a network of archeology of the Magna Graecia region.
c) Create theme parks related to archaeological sites through the construction of adequate facilities for their use.
d) Recovery, development, and reutilization of the most valuable elements of architectural and landscape heritage.
e) Redevelopment of historic centers through the recycling of abandoned buildings.
f) Construction of multipurpose centers for the integration of cultural activities and entertainment.
g) Protection of the landscape through projects aimed at recovery and enhancement of the landscape.

Each action had to take into consideration six sub-actions[5]. The sum allocated to this was 231 million Euro, and considering that the amount of funds mobilized was nearly double, there was a large amount for the valorization of the cultural patrimony of Calabria; but could hardly justify the complex articulation of the plan. From this clearly defined priorities did not emerge and the finely targeted economic plan became a discretionary program without any priority. This pro-

---

5 The six sub-sections are:

1. Promotion and implementation of innovative initiatives that enhance the cultural heritage and local identities.
2. Events of significant cultural and anthropological value.
3. Preservation of ethnic minorities who have maintained important features of the original cultures.
4. Activities related to the ancient tradition of craft production, music, the production of objects of culture of pastoral farmers, and local foods.
5. Preservation of the oral traditions.
6. Promotion and creation of cultural networks.

gram occurred on the basis that the Italian QCS 2000-2006 – following Council Regulation 1260/99. And both the QCS and Calabria's POR had the approval of the European Commission. The Italian Government and the EU, therefore, have been responsible for the fact that the regional bureaucracies and politicians could make discretionary choices, with support available in the cumbersome text of the POR.

4. Overview of the cultural heritage endowment of Calabria and of program implementation

Doubtless, Calabria is rich of cultural goods as many other Italian regions. The Ministry of Artistic and Cultural Goods (MIBAC) maintains 57 archeological sites on over 4,000 hectares of land with nine managing superintendants in the region. There are 19 museums of art, history, and important monuments of which only five require an admission fee. Among them is the National Archeological Museum of Reggio Calabria which has historically maintained the highest number of visitors.

The majority of sites are in the provinces of Cosenza and Reggio Calabria, with 14 and 12 sites respectively. In addition, there are 27 historically significant sites consisting of constructions in historical towns. Of them, 9 are still not officially protected. The remaining 18 historically significant sites – comprised of historical buildings and ruins – have been the object of registration for their protection.

As mentioned above, the most important historical sites consisting of constructions in Calabria are the "defensive systems" made of towers, fortresses and castles dating back to the Ninth century A. D. These tend to be located on hilltops and near the sea. There are 147 castles, 196 towers, and 43 fortified structures officially recorded and protected. But only a few of them are correctly preserved.

Officially in Calabria there are 35 "theaters": 80% of which are privately (non-state) owned. Of this, 50% are conducted by cooperatives, 20% by associations, and the remaining 30% by private companies. The only culturally relevant theater is in Reggio Calabria.

In some areas there are ethnic minorities (i. e. Albanians, Hellenistic, Occitan, and Gypsies) who have retained important features of their cultures of origin.

The multiplicity of cultural goods of Calabria may be disorienting. However a reclassification has been completed by two of the three authors of this paper, i. e. Forte and Mantovani, by referring to the national classification of the important museums, archeological sites and monuments (inclusive of churches) done by the Ministry of Artistic and Cultural Goods, integrated, as for the historical buildings.. with the list of the historical castles still preserved and, for the other cultural sites, with the most important theatres and libraries and archives if any (see Forte Mantovani Skepys 2011, p. 30 of the text and Table A, pag. 45 of the Appendix).

A year after the expiration of the programs, the three Axes relating to culture achieved more success in comparison with the other axes of the POR, but they too were not satisfactory. Axis II has an allocation ratio of about 50% of the fund, as did Axis V (Social and City Life), and Axis VI (Networks). The program for natural and environmental resources (Axis I), for which Calabria has a natural vocation, has a ratio of only 45%. Local systems for development (Axis IV) had a ratio lower than 25% and human resources lower still at below 5%.

At its accomplishment the Cultural POR allocated 63.4% of the available resources, with a share of the project finance abandoned before completion. We consider the situation in 2007, by the official accounting at the end of February 2008, when 50% of the funds was allocated, and a further 46.3% was "committed"; of them, only 82% were really spent. The total amount committed was 197 million Euro, whilst the total amount spent was 157 million. 539 projects had been approved for execution, for each of these the average amount committed was 365,000 Euro, and each project on average received 291,000 Euro. Considering this, clearly there was a dispersion of funds in initiatives with a minimal impact on the valorization of Calabria's important cultural patrimony.

There were only 3 projects exceeding 5 million Euro. They were for the two archeological parks of Solacium in Crotone and the plaster cast and picture gallery in Catanzaro. In the 3-5 million Euro category there were four projects for the restoration of historic buildings and the structural adjustment of the National Museum of Cosenza, and as well as an appropriation 3 million Euro for the promotion of anthropological heritage.

Only 25 projects approved had budgets from 1 to 3 million Euro. Among them, two projects for the preservation of the Albanian traditions and the creation of a network designed to enhance minority languages. Projects with a budget of 500,000 Euro were almost exclusively dedicated to construction and restoration of buildings.

Most projects were in the range between 1,000-250,000 Euro for the improvement of library systems, consolidation of buildings and churches, and the promotion of crafts in the process of "extinction" such as tailors, carpenters, goldsmiths. At the end of 2007, 60.7% of the total number of projects approved was incomplete. The complexity of the procedures and the fragmentation of the expenditure into small projects resulted in a large proportion of unfinished projects, seven years after the beginning of the plan. And a share of them has been abandoned before the completion.

Table 1 – Number of projects per Province.

Province	*Number of projects*	*Share of projects*	*Share of population*
Cosenza	208	38.8	36.5
Reggio Calabria	147	27.4	28.2
Catanzaro	93	17.4	18.3
Crotone	44	8.2	8.6
Vibo Valentia	44	8.2	8.4

Source: POR Calabria (2009).

As one can see from Table 1, the distribution of the 536 projects by provinces follows closely the provincial distribution of the population, and so one can assume that the voting weight of each province determined the number of projects assigned to it. The fact that the Governor of the centre-right regional Junta in power until 2004 and the Governor of the successive centre-left Junta were respectively of the provinces of Cosenza (Chiaravalloti) and Catanzaro (Loiero) did not substantially affect the distribution of projects by provinces.

Was the distribution of funds among the provinces affected by either the differing importance of their cultural goods, their ability to attract tourism or their differing needs of valorization. Therefore, the criterion that prevailed, among the provinces, was that of the distribution of the funds in proportion to their electors.

5. Econometric methodology, data and empirical results

In this section we show statistical and econometric analysis results to shed light on variables that determined the POR 2000-2006 Axis II fund allocation. The dependent variables considered are the number of projects and the amount of money allocated.

In Table 2 some preliminary descriptive statistics are shown.

Table 2 – Exploratory data analysis.

Variable	*Mean*	*Median*	*Standard Deviation*	*Skewness*	*Kurtosis*	*Range*
lnamounts_pc	4.3061	4.5545	1.7295	-0.4602	3.1263	9.4483
lnpayments_pc	4.0135	4.1609	1.6979	-0.3040	2.9617	9.0586
lncommitment_pc	4.2685	4.5367	1.7243	-0.4921	3.2440	9.5749
Projects	2.5524	1	3.6953	5.5770	41.9537	35
Votes	53.9711	54.0975	6.3680	-0.0132	4.3171	47.0650
Nonprofits	25.1667	10	73.2106	6.5077	47.9020	656
Province	0.0238	0	0.1528	6.2470	40.0244	1
Health structures	0.4619	0	0.4997	0.1528	1.0234	1
University	0.0762	0	0.2659	3.1949	11.2075	1
Nursery	0.3048	0	0.4614	0.8483	1.7196	1
Primary school	0.3238	0	0.4690	0.7531	1.5671	1
Secondary school	0.8524	1	0.3556	-1.9868	4.9474	1
Senior high school	0.3571	0	0.4803	0.5963	1.3556	1
T&C	0.0762	0	0.2659	3.1949	11.2075	1
Touristic attractors	0.2810	0	0.4505	0.9747	1.9501	1
TV&R	0.1952	0	0.3973	1.5377	3.3646	1
Soccer	0.0381	0	0.1919	4.8259	24.2896	1
A&C&A	0.7381	1	0.4407	-1.0831	2.1730	1
A&P	0.0524	0	0.2233	4.0182	17.1462	1
L&P	0.4762	0	0.5006	0.0953	1.0091	1
Museums	0.2048	0	0.4045	1.4633	3.1412	1
Cultural Sites	0.1143	0	0.3189	2.4247	6.8790	1
Criminal Hubs	0.2571	0	0.4381	1.1113	2.2350	1
Councillor	0.0714	0	0.2582	3.3282	12.0769	1

Sources: our calculations on POR (2009) and www.regionecalabria.it data.

The tested projects – those of POR 2000-2006 Axes II resulting from the regional Report of 29 February 2008 referring to end of 2007[6] – were considered "non continuous" projects, which means they had a specific end date. This specification allowed for simplified testing and analysis. The data set is available on the official website of the Calabria Region in the Reports on POR 2000-2006 and is synthesized in various other Tables. Statistical analysis was conducted only for the cross-section containing municipals that received POR funds. The focus on the amount per-capita in municipalities that received projects allows us to examine which priorities, if any, have been pursued in allocating the funds among them. We constructed a data set to analyze the relationship of the data about the projects in per capita amount for the various municipalities, and the variables described below regarding these municipalities.

6 See: http://www.regione.calabria.it/calabriaeuropa/index.php?option=com_content&task=view&id=120&Itemid=253.

A variety of regression techniques were used. First, we ran a *Stepwise* regression, always concentrating on the per-capita amounts, i. e. on the municipalities that received funds[7].

Afterwards, we ran a GLM model[8]. In particular, these estimators permit us to estimate GLM-like models involving mean-variance specifications that extend beyond those for known exponential family distributions, and to estimate models where the mean-variance specification is of exponential family form, but the observed data do not satisfy the distributional requirements (Agresti, 1990)[9].

As a third method of estimate, we choose a Robust regression[10]. Finally, we estimated a Quantile regression[11].

---

7 Stepwise methods provide ways to automate the process of model selection. They work either by subtracting predictors from a complicated model, or by adding predictors to a simpler one according to some pre-set statistical criteria. Stepwise methods cannot consider the substantive or theoretical implications of their choices, nor can they do much troubleshooting to evaluate possible weakness in the models produced at each step. They produce badly biased models in many instances due to over-fitting. Despite their well-known limitations, stepwise methods meet some practical needs and have been widely used.

8 Nelder and McCullagh (1989) describe a class of *Generalized Linear Models* (GLMs) that extends linear regression to permit non-normal stochastic and non-linear systematic components. GLMs encompass a broad and empirically useful range of specifications that includes linear regression, logistic and probit analysis, and Poisson models.
Crucially, the properties of the GLM maximum likelihood estimator depend only on these two moments. Thus, a GLM specification is principally a vehicle for specifying a mean and variance, where the mean is determined by the link assumption, and the mean-variance relationship is governed by the distributional assumption. In this respect, the distributional assumption of the standard GLM is overly restrictive. McCullagh (1983) offers a full set of distributional results for the quasi-maximum likelihood (QML) estimator that mirror those for ordinary maximum likelihood.

9 Alternately, Gourioux, Monfort, and Trognon (1984) show that consistency of the GLM maximum likelihood estimator requires only correct specification of the conditional mean. Misspecification of the variance relationship does, however, lead to invalid inference, though this may be corrected using robust coefficient covariance estimation. In contrast to the QML results, the robust covariance correction does not require correction specification of a GLM conditional variance.

10 An *Iteratively Reweighted Least Squares* (IRLS) procedure obtains robust regression estimates. The first iteration begins with OLS. Any observations so influential as to have Cook's distance D values greater than 1 are automatically set aside after this first step. Next, weights are calculated for each observation using a Huber function (which downweights observations that have larger residuals) and weighted least squares is performed. After several WLS iterations, the weight function shifts to a Tukey biweight (as suggested by Li, 1985), tuned for 95 % Gaussian efficiency (Street, Carroll, and Ruppert, 1988; Hamilton 1992).

11 As originally proposed by Koenker and Baxistt (1978), quantile regression provides estimates of the linear relationship between X regressors and a specified quantile of the dependent variable Y. One important special case of quantile regression is the *Least Absolute Deviations* (LAD) estimator, which corresponds to fitting the conditional median of the response variable.

We choose the log-linear functional form, and our dependent variable is the natural logarithm of per-capita amounts (*lnamounts_pc*), and it represents POR funds of each municipality, divided for its population. *Projects* is the number of approved projects; *Votes* is the electoral flows; *Nonprofit* is the number of nonprofit organizations of any kind in the given municipality; *Province* is a dummy variable, that is equal to 1 if municipal is a Province, and equal to 0 otherwise; *Health structures* is a dummy variable, that is equal to 1 if in the municipal area insists at least one hospital, psychiatric facility nuthouse or fitness centre, and equal to 0 otherwise; *University* is a dummy variable, that is equal to 1 if in the municipal area there contains an academic institution, and equal to 0 otherwise; *Nursery* is a dummy variable, that is equal to 1 if the municipality has got a nursery, and equal to 0 otherwise; *Primary school* is a dummy variable, that is equal to 1 if in the municipal area there is at least one primary school, and equal to 0 otherwise; *Secondary school* is a dummy variable, that is equal to 1 if in the municipal area there is at least one secondary school, and equal to 0 otherwise; *Senior high school* is a dummy variable, that is equal to 1 if in the municipal area there is at least one senior high school, and equal to 0 otherwise; *T&C* is a dummy variable, that is equal to 1 if in the municipal area there is at least one theatre or a cinema, and equal to 0 otherwise; *Touristic attractors* is a dummy variable, that is equal to 1 if in the municipal area there is at least one disco, aquapark, wine-tasting shop, sport-centre, or a beach, and equal to 0 otherwise; *TV&R* is a dummy variable, that is equal to 1 if in the municipal area there is at least one local TV or radio station, and equal to 0 otherwise; *Soccer* is a dummy variable, that is equal to 1 if in the municipal area there is at least one professional soccer team, and equal to 0 otherwise; *A&C&A* is a dummy variable, that is equal to 1 if in the municipal area there is at least one hotel, camping or farm holidays, and equal to 0 otherwise; *A&P* is a dummy variable, that is equal to 1 if in the municipal area there is at least one airport or seaport, and equal to 0 otherwise; *L&P* is a dummy variable, that is equal to 1 if in the municipal area there is at least one library or local publisher, and equal to 0 otherwise; *Museums* is a dummy variable, that is equal to 1 if in the municipal area there is at least one museum, and equal to 0 otherwise; *Cultural Sites* is a dummy variable, that is equal to 1 if the municipality might be considered as a cultural hub (see Table 1) and equal to 0 otherwise; *Criminal Hubs* is a dummy variable, that is equal to 1 if the municipality might be considered as a criminal hub according to Gratteri and Nicaso (2007) classification, and equal to 0 otherwise (see § 7 at the beginning, below) *Councillor* is a dummy variable, that is equal to 1 if the municipality has been represented by a councillor as a member of Regional Government during the period 2000-2006, and equal to 0 otherwise.

As is shown in Table 3, notices that there are very few differences in the estimated coefficients among four estimation methods applied. In fact, the coefficients are very similar, while standard errors present slight variations. The second column represents the output of Stepwise Backward Robust OLS estimate. Recall that we choose the log-linear functional form, and our dependent variable is the natural logarithm of per capita amounts (*lnamounts_pc*). In order to control for heteroscedasticity, we applied White's correction.

Table 3 – Regression Analysis, POR-Calabria (2000-2006).

Dependent Variable: (lnamounts_pc)	***Stepwise Backward Robust OLS***[a]	***Robust GLM***[a]	***IRLS***	***LAD with bootstrapping***
Constant	3.4999*** (.1633)	3.4999*** (.1606)	3.4994*** (.1431)	3.6130*** (.2058)
Projects	.2931*** (.0678)	.2931*** (.0666)	.3744*** (.0575)	.3244*** (.0774)
Nonprofit	-.0131*** (.0029)	-.0131*** (.0029)	-.0132*** (.0025)	-.0137*** (.0774)
University	.5930** (.2712)	.5930** (.2666)		
Touristic Attractors	-.4752*** (.1804)	-.4752*** (.1773)	-.4399** (.2002)	
L&P	-.3128* (.1676)	-.3128* (.1647)	-.3705** (.1690)	-.3607** (.1907)
Senior high school	-1.0574*** (.1911)	-1.0574*** (.1879)	-1.0791*** (.1893)	-1.0711*** (.1840)
Number of obs.	210	210	209	210
F test	43.70 (.0000)		45.19	
Log-Likelihood	-321.0666			
Pearson Dispersion		1.295		
R^2	.5874		.5731	
R^2_{adj}	.5834		.5604	
Pseudo R^2				.3385
BIC	684.9101	-818.4658		
AIC	658.1332			
RMSE	1.1381		1.1462	
Ramsey OV test	2.03 (.1107)			
Mean VIF	2.52			
Tolerance Ratio	.3968			
Skewness-Kurtosis test	.98 (.6129)	0.98 (.6129)	9.46 (.0088)	3.30 (.1920)
Shapiro-Francia test	(.6134)	(.6134)	(.0160)	(.0486)
Shapiro-Wilk test	(.5947)	(.5947)	(.0246)	(.0360)
IQR	1 mild outlier 0 severe outlier	1 mild outlier 0 severe outlier	3 mild outliers 0 severe outlier	9 mild outliers 0 severe outlier
Link test	f. v. significant $(f. v.)^2$ not Significant	f. v. significant $(f. v.)^2$ not significant		f. v. significant $(f. v.)^2$ not Significant

Notes: a: White correction for heteroskedasticity applied. Significance levels: * 10%, ** 5%, *** 1%. Robust Standard Errors in parenthesis.

Using regression analysis, as expected, the number of total projects (*Projects*) is statistically significant, and this explanatory variable tends to have a positive influence on per capita amounts of the individual municipalities. The presence of museums in the considered municipalities is not relevant for the allocation of per capita funds, nor are the presence of important cultural sites relevant. Also the presence of schools – whether of primary or secondary education – does not seem relevant, whilst the presence of senior high schools is relevant with a negative impact. It appears that in municipalities where there are already important public cultural institutions no attention is required in terms of the allocation of POR' s funds for culture. A similar consideration may explain the *L&P*'s negative influence on the allocation of these funds. *Touristic attractors* tend to have a negative impact on dependent variable, too; the reason could be the different kind of tourism that the attractors stimulate. On the other hand one should notice that they are not significant in the LAD estimate. The variables *TV&R*, *A&C&A* and *A&P*, which too may be relevant for tourism, are not significant. One can argue that the presence of relevant tourist facilities and services does not exert an appreciable influence on the allocation of the Calabrian POR's funds for culture, even if the development of tourism is among the official objectives of the program. Yet, the presence of an academic institution (*University*) increases the funds assigned. This result might provide evidence in support of the idea that where there is a University, the capability of presenting projects to be approved tends to increase – possibly due to the greater competence and intellectual prestige of the authors advocating the project, or their capabilities in lobbying procedures. On the other hand, one can notice that in LAD estimate *University* is not significant and that in IRLS estimate the explanatory variable *University* does not have a statistical relevance. This result implies that the presence of an University in a given town it is not important in the policy of the Region as for the allocation of the POR's cultural funds. As previously seen, there is a strong correlation between the presence of nonprofit organizations and the allocation of funds to the municipalities. So, those with nonprofit institutions have been favored on those without them. However, the variable *Nonprofit* shows a negative incidence on the per capita amounts for municipalities which received funds. One can explain this result arguing that the competition among the different nonprofit organizations for these public funds reduced the success of them.

6. Regression results: a comment

According to the diagnostic checks, the goodness-of-fit is acceptable (the coefficient of determination and the adjusted coefficient both are >56 %), while the

F-stat reveals that set of independent variables (jointly considered) significantly differs from zero, since we strongly reject the null hypothesis.

Ramsey' RESET test controls whether non-linear combinations of the estimated values help explain the endogenous variable (Ramsey, 1969). The intuition behind the test is that, if non-linear combinations of the explanatory variables have any power in explaining the endogenous variable, then the model is misspecified. Since we don't reject the null hypothesis that the model has no omitted variables, we might conclude that it is well-specified.

The mean Variance Inflation Factor is equal to 2.52. VIF gives a quick check for multicollinearity. 1/VIF tells us what proportion of an explanatory variable's variance is independent of all the other *X* variables. A low proportion indicates potential trouble. VIF values provide guidance but not direct measurements of the increase in coefficient variances. Nevertheless, Chatterjee and Hadi (2006) suggest a sort of "rule of thumb": if the mean VIF is considerably larger than 1, we could suspect the presence of multicollinearity. With our mean VIF less than 3, and our largest VIF close to 5.5, our regression clearly doesn't meet both criteria. Moreover, the tolerance statistics is >0.2, so there is not a multicollinearity problem (Menard, 1995).

Table 4 – Pairwise correlation matrix for our statistically relevant variables.

Variable	***lnamounts_pc***	***Projects***	***Nonprofit***	***University***	***Touristic Attractors***	***L&P***	***Senior high school***
lnamounts_pc	*1*						
Projects	*0.2138*	*1*					
Nonprofit	*0.0084*	*0.8890*	*1*				
University	*0.0274*	*0.5461*	*0.5995*	*1*			
Touristic Attractors	*-0.1156*	*0.3231*	*0.3474*	*0.3396*	*1*		
L&P	*-0.0818*	*0.2270*	*0.2422*	*0.2653*	*0.2313*	*1*	
Senior high school	*-0.2385*	*0.3304*	*0.3255*	*0.3104*	*0.3964*	*0.2843*	*1*

Note: Bonferroni correction applied.
Source: our calculations on POR (2009) and www.regionecalabria.it data.

As the Table 4 above shows, there is only a high correlation coefficient between *Projects* and *Nonprofit* (r=0.8890); the reason for this lies on the fact that municipalities with a great number of nonprofit organizations tend to elaborate a higher number of projects. Moreover, any other pairwise correlation value is below 0.6. This could also explain the absence of multicollinearity in our regression equation.

Moreover, the pairwise correlation coefficients matrix patently shows us that – either we use Bonferroni-adjusted significance level or Sidak-adjusted significance level – there exists only a troublesome correlation between amounts and payments, but that this collinearity does not distort very deeply our estimate (Abdi, 2007).

Yet, if our model is really well-specified and then if we were to regress *lnamounts_pc* on the prediction and the prediction squared, the prediction squared would have no explanatory power. This is what *linktest* does (Tukey, 1949; Pregibon, 1979). We find that the prediction squared does have explanatory power, so our specification is not as good as we thought. Although *linktest* is formally a test of the specification of the dependent variable, it is often interpreted as a test that, conditional on the specification, the independent variables are specified incorrectly.

Finally, we analyze the normality of residuals. We conducted three different tests check the Gaussian distribution of residuals: Jarque and Bera test (1987), Shapiro and Wilk test (1965), Shapiro and Francia test (1972). Since all these tests fail to reject the null hypothesis of normality, we are able to conclude in favour of normality assumption.

7. Criminal hubs

In this section we discuss the relevance of the municipalities with Criminal Hubs on POR funds allocation, considering their the presence of cultural sites and of non profits, the number of projects approved, the amount allocated and the amount received by each of them. The list of municipalities with criminal hubs is drawn from Grateri and Nicaso (2007), the data on the projects approved and on funds allocated and received by the municipalities are drawn from POR Calabria, the cultural sites are those listed in Forte Mantovani Skepys 2011, p. 30 of the text and Table A, pag. 45 of the Appendix. The collection of these data may be found in Forte Mantovani Skepis (2011), Table G page 49-50.

Criminal hubs. have been preferred over the other municipalities beneficiaries of projects not only for the total amount allocated to them, but also for the per capita allocation of the funds and the amount of funding per project. The difference of this result with that relating to nonprofits may be explained considering that these criminal organizations are oligopolistic groups, not very numerous, so only a small and imperfect competition exists when compared with most of the Calabria's nonprofits.

Table 5 – Amounts, Payments and Commitment for Calabrian municipalities that received POR funds (Averages for municipalities).

Variable	*With Criminal Hubs*	*Without Criminal Hubs*	*All Municipalities*
Amounts	2,312,680 123,703,269	549,135.5 92,836,847	1,002,618 210549843.7
Payments	1,676,048 90,506,584	427,097.2 81,905,239.01	748,256 156,759,973.2
Commitments	2,144,570 115,806,753	523,041.6 66,843,571	940,005.9 197027467.4
Amounts per capita	446.3187 122.9476	200.687 144.4543	263.8494
Payments per capita	293.7673 88.7985	157.5825 104.0087	192.6015
Commitments per capita	423.4145 113.6212	192.3203 127.4447	251.7445

Notes: total number of projects: 539; total number municipalities with approved projects: 210.
Source: our calculations on POR (2009) and Gratteri and Nicaso (2007) data.

So, we have 539 total projects, distributed as follows:

- 426 to Measure 2.1 (=79.04 %)
- 40 to Measure 2.2 (=7.42 %)
- 73 to Measure 2.3 (=13.54 %).

As part of the total projects:

- 252 to Municipalities with Criminal Hubs (=46.75 %)
- 287 projects to Municipalities without Criminal Hubs (=53.25 %).

Projects assigned to Criminal hubs as part of a single Measure:

- 191 projects of Measure 2.1 (=44.84 %)
- 20 projects of Measure 2.2 (=50.00 %)
- 41 projects of Measure 2.3 (=56.16 %).

As Table 5 above shows, per capita payments to criminal hubs are 86 % greater than those of the non criminal hubs, and the per capita commitments for the criminal hubs are 220 % greater than those for the non criminal hubs. Municipalities that are criminal hubs received an average of 2,312,680 Euro, while municipalities that aren't criminal hubs received an average amount of 549,000 Euro (i. e. about 24 % of the former). For commitments, the ratio is lower 20 %. Clearly, they were less able to obtain the commitment of the allocated sums to their projects. For payments, the ratio is about 25 %. The reason of this difference lies in the higher ratio of the payments to the commitments for the projects of the municipalities that aren't criminal hubs. Indeed, the projects of Measure 2.1 and 2.3 – that require an investment of money by the beneficiaries of the sums committed for the projects – they may maximize their gains and their employment of manpower by not non completing the projects. As for the first stage, they may present their expenses as the cost of the project, and the expense for the machinery that they already own, as well as for the wages of the activities that require a lot of manpower and a minimum of materials. Then they may abandon the projects, because they may not really be interested in the concrete results. It is also interesting to observe that criminal hubs have a larger share of the project in Measure 2.2 (which does not require a counter-part by the principals of the projects and consists in services, i. e. in employment) and in Measure 2.3, which consists in projects by private enterprises for the valorization of the cultural goods, in which the labor component might also be quite important.

The projects executed in the criminal hubs, as Table 7 clarifies, were 252. Each project, on average, therefore got 456,000 Euro. However, the total amount spent for the 252 projects allocated to the criminal hubs (see Table 7) was 90,500,000 Euro. Therefore, in criminal hubs each project, on average, received 359,000 Euro. Clearly, criminal hubs were able to get more from this POR, not only per municipality, but also per project.

8. Impact of Calabria's POR projects for culture on cultural sites and on tourism

POR funds for cultural investments finalized to develop tourism, as the statistical analysis has shown, have been mostly dispersed to purposes different from the valorization of the important cultural sites of the region, without any consideration of priorities. This POR might have even harmed the promotion of Calabria's cultural sites, because the unfinished projects are of a high percentage. Moreover, the Central government budget may have overlooked Calabria's cultural sites, assuming that they would be taken care of by the special budget of POR (see Table 6).

Table 6 – Visitors of museums and revenues for Calabria and Italy (2000-2007).

	Visitors in 2000	Visitors in 2007	% Change 2007/2000	Revenues 2000	Revenues 2007	% Change 2007/2000
Calabrian Museums	238,937	212,130	-11.0%	322,602	270,696	-15.8%
Italian Museums	10,873,054	10,727,703	-1.0%	33,383,807	31,384,733	-6.0%
Calabrian Archeological Sites	139,639	87,696	-37.0%	0	0	0.0%
Italian Archeological Sites	16,856,112	16,363,057	-3.0%	28,245,726	34,237,406	21.2%
Calabrian Museums and Monuments	378,576	299,826	-21.0%	322,602	270,696	-16.1%
Italian Museums and Monuments	30,175,826	34,443,097	14.1%	77,017,081	106,033,174	37.7%

Source: MIBAC and SISTAN data.

The lack of tourist development of the archaeological sites in comparison to the Italian Calabria

Despite the importance of the sites of high archaeological value, their value through funding of the POR Calabria did not receive money, as they were and still are, free of admission fees. But the phenomenon is more dramatic since 2000, the start of the POR, when visitors to the sites decreased dramatically from 140,000 in 2000 to 88,000 in 2007. As for the Italian archaeological sites, in 2000 they attracted 17 million visitors with revenues of 28 million Euro. In 2007 the number of visitors fell to 16 million – a decrease of 3 %. Despite this slight decline in visitors, revenues increased significantly, from 28 million Euro in 2000 to 34 million in 2007 – with a significant increase of 21 %.

The unsatisfactory situation of the touristic valorization of Calabrian museums in comparison to the Italian ones

The situation of museums in Calabria is not rosy. In 2000 the number of visitors to Calabrian museums was of 238,000, and it fell to 212,000 in 2007 – a drop of 11 %. The revenues declined from 322,000 in 2000 to 271,000 in 2007 – 16 % decrease. This is comparable the Italian archaeological sites, which have seen their revenues increase by 21 %, whilst the number of visitors to these sites fell by 6 %.

Visitors and revenues to Italian museums and monuments

In 2000, visitors to Italian museums and monuments were approximately 30 million with a revenue of 77 million Euro. In 2007, Italian museums and monuments attracted 34,443,097 visitors and produced gross revenues of 106 million Euro. There is an increase in the flows of visitors since 2000 of about 13 % for the visitors and of more than 38 % for the revenues. For the archeological sites at the national level, 2007 witnessed a decrease in visitor numbers of about 6 % when compared with the number of visitors in 2000. The revenue of thosi sites increased by 21 %, from 28.2 million in 2000 to 34.2 million Euro in 2007.

The coexistence of these two divergent trends between Calabria and Italy shows that the POR for the culture of Calabria missed the objective of attracting new visitors to Calabria's important cultural sites.

Furthermore the objective of connecting Calabria's archeological sites into a unique system – which appears among the objectives of the POR – has not been realized.

Tourism in Calabria and in Italy

On the other hand, tourism in Calabria between year 2000 and 2007 has experienced a great increase of arrivals (nearly 45 %) and presences (nearly 39 %), with a spectacular increase in those of the number of foreigners. Arrivals of foreigners in this period increased by 78.3 % more than the double the increase in Italians whose numbers increased by 40 % (see Table 7).

Table 7 – Tourist's flows in Calabria and in Italy (2000-2007).

Presences Italians/Foreigners	**2000**	**2006**	**% Change 2006/2000**	**2007**	**% Change 2007/2000**
ITALIA	338,885,143	366,764,778	8%	376,641,751	11%
CALABRIA	6,282,074	8,155,053	30%	8,731,335	39%
Presences Foreigners	**2000**	**2006**	**% Change 2006/2000**	**2007**	**% Change 2007/2000**
ITALIA	140,356,985	156,861,341	12%	163,465,680	16%
CALABRIA	882,837	1,479,247	68%	1,542,133	74%
Arrivals Italians/Foreigners	**2000**	**2006**	**% Change 2006/2000**	**2007**	**% Change 2007/2000**
ITALIA	80,031,637	93,044,399	16%	96,150,083	20%
CALABRIA	1,083,078	1,476,026	36%	1,568,519	45%
Arrivals Italians	**2000**	**2006**	**% Change 2006/2000**	**2007**	**% Change 2007/2000**
ITALIA	44,924,162	51,850,572	**15%**	53,276,961	19%
CALABRIA	946,977	1,244,549	**31%**	1,325,825	40%
Arrivals Foreigners	**2000**	**2006**	**% Change 2006/2000**	**2007**	**% Change 2007/2000**
ITALIA	35,107,475	41,193,827	17%	42,873,122	22%
CALABRIA	136,101	231,477	70%	242,694	78%

Source: ISTAT.

The Italian trend has also been positive but has been much less pronounced than that of Calabria both for the arrivals and the presence, of foreigners and italian. Arrivals, in Italy as a whole, had an increase of 20.4%, less than half the rise of Calabria's. Presence of tourists increased by 11.1%, i.e. less than one third of the increase witnessed in Calabria. The arrival of foreigners, in Italy as a whole, in the considered period increased by 20%, about a quarter of Calabria's percentage, whilst the arrivals of Italians increase by 18.6%, slightly less than half Calabria's rise. Considering that in the same period the number of visitors to the Calabria's cultural sites diminished substantially one can argue that the great increase in the flow of tourists – and particularly of foreign tourists – to Calabria was due to reasons not associated with the attractiveness of its cultural sites. Additionally, Calabria's POR 2000-2006 which had been conceived for the enhancement of cultural sites as an important factor for the development of tourism, has been irrelevant or negative from this point of view.

9. Coherent projects

Only a part of the available funds of Calabria's POR 2000-2006 was spent on programs. The remaining part was destined to other regional expenditures which could be considered coherent with the POR, thus increasing the funds available to the Region for its ordinary administration.

This result coincides with those of the other Italian Regions which benefitted from Objective 1 of the European Regional Programs 2000-2006.

Table 8 – Italian European Regional Program 2000-2006 Coherent Projects.

Axis	Absolute Values (mln €)	% Financial Endowment	% Identified Projects
Natural Resources	4,173	54.5	38.9
Cultural Resources	794	31.5	26.6
Human Resources	1,542	18.6	15.8
Local Development Systems	4,092	27.7	22.4
Towns	1,433	70.2	44.6
Infrastructural Investments	8,377	85.7	64.0
Technical Assistance	23	2.6	2.5
Total	20,434	44.5	34.7

Source: Svimez (2010).

Indeed only 55.5% of the 45.9 billion Euro allocated for this program was spent on projects (see Table 8). The remaining 44.5% was allocated to coherent projects. They represent a share of 34.7% of the value of the approved projects. The difference between the percentage of the value of the approved projects and the higher percentage of coherent projects – relative to the total executed projects – is explained by the fact that a share of the project approved remained unfinished, so that the value of the projects executed was smaller[12].

10. Concluding remarks and policy implications

Most research on the effectiveness of the European Regional Programs for the convergence of less developed regions analyze the issue by connecting the execution of these programs to the economic performance of these regions. Research, generally, concludes that the programs did not have satisfactory results, from the perspective of growth, except in particular cases. These studies, however interesting, are mostly macroeconomic studies. They do not focus on the institutions and procedures, and related performance of these plans in the context of the resulting projects. Here we consider the European-Italian process which has been originated and implemented under the Regional Operational Program of Calabria 2000-2006, in the area of valorization of cultural goods for the development of tourism. We have demonstrated that its complex targeted structure, with its apparent rigorousness, allowed for discretionary behavior of politicians and of the bureaucracy in charge of its execution. The result was a proliferation of projects that did not pursue any priority and that in a large proportion remained incomplete.

Our empirical analysis for Calabria's case study has shown that reasons connected with pressure groups, rather than cultural and touristic objectives explain the allocation of the funds. There is no significant statistical statistic relationship between the important cultural sites and the allocation of funds. Furthermore, the regression with the approved project has shown that the presence of at least one museum is not significant, as for the allocation of per capita funds to the municipalities. Also the presence of schools – whether of primary or secondary education – does not seem relevant, while the presence of high schools is relevant with a negative impact. It seems that since these municipalities are already some important public cultural institutions, they do not need attention as for the allocation of POR' s funds for culture. A similar consideration may explain the *L&P*'s (libraries and publishers) negative influence on the allocation of these funds. The presence of an academic institution (*University*) increases the funds assigned.

12 The analysis of the composition of the funds allocate to coherent project instead than to the European Regional Program for Sothern Italy shows that the highest percentage regards infrastructures and natural resources (mostly agriculture). The lowest percentage regards human resources and local systems. Clearly in these last areas the pressure groups minimized the amount of funds unspent out of the European Development Programs.

This result might provide evidence that where there is a University, the capability of presenting projects suited for approval tends to increase, likely because of the greater competence and intellectual prestige of their authors. On the other hand, one can notice that in LAD estimate *University* is not significant and that in IRLS estimate the explanatory variable *University* doesn't have a statistical relevance. Touristic attractors tend to have a negative impact on dependent variable, and are not significant in the lad estimate. The variables *A&C&A* (hotels, camping, farm-holidays), *TV&R* (television and radio stations), and *A&P* (aero-terminals and ports) which are relevant for tourism, are not statistically significant yet. On balance, one can argue that cultural goods as attractors of tourism were neglected in the allocation of Calabria's POR funds for culture. However, this had been possible because the program allowed discretionary powers to be granted to the regional bureaucracies and politicians. But one cannot put the blame primarily on them, since Calabria's POR was constructed in that way following the European and Italian guidelines and had the approval of the Italian Government and of the European Commission.

Consider the flow of visitors are money to the cultural sites in 2000 when the program was not yet operational and in 2007 after its completion it emerged that these flows, for the museums and other sites that were considered in the official statistics decreased by 11 % in terms of visitors and by 16 % in terms of revenues. The opposite happened in Italy, with an increase of about 14 % in the number of visitors and nearly 30 % in the amount of revenues. On the other hand, tourism in Calabria between 2000 and 2007 experienced a great increase of both arrivals (nearly 45 %) and presences (nearly 39 %), with a relevant increase of 78.3 % in the foreign tourists. Calabria's tourism thus grew at a rate much greater than the average Italian rate, in spite of the failure of the POR for culture to operate as a stimulus for its growth. And one may, therefore, argue that the taxpayers' resources were wasted.

11. Suggestions for future researches

Here we considered the institutions and effects of the European Policy for the development of the less developed regions via the Regional funds, focusing on Calabria's cultural sector and its impact on tourism, which is potentially a very important axis for the development of Calabria and, more generally, for Southern Italy. What emerged was that the excess of targeted planning allowed a discretionary behavior of the bureaucracy and of the politicians who were inefficient, demonstrated a lack of effectiveness, and fostered rent seeking.

More generally, there is a strong need for further detailed scientific research on the allocation and impact of European Structural Funds, also in relation to the new convergence and cohesion Program 2007-2013. It is paradoxical that on the one hand EU maintains that tax exemptions for the less developed regions economy of the community distort market competition, while on the other hand, the EU taxpayers' money finances projects supposedly promoting convergence and cohesion in these regions provided that they derive from a regional plan following EU planning guidelines.

References

Abdi H. (2007), Bonferroni and Sidak Corrections for Multiple Comparisons, in Salkind N. J. (ed.), *Encyclopedia of Measurement and Statistics*, Thousand Oaks: Sage.

Agresti A. (1990), *Categorical data analysis*, New York: Wiley.

Altman D. G., Andersen P. K. (1989), Bootstrap investigation of the stability of a Cox regression model, *Statistics in Medicine*, 8, 771-783.

Basile R., De Nardis S., Girardi A. (2001), Regional Inequalities and Cohesion. Policies in the European Union, *ISAE Working Paper*, 23.

Beugelsdijk M., Eijffinger S. C. W. (2003), The effectiveness of Structural Policy in the European Union: An Empirical Analysis for the EU-15 in 1996-2001, *Journal of Common Market Studies*, 43, 1.

Bjorvatn K., Coniglio N. D. (2006), Policy Design and Rent Seeking. Targeted versus Broad Based Interventions, *Review of Development Economics*, 10, 4, 577-585.

Bjorvatn K., Coniglio N. D. (2007), How Should Industrial Policy be Designed in Developing Countries, *S.E.R.I.E.S. Working Paper*, 14.

Borbalá-Szabó E. (2007), EU Programs and Funds and their Impact on the Development of the Hungarian Economy, www.euconsent.net.

Cancelo J. R., Faína J. A., López-Rodríguez J. (2009), Measuring the Permanent Impact of European Structural Funds on Peripheral Objective 1 Regions: The Case of Galicia, *European Planning Studies*, 17, 10, October, 1535-1558.

Cappelen A., Castellacci F., Fagerberg J., Verspagen B. (2003), The Impact of EU Regional Support on Growth and Convergence in the European Union, *Journal of Common Market Studies*, 41, 4, 641-644.

Chatterjee S., Hadi A. S. (2006), *Regression Analysis by Example*, New York: Wiley.

Cini M. (2007), *European Union Politics*, Oxford: Oxford University Press.

Colbert F. (2000), *Marketing delle arti e della cultura*, Milano: Etas Libri.

Cole I. M., Chawdhry M. A. (2002), Rent Seeking and Economic Growth: Evidence from a Panel of EU States, *The Cato Journal*, 22, 2.

Commission of the European Communities (2009), *Commission Staff Working Document. Accompanying the 20th Annual Report of implementation of the structural funds*, Brussels: Commission of the European Communities.

Congleton R. D., Hillman A. L., Konrad K. A. (eds., 2008), *Forty Years on Research on Rent Seeking*, Berlin: Springer.

Cook R. D. (1977), Detection of influential observations in linear regression, *Technometric*, 19, 15-18.

Cooper G., Fletcher J., Gilbert D., Shepherd R., Wanhill S. (1998), *Tourism. Principles and Practice*, New York: Addison Wesley Longman Publishing.

Derksen S., Keselman H. J. (1992), Backward, forward and stepwise automated subset selection algorithms: frequency of obtaining authentic and noise variables, *British Journal of Mathematical and Statistical Psychology*, 45, 265-282.

Dreger C., Rahmani T., Eckey H.-F. (2007), Economic Convergence and Rent Seeking in Iran, *DIW Discussion Paper*, 741.

Ederveen S., de Groot H., Nahuis R. (2006), Fertile soil for Structural Funds? A panel data analysis of the conditional effectiveness of European cohesion policy, *Kyklos*, 59, 1, 31-55.

Ederveen S., de Mooij R., Gorter J., Nahuis R. (2002), Funds and games: The economics of European cohesion policy, *CPB Discussion paper*, 3.

Ederveen S., Gorter J. (2002), Does European cohesion policy reduce regional disparities? An empirical analysis, *CPB Discussion paper*, 15.

Eggert, W., von Ehrlich M., Fenge R., König G. (2007), Convergence and Growth. Effects of the European Regional Policy in Germany, *CIE Center for International Economics Working Paper*, 3.

European Commission (1997), *Agenda 2000 for a stronger and wider Union*, Brussels: Commission of the European Communities.

European Commission (2001), *Unity, solidarity, diversity for Europe, its people and its territory. Second Report on Social Cohesion*, Brussels: Commission of the European Communities.

European Union Regional Policy (2008), *Cohesion Policy 2007-2013. National Strategic Reference Frameworks*, Brussels: Commission of the European Communities.

Fischer P. (2006), *Rent-Seeking, Institutions and Reforms in Africa*, Berlin: Springer.

Forte F., Mantovani M., Skepys (2011). Rent seeking, non profits and Criminal Hubs: the case of Calabria, *Journal of politics and Law* Vol. 4 No. 1 March 2011 *Canadian Center of Science and Education* P. 36-51 (print end on line)

Forte F., Mantovani M. (2004), *Manuale di economia e politica dei beni culturali*, Soveria Mannelli: Rubbettino.
Forte F., Mantovani M. (2009), Cooperatives' Tax Regimes, Political Orientation of Governments and Rent Seeking, *Journal of Politics and Law*, 2, 4, December, 44-57.
Diggles K. (1986), *Guide to Arts Marketing: the Principles and Practice of Marketing as They Apply to Arts*, London: Rhinegold.
Gelauff G., Grilo I., Lejour A. (eds., 2008), *Subsidiarity and Economic Reform in Europe*, Berlin: Springer.
Gelauff G., Stolwijk H., Veenendaal P. (2005), Europe's financial perspectives in perspective, *CPB document*, 101.
Goldoni D., Rispoli M., Troncon R. (eds., 2006), *Estetica e management nei beni e nelle produzioni culturali*, Bolzano: Il Brennero.
Golley Y. J. (2007), *The Dynamics of Chinese regional development: market nature, state nurture*, Cheltenham: Edward Elgar.
Gourieroux C., Monfort A., Trognon A. (1984), Pseudo Maximum Likelihood Methods: Theory, in *Econometrica*, 52(3), May, 681-700.
Grossi R., Debbia S. (eds., 1998), *Cantiere Cultura. Beni Culturali e Turismo come risorse di sviluppo locale*, Milano: Federculture/Il Sole-24 Ore.
Gratteri N., Nicaso A. (2006), *Fratelli di sangue*, Cosenza: Pellegrini.
Hamilton C. L. (1992), *Regression with Graphics: A Second Course in Applied Statistics*, Pacific Grove: Brooks/Cole.
Hirshmann E. C. (1983), Aesthetics, Ideologies and the Limits of the Marketing Concept, *Journal of Marketing*, 47, Summer.
Imbriani C., Giannola A. (eds., 2003), *Neo-dualismo: Istituzioni, mercati e politiche di intervento*, Soveria Mannelli: Rubbettino.
Jarque C. M., Bera A. K. (1987), A Test for Normality of Observations and Regression Residuals, *International Statistical Review*, 55, 163-172.
Koenker R., Baxistt G.Jr. (1978), Regression Quantiles, *Econometrica*, 46(1), 33-50.
Kotler P., Scott W. G. (1998), *Marketing Management*, Torino: Isedi.
Li G. (1985), Robust Regression, in Hoaglin D. C., Mosteller F., Tukey J. W. (eds.), *Exploring Data Tables, Trend and Shape*, New York: Wiley, 281-343.
Lo Cicero M., Reganati F. (2003), *L'economia del Mezzogiorno d'Italia. Nuovi caratteri del dualismo e le variabili per misurarlo*, in Imbriani C., Giannola A. (eds.), *Neo-dualismo: Istituzioni, mercati e politiche di intervento*, Soveria Mannelli: Rubbettino.
Loddo S. (2006), Structural funds and regional convergence in Italy, *CRENoS Working Paper*, 3.

Mantel N. (1970), Why stepdown procedures in variable selection, *Technometrics*, 12, 621-625.
Mantovani M. (2006), Alcune riflessioni sulla politica fiscale per i distretti turistici e culturali, in AA. VV., *Annali 2006 del Dipartimento di studi Geoeconomici, Linguistici, Statistici, Storici per l'Analisi Regionale*, Rome: Sapienza University.
Mantovani M. (2008), *Lezioni di economia pubblica dei beni culturali*, Torino: Giappichelli.
Mantovani M. (2010), Le politiche regionali della Calabria per i beni culturali e nel quadro degli incentivi dell'UE 2000-2006, Spadaro A. (ed., 2010), *Istituzioni e proposte di riforma. Un progetto per la Calabria*, Napoli: Jovene.
Mantovani M., Skepys (2011). Rent seeking, non profits and Criminal Hubs: the case of Calabria, *Journal of politics and Law* Vol. 4 No. 1 March 2011 *Canadian Center of Science and Education* P. 36-51
McCullagh P. (1983), Quasi-likelihood Functions, *Annals of Statistics*, 11, 59-67.
Midelfart-Knarvik K. H., Hoverman H. G. (2002), Delocation and European integration: Is structural spending justified?, *Economic Policy*, 17, 35, October, 321-359.
Nantel J. A., Colbert F. (1992), Positioning cultural arts products in the market, *Journal of Cultural Economics*, 16, 2, December, 63-71.
Nelder J. A. (1989), *Generalized Linear Models*, London: Chapman & Hall.
Pregibon D. (1980), Goodness of link tests for generalized linear models, *Applied Statistics*, 29, 15-24.
Puga D., European regional policies in light of recent location theories, *Journal of Economic Geography*, 2, October, 373-406.
Ramsey J. B. (1969), Tests for Specification Errors in Classical Linear Least Squares Regression Analysis, *Journal of Royal Statistic Society*, 31(2), 350-371.
Rodriguez Pose A., Fratesi U. (2003), Between development and social policies: the impact of European Structural Funds in an Objective 1 regions, *Grupo de Economia Europea Working Paper*, 28.
Shapiro S. S., Francia R. S. (1972), An approximate analysis of variance test for normality, *Journal of the American Statistical Association*, 67, 215-216.
Shapiro S. S., Wilk M. B. (1965), An analysis of variance test for normality (complete samples), *Biometrika*, 52, 591-611.
Spadaro A. (ed., 2010), *Istituzioni e proposte di riforma. Un progetto per la Calabria*, Napoli: Jovene.
Street J. O., Carroll R. J., Ruppert D. (1988), A note on computing robust regression estimates via iteratively reweighted least squares, *American Statistician*, 42, 152-154.

Svimez (2009a), *Rapporto 2009 sull'economia del Mezzogiorno*, Bologna: Il Mulino.
Svimez (2009b), *Dopo il rapporto Svimez 2009. Una riflessione per rilanciare la politica di sviluppo del Sud*, Roma: Svimez.
Svimez (2010), *Rapporto Svimez 2010 sull'economia del Mezzogiorno*, Bologna: Il Mulino.
Tugores J. (2008), Regional integration and public policy. Evaluation of the European experience and possible implications for Latin America integration, *Etudios y perspectivas*, 65.
Tukey J. W. (1949), One degree of freedom for non-additivity, *Biometrics*, 5, 232-242.
Van der Beek G. (2004), The Dilemma of Enlargement for the European Union's Regional Policy, *The World Economy*, 27, 4, April, 587-607.
Viesti G. (2003), *Abolire il Mezzogiorno*, Roma-Bari: Laterza.
Viesti G. (2009), *Mezzogiorno a tradimento. Il Nord, il Sud e la politica che non c'è*, Roma-Bari: Laterza.
Viesti G., Prota F. (2009), *Le politiche regionali dell'Unione Europea*, Bologna: Il Mulino.
Vision & Value, London School of Economics (2007), *EU Structural Funds and Economic Development of Southern Italy*, London: LSE.
White H. (1980), A heteroscedasticity-consistent covariance matrix estimator and a direct test for heteroscedasticity, *Econometrica*, 48, 817-838.
Zaostrovtsev A. (2003), Rent-Seeking Versus Rent-Setting: Government versus Competition. The Case of St. Petersburg, in Lane T. D., Oding N., Welfens P. J. J. (eds.), *Real and financial dynamics in Russia and Eastern Europe*, Berlin: Springer.

The Effect Of Social Structure Change On The Formation Of National Fiscal Deficit: The Case Of Taiwan

Chia-Jen Chang / Tai-Lung Chou

Abstract

According to the statistic figures of debts in which as far as either balance per year or accumulated unpaid debts are concerned, the fiscal conditions of government at every level in Taiwan are seriously worsening. Currently the actions government takes to address the fiscal deficit include increasing revenues and decreasing expenditures, privatization, deregulation, and limiting the issuance of government bonds and the debt ceiling, macro budgeting, entrepreneurial budgeting, etc. Despite all the efforts, the fiscal deficit seems not to slow down and keeps rising.

Fiscal sociology to the fiscal problem basically considers the whole society is an organic society and public finance is only part of the whole society, and they both exercise class (group) analysis to investigate the fiscal problem. In this kind of methodology, fiscal sociology considers fiscal deficit is just a syndrome. That is, the conflicts of economic benefits, no matter coming from social, production or environmental problems, will all result in the fiscal deficit, which means it is economical, political and social crisis that hides behind fiscal deficits. On the economical conflicts of classes (groups), we may use element of production or professional hierarchy as the differential criteria for fiscal interest groups.

After realizing the perspective of fiscal sociology on fiscal deficit, when we face Taiwan's fiscal deficit in the post industrial society, we may understand the forming basis for fiscal deficit by investigating the change of the basic lifestyle in Taiwan society and the transition of social organizational structure. Therefore, to systematically analyze Taiwan society's internal forming structure at this post industrial era can manage the crux of fiscal deficit.

I. Introduction

According to the recent statistical data on debts of government at all levels in Taiwan, there is a deficit of up to hundreds of billion NT dollars every year[1], which leads to the total unpaid balance of debts as high as NTD four trillion seven hundred and forty-eight billion and six hundred million as of the end of 2009, accounting for 36.7% of the average GDP of the previous three years[2] (31.9% for the central government and 4.8% for the local government). Therefore, both the flow (surplus and deficit through the year) and storage (unpaid balance of accumulated debts for government at every level) problems tend to be enormously exacerbated.

The foregoing financial difficulties not only hamper the government's enforcement capability but also have influences on various governance areas such as

1 Table 1-1, Yearbook of Financial Statistics, R.O.C., (2009).
2 Table 7, Yearbook of Financial Statistics, R.O.C., (2009).

national defense, diplomatic affairs, economic development, social security, education, science and culture, as well as environmental and natural resources. For this reason, how to mitigate the financial dilemma has become an urgent and vital issue for Taiwan.

The current attitude of Taiwan government toward fiscal deficits is based on the neoclassical economic theory and public choice theory; thus, the government's coping strategy focuses on the government budgeting aspect, including increasing revenues and decreasing expenditures, privatization, deregulation, limiting the issuance of government bonds and the ceiling of debts, macro budgeting, and entrepreneurial budgeting, etc. However, the strategy is merely a stopgap measure, because it seems not to be associated with more extensive economic, social or political systemic problems, nor can it link together with all interactions of numerous communities in the society.[3]

Fiscal sociology stresses on political, economic and social problems hidden behind from the perspective of national fiscal budget. It sees changes of fiscal revenues and expenditures as an approach to understanding the transformation of role and function of the nation. Namely fiscal sociology, emphasizing structural association among the parts which constitute the society, considers the whole society an organic society and public finance only part of the whole society[4]. Just as what is argued by Goldscheid who proposes fiscal sociology, the fiscal procedure should be placed as the center of national activities, and we should interpret

---

3 Backhaus, J. Fiscal Sociology: What for? American Journal of Economics and Sociology, Vol.61, no.1, (2002).
Bell, Daniel, The Public Household – On Fiscal Sociology and Liberal Society, in The Public Interest, No.35, (1974).
Hobson, John M. The wealth of states: A comparative sociology of international economic and political change, Cambridge: Cambridge University Press, (1997).
Hobson, John M. The State and International Relations. Cambridge: Cambridge University Press, (2000).
McLure, Michael, An Italian Foundation for New Fiscal Sociology: A Reflection on the Pareto-Griziotti and Pareto-Sensini letters on Ricardian Equivalence and Fiscal Theory, University of Western Australia, Economics Discussion Paper No.03.11, (2003).
McLure, Michael, Approaches to Fiscal Sociology, in: Jurgen G. Backhaus (eds), Essays on Fiscal Sociology, Frankfurt: Peter Lang, (2005).
McLure, Michael, The Fiscal Sociology of Gino Borgatta: Pareto, Extra-Economic Redistribution and Economic Growth, Cambridge Journal of Economics, Vol. 30, Issue 4, (2006).
Moore, Mick, Revenues, State Formation, and the Quality of Governance in Countries, International Political Science Review, Vol. 25, No.3, (2004).
Schumpeter, Joseph A. The Crisis of the Tax State, in Alan T. Peacock ed., International Economics Papers, no.4, MacMillan, (1954).

4 Goldscheid, Rudolf (1967), A Sociology Approach to Problem of Public Finance, in: Classics in the Theory of Public Finance, Musgrave, R. A. and T. Peacock (eds), Macmillan, London.

fiscal deficits through social and financial status of most households and their effect on the society.

With the acknowledgement, we regard fiscal deficit a "syndrome", what hide behind are social concerns derived from conflicts of economic interests among different social hierarchies. For the fiscal deficit, we should focus on economic, political and social problems resulted from the change of basic lifestyle and transformation of social organizational structure to examine reasons for fiscal deficits.

Undoubtedly, Taiwan has entered the post-industrial society[5], and basic lifestyle and social structure have changed. Therefore, the study approach, fiscal sociology, would be a proper paradigm[6]. In this article, we also examine the fiscal deficit of Taiwan in post-industrial society based on the theoretical foundation of fiscal sociology[7].

II. Analysis Structure Of Fiscal Deficits In Fiscal Sociology

This section first depicts the analysis structure of national fiscal deficits from the perspective of fiscal sociology and, next, explains that the paradigm of neo-classical economic theory is not suitable for analysis of Taiwan's fiscal deficits while the paradigm of fiscal sociology that considers the effect of social structural transformation on fiscal deficits is more applicable to the current status of Taiwan in the post-industrial society after democratization, and, at last, emphasizes that the increasing competition for financial resources in the post-industrial society is the conflict of economic interests between professional hierarchies and between professional and non-professional hierarchies.

---

5 Both Bell (1973) and Block (1990) take the number of employees and output value of the tertiary industry to characterize the post-industrial society. Thus, we may determine that Taiwan has entered the post-industrial society since 1988 when the number of employees in the service sector exceeded that of employees in industrial sector, or 1989, if we take the contribution of the service sector to GNP as the threshold. Wan-I Lin (2008) and Bih-Hearn Lee (1994) also consider that Taiwan has marched into the post-industrial society after 1988 or 1989.

6 The concept of paradigm is proposed by Kuhn (1962), who defines scientific paradigm as 'accepted examples of actual scientific practice, examples which include law, theory, application, and instrumentation together – [that] provide models from which spring particular coherent traditions of scientific research. Men whose research is based on shared paradigms are committed to the same rules and standards for scientific practice' (Suh-Der Tsen et al., 2005: 246).

7 For the methodology of fiscal sociology and study approaches for fiscal problems, please refer to the report by Chia-Jen Chang (2008: 35-55) for details.

2.1 Analysis Structure Of National Fiscal Deficits

According to fiscal sociology, fiscal deficit is a "syndrome", showing impacts on the transformation of social structure due to progress in production technology and changes in relations of production, as well as social problems derived from the conflicts of economic interests arising as a consequence of the social structural transformation.

In addition, fiscal deficits simply reveal the balance of revenue and expenditure in accordance with a number of laws and regulations, while these laws and regulations represent the exercise of governmental functions. What's more important, governmental functions are determined by social structure formed at a certain economic base, as indicated by the directional arrow of the dotted line in Figure 1 - - ➔ (fiscal deficit - - ➔ revenue, expenditure - - ➔ laws and regulation - - ➔ social structure - - ➔ economic base). Therefore, the problem of fiscal deficits is by no means solved through "increasing revenues and decreasing expenditures" proposed by neoclassical economic theory.

To examine the political, economic and social problems hiding behind fiscal deficits, we should first understand the economic base of social structure and the impact of social structural transformation, as well as its influence on laws and regulations, revenues and expenditures, as indicated by the directional arrow of the solid line in Figure 1 ⟶ (economic base ⟶ social structure ⟶ laws and regulations ⟶ revenue, expenditure ⟶ fiscal deficits). Besides, it is more than the association between fiscal deficits and economy, as indicated by the directional arrow of the dotted line in Figure 1 ··········➤[8]

Therefore, the key of the political, economic and social problems behind fiscal deficits lies in social structure formed by the economic base. To examine the change of basic lifestyle and transformation of social structure, especially to analyze the internal structure systemically in the post-industrial society, would help us understand reasons for fiscal deficits.

In general, social problems behind fiscal deficits are developed from social force under the social structure formed at a certain economic base. Through the outcome from political and economic systems, unquantifiable social relationship is reflected in government budget under the post-industrial society based on monetary transactions[9].

8 Huang, Shin-Hsin Social Development Strategies 2010 (Research report by Financial and Economic Section), Research valuation Commission, Executive Yuan, (2003), p. 100.

9 Huang, Shin-Hsin, Welfare State vs. Fiscal Deficit? 'Castrated' Contemporary Fiscal Theory, Seminar of Social Welfare and Economic Development, Taipei: Chinese Economic Association (1994.5.7).

Figure 1: Analysis structure of fiscal deficits.

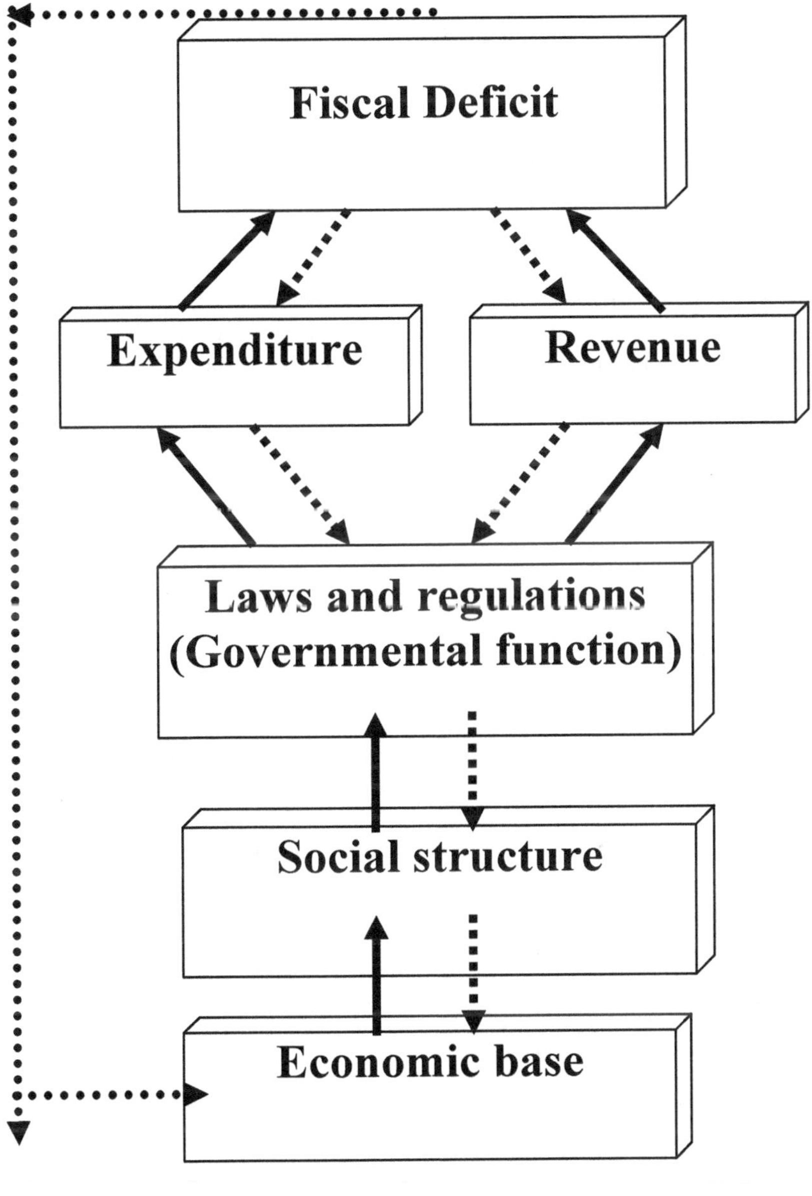

2.2 *Paradigm-Shift Of Study On National Fiscal Deficits*

From Figure 1, the study on neoclassical economic theory for fiscal deficit crisis merely focuses on the impact of revenues and expenditures on fiscal deficits, which explains the reasons for fiscal deficits with the gap between revenues and expenditures and addresses such problem by increasing revenues and decreasing expenditures. This kind of paradigm is suitable for an economic and social environment which is controllable by the government.

In terms of studies on fiscal deficits, the public choice theory, however, stresses on the effects of laws and regulations on revenues and expenditures, which thereby influences the formation of fiscal deficits. The theory considers how fiscal deficits are formed during the course of budget decision making under democratic system. Although the paradigm involves discussion about fiscal and budget systems in democratic society to identify causes of fiscal deficits, it ignores the impact of social structural factors on laws and regulations (governmental functions) and thus has no idea about how it came into being.

In the post-industrial society under democratization, fiscal sociology considers the impact of social structure on laws and regulations (governmental functions) and consequently the impact on revenues and expenditures, which bring fiscal deficits eventually. We may understand how the fiscal deficit develops with such paradigm, which is more suitable for addressing national fiscal deficits in Taiwan social and economic environment currently.

2.3 *Examining Taiwan's Fiscal Deficits By Professional Hierarchy As Fiscal Interest Groups*

Regarding the fiscal interest group in fiscal sociology, Goldschied suggests the group consists of the nation, capitalists and labors[10], Schumpeter, individual and collective[11], and Pareto, Griziotti and Borgatta, speculators and rentiers[12].

10 Goldscheid, Rudolf, A Sociology Approach to Problem of Public Finance, in: Classics in the Theory of Public Finance, Musgrave, R. A. and T. Peacock (eds), Macmillan, London, (1967).

11 Schumpeter, Joseph A. The Crisis of the Tax State, in Alan T. Peacock ed., International Economics Papers, no.4, MacMillan, (1954).

12 McLure, Michael, An Italian Foundation for New Fiscal Sociology: A Reflection on the Pareto-Griziotti and Pareto-Sensini letters on Ricardian Equivalence and Fiscal Theory, University of Western Australia, Economics Discussion Paper No.03.11, (2003).
McLure, Michael, Approaches to Fiscal Sociology, in: Jurgen G. Backhaus (eds), Essays on Fiscal Sociology, Frankfurt: Peter Lang, (2005).
McLure, Michael, The Fiscal Sociology of Gino Borgatta: Pareto, Extra-Economic Redistribution and Economic Growth, Cambridge Journal of Economics, Vol. 30, Issue 4, (2006).

Besides, O'Connor suggests the group is among different levels and organizations in society[13], while Musgrave argues that the fiscal interest group is affected by income sources, hobbies and types of household expenditures and age[14].

In consideration of change of basic lifestyle and transformation of social organizational structure in Taiwan society, these perspectives given above are not suitable for interpretation. As Perkin puts, competition for social resources in the post-industrial society does not lie between levels based on production factors but between professional hierarchies and between professional and non-professional hierarchies. As a result, the professional hierarchy can be used as standards for categorization of the fiscal interest group and also suitable for analysis of Taiwan's current fiscal deficits.

In Figure 1 "Analysis structure of fiscal deficits", the social structure is changed due to the variation of production technology in the post-industrial society; what's important is "the whole society is organized and controlled by professional elites", where the competition for fiscal resources emphasizes conflicts of economic interests between professional hierarchies and between professional and non-professional hierarchies, which is different from previous literature about Taiwan's fiscal deficits stressing the competition for fiscal resources between production factors or between labors and capitalists.

III. The Change Of Basic Lifestyle And Transformation Of Social Organizational Structure In Taiwan

The change of basic lifestyle and transformation of social organizational structure in the post-industrial society in Taiwan, including the progress in production technology, the trends toward the post-industrial society, structural corruption, and conflicts of economic interests between professional elites and the public, can be briefly described in Table 1.

---

13 O'Connor, James, The Fiscal Crisis of the State, ST. Martin's Press, (1973).
Loxley, John, Fiscal Sociology and the Fiscal Crisis of the State, Contemporary Crises, Vol.6, (1982).

14 Musgrave, Richard A. Theories of Fiscal Crises: An Essay in Fiscal Sociology, in Aaron, Henry J., Michael J. Boskin (eds), The economics of Taxation, Brookings Institution, Washington, (1980).
Musgrave, Richard A. Schumpeter's Crisis of the Tax State: An Essay in Fiscal Sociology, Journal of Evolutionary Economics, Vol.2, (1992).

Table 1: The change of basic lifestyle and transformation of social organizational structure in Taiwan.

Progress in production technology	The third social revolution is a revolution in human social organizations, which changes the relationship between people, resulting in transformation of social structure.
Trends toward the post-industrial society (the society is organized and controlled by professional elites.)	1 Enhancement of the living standard. 2 Transformation from agriculture and industry to service sector. 3 Transformation from class conflicts to conflicts between professional hierarchies. 4 The professional hierarchy adds new members through meritocracy. 5. Increase in female employment rate. 6 Governmental control power over the whole social economic resources. 7 Promotion of the concept of civil rights. 8 Expansion of higher education. 9 Emergence of larger-sized enterprises. 10 Influences of economic globalization.
Structural corruption	Professionals in public sector "cooperate" with professionals in private sector to exploit the public jointly.
Conflicts of economic interests between professional elites and the public	1 Conflicts of economic interests between individual and collective. 2 Conflicts of economic interests for distribution of tax burden. 3 Conflicts of economic interests for government expenditures. 4 Conflicts of economic interests for distribution of corporate profits.
Political, economic and social problems behind national fiscal deficits	Uneven distribution of "economic power" between professional elites and the public.

This section first depicts the trends toward the post-industrial society and the issue of structural corruption in Taiwan, while conflicts of economic interests between professional elites and the public will be discussed in Section IV.

3.1 Trends Toward The Post-Industrial Society In Taiwan

There are trends toward the post-industrial society in Taiwan social structure[15], including the enhancement of the living standard; professional elites (profes-

15 For details about these trends, please refer to the report by Chia-Jen Chang (2008: 60-74).

sional managers of cross-border companies and government officials) place at the top of social class controlling the economy of the whole society, distributing income and arranging social relationship; conflicts of economic interests between professional elites and the public; biased meritocracy brings about effects of factors (income, in particular) other than capabilities on the formation of professional elites; enhancement of female education and labor force participation rate; governmental control power over the whole economic resources appearing to be on the increase, however, declining in recent years; robust, but yet adequate, social security system; gradual increase in the number of persons receiving higher education; and steadily growing effects of professional elites from large or multi-national companies on the government. Of course, the most important is that Taiwan society organized and controlled by the increasing number of professional elites (most of whom are company managers and government officials). These trends justify[16] that Taiwan is now situating in the post-industrial era.

However, structural corruption between professional elites from public and private sectors is a vital factor during the course of conflicts of economic interests between the public and professional elite. For this reason, before examining conflicts of economic interests in Taiwan, we have to discuss about problems of structural corruption in Taiwan.

---

16 There ten trends are referenced from Perkin (1996: 8-20). Besides, Bell (1973) outlines ten trends in the post-industrial society as follows: 1. Importance of theoretical knowledge: Materialization of theoretical knowledge and material science as the basis for technology innovation; 2. Application of new intellectual technology: With new algorithms and economic methods, we may use model, simulation and systemic analysis to deliver a more effective and reasonable solution for economic and engineering problems; 3. Expansion of knowledge hierarchies: Technology and professional hierarchies saw the fast growth; 4. Professionalism and technology: Services in the post-industrial society refer to services to people (healthcare, education and social services) and professional and technological services; 5. Changes in types of work: In the post-industrial society, work is a competition among people; 6. Increase in female employment: In an industrial society, most job opportunities are provided to men, while in the post-industrial society jobs for women would be heavily promoted; 7. Transformation of science: Science is closely correlated with the needs of technology, military and society; 8. Working place is a unit of conflicts of political interests: In the post-industrial society, analysis focus on working places, the vertical hierarchy is a key target for politics; 9. Meritocracy: Reward in the post-industrial society is based on an individual's education and technology; 10. Abundance of goods: Despite abundance of goods, there are problems of lack of time and information in the post-industrial society. Block (1990) argues that there are trends in the post-industrial society such as the development of information technology, role of females and family structural transformation, rapid growth in service sector and professionalism.

3.2 Issue Of Structural Corruption In Taiwan

From the trends in the preceding paragraph that describe the post-industrial society of Taiwan, we may understand the transformation of the economic social structure in Taiwan. In the post-industrial society, the major conflict of economic interests would be the competition for the ideology "government vs. market" among professionals. The potential conflict could be: one side is the individualism enthusiastic about free market, while the other goes for dealing with social problems in a more collective way; or, alternatively, we may say that one side is against government interference while the other regards the government the protector of common interests. All professionals on both sides claim that they provide the best way for prosperity of the society and fair distribution of income.

This is a kind of competition between professionals from public and private sectors. Professionals from public sector intend to extend their services, because they are profoundly convinced that social justice and social cohesion are the optimal way to recall the cooperation will required for economic growth. By contrast, professionals from private sector (mainly managers of large companies and their right-wing media supporters) want fewer public expenditures and lower tax rates and uphold free market.

However, from the following discussion, it is found that, for distribution of social economic resources, professionals from public sector "cooperate" with professionals from private sector for joint exploitation of the public, which is namely a problem of structural corruption, leading to conflicts of economic interests among professional elites and non-professionals. The so-called structural corruption indicates built-in rewards; this system, to cooperate with elites so that exploitation and uneven distribution of income would carry on forever, provides politicians, officials and corporate managers with "profitable" positions or compensation for loss of job. It is the built-in rewards offered to the social elites through a system they have developed to ensure exploitation and uneven distribution of income[17]. The phenomenon exactly reflects Taiwan's unique heritage, social structure and political system.

Professionals from public and private sectors are not completely separated; there is a linkage connecting them to somewhat extent, showing how they exploit social resources jointly and turn public benefits into private interests (from direct bribery to legislative favoritism), where the public share all costs arising as a consequence. In Taiwan, professionals from public and private sectors are connected in the following manners, listed in Table 2, to bring about structural corruption problems.

---

17 Huang, Shin-Hsin, Chien-Chung Kuo (2006), Q&A for Debate on 18% and Measures for Reasonable Reform, Policy Research Journal, Vol.6, p. 34

Table 2: Issues of structural corruption in Taiwan[18]

Types of structural corruption	Current status in Taiwan society
Same ideology of professionals from public and private sectors	1 Ideology of free market 2 Freedom of professional elites
Political donation	1 Large companies provide economic support for politicians. 2 Penalty for violation of the conflict of *interest avoidance provision is excessively small.* 3 Currently election campaigns require large financial resources.
Fusion of professionals from public and private sectors	1 Legislators hold concurrent posts in profit-making businesses. 2 Business owners act as advisors to government decision-making.

1. Same Ideology Of Professionals From Public And Private Sectors

(1) Ideology Of The Free Market

Professionals from public and private sectors have the same ideology for free market, which is an obvious historical legacy for Taiwan. Politically there are left wing and right wing; Economically, however, most professionals from both public and private sectors are right-wing followers who, just as discussed earlier, propose strategies such as "increasing revenues and decreasing expenditures", "rational budget decision", and "limiting the issuance and ceiling of government bonds", etc to address fiscal deficits. Based on the theory of neoclassical economic theory, these strategies echo market-oriented economy and care about nothing but economic growth without reasonable distribution of economic resources.

(2) Freedom Of Professional Elites

Taiwan's free market has become a place where large conglomerates and their professional managers may freely do whatever they want. In Taiwan, these conglomerates replace market mechanism with management and coordination; they internalize transactions, use price negotiation between buyers and suppliers in place of planning between departments, and develop a multi-departmental struc-

18 Data source: Summarized by the authors.

ture instead of independent companies. What's more, they manage employees with fixed payroll scale, constant promotion period, additional benefits, and pension fund, etc.

The key to mass production and distribution is no more Adam Smith's "invisible hands" but the "visible hands" of professional managers, who plan every step from purchasing materials, fuels and parts to marketing. For managers who promote free market, what they have done is completely the opposite of what they have claimed to do; free market is just a mask that they use to conceal their greed[19].

2. *Political Donation*

Politicians participating in elections have direct connections with these conglomerates. With financial support from the conglomerates to the politicians (e. g. providing political donations to partisan candidates), the problem of structural corruption is growing worse. According to Taiwan's Political Donations Act passed in 2004, Article 8 states that "Political donations may not be contributed to ask for or in the expectation of undue benefits"; however, violators are only subject to administrative penalty, as specified in Article 26: "Penalty shall be twice the amount of the political donation". In addition, in accordance with the Legislators' Conduct Act promulgated in 2002, despite interest avoidance clause stated in Chapter 5, any legislator who violates the Act will be sent to the discipline committee for consideration. Therefore, how effective the Political Donations Act and the Legislators' Conduct Act are is questionable; or it is possible that these acts are simply tools for "endorsement" of the politicians.

While the political donations with special purposes blur political motives of the politicians, politicians have forgotten civil basic rights for reasonable distribution of economic resources. As described in the preceding paragraph, political parties in Taiwan are convinced of the superiority of market economy, lacking clear differences between their types of ideology. They can only highlight differences between the parties with marketing strategies. However, elections require "propaganda" through TV, newspaper and other electronic media, which is quite expensive and also strengthens political influences of enterprises. Eventually, politicians become the enterprises' "staff."

---

19 Perkin, Harold, The Third Revolution: Professional Elites in the Modern World, London and New York: Routledge, (1996), p. 29

Under such circumstances, the government actively gives support to enterprise, which can never be helpful for surveillance of the enterprise but allow them to affect government decision making instead[20].

3. Fusion Of Professionals From Public And Private Sectors

In addition to affecting professionals from public sector with money, professionals from private sector also use "fusion" to boost their ties. The case of Taiwan is introduced below.

(1) Legislators Holding A Concurrent Post In Profit-Making Enterprises

According to congress evaluation data released by the Taipei Society 2007, of all the legislators of the Sixth Legislative Yuan, there were 41 legislators holding a concurrent post in other profit-making enterprises, including 13 KMT (Kuomintang) legislators (Nan-Sheng Lin, Sheng-Liang Liu, Bing-Kun Chiang, Cheng-Yuan Tsai, Chun-Hsiao Chu, Hsien-Rong Lee, Ming-Tsai Lo, Chin-Long Tsai, Hsio-Ching Chen, Kuang-Shun Wu, Fu-Hsing Lee, Chih-Bin Chen, and Erh-Chang Tsao); 6 PFP (People First Party) legislators (Chun-Te Lin, Jung-Gi Chung, Hsueh-Chang Lu, Ding-Guo Fong, Chin-Ling Cheng, and Hong-Chun Lee); 15 DPP (Democratic Progressive Party) legislators (Wen-Lang Lin, Chien-Hui Huang, Chi-Fang Tsai, Shih-Chien Wang, Lai-Wang Tsao, Cheng-Liang Kuo, Hsio-Hui Chen, Ming-Chen Chen, Chao-Lung Chen, Huo-Sheng Tang, Kuo-Chung Cheng, Hsin-Ni Hsieh, Cheng-Dao Yu, Chin-Hsing Lin, and Ho-Tzu Chuang); 2 TSU (Taiwan Solidarity Union) legislators (Cheng-Che Huang and Tsong-Yuan Huang); and 6 non-partisan legislators (Ho-Shun Lee, Chin-Ting Chen, Ching-Piao Yen, Bing-Kun Lin, Li-Shan Chang, Tsong-Che Yang)[21]. In this case, it is obvious what kind of decision legislators will make when there's conflict between interests of profit-making businesses and public interests.

(2) Business Owners Acting Advisors To Government Decision-Makingg

Upon formulation of policies on tax or public expenditures, the *Six* big associations of industry and commerce are the first target for consultation for the Min-

20 For details about close ties between politicians and enterprises in Taiwan, please refer to the report by A-Rong Liu (2003).

21 This does not include the possible use of 'figureheads' that has substantial influences on profit-making businesses in private sector.

istry of Finance[22]. The six big association include Chinese National Association of Industry and Commerce (Chairman Mao-Hsiung Huang, also Chairman of Teco Electric and Machinery Co., Ltd), Chinese National Federation of Industries (Chairman Wu-Hsiung Chen, also Chairmen of Ho Tung Group), Central Chamber of Commerce ROC (Chairman Pen-Tsao Chang, also President of Taiwan International Securities Group), National Association of Small and Medium Enterprises (Chairman Ping-Pin Lin, also Chairman of Triad International Corp.), Taiwan Federation of Industry (Chairmen Cheng-Chia Lee, also Chairmen of Maywufa Group) and Taiwan Electrical and Electronic Manufacturers' Association (Chairman Yu-Cheng Chiao, also Chairman of Winbond Electronics Corp.). Since members of these six major associations are business owners, inevitably the negotiation results are favorable to these professional elites.

Figure 2: Agree that the government favors consortiums?[23]

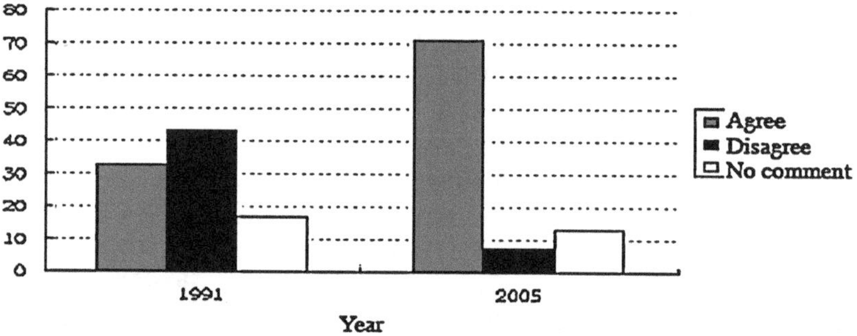

From poll surveys, we can also understand the public concern about the gradually increasing "influences of consortiums on the government". According to Figure 2, professionals from public and private sectors are fused together in one group. In 1991, only 30 % of Taiwanese people considered that the government favors consortiums, but in 2005 there were over 70 % of Taiwanese people believed that the government gives undue preferences to consortiums.

To sum up, there are few differences between public and private professional sectors. They share the same way of thinking and money flow. That is to say,

22 Integrated income tax system, land value increment tax 50 % cut, decrease in *financial* institutions sales tax rate, and formulation of the alternative minimum tax system are clear examples. For details, please refer to the reports by Chien-Cheng Yang and Chia-Jen Chang (2005) and Shin-Hsin Huang (2005).

23 "A full record of Transformation of Taiwan society", Institute of Sociology, Academia Sinica. http://www.ios.sinica.edu.tw/TSCpedia/index.php/%E8%B2%A1%E5%9C%98%E7%9A%84%E6%94%BF%E6%B2%BB%E5%BD%B1%E9%9F%BF%E5%8A%9B.

politicians, officials and entrepreneurs have close ties in many areas. It is hardly know who affects decision making.

Although professionals from public and private sectors are in confronting positions regarding tax and public expenditures, eventually the result always shows a win-win situation for both; namely, tax is reduced, but expenditures are not cut accordingly, and therefore fiscal deficits are inevitable. Just as we have proposed at the beginning of this section, for distribution of social economic resources, professionals from public sector "cooperate" with professionals from private sector for joint exploitation of the public. The next section, from an aspect of conflicts of economic interests, will explains how severe Taiwan's structural corruption problem is and its effect on governmental functions and fiscal revenues and expenditures.

IV. Conflicts Of Economic Interests And Changes In Governmental Functions Resulted From The Transformation Of Social Structure

From the discussion about structural corruption in the previous section, it is understood that in Taiwan society there exist conflicts of economic interests, which come from the conflict between professional elites and the public. With several key aspects such as "conflicts of economic interests for distribution of economic resources between individual and collective", "conflicts of economic interests for distribution of tax burden", "conflicts of economic interests for government expenditures" and "conflicts of economic interests for distribution of corporate profits", we intend to explain how the public are exploited by professional elites and the outcome of the exploitation.

Finally, we are going to explain that, under these conflicts of economic interests, governmental functions in society and economy are gradually limited, failing to provide a regulatory system for reasonable distribution of private property right and fair and free competition, in terms of conflicts of economic interests between professional elites and the public.

Besides, according to fiscal sociology mentioned earlier, how professional elites exploit the society and the outcome depends on Taiwan's unique historical heritage, social structure and political system. The conflicts of economic interests between professional elites and the public, major influential factors for social structure and actual outcomes and influences are listed in Table 3.

Table 3: The aspect of conflicts of economic interests between professional elites and the public, major influential factors for social structure, and actual outcomes and influences[24].

Aspect of conflicts of economic interests	Influential factor for major social structure in a society organized and controlled by professional elites	Actual outcomes and influence
Conflicts of economic interests for distribution of economic resources between individual and collective	1 Transformation from class conflicts to conflicts between professional hierarchies. 2 The professional hierarchy adds new members through meritocracy. 3 Expansion of higher education. 4 Emergence of larger-sized enterprises. 5 Influence of economic globalization.	1 Children in economic minority families are at a disadvantage in seeking investment opportunities for human capital. 2 Distribution of land and natural resources depends on distribution of income and wealth, same as an ordinary commodity 3 Capital completely privatized
Conflicts of economic interests for distribution of tax burden	1 Transformation from class conflicts to conflicts between professional hierarchies. 2 Governmental control power over the whole social economic resources. 3 Emergence of larger-sized enterprises. 4 Influence of economic globalization.	1 Constant decrease in tax rate 2 Huge amount of tax exempt due to Statute for Upgrading Industries. 3 Low real tax burden for high-income taxpayer 4 Low real tax burden for high-profitable enterprises 5 Decrease in tax burden rate.
Conflicts of economic interests for government expenditures	1 Transformation from class conflicts to conflicts between professional hierarchies 2 Promotion of the concept of civil rights 3 Emergence of larger-sized enterprises 4 Influence of economic globalization	1 Insufficient social security expenditures 2 Government subsidy for certain industries
Conflicts of economic interests for distribution of corporate profits	1 Transformation from class conflicts to conflicts between professional hierarchies. 2 Governmental control power over the whole social economic resources 3 Emergence of larger-sized enterprises 4 Influence of economic globalization	1 Labor force exploited by labor market 2 De-professionalization of the middle class 3 Economic recession attributed to labors 4 Absolute property

24 Data source: Summarized by the authors.

4.1 Conflicts Of Economic Interests For Distribution Of Economic Resources Between Individual And Collective

In the conflicts of economic interests for distribution of economic resources between individual and collective, there are several influential factors for social structure: "transformation from class conflicts to conflicts between professional hierarchies", "professional hierarchies adds new members through meritocracy", "expansion of higher education", "emergence of larger-sized enterprises" and "economic globalization".

In terms of "Transformation from class conflicts to conflicts between professional hierarchies", because of competition for ideology of professional elites, one side is the individualism enthusiastic about free market, while the other goes for dealing with social problems in a more collective way; or, alternatively, we may say that one side is against government interference while the other regards the government the protector of common interests. All professionals on both sides claim that they provide the best way for prosperity of the society and fair distribution of income.

In terms of "professional hierarchy adds new members through meritocracy", a society constituted by professional hierarchies requires a method that can add new specialists, especially those who are elites at the top of all structures with economic and political power. However, this system favors certain types of people, such as those who are loyal to a political party or have higher income, social status or eminent family background. As a result, social mobility facilitated by capabilities through school education is limited; reversely, unequal power domination among existing social classes is legitimatized. From a perspective of resource distribution, most economic resources are private, lacking economic resources shared by collective.

In terms of "expansion of higher education", a professional society needs well-trained labor force and a population, most of which are people with higher education. Therefore, the opportunity of investment in human capital has become a ripe target for economic competition between professional elites and the public.

In terms of "emergence of larger-sized enterprises", professional managers of large companies take initiative to expand their market share and thus make an utmost effort to privatize all national economic resources, so that they can become entrepreneurs who have influences on the government's decision making process.

In terms of "economic globalization", large conglomerates compete for market share, raw materials, and cheap labor force not only within the country; some multinational corporations may own factories, mines, oil wells and banks in a number of nations, and their business volume even exceeds a country's GNP. Hence, these market players also want to become multinational companies with decisive influences on government policy of privatization in many nations.

These social structure factors affect the distribution of economic resources between individual and collective and governmental functions, which is namely one of the effects of social structure on laws and regulations (governmental functions), stressed by fiscal sociology.

We may explain the conflicts of economic interests in Taiwan based on the deepening privatization of production factors (labor force, land and capital)[25], which has made a majority of economic resources belong to individuals.

1. Labor Force

Because in the post-industrial society the labor productivity is determined by the investment in human capital, whether opportunities of investment in human capital are equal is closely correlated with whether economic resources can be shared among contributing persons.

According to the Constitutional provisions (Taiwan), Article 159 specifies that "All citizens shall have an equal opportunity to receive an education"; Article 160 specifies that "All children of school aged from 6 to 12 years shall receive free primary education. Those from poor families shall be supplied with book by the Government"[26]; Article 161 specifies that "The national, provincial, and local government shall extensively establish scholarships to assist students of good scholastic standing and exemplary conduct who lack the means to continue their school education"; and Article 163 specifies that "The State shall pay due attention to the balanced development of education in different regions, and shall promote social education in order to raise the cultural standards of the citizens in general. Grants from the National Treasury shall be made to frontier regions and economically poor areas to help them meet their education and cultural expanse. The Central Government may either itself undertake the more important educational and cultural enterprises in such regions or give them financial assistance".

In the Educational Fundamental Act, Article 4 stipulates that "All people, regardless of their sexes, ages, abilities, geographic locality, ethnic groups,

---

25 Referring to the report by Shin-Hsin Huang (1998: 145-152).

26 Article 2 of the National Education Act stipulates that 'all children must attend six years of elementary school and three years of junior high school between the ages of six and 15. Exceptions to this rule are children with special needs and children receiving alternative forms of education.'

religious beliefs or political ideas, social or economic standings or other conditions, have equal opportunity for receiving education. Special protection on the education for indigenous peoples, the physically or mentally challenged or other disadvantaged groups shall be provided with considerations of their autonomy and special characteristics in accordance with relevant laws and regulations to support their development."

From the provisions of the Constitution and the Educational Fundamental Act, the opportunities of investment in human capital (i. e. accepting education) are equal in Taiwan. However, under the high education system with costly tuition, income has become a key factor for the right to education. In a situation where tuition rises without limitation, there will be more students in economic minority families at a disadvantage in seeking investment opportunities for human capital.

Besides, with a trend of professionalism in the post-industrial society, the technology level of labor force is upgraded, but intensive competition and rapid transformation of industrial structure are accompanied with unemployment or highly unsteady employment rate, in which case, the protection of employment opportunities has become more important.

According to the Constitution Taiwan, Article 15 specifies that "The right of existence, the right to work and the right of property shall be guaranteed to the people"; and Article 152 specifies that "The State shall provide suitable opportunities for work to people who are able to work". For policies on employment security, the Enforcement Measures for Unemployment Benefits was promulgated in 1998 and the Employment Insurance Act has been enforced since 2003.

2. *Land And Natural Resources*

Land and natural resources feature geographical characteristics and constraints; they cannot be freely transferred through transportation[27] and therefore belong to collective. Only when an individual demands for production of agriculture, industry or business, can these resources be private for transaction.

The land privatization in Taiwan is regulated in Article 143 of the Constitution, "All land within the territory of the Republic of China shall belong to the whole body of citizens. Private ownership of land, acquired by the people in accordance with law, shall be protected and restricted by law. Privately-owned land shall be liable to taxation according to its value, and the Government may buy such land according to its value. Mineral deposits which are embedded in the land, and natural power which may, for economic purpose, be utilized for

27 Huang, Shin-Hsin, Introduction to public finance, National Open University, (1998), p. 149.

public benefit shall belong to the State, regardless of the fact that private individuals many have acquired ownership over such land. If the value of a piece of land has increased, not through the exertion of labor capital, the State shall levy thereon an increment tax, the proceeds of which shall be enjoyed by the people in common. In the distribution and readjustment of land, the State shall in principle assist self-farming land-owners and persons who make use of the land by themselves, and shall also regulate their appropriate areas of operation".

From the Constitutional provision stated above, land and natural resources belong to all citizens. A citizen may acquire land ownership based on his/her need, on which there are constraints such as land value tax and land value increment tax. They are not ordinary commodities; where necessary, the government may expropriate or purchase a land by declared land value.

However, in Taiwan, land and natural resources are deemed ordinary commodities. Moreover, they are capitalized or securitized. If we treat land and natural resources as investment targets, then they will lose they're subject. In 2003, for example, real estate securitization began in Taiwan. Article 1 of the Clauses of Real Estate Securitization Act provides that "This Act is enacted for the purpose of developing national economy, improving the liquidity of real estate through securitization, providing additional fund-raising channels for real estate so as to efficiently develop and utilize real estate, promoting environmental quality, activating the real estate market, and protecting investment". In this regard, distribution of land and natural resources depends on distribution of income and wealth, same as an ordinary commodity.

Regarding farmland, there were two clauses of the Land Act deleted in January 2000, Article 30 "That transfer of ownership to private farmland may be made only to a transferee capable of cultivating the land by himself" and Article 30-1 "If a farmland heir is not capable of cultivating the land by himself, the farmland shall be divided to those capable of cultivating the land by themselves", in coordination with the Agricultural Development Act, under which non-owner-*farmers are entitled to purchase* farmland. Under Article 18 of the Agricultural Development Act, "Farmers, who had acquired agricultural lands after the enactment of this revised Act of January 4, 2000 and do not possess a farmhouse for their own use, may apply for the construction of a farmhouse in accordance with related construction laws and regulations of land use". In accordance with these regulations, farmland has become an ordinary commodity used for construction of high-end mansions. The distribution also determines distribution of income and wealth.

3. Capital Aspect

Capital is a tool created by people. If excessively concentrated, capital will become a tool for exploitation. Capital itself cannot be self-restraint and therefore should be regulated by the government.

According to the Constitution Taiwan, Article 142 specifies that "National economy shall be based on the Principle of People's livelihood and shall seek to effect equalization of land ownership and restriction of private capital in order to attain a well-balanced sufficiency in national wealth and people's livelihood"; Article 144 specifies that "Public utilities and other enterprises of a monopolistic nature shall, in principle, be under public operation. In cases permitted by law, they may be operated by private citizens" and Article 145 specifies that "With respect to private wealth and privately operated enterprises, the State shall restrict them by law if they are deemed detrimental to a balanced development of national wealth and people's livelihood".

In Taiwan which is affected by the theory of free market economy, generally the accumulation of private capital is encouraged. For example, decreasing income tax, security trading income *tax exemption, enforcement of* the Statute for Upgrading Industries, lowered estate or gift tax, and privatization of state-owned businesses[28] suggest that capital has been completely privatized.

Due to conflicts of economic interests for distribution of labor force, land and capital between individual and collective in Taiwan's current post-industrial society discussed above, most of the economic resources belong to private individuals while few belong to the nation (collective), and exploitation will arise from uneven competition because of unreasonable distribution of economic resources, thereby leading to unreasonable distribution of output.

4.2 Conflicts Of Economic Interests For Distribution Of Tax Burdenn

Regarding conflicts of economic interests for tax burdens, there are several social structure influential factors: "transformation from class conflicts to conflicts between professional hierarchies", "governmental control power over the whole

28 Although these corrupted elites become more accommodated and kind, they do not lose their greed for fortune; contrarily, they abuse and occupy the nation's property. Seemingly, privatization of state-owned businesses distribute national resources to people; however, improperly designed implementation processes and systems have turned privatization into conglomeration. The government's fiscal revenue increase though, a fiscal resource disappears, from a long-term perspective.

social economic resources", "emergence of larger-sized enterprises" and "economic globalization".

In terms of "transformation from class conflicts to conflicts between professional hierarchies", professional hierarchies demand lower tax rate and less government interference, while private companies also hopes that the government spends more on their products and services. Therefore, professional hierarchies propose the concept of the Laffer curve and the trickle-down theory as a theoretical basis for government subsidy to enterprises as well as tax abatement. The Laffer curve suggests that lower tax rate would generate more tax revenues; and the economic policy on trickle-down distribution argues that other people may benefit from the tax preferences for the rich, as corporate managers would distribute corporate profits to employees and the public.

In terms of "governmental control power over the whole social economic resources", the government gives tax preferences to support emerging strategic industries through the Statute for Encouragement of Investment and the Statute for Upgrading Industries. Regardless the ratio of government revenues to GNP, both the ratio of government employees to total labor force and from the structure of gross domestic fixed capital formation suggest that governmental control power over the whole social economic resources appear to be on the decrease; governmental functions are gradually limited. Despite this, tax preferences to professional hierarchies are always supported.

In terms of "emergence of larger-sized enterprises", professional managers of large companies and government officials keep proposing an intravenous model of capital investment as an excuse for tax rate reduction and tax preferences. They try to persuade the public of their views that a higher tax rate for profit-seeking businesses or individuals with higher income will prevent the capital from flowing in the economic system, and thereby impose an adverse effect on economic growth and productivity[29].

In terms of "economic globalization", power of a cross-border company may be far more than a sovereign state. Without military forces, a multinational company may have power to urge or guide the government (otherwise they would withdraw investment from the country). Therefore, regardless of in developing or developed countries, politicians are waiting in line to solicit foreign investment with free land resources, existing infrastructures and tax holidays. Therefore, with regard to conflicts of economic interests for distribution of tax burdens, they can always enjoy tax exempt or decreases in tax rate.

29 Block, Fred, Postindustrial Possibilities: A Critique of Economic Discourse, university of California Press, (1990), p. 152.

These social structure factors may affect the distribution of tax burdens and governmental functions, which meets the perspective of fiscal sociology, justifying the importance of social factors for the distribution of tax burdens.

Thus, we first describe current regulations on tax reduction and constant decreases in tax rate of the tariffs; next, we observe tax burdens between professional elites and non-professionals to explain a common situation. In conflicts of economic interests for distribution of tax burdens, non-professionals play a major role in fiscal burden of the nation. At the last part, we depict that tax rate reduction and tax reduction enable Taiwan's tax burdens to decline.

1. Decreases In Tax Rate And Tax Reduction

From observation of decreases in income tax, business tax, land value increment tax, estate or gift tax over the years and major tax reduction under the Statute for Upgrading Industries[30], it is clear that mostly individuals with high income and profit-seeking business enjoy the tax reduction and tax rate reduction[31].

(1) Decrease In Tax Rate

In terms of decreases in tax rate, the top marginal income tax rate for profit-seeking enterprises dropped from 35% to 30% in 1985, further down to 25% in 1986, 20% in 2009 and 17% in 2010. The top marginal consolidated income tax also declined from 60% to 50% in 1986 and then to 40% in 1990. In addition, the integrated income tax system began applicable to consolidated income tax and profit-seeking enterprise income tax in 1998.

Regarding business tax, the sales tax system which had been based commodity tax was transformed to be a system based on value-added business tax in 1987. This is a tax system where single-stage manufacturing tax was replaced by multi-stage net sales tax. In this system, business tax for the banking industry had dropped from 5% to 2% in 1999 and then was exempted in 2002[32].

Besides, there were three classes of land value increment tax rate, 40%, 50% and 60%.; however, from February 1, 2002 to January 31, 2005, the land value increment tax was cut by 50% and in 2005 was adjusted to be 20%, 30% and

30 Five-year tax exempt, accelerated depreciation, and investment tax credits, etc.

31 According to Table 18 Mean and Median Disposable Income of Income Recipients by Occupation, the report of household revenue and expenditure survey 2008 by the Directorate-General of Budget, Accounting and Statistics, Category I Legislators, government administrators, business executives and managers and Category II Professionals have highest income.

32 Cancelled in 2005.

40%[33]. Furthermore, the top marginal estate or gift tax rate was reduced from 50% all the way to 10% in 2009.

(2) Tax Reduction

In 1991 the Statute for Encouragement of Investment was substituted by the Statute for Upgrading Industries, Statute for Upgrading Industries, in which major tax reduction include accelerated depreciation, investment tax credits, and tax exempt, etc., as specified in Articles 5-19 and Article 70-1.

These tax reductions were amounted to 1,180 billion from July 1992 to the end of 2009, including income tax reduction of 1,160 billion approximately, from which we may understand that Statute for Upgrading Industries focuses on income tax. During the same period, the amount of income tax revenues was about 8,180 billion; the ratio of tax reduction under the Statute for Upgrading Industries to total income tax revenues appeared to be on the rise and reached as high as 30.65% in 2009, with an average of 14% above[34], as shown in Table 4.

33 For formulation of policies on decreases in consolidated income tax and the integrated income tax system for business income tax, business tax relief for banking industry, decreases in the land value increment tax, please refer to the report by Chien-Cheng Yang and Chia-Jen Chang (2005) for details.

34 Under the Statute for Upgrading Industries, formerly known as the Statute for Encouragement of Investment, the total tax reduction accumulated to NTD528.6 billion from 1961 to 2005, in which income tax reduction was about NTD380 billion, equal to 5.5% of the real amount of income tax. (Data source: Table 72, Yearbook of Financial Statistics 2005).

Table 4: Ratio of tax reduction under the Statute for Upgrading Industries to total income tax revenues[35]
Unit: Thousand NTD, %

Fiscal Year	Income tax revenue	Tax reduction under Statute for Upgrading Industries	Tax reduction under Statute for Upgrading Industries (income tax)	Ratio of tax reduction under the Statute for Upgrading Industries to total income tax revenues
1993	237,618,241	5,915,892	5,535,878	2.33
1994	266,020,141	12,226,216	10,110,313	3.80
1995	319,383,860	13,459,489	12,439,679	3.89
1996	343,550,020	14,511,349	13,352,281	3.89
1997	352,890,477	26,255,479	25,224,826	7.15
1998	398,390,232	34,717,336	33,245,655	8.34
1999	432,388,876	47,188,859	44,941,992	10.39
2000	610,580,021	83,677,344	81,348,275	13.32
2001	478,636,373	65,308,027	61,043,570	12.75
2002	392,939,078	36,263,935	34,557,584	8.79
2003	411,086,972	54,910,156	54,836,663	13.34
2004	455,913,822	53,139,368	52,314,562	11.47
2005	625,807,052	83,406,303	83,299,187	13.31
2006	646,217,799	119,462,825	119,356,561	18.47
2007	730,159,866	180,501,472	180,433,165	24.71
2008	834,988,400	151,261,020	151,228,500	18.11
2009	640,966,779	196,681,848	196,484,205	30.65
Total	8,177,538,009	1,178,886,918	1,159,752,896	14.18

Data Source: Table 72, Yearbook of Financial Statistics 2005.

35 Conversion according to Table 3-1 and Table 3-24, Yearbook of Financial Statistics 2009; and Table 2 and Table 17, Yearbook of Financial Statistics 2007. 1993-1999 are July fiscal years while 2001-2009 are calendar fiscal years (2000□July 1999 to December 2000).

2. Distribution Of Tax Burdens Between Professional Hierarchies And Non-Professional Hierarchies

According to the poll survey of "opinions on tax reform related issues" released by the Research, Development and Evaluation Commission of Executive Yuan on July 21, 2005, 85.9% of the respondents believed that successful enterprises and individuals with high income to whom tax reduction apply only pay relatively few tax, which is quite unfair.

(1) Lw Real Tax Burden For High-Income Taxpayer

From the observation of the ratios of individual's various types of income to total income 1995-2007, it is found that 70% of the consolidated income tax came from income from salaries and wages and only 20% from capital gains[36], in which income from interest was decreasing year by year, while income from stock dividend was increasing. According to the distribution of consolidated income tax income brackets in 2007, income from salaries and wages was concentrated on low-income levels while capital gains, especially income from stock dividend, on high-income levels, as shown in Tables 5 and 6.

Table 5: Ratios of individual's various types of income to total income 1995-2007[37]
Unit: %

Year	income from salaries and wages	business income	income from stock dividend	income from interest	income from lease and royalty	income from property transaction
1995	72.15%	5.50%		15.39%	2.23%	0.31%
1996	72.30%	5.26%		15.37%	2.22%	0.29%
1997	72.65%	5.95%		14.49%	2.21%	0.29%
1998	71.79%	7.48%		14.30%	2.16%	0.22%
1999	70.88%	2.86%	6.21%	13.87%	2.12%	0.20%
2000	70.40%	2.46%	8.63%	12.66%	2.09%	0.18%
2001	70.88%	2.03%	9.08%	12.26%	2.12%	0.13%
2002	74.12%	2.21%	8.00%	9.11%	2.17%	0.18%
2003	75.65%	2.54%	9.11%	6.18%	2.17%	0.20%
2004	75.83%	1.97%	10.32%	5.11%	2.12%	0.24%
2005	73.73%	1.92%	12.21%	5.38%	2.13%	0.24%
2006	73.31%	1.94%	11.95%	6.37%	2.18%	0.26%
2007	72.34%	1.88%	12.78%	6.80%	2.09%	0.26%

36 Most of which are income from interest, business income, income from dividend, lease and royalty, and income from property transaction.

37 Conversion according to Table 106, Yearbook of Tax Statistics 2007 and Table 3-11, Yearbook of Financial Statistics 2009, Ministry of Finance.

Table 6: Distribution of income brackets for consolidated income tax 2007[38]
Unit: Thousand NTD, %

Income bracket (NTD10,000)	Total income of the income bracket	Income from salaries and wages	Business income	Income from stock dividend	Income from interest	Income from lease and royalty	Income from property transaction
0	480,686,351	72.99	3.55	5.95	12.89	1.82	0.28
0-37	1,345,784,928	81.90	1.66	5.21	7.18	1.53	0.23
37-99	1,151,197,634	78.71	1.58	7.89	6.59	1.94	0.24
99-198	712,418,158	73.07	1.68	12.06	6.01	2.56	0.26
198-372	404,196,267	65.46	1.56	17.96	5.31	3.08	0.30
372-500	109,680,146	56.97	1.55	24.56	4.55	3.48	0.32
500-1000	97,377,487	46.85	1.44	33.85	3.68	3.53	0.35
1000 above	249,703,508	20.60	2.80	65.65	1.46	1.93	0.38

Besides, the tax system is also developed toward tax separation. For example, under Article 14-1 of the Income Tax Act, from January 1, 2010, the following income received by an individual shall not be added to the gross consolidated income, but withheld in accordance with the provisions of Article 88 at the rate of 10%:

1. The portion of the pecuniary amount realized by short-term commercial papers at their maturity in excess of the selling price at their initial issuance is deemed as income from interest.
2. The interest distributed from beneficiary securities or asset-backed securities issued in accordance with the Financial Asset Securitization Act and the Real Estate Securitization Act.
3. The interest derived from repo (RP/RS) trade whereby an individual purchases securities or short-term commercial papers as described in the preceding paragraph and Subparagraphs 2 and 3 in this paragraph shall be the net amount of the sale price at their maturity in excess of the original purchase price.
4. Income from transactions in structured products between individuals and securities firms or banks.

Income from transactions of securities and futures shall be suspended in accordance with Article 4-1 and 4-2 of the Income Tax Act

These regulations and figures show big victory of managers of high-income companies over low and middle income taxpayers whose income come from

38 Conversion according to Table 106, Yearbook of Tax Statistics 2007 and Table 3-11, Yearbook of Financial Statistics 2009, Ministry of Finance.

salaries and wages. As a result, in the post-industrial society of Taiwan, low and middle income taxpayers afford most of the consolidated income tax.

(2) Low Real Tax Burden For High-Profitable Enterprises

According to data of profit-seeking enterprise income tax return 2004, the number of companies applying for tax reduction was positively correlated with income throughout the year; 1/1000 high-income companies which earned nearly 500 million or more accounted for nearly 46 % of tax reduction under the Statute for Upgrading Industries.

With 61.80 % of profit of all companies, these companies had tax payable accounting for 62.22 % of total tax payables. These two percentages were almost the same. However, they enjoyed 86.03 % of total tax reduction, while they simply recorded a total actual tax rate paid of 45.71 %, representing a gap of 16.51 %. What's worse, in 1/1000 of these high-income companies (earning nearly 500 million or more throughout the year) in 2004, there were 63 companies enjoying tax reduction and paying no business tax actually under the Statute for Upgrading Industries[39].

In 2005, for example, TSMC (Taiwan Semiconductor Manufacturing Company) registered a net profit before tax of 93.8 billion yet an income tax expense of 200 million, representing a tax rate of 0.26 %. FPG (Formosa Plastic Group) had a tax rate of 12 %; however, (Formosa Chemicals and Fiber Corp.) paid no tax even it recorded a net profit before tax of nearly 40 billion. NPC (Nan Ya Plastic Corp.) also achieved a net profit before tax of 41 billion but only paid an income tax expense of only 1.1 billion, representing a tax rate of 2.76 %. Cathay *Financial* Holdings earned a net profit before tax of 21.9 billion and paid an income tax of 200 million, representing a tax rate of 0.91 %; Mega *Financial* Holdings made a net profit before tax of 22.1 billion with an income tax expense of minus 400 million; and Chinatrust *Financial* Holding earned a net profit before tax of 15.9 billion, with an income tax expense of about 152 million. There were 22 large companies with profit of more than 10 billion enjoying tax reduction and paying an average tax rate of merely 8.379 %[40]

39 Yang, Chien-Cheng, (2007), Tax Preference Measures under the Statute for Upgrading Industries, Review of Integrated Income Tax system and Minimum Tax, A research project 2006 commissioned by the Taxation Agency, Ministry of Finance ROC, p. 22.

40 Huang, Chun-Sheng, Who suffers from progressive tax rate? Who benefits from tax preferences? Taiwan needs a fair and just tax system, 'New trend, new concept for discussion over tax reform of new government' forum, Chunghua Public Finance Association (2008.06.14), p. 60.

3. Decrease In Tax Burden Rate

As shown in Figure 3, the tax burden rate (the proportion of tax revenues to the *GNP*) in Taiwan was around 16%-18% in early 1980s. After 1998, subject to the integrated income tax system, decreases in business tax rate for the banking industry and incentive measures such as tax reduction and tax preferences, the tax base was shrunk; the tax burden rate decreased year by year, declined to a record low of 11.5% in 2003 and saw a slight growth subsequently. In 2005, the tax burden rate rose to 13.7%, and then dropped a little bit to 13.5% in 2006 and increased to 13.8% again in 2007.

Figure 3: Tax burden rate in Taiwan[41]

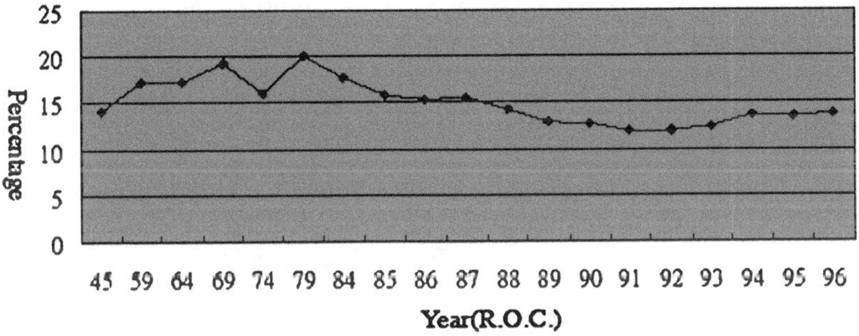

From the discussion in the three aspects, the Laffer curve and trickle-down distribution are simply a basis for rationalizing their benefits. In other words, decreases in tax rate and tax reduction are nothing but a kind of exploitation by professional elites in conflicts of economic interests for distribution of tax burdens.

4.3 Conflicts Of Economic Interests For Government Expenditures

In conflicts of economic interests for government expenditures, there are some major social structure influential factors: “transformation from class conflicts to conflicts between professional hierarchies”, “promotion of the concept of civil rights”, “emergence of larger-sized enterprises” and “economic globalization”.

With regard to “transformation from class conflicts to conflicts between professional hierarchies”, all professionals from public sector, regardless national defense, education or social welfare, wish to acquire more budgets. Alternatively,

41 Table 131, Yearbook of Tax Statistics 2007, Ministry of Finance.Table 131, Yearbook of Tax Statistics 2007, Ministry of Finance

professionals from private sector demand more government expenditures on economic development, because they think in a welfare state healthcare services and education are not human capital maintenance or creation of investment but costs for private businesses, and social welfare expenditures would affect the willingness to save money and work.

In terms of "promotion of the concept of civil rights", civil rights have evolved from equality before the law, equal rights to vote and to be elected, to equality in society, including survival rights, the right to education, right to medical treatment and right to demand a clean environment. The processes of all these changes require government social welfare expenditures.

In terms of "emergence of larger-sized enterprises" and "economic globalization", the government should provide land and infrastructures to solicit foreign and domestic investment; therefore, government expenditures have to focus on economic development.

These social structure factors affect the distribution of public expenditures and governmental functions, which exactly meets the views of fiscal sociology that argues the importance of social factors for the distribution of public expenditures.

There are also conflicts of economic interests for public expenditures between professional elites and non-professionals. In the post-industrial society of Taiwan, the biggest conflicts of economic interests for public expenditures are problems of social welfare expenditures and economic development, followed by problems of government subsidy for certain industries

1. Social Welfare Expenditure And Economic Developmen

Professional elites from Taiwan's private sector see welfare state, healthcare services and education as costs for private companies, instead of human capital maintenance or creation of investment. They believe that social welfare system will lower people's willingness to save money and work; they also argue that expansion of social welfare expenditures will have a crowding effect on economic construction expenditures, thereby affecting economic development.

Do social welfare expenditures affect national economic growth and competitiveness? Empirically, Nektarios[42] uses time series of macroeconomic variables to reason that increases in social welfare have significant effects on the willingness to save money and work. Using cross-border data for comparison, Cheng Wang and Wen-Hui Cheng[43] find a slightly negative correlation between social welfare

42 Nektarios, Miltiadis, Public Pension, Capital Formation, and Economics Growth, Westview Press, Boulder, (1982).

43 Wang, Cheng and Wen-Hui Cheng, Effect of social welfare system of economy – international comparison, Taipei: Council for Economic Planning and Development, Executive Yuan, (1995).

expenditure and economic growth. However, based on Taiwan research data, Chi-Yuan Tsai[44] and Chin-Sheun Ho[45] suggest that social welfare expenditures related to healthcare and education would help raise human capital, which may therefore boost economic growth. In conclusion, there's no consensus empirically due to different data and study approaches.

Professional elites from private sector do not know that unemployment is the result of control over inflation and poverty, the result of the increasing gap between the rich and the poor in uncontrolled free market, while crimes, drug abuse and mental disorders are results of poverty. The costs go far beyond the costs for implementation of a welfare state. Implementing a welfare state as investment in maintenance of human capital would be the cheapest and most rational solution, which is also the motivation for sustaining a professional society. That's to say, welfare state is part of the social system; it is not a cost for industries but investment in human capital and social harmony. This is a cheapest insurance against crime, drug abuse, disorders, misfortunate, and social discomfort. As the social welfare system stresses on income redistribution and functions as the guarantee for maintaining national basic survival rights, therefore a well-designed social welfare system would bring about fairness and justice, and a stable society in turn will secure investment and economic growth. For example, OECD countries, where social welfare expenditures make up a large proportion of government expenditures, often record acceptable economic performance[46].

Besides, Shin-Hsin Huang[47] also argues that under the social structure of democratic capitalism, an individual enjoys sufficient freedom in politics, economy and society. The formation of private property right system makes an individual a subject dominating economic resources. Therefore, whether an individual's economic safety is secured depends on the economic resource under his/her control.

A selfish individual with freedom and autonomy will manage to arrange his/her resources effectively; however, under uneven distribution of economic resources and unequal competitiveness, an individual with advantages will have sufficient motives and capabilities to exploit others (because of division of labor based on capitalism, market making between individuals enables a competitive

---

44 Tsai, Chi-Yuan, effect of social welfare expenditures on Taiwan's macroeconomics, Taipei: Research Center of Humanities and Social Sciences, SINICA, (1995).

45 Ho, Chin-Sheun, Macroeconomic effect of government social welfare expenditure, Taipei: Directorate-General of Budget, Accounting and Statistics, Executive Yuan.

46 Chan, Hou-Sheng and Yeun-Wen Ku, Integration of Social and Economic Policies, collected in Social Welfare Policy in New Century: The White Paper on Health – Social Welfare (Chan, Hou-Sheng and Yeun-Wen Ku eds), Taipei: Health, Welfare & Environment Foundation, (1999).

47 Huang, Shin-Hsin, Ren-Hui Hsu and Che-Chen Chang, (1994), government budget, National Open University.

market transaction relation). As a consequence, economic resources are wasted and an individual's economic security is also threatened. That is, social welfare expenditures are inevitable expenses under democratic capitalism; otherwise, people's social rights (basic living standard and economic security) cannot be protected. Only a reasonable distribution of resources is the foundation for economic growth.

In terms of Taiwan's social welfare expenditures, although the ratio of social welfare expenditures to net government expenditures rose from 6.6% in 1986 to 15.3% in 2005, and the ratio of social welfare expenditures to GNP also jumped from 1.2% in 1987 to 3.1% in 2006, there are still problems in Taiwan's social welfare system below (Executive Yuan, 2006).

First of all, Taiwan's social insurance system is not robust yet. Despite military insurance, government employee insurance, teacher insurance, labor insurance and farmer insurance in Taiwan currently, there are still 3,530,000 citizens aged between 25 and 64 without protection of economic security for the elderly[48]. Moreover, old-age benefits in labor insurance have not been annualized[49] and lack proper protection.

Second, there are chaotic payment standards for various social benefits; for the elderly, for example, have social benefits such as NTD5,000 per month for old-age farmers' welfare allowance, NTD 3,000 per month for elderly welfare benefits, NTD 6,000 per month for low-income elderly living allowance, and NTD 3,000 per month for middle-income elderly people living allowance. Besides, there are rent allowance, living allowance, medical benefits, birth allowance, and education grant, etc. for military, civil service and education personnel or their dependants.

Besides, benefits for military, civil service and education personnel are better than those for labors; in addition to various living allowances, there are pension funds for retired military, civil service and education personnel, interest subsidy for pension funds, tax exempt for military and civil service personnel, higher retirement benefit replacement rate, and health insurance subsidy for retired military personnel, etc.

In the national health insurance system, there are several problems: financial imbalances are exacerbated and the gap between premium costs is widened, health insurance revenues and expenditures lack linkage, the resource deployment mechanism is not robust yet, and medical care quality is not taken into account.

Also, because of the gradual rising ratio of elderly aged above 65, the declining number of persons per household, low birth rate, and the trend of working

48 Taiwan's National Pension Act took effect since October 1, 2008.

49 In Taiwan Labor pension began on January 1, 2009.

women, the need for long-term care system is increasing. In Taiwan, care services and education for pre-school children are going private. In 2005, the number of private nursery schools accounted for 91.9% of the total in Taiwan. The ratio of the number of children to the number of served persons was 72.1%, making child-care a heavy burden for families.

With these trends, there is still room for improvement in social welfare systems in Taiwan. This is also reflected in conflicts of economic interests for public expenditures, where professional elites have a victory over the public.

2. *Government Subsidy For Certain Industries*

Professional elites from private sector do not want government interference. Yet they demand tax relief and seek support from the government when they are in need of help.

In the post-industrial society of Taiwan, the most obvious example would be business tax of the banking industry for special use. Under Article 11 of the Business Tax Act, the current tax rate for the banking industry is still 5%, in which 3% is used to write-off of overdue debts or provision for allowance of doubtful accounts, while 2% is specially provided for the RTC (Resolution Trust Corporation) in dealing with problems of financial institutions. When the ratio of overdue debts of a financial institution is lower than 1%, write-off of overdue debts or provision for allowance of doubtful accounts will not be applicable. The fund for special use by the RTC shall be effective in 2011; however, the fund will be transferred to special reserve for insurance claims and other reserve.

The Resolution Trust Corporation (RTC) was established in July 2001. As of August 31, 2008, the RTC has dealt with 54 poorly managed financial institutions, at a total amount of NTD206.3 billion: including 36 community financial institutions in 2001, 8 community financial institutions in 2002, Fengshan Credit-Cooperative Association and Kaohsiung Business Bank in 2004, Credit Dept. of Sinpi Farmers' Association and Chung Shing Bank in 2005, Credit Dept. of Dapu Farmers' Association (merged with Chuchi Farmers' Association on March 8, 2007), Enterprise Bank of Hualien (business transaction completed on September 8, 2007), Taitung Business Bank (business transaction completed on September 22, 2007), China's *Trust* and Investment Corporation (business transaction completed on December 29, 2007) in 2007, and Chinese Bank (business transaction completed on March 29, 2008) and Bowa Bank (business transaction completed on May 23, 2008) in 2008.

By nature, as of August 31, 2008, there were 38 credit departments of farmers' associations or fishermen's association receiving funds of 49.5 billion (24%) from the RTC under applicable law; 9 credit-cooperative associations receiving about 43.3 billion (21 %); and 7 banks (including trust and investment companies) receiving about 113.5 billion (55 %)[50].

Obviously, it was a huge victory for professionals from private sector in competing for government expenditures. In addition to demanding tax relief for covering bad debts of banks due to poor management, they further expect the government to use tax revenues from the public for reconstruction of financial institutions

4.4 Conflicts Of Economic Interests For Distribution Of Corporate Profits

Principally conflicts of economic interests for distribution of corporate profits are affected by several social structure factors: “transformation from class conflicts to conflicts between professional hierarchies”, “governmental control power over the whole social economic resources”, “emergence of larger-sized enterprises” and “economic globalization”.

In terms of “transformation from class conflicts to conflicts between professional hierarchies”, professional hierarchies not only exploit labors but also “de-professionalize” the middle class”, and further attribute economic recession to employees.

In terms of “governmental control power over the whole social economic resources”, under the ideology of free market, the government takes a laissez-faire attitude toward the relation between professional hierarchies and workers in the labor force market.

In terms of “emergence of larger-sized enterprises” and “economic globalization”, the labor force at the bottom level is easily replaced by foreign labors. Furthermore, their job and income become more unsteady owing to less market demand. On the other hand, large corporations internalize transactions between buyers and sellers, replace planning and negotiation between departments with price negotiation between purchasers and suppliers, develop a multidivisional structure instead of independent firms, and manage occupational hierarchies with fixed salary scale, fixed promotion period, additional benefits and pension.

These social structure factors affect the distribution of corporate profits government functions, which exactly matches the perspective of fiscal sociology that argues the importance of social factors for the distribution of corporate profits.

According to conflicts of economic interests for corporate profits, it is found in the post-industrial society of Taiwan, professional elites use their advantage

---

50 Data References from the website of the Financial Supervisory Commission, Executive Yuan at http://www.cdic.gov.tw/ct.asp?xItem=843&CtNode=219&mp=1.

in industrial relation to privatize corporate benefits while sharing costs with the public.

1. Labor Force Exploited By Labor Market

The drastic struggle for income does not come from the poor and the middle class but the rich who sacrifice others to expand their wealth. It should be noted that some ruling elites show excessive greed. They also reduce employment of labors and cut their wages and work rights; furthermore, tasks are more often outsourced at a lower cost, resulting in the outsourced workers having to do the same amount of work but with less pay.

In a free market of capitalism, unskilled workers are the most miserable; they become a "commodity" that is easily replaced by foreign labors and their job and income are unstable. Such Blue collars are at the risk of "proletarianization", because they can be substituted by robots and cheap labors and are pushed down to the bottom unskilled hierarchy[51]

In Taiwan, average labor remuneration of each employee was NT538,658 in 2006, an increase of 7.1 % over the past five years, 15.3 % lower than that according to the census 2001. The industrial saw a growth of 11.5 %, higher than the service sector (3.8 %). Among the industries, manufacturing had the largest growth, 13.2 %, followed by real estate, 12.2 %, and then professional science and technology service, 12.1 %; support service showed a greatest minus growth of 9.2 %, as shown in Table 7.

Table 7: Variation in average labor remuneration of each employee per year in four recent Industry, Commerce and Service Censuses[52]
Unit: NTD, %.

Item	1991	1996	2001	2006
Average labor remuneration of each employee per year (NTD)	288,285	436,357	503,203	538,658
Compared with previous census (%)	71.69	51.36	15.32	7.05

51 Perkin, Harold, The Third Revolution: Professional Elites in the Modern World, London and New York: Routledge, (1996), p. 39.

52 Preliminary statistical results of Industry, Commerce and Service Census Taiwan, 2006.

By the end of 2006, there were 7,676 firms using dispatched workers. On average, there were 126,451 dispatched workers each month, in which 39,103 were used in manufacturing. In terms of the ratio of dispatch labors to employees, medical care and social work had the highest ratio of 8.6%. There were 1,409 firms engaged in dispatch business with 127,254 dispatched workers each month on average.

In terms of average labor remuneration per dollar of output and the average output value per employment over the past five years, the average output value per employee was NTD3.22 million, an increase of 30.8% over that in 2001; however, average labor remuneration per dollar of output declined by 15%. Please see Table 8.

Table 8: Productivity and labor cost for unit output in industry, commerce and services by trade[53].

Sector	Average output per employee (1,000 NTD)			Average labor remuneration per dollar of output (NTD)		
	2006	2001	Increase/ decrease rate (%)	2006	2001	Increase/ decrease rate (%)
Total average	**3 216**	**2 458**	**30.84**	**0.17**	**0.20**	**-15.00**
Industrial sector	**4 804**	**3 299**	**45.62**	**0.11**	**0.15**	**-26.67**
Mining and quarrying	4 263	2 712	57.19	0.16	0.23	-30.43
Manufacturing	5 169	3 473	48.83	0.11	0.14	-21.43
Power and fuel supply	13 412	10 508	27.64	0.09	0.12	-25.00
Water supply and pollution prevention	3 260	2 529	28.90	0.21	0.28	-25.00
Construction	2 249	1 910	17.75	0.21	0.23	-8.70
Service sector	**2 016**	**1 790**	**12.63**	**0.26**	**0.29**	**-10.34**
Wholesale and retailing	1 405	1 076	30.58	0.30	0.38	-21.05
Transportation and warehouse	3 082	2 275	35.47	0.19	0.24	-20.83
Accommodation and food services	1 185	1 239	-4.36	0.31	0.27	14.81
Information and communication	4 185	4 252	-1.58	0.19	0.20	-5.00
Banking and insurance	4 986	4 127	20.81	0.20	0.22	-9.09
Real estate	3 314	2 226	48.88	0.17	0.23	-26.09

53 Preliminary statistical results of Industry, Commerce and Service Census Taiwan, 2006.

Professional, science and technology service	2 068	1 988	4.02	0.31	0.29	6.90
Support service	843	1 138	-25.92	0.46	0.38	21.05
Compulsory social security	25 179	25 086	0.37	0.05	0.04	25.00
Educational service	686	...	...	0.48	...	...
Healthcare and social work	1 732	...	...	0.44	...	...
Healthcare service	1 987	1 993	-0.30	0.43	0.39	10.26
Residential care services	890	...	...	0.47	...	...
Other social work service	689	...	...	0.54	...	...
Art, entertainment and leisure	1 255	1 178	6.54	0.33	0.32	3.13
Other services	1 130	1 129	0.09	0.35	0.33	6.06

2. *"De-Professionalization" Of The Middle Class*

Professional elites at the top also try to break up the occupational hierarchy between "the safe middle class" and "labor force level". In a properly organized society, the middle class has steady job and high income. However, the middle class with income from salaries and wages is proletarianized. This is a world where top professional elites try to "de-professionalize" professionals they employ and increase profits by cutting labor force costs. These strategies, which have been used to fight against the Blue collars in traditional mass-production industry, are used to deal with White collars and middle-level managers of the middle class[54].

From the structure of labor remuneration and corporate rewards and the ever widening gap of income, we may find such phenomenon in Taiwan. The structure of labor remuneration and corporate rewards has shown evident changes over the past five years. The ultimate output of a corporation may be distributed by the contribution of each production factor, which can be further divided into human resource input (labor remuneration), fixed asset input (rent), capital input (interest) and corporate rewards. From the net value added for commercial and industrial factors of production 2006, labor remuneration accounts for the largest percentage (52.4%), decreased by 5.8% over 2001 (58.2%); followed by corporate rewards

54 Perkin, Harold, The Third Revolution: Professional Elites in the Modern World, London and New York: Routledge, (1996), p. 40.

(41.6 %), increased by 8.6 % when compared to 2001 (33.0 %); rent slightly rises by 4.6 %, while interest expense significantly drops to 1.5 % due to low interest rate and diversified financing tools. This indicates that when the added value created by the industry and commerce is distributed to various production factors, labor remuneration declines while corporate reward rises. Please see Table 9.

Table 9: Distribution structure of net value added for commercial and industrial factors of production by sector[55].
Unit: %

Sector	2006				2001			
	Labor remuneration	Corporate reward	Rental	Interest	Labor remuneration	Corporate reward	Rental	Interest
Total average	52.36	41.58	4.58	1.47	58.19	33.00	4.22	4.59
Industrial sector	51.04	44.54	1.44	2.98	60.09	31.05	1.58	7.28
Service sector	53.42	39.19	7.13	0.26	56.84	34.39	6.10	2.67

This shortsighted approach is self-destructive from a long-term perspective. A strategy lowering wages or dismissing employees without knowing how consumers earn money to buy their products in the future will lead to economic decline.

A laissez-faire attitude toward the labor market would widen the gap between incomes, therefore increasing unemployment rate, the poor and homeless people, crimes and violence, and tension among races, yet ignoring public infrastructures. The middle class will show their insecurity and resent, because they no longer believe they have a stable job and gradually increasing income.

However, right-wing politicians and neoclassical economic theory are trying to free themselves from responsibilities and attribute the responsibilities to victims (poor people, benefit beggars and foreign labors, etc.). Therefore, the ideology of free market has become one of tools that rationalize exploitation.

3. Economic Recession Attributed To Labors

Ruling elites are professional politicians, government officials, company managers as well as their academic partners. They attribute economic recession to labors, labor unions, growth in national expenditures and increases in social-

55 Preliminary statistical results of Industry, Commerce and Service Census Taiwan, 2006.

welfare burden; what they do not know is, it is these professional elites whose greed leads the country to annihilation. Unlike most west European countries and Japan where corporations hedge against profit squeezes by joint cooperation with labors in technology enhancement, Taiwanese businesses opt to use laborers as "scapegoats" and lower their wages with the excuse of economic struggle, or by using the weak labor union to accelerate work flow and shrink the number of in-house staff and hire low-wage workers or contracted labors instead.

4. Absolute Property

The concept, absolute property, is deeply rooted in Taiwan. Every object has its unique owner, while a company exclusively belongs to its shareholders. This situation is similar to what is in the USA and UK. Conceptually Taiwanese businesses are owned by their shareholders alone, therefore other stakeholders (employees, creditors, etc.) can be ignored.

Under such property right structure of companies, the ownership belongs to distant, anonymous shareholders. Thus, the corporate goal is not to acquire long-term growth or investment in future product but short-term benefits, giving high rewards to shareholders and executive managers in exchange of sustaining stock value to face merge and acquisition and challenges. Without continuing innovation to increase interests for stakeholders, managers only care about the next balance sheet and tomorrow's stock price.

An individual has an absolute property. With such concept of absolute property, market liberals deduct individualism and the theory of free market. Under the free market system, professionals from the private sector extract more resources from society. Besides salaries and year-end bonus, they have a great sum of stock options (leaders give themselves rewards) and transfer corporate ownership from shareholders to managers. In this way, a CEO of a company becomes an owner-manager in the post-industrial society. These managers are interested in changing what they control into permanent properties without paying any effort, which, of course, is done in an excuse of free market. For them, freedom of market represents the freedom to acquire corporate ownership without paying a price; however, legally they are just servants of their companies[56].

56 Perkin, Harold, The Third Revolution: Professional Elites in the Modern World, London and New York: Routledge, (1996), pp. 190-92.

4.5 Transformation Of Governmental Functions Under Conflicts Of Economic Interests

According to the four aspects of conflicts of economic interests discussed above, professional elites from public and private sectors gain a victory over other members in Taiwan. This suggests a dangerous tendency in a professional society; namely, elites who control cash flow and have the advantages of domination gather more resources for themselves. The danger is not only unfairness but many other social symptoms (crimes, drug abuse, homeless, or mental disorders) due to resentment or anger, which is also what Marx calls, "*contradiction* of *capitalism*", contradiction arising from unfair distribution of social resources.

Therefore, governmental function are gradually limited in the economy, failing to establish a regulation governing conflicts of economic interests for distribution of property between professional elites and the public as well as fair and free competition.

In terms of conflicts of economic interests for distribution of economic resources between individual and collective, since economic resources such as labor, land and capital are gradually privatizing, the nation's economic resources of collective ownership are declining. Such unreasonable distribution of economic resources will lead to unfair competition and then irrational distribution of output.

In terms of conflicts of economic interests for distribution of tax burdens, because tax base is shrunk and the tax rate is decreased little by little, the government's ability to raise funds is challenged. Under the principle of "revenues according to expenditures", the government fails to provide people with public goods and services from tax revenues, thereby relying on the issuance of government bonds.

In terms of conflicts of economic interests for government expenditures, because professional elites ignores positive effects of social welfare expenditure on economic growth and competitiveness of the nation, and they consider that social welfare expenditures only have crowding effects on economic development expenditures, social welfare expenditures will appear to be insufficient. As a result, there's much room for improvement in sustaining basic living right of the people for the government.

And in terms of conflicts of economic interests for distribution of corporate profits, as the ideology of free market prevails, both the labor class and the middle class take responsibility for economic recession, while corporations expect the government to liberalize labor market; consequently, the government's protection of labor's work right is becoming weaker over time.

V. Taiwan's Fiscal Deficit Problem From A Perspective Of Fiscal Sociology

Like the perspective of national fiscal deficits argued by fiscal sociology, reasons for national fiscal deficits shall be analyzed in the process: economic base →, social structure →, laws and regulations → , revenues, expenditures → , fiscal deficits. With discussion about the analysis process, we may identify reasons, specified as follows, for fiscal deficits in the post-industrial society of Taiwan. *5.1 ECONOMIC BASE* Since Taiwan entered the post-industrial society in 1988 or 1989, the progress in production technology has led to revolution in social organization that changes relationship between people and results in the transformation of Taiwan's social structure.

5.2 Social Structure

The progress in production technology changes production relation which, in the post-industrial society of Taiwan, brings about changes in basic lifestyle and transformation of social organizational structure in the following scenarios: enhancement of the living standard; professional elites (managers of multinational companies and government officials) at the top of social class dominate the whole economy, distribute income and arrange social connections; conflicts of economic interests between professional elites and the public; biased meritocracy brings about effects of factors (income, in particular) other than capabilities on the formation of professional elites; enhancement of female education and labor force participation rate; governmental control power over the whole economic resources appearing to be on the increase, however, declining in recent years; robust, but yet adequate, social security system; gradual increase in the number of persons receiving higher education; and steadily growing effects of professional elites from large or multi-national companies on the government. Of course, the most important is that the society of Taiwan gradually became organized and controlled by professional elites (most of whom are company managers and government officials).

5.3 Conflicts Of Economic Interests Under Structural Corruption

Under the transformation of social structure, the distributions of "economic resources", "tax burdens", "government expenditures" and "corporate profits" have shown a big victory of professional elites over the public.

1. Conflicts Of Economic Interests For Distribution Of Economic Resources Between Individual And Collective

According to results of conflicts of economic interests: (1) children in economic minority families are at a disadvantageous position in seeking investment opportunities for human capital; (2) distribution of land and natural resources depends on distribution of income and wealth, same as an ordinary commodity; and (3) capital is completely privatized.

In other words, under the post-industrial society of Taiwan, resources such as labor, land and capital are distributed between individual and collective, shrinking resources of the nation. Most economic resources are private; such unreasonable distribution of economic resources results in unfair competition and leads to irrational distribution of output.

2. Conflicts Of Economic Interests For Distribution Of Tax Burden

Results of conflicts of economic interests show: (1) constant decreases in tax rate (2) a huge amount of tax exempt due to Statute for Upgrading Industries (3) low real tax burden for high-income taxpayer (4) low real tax burden for high-profitable enterprises (5) decrease in tax burden rate.

Namely, under the post-industrial society of Taiwan, tax policies are formulated with consideration of economic efficiency in place of social goals; therefore, tax base is being eroded due to tax rate reduction and tax reduction demanded by professional hierarchies. To enhance corporate profitability, professional elites demand decreases in tax rate but ignore unemployment which labors and the middle class might face. In their opinion, restraints on tax should be removed to encourage multinational corporations; but they forget that labors and the middle class may also lose job opportunities. Although their production volume and profits keep rising, they do not fulfill their commitment to trickle-down distribution of wealth

3. Conflicts Of Economic Interests For Government Expenditures

Results of conflicts of economic interests show: (1) insufficient social security expenditures; and (2) government subsidy for certain industries. These tendencies suggest that there is room for improvement in social welfare system, indicating that, with respect to conflicts of economic interests for public expenditures, professional elites have a victory over the public. Professional elites from the private sector reject government interference but demand tax reduction when they are in need of help.

4. Conflicts Of Economic Interests For Distribution Of Corporate Profits

Results of conflicts of economic interests show: (1) labor force exploited by labor market (2); "de-professionalization" of the middle class (3); economic recession attributed to labors; and (4) absolute property.

Exploitation of labors and the middle class by professional elites will lead to a vicious circle of low consumption and problems of unemployment. In other words, the professional society is not capable of or is not willing to provide its core members with work and security protection. There is only one reason – an ideology of "extraction of residual value to a point of self-destruction". When the extraction increases, it can stop producers from procuring the quantity of products they produce, therefore sufficient employment is not available in the economic system; therefore unemployment, resent and disharmony in society.

Excessive exploitation is a disaster, from which resentful feelings will destroy the cooperative intensions which production and culture rely on. Some labors may therefore suffer from alcohol addiction or drug abuse, commit crimes or riot. When people want to regain previous living standards, the struggle for income will develop intensively. Eventually, when the producer is no longer able to procure goods they have produced, the economy begins to slow (if it is not absolute when compared with other countries). Professional elites attempt to fill the gap through over-consumption; however, inevitably they fail, because, by reducing effective demands, they intuitively turn to luxurious goods, land and big mansions and accumulate savings. The result is a downward vicious cycle and unemployment due to low consumption[57].

That is to say, pursue for free market policies and the final results will enable polarized development of population, and the gap is too big to accept. These different trends probably spoil the fruit of trade and investment.

5.4 Government Revenues And Expenditures

In the post-industrial society of Taiwan, government officials and company managers are the most important people who control the distribution of social resources. Besides, professional hierarchies insist the ideology of free market, thereby leading to a laissez-faire market. Emergence of larger-sized enterprises and economic globalization has weakened governmental functions. All these enable government officials and company managers to extract social resources

---

57 Perkin, Harold, The Third Revolution: Professional Elites in the Modern World, London and New York: Routledge, (1996), pp. 187-189.

excessively to satisfy themselves while leaving the costs to the public. As a result, most economic resources are private; tax base is eroded and lost; social security expenditures are insufficient, basic labors and the middle class shoulder the responsibility of economic recession and the problem of unemployment. There are reflected on government expenditures and revenues ultimately, while government fiscal deficits are one of the symptoms.

5.5 Reasons For Fiscal Deficits In Taiwan

Therefore, in the post-industrial society of Taiwan where professional elites exploit the public, the problem behind fiscal deficits is uneven distribution of "economic power" between professional elites and the public.

Professionals from public sector "cooperate" with professionals from private sector for joint exploitation of the society, making Taiwan enter a new pattern of government stage – company country. Just as what *Nan* Fangshuo says, "Company is the nation and vice versa. Politics should also serve the company. Various functions of a "country", which is known as relative autonomy, have been thoroughly changed. As companies control and take over the state mechanism (such as reduction in corporate burdens and grant of incentives with the intention to profit the rich class), while the nation's fiscal is shouldered by low and medium income citizens, announcing the coming of the era that robs the poor to the rich. When companies are free from surveillance and the government does not exercise its duty of control, company managers become the professional hierarchy with supreme power, and then fabrication of financial statements is just a matter of course. All the rhetoric, privatization, deregulation, and globalization, would be used for nothing but rationalization of corporate profits"[58]

The country becomes a vassal of companies, and a system where nationals are consumers has already been developed. Company is the dictator, while the role of the government is redefined, from the warden to a supporter of companies. The government no longer makes all efforts in guiding the market; contrarily, the government takes initiative to make policies favorable to enterprises. During the formulation of a policy, the government, waiving its right to setting agenda, prefers enterprises instead of individuals.

In general, in the post-industrial society of Taiwan, conflicts of economic interests arise from transformation of social structure, lacking a fair regula-

58 Hertz, Noreena, The Silent Takeover: Global Capitalism and the Death of Democracy. New York, NY: HarperCollins, translated by Yu-Wen Hsu(In Chinese), Taipei: EcoTrend Publications, (2003), p. 15.

tory system that governs the distribution of private properties with equal and free competition. In this way, professional elites who have dominant advantages exploit economic resources while leaving costs to the public, all of which will be reflected on government fiscal deficits. The exploitation of the public by professional elites from public and private sectors and the power of professional elites more than sovereignty of the state have reduced the nation's autonomy, imposing restrictions on governmental functions in the whole economic and social system, which would be the political, economic and social problems behind fiscal deficits in Taiwan.

VI. Conclusion

Just as landlords in the pre-industrial society and entrepreneurs in the industrial society, professionals in the post-industrial society of Taiwan also succumb to the temptation and exploit their people as far as possible. The exploitation is a symptom from a fiscal perspective. However, as Schumpeter puts it, "The public finance are one of the best starting points for an investigation of society, especially though not exclusively of its political life. The full fruitfulness of this approach is seen particularly at those turning points, or better epochs, during which existing forms begin to die off and to change into something new, and which always involve a crisis of the old fiscal methods."[59][60].

Therefore, as what the fiscal sociology argues, we should find out the root cause of Taiwan's fiscal deficits to address the dilemma. That is, in the post-industrial society of Taiwan, all social structures should be adjusted in response to the situation to address the problem of the fiscal deficit, because all conflicts of economic interests between professionals and the public (including conflicts of economic interests for distribution of economic resources between individual and collective, conflicts of economic interests for distribution of tax burdens, conflicts of economic interests for government expenditures, and conflicts of economic interests for distribution of corporate profits) will be reflected in the debt of the nation. In other words, the key to the problem of fiscal deficits lies in conflicts of economic interests from the exploitation of the public by professional elites.

Since these professional elites cannot resist temptation of power abuse, plus Taiwan has no regulatory system governing the distribution of private proper-

59 Schumpeter, Joseph A. (1954), The Crisis of the Tax State, in Alan T. Peacock ed., International Economics Papers, no.4, MacMillan, p. 7Schumpeter, Joseph A. (1954), The Crisis of the Tax State, in Alan T. Peacock ed., International Economics Papers, no.4, MacMillan, p. 7.

60 Schumpeter, Joseph A. The Crisis of the Tax State, in Alan T. Peacock ed., International Economics Papers, no.4, MacMillan, (1954), p. 7.

ties and equal and free competition for conflicts of economic interests arising from the transformation of social structure, there are privatization of benefits and socialization of costs, in terms of conflicts of economic interests between professional elites and the public, which will eventually be reflected in the fiscal deficits.

Reference

Backhaus, J. Fiscal Sociology: What for? American Journal of Economics and Sociology, Vol.61, no.1, (2002), pp. 55-78.

Bell, Daniel, The Coming of Post-industrial Society: a venture in social forecasting, New York: Basic, (1973).

Bell, Daniel, The Public Household – On Fiscal Sociology and Liberal Society. In The Public Interest, No.35, (1974), pp. 29-68.

Block, Fred, Postindustrial Possibilities: A Critique of Economic Discourse. University of California Press, (1990).

Chan, Hou-Sheng and Yeun-Wen Ku, Integration of Social and Economic Policies, collected in Social Welfare Policy in New Century: The White Paper on Health – Social Welfare (Chan, Hou-Sheng and Yeun-Wen Ku eds), Taipei: Health, Welfare & Environment Foundation, (1999), pp 3-20.

Chang, Chia-Jen, Examination of Taiwan's Fiscal Deficits from Fiscal Sociology, PhD Thesis, Department of Public Finance, National Chengchi University, (2008).

Chen, Cheng-Chang, Background of Social Hierarchies and Opportunity for Admission to Universities, "Social Theory and Education" seminar, Pingtung: National Pingtung University of Education (2005).

Executive Yuan, Three-year sprint program for economic development vision – social welfare option, Taipei: Executive Yuan, (2006).

Fu, Li-Yeh, Taiwan Social Welfare Development – Past and Future, Taiwan Future Development Seminar, National Taipei University (2005).

Goldscheid, Rudolf, A Sociology Approach to Problem of Public Finance, in: Classics in the Theory of Public Finance, Musgrave, R. A. and T. Peacock (eds), Macmillan, London, (1967), pp. 202-213.

Hertz, Noreena, The Silent Takeover: Global Capitalism and the Death of Democracy. New York, NY: HarperCollins, translated by Yu-Wen Hsu(In Chinese), Taipei: EcoTrend Publications, (2003).

Ho, Chin-Sheun, Macroeconomic effect of government social welfare expenditure, Taipei: Directorate-General of Budget, Accounting and Statistics, Executive Yuan, (1995).

Hobson, John M. The wealth of states: A comparative sociology of international economic and political change, Cambridge: Cambridge University Press, (1997).

Hobson, John M. The State and International Relations, Cambridge: Cambridge University Press, (2000).

Huang, Chun-Sheng, Who suffers from progressive tax rate? Who benefits from tax preferences? Taiwan needs a fair and just tax system, "New trend, new concept for discussion over tax reform of new government" forum, Chunghua Public Finance Association (2008).

Huang, Shin-Hsin, Ren-Hui Hsu and Che-Chen Chang, government budget, National Open University, (1994).

Huang, Shin-Hsin, Welfare State vs. Fiscal Deficit? "Castrated" Contemporary Fiscal Theory, Seminar of Social Welfare and Economic Development, Taipei: Chinese Economic Association (1994).

Huang, Shin-Hsin, Introduction to public finance, National Open University, (1998).

Huang, Shin-Hsin, Social Development Strategies 2010 (Research report by Financial and Economic Section), Research valuation Commission, Executive Yuan, (2003).

Huang, Shin-Hsin, General examination of minimum tax, unpublished, (2005).

Huang, Shin-Hsin, Chien-Chung Kuo, Q&A for Debate on 18 % and Measures for Reasonable Reform, Policy Research Journal, Vol.6, (2006), pp 19-50.

Kuhn, T. S., The Structure of Scientific Revolution, translated by Suh-Der Tsen, Da-Wei Fu, Dao-Huan Wang, Yung-Hsiang, Taipei: Yuan-liou Publishing (Ed.2), (2005).

Lee, Bih-Hearn, Post-industrial Transformation in Taiwan, Journal of Sun Yat-senism, Vol.12, (1994), pp 245-282.

Lin, Wan-I, Population changes and countermeasures in Taiwan, Annual conference of Taiwan Social Welfare Academic Association, and an international academic seminar: "Suggestion and Innovation for Social Protection System in New Century: Changes across Time and Multinational Comparison", Taiwan Social Welfare Academic Association (2008).

Liu, A-Rong, Political and Business Relation of the Century, Taiwan – 1990-, Journal of Culture and Society, Vol.16, (2003), pp. 97-126.

Loxley, John, Fiscal Sociology and the Fiscal Crisis of the State, Contemporary Crises, Vol.6, (1982), pp. 285-301.

McLure, Michael, An Italian Foundation for New Fiscal Sociology: A Reflection on the Pareto-Griziotti and Pareto-Sensini letters on Ricardian Equivalence and Fiscal Theory, University of Western Australia, Economics Discussion Paper No.03.11, (2003).

McLure, Michael, Approaches to Fiscal Sociology, in: Jurgen G. Backhaus (eds), Essays on Fiscal Sociology, Frankfurt: Peter Lang, (2005), pp. 38-50.
McLure, Michael, The Fiscal Sociology of Gino Borgatta: Pareto, Extra-Economic Redistribution and Economic Growth, Cambridge Journal of Economics, Vol. 30, Issue 4, (2006), pp. 521-539.
Moore, Mick, Revenues, State Formation, and the Quality of Governance in Countries, International Political Science Review, Vol. 25, No.3, (2004), pp. 297-319.
Musgrave, Richard A. Theories of Fiscal Crises: An Essay in Fiscal Sociology, in Aaron, Henry J., Michael J. Boskin (eds), The economics of Taxation, Brookings Institution, Washington, (1980).
Musgrave, Richard A. Schumpeter's Crisis of the Tax State: An Essay in Fiscal Sociology, Journal of Evolutionary Economics, Vol.2, no.2, (1992), pp. 23-47.
Nektarios, Miltiadis, Public Pension, Capital Formation, and Economics Growth, Westview Press, Boulder, (1982).
O'Connor, James, The Fiscal Crisis of the State, ST. Martin's Press, (1973).
Perkin, Harold, The Third Revolution: Professional Elites in the Modern World, London and New York: Routledge, (1996).
Schumpeter, Joseph A. The Crisis of the Tax State, in Alan T. Peacock ed., International Economics Papers, no.4, MacMillan, (1954), pp. 5-38.
Tsai, Chi-Yuan, Effect of social welfare expenditures on Taiwan's macroeconomics. Taipei: Research Center of Humanities and Social Sciences, SINICA, (1995).
Wang, Cheng and Wen-Hui Cheng, Effect of social welfare system of economy – international comparison, Taipei: Council for Economic Planning and Development, Executive Yuan, (1995).
Yang, Chien-Cheng and Chia-Jen Chang, Political Economy on Tax Abatement, Fairness and Justice of Tax Reform Seminar, Taipei: Chinatimes Foundation (2005).
Yang, Chien-Cheng, Tax Preference Measures under the Statute for Upgrading Industries, Review of Integrated Income Tax system and Minimum Tax, A research project 2006 commissioned by the Taxation Agency, Ministry of Finance ROC, (2007)

In Search of the Laws of Access and Survival of the Members of the Italian Parliament in Relation to their Party Affiliation (1946-2011)

Silvia Fedeli and Francesco Forte

Abstract

Drawing on Schumpeter and public choice theories on the political entrepreneurs and on the sociological theories of the political class as elites, we focus on the laws of access and survival of the members of the Italian parliament, from the beginning of the Republic to present period, in relations with their affiliation to the various political parties that differ for the sociological composition, the size, the political collocation, the organizational structure.

Keywords: Political enterprise, political class, survival analysis, Italian Parliament.

1. Introduction

The paradigm according to which the demand and the supply of politicians mimic the labour market paradigm appears a very partial and limited explanation of the phenomenon, even if we consider the candidates as individual suppliers of labour. The assumption that they are merely attracted by the wage they shall get for serving the electors appears too naïve. Besides what has been observed about the rent seeking as a negative sum game and the positive sum games that may therefore emerge in the political competition, as James Buchanan argues, politicians, like everyone else, if not constrained, tend to follow their own motivations, but these are not necessarily those of a narrow utilitarian *homo oeconomicus* paradigm. They may be different. While it is naïve to assume that they necessarily coincide with the interests (and values) of the generality of the electorate,[1] whatever this means, members of the parliament may be attracted by the prestige and reputation that they can get, by the

1 Here, we refer to the stream of research inaugurated by James Buchanan (1954a; 1954b; 1962) on the economics of the political exchange, i. e. on the basis of the public choice approach to public sector institutions and activities; see also Buchanan (1979) – which explains why the three papers mentioned above are at the basis of the public choice theory of politics as political exchange – and Buchanan (1976, 1993, 1986, 1996). See also Tullock (1965) on the entry barriers in politics and Buchanan and Tullock on the opportunistic behaviour of politicians caused by the pressure of rent-seeking groups of interest; on Buchanan and Tullock's contributions to the theory of rent seeking see Buchanan et at. (1980). This public choice approach has been dissected through the paradigm of opportunistic behaviour in the agency relations between politicians, their electors, their parties, and the interest groups behind them. Contributions

pleasure of exerting power,[2] by the satisfaction of pursuing their own ideological objectives. According to Max Weber (1918),[3] entrepreneurs are selected in the market struggle, whereas professional politicians and political leaders in the democratic system typical of capitalist society are selected through the struggle taking place within political parties, the parliament and the government. Therefore, the politician-entrepreneurs do not need to be experts in a particular sector of specialized knowledge, learnt through formal education. They must be experts in specific political work, which can be learnt only in the political arena. Both the market economy entrepreneur and the political leader fight for their power and for the success of the "cause" for which they are responsible. In this context, Weber (1919) deals with professional politicians, classifying them into those who live for politics (and have their own means, deriving from personal activity or inherited wealth or both) and those who make a living through politics. A number of professional categories may be of help in entering the political arena and achieving success. Among them, the legal profession appears particularly suited to *politik als beruf*.[4]

Besides Max Weber, a substantial body of research in the areas of the political and sociological science has developed the interpretation of the political class as an elite, and of the law of survival and circulation of politicians and of political enterprise. According to Pareto (1901-1902; 1906; 1916), political (and other) elites are composed of individuals of superior talent in their own activity. The distribution of their individual qualities is similar to that of the wealth curve, with a bell shape, but the distribution of talents that enables the elite to get into power does not (necessarily) coincide with the one behind the existing wealth distribution. In Gaetano Mosca's theory of circulation of the elites (1896, 1932, 1933), political elites are *organized* minorities. The more the masses predominate the more the middle class tends to absorb members coming from the lower class.

---

by Gary Becker and by Mancur Olson should also be mentioned here, although they focus on interest groups more than on the effect of rent seeking on public choices.

2 According to political science tradition, the chief aim of politicians is to exert power (see Dahl 1970).

3 See also Weber (1948).

4 Law experts are particularly important in left wing parties. This is so because the main business of the expert lawyer is to defend the interest of a party and to persuade people of its validity. Moreover, lawyers have an independent profession which allows them to fight more freely in the risky political arena. A second category suited to politics as a profession is that of journalists and, particularly, of political journalist. A third category is that of party bureaucrats as well as journalists working for party newspapers. These categories are also more important in left wing mass parties. A fourth category is that of union managers and bureaucrats, while a fifth is that of representatives of the interests of farmers, of industrial organizations, of artisans, and of the chambers of commerce. The last relevant category is that of white collar workers of the private and public sector employees.

Therefore in a complex democratic society the political elites tend to consist of individuals who reflect their (not high) average morality and average intellectual qualities.[5] Robert Michels (1911)[6] argued that the prevailing law relating to the political class is not that of circulation, but that of persistence of the political elites, because of the inherently oligarchic structures of political parties.[7] Robert Dahl (1990) strongly criticizes Pareto, Mosca and Michels, claiming that the real democracies among modern societies are polyarchic, reflecting their pluralistic structure. However, Dahl (1998) maintains that in a polyarchic society there is a defect of democratic influence on the decision making process, partly due to institutional barriers.[8] According to Charles Linblom (1977 and 2001), in a polyar-

---

5 However, according to Luigi Einaudi (1923; 1934; 1954) there are two political classes, those who may deserve the name of elite and those who do not: politicians who make public choices according to the "economic" model of public economy may deserve the name of elite. Those who are competent and know the laws of economic life shall survive in the long run, at least in societies which succeed in reaching the objectives of their individual members. The institutions which "good politicians" adopt when in power also last, while the institutions created by bad politicians perish. See Forte and Silvestri (2009).

6 Michels' view of the law of selection and circulation of the elites differs from that of Kautsky. Karl Kautsky (1892), referring to the German Social Democratic mass party, presented the structure of the mass organized party as a democratic structure, with a general assembly which chooses, among the most qualified individuals in relation to the tasks to be assigned, the elite that should rule the party and represent the assembly itself in parliament. Thus, the rulers of left-wing democratic parties and their parliamentary representatives are an elite, not only politically, but also from a cultural (and an ethical) point of view, though they are not oligarchic in structure.

7 Michels' analysis may complement that of Weber, with respect to the way in which the political elite is chosen. This occurs in so far as this type of party is relevant in a given democratic, developed country, because of its sociological and cultural characteristics and its institutional factors: an electoral system that favours the big organized parties; a labour market legislation and praxis that favours the big organized unions; a commercial law that recognizes the participation of the representatives of the workers to the supervisory boards of corporations; a legislation and policy that favour the development of cooperatives running parallel to mass parties; and so on...

8 However, the comparative table of institutions reported in his book contains broad mistakes and highly debatable indications. As far as Italy is concerned, the Senate is considered of unequal power with respect to the Chamber of Deputies, whereas in Italy there is a system of perfect bicameralism. Moreover, according to Dahl, the Italian Senate is elected with the same (or similar) rules as those applying to the other chamber – another wrong proposition. The electoral system is defined as proportional, but when Dahl's book was written in Italy there was a plurality system with a coefficient of proportionality. The jurisdictional control over laws is considered inadequate in Italy, but since the country has a Constitutional Court which, every year, produces several sentences on the constitutionality of laws, repealing any unconstitutional rules or interpretations, whether this control is efficient or otherwise is a mere subjective judgement (and a highly disputable one). The purpose of this note is to warn about empirical research based on cross-country information concerning institutional data, because

chic democracy there are basically three elites interacting among each other: the political class, the entrepreneurs and the military elite, with a predominance of the latter two. The survival of the political elites is conditioned by the others.

What emerges from many of these theories of the elite is that the issue of survival concerns not only the individuals, but also their "species/bunches", i. e., their political parties. [9] With this in mind, we shall examine the Italian case, considering all the members of the two chambers of parliament from the first elections held after the Second World War, in 1946, to 2010. We will pay particular attention to some features that might be relevant in explaining the survival of politicians inside their own political parties, i. e., education, profession.[10] We shall concentrate on the main political parties dividing the overall period into two sub periods of the first and the second republic, basically different because of the different electoral system used.

In section 3, after the description of the institutional frame in which our research is carried out, we shall give a general picture of the trends relating to the values of relevant variables in the period under examination. In Section 4, after presenting the data set (4.1), we examine the probability of survival for groups of politicians over time using the Kaplan-Meier method (4.2). Conclusions follow in section 5.

---

it may contain errors, even when it includes a limited number of developed countries, as in Dahl's case.

9 Combining this observation with the traditional postulate that the main objective of the political class and of political organizations is to obtain and maintain power, one may distinguish, as in Merlo *et al.* (2009), whether it is the politicians who condition their party to pursue their own interest or if the party constrains their behaviour in order to ensure electoral victory for the party itself, which then compensates the politicians in other ways.

10 Merlo *et al.* (2009) present an overview of the Italian political system aiming to highlight the way in which changes in the Italian electoral law have affected the candidates' selection process, the parties' internal organization and the overall structure of the party system. They also study the career profiles of Italian legislators taking into account their age, gender, education, occupation and income prior to entering the Chamber and considering the changes between the first and second Republic. However, their data set is incomplete because it contains information only on the individuals elected to the Chamber of Deputies (ignoring whether they were – either before or after – elected to the Senate) and only since 1948 (thus, overlooking the fact that the first recruitment – in the 1st legislature – was very much affected by the membership of the Constituent Assembly; see figure 1). Moreover, their analysis of the political labour market is relevant only for the limited period following 1981. Indeed only in 1982 did the Italian law require all elected officials to disclose their annual income tax returns, referring to the income earned in the previous calendar year. Therefore their data set contains information on the total reported income of all members of the Chamber of Deputies only between 1981 and 2006.

2. An overall picture of the Italian parliament

In 1948 the Italian Constitution set up a pure parliamentary system, under a perfect bicameral systems with a 630 members (since 1963) in the Chamber of Deputies (*Camera dei Deputati*) and 315 members in the Senate (*Senato della Repubblica*). A proportional electoral law was chosen for both chambers, with different rules about the age of the active and passive electorate, and the way of selecting the representatives for each electoral list (this law lasted until 1994). The results was a complex multiparty system that led to a variety of coalition governments.[11] In the early '90 several shocks affected Italian political institutions. As a consequence, most of the old parties disappeared and new parties emerged. Moreover, in 1994, Italy moved to a mixed electoral system, where, in the Chamber of Deputies, 75% of the representatives were elected by a plurality system and the remaining 25% according to the proportional system. For the Senate, 232 senators were elected by plurality rule, the remaining 83 by a proportional system. Before the 2007 political elections, the electoral system was again modified, going back to the proportional system, but with some differences from the previous one. For the Chamber there is a double threshold. In the Senate, the seats are assigned at regional level, with a premium of additional seats for the party with the relative majority within each region. In either branch, voters are only allowed to cast a ballot for their party of choice, but not for individual candidates. For all these reasons, we shall distinguish two sub periods in our analysis, the first goes from 1946 to 1994 and is named, according to common usage, "First Republic"; the second, starting in 1994, is known as "Second Republic".

On the basis of the theories of the political class discussed above, we shall consider, for the two sub periods, all members of parliament grouped with respect to their affiliation to the main political parties in order to study their education and profession. Education and profession, according to Pareto's theory of elites, may influence the non-logical and logical mix of public choices. They are also relevant in Weber's theory of politics as profession. Political affiliation, combined with education and profession, also helps to verify the relevance of the theory of political parties as elites formulated by Kautsky in comparison with that of Michels, because, according to the former, the politicians who emerge (in left-wing mass parties) are supposed to be the most qualified from the political

11 The constitutional mandate of a Legislature is five years. Elections may occur before the regular end of the legislature, if the President of the Republic acknowledges that there is no longer a majority capable of expressing a government. Early elections have been relatively frequent in Italy.

point of view in relation to the tasks assigned to them, whereas, according to the latter, politicians who tend to emerge are the most powerful in the parties' bureaucracies.

3. Empirical analysis of the determinants of the circulation of the elites in the post-war Italian parliament: a survival approach

We analyse the survival of the members of the Italian parliament belonging to different political groups, taking into account all the available information relating to the individual member of the parliament. The fact that the members of the parliament enter one branch and may be re-elected to the other is also taken into consideration. The re-election, the event of interest, might be "recurrent" for an individual member of the parliament and, therefore, it shall be approached taking into account also the order of re-election.

Fedeli and Forte (2011) have shown that the political groups do actually play a different but significant role circulation of the elites in the post-war Italian parliament. Here we further explore that issue, by using the same, unique and newly built, dataset that contains detailed information on all members of the two branches of the Italian parliament since 1946. The dataset contains recurrent event outcomes for 15,357 repeated observations referred to 7,127 subjects (the members of both branches of parliament since 1946),[12] followed by us as if they were "patients" in respect to their re-election to either branch. The summary statistics for the whole period are in table 1.

12 For each individual in the sample, the dataset contains, amongst others, date and place of birth, gender, education, profession, party affiliation, electoral district, and parliamentary group membership.
We draw this information from the official website http://www.parlamento.it and from *La Navicella*, an official publication edited at the beginning of each Legislature, which contains self-reported biographical information on all members of parliament.

Table 1 Summary statistics of the considered variables

DESCRIPTION	Freq.	Percent	Cum.
NUMBER_RE-ELECTION			
1	7,128	46.42	46.42
2	3,898	25.38	71.8
3	2,050	13.35	85.15
4	1,078	7.02	92.17
5	596	3.88	96.05
6	296	1.93	97.97
7	157	1.02	99
8	79	0.51	99.51
9	45	0.29	99.8
10	13	0.08	99.89
11	8	0.05	99.94
12	4	0.03	99.97
13	3	0.02	99.99
14	2	0.01	100
Total	**15,357**	**100**	
EDUCATION			
1 primary or elementary school	319	2.19	2.19
2 middle school, or junior high	442	3.03	5.22
3 high school	2,850	19.57	24.79
4 university	10,954	75.21	100
Total	**14,565**	**100**	
PROFESSION			
1 manual workers and farmers	408	2.7	2.7
2 medical doctors, pharmacists, veterinary doctors	735	4.87	7.57
3 journalists and writers	1,157	7.66	15.23
4 artisans and traders, army officers, architects and engineers, accountants, consultants, others	1,462	9.68	24.92
5 manager, industrialists, entrepreneurs	1,818	12.04	36.96
6 political managers	2,226	14.74	51.71
7 lawyers, judges, notaries	3,271	21.67	73.37
8 white collars workers and teachers, including university professors	4,020	26.63	100
Total	15,097	100	
GROUPS OF PARTIES OF THE FIRST REPUBLIC			
0 Others	596	5.61	5.61
1 DC	4,433	41.72	47.33
2 PCI (including DS and PRC)	2,880	27.1	74.43
3 PSI (including PSI and PSDI when unified)	1,418	13.34	87.78
4 MSI	479	4.51	92.28
5 PSDI	289	2.72	95
6 PLI	291	2.74	97.74
7 PRI	240	2.26	100
Total	**10,626**	**100**	
GROUPS OF PARTIES OF THE SECOND REPUBLIC			
0 Others	223	4.71	4.71
1 Centre Right	1,769	37.39	42.11
2 Centre Left	1,471	31.09	73.2
3 Lega	436	9.22	82.41
4 Former DC	443	9.36	91.78
5 Various left	318	6.72	98.5
6 La rete & IDV	71	1.5	100
Total	**4,731**	**100**	

Our approach to the circulation of the political class disentangled by political affiliation, studies the survivor curves for the members of parliament in relation to their different professional activities, education. They are obtained with the Kaplan-Meier (KM) method,[13] which gives the probability that a study subject might survive past a specified time. The general formula for the KM survival probability at a failure time $t_{(j)}$ gives the probability of surviving past the previous failure time $t_{(j-1)}$ multiplied by the conditional probability of surviving past time, given survival to at least time $t_{(j)}$. That is

$$S(t_{(j)} = S\, t_{(j-1)} \times \Pr(T > t_{(j)} \mid T \geq t_{(j)})$$

With this approach no model is actually used to fit survival data and the curves are plotted as step functions. This allows for a comparison of the various groups over time.

4.1 The First Republic

For the First republic we consider the two main governing parties (DC and PSI) and the two main opposition parties (PCI and MSI). For the Second republic, in the next section, we shall consider the two main parties alternating in government and opposition, i. e. Centre-Left and Centre Right. We shall consider the survivor functions of members of the parliament belonging to these political parties by distinguishing education and professions.

In accordance with the theories of Weber, Linblom, Einaudi and, to some extent, Kautsky – socio political changes requiring new professional qualifications for individuals to perform political activity were highly relevant for the composition of the political class by profession and degree of education. In Italy's new post-war democracy, the largest part of the members of the Italian Parliament had a university degree: 74.4 % in the Chamber and 74.8 % in the Senate; but there was also a substantial share of members of both branches with only elementary/primary[14] education (10.9 % in the Chamber and 2.1 % in the Senate): these were likely to be those politicians who had organized the parties participating in the new democracy. The percentage of deputies with elementary/primary education falls to about 1 % in the Chamber with the generational change occurring after 1968 (VI Legislature),

13 See Kaplan and Meier (1958).

14 The post-war Italian education system is based on a four-level structure. Compulsory education includes both *Scuole elementari* (primary or elementary school) and *Scuole medie* (roughly translatable as middle school, or junior high); individuals who continue their studies after compulsory education choose among a variety of high school paths (*Scuole superiori*) which, in turn, can lead to University.

and even below 1 % in the subsequent legislatures. In the Senate, the decrease in the number of members with a primary school qualification was slower, and it started with the X Legislature, because some senior deputies with lower education moved from the Chamber of Deputies to the Senate, thus supporting the thesis of Kautski that the professional politicians of the workers 's party have an inherently political qualification and that of Michels that in big and organised parties, the long lasting politicians' life mainly depends on their political role inside the party.

In figures 1 to 4 we consider the survival of groups of members of the parliament distinguished by education.

Figure 1. Kaplan-Meier survival estimates (PCI)

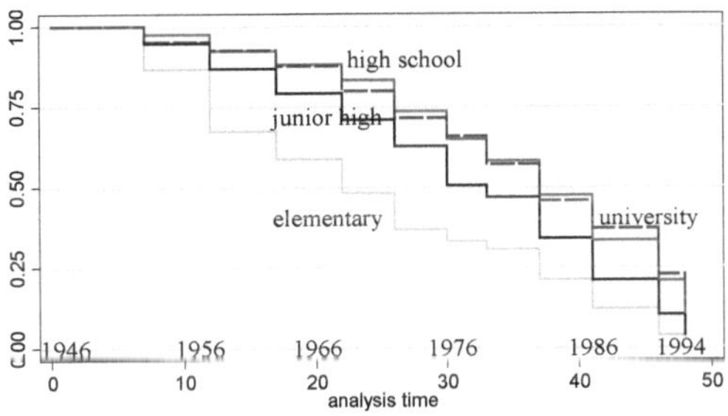

Figure 2. Kaplan-Meier survival estimates (DC)

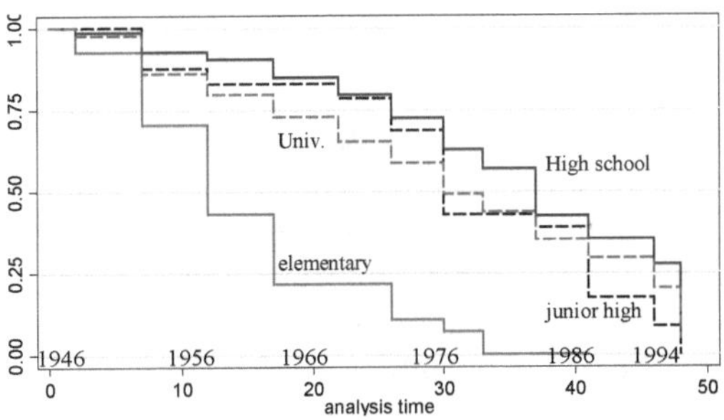

Figure 3. Kaplan-Meier survival estimates (MSI)

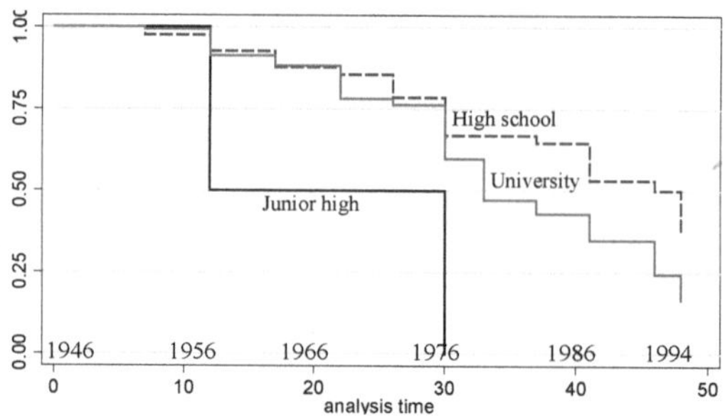

Figure 4. Kaplan-Meier survival estimates (PSI)

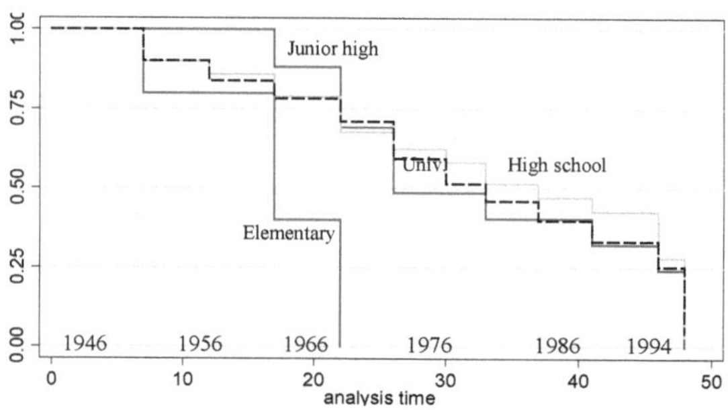

The highest survival in DC, PSI e MSI is for those members of parliament who hold a high school qualification, in spite of the fact that, as mentioned, those with a university degree form approximately 75 % of the total throughout the period. Only in the PCI the survival of those member with university degree goes together with that with high school qualification and is the highest. Notice that high school and graduate members of the parliament used to have the same survival in the first few legislatures in either party. These survival curves might suggest that the graduate members of the two chambers after their experience in parliament exploit their new political expertise outside it *via* the relationships with the interest groups which are connected with them (a thesis that may validate the public choice theories of rent seeking). Those with junior high and high school qualifications remain in parliament for a longer period because less qualified for the revolving doors. However, one may argue with Gaetano Mosca that individuals who hold a high school diploma are best suited to represent the voters in a mass society. Notice also the differences in the parties considered amongst the survival curves of the members of parliament with elementary qualifications only. The group with elementary qualifications has the lowest survival in either party. However this group persists all over the period in the PCI, for which it is confirmed the importance of the individual role in the hierarchical structure of the political party. The group with elementary qualifications gradually disappears from the other parties. In particular, the group of members with elementary/primary qualifications disappears, respectively, from the PSI with the general elections held in 1968, from the MSI in 1963, from the DC in 1983. On this basis, one might argue that the *petite bourgeoisie* class, that with a mere junior high/high school qualification, begins to emerge the more effectively the less organized are the political movements, mainly for PSI, DC and MSI, in which a variety of interest groups can exercise greater influence.

This inference might be confirmed also by looking at the very substantial differences and changes in the professions of the members of the republican parliament in the considered political parties. The overall picture shows that legal professions and teachers (mostly with a university degree) covered more than 40% of the universe considered since the beginning, both in the Chamber and in the Senate, with a net predominance of lawyers (see Fedeli and Forte, 2011). New professions emerged in later years. In particular, "managers, industrialists and entrepreneurs" remarkably increased their presence. On the other hand, the number of unions leaders and political managers constantly increased in both chambers. Considering for each profession the distribution within each of the parties studied here (PCI, DC, MSI and PSI) in the various legislatures, it turns out that the legal professions (Profession 1, including lawyers, judges, notaries, and legal consultants) had a low presence in the Communist Party (PCI) only. Their number was much higher for DC and PSI (although this tended to decrease after the first few legislatures), as well as for MSI (where however those belonging to the legal professions increased up to the eighth legislature). Profession 2, made up of clerks and teachers, including university professors, is highly represented mainly in the DC, where it declines in the last few legislatures. Its presence increased overall in the PCI, and was almost stable, with alternating phases, in MSI and PSI. Profession 3, which includes political managers of various kinds, is the highest in the PCI (with a trend towards overall increase), followed by DC and PSI, whereas the trend is decreasing in the MSI (with the exception of the last legislature). "Workers and farmers" represented quite a low share in almost all the parties considered, with the exception of the PCI during the first few legislatures. Afterwards their presence decreases even in the Communist Party, reaching the level of the other parties starting from the tenth legislature. "Journalists and writers" are dominant in the MSI during the early legislatures and in the '70s-'80s. Their percentage is quite stable in the PCI up to the tenth legislature and in the PSI up to the fifth. It is declining in the other periods for all parties with the exception of the DC, where "journalists and writers" are increasing, but their total always remains lower than 6%. Profession 8, referring to managers, industrialists and entrepreneurs, increases mainly in the DC, followed by the PSI. Their presence is always low in the PCI and in the MSI (the latter, however, shows two peaks in the sixth and tenth legislatures). The figures of the distribution of profession in various parties are available from authors on request.

Figures 5 to 8 show, for the same parties, the corresponding Kaplan-Meier survival curves. We should recall that the PCI has a predominance of professions 2 and 3 (e.g. "clerks and teachers, including university professors" and "political managers"); they also have the highest survival curve, whereas "workers and farmers" show the lowest. The importance of clerks, teachers and professors in PCI may be explained by the peculiar relevance of rent seeking in the (growth of) public expenditure in these areas for this party. In the DC, too, "workers and farmers" have the lowest survival rate, while political managers" and "journalists and writers" have the highest. In the MSI, where the legal profession is the dominant one, the highest survival is for Profession 3 (political managers) together with Professions 2 (clerks and teachers); again, "workers and farmers" show the lowest survival. Unexpectedly, in the PSI the legal profession shows the lowest survival, whereas "workers and farmers" followed by "journalists and writers" last longest.

Figure 5.

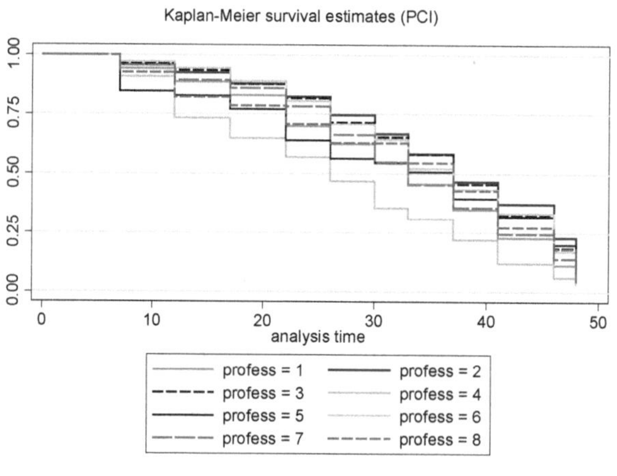

Figure 6.

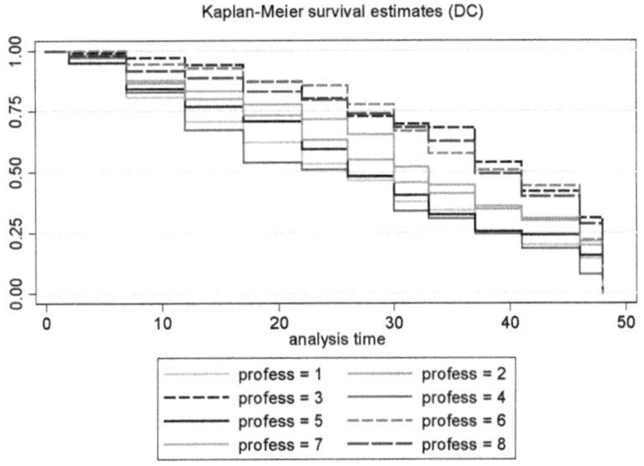

Figure 7.

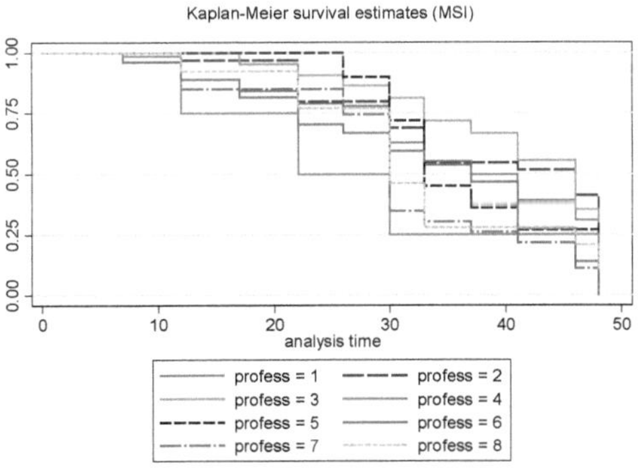

Figure 8.

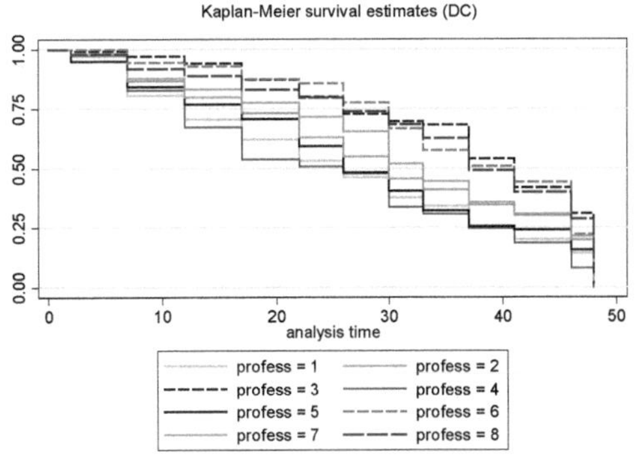

4.2 The Second Republic

As already mentioned, the main change in Italy's political class took place in 1994, with the disappearance of most of the historical political parties of the First Republic. For the Second republic we consider the two main parties alternating in government and opposition, i. e. Centre-Left and Centre Right.

The renewal of the political class initially did not cause a reduction in the share of members of both the Chamber and the Senate with a university degree. However, their percentage did fall in the XV and XVI legislatures in both branches, even though in Italy the share of citizens with a university degree had greatly increased in comparison with the period immediately after the Second World War. An interesting change relates to members of the parliament with a high school qualification. In the first Legislature they were about 12.11 % in the Chamber and 5.1 % in the Senate. In both the Chamber and the Senate the numbers continued to increase significantly and, in the Second republic, they reached 28.7 % in the Chamber of Deputies. The *petite bourgeoisie*, often with junior high and high school qualifications, active in the small businesses and minor activity, that has already emerged in the First Republic, predominates/consolidates in the new political situation of less organized political movements, in which a variety of interest groups could exercise greater influence. This occurs in particular in the Centre-Right group.

In figures 9 and 10 we consider the survival curve of the two main groups (centre-left and centre-right) distinguished by education. The centre right is characterised by the absence of members of parliament with elementary school qualifications. The highest survival is for those members with junior high school qualification, whose survival curve is almost stable on the median since 1996. From the beginning of the Second Republic, however, but only up to 2007, graduate members of parliament and those with high school qualifications survive longer than all other categories. In the centre left, the group of members of parliament with elementary school qualifications survive up to 2007, to disappear afterwards. The highest survival is for graduate members of parliament and for those with high school qualifications, whose curves go together. Notice here the negative change in levels of education determined by the new electoral law which results in the strengthening and actual predominance of the group with junior high qualifications, especially in the centre right. As we shall see below, a change of the dominant professions also emerges in 2007, both in the centre-left and in the centre right.

Figure 9.

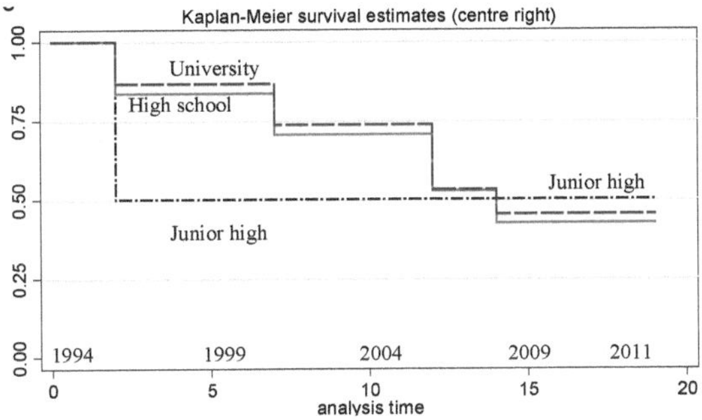

Figure 10.

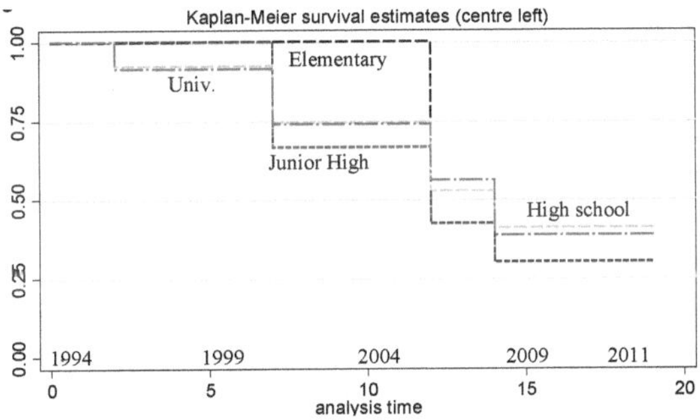

The legal professions and teachers (mostly with a university degree) covered more than 40 % of the universe considered, both in the Chamber and in the Senate of the First Republic, with a net predominance of lawyers. New professions emerged in the Second Republic, but most remarkable is the increase of "managers, industrialists and entrepreneurs". Likely the virtual disappearance of the organized parties, mainly affecting the centre right, and their reduced importance in the left allow for rent seeking by businessmen with their own members in the parliament. On the other hand, the number of unions leaders and political managers – whose share, in the First Republic, constantly increased in both chambers – after the initial period, diminishes substantially in the Second Republic, mainly due to a reduction in the Centre-left. The party model *à la* Kautsky or Michels becomes less influential over this period, in particular after the change in electoral system which became effective starting with the political elections in 2007. The Centre Right, in this new context, mostly requires organization and innovation. Thus the political managers increase in it, although in a limited number with respect to the past.

Considering the distribution of the professions for centre right and centre left, respectively, notice that the legal professions which dominate the centre right also remarkably increase their presence in the centre left beginning with the thirteenth legislature. "Clerks and teachers, including university professors" dominates the centre left, however its percentage reduces from 40 % to 30 %. The presence of this profession also decreases in centre right. Political managers, who are quite important for the centre left, nevertheless decrease from 25 % in 1994 to 15 % in the fifteenth legislature, though their numbers increase again after 2007. They represent a low share in the centre right, but the group increases in the fifteenth and sixteenth legislature. "Workers and farmers" represent a low share in both centre left and centre right parties and they disappear from the centre right with the fifteenth legislature, while their presence remains at about 1 % in the centre left. "Journalists and writers" increase in the centre left starting from 1996 and their presence matches the numbers in the centre right in the most recent elections. "Managers, industrialists and entrepreneurs" persistently increase in the centre left, going from 5 % to 15 %. Their numbers are more important in the centre right where, however, they show a reduction in 1996 (thirteenth legislature), only to then increase again, reaching approximately 30 % in the sixteenth legislature. The figures of the distribution of profession in various parties are available from authors on request.

Figures 11 and 12 show, for the same parties, the corresponding Kaplan-Meier survival curves relating to professions, in the centre left "journalists and writers", "managers, industrialists and entrepreneurs" and the legal professions show the highest survival. On the other hand, in the centre right, the highest survival is, unexpectedly, registered for "political managers", followed by "journalists and writers" and the legal professions. In both political groups "workers and farmers" have the lowest survival.

Figure 11.

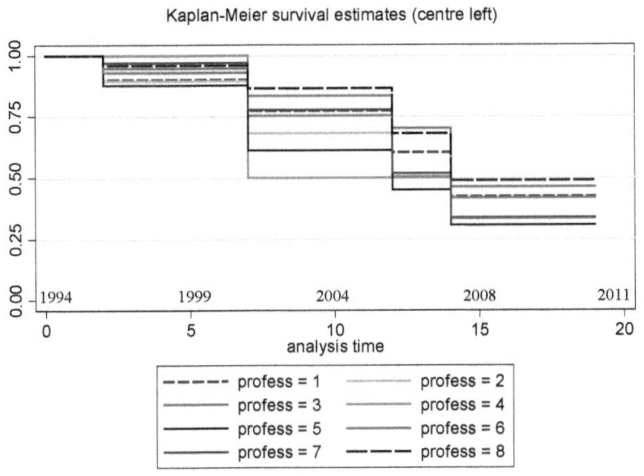

Figure 12.

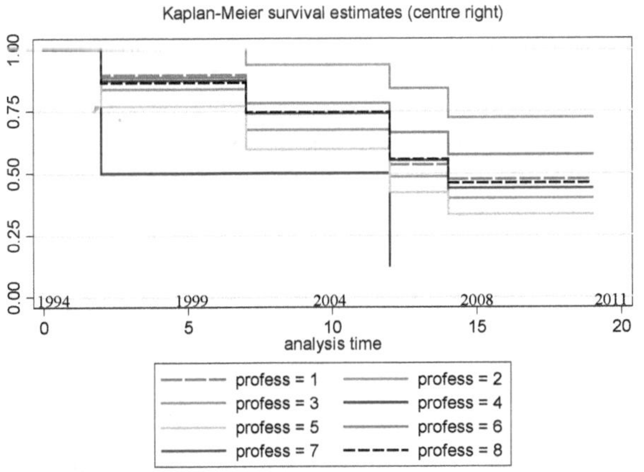

5. Conclusions

We have focused on the role played by the political parties as related to such variables as education and profession, which might be relevant according to one or more of the theories mentioned in Section 2. We tested these variables separately for two sub-periods corresponding to the so-called First and Second Republic.

The reason for this division into two sub-periods is that the number of 'shocks', intervened between the two, remarkably changed the political movements in Italy. On these bases we could analyse their role, joint with that of other elements.

Remarkable changes between the first and the second period unexpectedly emerged from our analysis. The first notable change is the emergence of a new class of politicians without a university degree, representing the broadening of the middle class due to the rise of the lower classes. In line with Gaetano Mosca's theory, the political elites become gradually characterised by those *talents* best suited to achieve power and to exert it in the society. Therefore, the more the masses predominate the more the middle class tends to absorb members coming from the less educated social categories and the political elites tend to consist of individuals who reflect their (not high) average morality and average intellectual qualities. This emerges more clearly in the Second republic, where the members of the biggest political movements are on average overall less educated than in the First Republic, and mainly the Centre Right. In this respect, we noticed the overall high share of members of parliament who hold a university degree, but also an appreciable reduction of this share in the second sub-period; moreover, almost no one, at the end of the second sub-period has elementary/primary school qualifications only. On the one hand, this seems to confirm that in order to become a member of parliament, skills acquired with education are required. On the other hand, it emerged that, in the First Republic, the members of parliament with, at least, a secondary school diploma, having on average the highest probability of survival, also increase through time. In the second sub-period, the skills and the intellectual qualifications that make the difference when it comes to survival, are more related to specific professions rather than education, for which the highest survival is for those member with a mere junior high qualification.

The results obtained when studying political affiliation, combined with education and profession, seem to support the rent seeking approach, mainly, for the most common profession in the Italian parliament, although declining, in either party considered: i. e., the white collar workers and teachers (inclusive of university professors). This, likely depends on the increased importance of the public sector thus supporting the public choice view of the relevance of rent seeking. It also emerges that the relevance of the theory of political parties as elites formulated by Kautsky according to whom, the politicians who emerge (mainly in left-wing mass parties) are supposed to be the most qualified from the political point of view in relation to the tasks assigned to them is declining with the end of the First Republic. In the Second Republic we noticed the revival of the role of political managers and lawyers for their specific skill as political entrepreneurs inside the parliament. In the Second republic, as noted, the political movements are less organised according to the hierarchical structure prevailing during the

First Republic. The share of political managers in the second sub-period has overall diminished, mainly in the Centre left. Although increasing, it is quite a low share in the Centre right, where, however, this group show the highest survival. In other words, the disappearance of the old, consolidated, parties increases the good chances of survival of career politicians as political entrepreneurs in the new Centre right, but in the absence of the previous hierarchical bureaucratic structure. The profession of "lawyers et al.", which was the most represented in the first period, was nevertheless declining during that same period. In the second sub-period, while no longer predominant, the legal profession rises again, showing a remarkable survival in both left and right movements. As in Weber's theory, these politicians, whether by their own profession or by option, have political skills, formed trough a mix of their original profession and their political experience. Thus, also the thesis of Michels that in big and organised parties, the long lasting politicians' life mainly depends on their political role inside the party is not longer verified in the Second republic. A more convincing explanation of this revival may be that legal professional skills give more room for manoeuvring for rent seeking when political parties are young and their structures not yet consolidated. This interpretation seems to be confirmed also by the results obtained for the profession of "managers, industrialists and entrepreneurs", that begins to emerge in the first sub-period and strongly consolidates in the second. Clearly, with the diminished importance of the organized parties the business class can enter into active politics, by its own members making directly their own rent seeking activities in the Italian Parliament.

References

Alchian, A. (1950) Uncertainty, Evolution and Economic Theory, *Journal of Political Economy*, 58: 211-221.

Becker G. S. (1982), *Competition Among Pressure Groups for Political Influence*, University of Chicago

Buchanan, J. M. (1954a), Individual choices in the market, reprinted in 1999, *The Logical Foundations of Constitutional Liberty*, volume 1 of *The Collected works of James M.Buchanan*, Indianapolis, Liberty Fund, pages75-88

Buchanan, J. M. (1954b) Social Choice, Democracy and the Markets reprinted in 1999, *The Logical Foundations of Constitutional Liberty*, volume 1 of *The Collected works of James M.Buchanan*, Indianapolis, Liberty Fund, pages 89-02.

Buchanan, J. M. 1962 Politics, Policy and the Pigouvian Margins reprinted in 1999, *The Logical Foundations of Constitutional Liberty*, volume 1 of *The*

Collected works of James M.Buchanan, Indianapolis, Liberty Fund, pages 60-74.

Buchanan, J. M. (1976) "Methods and Morals in Economics. The Ayres Knight discussion"; reedited in 2001, *Ideas, Persons and Events*, volume 19 of *The Collected works of James M.Buchanan*, Indianapolis, Liberty Fund,. pages 123-134 ;

Buchanan, J. M. (1993), Public Choice after Socialism"; reedited in 2001, *Ideas, Persons and Events*, volume 19 of *The Collected works of James M.Buchanan*, Indianapolis, Liberty Fund,. pages 276-85;

Buchanan, J. M. (1986), Can Policy Activism Succeed? A Public Choice Perspective ";reedited in 2001, *Ideas, Persons and Events*, volume 19 of *The Collected works of James M.Buchanan*, Indianapolis, Liberty Fund,. pages 331-343; 344-355.

Buchanan, J. M. (1996), Society and Democracy reedited in 2001, *Ideas, Persons and Events*, volume 19 of *The Collected works of James M.Buchanan*,, Indianapolis, Liberty Fund,. pages344-355.

Buchanan, J. M. 1979 Politics without Romance. A Search of Positive Public Choice Theory and its Normative Implications reprinted in 1999, *The Logical Foundations of Constitutional Liberty*, volume 1 of *The Collected works of James M.Buchanan*, Indianapolis, Liberty Fund, pages 45-59.

Buchanan, J. M., R. D. Tollison and G. Tullock,(eds.) (1980) *Toward a theory of the Rent-seeking Society*, College Station, Texas, A&M University Press.

Buchanan, J. M. and Vanberg, V. J. (1994) Constitutional Choice, Rational Ignorance and the Limits of Reason, *Economics as Social Theory*. New York: Routledge.

Besley, T., and S. Coate, 1997. An Economic Model of Representative Democracy, *Quarterly Journal of Economics*, 112, 85-114.

Caselli, Francesco and Massimo Morelli, 2004. Bad Politicians, *Journal of Public Economics*, 88, 759-782.

Dahl R.,(1971) *After the Revolution? Authority in a Good Society*, Yale University Press.

Dahl R.,(1971) *Polyarchy: Participation and Opposition*, Yale University Press.

Dahl R., (1998), *On Democracy*, Yale University Press

Dahl R. (1990), *Democracy and its critics*, Yale University Press

Di Lorenzo T. J. (1988) Competition and Political Entrepreneur ship: Austrian Insights into Public-Choice Theory, *The Review of Austrian Economics*

Einaudi L., (1923) *Parlamenti e classe politica*, in *Corriere della Sera*, 2 giugno 1923, in *Cronache*, VII.

Einaudi L., (1934) Prefazione a de Viti de Marco A., *Principi di economia finanziaria*, Einaudi, Torino, pp.XV-XXVII.

Einaudi L., (1954)*Il buongoverno. Saggi di economia e politica (1897-1954)*, a c. di Ernesto Rossi, Laterza, Bari.

Fedeli, S., and F. Forte (2011), "The law of survival of the political class: an analysis of the Italian Parliament (1946-2011) ", Working paper n.146 DIPARTIMENTO DI ECONOMIA PUBBLICA, Sapienza – Università di Roma: http://www.dipecodir.it/upload/wp/pdf/wp146.pdf

Forte, F: (1982), The Law of Selection in Public Economy as compared to the Market Economy, *Public Finance*, 37, 2.

Forte, F. (1993) *Principi di economia pubblica*, Giuffre; 3. ed. of "Principi di economia finanziaria"

Forte, F., (2010) *Principles of Public Economics: A Public Choice Approach*, Edward Elgar Pub

Forte F. and P. Silvestri (2009) Pareto's sociological maximum of utility of the community and the theory of the elites, mimeo.

Kaplan, E. L. and Meier P. (1958), Non parametric estimation for incomplete observation, *Journal Of The American Statistical Association*, 53, 457-481

Kautsky, K. (1892), *Das Erfurter Programm in Seinem Grundsatzlich Theil*, German Edition, 1920, Stuttgart Nachfr. Verlag, English translation as Karl Kautsky (1910), The Class Struggle (Erfurt Program 1888), 1892 Charles H. Kerr & Co, Italian Translation, 1971, Roma, Samonà &Savelli.

Leoni B. (1967), Rappresentanza politica e rappresentanza dei partiti, *Il Politico*, n.3. Reprinted in Leoni B. (2009) *Scritti di Scienza Politica e di Teoria del Diritto*, Rubbettino.

Linblom C. (1977) *Politics and Markets: The World's Political-Economic Systems*, New York: Basic, 1977.

Linblom C. (2001) *The Market System: What It Is, How It Works, and What to Make of It*, Yale University Press, 2001.

Mattozzi A. and A.Merlo (2007c) *Political Careers or Career Politicians,* PIER Working Paper 07-009, available at http://www.econ.upenn.edu/pier

McCormick E. and Tollison R. G.(1981) Politicians, legislation, and the economy: An inquiry into the interest-group theory of government, M. Nijhoff, Boston and Hingham, Mass..

Merlo A., V. Galasso, M. Landi, and A. Mattozzi (2009) "The Labor Market of Italian Politicians", PIER Working Paper 09-024

Messner, M., and M. Polborn, 2004. "Paying Politicians." *Journal of Public Economics*, 88, 2423-2445.

Mitchell, W. C. (1984), Schumpeter and public choice, Part II – Democracy and the demise of capitalism: The missing chapter in Schumpeter, *Public Choice* 42: 161-174

Michels R. (1911) *Zur Soziologie der Perteiwesens in der Modernen Demokratie. Untersuchungen uber die Oligarchischen Tendenzen des Groppensleben*, Leipzig Wrrner Klinkhardt; first Italian edition revised and increased by the author Torino, Utet, 1912, Second revised and increased German edition, 1925, Stuttgart, Alfred Kroner Verlag; Second Italian Edition on the second German edition, with an Introductory Essay of Juan I, Linz, Bologna, il Mulino 1966. English Translation (1999) Political Parties.

Montemartini G. (1900), Le basi fondamentali della scienza finanziaria pura, *Giornale degli economisti*, II. Translated in English in R. A. Musgrave and A. T.Peacock (1958), *Classics in the theory of public finance,* London, Macmillan as "The Fundamental Principles of the Pure Theory of Public Finance

Mosca G., (1932) *Lezioni di Storia delle istituzioni e delle dottrine politiche*, Castellani, Roma.

Mosca G. (1896) *La classe politica*, Bocca, Torino, second edition in 1923, the third and last in 1939 in Bari by Laterza.

Mosca G. (1933) *Storia delle dottrine politiche.*, Bari, Laterza.

Osborne, Martin J., and Al Slivinski, 1996. A Model of Political Competition with Citizen-Candidates, *Quarterly Journal of Economics*, 111, 65-96.

Pareto, V. (1906) *Manuale di Economia Politica Manuale di economia politica con una introduzione alla scienza sociale.* – Milano : Società Editrice Libraria, 1906. – xii, 576 p. – Altre edizioni nel 1909 e 1919.

Pareto, V. (1916). *Trattato di sociologia generale.* – Firenze : Barbera,. – 2 vol.

Pareto V. (1901-1902), *Les systèmes socialistes : Cours professé à l'Université de Lausanne.* – Paris : Giard & Brière, 1901-1902. – 2 v. (406, 492 p.). Further ed. in 1926 *I sistemi socialisti.* – Milano : Istituto Editoriale Italiano, and 1917-1920.

Schumpeter J. A. (1912 and 1934) *The theory of economic development – An inquiry into profits, capital, credit, interest, and the business cycle.* Harvard University Press, Cambridge

Schumpeter, J. A. (1942 and 1954), *Capitalism, Socialism and Democracy,* Unwin, London.

Tullock G. (1965), *Entry barriers in politics.* American Economic Review, Vol. 55 pages 458-66

Wagner (1966), Pressure groups and political entrepreneurs: A review article, *Public Choice*, 1, 161-170.

Wagner R. E (2007), *Fiscal Sociology and the Theory of Public Finance*, Centnham UK Elgar

Weber, M. (1918) *Parlament und Regierung im neugeordneten Deutschland. Zur politischen Kritik des Beamtentums und Parteiwesens*, Duncker & Humblot,

München, Leipzig 1918. (Ed. It. *Parlamento e Governo*" F.Ferrarotti (ed.) Editori Laterza Roma – Bari 2002)
Weber, M. (1919), *Politik als Beruf*, Berlin, Duncker & Humblot, Ed. It. *La politica come professione*, in *Il lavoro intellettuale come professione*, Torino, Einaudi, 1971
Weber, M. (1948) *From Max Weber: Essays in Sociology* Edited by H. H. Gerth, C. Wright Mills, Series: International Library of Sociology, Routledge, Publication Date: 29/01/1998 (first published in 1948 by Routledge and Kegan Paul Ltd, Great Britain))
Wohlgemuth, M. (2000), Political entrepreneurship and bidding for political monopoly, *Journal of Evolutionary Economics* 10, 273-295

Affiliations

Backhaus, Jürgen
Universität Erfurt, Krupp-Stiftungsprofessur für Finanzwissenschaft und Finanz-soziologie
Postfach 900 221 (Nordhäuser Str. 63)
99105 Erfurt
Tel: +49(0)361/737-4551
juergen.backhaus@uni-erfurt.de

Bharti, Nalin,
Assistant Professor (Economics), Department of Humanities and Social Sciences
Indian Institute of Technology Patna
nalinbharti@gmail.com
nalinbharti@iitp.ac.in
Ph. +91-0612-2552017
Fax: +91-0612-2277384/383

Boguslavski, Vladimir
Alexey Arkhipov, PhD
(Rostov State University)
Omvladimir@yahoo.com

Chang, Chia-Jen
Assistant Professor, Department of Public Affairs and Civic Education, National Changhua University of education, Taiwan
cjcj1862@cc.ncue.edu.tw
cjcj1862@gmail.com

Chou, Tai-Lung
Associate Professor, Department of Accounting and Information, Overseas Chinese University, Taiwan
jtl@ocu.edu.tw

Da Empoli, Domenico
University of Rome
Dipartimento di Teoria Economica e Metodi Quantitativi per le Scelte Politiche. Facoltà di Scienze Politiche, Università di Roma "La Sapienza", Piazzale Aldo Moro, 5.
00185 Roma, Italy
d.daempoli@dte.uniroma1.it

Ebner, Alexander
Goethe-Universität Frankfurt am Main
Institut für Gesellschafts- und Politikanalyse
Robert-Mayer-Straße 1
(Postfach 92)
D-60054 Frankfurt am Main
Telefon: +49 69 798 – 28388
a.ebner@soz.uni-frankfurt.de

Eusepi, Giuseppe
Sapienza University of Rome
Department of Law and Economics of Productive Activities
Via del Castro Laurenziano, 9
00161 Roma, Italy
Giuseppe.Eusepi@uniroma1.it
phone: +39-06-49766955
fax: +39-06-49766281
web-site: http://w3.uniroma1.it/ecspc/

Fedeli, Silvia
Professor of Public Finance
Sapienza – Universita' di Roma
Department of Economics and Law
Via del Castro Laurenziano, 9
00161 Roma, Italy
silvia.fedeli@uniroma1.it

Forte, Francesco
Emeritus Professor of Public Finance
Sapienza – Universita' di Roma
Department of Economics and Law
Via del Castro Laurenziano, 9

00161 Roma, Italy
E-mail: francesco.forte@uniroma1.it
micros.ricerche@vodafone.it

Ganesh, Gopal
Former Indian Administrative Service Officer, Ex-Member Secretary Disinvestment Commission
and an Advisior to the 12th Finance Commission
Government of India
gopal.ganesh@gmail.com

Leen, Auke R.
assistant Professor of Economics, Research Fellow Leiden University Law School, Faculty of Law, Department of Tax Law and Economics
Leiden University, The Netherlands
a.r.leen@law.leidenuniv.nl

Le Brun, Bénédicte
Centre de recherche sur la décentralisation territoriale
Université de Reims Champagne Ardenne
lebrunb@gmail.com

Magazzino, Cosimo
Department of Public Institutions, Economics and Society – Roma Tre University.

Mantovani, Michela
Lecturer in industrial Economics (SECS-P/06), Department of Economics and Law, "Mediterranea" University of Reggio Calabria
mantovani@unic.it

Peukert, Helge
Universität Erfurt, Krupp-Stiftungsprofessur für Finanzwissenschaft und Finanzsoziologie
Postfach 900 221 (Nordhäuser Str. 63)
99105 Erfurt
+49(0)361/737-4553
helge.peukert@uni-erfurt.de

Raudla, Ringa
Ringa Raudla is Senior Research Fellow in the Department of Public Administration at Tallinn University of Technology. She holds a doctoral degree in economics from the Faculty of Law, Economics, and Social Sciences, University of Erfurt, Germany. Her main research interests are political economy, public finance and post-communist transition. She has taught courses on public administration, public finance, law and economics, and research methods, and has worked as a consultant for several government institutions in Estonia. She has published numerous articles and book chapters in areas such as constitutional political economy, social insurance reform, public procurement, fiscal governance, and fiscal sociology. Her recent publications include articles in Governance, Constitutional Political Economy, European Journal of Law and Economics, Journal of Public Policy and Public Administration.
ringa.raudla@gmail.com

Scheuerer, Gerhard
Ltd. Ministerialrat i. R., Lehrbeauftragter der Universität Erfurt
Im Ziegelgarten 2b
99098 Erfurt
Phone ++49 361 4233475
gerhard-scheuerer@t-online.de

Schöbel, Enrico
Postdoctoral Research Assistant and Lecturer in Public Finance
Universität Leipzig
Institut für Öffentliche Finanzen und Public Management
Lehrstuhl Finanzwissenschaft
Neues Augusteum
Augustusplatz 10
04109 Leipzig
Phone +49-(0)341-97 33 581
schoebel@wifa.uni-leipzig.de

Silvestri, Paolo
Università di Torino
Dipartimento di Economia e Statistica "Cognetti de Martiis"
Campus Luigi Einaudi, Lungo Dora Siena 100A
10153 – Torino (Italy)
+39 011 6703895 (fax)
paolo.silvestri@unito.it

Wagner, Richard
Department of Economics, 3 G4
George Mason University
Fairfax, VA 22030
USA
rwagner@gmu.edu

Finanzsoziologie

Herausgegeben von Jürgen G. Backhaus

Band 1 Jürgen G. Backhaus (ed.): Essays on Fiscal Sociology. 2005.

Band 2 Jürgen G. Backhaus (ed.): Fiscal Sociology. Public Auditing. 2007.

Band 3 Helge Peukert: Rudolf Goldscheid: Menschenökonom und Finanzsoziologe. 2009.

Band 4 Ringa Raudla: Constitution, Public Finance, and Transition. Theoretical Developments in Constitutional Public Finance and the Case of Estonia. 2010.

Band 5 Jürgen Backhaus (ed.): Essentials of Fiscal Sociology. Conception of an Encyclopedia. 2013.

www.peterlang.de

FSC
www.fsc.org
MIX
Papier | Fördert gute Waldnutzung
FSC® C083411

Kolibri 360 GmbH
Ferdinand-Jühlke-Straße 7
99095 Erfurt, Deutschland
produktsicherheit@kolibri360.de